# SASKATCHEWAN

# John W. Warnock

# SASKATCHEWAN
## THE ROOTS OF DISCONTENT
## AND PROTEST

**BLACK
ROSE
BOOKS**

Montréal/New York/London

Black Rose Books No. HH328

National Library of Canada Cataloguing in Publication Data

Warnock, John W., 1933-

Saskatchewan : the roots of discontent and protest / John W. Warnock.

Includes bibliographical references and index.

Hardcover ISBN: 1-55164-245-X (bound)  Paperback ISBN: 1-55164-244-1 (pbk.)

1. Political culture--Saskatchewan.  2. Saskatchewan--Politics and government.
3. Saskatchewan--Economic conditions.  4. Saskatchewan--Social conditions.  I. Title.

HN110.S35W37 2004    971.24    C2003-905803-4

*Cover design: Associés libres*

*Cover art from a painting by Mike Steadman entitled "We Remain"*

| | | |
|---|---|---|
| **BLACK ROSE BOOKS** | | |
| C.P. 1258 | 2250 Military Road | 99 Wallis Road |
| Succ. Place du Parc | Tonawanda, NY | London, E9 5LN |
| Montréal, H2X 4A7 | 14150 | England |
| Canada | USA | UK |

To order books:

In Canada: (phone) 1-800-565-9523 (fax) 1-800-221-9985
email: utpbooks@utpress.utoronto.ca

In United States: (phone) 1-800-283-3572  (fax)  1-651-917-6406

In the UK & Europe: (phone) London 44 (0)20 8986-4854 (fax) 44 (0)20 8533-5821
email: order@centralbooks.com

Our Web Site address: http://www.web.net/blackrosebooks

A publication of the Institute of Policy Alternatives of Montréal (IPAM)

Printed in Canada

The Canada Council | Le Conseil des Arts
for the Arts | du Canada

# TABLE OF CONTENTS

*To the memory of my mentors*
*in political economy at the University of Saskatchewan*

*Ken Buckley, Vernon Fowke, and Irene Spry*

# PREFACE

**M**y wife and I arrived in Saskatchewan in August 1963. We were emigrating from the United States, moving to a new country and hoping to eventually become Canadian citizens. I was taking a teaching job in the Department of Economics and Political Science at the University of Saskatchewan. Fortunately, I was soon granted a long-term appointment at the university, which made this possible.

I was attracted to this department because of its tradition of political economy. As an undergraduate at Duke University I took an interdisciplinary program in social science which was political science, history, economics and sociology. I did not really get to study anthropology until the academic year I spent at York University, 1970-1. There was no discipline called political economy in the United States. Political economy was a British and European tradition. In the United States all the social sciences were deemed to be separate. American academics were absolutely certain that there was no connection between politics and economics. All the way through my studies at three universities I was protected from any radical social science theories like Marxism.

Sometime during my years in North Carolina I decided to try for a career in the U.S. Foreign Service. I enrolled for advanced study in the School of Foreign Service at Georgetown University in Washington, DC. On the positive side, its academic approach was interdisciplinary social science. Foreign service officers were expected to be "generalists." On the negative side, the university was dominated by right wing Jesuits, academics from Eastern Europe who had fled when the Soviet Army arrived at the end of World War II, and rich Roman Catholic students.

Not satisfied with Georgetown, I transferred to American University, also in Washington to do a masters degree and doctorate in interdisciplinary social sciences. In early 1961 I was accepted into the U.S. Foreign Service and assigned to the Latin American section of the Economics branch of the Department of State. My arrival coincided with the beginning of John F. Kennedy's administration. It was an important time in the history of U.S. foreign policy, and with my top secret security clearance I saw from the inside the Bay of Pigs invasion of Cuba, the Alliance for Progress approach to intervention in Latin America, the subversion of Patrice Lumumba's government in the Congo, the Cuban missile crisis, and the decision of the Kennedy administration to get directly involved in the civil war in Indochina. In Iraq in February 1963 there was coup by Saddam Hussein's faction of the Baath Party, supported by the Kennedy administration. They provided the new Baath government with a list of suspected Communists who were then killed. As early as 1959 Saddam was "Our Man in Bagdad," hired by the CIA to try to assassinate the prime minister. After two years I decided I did not want to spend my adult life "going abroad to lie for your country" as Metternich had once described the role of a diplomat.

Why did we choose Saskatchewan? Part of the reason was our love of outdoor activities, and we had travelled in Canada. I was impressed by the faculty in the Department of Economics and Political Science. It was not as pure a political economy department as at other Canadian universities. But the scholarly work of its faculty was clearly in the British tradition of political economy, it had political economy courses, and there was an honours course in political economy and history. I was also interested in the Co-operative Commonwealth Federation (CCF) government, the first social democratic government in North America.

When I arrived at the department in August 1963 the first person I met was Cy Gonick. He was in the process of moving to the Department of Economics at the University of Manitoba. We discussed his plan to create *Canadian Dimension Magazine*, and he invited me to contribute to it and be on the original board of directors. This was the beginning of my commitment to Canadian politics and journalism.

The second person I met was Ed Safarian, who had replaced the deceased George Britnell as chairman of the department. Safarian, who had a doctorate from the University of California, would begin the shift in the department away from political economy and toward an eventual split between economics and political science. He introduced me to Vernon Fowke. When my wife Betty and our young daughter arrived in Saskatoon, we spent our first weekend together in Saskatchewan at Fowke's cottage at Wakaw Lake.

Shirley Spafford has documented the early history of this department and its political economy tradition in her book, *No Ordinary Academics* (University of Toronto Press, 2000). There was an early conflict between William Walker Swanson, the first chairman, and those who followed. Swanson, born in Scotland, had a doctorate from the University of Chicago, and while he did important research on the wheat economy, he was a staunch free market liberal and was hostile to the Saskatchewan tradition of populist politics and the CCF.

The department changed under the new chairman, George Britnell. A local boy from Moosomin, he studied under Harold Innis at the University of Toronto. Vernon Fowke had been born at Parry Sound, Ontario, but his family had moved to Melville, and he attended the University of Saskatchewan. Ken Buckley, another leading figure in the department, was from Aberdeen, just down the rail from Saskatoon; he had also studied under Innis at the University of Toronto.

The most amazing person in the department, however, was Mable Frances Timlin. Born in Wisconsin, she graduated from Milwaukee state Normal School and in 1916 moved to Saskatchewan to teach school, first in Bounty and Wilkie, and then in Saskatoon. She earned a bachelor's degree in English at the University of Saskatchewan while at the same time reading economics and political science. In 1935 she was appointed instructor in economics. She was the real theorist in the department. She completed a doctorate in economics at the University of Washington at the age of 40, authored widely acclaimed works on Keynesian economics, was the first woman social scientist admitted to the Royal Society of Canada, and was the first woman elected to the executive committee of the American Economics Association. While she had retired in 1959, "Timmie" regularly came around the department to engage in wide ranging discussions. I well remember a conversation with her when she strongly attacked mathematical economics and neoclassical model building as contributing nothing to the understanding of the Canadian economy. It was far removed, she argued, from the reality of Canada's integration with the United States, dependence on resource extraction industries, and enormous size and pronounced regionalism.

It was under these four academics that the department earned its reputation as a Saskatchewan department devoted to the farm movement in western Canada and social democracy. The province was their home, they had lived here during the depression, and they well knew the problems of the farmer. They also believed that academics had an obligation to serve the people who paid their salaries. They gave lectures all around the province, worked for royal commissions, and advised governments. When Tommy Douglas' CCF government was formed in 1944, George Britnell, Vernon Fowke, and Dean F.C. Cronkite of the College of Law served as the members of the Economic Advisory Committee. Britnell became an adviser to the leftist government of Guatemala under Jacobo Arbenz (1950-4), overthrown by a U.S. government-sponsored military coup.

Unfortunately, Fowke died prematurely, and I only had the benefit of his kindness and knowledge for several short years. He introduced me to Innis, the metropolitan hinterland thesis of Canadian political economy, and always stressed that we should understand the power of capital in economic development. Ken Buckley's office was across from mine, and we had long discussions about the nature of capitalism and Canadian economic development. He introduced me to duck hunting. Norman Ward, the senior political scientist and resident humourist, introduced me to grouse and partridge hunting. Ward, one of Canada's best known political scientists at that time, was the first to tell me that George Britnell taught more political science courses than economics or political economy. Britnell insisted that "anyone can teach political science." Ward liked to say that being an academic was the next best thing to being a bum: you got paid well for doing what you really liked to do.

The other major influence on my development as a political economist came from Irene M. Spry, who only taught in the department for one year, 1967-8, before moving on to the University of Ottawa. She was a delightful woman, and as her office was adjacent to mine, I spent many hours there. She was still working on the Palliser books. But along with Helen Buckley, who was in the Centre for Community Studies, she was one of the very few academics who had any intellectual and political interest in the impact of the National Policy on the Aboriginal people in Western Canada. Spry was an impressive scholar with degrees in political economy from London School of Economics and Cambridge University, where she studied under John Maynard Keynes and the Marxist scholar, Maurice Dobb. She also had a masters degree in Social Research and Social Work from Bryn Mawr College. At the University of Toronto she worked with Harold Innis. She and her husband, Graham Spry, had co-founded Saskatchewan House in London. Graham Spry was the Agent-General for the province in London between 1946 and 1967. Like her husband she was a long time social democrat and member of the League for Social Reconstruction in the 1930s. It was a great loss when she moved on to the University of Ottawa. I was pleased to read that right up to her death at age 91 she was a political activist as well as a scholar. She encouraged me to be active in politics, insisting that if you hide away in the university you quickly lose touch with the views of ordinary people. I am still waiting for the book she was working on at the time of her death, *From the Hunt to the Homestead*, a political economy history of the prairies. She was an active supporter of the Associated Country Women of the World.

Over the years many well known scholars taught for a short time in this department including Frank Underhill, James A. Corry, Robert MacGregor Dawson, James Mallory, Bernard Crick, Hugh Thorburn, and Gordon Thiessen. While I was there Bruce Wilkinson, Ken Rae, Elias Tuma, John Cartwright, Don Rowlatt, and Robin Neill moved on to major careers elsewhere. Jack McLeod, who switched to the University of Toronto, wrote *Zinger and Me* on academic life in Saskatoon.

The University of Saskatchewan's tradition in Canadian political economy was a combination of Harold Innis and John Maynard Keynes. It was liberal social democratic and materialist. In the 1960s a new political economy was emerging in Canada which looked to the traditions of continental Europe. I spent the 1970-1 academic year at Atkinson College, York University. Daniel Drache and I shared an office and a year trying to find more radical materials to include in our teaching of Canadian political economy. The older tradition identified with Harold Innis was almost completely devoid of human content. There was absolutely no discussion of social class in Canada, nothing on the development of the trade union movement or the Communist Party, and precious little on the nature of the capitalist class. There was virtually nothing on the relationship between the capitalist class in Canada and the many dominant foreign-owned corporations. There was almost nothing on the relationship between the European settlers and the Aboriginal population nor on the role of women in the economy and society. All of those subjects are now very well covered by the new political economy.

The 1960s and 1970s were exciting times to teach in university. A large number of students were not only active in politics they were actually interested in reading, learning and trying to find the answers to the bigger questions. They were not satisfied with being spoon fed the usual liberal dogma. They wanted to read Marxism and study imperialism. Today most students focus on getting good grades hoping that this will land them a job after they graduate. Most go out of their way to avoid controversy. There are no active student course unions any more. Quite a few students do have a critical approach to their studies, but they are very cynical about changing anything. But there are still some who become active in the anti-war movement, the anti-globalization movement and Green politics. In my own early work and development as an instructor, researcher and writer in the new Canadian political economy I benefitted from a close relationship with Ed Mahood and Howard Adams, both of whom taught in the College of Education. They provided the critical intellectual support that was largely absent from my rather conservative colleagues.

The department changed under the direction of Ed Safarian and Bob Kautz. More Americans were hired as well as more Canadians who had received their advanced degrees in the United States. A crisis developed in 1971 when John Richards, a very popular professor, was not rehired. Richards was born and raised in Saskatchewan, had gone to the University of Saskatchewan, and was completing a doctorate at the University of Washington in St. Louis. It was widely believed that he was "fired" because he was a promoter of the Canadian tradition of political economy while the majority in the department wanted to move to the American tradition of completely separate disciplines of economics and political science. Others believed that he was not rehired because he was active in the Waffle group, the left wing organization within the New Democratic Party. Indeed, in the 1971 provincial election he was elected to the legislature from Saskatoon-Sutherland. He was a close personal, political and academic friend of mine at the time.

In any case, hundreds of students protested by occupying the department for weeks on end. Professors were blocked from getting to their offices. Student course unions demanded that Richards be re-hired. The department was deeply split, never really recovered from this conflict, chose to follow the American road, and formally divided. A few years after the occupation I decided to leave the department and move to British Columbia. The political economy tradition disappeared from the two new reconstructed departments but re-appeared as the new Canadian political economy in the Department of Sociology.

In British Columbia my wife and I were fruit growers in the Okanagan, but I was also a researcher and writer specializing in the political economy of food and agriculture. I became involved in the environmental movement. But I never lost touch with my friends in Saskatchewan. In 1986 John Conway and Joe Roberts asked me to return to the University of Regina as a special lecturer. It was natural that when I returned it would be to the University of Regina. Academics at this university had been major participants in the development of the new Canadian political economy. I found my home in the Department of Sociology which had developed a reputation in political economy, rural sociology, and continental integration, my major fields of interest.

## Looking Toward the Future

The policy shift from the more egalitarian Keynesian welfare state to the neoliberal order of inequality was not ordained by God. It is not a product of some biologically determined evolution. It was fashioned by political and economic forces who stand to benefit from the changes. We still live in a democracy, and people can and will mobilize to change government policy. During World War II Canadians demonstrated that we do not need depressions and high unemployment. A government with broad popular support brought full employment, higher standards of living, and a more egalitarian society. To have such a government again Canada would have to withdraw from the North America free trade agreements which greatly constrain the scope of government. But this is a real option open to Canadians.

Saskatchewan has also had governments which took the lead in Canada in introducing progressive social legislation that benefits the majority. Under the CCF government of T. C. Douglas great strides were made. The NDP government of Allan Blakeney began a process of gaining ownership and control over our own natural resources. That policy has been reversed by subsequent provincial governments. But there is no divine law that says that a future government could not decided to again take up that political goal. All it takes is a government with some imagination, the political will, and support from the general population.

This book is not a comprehensive study of the political economy of Saskatchewan. It is a series of essays that I have written over the past few years. They focus on the province's major continuing problems and issues, and in that sense I believe that they hang together. We have just entered the 21st century, and Saskatchewan is about to celebrate its centennial. Traditionally, human beings have used such occasions to reflect on the past, assess the present situation, and try to plan for the future. It is time to do this in Saskatchewan.

The essays in this book are designed to encourage people to look at the political economy and political culture of Saskatchewan in a meaningful way. Is this the best society we can create? How can we bring about change? Can we expand democracy? Can we once again establish a goal of a just society for everyone? This requires going to the root of long standing problems. We should all be concerned about the future of the economy, the persistence of patriarchy, and the reality of racism and discrimination. We have a long political tradition of popular change, represented by the grass roots agrarian movement and the social democratic ideal of social justice. We have ongoing and persistent problems and deeply held prejudices. But we also have the experience and ability to move away from the status quo and take another road.

From a political economy perspective, there is very little serious discussion of the state of the province. When economic growth rates are high, the government claims it is because of their policies. When they are low, the opposition parties claim it is because of bad government policies. The same thing happens when population figures come out. While in opposition the major parties always complain that kids have to leave the province because the government is not creating enough jobs or is scaring business away. They were arguing about that when I arrived in Saskatchewan in 1963.

The political right in the province, represented by the Saskatchewan Party, the Canadian Reform-Alliance-Conservative Party, the business organizations, and the Canadian Taxpayers Federation are insisting that economic growth and re-population can only happen if we move faster and farther down the road of the free market economy with very limited government. It is the "socialists" who are driving away investment and business activity. Most understand this as political rhetoric, but with strong support from the mass media, it has a major influence on people. Is the political economy of the free market and free trade the best option for Saskatchewan? The policies they advocate have been in place in North Dakota for quite a few years. What have they done for that state? Compared to North Dakota, Saskatchewan looks like the promised land.

There is almost no discussion about the nature of Saskatchewan as a resource hinterland within the Canadian and North American economy. In the past political and community leaders openly discussed the political economy of the metropolitan-hinterland relationship. Farmers were well aware of how the wealth they created was siphoned off by the farm supply industry, the financial sector, the food processing industry, and the wholesale and retail trade. No one discusses these issue in a serious way any more. There needs to be a real debate unless people just want to go along with business as usual. I have made this a central focus of this book.

To understand what is happening to Saskatchewan's economy it is necessary to understand how capitalism works. As long as people believe that the economy is just individuals and firms buying and selling goods and services in a market, where rational people all pursue their own self interest, people will remain mystified. It is necessary to look at Saskatchewan from a *political economy* perspective. People must recognize that the key to the operation of the capitalist system is the accumulation of capital. Those who own capital invest to make a profit and accumulate more capital. They shift their investments to maximize their returns. If businesses do not invest and expand they are squeezed out by competition. What happened to all the mom and pop neighbourhood grocery stores? Ask the owners of Seven Eleven and Mac's Milk.

Adam Smith was the first to demonstrate that this is the core of the capitalist system of production. He called it the Law of Accumulation.

It is also imperative that we understand how societies and economies create a surplus above the subsistence level, who controls that surplus, and how it is invested. The creation of an economic surplus and its investment in productive enterprise is what produces economic growth. Once we understand this, for example, we know why in a hinterland economy it is better for the majority when Crown corporations own and develop our natural resources rather than giant foreign corporations. That was the conclusion that Eric Kierans reached when he examined the resource extraction industries in Manitoba in 1973. It is still true today. Thus several essays at the beginning of the book address the differences between economics and political economy, how economic surpluses are created and controlled, the nature of capitalism, and how it operates in a hinterland resource community.

The people of Saskatchewan also must confront the historical origins of the province and the ongoing conflict between the European settlers and the Aboriginal population. This problem is not unique to Canada but is found in all those countries where a European white population settled during the period of colonial domination. The notion of European supremacy, and indigenous inferiority, is found in all white settler societies. It was the official ideology of the imperial government, the colonial society and all of its institutions. The ideology of European racial superiority served as a justification for taking the land from the indigenous population by force of arms and marginalizing and excluding those who survived.

Commentators often argue that Saskatchewan may be progressive when it comes to economic questions but at the same time it has a deeply entrenched "social conservatism." The term "social conservatism" is a code phrase used in place of "traditional patriarchal values."

What are the issues that are most commonly identified with social conservatism in Saskatchewan? They would include opposition to equal rights for gays and lesbians, including state rights which come from being officially married. Opposition to a range of rights for women, including the right to choice on whether or not to have an abortion. The right to own a firearm without having to register it with the government. Opposition to government-sponsored child care. Opposition to sex education in the schools and reading materials in libraries. Many social conservatives oppose the right of women to own farms, work outside the household, and object to government support for women who are victims of family violence.

One of the major concerns of social conservatives has been the rather dramatic rise in the divorce rate, and in particular, divorces initiated by women. Thus social con-

servatives in North America have been leading a campaign to make divorce more difficult. They have been very concerned about social assistance and their rates, for this
program has provided a social safety net for women who wish to leave their marriage.

Public opinion polls regularly show that on these issues Saskatchewan is more
conservative and traditional than Canadian opinion in general. Some attribute this
to the fact that people in this province are more committed to institutional religion.
Polls show majority support in Saskatchewan for using the Lord's Prayer in school.
One poll conducted by the Social Research Unit at the University of Saskatchewan
in 2000 reported that 40 percent believe that religion should be taught in the public
schools. Historically, the major Christian churches have been a foundation of patriarchal culture. They have been particularly influential in rural and farm communities. The rise of fundamentalist Christian churches in North America has re-enforced
traditional "family values."

Saskatchewan has a long history of radical and progressive politics. I have addressed this is several essays. It began with the farmers' resistance to their exploitation
by big business interests based in eastern Canada. From the formation of the Progressive Party, this movement evolved into the social democratic and populist Co-operative Commonwealth Federation (CCF). Not only did Saskatchewan elect the first
social democratic government in North America in 1944, the CCF-NDP became the
natural governing party of the province with a core support of around 40 percent of
the electorate.

The CCF was never a success on the federal level, and in 1962 it was transformed into the New Democratic Party. Following the tradition of social democratic
parties elsewhere, the new party was formed by an official alliance with the trade union movement. As the NDP it was elected to government in Saskatchewan in 1971.
Under the leadership of Allan Blakeney this government brought in a range of social
reforms and used the state to try to gain some control over economic development.

However, that social democratic policy tradition has all but disappeared. With
the election of Roy Romanow's NDP government in 1991, the party moved steadily
to the right. Today on basic issues it is hardly distinguishable from the conservative
parties. Thus any discussion of political economy or political culture in Saskatchewan
must include an analysis of the CCF-NDP tradition and why has it moved to the
right. Has the progressive tradition in this province come to an end?

Saskatchewan also has a long history of extra-parliamentary political activity,
beginning with the farmers' movements. During the CCF governments of T.C.
Douglas the Saskatchewan Teachers Federation, the Saskatchewan Farmers Union

and the Saskatchewan Federation of Labour worked together to try to influence government policy. During the NDP government of Allan Blakeney the Waffle movement worked within and outside the party to promote socialist policies. The Tory government of Grant Devine was confronted by a broad range of popular groups operating under the umbrella of the Saskatchewan Coalition for Social Justice. This extra-parliamentary political activity faded during the NDP governments of Roy Romanow and Lorne Calvert.

Will a new progressive tradition emerge within the NDP? Or outside the NDP? In the past in Saskatchewan when progressive movements became bureaucratized and stagnant, new movements emerged. Over the 1990s a growing sector of the Saskatchewan public lost interest in politics, became disillusioned with the NDP, and withdrew from political activity. The number of people even voting fell to less than 60 percent in 1999 and 2003. Does this mean that 40 percent of the population is no longer at all interested in politics? Or does it mean that they are just waiting for a new politics to develop?

The world is facing a number of serious crises as we begin the 21st century. Global warming and climate change is already a major problem. The world economy is stagnating and uncertain. The administration of President George W. Bush in the United States is pursuing a unilateralist policy which stresses militarism. There is widespread disillusionment and cynicism with liberal democracy as governments become more elitist and ignore the views of the majority of their citizens. Big business and corporations determine policy while at the same time corruption is widespread at the top. In most less developed countries governments are unable to meet the needs and demands of their own people. These countries are constrained by the rules imposed upon them by international institutions and First World governments.

The new world political economy system, known as "globalization" or neoliberalism, is facing a crisis of legitimacy. It has produced inequality, poverty and precarious working conditions in the industrialized countries. The structural adjustment programs imposed on the Third World have made things worse for the large majority, and this has undermined the credibility of capitalism. The new neoliberal political economy is highly undemocratic, with its stress on centralization, hierarchy and authoritarianism, decision-making behind closed doors, with emphasis always placed on giving first priority to the owners of capital over the needs of common people. Critics of the system, including the broad "anti-globalization movement," are growing in number and size. This is an environment that is ripe for political and economic change. It forms the background to any new analysis of the political economy of Saskatchewan.

## ACKNOWLEDGMENTS

It has taken me quite a few years to produce this book. I want to thank those friends and colleagues who took the time to read the manuscript and offer comments: Lorne Brown, Evan Carlson, Susan Ferren, Phil Hansen, John Keen, and Joe Roberts. I am, of course, completely responsible for the manuscript as it now stands. Two other close friends encouraged me in this project, Gail Youngberg and John McConnell. Sadly, they both passed away at a premature age. I want to thank the Boag Foundation for a grant to research some aspects of this study. Special thanks go to Ormond McKague, an old friend from the University of Saskatchewan, who not only read the manuscript to offer a critique of its content but who helped me with the final editing.

This book would not have been possible without the support I received from the staff at the University of Regina Library, and in particular those with the Interlibrary Loan and Government Publications sections. I also want to thank Linda Barton of Black Rose Books for her careful support in this project and the publisher, Dimitri Roussopoulos.

The cover art is from a painting by a friend, Mike Steadman, entitled "We Remain." Mike is a member of Sakewewak First Nations Artists' Collective in Regina and a founding board member of the Aboriginal Council of Regina.

Regina, Saskatchewan
April, 2004

# Chapter 1

———————○———————

# SASKATCHEWAN IN THE ERA
# OF NORTH AMERICAN INTEGRATION

What does it mean to be a Canadian? To be a "stubble jumper" from Saskatchewan? Historians and social scientists have argued that Canada is a "new country" meaning it is mainly inhabited by people who immigrated from other countries. Canada is not a nation in the traditional sense of the term. Social scientists describe a nation as a group of people who are born and raised in a particular culture. Their history and traditions are passed down through their language. They live in their own communities. They have their own religion. Their culture is tied to their agriculture and food, their land and ecology, and how they have organized themselves for production and reproduction. Thus, traditionally a "nation" has meant an historic people. The Maya, the Japanese, the Chinese and the French are nations.

Canadians do have some common experiences that identify us as a group. The majority have been born and raised in Canada. We are socialized to be Canadians by our family, our peers, our community, our educational institutions and our places of work. We absorb a Canadian culture.

In 1993 the *Globe and Mail* asked their readers to identify what it meant to be a Canadian. Here are a few of the responses. A Canadian: "Carries travellers cheques in a moneybelt." "Is convinced that democracy involves keeping your opinions to yourself." "Doesn't know anyone who has a flag." "Waits for the light to change before crossing a deserted intersection at 3 a.m." "Says 'no big deal' to a sidewalk cyclist who's just knocked him down." "Never sits in someone else's seat, even if the ticket-holder doesn't show." "Goes to hot-tub parties where people wear bathing suits." "Thinks the Free Trade Agreement is actually about free trade." Yes, we see ourselves as being modest, conservative, polite and respectful of authority. And that includes people who live in Saskatchewan. But why is that? (Clement, 1993)

## The Evolving Canadian Culture

There are a number of important factors which contribute to the construction of the Canadian culture. The most important characteristic that all Canadians share is that we live in a particular geographic space on this earth. We live in a territorial state which is recognized by international law and the United Nations. Our place on this earth, its geography and climate, is the most fundamental cultural characteristic that we all have in common.

Canada's historians, political economists and writers have emphasized the importance of our geography in our cultural development. A public opinion poll done for the *Globe and Mail* (July 1, 2003) found that 89 percent of Canadians say that the vast area of Canada defines the nation. In contrast to our neighbour to the south, we all experience long, cold winters. We have a huge northern region that stretches up to the North Pole which is almost unpopulated, a permanent frontier. We are a maritime country, with the longest coastline of any country in the world.

Margaret Atwood, one of our best known writers, has argued that many countries have a "single unifying and informing symbol at its core." This functions "like a system of beliefs which holds the country together and helps the people in it to co-operate for common ends." For the United States, she suggests, it is "The Frontier" and for England it is "The Island." For Canada, she argues, it is "survival." It is survival in the face of the harsh northern climate and environment. But it is more than this, it is also political survival. For those of French descent living in Quebec after conquest, it has been a question of cultural survival as a nation. But for the rest of Canada survival means "hanging on, staying alive." This was particularly true for Canada when we were a formal colony. In the more modern period, as we are overwhelmed by the United States, all we can do is try to survive as a people. (Atwood, 1972)

Canada began as a colony of France and then the United Kingdom. The indigenous people were organized as nations, but they became victims of European colonial and imperial expansion. Colonization in the age of imperialism involved the transplanting of Europeans to new territories which were claimed by military conquest. The Europeans who came to North America brought with them the Christian churches, and this has remained the dominant religious culture. But one of the most basic characteristics of Canada is that it is a white settler society. The indigenous, non-white population was decimated by diseases and imperial wars and eventually marginalized on small parcels of land called "reserves." As a white settler colony within the British empire, Canada was given special civil and human rights and self government which were denied non-white British colonies. When there were colonial rebellions against British rule, these new Canadians and their governments inevitably backed the imperial power.

The Europeans also brought with them capitalism as a mode of production. Within the world capitalist system today, we are among the most advanced and the richest. But capitalism is modified by the history and culture of different countries. We are part of the Anglo-American capitalist world, linked by language, culture and history. The free market tradition is stronger in the English speaking world. The Anglo-American countries work together very closely on the economic, political and military level. But Canada has a particular form of capitalism, which has included major government support for business development and even Crown corporations.

Canadians are very much aware of the fact that we live on the northern border of the United States. That makes us different from Australia and New Zealand, our Commonwealth partners. The central political issue in Canada has always been the degree to which Canada remains independent from the United States. At the time of Confederation our political and economic elites wanted Canada to be an independent country.

The structure of the Canadian economy has been heavily influenced by the fact that we border on the much larger and more powerful United States. Today 85 percent of our trade is immediately north-south. U.S. corporations, mass media, and popular culture dominate Canada. The goods we buy all seem to be what U.S. citizens want, increasingly sold by U.S. retail corporations operating in Canada. We have a relatively weak capitalist class, now pushing hard for even greater subordination of Canada into the U.S. continental economy. Years ago Ralph Allen, when he was editor of *Saturday Night* magazine, referred to Canada as the "northernmost banana republic." Today my students conclude that Canada is "Puerto Rico North." U.S. corporations have always treated Canada as a northern economic region, not a foreign country.

Canada's British political heritage helps to set us off from the United States. We cling to the monarchy and the Governor General. We are loyal to the Commonwealth. We support the British parliamentary system, even though it is a difficult system of government in a federal state. We keep the British first-past-the-post electoral system and strict party discipline, even though it encourages regionalism, inequalities in representation and discontent. The British parliamentary system is a top-down authoritarian system of government which enhances rule by elites. But it is not the same as the U.S. government.

Academics have tried to identify a Canadian culture. Seymour Martin Lipset and Louis Hartz, American social scientists, believe that Canada's character was set during the American war for independence. Upwards of 60,000 colonists moved north to the Maritime region or Ontario. They wanted to remain loyal to the British colonial government. With the defeat of the French in North America, Great Britain and their colonial elite formed an alliance with the conservative Roman Catholic Church and ruled over the French-speaking habitants. Thus Canada was founded by people who opposed the liberal revolution of the 18th century. For these commentators, this history explains our conservatism, deference and respect for authority, and our willingness to have greater government involvement in the economy. (see Lipset, 1963; McRae, 1964, Hartz, 1964, Clark, 1968)

John Porter, one of Canada's most respected sociologists, found Canada to be *The Vertical Mosaic*, where privileged white men dominate all the structures of power. Social inequality is the norm. The key to understanding Canada is the unequal distribution of wealth, prestige and power and how Canada's hierarchical, authoritarian system is maintained. (Porter, 1965)

Nevertheless, Canada has a long tradition of farm revolts, radical farmers movements and radical political parties. The trade union movement has a history of radical syndicalism and then industrial organization by a relatively strong Communist Party. We have had socialist parties and social democratic parties and governments. Collective action has long been a part of Canadian political culture, a resistance to rule by the privileged elite.

Culture is not a fixed phenomenon and constantly changes and evolves. In the post-World War II period immigrants to Canada have mainly come from non-Anglo Saxon countries. By the 1990s the majority of immigrants were non-Europeans and people of colour.

The Census of 2001 reported that Canada had 5.4 million people who had been born in other countries, accounting for 18.4 percent of the population, the highest of any other country other than Australia. "Visible minorities" (a term which officially excludes Aboriginal people) accounted for 73 percent of new immigrants in the 1990s and now account for 13.4 percent of the total population. Visible minorities mainly settled in our three largest cities: Toronto (with 43 percent), Vancouver (with 18 percent) and Montreal (with 12 percent). Toronto now ranks as first in the world with the highest percent of population which is foreign born, Vancouver third and Montreal seventh.

Like all those before, these new immigrants will become Canadians and absorb much of our cultural traditions. But they in turn will influence our cultural heritage. Some political commentators are arguing that the historic divisions in Canada between settlers and Aboriginal people and between English and French people are being replaced by the "cultural gap" between urban centres and rural hinterland areas and between older Canadians and newer Canadians. (Statistics Canada, 2003)

Michael Adams of the Environics research group argues that Canadians do not have to worry about the loss of Canadian independence because of free trade agreements, military integration with the U.S., and foreign ownership of the economy. Their research shows that the core values of Canadians and U.S. citizens are changing, and the differences between the two societies are widening. The average U.S. citizen is becoming more "materialistic, outer-directed, intolerant, socially conservative, and deferential to traditional institutional authority." There is an increasing level of xenophobia, acceptance of violence, sexism, demanding of conformity, and ostentatious consumption. Anti-feminism is rising fast. In 2000 49 percent of U.S. citizens said that the father should be "master in his own house" compared to only 18 percent in Canada. Canadians are becoming more like Europeans, Adams argues, more autonomous, less deferential to authority, more tolerant of individual differences, more accepting of social and racial differences. He cites an Ekos Research Associates' poll in May 2002 which found that 52 percent wanted Canada to be less like the United States; only 12 percent wanted Canada to be more like our southern neighbour. But Ekos has also regularly reported that Canada's political and economic elite have values that are at variance with those of ordinary Canadians. (Adams, 2003)

## Regions, Disparities and Different Political Cultures

The geography of Canada has made political union difficult, with the relative isolation of the Atlantic provinces, the Laurentian hills and the Canadian Shield, the dry prairies and the Rocky Mountains which block access to the Pacific coast. Canada has greatly benefitted from the vastness of the natural resources and the low population in relation to the land. Yet regionalism, the geographic barriers, our international isolation created by the Atlantic and Pacific oceans, and our cold climate have made it difficult to develop strong links with countries other than the United States. We have very high infrastructure costs, high energy costs, great distances from markets for our products, and a short summer season. Canadian culture starts with how we have adapted to our geographical and ecological space.

One of the basic characteristics of Canada is the existence of distinct regions and their inequality. Political and economic power has always resided in the Quebec City/Toronto corridor. Within the federal system, Ontario and Quebec have had the preponderance of the population and the representation in Parliament. Economic power has been centralized in Toronto and Montreal.

The Canadian prairie region has traditionally been known as "the West." The National Policy called for Confederation, the unification of the country from coast to coast, and the settlement of the prairies. After the indigenous population was removed and put on small reserves, the Homestead Act of 1872 brought in the white settlers. The political and economic elites who put together the National Policy saw the wheat economy as a way to build a manufacturing industry in central Canada. Wheat surrendered its position as the dominant staple to natural resource extraction after World War II.

The prairies are a particular ecological region within Canada, but they are also a classic hinterland area, dominated by metropolitan Canada. The three provinces remain fundamentally a resource extraction area which imports its manufactured goods from central Canada and the United States. This is how the prairies developed under Canadian capitalism.

Within the prairies there are differences created by the distribution of natural resources, the development of the capitalist economy and the political division into provinces. Manitoba always had Winnipeg as a regional city which grew with the wheat economy and the grain trade. It was the wholesale distribution centre for the prairies. Once Alberta began to develop its oil and gas resources Calgary and Edmonton grew to be strong regional centres. But Saskatchewan was always a hinterland region for Winnipeg, Calgary and Edmonton. It is a province different from Alberta and Manitoba. It has much in common with North Dakota, a hinterland agricultural area completely dominated by economic interests in Minneapolis-St. Paul. This hinterland status, and how people have tried to cope with it, are basic to the political culture of the province.

Saskatchewan was founded after the destruction of the plains buffalo and the military defeat of the Aboriginal people on the continent. The policy of assimilation or extermination of the Aboriginal people has failed. Not only have they survived, they are growing in numbers and political and economic strength. But the province was founded on racist policies made by people who had racist views towards the Aboriginal people.

J. Rick Ponting of the University of Calgary has been tracking public attitudes on race and racism for a number of years. He notes that "Native issues remain on the periphery of Canadians' consciousness." In a "sympathy for Indians" index he has used to measure public attitudes, Saskatchewan rates lowest of all the provinces. Louise Carbert suggests that racial attitudes in Saskatchewan may be partly due to the "relative homogeneity" of the population. The province has had "the highest percentage of immigrants from the United States (15 percent) and Great Britain (59 percent) in the country, and the lowest proportion of immigrants from Asia and elsewhere." This is reflected in the 2001 census, which found the province to have one of the lowest percentages of immigrants. Among Canadian cities, Regina and Saskatoon had the lowest percentages of visible minorities. (Ponting, 1988; Carbert, 1997; Canada, 2003)

Women have always played an unrecognized and often subordinate role in Saskatchewan's economic and political system. While a women's movement developed in the 1970s, it has virtually disappeared. Until 1991 very few women were elected to political office. Women are generally in the lower paying jobs. Alberta and Saskatchewan are the only two provinces without pay equity legislation. In the farm community women have worked very hard both on the farm and off but are not seen to be farmers and are normally not owners of land. Women have been basically excluded from the newer resource extraction industries.

Environics' survey of social values found that the highest support for traditional "family values" in Canada is found in Saskatchewan. Despite the province's radical political traditions, patriarchal values and social patriarchy are deeply entrenched in the political culture. This remains a key area of discontent. (Adams, 2003)

Many social scientists argue that Saskatchewan's political culture also reflects its political history. A number of observers have pointed out that Manitoba was basically settled by people from Ontario who brought a Tory tradition with them. The highest percentage of immigrant settlers from the United States ended up in Alberta. But Saskatchewan had the highest percentage of settlers from Great Britain. It is argued that they brought with them the British political traditions of co-operatives, trade unions and Christian socialism. (see Laycock, 1990; Friesen, 1987)

Saskatchewan had the first social democratic government in North America. This was the only place in Canada where a social democratic party became the dominant party and the natural governing party. The province is characterized by the "mixed economy," which includes a strong commitment to co-operatives and Crown corporations. This is widely seen as a basic part of the political culture.

But is this changing? Over the 1990s the social democratic NDP government moved strongly towards a liberal ideology and policy which is scarcely different from that of the more formally right wing parties. The original populist democratic political thrust of the farmers and their allies who formed the party was in opposition to the capitalist class and their political allies. But today Saskatchewan populism is usually identified with a right wing politics that focuses its attack on the most vulnerable sectors of our society: Aboriginal people, poor people and women. A number of social scientists have argued that under the onslaught of the ideological revolution brought by Margaret Thatcher and Ronald Reagan, the political culture of Saskatchewan is changing. The result has been a rise in discontent and new forms of political protest.

## We Have Come a Long Way from the Days of Sod House

On the whole things are pretty good for most of the people who live in Saskatchewan. The average standard of living has greatly increased since Tommy Douglas' social democratic government, the Co-operative Commonwealth Federation (CCF), took office in 1944. Statistics Canada reports that in mid-2002 the income of the average wage earner in Saskatchewan was 10 percent below the Canadian average. But the cost of living is somewhat lower, due mainly to the price of new homes, which in 2003 was only 50 percent of the Canadian average. The median income of a classic two-parent family in Regina and Saskatoon was above the national average in 2003. The cold, harsh climate has its advantages; we are not overpopulated. A national public opinion poll found Canadians listed Regina at the bottom of the list of places where they would want to live.

Like most places in Canada, the provincial economy goes up and down, and in recent years has been affected by the impact of the drought on farm production. But we set a record in 2001 with 38,352 vehicles sold. The major purchases were by men in their forties, with SUVs and half-ton trucks preferred. (Elliott, June 2002)

In March the provincial government introduces the budget. The budget papers always include a table entitled "Intercity Comparison of Taxes and Household Charges," which compares major Canadian cities according to provincial and munic-

ipal taxes, mortgage costs, home heating, electricity, telephone and automobile insurance for a family with an income of $75,000. Saskatoon, the provincial base, is almost
always the lowest cost city, even including the major cities in the Atlantic provinces.
In Saskatchewan you can survive on a lower income.

Over the years 2000-3 the mass media was full of stories about the effects of the
persistent drought on the Saskatchewan farmer. The drought may not be over, and
it has had a serious impact on farmers, particularly those with cattle and no pasture
or feed. The cattle industry was hard hit in 2003 by the loss of markets due to the discovery of bovine spongiform encephalopathy (BSE). The Farm Credit Corporation
has approved "postponement" of farm loan payments for farmers affected by the
drought and BSE. But they believe that this is a temporary problem, similar to what
hog producers faced in the late 1990s. The FCC reports that 96 percent of its loans in
Saskatchewan are in good standing. (*Leader Post*, June 17, 2003)

The original Saskatchewan homesteader received a quarter section (160 acres)
and the option to buy another. The number of Saskatchewan farmers peaked in 1936
at 140,000. The 2001 Census of Agriculture reported that the number of farms in the
province had declined from 60,840 in 1991 to 50,598 in 2001. But the average size of a
farm is now 1,283 acres or two square miles! Farmers are leaving the land, but few are
going bankrupt. In 1991 there were around 225 bankruptcies, but this steadily declined to only 64 in 2001. According to the Census, the average Saskatchewan farm
has $680,525 in capital investments, $10,852 in outstanding debt, leaving a net worth
of $571,641. The *Farm Financial Survey 2002* reports that the average farm in Sas-
katchewan has grown; it has assets of $774,000 and liabilities of $137,000, leaving a
net worth of $667,000. That is not bad. Capital rich and cash poor, as they say.
Farmers know how to capitalize income. The reality is that today farmers are perhaps
the wealthiest group of people in the province. (Statistics Canada, 2002; *Sask Trends
Monitor*, May 2002; Saskatchewan Bureau of Statistics, June 2002; *Western Producer*,
January 22, 2004)

However, there is another Saskatchewan. Poverty and inequality remain. It is a
very serious problem in the North and among Aboriginal people. In 2002 the child
poverty rate was higher than the Canadian average, higher than all but three other
provinces and 55 percent higher than it was in 1980. Whereas the province had the
highest minimum wage in the 1970s, by 2002 it had fallen to one of the lowest. One
result has been the proliferation of "low wage jobs," defined by the United Nations as
less than two-thirds of the median wage. In 2000 29 percent of the jobs in Saskatchewan were low wage compared to 25 percent for the United States, which had the

highest percentage of all the industrialized countries. (Campaign 2000, 2003; Hunter and Miazdyck, 2003)

This is very evident to those who want to see it. The property crime rate is the highest in Canada. The break-and-enter rate is the highest. The incarceration rate is the highest. When I lived in North Central Regina, a low income area with high unemployment and relative poverty, our house was broken into three times, and our food was stolen each time. Young Aboriginal women, many teenagers, work on the streets as prostitutes, waiting to be picked up by white men in their expensive half ton trucks. The traffic explodes during Agribition when the farmers come into the city. The cars, trucks and SUVs stream up the alleys buying drugs from local dealers, often youth gangs. Needles are in the streets and alleys.

My current house is on an alley next to a large food store. Youth gangs spray graffiti on the walls and garages. Kids sit and sniff gasoline in the summer. Low income men and women root through the dumpsters for bottles and food. Intoxicated men sleep in the caragana hedges next to my house. Men park in the alley at night and throw their condoms out the windows. This general situation of urban degeneration has become much worse over the past ten years.

Nevertheless, on the whole Saskatchewan is a good place to live. It is not overcrowded. There are all kinds of recreation opportunities. With a lower population and fewer vehicles, our air is less polluted. We have relatively few yuppies and no visible class of wealthy exploiters. The province still has a lot of the small town atmosphere and the progressive political tradition. No columnists from the *National Post* or the *Globe and Mail* would choose to live here.

## Continental Integration

World War II signaled a major change in Canadian political economy. There was a decided break with Great Britain and a shift towards economic, military and political integration with the United States. This was institutionalized during the Cold War, when the U.S. government was the unchallenged leader of the industrialized capitalist countries dedicated to the containment and elimination of communism. Canada was a junior partner of the U.S. government in a range of military organizations, from the North Atlantic Treaty Organization (NATO), to the North American Aerospace Defence Command (NORAD), the North American Defence Production Agreement, to the treaties promoting the development and manufacture of nuclear and chemical and biological weapons.

The Korean War brought a new U.S. policy. The administration of Harry S. Truman was concerned because the United States increasingly had to rely on the importation of strategic minerals for the war machine. The government's Paley Report, released in 1952, called on the United States to defend the "free world's economies" by opposing communism as well as the rise of nationalism. Countries should be encouraged to attract private investment in resource extraction, particularly through U.S. corporations. There was a fear expressed of nationalism and attempts by governments to try to preserve their key natural resources for their own use. The Paley commission was pleased to report that there was no "bad investment climate" in Canada. The role of Canada was to be the natural resource reserve for the U.S. military machine. The processing of natural resources should be done in the United States in order to maximize job creation. The report called for a continental agreement to guarantee U.S. access to Canadian resources, particularly oil and natural gas. (see Clark-Jones, 1987)

The U.S. government regularly asked for a continental energy agreement with Canada. But it wasn't until the election of President Ronald Reagan in 1980 that the U. S. Government began to push for a more formal and complete continental integration. In this he was supported by big business interests in both the United States and Canada. The opening came with the election of Brian Mulroney and the Progressive Conservative government in 1984. The result was the Canada-U.S. Free Trade Agreement (CUFTA) in 1987 and the North American Free Trade Agreement (NAFTA), including Mexico, in 1994. (see Warnock, 1988; Merrett, 1996; Cameron and Watkins, 1993)

Our political leaders, business organizations, economists and liberal academics all insisted that free trade would lead to a diversification of Canada's trade and less dependence on the United States. The political economists, popular groups, and the political left all denied this would happen. They feared that the regional agreements would lead to "Fortress North America," with Canada in a clearly subordinate relationship to the United States. This has certainly happened. Canada's trade with the United States increased from 78 percent of the total in 1984 to over 86 percent in 2001. Trade with other countries declined in importance. Even Canada's agricultural trade became more dependent on the U.S. market.

Foreign ownership of Canadian industry fell between 1971 and 1988, but that trend was reversed by the free trade agreements. By 1999 Statistics Canada reported that there were more than 6,800 U.S.-owned companies in Canada, and most were medium to large subsidiaries of American corporations. Their revenues were growing faster than those of Canadian companies. As in the past, 98.5 percent of new U.S. investment in Canada was for the takeover of existing Canadian companies. The United States accounted for 67 percent of foreign direct investment in Canada by 2000, and Canada's net liability to foreigners was $203.4 billion. (*Globe and Mail*, February 1, 1999; March 28, 2002).

In November 1996 the World Trade Organization released a special report which expressed concern over the structure of Canada's trade. Only 50 corporations accounted for around one half of Canada's exports. Furthermore, 45 percent of Canada's trade with the United States was intracompany trade between U.S. subsidiaries and their U.S. parents. This was not free trade but administered trade, subject to financial manipulation. The WTO also expressed concern about "the potential vulnerability of the Canadian economy deriving from such reliance on one large trading partner, on a handful of 'traditional' industries, and on relatively few large-scale plants." (Drohan, 1996)

## Advancing Continental Integration

The terrorist attack on the World Trade Center and the Pentagon on September 11, 2001 created new problems for Canada-U.S. relations. On the one hand, the U.S. had been promoting a policy of economic integration of Canada and Mexico into the U.S. sphere of influence. Canada provides the United States with cheap natural resources, including energy. Mexico provides U.S. corporations, sweat shop enterprises and farmers with cheap labour. This policy required almost free movement of professional and business people and goods across the international borders. But concern over terrorism led the U.S. government to greatly increase surveillance and control at border crossings, which quickly proved to be a major barrier to trade and economic integration. (McKenna, 2002)

The Liberal government in Canada co-operated with the U.S. government. In 2002 they adopted the Free and Secure Trade (FAST) initiative; this will allow shipments and drivers to avoid much of the border hassles. They adopted the NEXUS program to help "pre-approved" travellers cross the border. In 2003 the Bush administration announced that all visitors to the United States, including Canadians, will shortly have to present a passport and have their photo and fingerprints taken at the border; there was no protest from the government in Ottawa.

The U.S. government pushed the Canadian government to harmonize policies on the status of immigrants and refugees. In 2002 the Chretien government complied with Bill C-11. The Safe Third Country Agreement with the U.S. in September 2002 was also designed to co-ordinate policy on refugees. (Foster and Dillon, 2003)

Canadians were stunned when President Bush announced in April 2002 that the U.S. government was going to create a Northern Command (NORTHCOM), a new U.S. military zone which covered the entire North American continent, including the Canadian Arctic. NORTHCOM was to be operated completely under U.S. military command. The U.S. commander would also be in control of NORAD. Commentators noted that this was a major infringement on Canada's political sovereignty. The U.S. government is also pushing Canada to participate in a new anti-ballistic missile system, and the new Liberal government under Paul Martin has indicated that it will comply. (see Clarkson, 2002)

Major business interests in Canada have called for an even greater integration of Canada into the United States. They have proposed that the Canadian currency be replaced by the U.S. currency. The stated goal would be a customs union with the United States which would include harmonizing all business rules and regulations. North America would form a "common perimeter" rather than two separate countries. The border would virtually disappear. (see Clarkson, 2002; Hurtig, 2002)

The administration of George W. Bush also moved towards a unilateralist stance in foreign and military policy, ignoring the opinion of traditional allies. President Bush rejected the Kyoto Accord on climate change, expanded protectionism through the use of non-tariff barriers to trade, refused to seek United Nations' approval for the war against al-Qaeda bases and the Taliban government in Afghanistan, attacked Iraq without the support of the U.N. Security Council or its major NATO allies, announced the militarization of space and the cancellation of the anti-ballistic missile and non-proliferation treaties, announced opposition to treaties to control chemical and biological weapons, and declared that no American would ever appear before any international court of justice. They sabotaged the international treaty to control small arms and undermined the United Nations Convention against Terror in order to keep UN inspectors out of Guantanamo Bay. (see Clarkson, 2002)

The Liberal government under Jean Chretien changed Canada's policy during the U.S. and U.K. war against Afghanistan. They chose not to place Canadian forces under the policing and humanitarian operation headed by Great Britain. Instead, Canadian soldiers in Afghanistan were put directly under U.S. command for offensive military action. Furthermore, all individuals captured by Canadian forces during this military operation were turned over to the U.S. military who would screen them, and suspected terrorists were sent to the U.S. penal colony at

Guantanamo Bay, Cuba. This was of concern to many Canadians, for the Bush Administration had declared that these prisoners were not covered by the 1949 Geneva Convention on prisoners of war and that U.S. principles of justice did not operate there because it was foreign territory. (Leblanc and Mahoney, 2002)

Jean Chretien chose not to join with the Bush administration as part of the "coalition of the willing" in the invasion and occupation of Iraq in March 2003. However, Canada stepped up its naval forces in the Persian Gulf as part of the "war on terrorism" and expanded the commitment of Canadian forces in Afghanistan. The additional forces sent to Afghanistan were now placed under the International Security Assistance Force (ISAF), led by NATO but including non-NATO countries. This force was "sanctioned" by the U.N. Security Council but is not a UN operation. The ISAF was composed of military forces from 18 European countries and New Zealand, under NATO command. The entire force is there to protect Harmid Karzai, the U.S. proconsul hand picked by George W. Bush. In Afghanistan he is referred to as "the Mayor of Kabul." The rest of the country is controlled by the local "warlords." (*Globe and Mail*, January 2, 2002; February 13, 2003; Pilger, 2003)

Despite the militaristic character of the U.S. government of President George W. Bush, no one was quite prepared for the declaration of imperial status that came with the release of the U.S. National Security Strategy paper on September 22, 2002. The U.S. government declared that it would do everything in its power to sustain permanent military dominance over all other countries. The Bush Administration pronounced that it "has no intention of allowing any foreign power to catch up with the huge lead the United States has opened since the fall of the Soviet Union." A direct warning was given to China. Abandoning international law and the Charter of the United Nations, the U.S. administration declared the right to make "preemptive military strikes" against states deemed to be a threat. The U.S. government reserved the right of "regime change," direct intervention into the internal affairs of independent countries to change governments, even using military force. Iraq was seen as the first test case of the new doctrine. President George W. Bush declared that "America's values are right and true for every person in every society." (Text on the White House web site: www.whitehouse.gov)

Thomas Friedman is a columnist with the *New York Times* and is considered to be one of the key political supporters of the Bush administration. He summed up the new American political doctrine:

> The hidden hand of the market will never work without a hidden fist—
> McDonald's cannot flourish without a McDonnell Douglas, the builder of

the F-15. And the hidden fist that keeps the world safe for Silicon Valley's technologies is called the United States Army, Air Force, Navy and Marine Corps. Without America on duty, there will be no America On Line. (*New York Times*, March 28, 1999)

## Continentalism and Neoliberalism

The continental free trade agreements were part of a general policy shift in North America and around the world. Beginning during World War II, Canadian governments embraced a policy package now generally known as the Keynesian welfare state. This included the promotion of full employment, tax changes which had a goal of reducing the inequalities of income and wealth, the expansion of universal social programs, and the regulation of private industry for the benefit of society as a whole. With the onset of the first world recession in 1974-5, the owners of capital, the large corporations and their supporters in universities and "think tanks" began pressing for major changes. They wanted to go back to the days before the Great Depression of the 1930s and to revive the policies of the free market, free trade, and advancing the rights of private property.

The new policy package is commonly referred to as "globalization" in North America. Elsewhere around the world, including Mexico and Latin America, it is referred to as "neoliberalism," indicating it is a return to the policy of the early period of liberal capitalism. The goal of this new policy is to reduce government involvement in the economy, reduce the welfare state, reduce the power of trade unions, and to lower taxes on corporations and the rich. This has been the major thrust of governments since the election of Margaret Thatcher's Tory government in Great Britain in 1979 and Republican President Ronald Reagan in the United States in 1980. (see Shields and Evans, 1998; McBride and Shields, 1997; Teeple, 1995; Warnock, 1988)

There is no question that the move towards free trade, neoliberal economic and social policies, and continental integration has been beneficial to some. All of the big business organizations in Canada continue to strongly support the free trade agreements and the neoliberal model of minimal government. They have strong support from all of the right-wing "think tanks" like the Fraser Institute and the C. D. Howe Institute. This should come as no surprise, for the free trade agreements were designed to facilitate the movement of capital between countries, help corporations find cheaper labour, and reduce environmental, health and safety and other regulations. The volume of trade has increased significantly, as has foreign investment. But most people do not depend on investments for their living.

It is not surprising that other sectors of Canadian society have been much more skeptical of the free trade agreements, right from the beginning. As the Economic Policy Institute points out, the free trade agreements "explicitly excluded any protections for working people in the form of labour standards, worker rights, and the maintenance of social investments." And as they concluded in their review in 2001, the North American Free Trade Agreement (NAFTA) had "undercut the hard-won social contract in all three nations." Bruce Campbell, who wrote the Canadian section of the report, found that per capita income declined for the first seven years of NAFTA, there was an upward redistribution of income to the richest 20 percent of Canadians, a decline in stable, full time employment, and a major attack on Canada's social safety net. (Economic Policy Institute, 2001)

The agricultural sector of the economy was supposed to prosper under free trade. A study by Public Citizen Global Trade Watch in 2001 concluded that while Canadian agricultural exports grew by $6 billion between 1993 and 1999, net farm income to farmers fell by $600 million. This was confirmed in a study by the National Farmers Union which also found that net farm income had steadily declined under the free trade regime. The large agribusiness organizations were the main beneficiaries of increased exports under the free trade agreements. (Public Citizen, 2001; National Farmers Union, 2000)

Under the free trade regime from 1989 to 1999, personal disposable income per capita actually declined. For the bottom 20 percent of families with children, their earned income fell by 29 percent between 1984 and 1994. The biggest jump in inequality, using the Gini coefficient of income distribution as a guide, occurred after 1994, the year that NAFTA came into effect. (Graham, 2002; Jackson and Robinson, 2000; Curtis, 1999)

Wealth distribution is much more unequal in Canada. The latest *Survey of Financial Security* by Statistics Canada found that the top 20 percent of Canadians owned 68 percent of all wealth. The lowest 20 percent owned nothing; indeed, their debts exceed their assets by an average of around $7,000! On the prairies, the richest 20 percent of family units had assets worth on average $1.1 million while the poorest 20 percent had an average net debt of $5,655. The huge disparities in wealth belie the myth that Canada is a more generous and egalitarian country than the United States. (Kerstetter, 2002)

The neoliberal regime implemented by the governments of Brian Mulroney and Jean Chretien have used tax policies to increase the influence and power of corporations and the wealthy. Income taxes have been cut for people in the higher brackets.

Inheritance and gift taxes have been abolished. Capital gains taxes have been dramatically cut. Corporate taxes have been cut. The Conservative-Liberal governments have shifted to the goods and service taxes, property taxes, and increased users fees for services, all of which fall heaviest on middle and lower income Canadians. Unemployment insurance has been gutted, and the premiums paid by workers are now used to balance the federal budget and pay down the debt. We have seen a major reversal of the taxation regime of the Keynesian welfare state, which was founded on the principle of taxation based on ability to pay. (Jackson and Robinson, 2000; Curtis, 1999; Shields and Evans, 1998; McBride and Shields, 1997)

Under the new policy direction we have seen the privatization of Crown corporations and government services and an extensive deregulation of economic activity. Regional development programs and equalization grants to the poorer provinces have been cut. The federal government has cut back its financial contributions to and regulation of health care, post-secondary education and social services. Appropriations for cultural programs have been downsized. The general thrust of social policy is away from universality, or the right to a program on the basis of citizenship, to one of targeting special groups for inclusion or for exclusion. The Child Tax Benefit, for example, was designed to discriminate against lone parent families on social assistance. Across Canada the minimum wage has declined in real terms. (Jackson and Robinson, 2000; Shields and Evans, 1998; McBride and Shields, 1997)

The Mulroney and Chretien governments have been successful in their primary goal, to reduce the role of government in the economy. Federal program spending as a percentage of the gross domestic product has fallen from a high of 19.2 percent in 1983 to only 11.5 percent in 2002. This is a dramatic change. It explains why there seems to be a "shortage" of funds for health care, education and social programs needed to attack poverty. Total spending on income security programs by all three levels of government peaked in 1991 and since then has steadily declined. The economy certainly creates enough wealth for all these programs. Governments are simply not acquiring revenues through taxation. Instead, they have opted to increase the income and wealth of the upper 20 percent of the population. (Graham, 2002; Jackson and Robinson, 2000)

How have Canadians managed to cope with these changes? Families have worked longer hours and have added more family members to the paid work force. There are more people with multiple jobs, mainly women and youth. Overtime work has increased. At the same time, Canadians have had to cope with the decline in regular, full time jobs and the rise in non-standard or "precarious" work: part time employment, contract work, temporary work, casual labour, and the growth of self-employment, all of which normally pay less and have fewer benefits. The number of low paid jobs (a job that pays less than two-thirds of the median wage for all workers) has been rising, accounting for 25 percent of all workers in 1997. In Saskatchewan, low wage workers account for 29 percent of all employees. The hardest hit workers have been young workers (age 20-24) who have seen their average income fall by 24 percent during the period of free trade and neoliberalism. Families have more or less maintained their standard of living over the past fifteen years, but only by working harder and longer. (Jackson and Robinson, 2000)

## Persistent Economic Problems

Saskatchewan, as a resource based export economy, has always been particularly vulnerable to changes in the world economy. Those who promoted the shift in policy orientation to neoliberalism claimed that the changes would free up more private capital for investment, increase the rate of economic growth and boost employment. But this did not happen. For the rich countries which make up the Organization for Economic Co-operation and Development (Europe, U.S., Japan, Canada, Australia and New Zealand), annual per capita income growth rates during the period from 1960-79 averaged 3.4 percent; between 1980 and 1998, they fell to only 1.8 percent. For the developing countries (including China) the per capita income growth rate in the first period averaged 2.5 percent but fell to 0.0 percent in the second period. The era of globalization has produced lower general rates of economic growth. (Easterly, 2000)

One of the central effects of this change to neoliberalism has been the rise in inequality and the persistence of poverty around the world. In 1996 the United Nations Development Programme (UNDP) issued a major report on the rise in inequality. For the poorest 20 percent of the world's population, their share of the world's gross domestic product declined from 2.3 percent to 1.4 percent over the period from 1965-95. In contrast, the share which went to richest 20 percent rose from 70 percent to 85 percent. As the UNDP noted, "the assets of the world's 358 billionaires exceed the combined annual incomes of countries with 45 percent of the world's people." The gap in per capita income between the industrialized world and the developing world tripled from $5,700 to $15,400. The International Monetary Fund (IMF) reached a similar conclusion. Not only is the world's inequality greater than at any time in history, the inequality is steadily increasing. (IMF, 2000; UNDP, 1996)

But as the studies all noted, the rise of inequality is not just between the rich industrialized countries of the North and the less developed countries of the South. There is also a strong trend towards inequality in income, wealth and status *within* almost all countries, including the richest. The UNDP sees this as a major development during the neoliberal period of the 1980s and 1990s and attributes it to "jobless growth" over the period, "ruthless growth" where the "fruits of economic growth mostly benefit the rich," and what they call "voiceless growth," with the decline of democracy, lack of empowerment, the rise of political repression, authoritarian governments, and the decline of the trade union movement. The poor and women are the primary victims in this discrimination. Minority cultures are being swamped. The poor live in areas where they suffer from the loss of access to natural resources and resource destruction. This destruction "is increasing, driven overwhelmingly by demand in the rich countries." They note that even in the most advanced countries of the OECD, 100 million people live below the poverty line and five million are homeless. (UNDP, 1996, 2001; Cornia and Court, 2001)

One of the most widely cited studies of growing inequality was done by Branko Milanovic of the World Bank. Using household incomes, he covered 91 countries representing 84 percent of the world's population. He found world inequality very high. The richest one percent of the world's population receives as much income per year as the poorest 57 percent. Milanovic asks: "We can wonder how long such huge inequalities may persist in the face of ever closer contacts, not least through television and movies, where opulent lifestyles of the rich influence expectations and often breed resentment among the poor." He argues that this inequality promotes immigration, economic refugees, and "breeds terrorism." (Milanovic, 2002)

The international economic and financial institutions, controlled by representatives from the First World, have imposed a new economic regime on the weaker countries of the Third World. Mark Weisbrot and his associates at the Center for Economic and Policy Research in Washington, D.C. argue that for low and middle-income countries, the past twenty years under the policies of neoliberalism have been "the worst economic failure since the Great Depression." For Latin America and the Caribbean income per capita increased by only seven percent between 1980 and 2000. Africa experienced a 15 percent *decline* in per capita income over the past two decades. Progress also slowed on "major social indicators such as life expectancy, infant and child mortality, literacy and education." The key, Weisbrot and his colleagues argue, is the move away from pursuit of "country-specific development strategies" to the open market strategy supported by the "Washington Consensus:" the

U.S. government, the World Bank and the International Monetary fund. The most serious international economic problem at the end of the 20th century was the growing gap in income and wealth between the advanced, industrialized countries and the less developed world. (Weisbrot, 2001)

The disparity between the rich and the poor extends to the use of natural resources by the industrialized countries. Just before the World Summit on Sustainable Development began in 2002, the United Nations Environment Programme (UNEP) released a report condemning the consumer culture of North America. With only five percent of the world's population, the United States and Canada use 25 percent of the world's energy. The UNEP singled out the costs of urban sprawl, the shift towards bigger houses, and the popular automobile culture as major problems. While the size of families has declined in North America over the past 30 years, the average size of a new house has increased 48 percent. The U.S. uses nine times the world average of gasoline for automobiles and leaves an "ecological footprint" that is 4.4 times the world's average. For the United States, this can only be accomplished by sucking up resources from around the world, particularly energy. (UNEP, August 2002)

In the same month World Wildlife Federation International reported that the world was consuming natural resources at a rate that was 20 percent above the level of regeneration, and at the current level of population and economic growth, this figure would "skyrocket" over the next 50 years. This over consumption, primarily by the industrialized countries, is eating into the world's natural stock of fertile soil, fish, and forests, while dumping excess carbon dioxide into the atmosphere. Human expansion is leading to a steady decline in animal life. Their conclusion was echoed by a group of prominent California economists and ecologists associated with Redefining Progress. They found that in 1961 humans used 70 percent of the planet's annual potential for biological productivity, but by 1999 this had risen to 120 percent. The current levels of human economic development are not sustainable and it is not within the regenerative capacity of the biosphere. (WWF International, 2002; Wilson, 2002)

## A New General Economic Crisis?

The Canadian economy did very well in the first few years of the 21st century. It did much better than the U.S. economy while the speculative bubble of the U.S. stock markets was deflating from March 2000 into 2003. But there is still considerable uncertainty because of general developments in the world economy. Many political economists see the world capitalist economy as facing a number of ongoing serious problems.

The move towards neoliberalism produced one expected result: a dramatic increase in the amount of capital in the world. The wide-ranging reduction in taxation served to increase the share of the wealth created by the productive economy going to the class of owners of capital. The result was the creation of surplus capital and significant overinvestment in a whole range of industries, the creation of excess capacity in manufacturing and retailing, and unsold inventory. The rate of investment significantly exceeded the growth in final demand. As the *Far East Economic Review* (October 1, 1998) put it in the midst of the Asian economic crisis, the excess capacity was "stunning" and characteristic of "virtually every sector across the region." As they noted: "Supply far outstrips demand. Basic materials, steel, cars, petrochemical, semiconductors—the list rolls on." A few years later, in the middle of the U.S. economic slowdown, *Business Week* (April 9, 2001) proclaimed, "The U.S. economy is struggling with overcapacity as far as the eye can see."

Because there is a surplus of capital, and a surplus of industrial capacity, it is no longer possible for owners of capital to find good investments which yield the usual seven or eight percent return based on production and sales. Corporate profits were at their lowest levels since the Great Depression. Capital shifted from investment in enterprises to speculation in the financial markets. (*The Economist*, December 6, 2001)

The third major characteristic of the present economic system is the significant rise in personal and corporate debt. In the western industrialized countries, total debt (government, corporate and private) remained relatively steady between the end of World War II and 1980. Government debt declined, replaced by increased corporate and private debt. But beginning with the recession of 1980-1, private and corporate debt began to skyrocket. For example, in the United States in 1980 total outstanding debt was around 150 percent of gross domestic product. By the year 2000 it had risen to around 270 percent of GDP. Financial sector debt rose from 20 percent of GDP to 85 percent.

There has been a dramatic increase in private household debt over that period. As a percentage of personal disposable income, in early 2002 it had risen to 105 percent in the United States, 115 percent in Germany, 118 percent in Great Britain, and 132 percent in Japan. Household debt in Canada has been going up at a similar rate, around six percent per year. Annual personal savings, which had been at a rate of 2.5 percent of income per year, had vanished. (*Economist*, January 24, 2002)

Corporate debt has been rising at an unsustainable rate. The *Wall Street Journal* (January 1, 2002) reported that U.S. corporate debt was growing twice as fast as the growth in corporate asset values and twice as fast as output. Total U.S. corporate debt had reached 48 percent of GDP, the highest in history. This has now been matched by the rise of huge budget deficits and debt by the U.S. federal government, fueled by President George W. Bush's tax cuts for the rich.

This period of growth in debt has also been characterized by a series of major financial crises. There was Mexico in 1994, Asia in 1997, Russia and Long Term Capital Management in 1998, Argentina-Uruguay-Brazil in 2002, and the general collapse of U.S. markets in 2000-3 which was combined with widespread corporate and accounting scandals. The crisis of 2002 was described by *Fortune Magazine* (June 26, 2002):

> Phony earnings, inflated revenues, conflicted Wall Street analysts, directors asleep at the switch—this isn't just a few bad apples we're talking about here. This, my friends, is a systemic breakdown. Nearly every known check on corporate behaviour—moral, regulatory, you name it—fell by the wayside, replaced by the stupendous greed that marked the end of the bubble. And that has created a crisis of investor confidence the likes of which hasn't been seen—well since the Great Depression.

At the beginning of 2004, political economists, economists and Wall Street business economists were all discussing another major economic problem. The United States, by far the world's most powerful economy, has a persistent and growing trade deficit. Prior to 1988 the United States was a creditor nation lending more capital to others than it borrowed. But this has dramatically changed. Over the past 20 years the United States has run a deficit on its export-import account. By 2003 it had reached $6.3 billion or around 60 percent of U.S. gross domestic product. In 2003 the balance of payments deficit reached $500 billion. This is covered by borrowing $1.5 billion per day, which takes around 40 percent of the world's savings. (Roach, 2003; Greider, 2002)

On the surface, it appears that the U.S. and world economies are on the way back from the losses of the 2000-3 period. Investors are back in the stock markets. U.S. figures for economic growth are rising. But does this signal that the long term economic problems are over? Stephen Roach, chief economist for Morgan Stanley in New York, is skeptical:

> After all these years, a U.S.-centric world now makes for an increasingly dysfunctional global economy. Moreover, courtesy of SARS, runaway U.S. budget deficits, and lingering structural problems in Japan and Europe, the major risk is that the imbalances are about to get worse—possibly

a lot worse. There is nothing like the romance of postwar recoveries and cyclical revivals. For those of us who choose instead to remain cold, calculating, and unemotional, the world still looks like a very treacherous place. Call me a dreamcatcher. (Roach, 2003)

## The Changing Environment

In Saskatchewan people have always assumed a supportive environment. There is a low level of population, the wide open spaces, the friendly wind from Alberta, and lots of good clean fresh air. Urban smog is found elsewhere. There has always been some pollution from industrial agriculture, but it is deemed a price to be paid for a modern agricultural economy. But there may be limits to this tolerance. Recently there has been the SARS flu scare, the BSE problem, and avian influenza or bird flu. Chronic wasting disease has spread through the domesticated deer and elk herds in the province, the European Union has again stated that they don't want Canadian beef that has been fed growth hormones, scientists have confirmed that the genes from genetically engineered crops spread to other plants and create superweeds resistant to herbicides, organic farmers are seeking damages in court from agribusiness corporations for the loss of their canola markets due to genetic pollution, and local rural communities are fighting the expansion of giant hog barns.

People in urban Saskatchewan assume that they have clean water. But that complacency was broken in 2001 when 7,000 people in North Battleford became ill from drinking city water that was polluted by the parasite crypto sporidium. The previous year the city had to deal with coliform contamination of its water. The main cause of the problem was a combination of low levels of water in the North Saskatchewan River, animal and human waste contamination of the river, and the lack of government inspection of the plant and its operations. The North Battleford crisis brought attention to the general problem of the relative shortage of water in the province, its contamination from industrial agriculture, and the threat to supply in rural areas from the promotion of intensive livestock operations, particularly giant corporate hog barns.

The steadily increasing use of agricultural chemicals and fertilizers is starting to damage the water supply. For example, in 1999 Agriculture Canada released the results of a study of rainfall in the Lethbridge area, which found many common pesticides. In some of the samples the herbicide 2,4-D was found at "extremely high, unacceptable levels." A 1998 study of farm dugouts in Saskatchewan found herbicide and insecticide residues in all of them. A Canada-Saskatchewan Green Plan survey in 1997 found pesticides in many wells; the high was 45 percent of the wells in the Outlook-Davidson area. Nitrates from fertilizers and animal manure were found in 40 to 80 percent of the wells in different areas around the province. In 2001 and 2002 eighty-one small towns and rural municipalities in the province issued boil water warnings or were shut down because of contamination for E.coli bacteria. It finally became public knowledge that poor water quality is a serious problem on almost every Indian reserve in the province. (Sask Environment, 2002; Safe Drinking Water Foundation, 2002; Peterson, 2000)

Over a ten month period, Brij Verma took regular samples of water from the South Saskatchewan River for the National Hydrology Research Centre in Saskatoon. Tetracycline showed up in almost every sample. This antibiotic is widely used in intensive livestock operations. In 2002 the U.S. Geological Survey found pharmaceutical contamination in 80 percent of 139 streams monitored. Prescription drugs have become a serious water contamination problem in North America. (Warick, 2002)

The other major environmental concern in the province is the loss of forests due to clear cut logging. Over 90 percent of harvesting is done by clear cutting, and at best the forests are replaced with plantations that have no structural diversity. Forest fires become more frequent. Soil erosion increases, and soil quality declines. Fish habitat is destroyed. Lakes experience a rise in acidity and high rates of mercury contamination. Pest infestations increase. Water tables decline and wetlands dry up. Biological diversity declines. The carbon balance is changed. The provincial government's annual allowable cut, supposedly established to maintain the sustainability of the forest, had been set at 0.7 million cubic metres of wood. However, in 2002 the actual cut was around 4.5 million cubic metres. (Natural Resources Canada, 2002b)

## The Dark Cloud of Global Warming and Climate Change

Unfortunately, people living in Saskatchewan cannot hide from what is going on in the rest of the world. There is no way to avoid environmental problems that cross national and provincial boundaries. The biggest threat right now to Saskatchewan is from global warming and climate change. In January 2001 the United Nations' Intergovernmental Panel on Climate Change (IPCC) reported that the average surface temperature is increasing at a faster rate than they had projected five years earlier. They concluded that "we must move ahead boldly with clean energy technologies, and we should start preparing ourselves now for rising sea levels, changing rain patterns, and other impacts of global warming." The panel of world-renowned scientists had already concluded that to stabilize the world's climate we need a *70 percent reduction* in greenhouse gas emissions from the 1990 level. This requires a major shift from the use of fossil fuels.

Greenhouse gas emissions also reflect world power and domination by the industrialized, capitalist countries, led by the United States. Most of the world's pollution is being created by these countries. For example, the carbon dioxide emissions in metric tonnes per person in 1997 varied from 20.1 for the United States and 17.2 for Canada to only 2.9 for China and 1.1 for India. The United States now imports 60 percent of the oil it uses. Their dependence on imported fuels and raw materials helps us to understand U.S. foreign, military and economic policy. (Starke, 2002; Athanasiou, 1996; Brown, 1998)

At the 2002 World Summit on Sustainable Development in Johannesburg, the United States, Canada, Australia and Japan were identified as "an axis of environmental evil" for ignoring the plight of the environment and the world's poor. The delegates from the United States, Canada and the oil producing countries in the Middle East used their power to water down proposals to expand the use of clean, renewable energy technologies and opposed the resolution to require the industrialized countries to phase out their subsidies to the fossil fuel industries. (MacGregor, 2002)

The Canadian government, which signed and ratified the Kyoto Accord on global warming, has pledged to reduce our emissions by only six percent by 2012. Nevertheless, this modest proposal has faced strong opposition in Saskatchewan from the New Democratic Party governments of Roy Romanow and Lorne Calvert, the Saskatchewan Party, the provincial Liberals when aligned to the NDP, and of course the federal Reform-Alliance-Conservative Party. (Brown, 1999; Warnock, 2002)

However, Saskatchewan is already feeling the impact of global warming and climate change. Elaine Wheaton, a climatologist with the Saskatchewan Research Council, has argued that if governments continue to do nothing, we will face another dust bowl situation. David Schindler of the University of Alberta, who has done extensive research in this area, projects devastation to the boreal forests from increased forest fires, insect and disease infestations, and the failure to regenerate in hot, dry conditions. Boreal forests cover over half of Saskatchewan. (Schindler, 1998)

In July 2002 glaciologists at the University of Alaska reported that glaciers in Alaska and Canada are thinning much more rapidly than previously thought. The glaciers in the Rocky Mountains are melting, and the run-off which feeds the prairie rivers is starting to decline. In 2001 the flow of water in the Saskatchewan River was only 57 percent of normal. Natural Resources Canada projects that global warming will "significantly affect water resources in Canada, likely resulting in severe drought on the prairies and additional financial troubles for farmers." (Canada, 2002a; Mitchell, 2000; IISD, 2000; Pembina Institute, 1998)

The 2002 report from Natural Resources Canada predicted that with growing shortages, political jurisdictions would fight over water rights. As the drought spread through Alberta in that year, Premier Ralph Klein said it would probably be necessary to trap more water from the mountain runoff in Alberta rather than let it flow on to Saskatchewan. (Natural Resources Canada, 2002a)

Saskatchewan's forests are disappearing, and few seem to know or care. Environmental pollution is becoming a serious problem, but the province's political and business leaders prefer to look the other way. Global climate change is a major problem for everyone. The good life in Saskatchewan is threatened by the accumulated impact of over-consumption and environmental degradation, often described as the "culture of excess." Few want to face these challenges, hoping they will just go away. (see Roach, 2002)

## Political Changes Come to Saskatchewan

Saskatchewan has a long tradition of social democracy stretching back to the days of the Co-operative Commonwealth Federation (CCF) governments of Tommy Douglas and Woodrow Lloyd (1944-64). During the New Democratic Party (NDP) government of Alan Blakeney (1971-82) there was a general expansion of social programs. Ross Thatcher's Liberal government (1964-71), though ideologically committed to "free enterprise" and the promotion of business interests, made few changes in social programs. This was a recognition of widespread popular support for social democratic values throughout Saskatchewan society.

Since the formation of the province, there has been a left/right political polarization. The progressive farmers' movement was opposed by private business interests and those on the ideological right. The polarization intensified during the period of the CCF and NDP governments. Grant Devine's Progressive Conservative government was elected in 1982, just as the governments of Ronald Reagan in the United States and Margaret Thatcher in Great Britain were embarking on their neoliberal course. Devine's government took up the crusade attacking organized labour, privatizing most of the Crown corporations in the resource sector, and radically cutting the royalties and taxes on the resource extraction industries. With large budget deficits the result of the tax cuts, health and other social programs were cut. The political polarization intensified.

Grant Devine's Tories were crushed in the 1991 election. Public opinion polls clearly indicated that the Saskatchewan voters wanted a return to the social democratic mixed economy and the welfare state. However, there was no change in policy direction. Instead, the NDP government under Roy Romanow continued the policies begun by the Devine Tories. There was no return to the social democratic orientation of the Blakeney government. There was no change in policy direction when Roy Romanow stepped down as Premier and party leader and Lorne Calvert took his place.

This does not mean that the ideological polarization is gone. It is still there in the rhetoric of the leaders of the NDP and the opposition Saskatchewan Party. But in real terms, in key policy areas, there is very little difference between the two parties. Both advance the business agenda of cutting taxes and downsizing government. Both have pursued the privatization of Crown assets and contracting out government services. Both have stressed deregulation of the economy to make the investment climate more "business friendly." Both the Devine Tories and the NDP steadily reduced the taxation of natural resource extraction industries. Both supported a shift in taxation away from the ability to pay towards regressive taxes that fall heaviest on those in the lower income brackets. Both the Devine Tories and the NDP have come down hard on low income people and those forced to live on social assistance. Both have increased the rate of incarceration of Aboriginal and poor people.

One result of this has been a great deal of cynicism and disillusionment with politics. Since the 1991 election 40 percent of the eligible voters have stayed home and refused to vote. This is particularly the case for low income people who have concluded that the NDP no longer will support their needs. When in office, it is widely argued, the major parties all do the same thing. So the traditional political polarization has faded to a large extent.

The province now seems primarily polarized between the urban areas and the rural areas. Beginning with Grant Devine's election victory in 1982, NDP political support has declined in rural Saskatchewan. In office, the NDP adopted many policies which undermined their traditional supporters in rural Saskatchewan. The NDP now depends on the urban areas and the North for its electoral support.

As a result of the decline in the polarization on socio-economic policy, other issues have become more important politically. A new polarization has emerged around social issues. The political right strongly defends traditional patriarchal values. In this they have the support of the growing members of the Christian fundamentalist churches. The new right is opposed to abortion rights for women. They don't like sex education in schools. They do not like public sponsored child care. They are opposed to same sex marriage and the public rights which go with it. They want to curtail the Human Rights Commission which is seen as an institution promoting the rights of women and minorities. They strongly oppose gun registration which they believe is a conspiracy by women's groups to try to take away a basic right of men, the right to own and control weapons. There is a hostility to granting First Nations their land, resource and hunting and fishing rights as specified in the historic treaties.

On many of these issues the NDP has been silent. It does not advance women's rights, like pay equity and child care. It is silent on rights for gays and lesbians. The NDP took a strong public stand against gun registration. It has waffled on issues involving the rights of First Nations. It has acquired the reputation of being liberal on social issues largely by default; the Saskatchewan Party and other groups on the right only seem worse.

In the meantime, the more than 40 percent of the population who are disaffected with both the NDP and the Saskatchewan Party have dropped out of politics. The trend in Saskatchewan at this time is to move towards the U.S. political system: two major parties that are very similar on the important issues, they alternate holding office, and the majority of eligible voters do not think it is worth the time and effort to go to the polls.

This may be satisfactory for those people in leadership positions in the major parties. They have their time in office. Their supporters reap the benefits of good paying jobs for a number of years. But this system of government does not have the capability of dealing with major problems, whether they are economic or ecological. It may take a major crisis before people in Saskatchewan decide that this status quo needs to be changed.

# References

Adams, Michael. 2003. *Fire and Ice: The United States, Canada and the Myth of Converging Values.* Toronto: Penguin Canada.

Arscott, Jane and Linda Trimble. 1997. *In the Presence of Women: Representation in Canadian Governments.* Toronto: Harcourt Brace Canada.

Athanasiou, Tom. 1996. *Divided Planet: The Ecology of Rich and Poor.* Boston: Little Brown and Company.

Atwood, Margaret. 1972. *Survival: A Thematic Guide to Canadian Literature.* Toronto: Anansi.

Bradshaw, York W. and Michael Wallace. 1996. *Global Inequalities.* London: Pine Forge Press.

Brown, Lester *et al.*, eds. 1998. *Vital Signs 1998: The Environmental Trends That Are Shaping Our Future.* New York: W. W. Norton for the Worldwatch Institute.

Brown, Lorne A., Joseph K. Roberts and John W. Warnock. 1999. *Saskatchewan Politics from Left to Right '44 to '99.* Regina: Hinterland Publications.

Cameron, Duncan and Mel Watkins, eds. *Canada Under Free Trade.* Toronto: James Lorimer & Company.

Campaign 2000. 2003. *Honouring Our Promises: Meeting the Challenge to End Child and Family Poverty.* Toronto: Campaign 2000.; Regina: Social Policy Research Unit, University of Regina.

Canada. Natural Resources Canada. 2002a. *Climate Change Impacts and Adaptations: A Canadian Perspective.* Special paper on water resources. Ottawa: Natural Resources Canada.

Canada. Natural Resources Canada. 2002b. *The State of Canada's Forests 2001-2002.* Ottawa: Natural Resources Canada.

Canada. Statistics Canada. 2003. *Census of 2001.* Ottawa: Statistics Canada.

Carbert, Louise. 1997. "Governing on 'The Correct, the Compassionate, the Saskatchewan Side of the Border." In Arscott and Trimble, pp. 154-179.

Clark, S.D. 1968. *Canadian Society in Historical Development.* Toronto: McGraw-Hill Ryerson.

Clark-Jones, Melissa. 1987. *A Staple State: Canadian Industrial Resources in Cold War.* Toronto: University of Toronto Press.

Clarkson, Stephen. 2002. *Uncle Sam and Us: Globalization, Neoconservatism, and the Canadian State.* Toronto: University of Toronto Press.

Clements, Warren. 1993. "A Canadian is someone who carries traveler's cheques in a moneybelt." *Globe and Mail,* July 17, D-4.

Cornia, Giovanni Andrea and Julius Court. 2001. *Inequality, Growth and Poverty in the Era of Liberalization and Globalization.* Helsinki: United Nations University World Institute for Development Economics Research, Policy Brief No. 4.

Curtis, James *et al.*, eds. 1999. *Social Inequality in Canada: Patterns, Problems and Policies.* Scarborough: Prentice Hall Allyn and Bacon Canada.

Drohan, Madelaine. 1996. "Dependency on U.S. Leaves Canada 'Vulnerable': WTO." *Globe and Mail*, November 20, B-6.

Easterly, William. 2000. *The Lost Decade: Explaining Developing Countries Stagnation 1980-1999.* Washington, D.C.: World Bank, January. www.worldbank.org

Economic Policy Institute. 2001. *Nafta at Seven: Its Impact on Workers in All Three Nations.* Washington, D.C.: Economic Policy Institute.

Elliott, Doug. 2002. *Sask Trends Monitor*. Regina, Saskatchewan. www.sasktrends.ca

Foster, John W. and John Dillon. 2003. "NAFTA in Canada: The Era of a Supra-Constitution." In Hansen-Kuhn and Hellinger, pp. 83-115.

Friesen, Gerald. 1987. *The Canadian Prairies: A History*. Toronto: University of Toronto Press.

Graham, John R. *et al.*, eds. 2002. *Canadian Social Policy*. Toronto: Prentice Hall.

Greider, William. 2002. "The End of Empire." *The Nation*. September 23. www.thenation.com

Hansen-Kuhn, Karen and Steve Hellinger, eds. 2003. *Lessons from NAFTA: The High Cost of "Free Trade."* Ottawa: Canadian Centre for Policy Alternatives.

Hartz, Louis, ed. 1964. *The Founding of New Societies*. New York: Harcourt, Brace and World.

Hunter, Garson and Dionne Miazdyck. 2003. *Current Issues Surrounding Poverty and Welfare Programming in Canada: Two Reviews*. Regina: Social Policy Research Unit, University of Regina, SPR Working Papers, No. 21. August.

Hurtig, Mel. 2002. *The Vanishing Country: Is It Too Late To Save Canada?* Toronto: McClelland and Stewart.

International Institute for Sustainable Development. 2000. *Climate Canada: A Canadian Lens on Global Climate Change*. Winnipeg, International Institute for Sustainable Development.

International Monetary Fund. 2000. *World Economic Outlook*. Washington, D.C.: International Monetary Fund.

Jackson, Andrew and David Robinson. 2000. *Falling Behind: The State of Working Canada 2000*. Ottawa: Canadian Centre for Policy Alternatives.

Kerstetter, Steve. 2002. "Unequal Distribution of Wealth Rampant All Across Canada." *The CCPA Monitor*, Vol. 8, No. 9, March, p. 23.

Laycock, David. 1990. *Populism and Democratic Thought in the Canadian Prairies, 1910 to 1945.* Toronto: University of Toronto Press.

Leblanc, Daniel and Jill Mahoney. 2002. "Canada Opts for Combat Role." *Globe and Mail*, January 8, pp. A-1; A-6.

Lipset, Seymour Martin. 1963. *The First New Nation*. New York: Basic Books.

MacGregor, Karen. 2002. "UN Summit Begins with Canada, U.S. under Fire." *Globe and Mail*, August 27, A-1.

McBride, Stephen and John Shields. 1997. *Dismantling a Nation: The Transition to Corporate Rule in Canada*. Halifax: Fernwood Publishing, 2nd edition.

McKenna, Barrie. 2002. "Plans for a 'Modernized' Border Will Hit Canada Like a Freight Train." *Globe and Mail*, March 22, B-8.

McRae, Kenneth. 1964. "The Structure of Canadian History." In Hartz, pp. 219-274.

Merrett, Christopher D. 1996. *Free Trade: Neither Free Nor About Trade*. Montreal: Black Rose Books.

Milanovic, Branko. 2002. *True World Income Distribution, 1988 and 1993: First Calculation Based on Household Surveys Alone*. Updated to include 1998 data. Washington: The World Bank.

Mitchell, Alanna. 2000. "Prairie Today, Desert Tomorrow?" *Globe and Mail*, October 7, A-12-A-13.

National Farmers Union. 2000. "The Farm Crisis, EU Subsidies and Agribusiness Market Power." Presentation to the Senate Standing Committee on Agriculture and Forestry, February 17.

Pembina Institute. 1998. *Five Years of Failure: Federal and Provincial Government Inaction on Climate Change*. Calgary: The Pembina Institute.

Peterson, Hans G. 2000. "Rural Drinking Water and Waterborne Illness." Proceedings of the Ninth National Conference on Drinking Water. Regina: May 16-18.

Pilger, John. 2003. "Bush's Vietnam." *New Statesman*, June 22, 2003. www.newstatesman.org

Ponting, J. Rick. 1988. "Public Opinion on Aboriginal Peoples' Issues in Canada." *Canadian Social Trends II*, Winter, pp. 9-17.

Porter, John. 1965. *The Vertical Mosaic: An Analysis of Social Class and Power in Canada*. Toronto: University of Toronto Press.

Public Citizen Global Trade Watch. 2001. *Down on the Farm: NAFTA's Seven-Years War on Farmers and Ranchers in the U.S., Canada and Mexico*. Washington: Public Citizen Global Trade Watch. www.tradewatch.org

Roach, Stephen S. 2002. "The Costs of Bursting Bubbles." *The New York Times*, September 22. www.newyorktimes.com

Roach, Stephen S. 2003. "Dreamcatchers." Global Economic Forum, Morgan Stanley, April 21.

Safe Drinking Water Foundation. 2002. "Saskatchewan News Stories." See www.safewater.org

Saskatchewan Bureau of Statistics. 2002. *Economic Review*. Regina: Government of Saskatchewan.

Saskatchewan Environment. 2002. "North Battleford Water Inquiry." www.serm.gov.sk.ca

Shields, John and B. Mitchell Evans. 1998. *Shrinking the State: Globalization and Public Administration "Reform."* Halifax: Fernwood Publishing.

Schindler, David W. 1998. "A Dim Future for Boreal Waters and Landscapes." *Bioscience*, Vol. 48, No. 3, pp. 157-64.

Starke, Linda, ed. 2002. *State of the World 2002: A Worldwatch Institute Report on Progress Toward a Sustainable Society*. New York: W. W. Norton.

Teeple, Gary. 1999. *Globalization and the Decline of Social Reform.* Toronto: Garamond Press, 2nd edition.

United Nations Development Programme. 1996. *Human Development Report.* New York: Oxford University Press.

United Nations Development Programme. 2001. *Human Development Report.* New York: Oxford University Press.

United Nations Environment Programme. 2002. *North America's Environment: A Thirty-Year State of the Environment and Policy Perspective.* Washington, D.C.: UNEP Regional Office for North America, August.

Warick, Jason. 2002. "Drug Detected in Saskatchewan River." *Leader Post,* August 29, A-12.

Warnock, John W. 2002. "Kyoto and the NDP Government." *Briarpatch,* Vol. 31, No. 5, June, pp. 7-9.

Warnock, John W. 1988. *Free Trade and the New Right Agenda.* Vancouver: New Star Books.

Weisbrot, Mark *et al.*, 2001. *The Scorecard on Globalization 1980-2000: Twenty Years of Diminished Progress.* Washington: Center for Economic and Policy Research. www.cepr.net

Wilson, Edward O. *et al.* eds. 2002. "Tracking the Ecological Overshoot of the Human Economy." *Proceedings of the National Academy of Sciences,* Vol. 99, No. 14, July 9, pp. 9266-9271. www.pnas.org

World Bank. 2001. *World Development Report 2000/2001: Attacking Poverty.* New York: Oxford University Press.

WWF International. 2002. *Living Planet Report 2002.* Geneva: WWF International. www.panda.org

# Chapter 2

————————○————————

# ECONOMICS, POLITICAL ECONOMY AND HUMAN SOCIETY

There is a great deal of uncertainty in the world today. The international economy is anything but stable. Japan has been in a state of economic decline for a decade. The economies in Europe are stagnating. Many areas of the less developed world are characterized by widespread poverty and lack of steady economic growth. Even our NAFTA partner Mexico has had a stagnant economy for the past ten years.

Since the 1980s, the Canadian capitalist system has been going through a process of structural change. We have been moving away from a mixed economy to the free trade and free market economy associated with "globalization" or neoliberalism. Employment is no longer secure. More people are dependent on precarious work: part time, casual, temporary, contract or self-employment. The social safety net provided by the minimum wage, unemployment insurance, and social assistance is being taken away. Young people are even worried that they will not have any government-supported pensions when they retire. Businesses and factories are shutting and moving to low wage areas. The new economy has been quite good for the top one-third of income earners, but for the rest the last ten years has required more hours of work for an income that barely keeps up with inflation.

Canada is becoming more and more dependent on trade with the United States, and foreign, particularly American, investment is on the rise. We are so deeply entangled with the United States many believe that it is no longer possible for Canada to have anything which approaches an independent foreign policy. This concern has been elevated since the terrorist attack on the United States in September 2001 and the response of the U.S. government. Traditional civil liberties are under attack south of the border, and our government has been moving in the same direction. The U.S. government is putting enormous pressure on Canada to speed up the integration of Canada into the United States. This agenda is strongly supported by big business interests in Canada which want to see a customs union between the two countries. Given the large disparity in power and population, Canada would hardly be a separate country.

Since the collapse of the Soviet bloc, the United States stands alone in the world as a military superpower. The U.S. government has continued to dominate NATO and the Security Council of the United Nations. There is no country or bloc of countries to balance U.S. military and economic power. In October 2002 U.S. President George W. Bush issued a now famous National Security Paper which proclaimed that the United States is the dominant power in the world and that they will do everything possible to maintain that position. How far will the U.S. go in pursuing its now declared imperial policy? What are Canadians to do with this challenge?

Here in Saskatchewan our economy is becoming ever more integrated into that of the United States through trade and foreign investment. Saskatchewan used to benefit from a more diversified trade. We also used to have a rather large government and co-operative sector of the economy, under considerable local ownership and control, but that is steadily declining. While the agricultural sector is less important today, the province is more dependent on the extraction and export of non-renewable resources. Yet we have far less control over this sector of the economy than we did in the 1980s, and we are receiving a much smaller share of the value of this extraction and depletion. In the north the majority of Aboriginal people continue to live below the poverty line despite the annual export of billions of dollars of natural resources. In the larger urban centres, most of the Aboriginal population continues to live in poverty, confined to new ghettos.

Global warming and climate change may be academic issues for many, but in Saskatchewan and in northern Canada we can already see the changes. The rural population continues to shrink as farms disappear and people move to the larger towns and cities. No one knows what is going to happen in rural Saskatchewan in the future. But the trends do not point to better times. The move to free market policies may signal that we are abandoning the Canadian approach to hinterland development and moving towards the American model which we see in North Dakota.

In the past, there was a clear political split in the province. There were those on the moderate left, associated with the populist CCF and then NDP, who wanted greater ownership and control of our economy, the elimination of poverty and greater equality among all people. On the political right were the business interests who wanted less government control and the opportunity to make bigger profits. But today that division has all but disappeared. How can we understand these developments? What are the useful tools of analysis?

Much of the debate over these key issues in Saskatchewan has been paralyzed by the constraints imposed by the mass media, the political leadership, and the mainstream liberal academics at our universities. We have been cut off from the much more wide ranging discussion that takes place in Europe. For example, the debate over policies to deal with global warming and climate change differ radically. In Europe, where this issues is taken seriously, there have been major changes in energy policy which puts them far ahead of developments in North America. In Saskatchewan, there is strong elite leadership against even having a serious debate about the issue, let alone introducing effective policies.

The same would be true of the economic issues associated with the free trade and free market debates around globalization or continental integration. There is no serious debate now going on in Saskatchewan.

If we are to deal with these issues, which will greatly affect our children and grandchildren, then we have to understand the nature of capitalism. We also have to recognize the problems associated with this system of production and distribution. To address the issues of the province's relative depopulation and our persistent status as a resource dependent hinterland area, we have to fully understand the capital accumulation process. If you can't understand the problem, you can't come up with a viable solution.

This was not always the case. The first generation of farmers in Saskatchewan were able to identify their problems and advance alternatives. Workers understood why they were paid poverty level wages, had no benefits, and no job security. It did not take them long to come up with a range of solutions. When the Great Depression of the 1930s came, political movements sprang up which understood the problems and proposed viable alternatives. During World War II the role of government was changed radically, and quickly, to meet the needs of the time. In the post-war period, popular organizations, political parties, and governments adopted policies and programs that promoted full employment and the security of the welfare state. There was a broad consensus for this new program. The change was aided by a wide range of debate and political opinion which made it possible for people to identify problems and see the solutions.

But that is not the case today. There is no public debate. There is only a steady, numbing stream of exhortation to allow the free market and individual greed to address all problems. But to understand the ongoing issues which lead to our discontent, we must start by clearly examining how the capitalist system works. We must go beyond mainstream economics.

## Economics in the Saskatchewan Setting

What is economics? What role does it play in the development of Saskatchewan? What do we need to know about the economy? Does the approach of mainstream economics, taught in universities and presented to us every day through the mass media, help us understand what is going on in the world and in our province? Are there any alternatives to the free market and free trade policies being pushed on all of us by the U.S. government, big business leaders and our own political elite?

The local newspapers present us with these basic questions every day. Our political and business leaders always have something to say about the economy. Taxes are too high. The policies of the CCF and NDP governments have driven away investors and business interests. We need to privatize the Crown corporation utilities and use the cash to pay down the provincial debt. The minimum wage is too high and it is discouraging people from working. Lone parent women on social assistance should be forced to go out and get a job. The government is not giving enough aid to farmers. We need more tax holidays and assistance to attract investment in the natural resource area. Treaty Indians should pay provincial taxes. Trade unions and higher wages are forcing our businesses to move to Alberta. We can cut costs at the municipal level by contracting out a range of services to private companies and eliminate the higher labour costs of unionized government workers. Reserve land should be divided up among Indian band members so that they can learn to operate as individuals in the competitive market.

Will taking economics courses at university help us to understand what is going on in Saskatchewan? If you scan the textbooks used in university courses in economics you will soon find that they all play the same tune. Everyone and every society faces the same "economic problem," there are unlimited wants but limited resources. We must all make consumption choices every day, and this is economics. How do we distribute limited resources among alternate ends? Resources are scarce, we are told, and we can't have everything.

It doesn't take long to discover that the economics profession believes that these choices are best made by individuals and individual firms operating in as free a market as possible, unencumbered by government regulations. Introductory text books are full of examples which demonstrate that when people through their democratically elected governments decide to take actions to counteract the free market, or try to fix a "market failure," their attempts almost always never work. As one introductory text used at the University of Regina states, "Attempts to control the wants of large groups of people have tended to be spectacular failures." (see Scarth, 2000; Lovewell, 2002; Baumol *et al.*, 1994)

Alfred Marshall (1842-1924), the English mathematician, was Chair of Political Economy at Cambridge University for many years. He fought all his academic career to establish the discipline of "economics," separate from political economy and history. He finally achieved this in 1903. So Marshall is generally considered to be the founder of modern economics, often referred to as "neoclassical economics." He stressed that economics can be divided into three areas: the functioning of private markets, commonly referred to as micro economics; the functioning of the national economy as a whole, commonly referred to as macroeconomics; and world markets, originally referred to as "trade theory." Marshall's own economic analysis and theory concentrated on private markets. (Buchholz, 1989; Robbins, 1998)

The economic world as seen by mainstream economists has not really changed since the time of Marshall, what U.S. economist Joseph Stiglitz called "the Basic Competitive Model." This consists of three ingredients: rational self-interested consumers, rational profit-maximizing firms, and competitive markets with price-taking behaviour. Little attention is given to the fact that human beings all live in territorial states where governments, elected or not, implement legislation and policies seen to be for the common good of a community. (Stiglitz, 1993)

How does the Saskatchewan economy fit this timeless model? Do we live in the competitive free market economy? We have a forest industry completely dominated by one firm, Weyerhaeuser Corporation of Seattle. We have a uranium industry totally controlled by two trans-national firms, Cameco Corporation and Cogema, also foreign owned, who work together on joint projects. We have one completely dominating meat packing plant, Intercontinental Packers in Saskatoon, recently sold to Smithfield Foods of Virginia and then to McCains of New Brunswick. The coal industry, once owned by Sask Power, the Crown corporation which provides all our electrical power, is now owned by Sherritt International, a Canadian trans-national mining corporation. In the grain handling area, the farmers' co-operatives are fading with the invasion of Archer Daniel Midland, Cargill, ConAgra and Dreyfus, all giant foreign-owned agribusiness corporations. The Saskatchewan Potash Corporation, once a Crown corporation, dominates the market and is owned and controlled by American investors. On the municipal level, there is the invasion of the giant box stores, most of whom are part of American chains, which are driving local enterprises and Canadian national businesses to the wall. These firms all receive a range of government subsidies. The real world of the Saskatchewan economy seems far removed from that described in the textbooks of mainstream economics.

## Economics and Brainwashing

What should economists be doing? Robert Heilbroner and William Milberg argue that non-economists want at least three things. First, "economists are expected to provide a persuasive description of economic phenomena that makes sense of our current and past economic life-experience as individuals and communities." They conclude that the neoclassical economists, and those who dethroned John Maynard Keynes and the welfare state after 1975, have been "fundamentally deficient in this regard."

Second, "noneconomists seek guidance to the redress of specific economic problems." Here, they conclude, "there has been a marked failure across all mainstream strains of thought." In the Saskatchewan context we can think of one seemingly insoluble problem: the persistence of the province as a resource hinterland dominated by metropolitan political and economic forces. Mainstream economists have failed to come up with any program to deal with this situation. Part of the problem, Heilbroner and Milberg argue, "lies in their common belief in the irrelevance—worse, the impotence—of 'policy,' which is to say the uselessness of political (governmental) powers to affect the outcome of economic dynamics."

Third, we must recognize that for economists their complete acceptance of the free market as the only approach is a *choice*. The authors suggest that this may be an admission that "they simply do not know what to do." (Heilbroner and Milberg, 1995)

Others, however, argue that economists, who are very close to the centres of power in the private sector and the government, follow the prevailing view of the time. Today, economists line up with the neoliberal agenda being put forth by the business class and the political right. It was not long ago that mainstream economists were strong advocates of the economic theories of John Maynard Keynes and the government-sponsored welfare state. Keynesian policies had ended the Great Depression, mobilized the economy during World War II, and guided the post war economic boom that greatly improved the standard of living of most people. Before the Great Depression of the 1930s, mainstream economists were followers of Jean Baptiste Say and his law which insisted that "production creates its own demand" and that there could not be any such thing as a world depression and massive unemployment. (see Keen, 2001; Allen and Rosenbluth, 1992)

Douglas Dowd, the renowned American Marxist economist, argues that economists like everyone else have their ideological preferences. Adam Smith and Karl Marx both used empirical research to try to answer the question, "What do we need to know about the economy?" They also seriously addressed the question, "And what can and must we do to have the economy serve our human and social and ecological needs?" As Dowd argues, "both answered the questions, well and honorably." Both were "objective" in that they stretched neither fact nor logic. But they were not *neutral* because they spoke for different social interests. Smith was advocating for the rising capitalist class. Marx was advocating for the working class. (Dowd, 2000).

The way economics is taught in universities has changed over the years. When I was taking economics as an undergraduate student in the 1950s, we started looking at an issue by examining the data. We used an empirical approach. For example, when studying international trade we started by looking at the distribution and structure of trade and how it had changed over the years. What was the structure of trade between the dominant European states and the colonies and former colonies? What was the structure of the trade between Canada and the United States? What were the policies of different governments on issues like tariffs, quotas and foreign exchange controls? After this empirical analysis, we then looked at the different theories to try to determine which best explained what was in fact happening.

Economics text books today start by promoting a rather abstract theory of free markets and competition and assume a model of free trade as the ideal. This is always presented to students through a series of graphs sometimes accompanied by mathematical formulas. There is little emphasis on empirical research. There is no historical analysis. The simple models that are presented bear little resemblance to the real world. For example, most of the econometric models produced by economists around 1988 to support the Canada-U.S. Free Trade Agreement started with the assumption of full employment.

I well remember Joan Robinson, the famous economist from Cambridge University, who was a special guest to the Department of Economics and Political Science at the University of Saskatchewan when I was teaching there in 1967. She wrote around 30 books and hundreds of papers. In 1933 she wrote *The Economics of Imperfect Competition*. She argued that monopoly and oligopoly, and not free market competition, were the norm in markets, and the growth of conglomerate firms demonstrated that financial power, and not technical economies of scale, allowed large firms to get even larger. The pursuit of profit, she argued, does not necessarily allocate resources in a national economy to the benefit of society as a whole. Robinson also argued that free trade was a policy which was always promoted by the most dominant countries. It was only advocated by Great Britain after they had become the unchallenged world industrial leader. Robinson never received the recognition she deserved. Many say that was because she was a woman working in a man's world. Mainstream economists did not like her because she started out as a neoclassical economist and then became one of the greatest advocates of Keynesian economics. Others say it was because she once proclaimed: "Economics 101 as taught at universities is brainwashing." (Robinson, 1971)

So is the basic model of capitalism described by economists relevant to people in Saskatchewan? Farmers on the prairies have always known that the free market does not operate in the agribusiness sector. The farm machinery industry was historically characterized by price leadership by a dominant firm. The fertilizer and agricultural chemical industries had long histories of forming international cartels. The grain handling firms and flour mills operated as cartels. The large processing, wholesaling and retail firms in food production and distribution have always had far more power in the market than farmers, even when they were well organized. Governments did virtually nothing to promote competition. (Warnock, 1978; Winson, 1992)

Another example will illustrate the point. It seems as if all the introductory text books in economics use rent controls in housing to demonstrate that government policy cannot work when it confronts the real world of the market. When governments impose rent controls it is a policy designed to make affordable housing available to low income people. It is argued that if rents are kept low by a price freeze, then more people will choose to live in apartments rather than houses or condominiums and demand will go up. But with rent controls, and thus limits on landlord profits, investors will go elsewhere and apartments will not be built. Supply will not meet demand and there will be a shortage of apartments. (see Scarth, 2000; Lovewell, 2002)

We have an actual case study of how that has worked in Saskatchewan. Rent controls were imposed on older apartments by the NDP government of Allan Blakeney as an attempt to preserve affordable housing. When Grant Devine's Tory government was in office (1982-1991) there were pressures by business interests to eliminate these rent controls, but the government resisted. They listened to the anti-poverty activists on this issue. However, in 1992 the new NDP government of Roy Romanow gave in to business pressures and abolished rent controls. What happened?

First, Boardwalk Corporation of Calgary came to Saskatchewan and bought up most of the older apartments which had lower rents. They fixed them up to some extent and then raised the rent substantially. Affordable housing in the private market all but disappeared. But over the next ten years only a few apartments were built, all in the high rent category. At the same time, the federal government stopped funding social housing in 1992 and no new units were built. For low income people, a housing crisis developed across Saskatchewan. Rents for deteriorating houses in low income neighbourhoods went up substantially. Social assistance housing allowances had been frozen at 1982 levels, and recipients were forced to use food allowances to pay the rent. Demand on the food banks went up steadily even during good economic times. With the decision of the NDP government to let the real value of the minimum wage decline, many working poor households had to use the food bank as they did not earn enough money to pay for increasing rents. The free market approach to housing advocated by economists was a boon to slum landlords. But it did not in any way solve the problem of adequate affordable housing for low income people. (MacNeil and Warnock, 2000)

## Political Economy: An Alternative Canadian Approach

What is wrong with mainstream economics? What is missing from its method of analysis? Why does it have so few answers to the problems that we face in Saskatchewan?

The discipline of economics assumes that our economy is a "market economy" of individuals competing with each other for goods, services and employment. But there is no indication whatsoever that there are any differences between these individuals, between men and women, whites and Aboriginal people, those who come from poor families and those from well off families, people born and raised in Canada and immigrants, those who are physically fit and those who are disabled, etc. There is no indication that the structure of our society gives some people advantages that others do not have. Women work very hard on Saskatchewan farms, so why is farm ownership overwhelmingly in the hands of men? How is this dictated by the free market?

Economics today makes no mention of wealth and power. Indeed, William Scarth's text, *Economics: the Essentials,* used widely at the University of Regina, does not once use the terms "wealth" or "power." Mark Lovewell's text, *Understanding Economics,* also used at the University of Regina, does not mention "power" and uses "wealth" only to point out that different households have different amounts of accumulated savings. When you compare these two books to John Porter's *Vertical Mosaic; an Analysis of Social Class and Power in Canada* you would think they were describing different planets. Porter's book is soundly based on empirical data. It clearly demonstrates that some people have wealth and power and others do not. Canada is a very unequal society. (Scarth, 2000; Lovewell, 2002; Porter, 1965)

Economics as it is taught today has no history. Its time frame is limited to the present. There is no discussion of the Great Depression or how Canada was organized during World War II. There is no discussion of colonialism and imperialism. For example, in 1530 the Aztecs, Maya and other peoples of Mesoamerica were among the most advanced civilizations in the world. Their standard of living was well above that of the average European. Today what remains of these indigenous nations are among the poorest people in the Western hemisphere. In Mexico today the gross income and wealth inequalities are also reflected in an informal but dominant pigmentocracy: the descendants of the Spanish with their white skin are people of privilege. Those at the bottom of the social and economic hierarchy are the indigenous populations with their dark skin. How did this happen? What did it have to do with the free market economy?

All the economic texts start with a given: we have limited resources and endless wants. Douglas Dowd opens his latest book with the following observation:

As the twentieth century ended, two sets of economic facts stood in stark and disturbing contrast. First, for the first time in history, existing resources and technology taken together had made it possible for all 6 billion of the earth's inhabitants—now or within a generation—to be at least adequately fed, housed, clothed, educated and their health cared for. And second, instead, well over half of that population was malnourished (with numberless millions starving), ill-housed, ill-clothed, ill-educated, in precarious health, and stricken by infant mortality rates and average life-spans belonging to the era of the early industrial revolution—when there were no more than 2 billion people. (Dowd, 2000)

There is, of course, a fundamental problem with the unequal distribution of income and wealth. Many people experience "scarce resources" because they have very low incomes while others do not know what to do with all their money. But Dowd was also pointing out that there is no real scarcity. Scarcity, he argues, is primarily created by the irrational system of capitalism. There is tremendous waste in the system of production and distribution. And it is massive advertising and sales campaigns which create endless "wants." To survive, capitalism must constantly grow, it cannot exist in a steady state economy. It is a given that capitalism cannot create a society based on equality. It is also a given that it cannot create a society based on sustainable development. (see O'Connor, 1994)

Economics starts with the premise that there is and always has been "Economic Man." It assumes that the core of our being as humans is the pursuit of self interest. This is what economic theorists today call "rational choice theory." If so, then this must have existed for all human beings around the world and across time. But is this theory based on empirical knowledge or is it just an ideological supposition?

Human beings have always lived in communities. Contrary to what the early liberals proposed in their defence of capitalism, there was never a time in history when human beings lived like Robinson Caruso. They cannot develop without the support of other human beings. Children who are raised in feral conditions often cannot even learn to speak when placed in a community situation. Our knowledge and values are absorbed from our communities. All human beings as individuals are a product of their community. In fact, individualism as we know it was not possible before the capitalist industrial and urban revolution. Only in a society with a complex division of labour is individualism possible.

Furthermore, it is clear that people put a high priority on values other than pursuing their own self interest at all times. Human beings have a close and primary commitment to their families. Most people seem to place a very high priority on their sexual relationships. Many people make commitments of loyalty and support to friends. The evidence suggests to me that people prefer to live in communities of like people who share as a minimum their mother language. Many flee to other countries out of desperation, but they lament the loss of their homeland. In these important relationships people place values of love, commitment and solidarity above the values of Economic Man.

Economist Karl Polanyi has had considerable influence on Canadian political economists. His research was on economic systems in pre-capitalist societies, and he relied primarily on the work of anthropologists. He reminded us some time ago that "prior to our time no economy has ever existed that, even in principle, was controlled by markets." Gain and profit made on exchange "never before played an important part in human economy." The market for goods existed in all pre-capitalist economic systems. But it was quite marginal to the existence of human society. Market mentality did not exist. The primary concern of early peoples was family, kin, community and nation. Value systems stressed security and the preservation of the group. Reciprocity, sharing and redistribution were the norm, and trading was based on barter of roughly equivalent goods, not gain. The "market economy" and its value system did not exist. Nor did Economic Man. (Dalton, 1968)

The term "economics" has a Greek origin. It was defined as "the art of household management." Aristotle's *Politics* deals with economic questions. For him, economics went from household, to village, to city, and to state. If we move to the modern period, James Steuart wrote in 1761 that "economy is the art of providing for all the wants of a family, with prudence and frugality." He went on to add that "what economy is in a family, political economy is in a state." Adam Smith, in *The Wealth of Nations*, argued that "political economy is a branch of the science of a statesman or legislator." Following Turgot, Smith argued that political economy was the study of "the nature and causes of the wealth of nations." From the very beginning of social science in Europe what we now call "economics" was known as "political economy," a recognition that it was much more than just individuals buying and selling in the private market. Political economy was the process of production and distribution of wealth within the boundaries of national, territorial states, some even with elected governments. (Chattopadhyay, 1974)

James Caporaso and David Levine argue that political economy emerged in the eighteenth century "to help people understand and cope with a dramatic change in the system of want satisfaction, both in the nature of wants and in the manner of production and distribution of goods for satisfying them." The term "economics," as used by the Greeks, focused primarily on the household. Political economy emerges as an analysis of "the management of the economic affairs of the state." In pre-state societies, economic links were to family and kinship. This changed with the development of the modern territorial state. As they note, "the boundaries of want satisfaction are now political," and responsibility resides in the public authority. (Caporaso and Levine, 1992)

In addition, political economy is identified with the rise of capitalism as the dominant mode of production. Capitalism first replaces feudalism in Europe and then spreads around the world conquering and replacing other ancient modes of production. From the beginning the focus of political economy was on the rise of capitalism. As it is taught in universities in Great Britain and continental Europe, political economy includes economics, politics, history, sociology and anthropology. It is an integrated approach to studying human social problems. Following the British tradition, Canadian universities originally had departments of political economy which included economics, politics, sociology, anthropology and sometimes history. It sets forth an alternative approach to social analysis, one that is much more productive.

## Searching for Economic Man in Pre-Capitalist Societies

If we believe that the assumptions of mainstream economics are true, then Economic Man should have existed in all previous human societies. However, any examination of history and anthropology will reveal that this is not the case. Humans have historically been co-operative beings, and there is no reason to conclude that this cannot be the case in the future.

The earliest human beings on the Canadian prairies lived in groups now commonly referred to as bands and tribes. This form of human social organization is found at some period in the history in every country. Chieftainships did not exist on the Canadian prairies but were found elsewhere in the Americas. In addition, before the arrival of the Europeans, there were advanced state societies in the Americas, with hierarchical social classes and imperial systems. Most of us are familiar with the Aztec, Inca and Maya civilizations. There were others as well. Imperial state societies existed in all regions of the world before European expansion and colonialism.

Human beings are social animals. They have always lived in groups, never alone as individuals or as individual families. The first humans existed for thousands of years living in small bands of around 50 people or less, classified by anthropologists as "hunter-gatherer societies." This was their mode of production. The first concern of all human societies is to provide for material necessities: food, clothing and shelter. The second major task is to create a social order for the physical reproduction of the group, raising children and creating rules regarding sexual activity. These are the two most important tasks of any human society. From the beginning of human existence, these tasks have been socially organized. Furthermore, there is no uniform organization of these tasks on a worldwide basis and across time. Culture modifies genetic predispositions.

All human societies have some kind of political order to make group decisions, some form of government structure. They create a process of education to transfer culture and knowledge to new generations. Furthermore, all known human societies have had some form of religious order to provide social control and cohesion and to help resolve conflicts. Religion also provides psychological functions for individuals, explaining phenomena that we do not understand and giving emotional support to help deal with personal crises and anxieties.

Band societies are often classified as "primitive democratic," "primitive communistic," or "simple egalitarian" societies. They are small, between 25 and 150 people, and exist by hunting and gathering. They have bonds of common language and culture, and the only ties with other bands would be through marriage. The basis of community is kinship.

The most basic characteristic of band societies is that there is no private ownership of the means of production. In all band societies, land and other resources are common property. Closely linked to this is the fact that distribution of goods within the society is based on reciprocity. Everyone is guaranteed access to basic human needs. No one is allowed to go without food, clothing and shelter. Sharing and co-operation form the ethical and moral basis for band societies. Production of food by hunting and gathering wild food is a collective enterprise, although certain individuals may be better at this than others. Thus production is for use, not exchange as in a market-driven society. Bands may engage in trade, but it is marginal and certainly not central to their society. Political leadership is based on prestige, established by example. But in band societies in general, wherever they are to be found, women generally have a lower political status. It is the norm that political decisions are made by men. (Liebowitz, 1986; Harris, 1977)

The value system of band societies is quite different from what we know under capitalism. The priorities are the survival of the group, protection for the weak and the disabled, reverence for all the members of the group, and co-operation and not competition. There is no concept of individualism. There is respect for the work that women do and a recognition that it is of equal value to the society as the work of men. Contrary to popular belief, war is not widespread or common, as it was too costly to the group; they could not afford to have members of the band killed. The religious and moral values of the band reflect these material realities: the support for the equality of all members of the group. There is no Economic Man. (see Fried, 1967; Lewellen, 1992; Bodley, 1994; and Jolly and Plog, 1987)

Tribal societies are larger, having up to 500 members. They are based on alliances among bands, formed usually for political purposes, often to resist outside threats of war or competition for land and resources. The primary tie among tribes is kinship, a recognition that they all stem from a common ancestor. The Irish and Scottish clans are an example of more advanced tribes. As with the Celtic clans, warfare is more common. Other lineal tribes include the Iroquois, the Hopi, Zuni and Navajo. Composite tribes, amalgamations of peoples who are not linked by kinship, are very common in North America and include the Comanche, Cheyenne, and the buffalo-hunting tribes of the Great Plains.

Generally speaking, tribes are more sedentary, many rely on horticulture or swidden (slash and burn) agriculture for food production, others are known for domestication and pasturing of animals, and some rely primarily on fishing. When the Europeans arrived in North America almost all of the indigenous peoples they found were engaged in agriculture and fishing as well as hunting. On the Great Plains, the agricultural systems developed in Mesoamerica spread north and were even well established in the Missouri River basin in North Dakota.

Elman Service found that tribes which depend on hunting are more likely to have a patrilineal (or male) order of descent and are more likely to be based in patrilocal residence. In contrast, he found that matrilineal tribes (female order of descent) with matrilocal residence are more common among tribes dependent on rainfall horticulture where gardening is done by women. Matrilineal societies are found among horticultural tribes in North and South America, Melanesia, Southeast Asia and Africa. In matrilineal societies based on horticulture women have significantly more political influence and usually collectively control food in storage and households. Before being forced onto reservations, this was characteristic of the Hidatsa, Mandan and Arikara tribes which lived in the Missouri River Valley in what is now North Dakota.

Tribes have value systems which are similar to band societies. Production is still for use and not the market. The economic unit is the household, and the division of labour is along lines of sex and age. But the principle of equality still prevails, and those kinship groups or families who have a better economic situation are expected to share with those less fortunate. Everyone still has full access to the means of production. Economic Man is not found in tribal societies. (See Albers and Medicine, 1983; Service, 1962; Fried, 1967; Lewellen, 1992; White, 1959; Sahlins, 1968)

Chiefdoms are found in Central and South America, on the Northwest Coast of North America from Northern California to Alaska, in Asia, Oceania, Africa and Europe. These societies have larger populations, more advanced technology, and a system of agriculture which produces a significant economic surplus. In the era of European colonialism, chiefdoms were often created by the imperial countries to facilitate rule over colonized peoples in less developed areas. This form of social organization was not present on the Canadian prairies at the time of the arrival of Europeans.

The chiefdom is a more centralized and integrated society with a permanent political leadership. It is common that a kinship group has special political power, chiefs or kings rule on the basis of heredity, there are permanent government officials, and the heads of government have considerable power and authority.

The key difference between chiefdoms and band and tribal societies is the unequal access to the means of production, particularly land for agriculture. We also see the development of social stratification, the division of the society into different classes of people based on differential access to the means of production and the product. Aside from the chiefs and their followers, it is common to find the society divided between people who have a status similar to "nobles" and the majority who are "commoners."

But while chiefs and their followers have wealth and status, they also have significant obligations to the community at large. They may receive the agricultural surplus and live a life of leisure compared to the common people. But this wealth is not just for their own use. The chiefs still have a major obligation to redistribute. Thus the storehouse of food surpluses is there primarily to protect the nation against famine and war, and for ceremonies. It is still the obligation of the chief to ensure that none of the people in his community lacks food. (see Service, 1962; Herskovits, 1965; Fried, 1967, Lewellen, 1992; Balandier, 1970; Dalton, 1968)

Political economists, sociologists and anthropologists understand that every form of *production* has an integrated system of *distribution*. The system of production established by a band, a tribe, or even a larger chiefdom or kingdom is socially created and becomes deeply entrenched as part of the culture. For the members of the community, the system of distribution is unconscious behaviour because it is an unquestioned part of the culture. Production and distribution end with consumption. In these societies the process is completely different from exchange that happens in a capitalist market. Merchants operating in a market system, even under feudalism, are seeking a profit and consciously planning how to do so. This form of exchange requires the introduction of money, not only as a technique of exchange, but in the form of acquisition of wealth.

In band and tribal societies production was for use and distribution was based on equality. While trade developed in chiefdoms, it was not central to the operation of the economy. Distribution guaranteed that all members of the community had adequate provisions. The guiding ethical principles, reflected in their religions, were reciprocity and redistribution. There was no Economic Man.

## The Rise of the State and the Role of Ideology

The discipline of economics today does not include any discussion of the role of the state or ideological systems. There is no discussion of political structures. There is no discussion of political or economic power. These are deemed to be in the realm of politics, separate from economics. But they are central to the study of political economy.

One often hears people in Saskatchewan assert that the state was a European invention and did not exist in the western hemisphere. In some quarters it is popular also to put forth a contrast between the rapacious, imperial European systems of government and the relatively egalitarian and peaceful condition of the indigenous peoples of North America. But this is simply not true. Hierarchical and oppressive states existed in the western hemisphere before the arrival of the Europeans, in Mesoamerica and the Andes. They have basic characteristics that are very similar to state systems in Europe and elsewhere around the world.

Many anthropologists have described the nature of the early state societies. They are different from chiefdoms as people are grouped on a territorial basis. Identification according to blood ties is superseded by citizenship in a territorial state.

The second key characteristic of the state is the institution of a permanent public force over and above society. The state has at least a class of permanent military leaders, supported by public funds, which provide for internal policing and external war. The Aztec, Maya and Inca civilizations all had a permanent class of military leaders.

The state requires finances. Thus we have the central government bureaucracy, the key part of which is the tax collectors and financiers. This is a new political formation. In the Museum of Anthropology in Mexico City you can see the parchment papers on which are recorded the taxes that were collected by the Aztec government.

The state also requires an ideological structure. The authority of the kings and rulers is supported by the religious system. There is a class of priests which are part of the state structure, and religious ceremony is granted a status almost equal to that of political authority. In ancient state societies the male head of state is usually also the head of the religious order. These new institutions stand *over and above society*. They are not found in earlier human societies.

In the archaic state, a state religion provided the ideological justification for the class divisions and unequal access to the means of production. In the Americas, the

Aztec, Maya and Inca civilizations all had official state religions. Society was seen as a pyramid, hierarchical, based on inequality, with the king, royal family, and large landowners at the top and the slaves, peasants, serfs and cargo transporters at the bottom.

American anthropologist V. Gordon Childe argued that the key to the rise of "civilization" was the neolithic revolution, when humans began to cultivate plants and domesticate animals to gain control over their own food supply. Those societies adopted intensive cultivation, including irrigation and the introduction of staple foods such as rice, wheat, barley, millet, maize, yams and sweet potatoes. These great civilizations developed city states and empires. (Childe, 1951)

In his widely cited book, *The Evolution of Political Society*, American anthropologist Morton Fried argues that real physical force is the key to the state. "At the heart of the problem of maintaining general order is the need to defend the central order of stratification—the differentiation of categories of population in terms of access to basic resources." Once the states are well developed and established, one key task is maintaining the relations between such states and "their less well-organized hinterlands." All the city states were urban centres which dominated hinterland areas. Urban populations had to control the food and natural resources of the outlying areas. Militarism and colonialism went hand in hand with the state society.

Legitimacy is created through the use of an ideology. Thus the early state structures are in control of religion, sources of information and the means of communication. The class of political rulers control the priests, the bureaucrats, literacy and learning, and the scribes who write the official recorded history. The schools and universities teach the official ideology of the state. (Lewellen, 1992; Krader, 1968; Fried, 1967; Carneiro, 1970)

The model of the early state society is described by anthropologist Leslie White. Irrigated agriculture of cereals, as in the high civilizations in the Americas, and animal husbandry, permitted the production of an economic surplus. Population increased. Productivity of labour increased. Population density overrode kinship allegiances and created a new social division of labour. A state-church developed which co-ordinated and integrated the new increasingly urbanized society. Coercion was necessary "to cause a class of food producers to produce more than they needed or could consume. The result was a division of society into a dominant, ruling class and a subordinate class." This was a universal development. (White, 1959)

Social control is essential in any large human society, particularly one where there is a wide variation in the distribution of wealth, income, power and status.

States and their governments can use coercion to obtain consent. But an *ideological system* imposed through socialization is a much more effective system of social control. As Morton Fried argues, "the function of ideology is to explain and justify the existence of concentrated social power wielded by a portion of the community and to offer similar support to a specific social order." (Fried, 1967)

In pre-industrial state societies, the official religion was central to the ideological system designed to provide social control or social cohesion. As sociologist Emile Durkheim argues, the primary function of religion is to "instruct the humble to accept their lot in society," to keep the poor and oppressed in a relatively satisfied condition. As societies moved to a hierarchical basis, so did the pantheon of gods and goddesses. When state societies were headed by militaristic men, the religious orders downgraded the female goddesses of fertility and the moon and moved the Sun God and the warrior gods to the top of the hierarchy. The gods of defeated states were often integrated into the pantheon of gods of the imperial power, but on a lower order. One of the functions of religion for early states was to sanction imperial domination. This was clearly the role of religion in the early American states. (Durkheim, 1961; Collins, 1982; O'Toole, 1984; Pickering, 1988)

For thousands of years humans lived in pre-industrial societies. For most of that time they lived in small egalitarian bands where resources were held in common and production and distribution was based on reciprocity. In larger tribal societies equality still prevailed, and the chiefs were central to a process of redistribution. In the stratified societies called chiefdoms, there was differential access to the means of production and distribution. Yet there was still an important role for redistribution.

In state societies there was a significant division of labour, hierarchy and inequality, but at the same time there were the large warehouses for storing food for the purposes of redistribution. There were formal social classes, a ruling class, and the exploitation of a class of producers. But the basis for production remained what Aristotle called "householding," production for use rather than commerce and gain. Karl Polanyi was correct when he concluded that "all economic systems known to us up to the end of feudalism in Western Europe were organized either on the principles of reciprocity, or redistribution, or householding, or some combination of the three." Economic Man, rationally seeking to maximize profit, had yet to be found. (Dalton, 1968)

## Capturing the Economic Surplus

The key to the economic development of any society is the creation of an economic surplus. To understand what is happening in Saskatchewan it is important to know how the economic surplus is created, who controls it, and how and where it is invested. This requires the tools of analysis of political economy.

Economic growth and development occur when a society creates a surplus over and above what is needed for subsistence and invests it in productive enterprises. Creating an economic surplus, for example, and then investing it in large monasteries for priests may be popular, but it does not improve the standard of living of the community. The surplus may allow a society to expand its population or increase the well being of the existing members. Adam Smith described how the creation of the economic surplus increased the wealth of nations.

From a political economy perspective, what is termed the "economic surplus" is really "surplus labour." All societies require "necessary labour" for the purposes of production and reproduction, to ensure their continuation. Hunting and gathering requires human labour. In state societies based on irrigated agriculture, the labour of farm workers produces the "necessary labour" for existence.

Nevertheless, in all societies those who labour produce surplus labour. Every society has people who are unable to labour: children, the sick, and the elderly. There may be others who do not labour but must receive social support. Religious figures, for example, do not normally engage in productive labour. If there is no surplus created, and people were forced to live on a level of biological subsistence, then the society would not survive because it would not be able to produce the tools needed for production.

Over thousands of years humans existed in small band societies where they constantly faced famine situations because they had no ability to store food. Even in the mid-nineteenth century, John Palliser's expedition recorded times when Indian communities on the Canadian prairies, dependent on the buffalo, were seriously suffering from lack of food, particularly in the winter. (Spry, 1963)

Thus even in hunter-gatherer societies, those who provide food must produce a surplus to support others. In these egalitarian societies, the surplus is appropriated by the collective. In more advanced societies, there are necessary functions provided by people who do not produce goods. Even if there were no class society, and no class of idle non-producers, there is a necessity for administration, systems of justice, education, health, etc.

What is central here is how any society is *socially organized* for the purposes of production and distribution. Political economists have use the term "mode of production" to describe this phenomenon. When a society produces an economic surplus, who has control over or ownership of that surplus and how is it distributed? This is a central question. The mode of production is the foundation of any society. While Karl Marx was the first to use this term, it is now widely accepted in political economy and other social sciences, although not in the discipline of economics.

An economic surplus is created by the application of labour, using tools, to natural resources. Thus a peasant farmer (who is almost always a male, the head of the household) will create an economic surplus in food production through a process of applying his labour and the labour of his family, using the tools he has acquired, and using the land and other natural resources like water that are available to him. This farmer, using these *forces of production*, can create an economic surplus. Who owns and controls his economic surplus is directly linked to the mode of production of his community. These differ, depending on the class structure of the society.

If the farm worker is a slave, he/she surrenders all their product to the slave owner, who also owns the land and the tools of production. If he is a serf in feudal Europe, he surrenders his family's surplus to the lord of the manor. If he is a tenant farmer in Asia, he surrenders at least fifty percent of his family's crop to the landlord. If he is an independent farmer, who owns his own land, under Imperial Rome he surrenders most of his family's surplus to the state in the form of taxes. If he is a peasant in a capitalist "market economy," he surrenders much if not all of his family's surplus to the financial institutions, the farm supply industry and the "middle men" who control the marketing system for his product. In all these social situations, farmers have considered themselves to be exploited by political and economic forces largely beyond their control. The economic surplus that they and their families create is taken from them and they have no control over how it is used. (Childe, 1951)

Why should we be concerned with pre-capitalist modes of production? One of the basic differences between economics and political economy is the recognition of the importance of history. For example, how can we understand the plight of the peasants in Peru today if we don't know that in the early 16th century the Inca civilization in Peru, which was one of the most advanced in the world, was devastated by Spanish imperialism? How can we understand the status of Aboriginal people in Saskatchewan if we have no knowledge of the history of the region and the impact of mercantilism and English colonialism?

But there are other reasons. In contrast to economics, political economy under-stands that the world is constantly changing. Nothing is static. As we look at history we can see how it has evolved. We can see certain patterns of states and their econo-mies which are still with us today. Understanding the past helps us understand what is currently happening. How social classes and states operated in pre-capitalist societ-ies helps us understand how they operate under capitalism. The flow of history helps us make predictions of what might happen in the future.

## Imperial Systems and the Economic Surplus

Canada developed as a colony within the French and then British empires. Saskatch-ewan developed within an imperial system controlled by the governments in Ottawa and London. The opening of the Canadian west was an imperial commercial ven-ture, directed by capitalists in Canada, the United States and Great Britain, in alli-ance with their political allies. Empires have all had a great deal in common. Colonies and hinterland areas have all experienced similar exploitation. They have been domi-nated politically, economically and culturally by more powerful outside forces. We can learn a great deal that is relevant to our experience in Saskatchewan by examin-ing the history of empires. Empires all operate in a similar manner. Furthermore, we have some very good examples of empires right here in the America hemisphere, op-erating before the arrival of the Europeans.

All of the city states that developed around the world were characterized by a large population, the development of urban centres, a bureaucracy, citizenship, hier-archical social stratification into formal classes, public works, and a proliferation of non-agricultural occupations. The early states were patriarchal societies, with men as hereditary rulers, a professional class of military officers, and they all developed impe-rial systems which dominated hinterland areas. They engaged in long distance trade, but it was not a market trade but a state administered trade, often formalized in trea-ties, and closely linked to their systems of collecting tribute. The extraction of tribute from subjugated peoples was central to maintaining the empire.

The Andean civilization in South America is a good example. It lasted for around 3,000 years, reaching a peak as an empire between 1476 and 1532, when the Spanish arrived. It covered around 940,000 square kilometres and included the pres-ent states of Peru, Ecuador, Bolivia and much of Argentina and Chile. Estimates of its population vary between six and 32 million.

The Inca Empire had a highly stratified class system. The ruling Inca was the di-rect descendant of the Sun, an absolute ruler. Everything in the imperial realm belonged to the Inca. The nobles who surrounded him were also hierarchically based on how close their family was related to the Inca. Below this class were the state and imperial bureaucrats, then the specialized labourers, the *mitima* who were groups that moved around the empire to work on large-scale public works projects. At the bottom were the commoners, who provided free labour on agricultural land, public works, and in the mines. Their labour produced the economic surplus accumulated by the political-religious ruling class.

The productive land was all owned by the Inca state. But within the empire, landholding was more complex, often divided among military leaders and local ruling classes. The commoners, who farmed their state land as a family, were also required to provide *mita* (obligatory labour) on the land of the religious and political elite. As John Murra points out, "the governing idea of the system is labour time. Nowhere is there mention of contributions in kind or in any medium of exchange." (Murra, 1980)

Food was the basic form of tribute or tax imposed on the subjugated peoples. But this took the form of labour time. What the farmer, craftsman, weaver, miner or construction workers gave was labour—but what was received by the rulers was product. Labour was the only measure of value. (Moore, 1958; Carrasco, 1982)

The Inca empire was a powerful military force. When Lord-Inca Huayna Capac set out to conquer Quito, he mobilized an army of 300,000 warriors plus an entourage to provide support. After they defeated an enemy, they slaughtered all the wounded and captured warriors in the field. There was an additional ceremonial slaughter afterwards. The Inca engaged in a policy of state terrorism, designed to teach their vassals a lesson: if they rebelled or refused to pay tribute, they would pay a high price. (von Hagen, 1961)

The outlying vassal areas were the key to providing natural resources for the centre of the empire. The key to the empire was the extraction of an economic surplus from subjugated peoples, enforced by military action. While markets existed, they were not important to production and were part of state-directed trade. (Schreiber, 1992; Carrasco, 1982; Rowe, 1982; Gledhill, 1989)

Mesoamerica is always listed as one of the sites of original pristine states. And of the archaic civilizations in that area, that of the Aztecs is seen to have been the most advanced. The Aztecs saw themselves as the defenders of the Sun against the night, and to feed him, human sacrifice and blood was necessary.

The Aztecs built their civilization on a very advanced system of irrigated agriculture and the famous chinampa "floating gardens." Around 1430 the Aztecs formed a political alliance with the city-states of Texcoco and Tlacopan to rule the

Valley of Mexico. Despite very productive agriculture, the land base was not enough to provide food to meet the growing population. By the middle of the 15th century Tenochtitlan (now known as Mexico City) had a population of at least 150,000. The Triple Alliance carried out a program of military expansion to gain tribute and acquire land. In 1500 the Aztecs established hegemony over the Triple Alliance and became the central point for the collection of imperial tribute. (Wolf, 1959; Peterson, 1962; Townsend, 1992; De Lameiras, 1988)

The Aztec state was divided into 20 subgroups called *calpulli*. These divisions served as administrative units, but they also roughly corresponded to kinship groups. Within each *capulli* there was a hierarchical class system. At the top was a class of nobles who owned rights to kinship land which was then worked by serfs who were tied to the land. The other land was owned by the Aztec rulers and distributed to the most prominent warriors, worked by peasants who paid rent in the form of share crops. The Aztec rulers were a permanent hereditary class who claimed descent from Toltec times.

In areas in the Valley of Mexico conquered by the Aztecs, land was distributed to nobles. The land was worked by the *mayeques*, local people tied to the soil like European serfs. They worked on a crop sharing basis with most of the crop going to the noble. The Aztec rulers also kept land farmed by *mayeques*. The Palace Lands were cultivated by palace serfs. The economic surplus from these lands was used to support the bureaucrats, priests, teachers, entertainers, scribes, etc. Another class of land, also worked by serfs, supported the armies and soldiers. The merchant class also had its own lands and serfs.

At the bottom of this social structure were the slaves. Some of these were people who sold themselves or their families into slavery when they were in debt or during the famines in order to get food. Others were criminal slaves. Slaves taken in war were women and children, for male prisoners were always sacrificed to the Sun god. Women slaves were exploited as weavers, labourers and concubines.

For administrative purposes, the empire was divided into 38 tributary provinces. Each had a central town for the purpose of collecting tribute. Treaties defined the rights and obligations of the defeated peoples. As in the Inca empire, local rulers were expected to spend months each year at the imperial centre, send their sons to schools there, and then embrace the Aztec deities.

Considerable local autonomy was permitted as long as the tribute was paid. The tribute included agricultural products, crafts, clothing, natural resources, as well as luxury goods for the ruling classes. But all vassal states were also required to provide humans as tribute, women for concubines and workers and men for religious sacrifice. Provinces were expected to provide military forces in time of war. Labour was required for building and maintaining the system of irrigation, terracing and road building, as well as the construction of temples. There was a long-distance trade which was closely linked to the imperial system. (Calnek, 1982; Wolf, 1959; Townsend, 1992; Peterson, 1962; Gledhill, 1989)

Pedro Carrasco has described the Aztec empire, and its characteristics are similar to other archaic empires around the world:

> The means of increasing and maintaining the extension of the empire was always war and military imposed control. Occasionally booty may have been the principal object of a campaign, but there was always something more at stake than immediate plunder. A system of controls was set up that permitted the regular extraction of the economic surplus of conquered regions through the payment of tribute and labour services. (Carrasco, 1982)

The tribute imposed by the Aztecs was very heavy. When the Spanish arrived it was easy for Hernan Cortez and his 500 men to form alliances with subjugated peoples who wished to escape the exploitation of the Aztecs. They could not possibly have defeated the Aztecs without their local allies. Little did the people of Mexico know that the rule of the Spanish and the Christian Church would be even more horrendous.

An examination of the structure and operation of the Inca and Aztec empires reveals that they had much in common with the British and other European empires. The key to their survival and expansion was always the extraction of an economic surplus in the form of tribute from the colonized peoples living in the hinterland areas.

## Conclusion

Economic growth and development depends on the creation of an economic surplus. In agricultural societies, which are all characterized by the existence of the political state, class societies develop. In these class societies the ruling class of landowners extracts the economic surplus from the agricultural producers, whether they are peasants, farm labourers, independent farmers, serfs or slaves. Economic surplus is also extracted from other producers.

In these pre-capitalist societies, production is for use. Very little production is commodities for exchange. Where markets exist, they are not the "free markets" we associate with the development of capitalism. Most of the markets operate within administered prices established by the state. Long distance trade is closely linked to the state, if not a state operation.

There are local markets where peasants meet to exchange goods, mostly on a barter basis, as money or currency is normally not available. As states emerge we see the development of an independent class of craftsmen who exchange their product for the food, clothing and other necessities that they do not produce. When trade takes place within a village or tribal community, there are usually rules which govern such exchanges. Farmers' markets emerge in pre-state societies where agricultural producers can independently dispose of their small surplus production, what they produce over and above their needs and the rent. In these markets goods are exchanged because they have a use-value. While engaging in such an exchange, how does a person in a pre-capitalist society calculate the difference in goods? How does one establish the value of potatoes in relationship to cloth or clothes? In all these societies, this value is established by the labour time needed to produce the product. Furthermore, this exchange is on the basis of reciprocity or equivalence; there is no attempt to maximize gain at the expense of the other producer. Economic Man had not yet been discovered.

In 2000 when I was in Mexico friends took me to the central market in San Cristobal, Chiapas. These markets exist all across Mexico. I was looking at the blouses, dresses and shawls produced by a local Mayan woman. A young girl around the age of 10 was explaining to me the price of each item, created by her mother who was sitting there observing our interchange. The girl explained just how many days her mother had taken to produce each item. The value of her work was still being expressed in labour time.

In the period before the rise of the modern territorial state, all the state societies were in fact city states surrounded by hinterland areas. Cities cannot exist without hinterlands to provide food and natural resources. But these city states almost immediately became imperial states, using their military power to subjugate other peoples in order to exploit them, to extract an economic surplus under duress. People in the rural areas laboured, but much of what they produced was siphoned off by the military and political classes which ruled the city states. As Eric Wolf, the well known American anthropologist points out, this leads to disparity in growth, an imbalance between town and hinterland, between city and provinces:

> The growing gap between centre and hinterland was not based on an absolute enrichment of the centre while the countryside remained absolutely impoverished. Both grew in their involvement with each other; but the centres grew more quickly, more opulently, and, more obviously.

Wolf goes on to add that there are political repercussions from this disparity in development and the loss of hope in rural producers. It results in a history of peasant, serf and slave revolts:

> In complex societies, this confrontation of hope with the denial of hope pits rulers against ruled, rich against poor, and hinterland and periphery against core area and centre. The periphery suffers by comparison while the centre grows bloated with wealth and power. It is at the periphery that the controls of government and religion tend to be at their weakest; it is here that the forces of dissatisfaction can easily gain both strength and organization. (Wolf, 1959)

Can we in Saskatchewan learn anything from this history of human development? Is the history of the Aboriginal people on the Canadian prairies that much different from indigenous peoples in other areas of the world? How different in operation were the ancient empires and the more recent British empire? The development of all state societies originally rested on the exploitation of people who worked the land to produce agricultural products. Their economic surplus is siphoned off by a ruling class supported by a state structure. How much different is that from the development of agriculture on the Canadian prairies?

The rise of the city states around the world has always included the domination of hinterland areas. Agricultural products, natural resources and labourers have been extracted from hinterland areas to serve urban areas. There is a long history of rebellion in hinterland areas against urban exploitation. Does this have any relevance to our experience in Saskatchewan?

The early city states and empires were all founded on a class divided society. There was a ruling class which owned the means of production, mainly the land. There were other classes of workers, agricultural and craft, who did not own the means of production. Their labour was exploited by the ruling class, which had the support of the state apparatus. Does this model have any relevance to Canada and Saskatchewan?

Within all imperial systems, there are constant rebellions, by farmers, peasants, serfs, slaves and other workers. Empires must always use military force to maintain control over colonies and vassals that they have subjugated. Resistance to empires is widespread throughout history. Does this have any relevance to political developments in Canada and on the prairies?

Within empires, the ideological structure, the state religion, the educational system, the imperial culture, flows from the centre to the hinterland areas. It is always assumed that the culture of the centre is the most advanced, represents civilization, and must take priority over all local cultures. Is there any history of this in Canada? In Saskatchewan? These developments may be ignored by the discipline of economics as it is taught today. But they are central to political economy.

## References

Adams, Robert McC. 1966. *The Evolution of Urban Society: Early Mesopotamia and Prehispanic Mexico.* Chicago: Aldine Publishing Company.

Albers, Patricia and Beatrice Medicine, eds. 1983. *The Hidden Half: Studies of Plains Indian Women.* New York: University Press of America.

Allen, Robert C. and Gideon Rosenbluth, eds. 1992. *False Promises: The Failure of Conservative Economics.* Vancouver: New Star Books.

Balandier, Georges. 1970. *Political Anthropology.* London: Allen Lane the Penguin Press.

Baumol, William J., Alan S. Blinder, and William M. Scarth. 1994. *Economics: Principles and Policy.* Toronto: Harcourt Brace & Co. Canada.

Bodley, John H. 1994. *Cultural Anthropology: Tribes, States, and the Global System.* Toronto: Mayfield Publishing Company.

Bose, Arun. 1975. *Marxian and Post-Marxian Political Economy.* Markham: Penguin Books.

Buchholz, Todd G. 1999. *New Ideas from Dead Economists: An Introduction to Modern Economic Thought.* New York: Penguin Books.

Calnek, Edward E. 1982. "Patters of Empire Formation in the Valley of Mexico, Late Postclassic Period, 1200-1520." In Collier *et al.*, pp. 43-62.

Caporaso, James A. and David P. Levine. 1992. *Theories of Political Economy.* Cambridge: Cambridge University Press.

Carneiro, Robert L. 1970. "A Theory of the Origin of the State," *Science,* Vol. 169, No. 3947, pp. 733-8.

Carrasco, Pedro. 1982. "The Political Economy of the Aztec and Inca States," in Collier *et al.*, pp. 23-40.

Chattopadhyay, Paresh. 1974. "Political Economy: What's in a Name?" *Monthly Review,* Vol. 25, No. 11, April, pp. 23-33.

Childe, V. Gordon. 1951. *Man Makes Himself: The Rise of Civilization.* New York: The New American Library of World Literature.

Collier, George A., Renato I. Rosaldo, and John D. Wirth, eds. 1982. *The Inca and Aztec States 1400-1800.* New York: Academic Press.

Collins, Randall. 1982. *Sociological Insight.* London: Oxford University Press.

Coontz, Stephanie and Petea Henderson, eds. 1986. *Women's Work, Men's Property: the Origins of Gender and Class.* London: Verso Books.

Dalton, George, ed. 1968. *Primitive, Archaic and Modern Economies: Essays of Karl* Polanyi. Garden City: Doubleday and Company.

De Lameiras, Brigitte Boehm. 1988. "Subsistence, Social Control of Resources and the Development of Complex Society in the Valley of Mexico." In Gledhill, Bender and Larsen, pp. 91-102.

Dowd, Douglas. 2000. *Capitalism and Its Economics: A Critical History.* London: Pluto Press.

Durkheim, Emile. 1961. *The Elementary Forms of the Religious Life.* New York: Collier-Macmillan.

Fried, Morton H. 1967. *The Evolution of Political Society: An Essay in Political Anthropology.* New York: Random House.

Gledhill, John, Barbara Bender and Mogens Trolle Larsen, eds. 1988. *State and Society: The Emergence and Development of Social Hierarchy and Political Centralization.* London: Routledge.

Gledhill, John. 1989. "The Imperial Form and Universal History: Some Reflections on Relativism and Generalization." In Miller, Rowlands, Tilley, pp. 108-126.

Harris, Marvin. 1978. *Cannibals and Kings: The Origins of Cultures.* New York: Random House.

Heilbroner, Robert and William Milberg. 1995. *The Crisis of Vision in Modern Economic Thought.* Cambridge: Cambridge University Press.

Herskovits, Melville J. 1965. *Economic Anthropology: The Economic Life of Primitive Peoples.* New York: W.W. Norton.

Jolly, Clifford J. and Fred Plog. 1987. *Physical Anthropology and Archeology.* New York: Alfred A. Knopf.

Keen, Steve. 2001. *Debunking Economics: The Naked Emperor of the Social Sciences.* London: Pluto Press.

Krader, Lawrence. 1968. *Formation of the State.* Englewood Cliffs, N.J.: Prentice-Hall.

Lewellen, Ted C. 1992. *Political Anthropology: An Introduction.* London: Bergin & Garvey.

Liebowitz, Lila. 1986. "In the Beginning: The Origins of the Sexual Division of Labour and the Development of the First Human Societies," in Coontz and Henderson, pp. 43-75.

Lovewell, Mark. 2002. *Understanding Economics: A Contemporary Perspective.* Toronto: McGraw-Hill Ryerson.

MacNeill, Della and John W. Warnock. 2000. *The Disappearance of Affordable Housing in Regina.* Regina: Council on Social Development Regina.

Miller, Daniel, Michael Rowlands and Christopher Tilley, eds. 1989. *Domination and Resistance.* London: Unwin Hyman.

Moore, Sally Falk. 1958. *Power and Property in Inca Peru.* New York: Columbia University Press.

Murra, John Victor. 1980. *The Economic Organization of the Inca State.* Greenwich, Conn.: JAI Press.

O'Connor, Martin, ed. 1994. *Is Capitalism Sustainable? Political Economy and the Politics of Ecology.* New York: Guilford Press.

O'Toole, Roger. 1984. *Religion: Classic Sociological Approaches.* Toronto: McGraw-Hill.

Peterson, Frederick. 1962. *Ancient Mexico: An Introduction to the Pre-Hispanic Cultures.* New York: Capricorn Books.

Pickering, W.S.F. 1988. *Durkheim's Sociology of Religion: Themes and Theories.* London: Routledge & Kegan Paul.

Polanyi, Karl, Conrad M. Arensberg, and Harry W. Pearson, eds. 1957. *Trade and Market in Early Empires.* Glencoe, Ill.: Free Press.

Porter, John. 1965. The Vertical Mosaic: An Analysis of Social Class and Power in Canada. Toronto: University of Toronto Press.

Robbins, Lionel. 1998. *A History of Economic Thought: The LSE Lectures.* Princeton: Princeton University Press.

Robinson, Joan. 1971. *Economic Heresies: Some Old-Fashioned Questions in Economic Theory.* London: Macmillan.

Rowe, John Howland. 1982. "Inca Policies and Institutions Relating to the Cultural Unification of the Empire." In Collier *et al.*, pp. 93-118.

Sahlins, Marshall D. 1968. *Tribesmen.* Englewood Cliffs, N.J.: Prentice-Hall.

Scarth, William M. 2000. *Economics: The Essentials.* Toronto: Harcourt Canada.

Schreiber, Katharina J. 1992. *War Imperialism in Middle Horizon Peru.* Ann Arbor: Anthropological Papers, University of Michigan, No. 87.

Service, Elman R. 1962. *Primitive Social Organization: An Evolutionary Perspective.* New York: Random House.

Spry, Irene M. 1963. *The Palliser Expedition: the Dramatic Story of Western Canadian Exploration 1857-1860.* Calgary: Fifth House.

Stiglitz, Joseph E. 1993. *Principles of Microeconomics.* New York: W. W. Norton.

Townsend, Richard F. 1992. *The Aztecs.* London: Thames and Hudson.

von Hagen, Victor W. 1961. *Realm of the Incas.* New York: The New American Library.

Warnock, John W. 1978. *Profit Hungry: The Food Industry in Canada.* Vancouver: New Star Books.

White, Leslie A. 1959. *The Evolution of Culture: The Development of Civilization to the Fall of Rome.* New York: McGraw Hill.

Winson, Anthony. 1992. *The Intimate Commodity: Food and the Development of the Agro-Industrial Complex in Canada.* Toronto: Garamond Press.

Wolf, Eric R. 1959. *Sons of the Shaking Earth.* Chicago: University of Chicago Press.

# Chapter 3

————————O————————

# THE WORLD OF CAPITALISM

The world economy today is a capitalist economy. Almost all of the countries in the world have a capitalist mode of production. A few claim to have some form of socialism, but they are not strong enough to exist outside the world system. China, which was the largest centrally planned economy in the world at one time, is now reversing its socialist revolution and is moving quickly to become another capitalist economy.

As we all know, Canada is an advanced, industrialized, capitalist economy, and the average standard of living is one of the highest in the world. We have extensive natural resources, including water, that most of the world envies. But we are also a rather unusual capitalist country. We have a relatively weak capitalist class, reflected in the fact that so much of our economy is owned and/or controlled by foreign corporations. We have by far the highest level of foreign ownership of any industrialized capitalist state. Compared to Canada, Mexico has a more powerful capitalist class and greater control of its national economy.

Canada is also heavily dependent on trade with one country, the United States. In 2002 over 86 percent of our trade was with the United States. Furthermore, the structure of our trade is different from other advanced capitalist states. We are major importers of manufactured goods, particularly end products, and major exporters of natural resources and semi-processed goods. The structure of our trade is more like that of a colony or a semi-colony. We suffer from this by having a generally higher level of unemployment and underemployment.

Our communications industry is heavily dominated by U.S. corporate interests. No other advanced country has such a high level of foreign domination of advertising, television, movies, popular music, magazines and newspaper content as Canada. This ideological control re-enforces the U.S. corporate and political goal of general economic domination of Canada. Our major corporations, financial institutions, our economic elite, and most of our economists see nothing wrong with this situation. Our political leaders promote this development.

This economic integration is reflected in our political institutions. Our military is deeply integrated into the much larger U.S. military system. Our companies which manufacture arms are heavily dependent on subcontracting with major U.S. firms. At the United Nations, in NATO, and in the range of other international political organizations, we have a long history of close association with the U.S. government. During the Cold War with the Soviet bloc, the Canadian government usually acted as the "front man" for the U.S. government at the United Nations. The Canada-U.S. Free Trade Agreement and the North American Free Trade Agreement tie us closely to a much more powerful state, in a subordinate position, and as a result surrender considerable state sovereignty. Our political leaders have chosen a role for Canada as a "junior partner" to the most powerful military country in history, the world's leading capitalist country.

While we have a world capitalist economy, it is patently obvious that there are significant differences in how capitalism operates in different countries. Political economy recognizes that this is a product of history. Capitalism first developed in western Europe. It spread overseas as part of European imperialism and colonialism. Less developed countries around the world found capitalism imposed on them by foreign powers.

One of the most striking features of the world economy today is the uneven level of economic development between continents, nation states and regions within countries. The inequality between the advanced capitalist countries and the less developed countries continues to increase. Inequality is also increasing within countries. Inequality is a deeply rooted characteristic of capitalism.

Capitalism rose in Europe according to a similar model. There was the development of a national capitalist class which received strong support from the political leadership and the state. High tariffs and protections were established to develop an industrial state. Most of these countries benefitted from the inflow of capital from overseas colonies. They developed national economies, and international trade was a secondary phenomenon. Agricultural productivity increased, releasing farmers and farm workers for the urban, industrial economy. Capital was accumulated and invested in the national economy.

But this was not how capitalism emerged in most less developed countries. Almost all of these countries began as colonies or semi-colonies controlled by European imperial states. They did not have political control of their own development. They had a weak and dependent capitalist class. Their national cultures were subordinated and fragmented. They experienced widespread racial discrimination. They were invaded by Christian missionaries who degraded and tried to replace their indigenous religions.

The capitalist economy that arose in the colonized areas was distorted. The colonizers stressed the development of natural resources and agricultural products for export. They imposed a variety of taxes to finance the colonial administration. The best land was taken by European settlers. The indigenous populations were required to perform compulsory labour on colonial projects. Most of the economic surplus which was extracted from the labour of this production process was transferred to the imperial centre. There was no national economy.

Canada began its development as a colony within the French and then English mercantile imperial systems. But Canada was a special colony. It did not take long before the settlers from Europe came to outnumber the indigenous population. Within the British Empire, Canada was granted a special status as a Dominion. We were allowed to have political rights long before the non-white colonies. We achieved almost complete independence before World War II. The non-white colonies did not gain independence until into the 1950s and 1960s.

Today Canada is recognized as one of the most powerful capitalist states. We are a member of the Group of Eight leading capitalist countries. But in many ways we are different, and our history links us more with Australia, New Zealand, Argentina, Chile, Uruguay and Costa Rica as former colonies that evolved into white settler societies. Our particular history as a capitalist state within the British empire has been a determining factor in the development of Saskatchewan.

There is no need to repeat here the history of Canada as a colony and a Dominion within the British empire. What is important is to remember that the development of Canada, and the prairies and Saskatchewan, was a part of the world inter-imperialist rivalry between European capitalist states. This included the continued expansion of formal colonies well into the latter part of the 19th century. Saskatchewan emerged in the competition between the U.S. government and economic interests and the British and Canadian interests for the control of the western part of the North American continent. The political inclusion of Saskatchewan into the Canadian federal state followed definite patterns that had been established elsewhere within the British empire. (see Ryerson, 1960; Easterbrook and Aitken, 1956; Norrie and Owram, 1996; Nash, 2000)

While it is not possible to cover the development of capitalism here, it is very important to understand those elements of capitalism that are key to the development of Saskatchewan. From the beginning of the mercantile, colonial invasion, the Canadian prairies were a hinterland resource area operating within an imperial and colonial economy. That is still our general lot today. But Saskatchewan is part of an advanced industrial capitalist state, and we benefit from having one of the highest standards of living in the world.

Political economy was the first social science. It emerged in the eighteenth century, a product of the enlightenment and the rise of liberalism. It focused on the development of the modern territorial state and the expansion of imperialism and colonialism. It examined the rise of capitalism and the beginning of the industrial, factory economy. It is the best tool for understanding the development of capitalism in Canada and on the prairies.

## The Rise of Capitalism in Europe

Capitalism is a particular mode of production. It requires the private accumulation of wealth for investment, a large labour force of people who have no ownership of the means of production and can only survive by selling their labour in a free market, and the private ownership of land and resources. But it is much more than just a system of accumulating the economic surplus and investing it in productive enterprises. It is also a radically different social system which breaks down traditional human relationships of solidarity. All the institutions in society must change to embrace a new system and a new ideology. Capitalism could not have developed without its control over the government and the state. It also required control over trade and investment and a world economy.

Europe was the first part of the world to make the transition from the ancient modes of production to capitalism. The transition was a long process that stretched over several centuries. Some identify its beginning with the Christian Crusades in the eleventh century. While ostensibly a crusade of Christians against an evil Islam, the Crusades were manipulated by Venetian merchant capitalists and were primarily an organized scheme of piracy—sacking, looting, and seizing goods and capital. (Heilbroner, 1968)

Merchant capitalism began with the long distance trade between Asia and Europe and the great European trade fairs. By the fifteenth century the trade fairs had been replaced by cities, mainly along the Mediterranean, which were year round commercial centres. With this came the introduction of money, credit, commercial debt, and laws to regularize commerce.

With the expansion of trade, the European feudal system began to change. Serfs and peasants began to exchange their household surpluses in the city markets. The rent they owed their lords or the Church shifted from labour or goods in kind to money. Crafts developed in towns, undermining the dominance of craft production within the manor. Lords began to move into the new cities and became absentee landlords. There were technological changes in agriculture which increased productivity, led to the consolidation of farms, and the percentage of workers in farming began to steadily decline. (Heilbroner, 1968; Hunt, 1995; Warnock, 1987)

In 1600 the population of Europe was around 75 million people, of whom only around 3.5 million lived in anything approaching a city. Average life expectancy was around 23 to 25 years. Between 25 and 40 percent of all children died at birth. Poverty was widespread. Paul Bairoch estimates that the average consumption in the United Kingdom was only around 1800 kcal per day. Gregory King's social survey of 1688 concluded that over half the total population in the United Kingdom could not earn enough to support themselves and had to rely on charity and poor relief. (Bairoch, 1969; Mathias, 1969; Braudel, 1967)

The rise of capitalism was linked to the development of the national territorial state and a state economy. It is no surprise that capitalism developed first in England with its unified political state and internal market. Only with the development of the territorial state, a national economy, and a national government, was it possible to have a navy and merchant fleet and with it international trade, imperialism and colonies distant from Europe.

Robert Heilbroner has stressed that capitalism required the creation of Economic Man. [At last! He appears!] In all the pre-capitalist societies economics was subordinate to other allegiances. The state religions supported hierarchy and authority and subservience. Feudal ideology had to be replaced. The Christian Church taught that avarice or greed was a sin. Usury, lending money for a profit, was a mortal sin. Lending money was condemned as a parasitic activity. A lender could not claim as a payment for debt the tools or land of the worker, as this would impoverish him. As St. Thomas Aquinas proclaimed, "property is theft" from the producer. The Church often set the "just price" to try to prohibit profit taking. As the Church proclaimed, "the merchant can scarcely or never be pleasing to God." (Heilbroner, 1968)

As trade developed, so did manufacturing. By the sixteenth century the small craft operations were disappearing, replaced by the "putting-out system." Merchants, who sought goods to sell, used their capital to purchase inputs to manufactures and then contracted them out to independent workers who did the labour for a fee. As this system developed, the merchant-capitalist came to own the tools and machinery as well. It was only a short step to the creation of the mill or factory, a separate building where these workers now came to sell their labour for a wage. (Dobb, 1963; Hunt, 1995)

As agriculture moved from the feudal system, land became a commodity to be bought and sold. Lords, wealthy merchants and landlords began to fence off and claim the pastures and forests that were held in common for the use of peasants and serfs under the feudal system. Between three quarters and ninety percent of peasants were forced off the land in the United Kingdom by the enclosure movement in the sixteenth century. The result across Europe was the creation of a large class of unemployed workers who roamed from city to city looking for employment. The working class was being created. By the early nineteenth century, England had established capitalist farming: land ownership by a landlord class, their farms operated by tenant farmers, and hired labour to do the actual farm work. (Warnock, 1987)

## Mercantilism and the Primitive Accumulation of Capital

The early period of capitalist development is often called the era of mercantilism, and it is generally said to have covered the years between 1500 and 1750. This era in Europe saw the rise of the territorial state and the development of national economies. It was also characterized by overseas exploration, the first world trading economy, the development of European colonialism, and the slave trade.

Canada began as a European colony during the period of mercantilism. This early system of capitalism, imperialism and colonialism made its appearance on the Canadian prairies through the fur trade, the Hudson Bay Company, and the North West Company. It introduced a new value system, based on the production of commodities for a commercial market instead of use.

Gustav Schmoller, a noted German political economist, has argued that mercantilism was primarily concerned with state building. The absolute monarchs introduced a series of policies all designed to enhance the power of the territorial state. The internal state was firmly established with the creation of a military and police force, a penal system, a treasury and a bureaucracy, and the shift towards a national official religion, first established in England. It was the triumph of the centralized national state over the town, agricultural interests, and the Estates.

Most of the new European states imposed similar regulations. Power depended on the creation of a manufacturing industry. Tariffs and outright prohibitions blocked the importation of manufactured goods, and there were prohibitions on the export of raw materials. Exports were always to exceed imports. Protection and subsidies were given to the fishing and maritime industries. Foreign trade was confined to the national fleet. A national currency and banking system was created. A large population, and full employment, was considered basic to state power, and thus a national agriculture and food supply was stressed. All of these developments were seen as part of mercantilism. (Minchinton, 1969)

Colonies were needed to support the development of the "mother country." Non-European areas were seized by military force and put under direct colonial control. Regulations restricted the development of manufacturing in colonies, stressed the development of agriculture and primary commodities, and restricted trade to the imperial country. Tax systems were introduced to pay for the colonial administration and to promote dependent trade with the imperial centre. Eli Heckscher describes the political economy of mercantilism: "For if power was the object of economic policy and if the total fund of economic power was given once for all, the only method of benefitting one's own country was to take something away from someone else." Great Britain, France, Spain, the Netherlands and Portugal all operated their American colonies along these lines. (Minchinton, 1969)

The mercantile period stressed state and private monopoly power. The crown would grant permits to favoured people for monopoly control of trade in certain colonies. Examples include the Dutch East India Company, the East India Company, and of course the Hudson Bay Company. (Minchinton, 1969; Hunt, 1995)

Capitalism is a mode of production where the accumulation of the economic surplus is done by a class of private individuals and companies. The division of society between a class of producers and a class of owners had existed for thousands of years. The new ruling class was different in that it accumulated wealth for the purposes of investment in order to make even larger profits. The capitalist class may desire a life of luxury, but this is not its central focus or role. Thus political economists make a distinction between "wealth," used primarily to create personal luxury, and "capital," accumulated profits which are invested to earn additional profits. In the period of mercantile capitalism such a class was developing.

Imperialism and colonialism have also existed since the rise of the state in the Near East around 3,000 B.C. Trade and commerce are nothing new and can be found in almost all human societies since the beginning of time. But they do not describe a *mode of production*. Trade in itself is not a revolutionary phenomenon. It does not provide the difference between European feudalism and capitalism.

For most political economists, capitalism as a mode of production does not really begin until it supplants the agricultural and merchant economy identified with mercantilism. Thus, while it is argued that the industrial revolution began in England around 1750, it was not until around 1850 that the capitalist class was firmly in control and capitalism had become the mode of production.

Mercantilism was the beginning of the period of "primitive capital accumulation" in Europe. There had to be a growth in the claims or titles to capitalist property, the ownership of productive assets, and a concentration of these assets in the hands of an entrepreneurial capitalist class. This was a precondition to the development of capitalism.

The state also had a key role to play in the accumulation of capital. State funds were used to develop the infrastructure, ports, the navy, and even royal manufacturing. In the domestic economy, capital came from the price revolution, buying and selling goods and services, land speculation, banking and finance, usury from state debt, tax farming, and manufacturing. The profits from manufacturing were very high as workers were paid at a minimum subsistence level. (see Dobb, 1963; Hoffman, 1958; Mathias, 1969; Hobsbawm, 1968; Mandel, 1968)

But the most important source of early capital accumulation was trade and colonialism. The policies of the European countries in the Americas have been described as "conquest, pillage, extermination." Gold and silver were extracted mainly by slave labour. Sugar, cotton, tobacco and rice were produced on slave plantations on land stolen from the indigenous people, the majority of whom were exterminated. Colonial policies produced a very favourable balance of trade, maximizing the extraction of the economic surplus from the subjugated peoples. This led to seemingly endless imperial wars, for as William Pitt, the British Prime Minister stated in 1756, "When trade is threatened retreat is no longer possible." (see Beaud, 1983; Dobb, 1963; Williams, 1966; Mannix, 1962)

Because the domestic market was so depressed, as workers were paid only a subsistence wage, trade and colonialism were essential markets for manufactured goods. The terms of trade were more or less fixed by monopoly power, particularly trade between the European countries and their colonies. The success of the British textile industry not only depended on high tariffs and import prohibitions, it also rested on colonial power which destroyed the more advanced textile industry in India. Ireland, under British domination, was forbidden to export wool products to England. Under colonial rules, everything was done to discourage the development of an Irish clothing trade. As Maurice Dobb has argued, the imperial political power "often sufficed to make colonial trade forced trading and the profit on it indistinguishable from plunder." (Dobb, 1963)

The colonies, like those in North America, were also important for dealing with the problem of high unemployment. It was regular practice to sell convicts, pauper children, vagabonds and others who were often kidnapped to the Americas as indentured servants. They provided a needed labour force and helped solve the problem of "surplus population." (Dobb, 1963)

The new mode of production had a revolutionary impact on pre-capitalist societies. Anthropologist Alan Klein examined the changes which came to four prairie tribes, the Teton Dakota, Assiniboine, Gros Ventre and Blackfoot. Mercantile capitalism began the transformation of the "nomadic mode of production" with its egalitarian value system. Their traditional life was changed with the introduction of the horse and the gun, which became the private property of individual men. Hunting became individualized. Men took control of the trade in buffalo robes, which created greater inequalities within the tribe. The status of women was downgraded, and men with greater wealth began to purchase more wives who were needed to prepare the hides. Astohkomi (Crowfoot) of the Blackfoot personally owned a herd of 400 horses. Mercantile capitalism was introducing an entirely new political economy and value system. (Klein, 1983; Jenish, 1999)

Mercantilism describes the intermediary period between the collapse of feudalism and the rise of industrial capitalism. In the early period it stressed the development of the national, territorial state, with extensive government intervention in the economy. The development of large navies and merchant ships, world trade, and colonialism were essential. But as the European states moved to industrial capitalism, state regulations became an impediment to the expansion and accumulation of capital. The new bourgeois class challenged the old state and feudal ruling classes, demanding a move to the free market and a freer system of trade.

It is not possible to trace the history of capitalism here. Neither is it possible to show how economists and political economists have recorded and interpreted this history. But it is important to point out the developments and theories which have had the greatest impact on the development of Saskatchewan. Without an understanding of this historical process, it is difficult to find solutions to continuing problems.

## The Right to Steal Land

Canada and Saskatchewan were founded when agents of European governments claimed the continent for their countries, used military force and the threat of force to drive the indigenous people off their land, and brought in European settlers. Thus, Canada and Saskatchewan were both created by military conquest and the theft of land. For the British, it was important to construct an official ideology which justified the seizure of land by force from its original owners. John Locke performed this service for the empire. His arguments are still used today in Saskatchewan.

Political economy is always identified with the rise of liberalism and capitalism in western Europe. The first political economist with widespread influence was the English writer, John Locke (1637-1704). He is of particular importance to North America. He set forth the ideological justification for taking the land from the indigenous population. In addition, he was the first to clearly set forth the labour theory of value, which became the value system of classical political economy from Adam Smith through Karl Marx. He also established the theory of economic rent for the use of land and other resources which has been used by mainstream liberal political economists and economists down to the present day.

Locke's major work *The Second Treatise of Government* (1690) and *Some Considerations of the Consequences of the Lowering of Interest and Raising the Value of Money* (1691) had an enormous impact on the founders of the American government. He was the major propagandist in support of the English revolution of 1688, which put William of Orange on the British throne, and introduced the principle of the supremacy of the Parliament over the Monarchy. He is widely identified as the founder of political liberalism. All of the early political economists carefully studied his work and were greatly influenced by him. (Locke, 1966; 1976)

John Locke was born into a family of lawyers and merchants who lived in the West counties of England, where the local merchants and gentry had been trying for hundreds of years to subjugate Ireland and seize their land. In 1667 he abandoned a career as an Oxford Don and became secretary to Lord Ashley, Chancellor of the Exchequer under Charles II and later the Earl of Shaftesbury and Lord Chancellor. Along with Ashley, Locke was a partner in the New Royal African Company which was engaged in the slave trade. He invested in sugar plantations in Barbados where slavery was the mode of production. He served on the Board of Trade and Plantations where he dealt with matters like the Irish textile industry, problems in the Virginia colonies, and supervised other colonial holdings. He also served as secretary to the Proprietors of Carolina, the company given land by the Crown for a colony, and in 1669 he drew up The Fundamental Constitution of Carolina. He was personally involved in the expansion of the English empire. (Arneil, 1996; Cranston, 1957)

Locke was well aware of issues around property ownership through his work. He knew that in Scotland, Ireland and North America tribal property was communally owned. But he was first of all a protagonist for the expansion of capitalism and individual ownership of property. As Barbara Arneil points out, his primary goal was to justify English colonialism in the Americas. The Spanish had justified their seizure of land from other nations on the historic "right of conquest." Locke was looking for a different justification, one which might be judged to be more in tune with Christianity and natural law.

As Arneil documents, Locke first builds his argument on Genesis, where God orders men to "replenish the earth and subdue it." This requires that men cultivate the land and enclose it. (The liberals did not considered women to be citizens and completely left them out of their analysis.) Thus Locke, and the other defenders of English colonialism, justify England's right to take the land by the fact that the colonists are engaging in "pasturage, tilling and planting."

The indigenous population, Locke argues, can only claim the land that they are in fact cultivating. They have no claim to the "waste land" not under cultivation and land that is not enclosed. Furthermore, Locke was firmly committed to a capitalist system of agriculture. Land that is claimed from the unused commons and is cultivated becomes the private property of the man doing the farming. Since the indigenous population farmed on a collective basis, on collectively owned land, and did not enclose the land with fences, Locke argues that they do not even have a claim to land they are actually farming. They cannot establish ownership rights under law until their land is owned by individuals. This view is still widely held in Canada today.

Locke was also the first to logically set forth the classical political economy theory of value. It is labour, applied to natural resources, that produces value. Locke first argues that no consent is required of the rest of mankind for the seizure of land from the commons as long as there is "good left in common for others." There is no moral reason to preserve any wilderness or any land for other species. Thus it is morally right to seize the land of the Americas which is "wilderness," the "vacant places," and not being used for any productive purpose. This is the same argument that the English imperialists and colonists used in Ireland.

From earliest times, Locke argues, men have always acquired land and resources needed for survival. It is not necessary to make any payment to mankind in general for the appropriation of common property. This becomes the capitalist view of rent in resources. It was also accepted by Karl Marx and his followers.

However, there were at the time several widely recognized Christian natural law positions which put limitations on how much common property an individual man could seize, and Locke believed these had to be considered. Natural law took the position that a man could not justify taking more than he could use before it spoiled. The indigenous people claimed a great deal of land that was not being used for cultivation, and the natural product of this land was just left to spoil. Locke argues that they cannot justify keeping this land. There can be no justification for wilderness or "waste land" as the liberal capitalists called it.

The original natural law position of the Christian church was that an individual could not take more land than he could appropriate with his own labour. Locke stresses that this theoretical limitation on personal ownership under natural law was established before the introduction of money. Holding natural resources in the form of money overcomes the limitation on the amount of land that can be appropriated. Agricultural products can be sold in the market and transferred to gold and silver which do not spoil. Locke sees money as capital and as a substitute for land and natural resources. Locke justifies the unequal ownership of land and property, a basic characteristic of capitalism. Since the indigenous population had no money system (that Locke would recognize), only colonists could overcome the restrictions of the law of spoilage. European colonists had a moral claim to indigenous land.

Under Locke's defence of colonialism, the indigenous people of the Americas only had a right to the land used for subsistence. Large tracts of land, he argues, can only be held if the product of the land is sold to the rest of the world. Since the Amerindians had no money, they could not engage in world trade. Only the colonists had this ability and the right to own land beyond the subsistence level. Of course the indigenous peoples traded their surpluses, had their own system of barter and money, and through treaties had established their territorial boundaries, reflected in their own systems of government and law. But this was ignored by Locke. In his unpublished notes, he writes: "The chief end of trade is riches and power... riches consist in plenty of movables that will yield a price to a foreigner...especially in plenty of gold and silver." (Cited in Arneil, 1996)

But what about the natural law position on the labour theory of value? In *Considerations* Locke argues that every man has a right to sell his own labour. The appropriation of an economic surplus from the labour of another worker is not an act of exploitation. Through a free contract to work for someone else the worker gives consent to the appropriation of his share of the product created from his own labour. In the circulation process of the market this takes the form of money. Furthermore, Locke argues that by accepting the capitalist system of political economy mankind has voluntarily agreed to "disproportionate and unequal possession of the earth." (Macpherson, 1962)

Central to all of Locke's writings is his belief that the most important right of any man is the right to own property. He fully understands the class base of society, noting that England is divided between those who own land, merchants, and the labouring class which is poor and owns no property. It is from this position that he formulates his theory of government.

All governments are founded on the consent of those who are citizens. Citizens are defined by the liberals as those who own productive property. Each individual citizen cannot protect his property from the vast number of people who have none. Therefore it is necessary for individual property owners to consent to grant certain powers to government. As Locke argues, this new government has been constructed by property owners, it will be run by them, and it will serve their interests. At all times it will be subservient to "civil society" which he defines as the collective of property owners. This surrender of individual rights is necessary to obtain the guarantee that the government will protect private property rights. It is the only rational basis for forming a government. (For a detailed discussion of Locke and property rights, see MacPherson, 1962; Arneil, 1996)

The colonists, however, were not going to be limited by Locke's labour theory of value and his view of the right to property. This was settled in a famous case in 1823 where the U.S. Supreme Court, with Chief Justice John Marshall writing the decision, ruled that the English had the right to land they claimed in the Americas only because they had conquered the indigenous population. "Conquest gives title which the courts of the conqueror cannot deny." This ruling became the foundation for subsequent decisions on Aboriginal land claims. (Arneil, 1996)

## Capital Accumulation Drives the System

The key to understanding capitalism as an economic system is to understand the nature of capital and how it is accumulated. We know that all urban societies in the past have depended on the creation of an economic surplus and its investment in productive enterprises. This process is crucial to understanding economic development in Saskatchewan. What is capital? How is it created? Who has ownership and control?

Who decides how and where it is invested? If the economic surplus created by the labour of people in Saskatchewan is accumulated and invested outside the province, then economic development will lag compared to the rest of the country.

Adam Smith (1723-1790) is the best known of all the classical liberal political economists. He was Professor of Moral Philosophy at the University of Glasgow, a close friend of David Hume, and he traveled to Europe to consult with Voltaire and Quesnay on political and economic issues of the day. *The Wealth of Nations*, published in 1776, took ten years to write and was an attempt to pull together liberal thought into a broad overview. He is seen as the most important early defender of capitalism.

Central to Smith's political and economic argument is his view of human nature. As a classic liberal, he believes that egoism is the driving force behind all human activity. It is "the uniform, constant, and uninterrupted effort of every man [sic] to better his condition." This is Economic Man. Thus society is nothing more than a collection of individuals seeking to maximize their own economic well being. Smith concludes that this will produce a balanced and harmonious society, the result of the "invisible hand" of the market operating for the interest of all. It is competition which regulates this society. In the economic area, every entrepreneur, every businessman, is in constant competition with every other businessman. (Smith, 1967)

As Robert Heilbroner has pointed out, it is "curious" that Smith could conclude that such a system of political economy could produce harmony. This was not the real world of England: "Outside the drawing rooms of London or the pleasant rich estates of the counties, all one saw was rapacity, cruelty and degradation mingled with the most irrational and bewildering customs and traditions of some earlier and already anachronistic day." Men worked long hours under horrendous conditions for a pittance. Women and children worked in the mines and the new textile factories for 12 to 14 hours a day. The poor wandered the country in bands desperately seeking employment. It was England between the collapse of feudalism and the future industrial capitalist system. (Heilbroner, 1961)

Smith agrees with Locke and the other classical political economists: *productive labour* is the source of all value and wealth. "Labour is the real measure of the exchangeable value of all commodities," he argues. "The annual produce of the land and labour of any nation can be increased in its value by no other means but by increasing either the number of productive labourers, or the productive powers of those labourers who had before been employed." Machines and instruments are used to increase labour productivity, but this is "labour stocked and stored up." Smith also makes the distinction between "direct labour" which is the current labour being used and "indirect labour" which is the labour stored up as capital. Capital, seen by most economists today as an independent factor of production, is in reality only the stored value of previous labour. This capital (often called "stock" by Smith) can be lent by owners to others for an annual interest. These loans are made in money, either in paper, gold or silver. Capital and stock, therefore, is commonly expressed as money. But capital only comes "from the ground or from the hands of the productive labourers."

The labour theory of value was viewed as common sense. Minerals in the ground, trees in the forest, fish in the oceans, hay in the fields have no value until human labour is applied and the raw materials are transformed into some product for use or commodity for sale in the market. Buildings, machinery and instruments used in production were created by previous labour that was applied to resources.

Smith focuses on the accumulation of capital. This is the key to progress and development in a capitalist society. Productive labour applied to agriculture or to manufacturing produces the economic surplus. When labour is applied to land, the economic surplus is called "rent" which is paid by the English tenant farmer to his landlord. When the economic surplus is extracted from the labour of those who are employed in manufacturing, it is called capital. This rent and capital is then invested in enterprises to produce more capital.

This is what distinguishes capitalism from previous economic systems. The private owners of capital, the capitalist class, are always seeking to invest their capital to accumulate more capital. All capitalists are doing this in competition with all other capitalists. If a man does not always pursue the goal of maximizing profit he will fall by the wayside, be driven out of business, lose his markets, be pushed aside by his competitors and most likely go bankrupt. This is the necessary *role* of capitalists within the system, and Smith argued that it benefits society as a whole. Political economists refer to this as Adam Smith's *Law of Accumulation*. It is the root of capitalism.

Smith also believes that the system works best when there are no constraints on the capitalist. They must be free to invest wherever they can maximize their profits. Therefore, Smith, like all liberals, wanted a limited government. There are only three legitimate functions for governments: protection of the country against invaders, a system of law and order which protects individuals and private property rights, and certain public works which while necessary for a nation state would not be profitable investments for capitalists. That is the abstract theory. The real world is also described in *The Wealth of Nations*: "Civil government, so far as it is instituted for the security of property, is in reality instituted for the defence of the rich against the poor." (Smith, 1967)

There is an enormous gap between the ideal model of competitive capitalism as described by Smith and the actual world of capitalism. The small firm gives way quickly to the large firm. The entrepreneur gives way to the corporation run by a management that is a salaried class. The competitive market gives way in the 19th century to markets dominated by monopoly firms, oligopoly markets of a few firms following a recognized price leader, the formation of national and international trusts and cartels, and extensive government support and protection for their nationally-based firms. In the 20th century monopoly power becomes rooted in massive advertising and "product differentiation," style changes that create artificial competition and drive up the price of commodities.

For small business, they are now confronted by competition from large transnational corporations which have the economic and political power which comes with size, capital and government support. When Home Depot moves into Regina, almost all of the local and Canadian owned lumber yards are driven out of business. When Office Depot moves into Regina, all of the small, locally owned stationery stores go out of business. When Chapters arrives, many of the small book stores decide to close up shop. The Seven Eleven chain eliminates the mom and pop local grocery stores. The local drug stores face stiff competition from the national and international supermarkets and chain stores.

These large corporations come to Saskatchewan for only one purpose: the accumulation of capital. They triumph through the power that comes with economies of scale, they pay their workers less, and they sell a wide range of goods that are produced in low wage areas of the less developed world. Wal Mart is welcomed to Regina by the provincial and municipal governments, who virtually exempt them from paying local taxes. As we know from studies in the United States, for every two jobs they create, they eliminate three. A survey in 2000 found that 83 percent of their ticketed items were made offshore and 53 percent came from China, where there is virtual slave labour. These transnational corporations form a huge black hole which sucks the economic surplus out of Saskatchewan and sends it back to their head offices. (see Kunstler, 1998; Stone, 1995)

But the worry and discontent of local businesses is articulated by the Canadian Federation of Independent Business and the Saskatchewan Chamber of Commerce. They blame their plight on "socialism," "big government" and of course high taxes. Because of their commitment to the system, they cannot admit that their biggest threat comes from international capital.

The process of capital accumulation is central to understanding how the economic system works in hinterland areas like Saskatchewan. Ownership and control does matter. In his time Adam Smith believed that capitalists would have a loyalty to their own country and that they would not invest abroad unless they had no other choice. In the era of free trade, strongly supported by Smith, the loyalty of capitalists is only to maximizing profit.

## Free Trade in Theory and Practice

Free trade, of course, has been high on the political agenda in Canada since the early 1980s when the Tories under Brian Mulroney were running the country. Now that Canada is deeply entangled in continental free trade agreements with the United States, there is considerable debate over whether the free trade regime has been good for Canada or Saskatchewan. Political economists always raise the other questions: Who benefits from free trade? Who does not?

From the beginning of European settlement of the Canadian prairies, farmers and others have been keenly interested in the issues around trade policy, including tariffs and the concept of free trade. Beginning in the 19th century Canadian capitalists argued for high tariffs and other protections of "infant industries." Farmers in western Canada wanted a policy of free trade, hoping it would undermine monopoly pricing by the corporate sector. Over the years tariff policy remained an important political issue.

Free trade and free markets are central tenets of mainstream economics today. They are a given, like a fundamental religious principle. Those who question this commitment are seen to be either ignorant or fools. Since this is such a key issue in Canada and Saskatchewan, it is important to briefly look at the origin and development of this theory and actual state policy.

Of all the early political economists, David Ricardo (1772-1823) had the most lasting impact on both economics and political economy. Ricardo was the son of a wealthy banker and became a stockbroker. He first worked for his father and then set up his own company when he was twenty-five. Through his market speculations he was able to buy a country estate and retire as a wealthy man at the age of forty-two. He also taught political economy at the college at Haileybury founded by the East India Company. His major work, *On the Principles of Political Economy and Taxation*, was published in 1817. Elected to Parliament in 1819, he was famous for legislation he introduced proposing that government debt be paid off by a one time tax on capital. (Heilbroner, 1961; Hunt, 1995; Buchholz, 1989; Robbins, 1998)

Like John Locke and Adam Smith, Ricardo supports the labour theory of value. He argues that "the value of a commodity, or the quantity of any other commodity for which it will exchange, depends on the relative quantity of labour which is necessary for its production, and not on the greater or less compensation which is paid for that labour." Capital is "the labour which is bestowed in the implements, tools and buildings." But unlike Smith and the other liberals, he did not believe that capitalism is an economic system that produces harmony. He saw conflict between the major classes as one of its basic characteristics. (Ricardo, 1962)

Ricardo was a propagandist for the new bourgeois class in their political conflict with the landed aristocracy. The landlord class dominated Parliament and passed legislation known as the Corn Laws which blocked the import of cheaper cereal grains. Since workers were paid at a subsistence wage, when the price of bread was high, wages had to be higher than necessary, and this cut into profits. Cheap grain, Ricardo and the capitalists argued, would allow wages to be lowered and profit to increase. This was the main reason why Ricardo supported free trade, trade without barriers of tariffs and quotas on imports.

Ricardo is widely known as the intellectual source of the theory which supports the policy of free trade. Each country, he argues, should specialize in the production and export of those products that use the lowest amount of labour time relative to the competition. As well, a country should import those products which require the highest amount of labour time. Thus in his famous model he argued that Great Britain should specialize in manufacturing and Portugal should give up manufacturing and specialize in producing wine. (Ricardo, 1962)

But this policy was not readily accepted in other countries. Alexander Gerschenkron argues that the classical liberal political economy of the free market and free trade suited the interests of Great Britain, which was the most powerful and most highly developed industrial state. This policy was rejected by the "late developers"who wanted to pursue a policy of industrialization. These countries all relied on high tariffs and other state interventions in the economy in order to promote their own industrial strategies. (Gerschenkron, 1963)

The first major challenge to the theory of free trade came from the United States. When the first U.S. Congress met in 1786, petitions came from most of the states to establish a policy of protection. One of the first acts of the Congress was to impose protective tariffs. However, these tariffs were not high enough to block out English goods. The Congress asked Alexander Hamilton, Secretary of the Treasury, to prepare a report, which was presented in 1791. The *Report on Manufactures* has been seen as one of the most complete statements on why countries should strive to industrialize. (Hamilton, 1934)

Hamilton argues that manufacturing is important because it has a greater division of labour. It employs more workers and in many different areas. It increases skills and technology. It attracts immigrants and capital for investment. It employs a great many people all year round and twenty-four hours a day. It creates a demand for agricultural products. It nurtures the "spirit of enterprise."

For a country emerging from colonialism, the development of manufacturing could not be left to the free market and entrepreneurs. Who would try to invest in an area where the market was dominated by good, cheap imports from the most advanced industrialized country? Thus Hamilton proposes a list of ways that a government could intervene in the economy to support the development of manufacturing. These include tariffs, quotas, limitations on the export of key natural resources, export subsidies, drawback duties on imported raw materials used in manufacturing, support for research and development, promoting the immigration of skilled workers, quality controls on exports, development of infrastructure, and state support for financing private industry. The government steadily increased protective tariffs until the 1930s, by which time the United States had become the world's dominant economic power. It then adopted a policy of free trade. (Alam, 2000; Hamilton, 1934; List, 1991)

The most influential political economist to follow Hamilton's position was Frederich List (1789-1846). Born in Germany, List was a professor of political economy at the University of Tubingen and editor of several periodicals. He was elected to the legislature in Wurtemberg in 1820. He was jailed for ten months for advocating local self government and open judicial proceedings. He was arrested again and forced to emigrate to the United States. While in Pennsylvania, he developed a coal mine and a small railroad and became an advocate of economic nationalism. He studied the economic development of England and the United States, and in 1841 published *The National System of Political Economy*. This work was much more influential in Germany and Japan than the work of Smith and Ricardo. (List, 1991)

List was a traditional conservative. On a fundamental level he disagreed with the liberals. He argues that people do not always pursue their own self interest at the expense of everyone else. This is not basic human nature. He attributes this "cosmopolitan liberalism" to a particular group of middle class, intellectual men. Most people's primary attachment, he argues, is to their families, their kinship group, their friends, and their nations. Thus he argues that people are basically more co-operative than competitive. In the era of industrial nation states, a person's highest allegiance would be to their country.

List sees territorial states all going through three stages of economic development. First they are agricultural. Then when they are new countries without manufacturing, they need a political economy system that sustains the development of manufacturing. Once they have a well developed industrial economy, then they can adopt policies of free trade.

List points out that England did not adopt free trade until between 1846 and 1849. Before this high tariffs were imposed on manufactured imports. In 1700 British manufacturers had secured the complete prohibition of Indian cotton imports. Indian cottons could only be imported if they were further manufactured and then exported. While England was by far the technological leader in the iron and steel industry, high tariffs nevertheless protected this particular industry until 1825. The United States under Hamilton was only following the British precedent. In contrast, List argues, the collapse of Portugal's industry was due to the fact that Great Britain had forced them to adopt policies of free trade. (List, 1991)

In his major work List places considerable emphasis on a country's "productive powers." A modern state has to have a good system of universal education, technical and post secondary institutions, research and development, and a well developed infrastructure. He also refers to "mental capital," which comes with urbanization and manufacturing; it is not found in an agricultural society. Manufacturing societies produce municipal liberty, intelligence, arts and science, internal and external commerce, navigation and railway transport, civilization, and political power. Agricultural societies in general are found by List to reflect "caprice and slavery, superstition and ignorance" and "want of means of culture." (List, 1991)

Douglas Dowd reminds us that the countries which rejected free trade as a policy of economic development, Great Britain, the United States, Germany, France, Japan, Italy and Canada, now make up the Group of Seven or G-7, the most powerful industrialized countries in the world. Shahid Alam demonstrates that the success of "late development" is the ability of countries to have control over their trade and investment policy. Those countries which had a long history of a lack of sovereignty because of external control through colonization, or were "quasi-colonies" dominated by imperial countries, fell far behind the others and today have the most desperate economic and social conditions. (Dowd, 2000; Alam, 2000)

The question of protection of industry and support for free trade has long been a central political issue in Canada. During the rise of manufacturing in Canada in the

19th century, the industrial capitalists in central Canada, usually linked politically to the industrial working class, supported high tariffs and other protections. The farmers in western Canada were strong supporters of free trade, hoping that imports from other countries would undermine the monopolistic power of the Canadian manufacturers.

Beginning in the 1980s the capitalist class in Canada shifted its position. It now calls for free trade with the United States and the elimination of government regulations and controls on the movement of capital. Whereas the policy of protection in the 19th century supported the political goal of an independent Canada, the policies of continental integration, supported by the Canadian capitalist class over the last 20 years, has promoted Fortress North America and the virtual disappearance of Canada as an independent country. (see Clarkson, 2002; Hurtig. 2002)

## Karl Marx, Class Conflict and the Rise of the Socialist Movement

For most people in Canada, Karl Marx's analysis of capitalism was proven false by the decline and fall of the Soviet system of centrally planned economies. Today there are no strong communist parties in any industrialized states and few elsewhere. The moderate social democratic and labour parties have also renounced Marxism. Those who are now challenging the capitalist system, the relatively small new left parties, the Green parties, and the anti-globalization movement, do not generally identify with the class struggles of the 19th century. So why would anyone bother examining Marxism and its analysis of capitalism?

First it is important to recognize that the major political, economic and industrial conflicts of the present period are not found in the advanced capitalist societies. In First World countries the broad, organized working class has found its place within the capitalist system. The working class in these countries has for the most part given up any dream of a different society and has settled for a consumer society. Those who are poor and marginalized are a minority in all the industrialized capitalist countries and are rather easily controlled by the power of the state. For the most part, they are not politically active.

The real political and economic conflict today is in the less developed countries, where the large majority of the world's population lives. Here the conflict between the domestic and international capitalist class and the working class and the poor is an every day reality.

Furthermore, many would argue that the primary economic and political conflict today is between the rich capitalist countries and the poor capitalist countries.

The major conflict is an international conflict, between the countries which are the core of the new imperialism and the dependent less developed capitalist countries.

Class conflicts, along with national and international conflicts, are very much part of the world capitalist system today. To understand why this conflict persists in its present form, it is necessary to look at the historic critique of capitalism as a system. Here we are guided by the political economy of Marxism. It is quite relevant to any discussion of the economic status of Saskatchewan.

For the vast majority of people, the capitalist industrial revolution was no picnic. The standard of living of the poor majority fell in relative terms. Workers were no longer skilled craftsmen with their own tools and workplaces but unskilled humans attached to machines in dirty and noisy factories. The division of labour in the factory made it possible to employ women and children for even lower wages. Children were indentured to companies for seven years, where they worked 14 to 18 hours a day for only a meal. Women worked in the mines from 14 to 16 hours a day. In the new cities workers lived in filth and misery in working class districts, with no sanitary facilities, many to a single room. Most did not live to see thirty years of age. (see Hobsbawm, 1968; Engels, 1958)

Given the horrors of industrial capitalism, it is not surprising that there was a flowering of political writers condemning the system. William Thompson denounced the evils of competition and the pursuit of wealth. Robert Owen advanced a Christian, co-operative alternative to the capitalist system based on exploitation. William Godwin denounced the corrupt and unjust institutions and argued that capitalism, based on greed, made fraud and robbery inevitable. Henri de Saint-Simon condemned the idle rich who live off the labour of the poor. Charles Fourier argued that capitalism was inevitably destructive of human beings and called for a retreat to co-operative, agricultural societies. Pierre Joseph Proudhon, reviving St. Thomas Aquinas, declared that "property is theft" under capitalism, theft from the workers, and all states were tyrannies. (see Gray, 1963; Hunt, 1995)

Throughout the early nineteenth century rebellions against the new capitalist system occurred on a regular basis. This peaked in 1848 when across the European continent workers and peasants rose in revolt. For the most part, the workers were only demanding the right to vote and a job. The uprisings in France, Austria, Germany and Italy were met with bullets from the armed forces which killed and wounded thousands, laws against workers and their organizations, and the imprisonment of political activists. In February 1848 *The Communist Manifesto* made its appearance. (see Abendroth, 1972; Caute, 1966)

Radical political economy begins with Karl Marx (1818-1883) and Frederick Engels (1820-1895). As Alexander Gray notes "The collaboration of Marx and Engels is surely something that is unique in literary history." It lasted for almost forty years. Marx studied philosophy under Georg Hegel in his native Germany but was active in revolutionary organizations for all of his adult life. In 1848 he was exiled to London where he did his research, writing and work with the international working class political movements. His friend and colleague Engels gave him financial support.

August Comte is usually cited as a founder of sociology, for he was the first to use the term. But Engels' *The Condition of the Working Class in England in 1844* is the first real sociological work. There was a loose division of labour between the two, with Marx concentrating on political economy and Engels on sociology, anthropology, dialectics and nature, and the family. But they collaborated on everything, and thus the term "Marxism" includes the work of both Marx and Engels. Marx died before completing volumes II and III of *Capital*, and they were edited (and some say modified) by Engels. (see Bose, 1975; Freedman, 1963; Mandel, 1968)

Marx studied and appreciated the work of the liberal political economists. First, they had introduced the scientific method. To understand any social system it is absolutely necessary to have an empirical approach. Political economy must be based on the facts as they are, not on abstract philosophical speculation or ideological pronouncements. Secondly, it is essential to study history. Political economy must describe how social systems actually work.

One of Marx's important works was *A Critique of Political Economy*, published in 1859. Classical liberal political economy, he argues, was very much a part of the world of the new capitalist class. They were its advocates. Any analysis of capitalism has to start with the class structure of production and how the capitalist class accumulates capital. Marx and Engels were critical of the view that capitalism was the end of history. Just as the liberal political economists of their time ignored the history of pre-capitalist human experience, they refused to recognize that capitalism was an historical creation. It is not permanent, and it is not the end of history. Change is an unending process. Thus, because of its empirical approach, Marxism came to be known as "scientific socialism." (Marx, 1970)

It is not possible to cover here the contribution of Marxism to political economy. But it is important to mention the most central concepts which are key to understanding capitalism, whether it is in Great Britain in the 19th century or Saskatchewan in the 21st century.

Perhaps the most important contribution of Marxism to social science was "historical materialism." The goal of political economy is to understand the world. This means looking in depth at the history of human existence. How was society ordered in the period before the rise of the state? What was the mode of production of specific communities? What was the class structure of early state societies? How was the economic surplus accumulated? How was it distributed? What was the relationship between the ideological structure and the system of production?

From this analysis, Marx and Engels conclude that the history of human beings in class societies is a history of class struggle, a virtual war between the owners of the means of production, the rich, privileged classes, and the workers who perform the labour: the slaves, the serfs, the peasants, the industrial workers, and the colonized peoples. Social class and class conflict is the fundamental contradiction in all class-based societies, and this conflict is the dialectical process that moves history.

The core of any society is how it is socially organized for the purposes of production. Marxists call this the "base" of the society. Thus, for example, in the American South in 1860 the system of production was plantation agriculture with labour by African slaves, directed by the class of large land owners. While there were many small independent farmers and urban manufacturing operations, the society was run by a ruling class of slave owners. Many small farmers and businesses also used slave labour. The South was a capitalist society, but a specific capitalism based on slavery as a mode of production. It was slavery that defined this society, not the fact that it was an agricultural society or that it was a commodity exporting society.

Thus with slavery as the basic mode of production, the "superstructure" of the society had to follow. The value system of the society at large, and its institutions, must mirror the values of the base, Marx and Engels insist. No society can survive if there is a fundamental contradiction between the values of the economic base and the value system of the superstructure. Thus in the American South the legal system, the police and penal system, the government, the educational system, the mores of the society, the religious organizations, and the ethical rules had to follow the basic principles of support for slavery. And they did. For example, all the Christian churches in the South supported slavery, even when their Northern branches opposed slavery. (see Foner and Genovese, 1969; Elkins, 1976)

Marx and Engels also stress the role of the market in capitalism. Under capitalism production of commodities is not for use but for exchange. The means of production also become commodities: factories, machinery, tools, land, buildings, technology, etc. The labour power of workers also becomes a commodity. The majority of people under capitalism can only support themselves by selling their labour in the market. Relations between workers, and between individuals, becomes a commodity relationship.

In his major work *Capital* Marx details his moral critique of capitalism. The system produces profound *alienation.* "Work" is central to the existence of humans, Marx argues, the productive process over which they have control and find their own expression. A truly democratic society allows everyone to develop their full potential, doing the work that is their own choice. Under the capitalist system a human being is forced to do "labour" for another person simply to survive. Workers have little choice in this; they must take whatever jobs are available or face starvation. Increased remuneration, which would come with increased productivity, would allow many workers to have better clothing, food, and treatment. But higher incomes do not change the system of exploitation, whether one is a slave or a wage labourer. Under capitalism, workers have no control over the workplace or how commodities are produced. They have no control over what they produce. Workers under capitalism are alienated from their fellow workers, those workers who have gone before, the natural world which gives up the resources, and the other species on the planet. Marx and Engels argue that a worker can never be free from this alienation until the capitalist system of exploited labour is ended and replaced with socialism.

The class structure of society is central to the analysis of modern political economy. The ruling class today are those who own the means of production. The capitalist class is divided into class fractions: land, resources, merchant, finance and industrial groups. They often clash but they are united in their determination to maintain the capitalist system.

The Marxist model of capitalism identifies the largest class as the working class, those who sell their labour in the market. This class is also characterized by class fractions, which became more important in the twentieth century. The third class is the petit bourgeois class, those independent farmers, small businessmen and professionals who labour but also own their own means of production. Marx and Engels believe that this class will decline over time as the capitalist system evolves toward a monopoly period.

Finally, there is a fourth class, which Marx and Engels called the lumpen proletariat. This class of people are outside the main labour force, either unable to work, or discriminated against, marginally in the labour force, dependent on private and state charity to survive. This class is the largest class in most less developed countries. Conflict between the classes, whether in the private sector of production or in the political area, is fundamental to capitalism. In Saskatchewan it takes the form of industrial and government labour disputes and competition in the electoral process. In many less developed countries it takes the form of state repression and armed resistance.

The creation of the economic surplus is different under capitalism. In pre-capitalist societies most of the economic surplus is extracted from agricultural labourers, through tribute under imperialism, through price manipulation in trade, and through usury. Under capitalism the primary source of the economic surplus is through the extraction of the "surplus value" from the worker in the production process. The surplus value is the difference between the wages received by the worker who creates the product and the price that the owner receives from the sale of the product. This surplus becomes known as "capital" when it is accumulated by the owner. Capital is not a "factor of production" as claimed by liberal economists. "Capital," Marx argues, "is dead labour, that vampire-like, only lives by sucking living labour, and lives the more, the more labour it sucks." (Marx, 1961)

In contrast to the liberal political economists, Marx and Engels insist that workers do not voluntarily agree to grant part of the value of their labour to the employer. They have no option in the matter. It is not a free contract. For the workers, it is either sell your labour or starve. Wage labour under capitalism is a form of wage slavery. The exploitation of the worker can only be resolved through the overthrow of the capitalist system and its replacement by a socialist system of workers' ownership and control of the means of production.

Marx had a vision of a socialist future. In 1870 the workers in Paris seized power and proclaimed the Paris Commune. It was soon crushed by the state and thousands of workers were killed, tortured, imprisoned, and sent into exile. Yet during that short period of political control, they established a new society. Factories were owned and operated by the workers as co-operatives. The state was abolished, replaced by the locally-controlled militia. Decentralized, direct democracy was instituted. Local districts elected delegates to the central government, and delegates met weekly with their constituents and were subject to regular recall by their electors. The central city government represented a wide range of political opinion, a pluralist government, led by the working class. The mass media was locally owned and controlled by workers. People from all over the world were accepted as citizens. It was the opposite of a totalitarian state.

The new political economy of the left, set forth by Marx and Engels, identified the contradictions that would always exist under capitalism. Competition leads to monopoly control by the largest capitalists and corporations. The unequal distribution of income and wealth produces the business cycle and regular depressions. Workers are alienated from the product of their labour and other workers. The introduction of labour saving equipment may raise profits but does not increase the ability of workers to buy goods. Employers always want to pay the lowest wage possible, but this undermines the purchasing power of the workers in general. People are poor and hungry while capitalist economies have a problem with overproduction of food, which is distributed according to ability to pay. Technology is controlled by the capitalists and is always used to increase profits not the well being of workers or society as a whole. Unemployment and under employment are found everywhere. The major capitalist countries unite to defend the system, but there is always competition among them, often leading to major wars. Capitalism has always been linked to colonialism, imperialism, war, and the domination of the poor countries by the rich countries. Adam Smith was wrong. It is not a harmonious system but one characterized by endless conflict. (Marx, 1961, 1970; Mandel, 1968; Heilbroner, 1961; Hunt, 1995)

Marxism has always been seen as a radical political movement, usually led by the organized working class and/or the poor. These political movements today are found mainly in the less developed world. But Marxism is also an approach to social science. Today it is the dominant theory within the discipline of political economy. Marxism provides a powerful explanation as to why Saskatchewan continues to be a hinterland economy.

## Social Democracy as the Alternative to Class Conflict

In the 20th century social democracy appeared as a political alternative to Marxism and socialism, movements committed to replacing the capitalist system. Social democracy has advocated the reform of capitalism through progressive taxation and the expansion of the welfare state. It was most successful in Great Britain, Australia, New Zealand and the Scandinavian countries. Social democracy had a profound impact on political developments in Saskatchewan, where it emerged as the basic ideology of the Co-operative Commonwealth Federation (CCF) and its successor, the New Democratic Party (NDP). General social democratic policies were also adopted in Canada by Liberal and Progressive Conservative federal governments in the post World War II period.

In Saskatchewan, the CCF and then the NDP became the dominant party. The principles and values of social democracy were widely supported. The mixed economy—private, co-operative and state owned—was broadly accepted. But the commitment of the NDP to the basic principles of social democracy and the mixed economy have been questioned since the 1980s. Indeed, throughout the First World social democratic parties and governments have been steadily moving to the political right, repealing the welfare state and abandoning the goal of full employment and a more equal distribution of income and wealth. Is there a future for social democracy?

In the area of political economy, the social democratic approach was originally identified with John Stuart Mill (1806-1873). Mill is generally viewed as the liberal who reformed liberalism, moving it away from its *laissez faire* economic approach to embrace government policy reforms to promote greater equality. He was the son of James Mill, the famous English historian and liberal propagandist. He was a child genius, mastering Latin and Greek before he was ten, then taking on mathematics and history. As Heilbroner writes, "At thirteen he made a complete survey of all there was to be known in the field of political economy." He met and fell in love with Harriet Taylor. "It was a superlative match. Harriet Taylor completed for Mill the emotional awakening which had begun so late; she opened his eyes to women's rights and, even more importantly, to mankind's rights." (Heilbroner, 1961)

His two volume work, *The Principles of Political Economy*, was published in 1848, the year of the workers' rebellion across Europe and the publication of *The Communist Manifesto*.

It is widely considered to be the most comprehensive and best written of all the classical liberal works on political economy. It is a broad survey of all the major topics covered by the early political economists. His central core view is that the key to understanding economics and political economy is to focus on *production*, not distribution. Production is the application of labour to natural resources. He is one of the first political economists to stress that nature is not without its real limits; there is such a thing as scarcity. Furthermore, nature is stubborn and cannot always be manipulated by human beings. (Mill, 1965)

Mill broke with many of the liberal ideologues and argued that distribution of wealth is a political matter. There are no universal laws on distribution. A democratic society can always decide how it wants to distribute the wealth it creates. This is a question of moral values.

Thus his theory of economic progress argues for the elimination of poverty, "the first among existing social evils." This is a precondition for progress. It then depends on developing a working class that is well-paid and well-educated. This would be accomplished through land reform, the emigration of surplus labour to colonies, creating a class of "labour aristocracy" which would be well educated, support for new poor laws, and taxation policies. Thus economic growth is not an end in itself; equally important is a just and more equitable distribution of wealth and income. These became the core principles of social democracy.

In his later years Mill became a critic of unregulated free enterprise capitalism. Capitalism creates great inequalities, it breeds egoism and class conflict, it erects huge barriers to the development of the individual. As a rational liberal, he did not like the fact that under capitalism people are rich or poor regardless of their own individual merit. He carefully studied the early socialists, but there is no evidence that he studied or understood Marxism. As a member of the privileged elite, he feared class rule by the poor majority. (see Kurer, 1991; Mill, 1962)

One of his innovations is the call for a stationary state. There is no need to continue economic growth endlessly. Indeed, he argues that by 1848 Great Britain already had created enough wealth; all it really needs is a better system of distribution. He argues that human beings would be much better off if they give up the pursuit of greater wealth and shift to promoting leisure and a better quality of life.

Mill was not a socialist. He did not really understand the drive to accumulate which is central to the existence of capitalism. He did not see capital as theft from workers; following Jean Baptiste Say, he argued that capital is just a factor of production. He saw no exploitation of workers as it is explained by Marx and Engels and other socialists. For the working class all that was needed was full employment and increased wages, a good standard of living. Mill was not concerned about English imperial and colonial policy in Ireland or in the "new countries" where he believed there was much "unused land." (Kurer, 1991)

In *On Representative Government* Mill sets forth his liberal, social democratic political views. Government is necessary to provide security of person and property. There cannot be an increase in production if there is no security of private property. Private property are the goods and capital used in production. Personal property is different, consumption goods which are not used to earn a living or produce a profit. Security of property can be protected by having a two house legislature with the upper house representing men of property, and by having a weighted system of voting, giving plural votes to men with property and education. In a radical break with the liberals of his time, he argues that women should have the vote if they "can give all the guarantees required from a male elector." (Mill, 1962)

As Heilbroner concludes, Mill was "English to the core: gradualist, optimistic, realistic, and devoid of radical overtones." He was one of the first prominent political economists to reject the laissez faire economy advocated by classical liberalism. He was the intellectual mentor of the British Labour Party and the other social democratic parties in the industrialized world, including Canada and Saskatchewan. (Heilbroner, 1961)

## The Age of Imperialism

John Stuart Mill died in 1873. Profound changes were underway in the world at the time and in political economy. In 1870 the workers in Paris revolted and seized control of the city and created the first socialist state, the Paris Commune. After only a few months it was crushed. But the Working Men's International Association called for the creation of socialist workers parties in all the European countries. A high priority was placed on organizing trade unions. The working class was on the rise.

The first great economic depression began in 1873 and lasted until 1896. The depression was particularly hard on less developed countries, as the prices for primary products fell dramatically. The depression hit Great Britain very hard. Many see this as the beginning of the decline of British world hegemony, with the rise of the United States and Germany to the status of world powers.

Capitalism began to change, just as Marx and Engels had predicted. There was a shift to concentration of production in all major industries and the growth of the large corporation. There were many attempts to create international cartels. Income and wealth became concentrated in the hands of a small group of capitalists who had inordinate political power.

With the onset of the world depression, and the rise of working class militancy, the political leadership in the European countries intensified their search for colonies and foreign trade. National chauvinism increased. The European countries divided up Africa, the last major area of the less developed world that was not under imperial and colonial control. There was a revival of mercantilist policies. A new age of imperialism emerged as European corporations and capitalists expanded their investments in the less developed areas of the world.

This period also saw the beginning of the National Policy and the wheat economy in Canada. Blocked from a greater integration into the U.S. economy by the U.S. government, Canadian capitalists sought an alternative, a united Canada, coast to coast, and the creation of a new hinterland for economic exploitation and capital accumulation in western Canada.

There was a new development in classical liberal political economy. Herbert Spencer (1820-1903) re-asserted the view of unregulated capitalism but based it on the social interpretation of Charles Darwin's theory of evolution and natural selection. He was also a strong supporter of traditional patriarchal values. The Social Darwinists argued that there should be no social policies to protect the poor and the weak; they should be allowed to die, with the fittest surviving. Monopoly power was a natural result of competition, and the corporate world should not be regulated by government.

This period also witnessed the split between political economy and those who chose to call themselves economists. The economists continued to insist that Jean Baptist Say was correct, that depressions were impossible under capitalism. They held this position right into the Great Depression of the 1930s.

Economists shifted away from political economy to concentrate on the role of the individual and the corporation in making economic decisions. What became known as neoclassical theory of utility and consumption was set forth by William Stanley Jevon, *The Theory of Political Economy* (1871), Karl Menger, *Principles of Economics* (1871), and Leon Walras, *Elements of Pure Economics* (1874). This new approach was synthesized by Alfred Marshall in *Principles of Economics* (1890). Neoclassical economics abandoned empirical research to stress abstract models, algebra and calculus.

Yet the real world was far removed from the abstract models created by Marshall and the neoclassical economists. While Marshall was insisting that the capitalist market was characterized by a steady equilibrium, he witnessed the first great world depression, the rise of the socialist parties and trade unions, World War I, and the Bolshevik revolution in Russia. While he held the chair in political economy at Cambridge University, Marshall fought to introduce courses in "economics" that would be separate from "history and the moral sciences." (Buchholtz, 1989; Robbins, 1998)

## Conclusion

Capitalism is the mode of production which dominates the world. One can find a few enclaves around which still operate on the basis of pre-capitalist modes of production, but they are subsumed under the world system. Beginning with the revolution of workers and peasants in Russia during World War I there was an attempt to create a Soviet system of centrally planned economies. Those attempts in the Union of Soviet Socialist Republics and eastern Europe collapsed after 1989. The re-introduction of capitalism in these countries has resulted in a dramatic decline in the standard of living of the vast majority to almost Third World levels. Politically, there has been a rise of nationalism, racism and constant conflict. The Peoples Republic of China, created in 1949 at the end of the peasant and workers revolution, is now a totalitarian state re-imposing capitalism, with gross exploitation of labour and the denial of basic human rights. Only Cuba, North Korea, Laos and Vietnam remain nominally centrally planned economies, and they are all adopting market reforms. It seems like capitalism has triumphed, and there is no indication that the socialism that was posed for years as the logical alternative has any life.

Yet as we have seen, there are different capitalisms. First World capitalism, now with broad support from the working class, is characterized by gross consumerism, a system of production based on creating massive waste, and widespread destruction of resources and the environment. It is creating global warming and climate change, which poses a major threat to the world as we know it. It can only exist in its bloated form by the extraction of resources from the Third World and the export of its pollution.

Most of the countries of the capitalist less developed world are stagnating, particularly since the onset of policies of neoliberalism after 1980. Africa has experienced a shocking decline in the standard of living of the average person, and famine is persistent. Within this capitalist world there is a steadily growing gap in income and wealth between the advanced industrialized countries and those who are "less developed." Given this reality, it is no surprise that discontent is widespread and taking the form of protest, violent dissent and armed conflict. The advanced industrial countries use the military power of the U.S. government and the financial and economic power of large transnational corporations and financial wealth to dominate and control the large majority of people who live in the less developed world. Capitalism has not produced a harmonious world. It has created the exact opposite.

Canadians have been privileged. We have one of the highest standards of living in the world. But discontent persists. Canada developed as a colony within the French and then British imperial systems. But by the time we became independent of Great Britain we were an economic and political satellite of the United States. Canada has never been an independent country, running its own affairs, masters of its own house. That is one of our discontents. It has nothing to do with our cold climate.

Living in a capitalist country, we experience the same alienation as others. People are here to serve the economy, the economy does not serve us. And of course we mean the capitalist economy. We know the insecurity of booms, busts, inflation and depressions. In our workplaces we experience the kind of alienation detailed by Karl Marx. Those who labour for governments endure alienation in a slightly different way from industrial workers. We must try, with limited resources, to help those whose health and spirit have been damaged by the system; we do not help people become healthy individuals. We are forced to teach the capitalist ideology of exploitation rather than human co-operation and liberation. We administer social services which keep people poor and depressed rather than helping them enter the mainstream of society. We labour in hierarchical, authoritarian situations; democracy does not exist in our daily lives, for capitalism is a command society. Canadians are to work harder and longer to buy another new car. Is endless consumption of non-essential products enough to compensate for alienation? Is labour only to provide for our subsistence, or should it be work which is creative and fulfilling? The system simply rules out such questions.

From the beginning, Saskatchewan was born of discontent. The English empire used military force to steal the land from the original inhabitants and condemn those who survived to poverty and despair. The Europeans who settled on the land as farmers were exploited by the capitalist system. The concentration of economic and political power in central Canada meant people in the west had little influence over government decision making. The citizens of Saskatchewan watch as their natural resources leave the province and make capitalists elsewhere wealthy while people in the North live in seemingly endless poverty. Capitalism as we know it is characterized by Social Darwinism: the rich get richer and the poor suffer and die at an early age. In the era of "free trade" since 1989 we have seen a major increase in foreign ownership and control of the economy of Saskatchewan. Citizens seem to have no control over this process. Whatever political party we elect, the resulting governments all do the same thing, catering first to the interests of big business. Is there nothing better than this? Is rapacious capitalism and political systems which are anti-democratic the best we can hope for?

## References

Abendroth, Wolfgang. 1972. *A Short History of the European Working Class*. New York: Monthly Review Press.

Alam, M. Shahid. 2000. *Poverty from the Wealth of Nations: Integration and Polarization in the Global Economy since 1760*. New York: St. Martin's Press.

Albers, Patricia and Beatrice Medicine, eds. *The Hidden Half: Studies of Plains Indian Women*. Lanham, MD: University Press of America.

Arneil, Barbara. 1996. *John Locke and America: The Defense of English Colonialism*. New York: Oxford University Press.

Bairoch, Paul. 1993. *Economics and World History*. Chicago: University of Chicago Press.

Beaud, Michael. 1983. *A History of Capitalism 1500-1980*. New York: Monthly Review Press.

Bose, Arun. 1975. *Marxian and Post-Marxian Political Economy*. Harmondsworth: Penguin Books.

Braudel, Fernand. 1967. *Capitalism and Material Life, 1400-1800*. London: Weidenfeld and Nicolson.

Buchholz, Todd G. 1990. *New Ideas from Dead Economists: An Introduction to Modern Economic Thought*. New York: Penguin Books.

Caute, David. 1966. *The Left in Europe Since 1789*. London: Weidenfeld and Nicolson.

Clarkson, Stephen. 2002. *Uncle Sam and Us: Globalization, Neoconservatism, and the Canadian State*. Toronto: University of Toronto Press.

Cranston, Maurice. 1957. *John Locke: A Biography*. Oxford: Oxford University Press.

Dobb, Maurice. 1963. *Studies in the Development of Capitalism*. New York: International Publishers.

Easterbrook, W.T. and Hugh G. J. Aitken. 1956. *Canadian Economic History*. Toronto: Macmillan of Canada.

Elkins, Stanley M. 1976. *Slavery: A Problem in American Institutional and Intellectual Life*. Chicago: University of Chicago Press.

Engels, Frederich. 1958. *The Condition of the Working Class in England in 1844*. London: Weidenfeld & Nicolson.

Foner, Laura and Eugene D. Genovese, eds. 1969. *Slavery in the New World*. Englewood Cliffs, N.J.: Prentice-Hall.

Freedman, Robert. 1963. *Marx on Economics*. Harmondsworth: Penguin Books.

Gerschenkron, Alexander. 1962. *Economic Backwardness in Historical Perspective*. Cambridge: Harvard University Press.

Gray, Alexander. 1963. *The Socialist Tradition: from Moses to Lenin*. London: Longmans.

Hamilton, Alexander. 1934. *Papers on Public Credit, Commerce and Finance*. New York: Columbia University Press.

Heilbroner, Robert L. 1968. *The Making of Economic Society*. Englewood Cliffs, N.J.: Prentice-Hall.

Heilbroner, Robert L. 1961. *The Worldly Philosophers: The Lives, Times and Ideas of the Great Economic Thinkers*. New York: Simon and Schuster.

Hobsbawn, E.J. 1968. *Industry and Empire: An Economic History of Britain Since 1750*. London: Weidenfeld & Nicolson.

Hunt, E.K. 1995. *Property and Prophets: The Evolution of Economic Institutions and Ideologies*. New York: Harper Collins College Publishers.

Hurtig, Mel. 2002. *The Vanishing Country: Is It Too Late To Save Canada?* Toronto: McClelland and Stewart.

Jenish, D'Arcy. 1999. *Indian Fall: The Last Great Days of the Plains Cree and the Blackfoot Confederacy*. Toronto: Penguin Books.

Klein, Alan. 1983. "The Political Economy of Gender: a 19th Century Plains Indian Case." In Albers and Medicine, pp. 143-174.

Kurer, Oskar. 1991. *John Stuart Mill: The Politics of Progress.* New York: Garland Publishing.

Kunstler, John Howard. 1993. *The Geography of Nowhere.* New York: Simon and Schuster.

List, Frederich. 1991. *The National System of Political Economy.* Fairfield, N.J.: Augustus M. Kelley.

Locke, John. 1966. *Second Treatise of Government.* New York: Barnes and Noble, 1966

Locke, John. 1976. *Some Considerations of the Consequences of the Lowering of Interest, and Saving the Value of Money.* London: Anwsham and Churchill.

MacPherson, C.B. 1962. *The Political Theory of Possessive Individualism: Hobbes to Locke.* New York: Oxford University Press.

Mandel, Ernest. 1968. *Marxist Economic Theory.* London: Merlin Press.

Mannix, Daniel P. 1962. *Black Cargoes: A History of the Atlantic Slave Trade.* New York: The Viking Press.

Marx, Karl. 1961. *Capital.* New York: International Publishers.

Marx, Karl. 1970. *Critique of Political Economy.* New York: New World Paperbacks.

Mathias, Peter. 1969. *The First Industrial Nation.* London: Methuen.

Mill, John Stuart. 1962. *Consideration on Representative Government.* Chicago: Henry Regnery.

Mill, John Stuart. 1965. *Principles of Political Economy.* New York: Augustus M. Kelley.

Minchinton, Walter E. 1969. *Mercantilism: System or Expediency?* Lexington, Mass.: D.C. Heath.

Nash, Gary B. 2000. *Red, White and Black: The Peoples of Early North America.* Upper Saddle River, NJ: Prentice Hall.

Norrie, Kenneth and Douglas Owram. 1996. *A History of the Canadian Economy.* Toronto: Harcourt Brace Canada.

Ricardo, David. 1962. *Principles of Political Economy.* London: Dent.

Robbins, Lionel. 1998. *A History of Economic Thought: The LSE Lectures.* Princeton: Princeton University Press.

Ryerson, Stanley B. 1963. *The Founding of Canada: Beginnings to 1815.* Toronto: Progress Books.

Smith, Adam. 1967. *An Inquiry into the Nature and Causes of the Wealth of Nations.* New York: Modern Library.

Stone, Kenneth. 1995. "Competing with the Discount Mass Merchandisers." Department of Economics, Iowa State University. www.walmartwatch.com

Williams, Eric. 1966. *Capitalism and Slavery.* New York: Capricorn Books.

Warnock, John W. 1987. *The Politics of Hunger: The Global Food System.* Toronto: Methuen.

# Chapter 4

————————○————————

# SASKATCHEWAN
# AS A PERMANENT HINTERLAND AREA

I arrived in Saskatchewan in 1963. The following year there was an election, and the opposition Liberal Party attacked the CCF-NDP government for forcing young people out of the province, for driving entrepreneurs and other businessmen out of the province, and for failing to develop resources and manufacturing. High taxes were identified as a key barrier to economic development. Ross Thatcher, to be elected premier, proclaimed that the Liberals had a constructive program which would "halt the population exodus, attract new industries, and obtain jobs for our young people." (quoted in Eisler, 1987)

Fast forward to 2003. The Saskatchewan Chamber of Commerce launched *Action Saskatchewan: A Blueprint for 2005*, and Paul Martin wrote a series of full page stories for them in the main newspapers promoting new economic innovations which would "grow Saskatchewan" and provide jobs for our kids. Business interests and the University of Saskatchewan held a conference in June 2003 to discuss strategies for "doubling the province's population." The provincial branch of the Canadian Taxpayers Federation repeated Ross Thatcher's message from 1964: the NDP government, co-operatives, Crown corporations, and government intervention in the economy were driving businesses and our kids away. The alternative vision remained the same: cut taxes and free up the economy for private enterprise.

A similar message came from Graham Parsons of the Organization for Western Economic Co-operation. He urged the privatization of Crown corporations and promoted the low-tax free market policies of Ireland as the answer to Saskatchewan's problems. He denounced the decision by the NDP government of Allan Blakeney to take over part of the potash industry in the mid-1970s. Saskatchewan was condemned to being a have not hinterland province because of 60 years of provincial government intervention in the economy. (*Leader-Post*, October 22, 2003)

Then came the provincial election in the fall of 2003. The opposition Saskatchewan Party proclaimed that if elected they would "grow Saskatchewan by 100,000 people in ten years." They would lower taxes and create more jobs and more investment. The NDP and the Liberals replied with a series of promised policies designed to create jobs so that our kids could stay. Nothing seems to change. Saskatchewan is always portrayed in a poor light compared to oil-rich Alberta. The province is never compared to North Dakota or South Dakota, those two free market, Republican states. Their citizens think of Saskatchewan as some sort of an economic miracle.

This debate has gone on for years. The NDP, in opposition from 1982-91, regularly attacked the Tory government of Grant Devine when the population figures dropped. The issue is never resolved, and the "debate" sheds little light on it. There is no serious attempt to try to understand why Saskatchewan is a hinterland province or why the prairies remain so dependent on agriculture and resource extraction.

Regions, regionalism and regional disparities are part of the psyche of anyone who lives in Saskatchewan. The province is far from Vancouver and the Pacific Ocean and even farther from Ontario. South across the border has even greater open spaces. There was a great deal of trauma in Regina when Via Rail canceled the last passenger train service. Air service is limited. Flying to Vancouver means an inevitable long stopover in the awful Calgary airport. It costs about 40 percent more to fly to Toronto or Ottawa than it does to take a charter flight to England. Everyone talks about their kids who now live in Calgary, Edmonton or Vancouver and the grandchildren that they rarely see. Saskatchewan is an isolated place

In the early days of the prairie wheat economy, the freight rates took around one half of all the farmer's gross income. The *Western Producer* today is still filled with the debate over freight rates and who should control the railways. The Crows Nest Pass agreement provided government subsidized freight rates for grain "in perpetuity" in return for huge land and other grants to the Canadian Pacific Railway Company. The Crow Rate was abolished as part of the Canada-U.S. Free Trade Agreement. In 2001 the new freight rates took around one-third of the gross income from the sale of a bushel of wheat, by far the largest single cost of production for farmers. Western alienation continues.

Brian Mulroney promised that the Canada-U.S. Free Trade Agreement would "end regional disparities in Canada." But the unregulated free market, and internal Canadian free trade, has done nothing to change Saskatchewan. It has, however, pushed the standard of "efficiency" to the top of the list.

The economists and the other experts insist that the policies of the past were wrong. Saskatchewan doesn't need legislation requiring beer to be manufactured in the province or provincial marketing boards which require poultry, eggs and milk to be processed in the province. It doesn't matter if bread is baked in Regina or Winnipeg. Those giant American grain handling companies offer better service than the farmer-owned prairie pools. Who needs consumer co-ops when Wal Mart can bring cheaper goods. Consolidated schools are better than local, community schools. Those 52 rural hospitals that were shut down by the NDP government were inefficient. The virtual bank in the chain grocery store pays a higher rate of interest on a savings account than the local credit union. The provincial governments were right to sell off all those provincial Crown Corporations. The NDP was right to put a high priority on cutting taxes and downsizing the role of government in the provincial economy.

There are still those populist parties denouncing "central Canada" for its political domination and neglect of the West. But their tune has definitely changed. The attack on big business has disappeared. The Reform Party, started in Alberta by Preston Manning, proclaimed in its constitution that the west had been "subjected to systematic injustice or inequality of treatment." Reform and its successor, the Canadian Alliance Party, demanded the Triple E Senate ("Equal, Elected and Effective"). The prairie provinces should be able to veto important legislation, not just Quebec. Changes to the Constitution were necessary to make all provinces equal. The latest bumper sticker calls on us to "Defend the West" by opposing the Canadian Wheat Board, the Kyoto Agreement on Climate Change, and federal gun control legislation.

The National Farmers Union carries on the older populist tradition. They denounce the free trade agreements for having increased monopoly control of agribusiness which has resulted in the further decline of the share of the consumer's dollar that is going to farmers. With increased control of agribusiness by transnational corporations, even more of the value of the labour and investment of the prairie farmer is going to central Canada and the United States. Globalization has intensified regional disparities. (see NFU, 2000; Boyens, 2001; Epp and Whitson, 2001; Laycock, 2002)

The radical Co-operative Commonwealth Federation (CCF) government headed by Tommy Douglas was elected in 1944. Since then there has been significant change on the prairies and in Saskatchewan. The majority of farmers and farms have disappeared. King Wheat has been replaced by a wide variety of crops. The livestock industry has boomed. But this consolidation of farms has devastated the rural area. The population that remains in Saskatchewan is becoming polarized between an older generation of people with a European background approaching retirement and a younger, less educated, Aboriginal population which has been largely excluded from many areas of employment. The resource extraction industries have been fully developed, but unemployment and poverty remain very serious problems in the province's North. The economy still relies on the export of primary products, but with the free trade agreements, is much more dependent on one market, the United States. Saskatchewan still imports almost all of its manufactured goods. As Robert Roach of the Canada West Foundation has concluded, "The West stands out in Canada as a resource and agricultural producing region. Despite significant increases in value added (i.e., manufactured) exports, the West remains in many ways a 'hewer of wood and drawer of water.'" (Roach, 2002)

## What Is a Region?

In our schools we learn that Canada has six regions: the Atlantic area, Quebec, Ontario, the West, British Columbia and the Arctic. This is a geographical approach. There are the differences of the land, the topography and the climate. The regions in Canada tend to be separated from each other by some topographical barrier. The West, for example, is cut off from the East by the Canadian shield. Within such regions, there is some degree of sameness.

Traveling west through Ontario one reaches Kenora, crosses the border into Manitoba, and then passes through the provincial forest and onto the Canadian prairies. The grasslands stretch across to the Rocky Mountains. North of the grasslands is the Boreal Forest, which seems identical across the three prairie provinces. It certainly appears that this is a geographic region. There is considerable economic homogeneity as well, first with the buffalo economy, then grain and livestock, followed by natural resource extraction. Not just Saskatchewan but all of the prairie economy has remained dominated by the extraction of natural resources and agriculture. And of the three provinces, Saskatchewan is the most dependent. (see Roach, 2002)

But are these mere geographic phenomena? They did not exist in what was Canada before the arrival of Europeans. Canada at that time was populated by various indigenous nations who occupied their own historic lands, but there was no border between Canada and the United States. There were differences determined mainly by how each indigenous nation adapted to the environment where they lived. There were obviously still geographical regions, but it is doubtful if the indigenous people ever discussed regions, regionalism, or economic and political disparities within the North American continent. These are historical, human creations.

Most of the studies of regions and regionalism in Canada in recent years focus on the differences between the geographic areas. This is usually done through an analysis of differences between *provinces*, which are not the same as geographical regions. Most concentrate on economic criteria like per capita income, unemployment rates, or the extent of manufacturing industry. An early study by Jeffrey G. Williamson concluded that of six developed countries (Canada, United States, United Kingdom, Sweden, New Zealand and Australia) Canada had the highest degree of regional economic differences. Even in the period of high levels of economic growth (1945-1960), Canada was the only country which did not achieve a reduction in inequality in per capita income or levels of unemployment. S. E. Chernick, writing for the Economic Council of Canada, recorded that over the period between 1926 and 1964 disparities in personal income were a notable feature of Canada, and despite various government policies, nothing really changed. Regional differences persisted. (Kerr, 1968; Williamson, 1965; Chernick, 1966)

Paul Phillips, a political economist at the University of Manitoba, has concluded that economic policy was fairly stable in Canada after World War II down to the changes brought in by the government of Brian Mulroney after 1985. He also believes that there is no evidence that the federal programs to counteract regional disparity made any difference. They may have helped in containing disparities. But "these measure have had minimal effect on the root causes, industrial structure and resource dependence." (Phillips, 1982)

The term regionalism is widely used in Canada without ever being carefully defined. In popular terms, it seems always to mean a relationship between geographic areas. It generally is used without reference to people. Thus, as we hear all the time in Saskatchewan, "the West" is being shortchanged by "central Canada." As Janine Brodie has pointed out, in this approach "conflict revolves around the allocation of power and resources across geographic units rather than, for example, among social classes." The emphasis is on spatial inequalities. (Brodie, 1990)

Ralph Matthews, who has written extensively on regional disparities from the perspective of Atlantic Canada, has defined regionalism as "essentially the social-psychological" factor where "people come to define their situation and to identify themselves as belonging to a particular region and develop an identification with the majority of other residents in it." This is an evolving process and will be influenced by migration. (Matthews, 1983)

J.M.S. Careless, one of Canada's most distinguished historians, has stressed the integration of geographical and social factors in regional development. The regions of Canada "were not necessarily, or even mostly, co-terminus with natural regions, but emerged in history." A historical region "displays the interaction of human and geographic elements over time." Thus there is the common identification of regions with provinces, which are very much historical creations of humans. "Physical factors thus interfused with human—with ethnoculture, metropolitan input, economic effort, and political organization—to delineate regionalism, which is to say, the community fabric and group consciousness that mark historical regions." The material aspects are combined with characteristic mind sets and behaviour, which produce "the collective sense of common qualities of life and interests." (Careless, 1954)

The early Canadian political economists and historians described Canada as a frontier society. The development of Canada took place within the political and economic context of European imperialism and colonialism and was a succession of occupations of frontier lands taken from the indigenous peoples. These included fishing on the East coast, the fur trade, the move to the forest industry, the push to central Canada and the first agriculture frontier, mining, and then the settlement of the West by European farmers. British Columbia combined the fishing, lumber, mining and agriculture frontiers. This process was driven by metropolitan centres of commercial power. Thus, the exploitation of the land and natural resources, and the extraction of "economic rent," was at the heart of the earliest development of Canada.

For many commentators in the liberal tradition, this was a complementary relationship. The metropolitan interests gained natural resources, agricultural commodities, and markets for their manufactured products. Those living and working in the frontier or hinterland areas were dependent on those in the urban centres for finance, manufactured goods used in resource extraction, technology, transportation, and the marketing of natural products. The powers in the urban centres mobilized the immigrant settlers and labour force. Political and military power was necessary to remove the obstacle of the indigenous population. (Careless, 1989; Creighton, 1970; Lower, 1938)

The westward move in the United States has been described and interpreted in the work of Frederick Jackson Turner, particularly in *The Frontier in American History*.

It is the classic interpretation of the foundation of white settler societies. The frontier was always moving, he argued, between land that was settled and the wilderness. It was a political and military border. For the indigenous population of North America, it was certainly that, a zone of warfare which steadily pushed westward. But for Turner it was more than that. It was the marginal zone between "civilization" and "savagery." Like all imperialists of his day, he believed that this expansion was inevitable because of the moral, economic and political superiority of western, European civilization. In this specific case, the American settler was viewed as the embodiment of civilization, bringing work and profit to the wilderness land. The indigenous population, which was "not cultivating the land," and who did not share the liberal, capitalist spirit, were a barrier which had to be removed. (Turner, 1920)

Canadian commentators on the Turner thesis note the differences with Canada. There was no steady march to the west because of Canada's geographic barriers. There was no continual expanse of land to be settled by farmers. There was no easy transportation route. The push for expansion in Canada did not come from yeoman farmers but the commercial and financial interests who wished to profit from resource extraction. In Quebec, the seigniorial system was in opposition to the liberal ideal of independent family farmers. After the end of the fur trade, colonial expansion required the displacement of the indigenous population. But this could be done more efficiently by threat of force, the spectre of starvation, and treaty negotiations rather than the U.S. approach of imperial war.

## Metropolitan Domination

There is a long tradition of describing Canadian development within a framework of metropolitan domination of hinterland areas. It has been central to geographical analysis and theory. The common approach is to contrast the industrial heartlands with the resource extraction hinterlands. The heartlands are described as having good geographic locations, access to cheap transportation, a large population, a developed industrial and manufacturing sector, finance capital, and a good social infrastructure. The hinterlands are condemned to providing surplus labour, raw materials and primary agricultural products and are subject to boom and bust periods. (McCann, 1982; Reed, 1995)

The metropolitan-hinterland perspective has always been a major approach used by political economists. The work of Norman S. B. Gras, a Canadian who taught economic history at Harvard University, was most influential. In 1922 he published *An Introduction to Economic History* which stressed the importance and power of metropolitan centres to economic development. Athens set the pattern here as the imperial centre dominating the colonies that it had created. Indeed the term "metropolis" comes from the Greek, meter (mother) plus polis (city), signifying the imperial centre of a large city state. Imperial Rome was similar, dominating not only peoples around the Mediterranean but the other smaller centres and hinterland areas of Italy. In the Christian period, the centre of the Church was called the metropolis, the city of the administrative centre, usually headed by a bishop. All of the early city states in the pre-capitalist period established political and economic control over subjugated peoples for the extraction of economic tribute.

Gras referred to the metropolitan centre as the controlling point and argued that all large cities were only possible because they were able to dominate large hinterland areas. Metropolitan centres within capitalism, he argued, went through phases. First they become a commercial power. Next there is the development of manufacturing. Then they extend their control over transportation and communication. Finally they become centres of capital accumulation, dominating hinterland areas through finance and the stock market. Gras viewed metropolitan domination as an inevitable development under capitalism and concluded that it served the interests of the nation state as a whole. (Gras, 1920)

S. Delbert Clark, usually identified as Canada's first prominent sociologist, devoted his life to studying frontier communities. In his most famous work, *The Social Development of Canada*, Clark argued that the new frontier communities in Canada were opened up solely for the purpose of economic exploitation, to extract new natural resources for export. In Canada this was done by political and economic forces in metropolitan centres, recruiting labour and capital for this form of development. The communities where these resource staples were extracted were generally horrible places to live. The result was not only economic exploitation of labour and resources and the political domination of hinterland regions but the rise of industrial and political dissent, confronting capital, the state, the military, and the established churches. However, the power imbalance was too pronounced, and these frontier regions were eventually brought into conformity with the rest of Canadian society. (Clark, 1942)

In the *Commercial Empire of the St. Lawrence*, historian Donald Creighton describes the Anglo-Canadian merchant interests in Montreal that built the early political state within the British Empire. While Creighton saw this group of capitalists as key to the development of the country, A. R. M. Lower, political economist and historian, concluded that the metropolitan power they represented was exploitative of hinterland regions and their people. He was one of the few historians who under-stood that the metropolitan-hinterland relationships was a *process of capital accumulation*. In his famous study of British capital and the forest industry in Canada, Lower concluded this relationship was one of imperial exploitation, as the metropolitan centres of power in Canada were only intermediaries with the real centres of imperial power. W. L. Morton, the historian with roots in Manitoba, also saw the metropolitan hinterland relationship as imperial in form, extracting capital much as the older imperial states had extracted tribute. (Creighton, 1937; Lower, 1937; Morton, 1950)

Canada's most prominent political economist and one of the founders of the staple theory of Canadian development, Harold Innis, did not focus his work on the metropolitan hinterland issue. But in *The Bias of Communication* and *Empire and Communications* he records that in all the historic empires, the metropolitan centre was the centre of ideological power. It had control over religion, culture and communications, and these institutions played a very important role in the domination of colonized areas and peoples. Innis's view was endorsed by historian D. C. Masters in *The Rise of Toronto, 1850-1890*. Toronto arrived at metropolitan status when it established domination over adjacent hinterland areas. Not only was Toronto the centre of economic power, it was also able to exert control through its political, cultural and social power. (Innis, 1950; 1951; Masters, 1947)

A parallel U.S. example illustrates the Canadian theory. Minneapolis-St. Paul came to be a regional metropolitan power that dominated the hinterland area known as the U.S. Central Northwest. By 1823 the steamboats were coming up the important trading route of the Mississippi River to the conjuncture of the Minnesota River, the site of the city. This broke the control of St. Louis over the region. The Twin Cities became a major fur trade centre after 1816 when the Hudson Bay Company was banned from operating in the United States. It was the headquarters of the American Fur Company after 1849. From there it moved into the lumber trade as a milling centre, became a regional centre for wholesale and retail distribution, and then became a major centre for flour milling, the home of Robin Hood, General Mills and Cargill. Railroads were built to Chicago, and the Sault Ste. Marie line, built by the CPR, opened trade through Montreal. (Fay, 1927)

With the expansion of the wheat economy in the Central Northwest, the Twin Cities became a major centre for banking and finance and the source of its own investment capital. This broke their dependence on the capital markets of Chicago and New York. The hinterland area of the city today roughly coincides with the Ninth Federal Reserve area, created by the U.S. central bank, covering North and South

Dakota, Montana, Minnesota and part of Michigan and Wisconsin. In commenting on the development of the Twin Cities as a dominant metropolitan power, Gras concludes "both the policy of mercantilism and that of liberal free trade were based upon an emphasis on material wealth. Both stressed the accumulation of goods, forgetting the welfare of human beings." (Gras, 1929)

## Domination by Ruling Elites or a Ruling Class?

The traditional metropolitan-hinterland model of regionalism has been subject to much criticism. Many social scientists have pointed out that it is a geographic description of spatial differences. It is not a case of Toronto exploiting the prairie hinterland, for example. It is a question of political and economic power exercised by human beings. Some commentators argue that the real relationship is between the *ruling elites* who reside in the metropolitan centres and those who labour to produce wealth in the hinterland areas, whether they are farmers, workers in the resource industries, or workers in industrial plants. Other sociologists and political economists argue that the political and economic elites in the metropolitan centres not only work together, they form a *ruling class.*

The close ties between the economic and political elite were detailed in the work of Gustavus Myers and Libbie and Frank Park. All the major decisions on the early development of Canada were made by an interlocking group of very wealthy men and their political allies. Most of the political leaders were also direct investors in the companies that bought and sold land, the construction industry, the railroad companies, and the large corporations that appropriated coal, timber, minerals and other resources. They were closely linked to British and American capitalists. But very few Canadians ever saw this literature, and it certainly was not assigned reading in Canada's schools and universities. (Myers, 1914; Park and Park, 1962)

This changed with the publication of John Porter's *The Vertical Mosaic* in 1965. Porter, a sociologist at Carleton University, conducted an exhaustive study of the relation between social class and political power in Canada. He detailed how a privileged group of powerful men controlled all the basic institutions in our society: the corporations, the political system, the federal bureaucracy, the mass media, and even the universities. Porter's research methodology was liberal, and he firmly rejected the Marxist analysis of capitalism. Yet he reported the facts. Inherited wealth and status gave certain people, particularly Protestant men with a British background, better access to elite positions of power than the rest of Canadians.

While Porter rejected the Marxist concept of a ruling class, he nevertheless showed that the wealthy economic elite in Canada is composed of a close group of men. First of all, they live in the metropolitan centers of economic and political power where one finds the corporate head offices and the stock exchanges. The owners and top managers of the financial institutions and the dominant corporations sit on various boards of directors, live in the same upper class neighbourhoods, go to the same private schools and elite universities, attend the same churches, are fund raisers for the Conservative and Liberal parties, belong to the same charitable organizations, are members of the same private men's clubs and country clubs, and have vacation homes in the same special areas in the Caribbean and Florida. They have "coming out" parties for their daughters so that they will be encouraged to marry men of their own social background. Porter called this group of men "elites." (Porter, 1965)

Wallace Clement, a sociologist and political economist also at Carleton University, expanded on Porter's empirical work, providing even greater detail. Furthermore, Clement undertook a major study of the relationship between Canadian capitalism and corporations and their ties to the large American corporations, dominant in so many sectors of the Canadian economy. In contrast to Porter, Clement employs a Marxist analysis, concluding that those who own and control the major sectors of the economy constitute a ruling class. (Clement, 1975; 1977)

## Atlantic Dependency—Parallels with Saskatchewan

A radical analysis of regions and regional disparity has emerged in the Atlantic provinces. It has had considerable influence on social scientists on the prairies. The theoretical analysis developed on the East coast has much to offer those seeking answers in Saskatchewan. The two regions share many of the same problems. For political economists and sociologists, it is not enough just to describe how conditions are. The facts are not enough. It is necessary to develop a theory to explain how the system works and why. Theory also helps us see what changes can be made and how people should mobilize to produce change. (see McCrorie and MacDonald, 1992)

From the end of the American war for independence to the U.S. civil war, the economies of the Atlantic area grew rapidly along with its population. Newfoundland developed with the fishing and sealing industries. Shipping interests expanded with the carrying trade to the West Indies and the United States. The square timber trade with Great Britain became a basic staple export for the region, but sawmills and the lumber trade soon followed. Shipbuilding and the export of ships became the major manufacturing industry. Local agriculture provided for the local economy, but in Prince Edward Island an agricultural surplus was created for export. Mining began with coal in Nova Scotia. In the 1850s and 1860s railways were built to link the Maritime provinces to the St. Lawrence sea and river route.

At the beginning of the U.S. civil war the Maritime provinces were moving into the era of manufacturing. They dominated the ship building industry and the lumber industry. There were flour mills, iron foundries, and metal trades. On a relative basis, New Brunswick and Nova Scotia were as developed in manufacturing as the Province of Canada. (Easterbrook and Aitken, 1956; Marr and Paterson, 1980; Norrie and Owram, 1996)

In the talks leading up to Confederation, business and political interests supported a railway link between central Canada and the Atlantic coast. The St. Lawrence was closed in the winter, and railways were taking trade through American ports. It was hoped that an all-weather route would increase exports to central Canada and channel more trade through the Atlantic ports. Confederation, internal free trade, the Intercontinental Railway, and the high tariffs on imported manufactured goods were to have the opposite effect. Manufacturing shifted to central Canada, and the Atlantic provinces began their relative decline.

This decline has been the source of ongoing discontent in the Atlantic region. It is the subject of wide debate and academic inquiry. In the 1960s and 1970s scholars in the Atlantic region were influenced by the writings of the Latin American school of dependency political economy. Bruce Archibald used the model developed by the Chilean political economist Andre Gunder Frank, who taught at Concordia University in Montreal for a short time, to try to explain the relative economic decline of the Atlantic provinces. The dependency school interpreted the metropolis-satellite dichotomy using the capital accumulation approach of Adam Smith and later Marxists. The key was seen to be the expropriation of profits (or the economic surplus) created in the peripheral areas through monopoly control and political power exercised by economic interests in the central core area. Archibald argues that the same process operates within Canada. With internal free trade following Confederation, manufacturing shifted to central Canada and the Atlantic provinces were forced to rely once again on resource extraction. This process was intensified in the more recent period by U.S. corporate domination of Canada. The economic surplus for investment in Canada was reduced by the repatriation of profits to the head offices in the United States, leading to a "deepening underdevelopment of the Maritimes." (Archibald, 1971)

Others in Atlantic Canada have expanded on this beginning. Henry Veltmeyer points out that there is a tendency in the capitalist system to the concentration of capital and capitalists in metropolitan centres. Hinterland areas appear to be trapped in the growing polarization, finding it difficult to break out of the pattern of production of agricultural goods, extracting natural resources, and exporting populations. The main role for Atlantic Canada within the capitalist system has been to produce a reserve army of labour which is drafted by the manufacturing sectors in Central Canada when it is needed. (Veltmeyer, 1979)

The differences in class structure are stressed by James Sacouman. He attributes the disparities between Atlantic Canada and central Canada to the differences in the mode of production. Central Canada has developed to the stage of monopoly capitalism and is the home of the capitalist class. In contrast, in Atlantic Canada there has been the long persistence of the old petit bourgeois class, the original family production units which are characteristic of farming, fishing, and small woodlot operations. As capitalism develops, this class of independent producers is squeezed out of business. The monopoly power of big capital is able to extract the economic surplus from these economically weak family production units and transfer the surplus to central Canada. This is a key part of the capital accumulation process. There are strong parallels here with the development of the prairies. (Brym and Sacouman, 1979)

## Capitalism and Metropolitan Domination

The more recent political economy answer to regions and disparities has been to see spatial polarization as an inevitable aspect of the development of the capitalist system. It is rooted in the Law of Accumulation as set forth by Adam Smith and expanded upon by Karl Marx. The accumulation of capital is the engine which drives the capitalist system. Individual capitalists have no choice in the matter. All entrepreneurs, corporations or businesses face competition from others, domestic and foreign. This is the "external coercive law" that keeps all capitalists seeking to accumulate more, to preserve what they have. Survival cannot be achieved except by further accumulation. It is the law of "grow or die." A stationary state, such as that proposed by John Stuart Mill and many more contemporary economists with an ecological orientation, is not possible under the system. There cannot be a "no growth" system of capitalism. Expanding on Smith, Marx put it well: the system is driven by "accumulation for accumulation's sake; production for production's sake." (see Harvey, 1977; Massey, 1978; Webber, 1982)

How does Marxist political economy explain the geographic phenomenon of metropolitan domination of hinterland regions? There is the need for capital and capitalists to congregate in centres. The expansion of capital requires the development of pools of capital, financial institutions which mobilize capital from small savings, stock exchanges, and a decision-making process for investment. Capitalists need to meet regularly to plan investments and marketing. This is best served by the concentration and centralization of appropriate institutions, including the head offices of financial and other corporations. Research and development is concentrated in urban centres around universities, institutes, government agencies, and the head offices of corporations. Thus it is the norm for each industrialized country to have one centre where this activity is concentrated. Canada is one of the few countries with two financial centres, reflecting the historic development of Montreal and then the rise of Toronto. (Pomfret, 1993)

The drive to accumulate more capital and to reach new markets requires capital to push into the most distant markets. Thus, transportation and communication are key elements. Marxists have included them in the production process itself, arguing that the end product is only really finished when it is for sale on the local market. Thus capitalist production is sensitive to the costs of transportation and the ability to bring raw materials to production centres.

As a result, there is the drive by capitalists to introduce cheaper and faster means of transportation and communication. This enables extensive penetration of distant markets. New areas of accumulation are opened. Capitalists are very interested in how quickly they can realize a profit on their investment. The "velocity of circulation of capital" is very important to the accumulation process. The turnover of capital is slower in distant markets. As Marx put it, speed in transportation and communications is necessary "to annihilate this space with time." (Marx, 1973; Harvey, 1977)

Marx and those who accept his basic analysis agree that in order to minimize the costs of this circulation process (production and then distribution to distant markets) it is useful to concentrate production, labour, credit and capital in a few metropolitan centres. Thus *metropolitan concentration is a natural characteristic of capitalism*, and improvements in transportation tend to support already existing market relationships. Marx noted that for capital the development of the steam engine, railways, and steel ships enhanced the process of agglomeration and concentration in large urban centres. The centres of capital and manufacturing are always found where there is good, cheap transportation.

In the world of capitalist competition, imperial centres may rise and fall. Government policies may induce shifts from one urban centre to another. The centre of capital in Canada moved from Montreal to Toronto. The most important world centre of capital moved from London to New York. Within a country, particularly one which is relatively small (like Great Britain), government policies may shift production from one regional centre to another. *But there is no evidence that hinterland areas ever change into metropolitan centres.*

On a world basis, Marx argued that an international division of labour under capitalism suits the interests of the main centres of modern industry. The capitalist system "converts one part of the globe into a chiefly agricultural field of production, for supplying the other part which remains a chiefly industrial field." Capitalists can usually get a higher rate of profit by selling products in peripheral areas where local competing products are handicapped by inferior production methods. These excess profits are usually the result of a "technology-gap" which can become permanent. (Marx, 1973; Harvey, 1977)

Thus for those who have adopted Marxist political economy, the existence of metropolitan domination of hinterland areas is a natural development of capitalism. The concentration of capital's institutions and production in central areas follows the logic of the system and the unending competition for markets. Capital is accumulated by extracting the surplus value from workers in manufacturing, generally found in or near the metropolitan centres, but also in regional centres. Hinterland areas are necessary to provide raw materials, agricultural production, the reserve army of labour, and markets for manufactured goods. Those who are engaged in domestic commodity production in hinterland areas, such as independent family farmers, fishers, and small forest operators, will contribute their economic surplus through the process of finance and where they buy their inputs and sell their products. They operate in a highly competitive market of small producers and sell to a highly monopolized corporate market.

## Capitalist Centralization and Ecology

The Marxist view of metropolitan domination focuses on the accumulation process of capitalism. But the new ecological approach to the dichotomy brings us back to the geographical model. The case is well put by William Rees, who teaches in the School of Community and Regional Planning at the University of British Columbia. (Rees. 1992; 1994)

The mainstream and Marxist economic models both assume that the natural world will always be here and functioning as we know it. If there are shortages of natural resources, for example, higher prices will lead to conservation and new technologies will find substitutes. Robert M. Solow, Nobel Prize winning economist at Massachusetts Institute of Technology, has argued that "the world can, in effect, get along without natural resources." (Solow, 1974)

The natural system, or "natural capital" as our economists call it, provides three basic services for human beings and all other species. First, it produces and provides for our material resources: air, water, food, and other raw materials. Second, the ecosphere recycles our organic wastes and absorbs our industrial wastes and end products. Third, it provides basic services which are of general benefit to humans, including space for living, nature to enjoy, and functions which are essential to life, including maintenance of the atmosphere, stabilization of the climate, and regeneration of the ozone layer. (Rees, 1994)

In the period since World War II, most of the followers of Karl Marx have argued that ecological destruction is inevitable under capitalism but in a socialist, democratically controlled society, there would be no problems. The position of Marxist political parties during the Cold War was that technologies under socialism would overcome any ecological problems. Central planning would overcome urban-rural conflicts and end regional disparities. But that optimism stood in stark contrast to the ecological destruction within the Soviet bloc of countries. (see Redclift and Benton, 1994)

In contrast to the Marxists, Rees and other ecologists and ecological economists focus on the earth's carrying capacity. This is defined as "the population of a given species that can be supported indefinitely in a given habitat without permanently damaging the ecosystem upon which it depends." And for humans, this means "the maximum rate of resource consumption and waste discharge that can be sustained indefinitely in a given region without progressively impairing the functional integrity and productivity of relevant ecosystems."

The key question for urban areas is how much land is necessary to support the people who live there. What is needed to provide the food, fuel, wood products, etc., and all the waste-processing required? Obviously this cannot be provided in the land available in an urban area. As Rees argues, "however brilliant its economic star, *every city is an ecological black hole* drawing on the material resources and productivity of a vast and scattered hinterland many times the size of the city itself." Urban areas, regardless of the mode of production under which they operate, must "appropriate carrying capacity from distant elsewhere." (Rees, 1992)

As an example, Rees does some calculations on this for the lower Fraser Valley of British Columbia (Vancouver to Hope). Assuming the average Canadian diet and standard of living, the land equivalent needed for each resident of this area is around one hectare for food, 0.5 hectares for wood, and 3.0 to 4.0 hectares for forests and fields needed to absorb carbon dioxide from fossil fuel consumption. To support only these few services requires a land base of 8.5 million hectares for the region's 1.7 million people. But the Fraser Valley is only 400,000 hectares. Thus the region must "import" the needed productive/absorbive capacity from hinterlands in Canada and elsewhere. (Rees, 1992; 1994)

The reality is that all urban areas and many nations "already exceed their territorial carrying capacities and depend on trade for survival." Rees points out that "northern urbanites, wherever they are, are now dependent on the carbon sink, global heat transfer, and climate stabilization functions of tropical forests." The system of international trade permits the wealthy nations of the First World to export their "ecological and social malaise" to the Third World. Many hinterland areas and Third World countries rely on the export of agricultural and primary products and in return absorb the pollution of the urban First World. Rees argues that urban people in the north are isolated from the negative effects of high level consumerism. They do not equate their consumption of coffee, tea, bananas, cocoa, sugar, wood, fruits, vegetables, meat, and oil with erosion, desertification, deforestation, climate change, pollution and the horrendous living conditions of a great many people in the Third World.

Ecologists in general are deeply concerned about the destruction of our natural capital and the inequalities which often take the form of urban and hinterland disparities, both within countries and between countries. As Rees argues, the world capitalist system at present depends on the "appropriation of a vastly disproportionate share of the 'net planetary product' by wealthy industrialized nations." This helps us understand why business interests and capitalists in general are pushing so hard for free trade agreements. As one example, the rich capitalist countries are changing the rules of the World Trade Organization to include a ban on any government prohibitions of exports of agriculture and primary products. (Rees, 1994)

Canada is part of the world capitalist system. We do not have a centrally planned economy. Thus it is inevitable that we will have the centralization of economic and political power in the industrial and financial centres of Canada. That is simply how the system works. All urban centres, from earliest times, have required hinterland areas to provide agricultural products, natural resources, population, and to absorb excess production. Historically, these relationships have been imperial in nature, with political, military, economic and ideological domination emanating from the urban centre. Canada has been no different. Since the arrival of European immigrants, power has resided in the central urban areas, exercised by a small group of men.

From an ecological perspective, urban areas require hinterland areas. They cannot exist without them. Even the city-states of Hong Kong and Singapore survive because they have their hinterland areas. Without the appropriation of carrying capacity, by both trade and the natural processes of the globe, they would not be able to survive. This explains the persistence of Saskatchewan as a hinterland within Canada and within the prairies. The question has to be whether this exploitation is inevitable. Are there no alternatives possible?

## The Politics of Discontent

The prairies have been home to discontent and protest. Writers often allude to the "rebellious West." The indigenous population resisted colonialism, but they were overwhelmed. There was the resistance of the Métis in 1969-70 and then again in 1885. The political agitation by the prairie grain farmers is well known. The west also produced the militant One Big Union, radical trade unions in the resource extraction industries, and the Winnipeg General Strike. The Progressive Party, the Co-operative Commonwealth Federation, the Social Credit movement and the Reform Party are more restrained expressions of western alienation and discontent. When John Diefenbaker, the rural Saskatchewan lawyer, became Prime Minister in 1957, the eastern Liberal establishment and big business turned on him, attacking him in every possible way. This confirmed the prairie view of central Canada. The Western Canada Concept and a few other parties proposed that western Canada separate from confederation and form an independent country. S. D. Clark went as far as stating that these rebellions against political and economic power in central Canada were the expressions of a "separate people." (Clark, 1950; Pratt and Stevenson, 1981)

Regionalism also includes some sense of community, of common experience. Ed McCourt, who taught English at the University of Saskatchewan, argued that there is a common theme in the writing that came from the prairies. Writers on the prairies are heavily influenced by the landscape and the struggle to survive in a hostile environment. Eli Mandel agrees that the geography of the prairies has had an impact on the writer. But the view depends on their interpretation of the wide open spaces, the cold climate, the isolation, rural and small town life, the drudgery of farm work, and the patriarchal domination of the family farm culture. Some see the land as a source of strength, others as a barrier to personal development. (McCourt, 1970; Mandel, 1973)

Saskatchewan has a political culture that is different from other parts of Canada. It includes a deep commitment to the principle of the individual family farm, owned and operated by the man as the head of the traditional patriarchal family. The family is a unit of production, with common interests. With this goes a strong belief in private ownership of production by small operators, and a hostility to both corporate and co-operative farms. Perhaps because so many immigrants came from the United States and European countries, there is little support for the view of Canada as "two founding nations." This led to strong opposition to Pierre Elliott Trudeau's project of bilingualism. The people of the prairies speak English and do not want to learn French. This cultural tradition brought support to the Reform Party and its successor, the Canadian Alliance, for their insistence that all provinces are equal, and that Quebec should not have any special status, particularly the right to a veto over changes to the Constitution.

From the beginning of the farm protest movement, there was a recognition that the British system of parliamentary government and party discipline, combined with the first past the post electoral system, meant that the federal government would always be controlled in Central Canada, with either a Tory majority from Ontario or a Liberal majority from Quebec. Proportional representation was advocated by the western "third parties" as one way to break this domination.

There is a strong belief on the prairies that the provinces must have the right to control their own natural resources. Many see this as the only area where the West has been given any real rights under the Constitution. In the 1970s, the NDP government of Saskatchewan joined forces with the Tory government of Alberta to fight for control over resources in the courts.

In the past "the West" meant the Canadian prairies. British Columbia was a different province, cut off from the prairies by the mountains, and it did not share the history of the settler farmer. Today the prairies seem a far less homogeneous region. Alberta, with the bonanza which came with the discovery of the oil and gas resources, is one of the "have" provinces, with its conservative political leaders usually aligning themselves with Ontario on federal-provincial matters. British Columbia, with its high general standard of living, is commonly aligned with Alberta. Manitoba and Saskatchewan are "have not" provinces, with relatively low general standards of living, regular recipients of "equalization" payments from Ottawa. Political leaders from Alberta and British Columbia complain about having to pay to support their poor cousins on the prairies.

In the 1970s, the Prairie Economic Council was replaced by the Western Premiers Conference, now including British Columbia. Because there were so many differences among the four provinces, the forum served mainly as an institution to try to gain political and economic concessions from Ottawa. The unity among the four premiers was a sense of isolation from the decision making centres in Ontario, what David Elton calls "shared disaffection." (Elton, 1988)

## Conclusion

There is no question but that geographic areas form the basis for regions and regionalism. But human activity over time creates historic regions, regionalism and regional disparities. Common sense and the empirical record are in accord here: within the capitalist mode of production, metropolitanism and regional disparities are a given. They are always there. They are normal. They are a byproduct of the capital accumulation process. Capitalists and their institutions collect surplus value from workers and economic rent from others and concentrate it in their institutions in centres of power. That is the way it is around the world.

Hinterlands have existed since the rise of the city state. They will continue to exist. The ecology of cities necessitates the existence of hinterlands. But this does not mean that people who live in hinterland areas are forever condemned to living in a situation of inequality and/or deprivation. But to overcome this problem it is necessary to resist and overcome the centralizing aspects of the capitalist accumulation process and the "market economy."

We do know that centralization and inequality can be overcome in a centrally planned economy. For example, in Bulgaria prior to the collapse of the Soviet regime, the Agro-Industrial Complex system was undergoing the process of decentralization of production. Rural areas were being re-populated. That ended with the collapse of the governments in the Soviet bloc and the restoration of a capitalist economy. Very few people in Canada would opt to live under a planned economy which was part of a totalitarian state. But that does not mean that other alternatives are not possible. (Warnock, 1987)

The environment of a region does impact on human behaviour. The fact that wheat is grown on the prairies and not corn and soybeans is due to geography and the climate. Nikita Khrushchev was impressed by the corporate corn-hog farms he visited in Iowa and tried to import the system into the Soviet Union. The experiment failed because the climate was not favourable and the growing season was too short.

Regions are historical creations, the products of actions of human beings. The Canadian and British governments, and the European settlers who came, created a modern agricultural economy on the prairies. It was designed by political and business leaders in central Canada as a system for capital accumulation. But the National Policy, as it was called, created much discontent and protest.

In Saskatchewan today business interests, the capitalist class in general, the political right, and the vast majority of economists promote the ideology of individualism, consumerism, the free market and free trade. They argue that people should have the right to buy any product, wherever and however it is made, at the lowest possible price. Following Margaret Thatcher, they are really arguing that there is no Saskatchewan community. This provincial territory just contains a collection of one million individuals all pursuing their own self interest. The government should be limited and not actively pursuing a common interest. There is strong opposition to government-backed regional development policies. It is argued that we no longer need collectivist institutions like the Canadian Wheat Board. We no longer need co-operatives. Even the provincial Dairy Co-operative has been sold to a private corporation based in Montreal. Our system of taxes is being changed to shift the burden from corporations and those with high incomes to consumption taxes and users fees imposed on all equally. This policy actively and consciously promotes inequality of wealth and income. The provincial governments encourage foreign ownership and control of the economy. This free market strategy will not in any way reduce regional disparities. It will inevitably lead to more discontent and protest.

## References

Acheson, T.S. 1977. "The Maritimes and 'Empire Canada.'" in David J. Bercuson, ed. *Canada and the Burden of Unity*. Toronto: Macmillan.

Allen, Richard, ed. 1973. *A Region of the Mind: Interpreting the Western Canadian Plains*. Regina: Canadian Plains Research Center.

Archibald, Bruce. 1971. "Atlantic Regional Underdevelopment and Socialism." In Laurier LaPierre *et al.*, eds., *Essays on the Left*. Toronto: McClelland and Stewart, pp. 103-128.

Boyens, Ingeborg. 2001. *Another Season's Promise: Hope and Despair in Canada's Farm Country*. Toronto: Penguin Books.

Brodie, Janine. 1990. *The Political Economy of Canadian Regionalism*. Toronto: Harcourt Brace Jovanovich, Canada.

Brym, Robert and R. James Sacouman, eds. 1979. *Underdevelopment and Social Movements in Atlantic Canada.* Toronto: New Hogtown Press.

Burrill, Gary and Ian McKay, eds. 1987. *People, Resources and Power: Critical Perspectives on Underdevelopment and Primary Industries in the Atlantic Region.* Fredericton: Acadiensis Press.

Careless, J.M.S. 1967. *The Union of the Canadas: The Growth of Canadian Institutions, 1841-1857.* Toronto: McClelland and Stewart.

Careless, J.M.S. 1954. "Frontierism, Metropolitanism and Canadian History." *Journal of Canadian History,* Vol. 35, No. 1, March, pp. 1-21.

Clark, S.D. 1950. "Foreword." In W. L. Morton, *The Progressive Party in Canada.* Toronto: University of Toronto Press.

Clement, Wallace. 1975. *The Canadian Corporate Elite: An Analysis of Economic Power.* Toronto: McClelland and Stewart.

Clement, Wallace. 1977. *Continental Corporate Power: Economic Linkages between Canada and the United States.* Toronto: McClelland and Stewart.

Creighton, Donald. 1937. *The Empire of the St. Lawrence.* Toronto: Macmillan of Canada.

Easterbrook, W.T. and Hugh G. J. Aitken. 1956. *Canadian Economic History.* Toronto: Macmillan Co. of Canada.

Eisler, Dale. 1987. *Rumours of Glory: Saskatchewan and the Thatcher Years.* Edmonton: Hurtig Publishers.

Elkins, David J. *et al.* 1980. *Small Worlds: Province and Parties in Canadian Political Life.* Toronto: Methuen.

Elton, David. 1988. "Federalism and the Canadian West." In R. D. Olling and M. W. Westmacott, eds. *Perspectives on Canadian Federalism.* Scarborough: Prentice-Hall Canada.

Epp, Roger and Dave Whitson, eds. 2001. *Writing Off the Rural West: Globalization, Governments, and the Transformation of Rural Communities.* Edmonton: University of Alberta Press.

Fay, C.R. 1927. "The Metropolitan Market." *Canadian Banker,* Vol. 34, January, pp. 181-92.

Gibbons, Robert. 1980. *Prairie Politics and Society: Regionalism in Decline.* Toronto: Butterworth.

Gras, Norman S.B. 1922. *An Introduction to Economic History.* New York: Harper & Brothers.

Gras, Norman S.B. 1929. "Regionalism and Nationalism." *Foreign Affairs,* Vol. 7, No. 3, April, pp. 454-67.

Harvey, David. 1977. "The Geography of Capitalist Accumulation: A Reconstruction of the Marxian Theory." In Richard Peet, ed. *Radical Geography: Alternative Viewpoints on Contemporary Social Issues.* London: Methuen, pp. 163-92.

Higgins, Benjamin and Donald J. Savoie. 1997. *Regional Development Theories and the Application.* New Brunswick, N.J.: Transaction Publishers.

Innis, Harold A. 1950. *Empire and Communications.* Toronto: University of Toronto Press.

Innis, Harold A. 1951, *The Bias of Communications*. Toronto: University of Toronto Press.

Kerr, Donald P. 1968. "Metropolitan Dominance in Canada." In John Warkintin, ed., *Canada: A Geographical Interpretation*. Toronto: Methuen, pp. 531-55.

Laycock, David. 2002. *The New Right and Democracy in Canada*. Don Mills: Oxford University Press.

Leslie, Peter M. 1987. *Federal State, National Economy*. Toronto: University of Toronto Press.

Lower, A.R.M. 1938. *The North American Assault on the Canadian Forest*. Toronto: Ryerson.

Mandel, Eli. 1973. "Images of Prairie Man." In Richard Allen, ed. *A Region of the Mind: Interpreting the Western Canadian Plains*. Regina: Canadian Plains Research Center.

Marr, William L. and Donald G. Patterson. 1980. *Canada: An Economic History*. Toronto: Macmillan of Canada.

Marx, Karl. 1973. *Grundrisse*. Harmondsworth: Penguin Books.

Massey, Doreen. 1978. "Regionalism: Some Current Issues." *Capital and Class*, No. 6, Autumn, pp. 106-25.

Masters, D.C. 1941. "Toronto Versus Montreal: The Struggle for Financial Hegemony, 1860-1875." *Canadian Historical Review*, Vol. 22, No. 2, June, pp. 133-46.

Masters, D.C. 1947. *The Rise of Toronto, 1850-1890*. Toronto: University of Toronto Press.

Matthews, Ralph. 1983. *The Creation of Regional Dependency*. Toronto: University of Toronto Press.

McCann, L.D. 1982. "Heartland and Hinterland: A Framework for Regional Analysis." In L. D. McCann, ed. *Geography of Canada: Heartland and Hinterland*. Scarborough: Prentice-Hall Canada, pp. 2-35.

McCourt, Edward A. 1970. *The Canadian West in Fiction*. Toronto: Ryerson.

McCrorie, James N. and Martha L. MacDonald, eds. 1992. *The Constitutional Future of the Prairie and Atlantic Regions of Canada*. Regina: Canadian Plains Research Centre, University of Regina.

Mitchell, Bruce. ed. 1995. *Resource and Environmental Management in Canada*. New York: Oxford University Press.

Morton, W.L. 1950. *The Progressive Party in Canada*. Toronto: University of Toronto Press.

Myers, Gustavus. 1914. *A History of Canadian Wealth*. Toronto: James Lewis & Samuel. [First published in 1914.]

National Farmers Union. 2000. *The Farm Crisis, EU Subsidies, and Agribusiness Market Power*. Paper presented to the Senate Standing Committee on Agriculture and Forestry. Saskatoon: National Farmers Union.

Norrie, Kenneth and Douglas Owram. 1996. *A History of the Canadian Economy*. Toronto: Harcourt Brace Canada.

Owram, Doug. 1981. "Reluctant Hinterland." In Larry Pratt and Garth Stevenson, eds. *Western Separatism: The Myths, Realities and Dangers.* Edmonton: Hurtig Publishers.

Park, Libbie and Frank Park. 1962. *Anatomy of Big Business.* Toronto: James Lewis & Samuel.

Phillips, Paul. 1982. *Regional Disparities.* Toronto: James Lorimer & Co.

Pomfret, Richard. 1993. *The Economic Development of Canada.* Scarborough: Nelson Canada.

Redclift, Michael and Ted Benton, eds. 1994. *Social Theory and the Global Environment.* New York: Routledge.

Reed, Maureen G. 1995. "Implementing Sustainable Development in Hinterland Regions." In Bruce Mitchell, pp. 335-357.

Rees, William E. 1994. "Pressing Global Limits: Trade as the Appropriation of Carrying Capacity." In Ted Schrecker and Jean Dalgleish, pp. 29-56.

Rees, William E. 1992. "Ecological Footprints and Appropriated Carrying Capacity: What Urban Economics Leaves Out." Paper presented to Urban Development Stream, Vancouver, B.C., March 16-20.

Roach, Robert. 2002. *Beyond Our Borders: Western Canadian Exports in the Global Market.* Calgary: Canada West Foundation.

Robinson, Elwyn B. 1995. *History of North Dakota.* Fargo: The Institute for Regional Studies, North Dakota State University.

Savoie, Donald J. 1986. *Regional Economic Development: Canada's Search for Solutions.* Toronto: University of Toronto Press.

Schrecker, Ted and Jean Dalgleish, eds. 1994. *Growth, Trade and Environmental Values.* London, ON: Westminister Institute for Ethics and Human Values.

Solow, Robert M. 1974. "The Economics of Resources or the Resources of Economics." *American Economics Review,* Vol. 64. pp. 1-14.

Turner, Frederick Jackson. 1920. *The Frontier in American History.* New York: Holt, Reinhard & Winston.

Veltmeyer, Henry. 1979. "The Capitalist Underdevelopment of Atlantic Canada." In Robert J. Brym and R.J. Sacouman, pp. 17-35.

Webber, M.J. 1982. "Agglomeration and the Regional Question." *Antipode,* Vol. 17, No. 2, pp. 1-11.

# Chapter 5

─────○─────

# SASKATCHEWAN
# AND THE WHEAT ECONOMY

The wheat economy has played a central role in constructing the political culture of Saskatchewan. It is a perfect example of how regions and regionalism are a blend of the specifics of geography and historic human activity. The Canadian prairies are without doubt a distinct geographical region. The flat dry lands with extremes in temperature are cut off from the Pacific Ocean by the Rocky Mountains and from eastern Canada by the Canadian Shield.

The province of Saskatchewan was created as part of the National Policy and the wheat economy. The National Policy demonstrated that economic development is closely tied to political development. It also confirmed that basic decisions within the capitalist mode of production are made by capitalists seeking new investment areas that can produce a profit or economic rent to be appropriated. The decision to create a Canadian territorial state, construct the railways, and populate the prairies with European settlers on largely "free land" as independent farmers, was made by our political leaders working closely with the most important capitalists in central Canada. Many of the political leaders themselves were involved in the companies which were to benefit from the policy. These facts often escape mainstream economists today who are conditioned to believe that what happens within the capitalist system is determined by individuals making rational choices in the market.

It doesn't take much reading of history to learn that the creation of Canada was a conscious attempt by our political leaders at that time to thwart continental integration. The National Policy was a plan to create a country linked east to west by transportation, communications and a separate market for investment and the sale of goods. Saskatchewan was created by people who were endeavoring to create a country independent of the United States.

Most economists today, following the leadership of big business and their propaganda organizations, are active supporters of continental free trade and call for closer integration of Canada into the United States. In contrast, the vast majority of political economists believe it is better to maintain Canada as an independent country. This political orientation can be seen in how they approach the issue of the National Policy and the wheat economy.

The original National Policy produced political and economic dissent. Over the years Saskatchewan's wheat economy has evolved, diversified into other agricultural crops and livestock and the extraction of natural resources. There has been a shift from goods production and export to an expanded tertiary or service sector. But discontent and protest remains, now taking a different form.

## The National Policy and Saskatchewan

The term "National Policy" was first used by John A. Macdonald in the House of Commons on March 7, 1878. As leader of the Conservative opposition, he introduced a resolution that called for a National Policy "which, by a judicious readjustment of the Tariff, will benefit and foster the agricultural, the mining, the manufacturing and other interests of the Dominion." This was to be the platform on which they fought and won the 1878 federal election. But as Vernon Fowke and most other political economists have argued, the National Policy really began much earlier, before Confederation. (Fowke, 1957)

The roots of the National Policy go back to developments in the 1840s. This was a period before the extension of the franchise, when only men of property had the vote, and only men of property were found in the legislatures. The important capitalist class was a relatively small group of Anglo-Canadian men who operated out of Montreal, the centre of finance and merchant trade. Upper and Lower Canada had been united in 1841 to help complete the canal system to the St. Lawrence River, to allow these merchants to capture the trade in agricultural and primary products going to Great Britain. Canadian wheat and flour had preferential status in Great Britain under the Corn Laws of 1815, 1822 and 1828.

But there was a political war going in Great Britain between the landed aristocracy, which supported the Corn Laws, and the rising industrial capitalist class, which was pushing for free trade. The new bourgeois class was to win this war, and the Corn Laws were repealed in 1846 and the Navigation Acts in 1849. Canadian agricultural products, timber and ships lost their preferential markets. In panic, the Montreal business leaders produced the Annexation Manifesto in 1849, demanding immediate union with the United States. (Easterbrook and Aitken, 1956; Fowke, 1957; Marr and Paterson, 1980)

At the same time, business interests in the Canadian colonies began to push for a reciprocity treaty with the United States, and a treaty was finally signed in 1854. Free trade was permitted for agricultural products, lumber and fish and a range of other natural products, but manufacturing was excluded. Much to the consternation of maritime interests, the fisheries in Canada were now open to American fishers. The treaty was to last for ten years. Many of the new Canadian economic historians have argued that trade with the United States would have expanded in any case and that the loss of the British preference would not end that market. However, for the Canadian capitalist class at the time, the fears were real. (Norrie and Owram, 1996; Pomfret, 1993)

In the 1850s Canadian business interests began to discuss a third option. Investment could be made in railways, and trade would expand within the British North American colonies themselves. Much of this would depend on increased immigration and the expansion of agriculture. By 1847 it was already evident that the repeal of the Corn Laws would not adversely affect the export of Canadian grain. Furthermore, the cost of transporting grain in Canada fell with the completion of the canal system between Toronto and Montreal. Railway construction was stimulated with government and municipal guarantees and bonuses. Many of our most important political leaders were involved in companies building railways and speculating in land. In 1858 Alexander Galt, minister of finance in united Canada, introduce a tariff to protect manufactures. The third option was beginning to take shape.

But there were other forces that pushed for Confederation and the National Policy. The U.S. Civil War broke out in 1860, and Great Britain was openly sympathetic to the South. The British wanted to maintain cheap imports of cotton and other agricultural products, and they were fearful of the growing industrial power of the northern United States. The U.S. government, angry with Great Britain, announced that they would not renew the Reciprocity Treaty of 1854. In 1862 the U.S. government passed the Homestead Act to encourage immigration and settlement in the west. The first trans-continental railway was under way and was completed in 1869. Montreal and Toronto business interests feared they were going to be left behind as the new western agricultural frontier came under U.S. domination.

Vernon Fowke has stressed the political goals which were behind the National Policy and Confederation. Immigration and U.S. government policy was pushing the agricultural frontier west without any regard for political jurisdictions. American nationalism and "Manifest Destiny" was reflected in the rhetoric of the publicists and politicians. The continent, indeed the whole of the hemisphere, was to be under the control of American liberal capitalism.

The St. Lawrence commercial capitalist class realized that if it were to secure any of the economic benefits from the opening of the west, it was necessary to develop a railway across the Precambrian Shield. A railway between the British territories in the west and Minneapolis-St. Paul, plus the rush of settlers from the United States into this new agricultural land, could lead to the dismemberment of British North America and a lost economic opportunity.

In 1857 both the British Parliament and the legislature in United Canada appointed special committees to examine how to acquire Prince Rupert's Land from the Hudson Bay Company. The purchase of the land was considered too great an undertaking for the British North American colonies.

It was also agreed that a trans-Canadian railway was necessary to link the colonies together and cement a political arrangement between them. The U.S. government was using land grants and subsidies to encourage the expansion of railways into the west. Canada would have to do the same. The Atlantic colonies were also urging a railway to overcome the handicap of the winter months when the St. Lawrence River was frozen. The railway project was seen to be too large a task for the separate colonies.

There were other arguments in support of the National Policy and a future wheat economy. The are summarized by Vernon Fowke, who studied the proceedings of the Charlottetown conference of 1864, the Quebec Conference of 1864, the Confederation Debates in the legislature of Canada in 1865, and the discussions in the press at the time. As he notes, these represented "the first of a series of debates on national policy." The push for Confederation reflected a combination of interests and political, military and commercial objectives. (Fowke, 1957)

The development of a national market, tied together by a transcontinental railway, would provide economic expansion for agriculture, merchant trade, investment opportunities, and industrialization. It would encourage the development of manufacturing and a more diversified economy. As Fowke notes, these were the central arguments of the Anglo-Canadian merchants of Montreal.

There was consensus that Canada needed to attract more immigrants, to halt the emigration of Canadians to the United States, and to settle the agriculture frontier of the prairies. Between 1850 and 1860 the population of Minnesota had risen from 6,000 to 172,000, statehood was granted in 1858, and during the Civil War representatives from that state introduced resolutions in the U.S. Congress calling for the annexation of western Canada. In 1868 the U.S. Senate passed such a resolution.

The British government was also concerned about its possessions on the Pacific coast. They had lost the Oregon Territory to the United States in 1846. The gold rush of 1857 brought around 30,000 Americans to British Columbia, then just a fur trade colony of the Hudson Bay Company. In 1859 a new colony of British Columbia was created. The separate colony of Vancouver Island was merged with it in 1866. But without a link to the other North American colonies, the British government and Canadian political leaders believed that it would eventually link with Washington, Oregon and California.

There was a need to build Canada as a new national state. The railway was the necessary link. We could not protect the Northwest Territories from U.S. immigration, and de facto control, without a railway close to the U.S. border, running across Canada to the Atlantic Ocean. In 1864 the U.S. government chartered the Northern Pacific Railroad, with the express purpose of capturing any future grain trade from the northern plains area, including the British Northwest Territories. To counter the U.S. political and economic strategy required a strong central government, with control over trade and commerce, banking and money, strong enough to raise capital internationally to finance these projects. A strong central government was needed to ease the burden of debt acquired by the individual colonies in the construction of railroads. Confederation was achieved in 1867, Manitoba was admitted in 1870, British Columbia in 1871, and Prince Edward Island in 1873. (Fowke, 1957)

## The Transformation of the West

The new Dominion government set forth on its plan to create a new "investment frontier" on the Canadian prairies. The first task was to acquire Rupert's Land from the Hudson Bay Company. An agreement was reached in 1870. The company was given a cash grant of £300,000, land adjacent to its trading posts, and one-twentieth of the land in the "fertile belt" of the Canadian prairies south of the North Saskatchewan River, plus extensive land in the Lake Winnipeg and Lake of the Woods area. This amounted to around 6.6 million acres.

In 1811 Lord Selkirk had received a grant of 115,000 acres from the Hudson Bay Company to create a colony at Red River. The settlers who came to farm clashed regularly with the Hudson Bay Company. The Métis who dominated the area regularly challenged the monopoly power of the company. Conflicts expanded between the Métis and the new European settlers. Most of the Métis in the Red River colony were of French Canadian background and were Roman Catholic. The settlers from Ontario were mainly English speaking and Protestant, many of them Orange Presbyterians.

By the time of Confederation there were over 5,000 permanent settlers in the Red River colony farming over 6,000 acres. Following Confederation European immigration increased as did conflict over land rights, titles, religion and ethnic background. The Métis were particularly concerned over the rumours that the Hudson Bay Company was selling Rupert's Land to the Canadian government.

A confrontation occurred in 1869 when land surveyors arrived from the Canadian government. In December 1869, Louis Riel and the Métis, who were a majority of the people living in the colony, announced the formation of a government and control over their historic lands. They asserted the right to negotiate with the government of Canada for admission to Confederation. A democratic convention endorsed their position. But John A. Macdonald was determined to set his own course for the development of the prairies. The Manitoba Act of 1870 created a small province of Manitoba, but an Imperial military force was dispatched to the Red River, the 60th Rifles under Col. Garnet Wolseley, to enforce the position of the Dominion government. Louis Riel went into exile into the United States, and metropolitan domination of the prairies was confirmed. (Friesen, 1987; Easterbrook and Aitken, 1956)

Before the Northwest Territories could be opened to European settlement and agricultural production it was necessary to remove the indigenous population from their land. In 1870 there were around 35,000 Indians, 10,000 Métis and only around 2,000 European Canadians in the territories. The traditional means of livelihood, the buffalo, was being exterminated through the commercial harvest for buffalo robes, outright slaughter, and the introduction of European diseases. Between 1871 and 1877 seven numbered treaties were signed with the Indian nations of the Canadian prairies. The land was surrendered, the indigenous peoples were assigned to small reserves, and the Dominion government made various promises to support a transition to agriculture. Under the Manitoba Act and the Dominion Lands Act the Métis were to be given land script or a cash equivalent.

The North West Mounted Police was formed in 1873 to oversee the transfer of land from the Indians to the Dominion government. As early as 1869, John A. Macdonald argued for the creation of the force as a military body, riflemen trained as cavalry, similar to the Irish Constabulary that the British used to support colonial control of Ireland. The rebellion of the Métis at Red River had convinced the government that a military force was necessary. None of the major studies of the wheat economy, or our texts on Canadian economic history, cover this important part of the National Policy. But it is the foundation of the political culture of Saskatchewan, and I will discuss it in more detail in Chapter 7. (see Frideres, 1998; Wotherspoon and Satzewich, 1993; Carter, 1999; Buckley, 1992)

The transcontinental railway was central to the National Policy, and a high priority for John A. Macdonald. In 1868 the U.S. Senate backed the building of the Northern Pacific Railway for the purposes of "draining the agricultural products of the rich Saskatchewan and Red River Districts" and to encourage U.S. settlement so that the area "will in effect be severed from the new Dominion and the question of their annexation will be but a question of time." The transcontinental train on this route today is appropriately named the "Empire Builder." (Fowke, 1957)

Who would control the Canadian Pacific Railway? Sir Hugh Allan and the Montreal business committee created a consortium. Senator D. L. Macpherson and a group of capitalists from Toronto put up a challenge. Macdonald and his political ally, Sir George-Etienne Cartier, created a company in 1873 with Allan as president. But political contributions, bribes and skullduggery resulted in the Pacific Scandal of 1873, which brought down the Conservative government. The Liberal government of Alexander Mackenzie prepared the way for the CPR, but a new consortium did not emerge until after Macdonald was re-elected in 1878.

The Canadian Pacific Railway was finally incorporated in 1881. It was an alliance of capitalists with political connections, including fur trader Norman Kittson, U.S. railroad magnate James J. Hill, Donald A. Smith of the Hudson Bay Company, George Stephens of the Bank of Montreal, and John S. Kennedy, a New York financier. Other key capitalist were connected with the railways in Ontario and Quebec. Only one-sixth of the stock was held by Canadian interests, the rest being American and British.

The CPR was a state capitalist enterprise. It received a direct government grant of $25 million plus 25 million acres of prairie land. Sections already built by government grants were given to the company, 713 miles, which had cost $37.8 million. Until the CPR was making a return of ten percent on their investment, there would be no regulation of rates. They also received a tax exemption for its prairie section in perpetuity, exemption from import duties, exemption of property taxation for twenty years for the land granted, and a "monopoly clause" guaranteeing that for twenty years no other railway would be built. While most believed that the route was to go through the more northerly fertile belt and through the Yellowhead Pass, the owners chose the quicker southern route, closer to the U.S. border, to undermine the Northern Pacific Railroad. John Macoun, a botanist, convinced the company that the southern, "desert" land in the Palliser's Triangle could be developed for agriculture.

Construction began quickly. By 1881 they had reached Brandon, by 1882 they were past Swift Current, and by 1883 they had passed Calgary and were close to the Kicking Horse Pass. The major Lake Superior section was completed in 1883. On November 7, 1885 the last spike was driven at "Craigellachie" in the B.C. Rocky Mountains. (Fowke, 1957; Friesen, 1987; Pomfret, 1993)

The "new investment frontier," the Canadian prairies, depended on the labour of farmers. Thus the Dominion government retained control over land and resources on the prairies, even after the provinces were created. The Dominion Lands Act of 1872 opened the land to homesteads, based on the precedent set in the United States. For a fee of $10 a settler could acquire one quarter section (160 acres) if he (women were basically excluded) was able to stay on the land for three years and begin farming. A settler could "pre-empt" another adjacent quarter section, indicating that he would purchase it when he had the funds. The free land was available only outside the belt of twenty miles on either side of the CPR. Within this belt land retained by the government would sell for $2.50 per acre. The CPR and the Hudson Bay Company also sold its land to new settlers. Paul F. Sharp reminds us that the CPR offered its land at 10 percent down with twenty years to pay. Given that farmers had to haul their grain to the railroad by horse and wagon, land development was slow pending the expansion of branch lines. While most settlements were of an individual nature, a number of colonies and "reserves" were created for specific religious and ethnic groups. For example, in 1874 around 4,800 French Canadians were repatriated to ten colonies in Manitoba. By 1876 there were 6,150 colonies and reserves in that province. (Fowke, 1957; Friesen, 1987; Norrie and Owram, 1996; Pomfret, 1993; Sharp, 1997)

For many Canadians, the Tariff of 1879 was the National Policy. It should be remembered that the Dominion government wanted to retain the Reciprocity Treaty with the United States. In 1866, 1869, 1870, and 1874 official delegations went to

Washington to try to negotiate a similar treaty. But the U.S. government was not interested; following the Civil War it enacted a high tariff policy to promote industrialization.

Tariffs had for some time been the primary source of revenues for the Canadian colonies. But as the depression of 1873 dragged on, business interests in both Canada and the United States began demanding higher tariffs for protection. Since exports were restrained by the U.S. tariffs, Canadian businesses felt they should at least dominate the Canadian market.

John A. Macdonald promoted a new tariff policy during the election campaign of 1872. The Canadian Trade Union Act, which the Conservative government passed in 1872, was part of his vision of a National Policy. The tariff would protect Canadian industry, and the Trade Union Act would allow workers to form unions and bargain for higher wages. This would slow the emigration of workers to the United States. (Craven and Traves, 1979; Parker, 1979)

The Tariff of 1879 introduced by Macdonald's Conservative government was designed to give assistance to the creation of a manufacturing economy in central Canada. The building of the railways was the key starting point. The backward linkages would promote the coal, steel and the rolling stock industry. The settlement of the prairies would promote the agricultural machinery industry, tools, hardware, home furnishings and textiles. Forward linkages would be created by the grain handling system, flour and baking industries, and meat packing. (Fowke, 1957; Marr and Paterson, 1980)

The new investment frontier and the Tariff of 1879 were designed to assist industrialization, which was centred in Ontario and Quebec. Vernon Fowke argues that "regional specialization rests on acquired as well as natural advantages." Thus the National Policy intensified regional disparities. The fact that industrialization started in central Canada has given that region a seemingly permanent superiority over the prairie provinces. (Fowke, 1957)

## The Wheat Boom

The wheat economy did not develop as rapidly as expected. Between 1881 and 1901 the land occupied on the prairies rose from 2.7 to 15.4 million acres. The real boom period was between 1901 and 1911 when land occupied rose to 57.6 million acres. In 1895 there were only around 2,000 homesteads registered, and the annual number peaked at around 45,000 in 1911, of which 25,000 were in Saskatchewan. In the end a total of 675,000 homesteads had been registered by 1930.

The population of the prairies tripled between 1901 and 1911. This settlement was directly related to the development of railway branch lines, which rose from 4,100 miles in 1901 to 11,600 miles in 1914. The Dominion government actively promoted immigration, first through the Department of Agriculture and then the Department of the Interior. Agencies in Europe actively distributed literature advertising "free land" in western Canada. The railroads also carried out a campaign to recruit settlers. (Fowke, 1957; Marr and Paterson, 1980)

A number of the economic historians have questioned whether or not this was an appropriate policy and whether there even was a "wheat boom" that spurred Canadian economic development. It has been argued that for most settlers there was little likelihood of making a profit from farming. But Europeans knew that land was a scarce commodity and money could be made on capital gains. For immigrants like my own ancestors, who were tenant farmers in Ireland and landless peasants in Germany, getting land in either the United States or Canada was a great opportunity. As American humourist Will Rogers put it, "buy land—they aren't making any more of it!" Paul Sharp notes thatl "land hunger is a relentless force." There was good land in Canada well after it had disappeared in the United States. "That this land lay under the Union Jack and not under the Stars and Stripes made little difference to land-hungry Americans who poured into the Canadian prairies after 1896." (Sharp, 1997)

The wheat economy was certainly a boon to the prairies. As Vernon Fowke and Ken Buckley have pointed out, it was a "concrete expression in the process of real-capital formation." There was construction on the farm in dwellings, the machinery for cultivating, seeding, harvesting and threshing, furnishing the households, thousands of miles of railways, hundreds of new towns with their marketing centres and financial institutions, the grain elevators and loading platforms, and the stockyards. (Fowke, 1957; Buckley, 1958)

The expansion across the southern part of the prairies came with new dry farming techniques, the development of early maturing varieties of wheats and other grains, and the expansion of the livestock industry. The production of wheat grew from 56 million bushels in 1901 to 224 million bushels in 1913. Between 1901 and 1921 wheat rose from four percent of all exports to 25 percent. Europe came to rely more on imported grain. The improvement in shipping greatly reduced transportation costs. The wheat boom was important to the entire economy, and it drew in people from all over Europe. The population of Saskatchewan grew from 91,279 in 1901 to 931,547 in 1936. The number of farms peaked in Saskatchewan in 1936 at 300,500. (Easterbrook and Aitken, 1956; Marr and Paterson, 1980)

## The Development of Class Conflict

It was not just the capitalists and their political allies who played a role in the wheat economy. Paul Craven and Tom Traves have reminded us that during the period of the National Policy, which they ascribe to the period between 1872 and 1933, there developed three major classes in Canada and they co-operated on some issues and were in conflict on others. In addition to the capitalist class, there was a large agrarian *petit bourgeois* class of independent farmers, those who owned their own means of production, beginning with land. Then there was, of course, the development of the industrial working class in Canada, those who survive by selling their labour in the market. They were known as the *proletariat* after the Roman class which owned no land or other property used as means of production.

The organized workers, represented by the Canadian Labour Union and the Knights of Labour in the 19th century, co-operated with the Conservative government and its capitalist class allies when it came to protection of industry. They supported the high tariff policy as a means of protecting their jobs and wages. This more dominant labour movement in central Canada resisted the open immigration policy supported by the manufacturers.

The labour movement worked with the farm organizations like the Grange to promote certain social policies. But the farm movement was strongly opposed to the high tariff policy. The farm movement, strongly committed to private ownership of the means of production, was unwilling to support policies of socialism advanced by the more radical wing of the labour movement. In 1886 the Trades and Labour Congress met with the Grange, but the attempt at a political alliance collapsed when the farm leaders refused to endorse the eight hour work day.

In western Canada the labour movement grew in the larger cities: Winnipeg, Vancouver, and then Calgary and Edmonton. The trade union movement was greatly influenced by the development of craft unionism in the United States. Ross MacCormack argues that the trade unions in Canada were heavily influenced by workers from Great Britain who were in the tradition of reform labourism. In the mid-1890s, they "revitalized Winnipeg's moribund unions." (McCormack, 1977; Young, 1969)

On the prairies the local businesses, which were mainly merchants involved in "forwarding, retailing, and service functions," demonstrated "the merchant's concern for immediate profit and rapid growth" and fought trade unions. Labour resisted the immigration policy which undermined wage levels. (McCormack, 1977)

The labour force in western Canada worked in the mines and forests, worked on the railways, were migrant farm workers, and were construction workers in the small cities. In the resource extraction industries they had to live in towns and camps, work long hours, usually without family, friends and community. It was here that the radical syndicalism of the One Big Union and Marxism took root.

In the period of the development of the wheat economy wage labourers in Saskatchewan were greatly outnumbered by farmers. The 1911 census recorded a total labour force of 208,000, of which 133,000 were in agriculture (farmers and farm workers) and 36,000 in the tertiary sector, living in towns and cities. Very few were organized into trade unions. Political radicalism was led by the agrarian sector. (Conway, 1994)

Americans rushed across the border to get cheap land. Paul Sharp has reminded us that in 1909 land sold for $50 an acre in North Dakota but only $2 per acre in Saskatchewan. Farmers in Iowa sold their land for $65 to $150 an acre and either bought land or homesteaded in Alberta or Saskatchewan. After three years on a Saskatchewan homestead the land could be sold for $20 an acre. Settlers from American farms understood the concept of economic rent in land and were much more successful than European immigrants. (Sharp, 1997)

Europeans fled to North America to get free land. But it was not easy to acquire title to the land claimed in a homestead. Vernon Fowke stresses that there were capital requirements for settlement on the prairies. Many relied on the support of family and friends. Others struggled in wage labour to be able to equip themselves for a settlement. The European settler was "engaged in a clearly recognizable task of creating capital," Fowke concludes. A settler had to remain on his land for three years as a minimum. But breaking sod was difficult, grasshoppers were very common, and there was hail, drought and frost. It cost between five and fifteen dollars an acre to take a crop off new land. Costs were higher than in the United States and wheat prices were lower. Many failed. Chester Martin and Vernon Fowke provide data showing that around 40 percent of all homesteaders failed to secure title to their claim. In Saskatchewan in the period between 1911 to 1931, around 57 percent abandoned their claims. (Fowke, 1957; Martin, 1973; Sharp, 1997)

American sociologist Seymour Martin Lipset, in his classic study of the rise of the Co-operative Commonwealth Federation (CCF) party, argues that rural Saskatchewan was socially a "one-class community." There were differences in income and status, but they were "not large enough to bring about the emergence of distinct social classes." (Lipset, 1971)

However, the amount of capital that a homesteader could bring with him had an enormous impact on his ability to stay on the land. Gerald Friesen concludes that a settler really needed an outlay of several thousand dollars to make a go of it. Those with little capital were usually the first to fail. But numerous settlers stayed on the land long enough to obtain title and then sold out, took their capital gains, and went on to other work or professions. (Friesen, 1987)

It was not long before stratification of settlers developed. Friesen argues that there were roughly three eras of prairie development. The first found settlers living in log and sod shacks, and equality was a social rule. The second period, which began around the turn of the century, saw the development of wealth differences and "a version of English or Australian class relations seemed to be developing." World War I saw big changes with the pressure to increase grain production, the growth in farm size, and the adoption of expensive new agricultural machinery. Before 1930 "there were clear social and economic distinctions within rural communities." Those with larger farms, often farmers with English-Canadian backgrounds, recruited men and women as "hired hands." Thus by the early 1930s there were pronounced distinctions between settlers according to farm size and net worth. (Friesen, 1987)

The towns, villages and small cities were also characterized by social stratification. Friesen points out that the merchants and professionals were the men of status, and they dominated the local government and were the executives on the local associations. A "better class" of teachers, clergymen, policemen, and civil servants "upheld the values of the status quo." The town was the "patriotic outpost of British-Canadian civilization" and the home of businesses which lived off the farmer. Conflict quickly developed between farmers and the private interests in the towns. One result was the development of consumer co-ops and credit unions. Lipset's figures show that farmers were dominant figures in elective positions in the Wheat Pool, co-operative stores, credit unions, rural municipalities, rural school boards and community centres. (Friesen, 1987; Lipset, 1971)

## The Struggle for the Economic Surplus

Economic rent is extracted from natural resources, including land, by the application of human labour. In many systems of agricultural production it is easy to see how the rent is extracted from the agricultural labourer as it takes the form of a share of the crop or unpaid labour time, slavery, taxation, or usury. Where there is a mode of agricultural production based on independent farmers, who at least nominally own the land they farm, it is not as clear. Usury becomes one form of exploitation, lending money to farmers for an interest. In Imperial Rome the mode of production in the Italian peninsula was predominantly independent farmers. They were eventually driven out of business by high government taxes, replaced by large land owners relying on slave labour. In Japan there was a fixed land tax on serfs under feudalism and then on independent farmers and landlords following the Meiji restoration in 1868. After 1873 the land tax amounted to about 33 percent of the crop.

The transformation in Russia revealed different ways of extracting the economic rent from farmers. Feudalism was ended in 1861, but the "liberated" serfs ended up as peasants working for large landowners or renting land. Under capitalism the Tsar's Stolypin Plan of 1906 promoted individual farm ownership, but the system reverted to the landlord-peasant system when farmers could not keep up mortgage payments and payments to money lenders. In 1918 the new Soviet government seized all landlords' land and redistributed it to the peasants. But little agricultural surplus was produced by the small farms, and food shortages for urban people remained a central problem.

In 1928 the Soviet government introduced a new policy, where the economic surplus needed for investment would be raised by "internal accumulation." This would be accomplished by keeping workers wages low (extracting an economic surplus from labour) and by imposing an agricultural "tribute" on farmers. The agricultural surplus (or rent) was to be extracted according to the system which operates under capitalism: prices for farm products would be kept low and the prices for farm supplies high. This was known as the "scissors effect," described by sociologist E. A. Preobrazhensky as "unequal exchange." (Plotted on a graph, prices for farm products drop while prices for farm inputs rise, and the two lines would cross, creating a "scissors" on the graph.) The extraction of the economic surplus from farmers would be called "original socialist accumulation" because the mode of production was not capitalism and the economic surplus would go to the state and be used for general purposes determined by the socialist government. This was not exploitation, it was argued, for the economic surplus was not being accumulated by a capitalist class. This forced accumulation depressed wages and farm income for many years, but it provided an enormous stock of savings for investment during the period of industrialization. (Warnock, 1987)

The scissors effect operates in Canada, although not during World War II when farm prices were set by the government and input prices were frozen. For example, between 1929 and 1933 farm prices fell by 50 percent while output rose by four percent. Agricultural machinery prices fell by only four percent. The farm machinery industry cut back production instead of lowering prices. (Warnock, 1978)

Farmers on the prairies were well aware of how the economic surplus was being extracted. It did not take long for them to join together to form organizations and political parties to advance their interests and try to keep some of the surplus. As farmers moved across the border to take up land in Canada, so did farm organizations. With the onset of the first great world depression in 1873, the Patrons of Industry (or Grange) entered Canada and moved to the west. The National Farmers' Alliance in the United States led to the People's Parties or Populist Parties in the late 1880s, and their members and ideas swept over the border. The Northern Alliance called for farmer-labour political unity to take control of government. The Society of Equity, founded in the United States, formed an organization in Canada in 1908.

The Territorial Grain Growers Association was created in 1901 and evolved to the Manitoba, Saskatchewan and Alberta Grain Growers Associations. The Canadian Council of Agriculture was formed in 1909 to unite farmers across the country.

The U.S. Socialist Party was very strong in the American grain belt, particularly in Oklahoma and Minnesota. They organized the Non-Partisan League during World War I, elected the governor of North Dakota in 1916, and took control of the legislature in 1918. This radical agrarian government implemented state ownership of grain elevators, flour mills, packing houses, and created state-owned banks. The Non-Partisan League moved into Saskatchewan and Alberta urging radical changes in the food production and distribution system. (Lipset, 1971; Sharp, 1997; Morton, 1950)

The central political thrust of all these organization was the *reform* of the capitalist system, to take power away from the monopoly capitalists and to place it in the hands of the ordinary people. There was a strong commitment to direct democracy. The attack focused on "plutocracy" and the "new feudalism." As Charles Schwartz puts it, by 1900 the western Canadian farmer "was confronted by what he considered to be monopolies at every turn: railway monopolies, banking monopolies, country-elevator and terminal monopolies, and farm implement monopolies, whose centre of power was in Eastern Canada." (Schwartz, 1959)

There was little pressure to replace capitalism with socialism, for this might logically lead to social ownership of land. There was a faith that if there were true competition, farmers would benefit. As the followers of Social Credit in Alberta were to stress, it is a case of "free enterprise" versus "capitalism." This can be seen in the support farmers gave to free trade, competition in railroads, co-operative ownership of grain elevators, and government regulation of the grain trade and corporate monopoly practices. The Christian social gospel played a key role in the agrarian political ideology, not the analysis of capitalism by Karl Marx and Frederick Engels.

The Manitoba and North-West Farmers' Union was formed in 1883 and demanded an end to the CPR's rail monopoly, provincial government "absolute" control over land and other resources, the abolition of tariffs on agricultural implements, a rail line to Hudson Bay, the creation of publicly owned grain elevators, warehouses and mills, and the establishment of a government grain inspection system.

The transportation system was the first order of business. Under the federal government's policy of "fair discrimination," rates were low in competitive areas (like Ontario) and were high where there was a monopoly situation, as on the prairies. Rates for shipping wheat from the west were three times as high as comparable distances in the east. In 1886 the grain elevator at Brandon would buy a bushel of No. 1 Northern wheat for 54 cents, sell it for 83 cents at Fort William and $1.00 at Liverpool. It cost about twice as much to ship a bushel of wheat by the CPR to Liverpool as it did to use the U.S. railroad system through Duluth. (Conway, 1994; Regehr, 1977)

Farmers elected a Liberal government in Manitoba in 1887 and it chartered two railways to provide competition with the CPR. The laws were disallowed by the Dominion government, but by April 1888 the CPR was negotiating an end to the "monopoly clause" in return for a guarantee of the interest on a new issue of bonds. In 1897 the CPR negotiated the Crows Nest Pass freight rate agreement with the Dominion government. In return for large cash grants, and access to mineral resources, the CPR agreed to reduce rail rates "in perpetuity" for grain exports and imported goods that farmers needed. After 1900 the Dominion government began promoting two new transcontinental railways. Competition, it was hoped, would reduce rates further. There was no need to nationalize the railways and run them as a public service.

The CPR granted monopolies to individual grain handling companies at towns along its line. Farmers charged the grain companies with a range of monopoly actions, including unfair weights, downgrading the grain, mixing lower grades of wheat with higher grades and selling the mix at the higher price, setting the dockage fees too high, monopoly storage fees, and paying farmers below market prices for their grain. In 1902 the Territorial Grain Growers Association brought suit against the CPR for preferential allocation of rail cars for loading grain and won the case in court. In response to farm pressure, the Dominion government enacted a federal law, revised a number of times, to provide general government inspection and grading of grain.

In 1899 and 1906 the Dominion government appointed Royal Commissions to investigate the grain trade. They both confirmed the charges made by farmers. The Manitoba Grain Act was passed to start government regulation of the grain handling industry. The Grain Inspection Act of 1904 was designed to regulate the industry from the farm gate to the export terminal.

The second major campaign by farmers was to reduce tariffs. The National Policy Tariff had imposed duties of 20 percent on agricultural implements, and this had been raised to 35 percent in 1884. Similar duties existed on coal oil, corn for feed, wire fencing, binder twine, salt, iron, cottons, tweeds, woolens and tools. The farmers' campaign in support of the Liberals and Sir Wilfrid Laurier did not pay off. Once in office, the Liberals came under the influence of big business and only modest changes were made. Farmers mobilized again for the election of 1911. The Canadian Council of Agriculture pressed the Farmers Platform of 1910 on members of Parliament. Not only did the tariff punish farmers, they argued, it resulted in the concentration of the population in very large urban centres. In January 1911 Laurier signed a new Reciprocity Treaty with the United States which lowered tariffs on a range of goods, including farm machinery. Business interests denounced the agreement as the first step towards continental free trade and the absorption of Canada into the United States. They were backed by the trade union movement in Eastern Canada. Laurier and the Liberals lost, and the National Policy was endorsed by the electorate. Continental free trade would come but much later. (Conway, 1994; Morton, 1950; Fowke, 1946)

While there was some pressure for state ownership of grain elevators, and an experiment with the system in Manitoba, the farm movement settled on the proposal of E. A. Partridge for a system of farmer-owned co-operatives. The Grain Growers Grain Company was organized in 1906 and the United Grain Growers Company in 1917. The farmers pressed the Dominion government to take ownership of the grain terminals and to operate them as a public service. After a Royal Commission confirmed the farmers' charges against the private grain trade, the Dominion government agreed to build terminal elevators at the Lakehead and interior elevators at Moose Jaw, Calgary, Saskatoon and Edmonton. The Grain Growers' Grain Company leased a terminal at Fort William. In the 1920s the farmers' movement created the Manitoba, Saskatchewan and Alberta Wheat Pools, which came to dominate the prairie grain trade. (Fowke, 1957; Lipset, 1971; Conway, 1994; Knuttila, 1994 )

Grain farmers also carried out an attack on the grain handling cartel and their domination of the Winnipeg Grain Exchange. The private grain companies had formed a cartel, the North West Grain Dealers' Association, to fix prices at elevator points, control the grain exchange, and to lobby government. During World War I the Canadian government became more involved in the industry. When the price of wheat rose dramatically in 1917, the Dominion government responded by creating the Board of Grain Supervisors with a monopoly control over the marketing of wheat. They fixed prices during the war but permitted the reopening of the private market in 1919. When prices rose again, the Canadian Wheat Board was created, based on the model advanced by the Canadian Council of Agriculture. Similar boards had been created in the New Zealand and Australia.

The Canadian Wheat Board was abolished after the 1920 crop. This coincided with the post war depression of 1920-3. The prices for grain fell. As Vernon Fowke reports, throughout the inter-war period grain growers protested the private grain trade and speculation by traders, believing they were responsible for low prices and price instability. Several Royal Commissions reported the problems with the private grain trade. Almost all the farm organizations demanded a compulsory government-run national wheat board. In 1935 the Tory government of R. B. Bennett created a voluntary Canadian Wheat Board, but it was not until 1943 that the compulsory board was created. At the end of World War II farm organizations across western Canada demanded the retention of the compulsory board. Saskatchewan passed supporting legislation, and referendums held in Manitoba and Alberta showed strong farmer support. In their drive to try to create orderly marketing of wheat, the Canadian government signed a wheat agreement with Great Britain in 1946 and then participated in the International Wheat Agreement of 1949, but this approach was abandoned when world prices for wheat rose above the negotiated prices. (Fowke, 1957; Britnell and Fowke, 1962; Phillips, 1990; Fairbairn, 1984; Schwartz, 1959)

The Wheat Board was a particular kind of marketing board. Throughout the Commonwealth, producer controlled marketing boards were being introduced. In 1926 the tree fruit growers in British Columbia created the first compulsory marketing system, endorsed by a producer referendum and passed by provincial legislation. Court decisions backed the food corporations, but in 1934 the federal Tory government passed the National Products Marketing Act, legislation similar to that which existed in Great Britain and elsewhere. However, corporate interests and federal Liberals challenged the legislation, and it was ruled unconstitutional by the Court of the Privy Council in London. In 1949 new federal legislation was introduced and upheld by the Supreme Court of Canada. Producers soon approved marketing boards for milk, poultry, eggs, potatoes, tree fruits, vegetables, and hogs. In Saskatchewan, producer pooling systems for marketing were established for eggs, dairy, poultry and live-stock in the mid-1920s, and they later became marketing boards. (Fowke, 1957; Lipset, 1971; Schwartz, 1959)

Farmers have always been very well aware of how much interest they pay on their mortgages, machinery loans, and operating loans. For most, this is the largest single cost of production. Prairie farmers had to turn to the chartered banks, loan companies and other lending institutions. Interest rates were higher on the prairies than in eastern Canada. Farm groups attacked the "banking monopoly" and the "pirates of St. James Street." The Progressive Party in the 1920s demanded a new national banking system and easy credit for farmers. They pushed for long term loans from federal government institutions. The Canadian Farm Loans Board and the Farm Improvement Loans Act were passed, but even they were attacked for not making loans to farmers who lived in areas where weather conditions resulted in unstable crops. The Farm Credit Corporation was not created until the Tory government of John Diefenbaker. (Britnell and Fowke, 1962; Skogstad, 1987; Macpherson, 1953)

Farmers are always looking for a way to eliminate the cost-price squeeze. When they go into the supermarket they are appalled when they see the prices consumers must pay while they know how little they get. And they know that their share continues to decline. Canadian farmers looked longingly at the Agricultural Adjustment Act passed by the U.S. Congress in 1938 which established a system of parity pricing. The basic principle was stated in the legislation: "Gross income from agriculture will provide the farm operator and his family with a standard of living equivalent to that afforded persons dependent upon other gainful occupations." Federal government payments would help correct the growing gap in the cost price squeeze. Prices for farm products were guaranteed during World War II and prices for inputs were frozen. This was a banner period for farmers in both the United States and Canada. When they went into the growing season they knew the price they would get for the crop and that it would all be sold. It was easy to plan. But this policy was dropped after the war. The U.S. government continued to provide extensive farm subsidies. In Canada, the Agricultural Stabilization Act was established in 1951 to provide supports for some commodities, including cattle and hogs. But in the era of free trade, governments are not supposed to provide subsidies for farm products which are exported.. (Schwartz, 1959; Marchildon, 2000)

## The Transformation of the Wheat Economy

There has been a radical change in the structure of the farm economy on the prairies over the past forty years. Saskatchewan's farm population peaked at 564,000 in 1931. Between 1961 and 2001, it fell from 306,000 to 135,000. The number of farms peaked in 1936 at 140,000 and fell to 94,000 in 1961 and then to 50,500 in 2001. Closely connected to the drop in farms was the abandonment of rail lines and the closure of grain elevators. In Saskatchewan between 1980 and 2000 the number of grain elevators declined from 1805 to 437. This had a devastating impact on rural communities and small towns. In addition, since the implementation of the Canada-U.S. Free Trade Agreement, government financial support for agriculture has fallen by around 25 percent while it has increased in Australia, Europe and the United States. In contrast to Canadian policy, the European Economic Community has made the continuation of a stable rural population a high priority social goal. As a result, rural population hardly declined in Europe between 1970 and 2000. (Acre, 2002)

Urbanization has been a steady development. By 2001 Saskatoon had reached 226,000 and Regina 193,000. Small towns are continuing to decline in population. Doug Elliott and Ken Perlich argue that a community of 1500 ought to be large enough "to support public and private sectors services such as a school, health clinic, financial institution, and a varied retail and wholesale trade sector." But in 2001 there were only 33 such communities left in the province. There were 14 rural communities with populations over 4,000 and even six of these experienced population decline between 1981 and 2001. Employment outside the two large metropolitan areas, in the rural south and the north, has been stable over the past twenty years, ranging between 250,000 and 265,000. (Elliott and Perlich, 2002)

The departure of so many farmers has led to a consolidation of land into larger units. According to the 2001 census, the average farm in Saskatchewan is now 1,277 acres, or almost two square miles of land, and of this total, 40 percent is leased. Average gross farm receipts were $116,497. The capital value of this average farm was $661,368, and the average farm debt was $120,333. Thus the average net worth of farm property alone was $541,035. Compared to other working families in the province, farmers are quite wealthy. The 1992 Farm Debt Advisory Committee reported that the top 20,000 farmers (or the top third of farmers at that time) held only two percent of farm debt, and the average debt they held was only one percent of their assets. In addition, these "high equity" farmers had on average $57,000 in cash, bonds and savings on hand. (Statistics Canada, 2002; Farm Debt Advisory Committee, 1992)

The other important characteristic of prairie farms today is their diversification away from a dependence on wheat. In the early 1980s around 70 percent of all land seeded to crops was in wheat; by the year 2000 this had dropped to 40 percent. The number of farms where wheat is the primary source of income dropped to 13,000 in the latest census. Farmers are shifting to oilseds, other grains, and specialty crops. The number of farms where the primary source of income is from cattle has risen to 12,800. With the shift to corporate hog operations, the number of hogs produced has risen steadily but the number of farms producing hogs has dropped from 26,000 in 1971 to only 1,577 in 2001. (Elliott, 2002)

Over the 1990s there was a push in Saskatchewan towards the development of large scale feed lots for cattle and giant hog barns. Most are operated as capitalist operations with owners holding shares representing their investment. Some are operated as so-called "new generation co-ops," which are not really co-ops because a farmer's votes or shares are based on the size of his contribution, whether it is capital or farm product. These new capitalist operations have had strong support, including financing, from the provincial NDP government. They have classified these operations as "farms" in order to allow them to bypass environmental and labour legislation which applies to "industrial developments" in rural areas. They actively opposed court actions by local farmers and rural residents who did not want these developments because of their history of environmental pollution and degradation. (Warnock, 1999)

But the trend to capitalist agriculture is not limited to industrial developments. There is a transformation happening on the family farm. *Western Producer Farming* magazine, with historic links to the Saskatchewan Wheat Pool, is designed for the modern commercial farmer. In 1998 it ran an article which featured one of the many successful large farmers, businessmen who are the target of their magazine. Ron operates a 8,500 acre farm which concentrates on grain and special crops. He has three large John Deere 4-wheel drive tractors which he trades every three years, four John Deere combines which he trades every year, one small field tractor which he trades every year, and a fleet of trucks and several semi-trailers to haul grain. He has two full-time employees who work year round and another four employees who work during the crop year. It costs him $1 million to put his crop in every year. Of the 8500 acres he farms, he rents 4500 acres. The only difference between this farm and the ones described by Karl Marx in his analysis of capitalist farming in England is the size of the capital investment. (Siemens, 1988)

The food processing sector of the economy has been growing across the prairies and in Saskatchewan throughout the 1990s. The meat packing industry has expanded, fed by the expansion of capitalist-style feed lots for cattle and corporate hog operations. More wheat is being milled into flour. Canola is being processed into oil. In Saskatchewan there is still processing of poultry, dairy and eggs, covered by marketing boards and supply management. In addition, there has been a proliferation of small size plants for processing fruits, herbs and spices, pulses, and organic and health foods. Feed manufacturing has expanded with the livestock industry. (see Wilderman *et al.*, 2001)

The economies of the prairie provinces have diversified over the years, and exports of wheat and barley are no longer that important. Around 60 percent of the value of Alberta's exports are oil and gas. In dollar value, wheat only accounts for two percent of Alberta's exports. Wheat accounts for less than six percent of Manitoba's exports. Wheat still accounts for 17 percent of Saskatchewan's exports, but is exceeded by oil and gas (22 percent) and other minerals (18 percent).

While the mass media may concentrate on the plight of farmers, the Saskatchewan economy has diversified over the years. In 2001 agriculture only accounted for 7.4 percent of the provincial gross domestic product. Government services accounted for 17.4 percent, financial services 16.3 percent, oil and gas extraction 8.9 percent, and manufacturing 7.1 percent. Thus when there were two years of drought in Saskatchewan in 2001 and 2002, and farm incomes were down, it did not have that much of an impact on the economy.

The structure of trade has also changed since the implementation of the Canada-U.S. Free Trade Agreement and the North American Free Trade Agreement. Canada has become even more dependent on trade with the United States. For Saskatchewan the percentage of merchandise exports going to the United States has increased from 45 percent in 1990 to 59 percent in 2001. Manitoba and Alberta are more dependent on the United States.

On the surface it may seem that those who have survived in farming have been the big winners. But there are some problems. The changes in agriculture have involved moving away from marketing boards and towards the free market. Farmers face a very highly concentrated agribusiness industry with little hope of bargaining power. Indeed, the general shift in farming is towards vertical integration with agribusiness through contract, not only in livestock production but also in field crops. (see Acre, 2002; Qualman and Wiebe, 2002; NFU, 2000; Martz and Moellenbeck, 2000; Warnock, 1999)

In constant 1996 dollars, the international market price for wheat has fallen from around $12 per bushel in 1916 to around $5 in 2000. The cost price squeeze has increased. This can be seen in the change in farm margins, the differences between gross farm cash receipts and net farm income. In Saskatchewan in the 1970s farmers' net income was around 50 percent of their gross sales. This has declined steadily to 10 percent or less over the 1990s. The latest Census reports that in 2000 the Saskatchewan farmer had to put up 87 cents for operating expenses for every dollar in cash receipts. These costs do not include depreciation. The margins have been tightest in the livestock area where the "free market" prevails and the corporate power of the packing plants is most concentrated. The highest margins for farmers have been in poultry, eggs and milk, where farmers retain some collective power through marketing boards. (Acre, 2002)

In order to cope with the decline in prices for farm commodities and the rise in farm expenses, members of farm families have been forced to work off the farm. In the 1970s, around 70 percent of farm family income came from the farm operation. This declined to less that 40 percent by 2000. (Elliott, 2002)

With the shift to larger corporate-style farming, there has been a major increase in the use of pesticides and manufactured fertilizers. This is resulting in air and water pollution across the province. One particular problem is herbicide use. In 1971 eight million acres of farmland were treated with herbicides; this rose to 30 million in 2001. Herbicide residues are common in water sources and even in rain. The expansion of livestock on corporate-style farms has increased the problem of pollution of surface and ground water from animal wastes.

The shift to newer crops, the expansion of trade with the United States, and the closure of railway branch lines has resulted in a major increase in truck transportation in Saskatchewan. The large transport trucks, of which grain trucks are only one example, are destroying the system of rural roads. The cost of the transportation system has been shifted from the railways to the farmers and rural communities. Trucking increases pollution and makes a greater contribution to the problem of global warming and climate change. This shift is encouraged by the extensive government subsidy to the fossil fuel industry and automotive transportation. The Organization of Economic Co-operation and Development (OECD) has called for the introduction of full cost pricing to eliminate the policy distortion. (Jones and Taylor, 2003)

There are some general problems posed by the shift in farming and the changes in the Saskatchewan economy. How sustainable is the system of industrial farming with its large fossil fuel subsidy and its widespread use of manufactured chemicals and fertilizers? Over the long run, the province's non-renewable resources are going to be depleted. Our natural gas, which is now privatized, is being shipped to the United States as fast as possible, and it is quickly being depleted. Our forests are not being harvested on a renewable basis, with Weyerhaeuser shipping the cheap wood off to the United States as fast as possible. Foreign ownership and control is on the rise in Saskatchewan, particularly in the natural resource and agribusiness sector. Under the policies of "free trade," government involvement in the economy has been in steady decline since the early 1980s. We have seen a dramatic increase in agri-food exports since 1990 but net farm income has remained flat. The corporate sector has captured almost all of the value of the increase.

Grain farmers in Saskatchewan have seen the federal government cut back support programs while their competitors in the world markets have benefitted from increased government spending. Farmers have lost the transportation subsidy of the Crow Benefit, which was terminated in 1995; the Feed Freight Assistance Program, also cut in 1995; the Special Canadian Grain Program, ended in 1998; Tripartite Stabilization, ended in 1994; the Western Grain Stabilization Program, terminated in 1991; and the Dairy Subsidy, which was phased out in 2001. The NDP government in Saskatchewan eliminated the Gross Revenue Insurance Program (GRIP) in 1993.

These program cuts were accompanied by a move to deregulation. The Two-Price Wheat Program was ended. The federal government ended controls on branch line abandonment, and the Saskatchewan government went along with this policy. The railway rate cap was eliminated. The Canadian Grain Commission lost its role in regulating grain company handling and elevator charges. These programs were replaced with a policy of encouraging and helping to fund foreign ownership and control of the agribusiness sector. Under the free trade regime Canada is being swallowed up in Fortress North America, and farmers are losing offshore markets. Is this a healthy development? (Qualman and Wiebe, 2002)

## Conclusion

Confederation was part of a broader political-economic strategy to create an independent Canadian state and develop a "new investment frontier" on the prairies. This policy has been very successful. The prairies were settled by immigrants and the new wheat economy was built. The manufacturing industry in central Canada grew rapidly. The economic surplus or economic rent produced by independent farmers is captured in a number of ways. The financial institutions collect the interest on their loans. The farm supply industry extracts a share of the surplus when they sell farmers goods, often at prices higher than the general world market. In the downstream area economic rent and surplus is extracted by the grain handling companies, the brokers, the truckers, the railroads, the steamship lines, the food processors, and the wholesalers and retailers. When consumers today pay two dollars for a loaf of bread at Safeway the farmer gets around twelve cents. (Martz and Moellenbeck, 2000)

It has always been said in Canada that the farmer "lives poor but dies rich." The farmer gets relatively little out of the food that is produced. However, he is compensated in the increase in the value of farm land, a result of what is known as "absolute rent," the monopoly created by private ownership of land. In the cost-price squeeze, and the desire of existing farmers to acquire ever more land, the number of farmers in Saskatchewan has fallen from 300,000 in 1936 to only 50,500 in 2001. However, the average farm is now over 1,200 acres and net farm equity is over $500,000. This is offset to some degree by the trend towards more land leased from absentee landlords.

In the post-1980 era of free trade and the free market, the corporate agribusiness sector, both the farm supply and the food processing industry, continues to become ever more monopolized. Every industry is controlled by a few large corporations. This is not only the case in Canada but also in the United States and Europe. (Magdoff, 1998; Bonanno, 1994; Goodman and Watts, 1997; Martz and Moellenbeck, 2000; National Farmers Union, 2000)

Since the implementation of the Canada-U.S. Free Trade Agreement in 1989, Canadian farmers have been losing the few institutions they had created to try to gain some bargaining power with the monopolized agribusiness sector. Farm supports have been radically cut. Marketing boards are under attack and being eliminated, replaced by vertical integration with large corporations. Consumer and producer co-operatives are disappearing. Governments are deregulating their rules governing corporate behaviour. Government financial assistance is shifting from farmers to agribusiness. Research is shifting from support of farmers to the support of agribusiness. The University of Saskatchewan, which used to be known for research and development which was public and aided farmers, has now shifted to doing private research for private corporations. The College of Agriculture sees its role as the promoter and defender of corporate agribusiness. Government has once again placed its highest priority on assisting capital accumulation by private interests.

The system works well for those who are in the business of accumulating capital. Profits are made at all levels of the corporate food system. Capital is accumulated by the finance industry. In times of financial stress, farmers ask for welfare payments from the federal and provincial governments. This assistance comes out of revenues that are raised through a regressive tax system where the burden falls heaviest on those in the lower income groups. Increasingly in Canada and Saskatchewan, the owners of wealth, natural resource extractors, and those in the higher income brackets are paying less and less tax. Farmers receive a range of tax expenditures from the provincial government, pay very little to the provincial treasury, and benefit greatly from the $500,000 lifetime capital gains exemption. Farmers pay around 10 percent of their income in taxes, well below the rate of the general population. The number of farmers in the business continues to decline, but precious few go bankrupt. They sell out and take their capital gains. This system is working so far, but it destroys rural communities, creates an unsustainable level of environmental degradation, and creates greater inequalities in income and wealth. The radical movements of the wheat farmer are gone. The days when a majority of Saskatchewan farmers were members of the Saskatchewan Farmers Union are gone. But discontent and protest remain.

## References

Action Committee on the Rural Economy. 2002. *Final Report to the Government of Saskatchewan*. Regina: Action Committee on the Rural Economy, March.

Aitken, Hugh G.J., ed. 1959. *The State and Economic Growth*. New York: Social Science Research Council.

Bercuson, David J., ed. 1977. *Canada and the Burden of Unity*. Toronto: Macmillan of Canada.

Bonanno, Alessandro *et al.*, eds. *From Columbus to ConAgra: The Globalization of Agriculture and Food*. Lawrence: University of Kansas Press.

Britnell, George E. 1962. *The Wheat Economy*. Toronto: University of Toronto Press, 1939.

Britnell, George E. and Vernon D. Fowke. 1962. *Canadian Agriculture in War and Peace, 1935-1950*. Palo Alto, Calif.: Stanford University Press.

Buckley, Helen. 1992. *From Wooden Ploughs to Welfare: Why Indian Policy Failed in the Prairie Provinces*. Montreal: McGill-Queen's University Press.

Buckley, Kenneth A. H. 1958. "The Role of Staple Industries in Canada's Economic Development," *Journal of Economic History*, Vol. 18, December, pp. 439-50.

Canada. Statistics Canada. 2002. *2001 Census of Agriculture*. Ottawa: Statistics Canada.

Carter, Sarah. 1999. *Aboriginal People and Colonizers of Western Canada to 1900*. Toronto: University of Toronto Press.

Conway, John F. 1994. *The West: A History of a Region in Confederation*. Toronto: James Lorimer & Co.

Craven, Paul and Tom Traves. 1979. "The Class Politics of the National Policy, 1872-1993." *Journal of Canadian Studies*, Vol. 14, Fall, pp. 24-38.

Craven, Paul and Tom Traves. 1987. "Canadian Railways as Manufactures, 1850-1880." In McCalla, pp.254-81.

Creighton, Donald G. 1972. *Towards the Discovery of Canada*. Toronto: Macmillan of Canada.

Diaz, Harry P., Joann Jaffe and Robert Stirling, eds. 2003. *Farm Communities at the Crossroads: Challenge and Resistance*. Regina: Canadian Plains Research Centre, University of Regina.

Easterbrook, W.T. and Hugh G. J. Aitken. 1956. *Canadian Economic History*. Toronto: Macmillan of Canada.

Elliott, Doug. 2002. "2001 Census of Agriculture." *Sask Trends Monitor*. Vol. 19, no. 5, May, pp.1-6.

Elliott, Doug and Ken Perlich. 2002. *Growing the Rural Economy*. Regina: Action Committee on the Rural Economy, July.

Fairbairn, Garry Lawrence. 1984. *From Prairie Roots: The Remarkable Story of Saskatchewan Wheat Pool*. Saskatoon: Western Producer Prairie Books.

Farm Debt Advisory Committee. 1992. *Report*. Regina: Farm Debt Advisory Committee, March.

Firestone, O.J. 1958. *Canada's Economic Development, 1867-1953*. London: Bowes & Bowes.

Fowke, Vernon C. 1946. *Canadian Agricultural Policy: The Historical Pattern*. Toronto: University of Toronto Press.

Fowke, Vernon C. 1957. *The National Policy and the Wheat Economy*. Toronto: University of Toronto Press.

Frideres, James S. 1998. *Aboriginal Peoples in Canada: Contemporary Conflicts*. Scarborough: Prentice Hall Allyn and Bacon Canada.

Friesen, Gerald. 1987. *The Canadian Prairies: A History*. Toronto: University of Toronto Press.

Glazebrook, G.P. DeT. 1967. *A History of Transportation in Canada*. Toronto: McClelland and Stewart. First published in 1938.

Goodman, David and Michael J. Watts, eds. 1997. *Globalizing Food: Agrarian Questions and Global Restructuring*. London: Routledge.

Jones, Chris and Robert Taylor. 2003. "Take the Train Please." *Globe and Mail*, February 24, A-11.

Knuttila, K. Murray. 1994. *"That Man Partridge": E. A. Partridge, His Thought and His Times*. Regina: Canadian Plains Research Centre, University of Regina.

Knuttila, K. Murray and James N. McCrorie. 1980. "National Policy and Prairie Agrarian Development: a Reassessment." *Review of Canadian Sociology and Anthropology*, Vol. 17, No. 3, pp. 263-272.

Laycock, David. 1990. *Populism and Democratic Thought in the Canadian Prairies, 1910-1945*. Toronto: University of Toronto Press.

Lipset, Seymour Martin. 1971. *Agrarian Socialism: The Co-operative Commonwealth Federation in Saskatchewan, A Study in Political Sociology*. Berkeley: University of California Press.

Mackintosh, W.A. 1964. *The Economic Background of Dominion-Provincial Relations.* Toronto: McClelland and Stewart. First published in 1939.

Mackintosh, W.A. 1934. *Prairie Settlement: The Geographic Setting.* Toronto: Macmillan of Canada.

McCalla, Douglas, ed. 1987. *Perspectives on Canadian Economic History.* Toronto: Copp Clark Pitman.

McCormack, A. Ross. 1977. *Reformers, Rebels and Revolutionaries: The Western Canadian Radical Movement, 1899-1919.* Toronto: University of Toronto Press.

Macpherson, Crawford B. 1953. *Democracy in Alberta: Social Credit and the Party System.* Toronto: University of Toronto Press.

Magdoff, Fred *et al.*, eds. 1998. *Hungry for Profit: Agriculture, Food and Ecology.* New York: Monthly Review Press.

Marchildon, Gregory P., ed. 2000. *Agriculture at the Border: Canada-U.S. Trade Relations in the Global Food Regime.* Regina: Canadian Plains Research Centre, University of Regina.

Marr, William L. and Donald G. Paterson. 1980. *Canada: An Economic History.* Toronto: Macmillan of Canada.

Martz, Diane J.F. and Wendy Moellenbeck. 2000. *The Family Farm in Question: Compare the Share Revisited.* Muenster, SK: Centre for Rural Studies and Enrichment.

Martin, Chester. 1973. *Dominion Lands Policy.* Toronto: McClelland and Stewart.

Martin, Ged, ed. 1990. *The Causes of Canadian Confederation.* Fredericton: Acadiensis Press.

Mercer, L.J. 1982. *Railroads and Land Grant Policy.* New York: Academic Press.

Morton, Arthur S. and Chester Martin. 1938. *History of Prairie Settlement and "Dominion Land' Policy.* Toronto: Macmillan of Canada.

Morton, W.L. 1964. *Canada 1857-1873: The Critical Years.* Toronto: McClelland and Stewart.

Morton, W.L. 1950. *The Progressive Party in Canada.* Toronto: University of Toronto Press.

National Farmers Union. 2000. *The Farm Crisis, EU Subsidies, and Agribusiness Market Power.* Saskatoon: Presentation to the Senate Standing Committee on Agriculture and Forestry, February 17.

Naylor, R.T. 1976. *The History of Canadian Business, 1867-1914.* Toronto: James Lorimer & Co.

Norrie, Kenneth and Douglas Owram. 1996. *A History of the Canadian Economy.* Toronto: Harcourt Brace Canada.

Owram, Doug. 1992. *Promise of Eden: The Canadian Expansionist Movement and the Idea of the North West, 1856-1900.* Toronto: University of Toronto Press.

Parker, Ian. 1979. "The National Policy, Neoclassical Economics and the Political Economy of Tariffs." *Journal of Canadian Studies*, Vol. 14, Fall, pp. 95-110.

Phillips, Paul. 1990. "Manitoba in the Agrarian Period: 1870-1940." In Silver and Hull, pp. 3-24.

Phillips, Paul. 1977. "National Policy, Continental Economics, and National Disintegration." In Bercuson, pp. 19-43.

Phillips, W. G. 1956. *The Agricultural Implement Industry in Canada*. Toronto: University of Toronto Press.

Pomfret, Richard. 1993. *The Economic Development of Canada*. Scarborough: Nelson Canada.

Qualman, Darrin and Nettie Wiebe. 2002. *Structural Adjustment of Canadian Agriculture*. Ottawa: Canadian Centre for Policy Alternatives, November.

Regehr, T.D. 1977. "Western Canada and the Burden of National Transportation Politics." In Bercuson, pp. 45-71.

Roach, Robert. 2002. *Beyond Our Borders: Western Canadian Exports in the Global Market*. Calgary: Canada West Foundation, May.

Ryerson, Stanley B. 1968. *Unequal Union: Confederation and the Roots of Conflict in the Canadas 1815-1873*. New York: International Publishers.

Satzewich, Vic and Terry Wotherspoon. 1993. *First Nations: Race, Class and Gender Relations*. Toronto: Nelson Canada.

Schwartz, Charles. 1959. *The Search for Stability*. Toronto: McClelland and Stewart.

Sharp, Paul F. 1997. *The Agrarian Revolt in Western Canada: A Survey Showing American Parallels*. Regina: Canadian Plains Research Centre, University of Regina. First published in 1948.

Siemens, Harry. 1998. "Records Essential When Managing a Big Farm." *Western Producer Farming*, Vol. 1, No. 1, October, pp. 28-29.

Silver, Jim and Jeremy Hull, eds. 1990. *The Political Economy of Manitoba*. Regina: Canadian Plains Research Centre, University of Regina.

Skogstad, Grace. 1987. *The Politics of Agricultural Policy-Making in Canada*. Toronto: University of Toronto Press.

Stirling, Bob and John W. Warnock. 1993. *Agriculture and Free Trade: What is the Alternative?* Regina: Paper presented to the hearing of the Citizen's Inquiry on the Multilateral Agreement on Investment, October 7.

Tulchinsky, Gerald J. J. 1976. *The River Barons: Montreal Businessmen and the Growth of Industry and Transportation 1837-53*. Toronto: University of Toronto Press.

Warnock, John W. 1999. "Industrial Agriculture Comes to Saskatchewan." In Diaz *et al.*, pp. 303-22.

Warnock, John W. 1987. *The Politics of Hunger: The Global Food System*. Toronto: Methuen.

Warnock, John W. 1978. *Profit Hungry: The Food Industry in Canada*. Vancouver: New Star Books.

Wildeman, Brad *et al.*, 2001. *Agri-Value Subcommittee Report*. Regina: Action Committee on the Rural Economy, May.

Young, Walter D. 1969. *Democracy and Discontent: Progressivism, Socialism and Social Credit in the Canadian West*. Toronto: Ryerson Press.

# Chapter 6

————○————

# THE POLITICAL ECONOMY OF RACISM

Racism is deeply embedded in the political culture of Saskatchewan. Yet there is almost no discussion of this major problem. There are individual horror stories which sometimes reach the news media, but there is no attempt to link a particular case to a general situation. In addition, Canadians with a European background generally take the position that racism is not a problem. We are different from the United States, where there has been a long history of political conflict between whites and blacks.

When racism emerges as an issue to discuss, it is almost always put in the context of cultural misunderstanding. Or it is seen as a problem of individual racial prejudice. Racism in Saskatchewan is rarely seen as a social problem that developed in the historic differences between a dominant group, the white settlers, and the subordinate group, the indigenous population. It is not seen as an institution that gives one group of Canadians social advantages and economic benefits over other groups in society. As the UNESCO declaration on race and racism proclaimed, racism is an ideology used by dominant groups to try to justify social inequalities. (UNESCO, 1978)

In Saskatchewan the dominant order of racism is directed at the indigenous population. It serves to ideologically justify the seizure of land from the indigenous people by force and threat of force. The National Policy and the wheat economy were founded on the removal of the indigenous people from their land and its transfer by the Canadian government to European settlers who acquired the land to begin commercial farming. There was clearly a *material base* to the origin of racism in Saskatchewan.

Anyone who has lived in Saskatchewan is aware of the tension between the white and the Aboriginal community. To understand the roots of this ongoing conflict, it is necessary to employ an historical and political economy approach.

In the 19th century Canada, a white settler Dominion within the British empire, was evolving towards an independent country in an age of unprecedented international imperialism and colonialism. The western European powers were occupying and dividing up the world into colonies and spheres of influence. The European white societies were imposing their will on what was almost exclusively a non-white world. Thus colonialism, and the flight of fifty million white Europeans to other countries, inevitably resulted in racial conflict. The creation of Canada was a part of this world development.

Confederation in 1867 did not produce an independent country. Our foreign and defence policies were still dominated by the British. The Court of the Privy Council in London still had final say over Canadian legislation. Furthermore, our governments were profoundly influenced by English politics and what was going on within the British Empire. As Laura Macdonald has reminded us, when conflict arose within the British Empire, the Canadian government (and the general public) were always on the side of imperial Great Britain and against the movements for independence in the non-white colonies. (Macdonald, 1995)

For the corporate and political leaders behind the Canadian government's National Policy the main problem was what to do with the Indian and Métis communities that stood in the way of developing a new frontier for investment on the prairies. The Canadian government looked to the mother country for guidance. England had the experience of managing the huge British Empire, which began with over five hundred years of colonialism in Ireland. By the mid-nineteenth century, the British and American governments had evolved an Aboriginal policy for North America. In the end, the development of western Canada followed the world wide pattern of European colonialism and in particular the experience of the British empire. Racial policy was central to colonial policy. It was based on political domination and economic exploitation. But racism did not end with the overthrow of western European colonialism or complete independence for Canada. (see Bodley, 1999; Blaut, 1993)

## The Scope of the Problem

The Saskatchewan Human Rights Commission has classified Aboriginal people as a "designated group" which has experienced "historical inequities that have become entrenched within education, economic and other systems." This is reflected in some basic facts concerning the status of Aboriginal people in Saskatchewan. Unemployment is much higher than it is for whites. Their participation in the labour force is much lower. Aboriginal people have much lower average incomes. Around seventy-five percent of young Aboriginal people do not graduate from high school. Ninety percent of the women in prison in Saskatchewan are Aboriginal, and seventy-five percent of the men. Saskatchewan has the highest rate of youth incarceration of any province in Canada, and around 90 percent of those in custody are Aboriginal. Saskatchewan has the highest infant mortality rate of any province, and this is due to the high rate in Northern Saskatchewan, where Aboriginal people are the majority. As the Saskatchewan Human Rights Commission points out, in Northern Saskatchewan Aboriginal people endure "lack of adequate affordable housing, poor access to health care services, insufficient education resources to address the special needs of Northern students, difficulties with police services and the need for community services for young people." This is no accident. (Saskatchewan Human Rights Commission, 2001)

The Saskatchewan Human Rights Commission has tried to get the University of Regina and the City of Regina to change their hiring practices, to bring the levels of employment of females, Aboriginal people, employees with a disability, and visible minorities up to the level of the workforce in society as a whole. To date this process of voluntary affirmative action has failed. The City of Regina has the worst record. The Employment Equity Monitoring Report found that all four groups were significantly under represented, and no Aboriginal people or visible minorities were employed in the middle or upper management ranks at City Hall. (*Leader-Post*, June 11, 2003)

In October 2002 Sigma Analytics conducted a poll for the *Regina Leader-Post*. Almost one-half of the respondents thought that "economic and social differences" between Aboriginal people and non-Aboriginal people were "becoming greater." The poll also reported that 56 percent of respondents felt that Aboriginal people "do not have a right to self-government." *Maclean's Magazine's* annual poll in December 2002 asked Canadians what their major concerns were and where their taxes should be spent. Only three percent favoured increased funds to help solve the problem of Aboriginal poverty. (*Leader-Post*, October 23, 2002; *Maclean's Magazine*, December 30, 2002)

For many year, Doug Cuthand has written a column on Aboriginal issues for the *Regina Leader Post* and the *Saskatoon Star Phoenix*. In January 2002 he submitted his column which compared the plight of the Palestinians to that of the First Nations people in Canada. Both lost their land to imperial forces. The Palestinians, he noted, were put in "camps similar to reservations and they have been colonized and controlled by an outside force." The editors of the two Saskatchewan newspapers refused to print his column. (Cuthand, 2002)

First Nations people have rights guaranteed under the Constitution which go back at least to the British Royal Proclamation of 1763, which recognized them as independent nations whose rights could not be taken away except through a negotiated treaty. These rights were entrenched in the Constitution Act of 1982, which also recognized Inuit and Métis as having Aboriginal status under Canadian law. Yet the political forces on the right in Canada have been carrying out a campaign against treaty rights for Aboriginal people and have gained support well beyond their political allies. The Reform Party and the subsequent Canadian Alliance have called for the assimilation of Aboriginal people into white society. Along with the Canadian Taxpayers Federation, they have argued that Aboriginal people in Canada are just another "minority group" and should not have any special legal status. They have insisted that Aboriginal people should not be exempt from taxation, even though this was part of the treaty settlements where they surrendered their land to the Canadian state. They describe government policy towards Aboriginal people as "racist" for granting First Nations people treaty rights and argue that all Canadians should have the same rights and duties. In April 2002 Brian Pallister, the Canadian Alliance critic on Aboriginal affairs, argued that Native people should have to work for welfare, while at the same time admitting that those who live on reserves and in rural and northern parts of Canada have few job opportunities. These views have widespread support in Saskatchewan. (see Laycock, 2002)

The Red Pheasant First Nation used some of its money from the Treaty Land Entitlement Framework Agreement to buy 327 acres of farm land adjacent to the city of North Battleford. Between May 1995 and December 2002 they repeatedly tried to sign a municipal services agreement with the city. The city refused to accept any of the five different proposals. One of the strongest opponents of any agreement was Senator Herb Sparrow, once the leader of the provincial Liberal Party. He described urban reserves as "ghettos" plagued by unemployment and welfare dependency. Yet urban reserves have been signed in other cities, and they are the base for successful business operations. In the end, the band declared the land an urban reserve without the approval of the City of North Battleford. (Cuthand, 2003)

In Saskatoon Aboriginal women disappear. Little effort is made to find out what has happened to them. The police in Saskatoon are found guilty of taking Aboriginal men out of town in the middle of winter and dumping them. Several Aboriginal men have been found frozen to death in one particular area. In Regina an Aboriginal man has an epileptic seizure at a soup kitchen for poor people, becomes disoriented, and when the police arrive they give him a dose of pepper spray, and he dies. An Aboriginal woman in Regina is beaten to death by two middle class white high school boys who receive minimum sentences.

In the summer of 2002 three white men in their twenties pick up a young Aboriginal girl in Tisdale, push beer on her, take her in a truck out on a rural road, and sexually assault her. The girl, age 12, is less than five feet tall and weighs less than 90 pounds. Two of the men are acquitted, and the third is convicted but gets only two years of house arrest. The judge rules that the victim may have been a "willing participant" or even "the aggressor" in the case. The Aboriginal community is outraged. But there is a deafening silence from the men who are Saskatchewan's community leaders. There is not a peep from the elected leaders of the three major political parties. (Warick, 2003a)

For twenty years the six bands of the Qu'Appelle Valley north of Regina have been trying to get compensation for the flooding of their land. The federal government, without permission or consultation, built a dam to control water and promote cottage development on the lakes for urban whites. Frustrated after 60 years of no response from governments, the bands refused to allow government workers on their land to manage the dam and water levels. Water levels dropped, and cottage owners were outraged. Racist graffiti was sprayed at the site of the dam. At a public meeting with cottage owners, racist taunts were shouted at Aboriginal leaders. Whites called for the Army. Many insisted that not one penny should be given to the six bands. (Warick, 2003b)

Are these unusual cases? The Aboriginal people I know all say that they regularly experience racial discrimination. Some have told me they think Saskatchewan is the most racist place in Canada. Furthermore, this is not changing. Racism is on the increase across Canada as Aboriginal peoples pursue legal and political actions on land claims, demand access to natural resources now almost exclusively under the control of whites, and insist on the right to self government. Presently Aboriginal people are largely confined to the more marginal jobs. We should expect to see a further increase in racism as greater numbers of First Nations people finish high school, go through university and seek employment in jobs which have been the domain of people with European backgrounds.

In order to understand this problem, we need to understand the *roots of racism* and how it became so much a part of Saskatchewan's popular culture. We have to understand the origins and roots of English racism and how it was brought to Canada and Saskatchewan.

## What Do We Mean by Race and Racism?

The terms race and racism have been historically constructed. Michael Banton divides the history of race and racism into three general periods. From the 16th to 19th century, race was seen as lineage: "a group of persons, animals, or plants, connected by common descent or origin." The second phase "was signaled by the use of race in the sense of type, in which the word designated one of a limited number of permanent forms." This phase began in the early 1800s but did not reach full acceptance until Darwin's theory of natural selection. Race was subspecies, with each defined by a common genetic pool, the approach taken by Nazi Germany, the American south in defence of a policy of human segregation, and the apartheid system in South Africa. (Banton, 1987)

The third phase of Banton's classification comes in the 1930s, when social scientists and other scholars concluded that the role of race was associated with social division and how those divisions are constructed to give advantages to one group of humans at the expense of others. Genetics was replaced by socio-economic status. Sociologists, anthropologists and scientists agreed that there is no genetic difference between human groups. Many, like Banton, insist that the term "race" should not be used at all because it is false.

Political and non scientific concepts of race and racism are also strongly associated with the expansion of European imperialism and colonialism. The initial position of the English and other Europeans was that the other peoples of the world were human beings. However, it was also clear to the Europeans that they were backward and needed to be brought under the control of those who would Christianize them and help them adjust to the world of private property and capitalism. In this period, the Europeans knew that they were superior, but the differences were seen as an outgrowth of the uneven development of history.

In the second phase of imperialism and colonialism, the English and the other Europeans saw themselves as being a superior race. It was assumed that over the course of history and economic development the inferior races would disappear. They would either die out or would be completely assimilated.

In the third phase, race was identified as a recognizable social group based on physical characteristics. These groups of humans had a common history and territory. The differences were not genetic but due to their status in society.

But while academics may overwhelmingly agree that race does not exist as a biological fact, there is no question but that it continues in popular culture. Attitudes of race superiority and race inferiority are "common sense" in a great many communities. This is now referred to as racial prejudice or racism.

The definition of race and racism has caused theoretical problems. For example, during the Nazi period "race" was used to support the genocide of the Jews and other sections of the German population. While the famous anthropologist Ruth Benedict denounced racism, she also embraced the view that "race is a classification based on traits which are hereditary." While she attacked the dogma that one group is superior and another inferior, she supported the idea that race was a legitimate field of science. (Benedict, 1942)

American anthropologist Ashley Montague rejected Benedict's view of race as a biological reality. He defined racism as an ideology and argued that the term "race" should be dropped entirely from the vocabulary of all scientists. (Montague, 1964)

John Rex, who was a member of the UNESCO group of experts who met to evaluate race and racism in 1967, set forth the position of mainstream liberal sociologists. Racism is an ideological argument used to legitimize inequality between two group of people. In this situation, a dominant group will identify another group by a variety of biological and/or cultural characteristics in order to justify unequal treatment. Robert Miles objects to this definition as being too broad and inclusive; he believes it could be used to cover sexism as well. (Rex, 1970; Miles, 1987)

David Wellman, an American sociologist, argues that racism is personal prejudice. Essentially, it is "the defence of a system from which advantage is derived on the basis of race." It is a "structural relationship based on the subordination of one racial group by another." Therefore, "racism is determined by the consequences of a sentiment, not its surface qualities. White racism is what white people do to protect the special benefits they gain by virtue of their skin colour." Racism, he adds, is a psychological disorder "which is deeply embedded in white people from a very early age." (Wellman, 1977)

In the 1970s it became common to view racism as an outgrowth of colonialism. Franz Fanon was a key advocate of this position. Racism, he argued, was not a static phenomenon but changed and was transformed. Racism became a world wide problem as a result of European colonialism The biological arguments used in the 19th century served to justify European domination of non-white colonized peoples. Indeed, in the administration of the colonies, racism was a central policy. It justified subordination and exploitation. (Fanon, 1970)

Racism is central to a system of social stratification. But can we assume that it is the primary division within a society? What about class or gender divisions? Are they less significant? Can it be said to be a system of domination if the people who are advancing racism, as we can see in Europe today, are primarily powerless white men?

In popular culture in North America the idea of race is primarily seen as differences between people according to skin colour. In the past certain populations now seen as "white" were differentiated according to racial categorization. For example, Slavic people were considered as a racial group as were Southern European Mediterranean peoples. These categories were even specified in immigration legislation. Despite the fact that social and physical scientists insist that "race" does not exist as a biological fact, it remains as "common sense" when it is used for practical purposes, for exclusionary practices.

Today academics normally use the term "racialization." Despite our scientific rejection of the concept of race, there has to be a recognition that in the popular culture certain groups of people who share some phenotypical human features are categorized as a group. This is an ideological process. The term "racism" is always used as a concept of exclusionary practice, both intentional and unintentional. While "race" is a scientifically invalid term, we can use "racialization" in our sociological research. Furthermore, we can't ignore the fact that racism is a real experience for a great many people. (Barot and Bird, 2001)

A common approach to the question is to reposition "race" under the general category of ethnic studies, a form of cultural differentiation. Ethnicity has been generally seen as the social organization of cultural differences. It is also a way to socially construct what is "us" and "them." Richard Jenkins argues that ethnicity is "a way of talking about one of the most general and basic principles of human sociability: collective identification." (Jenkins, 1999)

But there are some strong objections to subsuming race and racism under ethnicity. Ethnicity tends to ignore history and structural differences between groups. As Bill Rolston argues, in the context of Irish history it appears as a way of looking at a conflict "with little more than a polite nod in the direction of imperialism, colonialism, state power and 'ethnic stratification.'" The official state approach to dealing with such conflicts is to invoke policies of "multiculturalism." This strategy employs psychological approaches which try to avoid politics, places emphasis on personal prejudice, denies the importance of history, avoids the structural levels of inequality, and engages in wishful thinking. Within the context of the conflict in Northern Ireland, the approach of "multiculturalism" obscures the inequalities of power. The ongoing conflict between Protestants and Catholics is much more than just ethnic differences. (Rolston, 1998)

This can be compared to the official Canadian policy of multiculturalism which has been in place since 1971. The stated objective of the policy is "to break down discriminatory attitudes and cultural jealousies." But the policy has not succeeded in countering racism and discriminatory practices. As University of Saskatchewan sociologists Peter Li and Singh Bolaria argue, it "furnishes Canadian society with a great hope without having to change the fundamental structures of society." (Bolaria and Li, 1988)

Stuart Hall argues that poor whites in the British working class find racism to be an ideological explanation for their status within an unequal capitalist system. It arises "because of the concrete problems of different classes and groups in society." It helps people without power to understand and deal with their problems, to make sense of the world and to provide a strategy for political action. It does not matter that it is a mistaken ideological position. (Hall, 1978)

The classic Marxist position on racism was articulated by American sociologist Oliver C. Cox of Lincoln University. He argued that racism as we know it did not develop in Europe until the crossing of the Atlantic and the push into the Caribbean, a development that was driven by mercantile capitalism. Aside from the extraction of natural resources, the goal of the European colonists was to acquire land. The conflict which developed was between the white Europeans who had seized the land and the native tribes and African slaves who provided the labour. As Cox argues:

> Hence, racial antagonism is essentially political-class conflict. The capitalist exploiter, being opportunistic and practical, will utilize any convenience to keep his labour and other resources freely exploitable. He will devise and employ race prejudice when that becomes convenient.

The capitalists exploited "coloured workers" and employed conditions, treatments and punishments that were humanly degrading. "In order to justify this treatment the exploiters must argue that the workers are innately degraded and degenerate, consequently they naturally merit their condition." (Cox, 1948)

However, racism develops in Europe before the emergence of mercantile capitalism. Racism has been found in non-capitalist modes of production. In addition, racism is found in capitalist societies where it does not serve the interests of the capitalist class. Therefore, the classic Marxist conception of racism does not appear to be adequate.

Some of the problems with the issue of race and racism can be illustrated by looking at the current situation in Northern Ireland. The English view the Irish as inferior, and most consider this to be a form of racism. The British Commission for Racial Equality classifies the Irish as "Britain's largest ethnic minority group" that they serve. The Protestants in Northern Ireland consider the Roman Catholic people of Ireland to be inferior and discriminate against them in every way possible. This is seen as a form of racism. In Northern Ireland, almost all of the Protestants are Unionists, identify strongly with England and the Monarchy, and want Northern Ireland to remain as part of the United Kingdom. Yet when they go to England they are treated as "Irish." The English in their racism do not distinguish between Protestant and Catholic people from Ireland. However, in Northern Ireland visible minorities claim they are discriminated against by both Protestant and Roman Catholic whites. They do not want to be linked with the cause of the nationalists and republicans in anti-racist coalitions. (McVeigh, 1998)

In contemporary Northern Ireland, liberals have declared that the conflict is sectarian, just a conflict between different religious groups with long histories. The solution is to promote understanding between the two groups. But this approach ignores the fact that the British state is a very important factor in the conflict and that it is on the side of the Protestant group. The "sectarian" argument fails also because the roots of conflict were deeply established before the Protestant reformation. For example, the infamous Statutes of Kilkenny, which the English imposed in 1366, defined the Irish as inferior and tried to prohibit social contact between them and the English settlers. The historic source of racism towards the Irish is rooted in English colonialism. (McVeigh, 1998)

The Irish example raises an important question: how can the term race or racism be used when all the people involved are white? Liberals do not see this as racism but "ethnic" differences. Pamela Clayton argues that "Racism can exist separately from notions of race; and only the term 'racism' adequately implies the viciousness of the stereotype of the inferior group and the peculiar mixture of contempt, hatred and fear that characterizes the feelings of members of the dominant (but insecure) group towards the inferior (but threatening) group." (Clayton, 1998)

Anyone can see this just driving around Belfast looking at the graffiti and murals in the Protestant neighborhoods. "Kill all Irish." "Any Catholic will do." "Kill all taigs." Taigs is a pejorative term widely used to demean Irish Catholics, similar to whites in the United States calling black people "niggers."

Many Protestants, Clayton argues, "see Catholics as the Other, the eternal enemy, always a threat. Not only do Catholics have no right to regain their lands, they have no right to complain." In the eyes of the Protestants, the Irish Catholics are "lazy, dirty, devious, treacherous, violent, over-fecund, irrational, emotional, inferior in education and skills, ungrateful, easily manipulated, superstitious, priest-dominated and in thrall to manipulative leaders." In contrast the Protestants portray themselves as "hard-working and competent, independent in deed and thought, peaceful and law-abiding, but manly and resolute." As Clayton notes, these are the stereotypes found in other colonies. One of those could be Saskatchewan. (Clayton, 1998)

## Origins of European Racism

European ideas of superiority/inferiority were developed before the onset of world colonialism. The Greeks and Romans had a conception of "barbarians" who lived beyond the boundaries of their civilizations. In both of these advanced cultures "whiteness was positively evaluated and blackness negatively evaluated. Blackness was associated with death and the conception of an underworld." But this did not carry over to characterizing Africans as inferiors. Differences were considered to be cultural and not biological. It was assumed that human physical differences came from environmental factors like climate, topography, and hydrological conditions. African skin colour and hair type were seen to be due to long exposure to the hot sun. (Miles, 1989)

But this was altered during the early Christian period. In the symbolism of this European religion, there was the white/black dichotomy including good/evil, pure/diabolical, spiritual/carnal, and Christ/Satan. This resulted in a hierarchical religious evaluation. As Miles concludes, "Monstrousness, sin and blackness therefore constituted a rather different form of Trinity in European Christian culture in this period." From this came the European view of the Other: the non-European, the "wild man," the human who lived in the woods, lacked civilization, had no moral sense, wore few clothes, lived by hunting animals, and was prone to violence. In particular, the wild barbarian was characterized by "untamed sexuality." The Other, the "wild man," is "desire incarnate, possessing the strength, wit and cunning to give full expression to all his lusts." (Miles, 1989)

Adam of Bremen, an 11th century bishop, wrote of those who lived outside his area of civilization, in the more northerly regions. They were categorized as "monstrous races" who were "ferocious barbarians." The most barbarous were the Amazons said to live near the Baltic Sea, a land inhabited only by women. They were fierce women who drove away men. Others who lived in this region were called the Anthropophagi, those who survived by eating human flesh. (Jahoda, 1999)

In the feudal period, before the discoveries of the navigators, the European view of the Other, the foreigners, was based on their relationship to the Arab world. The world of Islam was portrayed as "barbaric, degenerate and tyrannical," and this was seen to be rooted in their character and their false and heretical theology. Muhammad was represented as "an impostor by claims that his life exemplified violence and sexuality." Islam was said to spread "polygamy, sodomy and a general sexual laxity." (Miles, 1989)

Thus in the eleventh century the Christian clergy and their supporters urged a Crusade against the infidels who occupied the Holy Land. Murderous acts in the defence of Islam were seen as examples of their inherent violence and cruelty. When Christians performed the same acts, it was to glorify the only true God. In sum, down until the late 17th century, Arabs and Islam were seen as "the negation of Christianity, and Muhammad an Antichrist in alliance with the Devil." (Miles, 1989)

Ashley Montague argues that Christianity promoted racism. He notes that in 1455 there was the papal decree that approved the subjugation of infidels by Christians. "The net effect of this decree was the official sanction for the enslavement of Blacks, indigenous Americans, and other 'infidels,' for their benefit, of course: the salvation of their souls and their admission to God's Kingdom." (Montague, 1997)

The "Wild Men of the Woods" were savage, hairy and always "characterized by their unrestrained licentiousness." These evil men were said to be the descendants of Noah's youngest son, Ham, and they were black. St. Augustine wrote that Nimrod, a descendant of Ham, built the tower of Babel, and was responsible for the fragmentation of humanity. (Jahota, 1999)

The Other in this early period were regularly portrayed as living with animals, looking closely like apes, and having an unrestrained sexual appetite. Edmund Spenser's *Faerie Queene* portrayed them as slaves to passion, who raped women, carried them off, and then ate them. The females were cursed by "an irrepressible desire to copulate with ordinary men." It was common knowledge that the savage Other was close to an ape, was linked with the devil and later identified with sin. (Jahota, 1999)

Gustav Jahota points out that it was widely believed that apes desired to rape women. It was reported that women who were shipwrecked were raped by apes and produced barbarous creatures. This strange myth was even believed by Thomas Jefferson, the scholarly president of the United States. Jefferson, who owned a large plantation with slaves, believed that it was a case of inferiors preferring to mate with superiors. "Just as the orangutan prefers black women to females of his own species," Jefferson argued, "so blacks prefer whites." He may have been following the distinguished French philosopher Voltaire who had written that "in the hot countries apes subjugated girls." (Jahota, 1999)

In the period of mercantile colonial expansion, the focus was on the contrast between civilization and barbarism. The inhabitants of the new worlds were "savages" and "monstrous people." The travelers consistently portrayed the newly discovered people as the Other. They were barbarous, tyrannical, infidel, naked, having a dark skin colour, long hair, and cannibals. Martin Frobisher described the people he discovered in northern Canada as fierce and cruel, "devourers of man's flesh." Christopher Columbus saw the Carib Indians as kind and gentle but also cannibals. Europeans were superior by civilization. The dark people were heathens and barbarians. (Miles, 1989)

As Jahoda stresses, the Other were commonly said to be cannibals. And this was not limited to non-Europeans. The English insisted that the Irish were cannibals. So were the Scottish Highlanders. When the army of Bonnie Prince Charles marched on London in 1745, the English journals tried to rally the people to resist the invaders by insisting that if the Scottish Highlanders were victorious, they would eat their babies as they were cannibals. (Jahoda, 1999)

In the 14th century European explorers discovered the Canary Islands. Reports focused on these "wild people." The were naked, lacked any interest in gold and silver, and were happy with their idyllic life. But they were said to have faces like monkeys, howl like dogs, eat raw meat, and have sexual intercourse in public with shared women. (Jahota, 1999)

John Mandeville, one of the early 14th century explorers, reported that the Other foreigners were "giants, horrible and foul to the sight" who "eat raw flesh and raw fish." (Jahoda, 1999) This was the general, popular view of non-Europeans at the beginning of the expansion of European mercantile colonialism. It was closely tied to the view expressed by institutionalized Christianity.

## The English, the Irish and the Establishment of an "Inferior Race"

For Canadians it is most important to understand the development of the idea of racial superiority and inferiority in English society. The English version of racial domination became central to their colonial policy around the world including their colonies in North America. The general attitudes towards Aboriginal people developed in Canada under English colonialism. The basic Christian attitude of Europe as the foundation of "civilization" and the non-white non-Christian world as "barbarian" was also brought here by the colonists. It became a central focus of the relationship between white immigrants and Aboriginal people in Saskatchewan.

What is the origin of English racism? It develops as England tries to subjugate its first colony, Ireland. The Celtic areas of Scotland and Wales were absorbed into Great Britain. This was not an easy process, but over the years it was accomplished. In contrast, the Irish people strongly resisted English imperialism and colonialism.

England developed its imperial and colonial policy in Ireland. The colonization process began during the feudal period, well before the development of mercantile capitalist colonialism. During this long struggle, the English and the English-speaking colonists who went to Ireland developed a deeply rooted anti-Irish sentiment that still persists. It constitutes a form of racism.

The English experience of imperialism and colonialism in Ireland is most important to Canada. The English were late in becoming a colonial power in North America, but it did not take long for them to become the dominant power. The people who first established English colonies in North America had direct colonial experience in Ireland. Furthermore, the racist policies and attitudes of the English towards the Irish were carried over to North America and applied to the Aboriginal people. The settlement of western Canada follows this script.

At the core of imperial policy toward Ireland was the goal of the English ruling class to *seize the agricultural land*. Over a period from 1189 to 1700 they gradually removed ownership of land from the Irish and granted it to English landlords. At the same time, they expected that the labour on their newly acquired land would be performed by the Irish. The colonial project was pushed by the west country gentry which wanted to capture economic rent from the labour of a subjugated Irish labour force.

The conquest of Ireland required almost constant warfare and military occupation. In this effort the English adopted a policy of total war against the Irish which included burning their crops and houses, killing their livestock, slaughtering the garrisons that surrendered, paying a bounty for the heads of Irish killed, and slaughtering civilian men, women and children. This was often described by the English rulers as a "policy of terrorism." They regularly made agreements with the chiefs of the Irish clans and then broke them. They passed a range of laws designed to destroy the Irish as a distinct culture in order to convert them by force into Englishmen. (see Canny, 1973, 1976; Ranelagh, 1983; Frame, 1998; Curtis, 1950, 1968; de Breffny, 1977)

But it was not enough to justify this seizure of land simply in terms of an imperial and colonial war and the "right of conquest." The Irish were Europeans, and their style of living was not that much different from the people living in rural England. They were not heathens but Christians. Indeed, for hundreds of years the Irish were the leading Christian scholars. There had to be a *moral and ideological justification* for this policy, one that could be accepted by the rulers, the Christian church and the people as a whole.

In the period of the Anglo-Norman invasion after 1169, the case for English occupation of Ireland was made by Gerald de Barry, a monk who was also known as Giraldus Cambrensis or Gerald of Wales. He wrote the official account of the invasion, *The History of the Topography of Ireland* and *The Conquest of Ireland*. His writings were propaganda, much of it fiction, designed to promote the interests of the new Anglo-Irish landlords. Gerald described the Irish character as lazy, treacherous, engaging in blasphemy and idolatry, ignorant of Christian beliefs, and promoting incest and cannibalism. (see Rolston, 1993)

Thus, the English kings of this period believed they had a mission to bring the Irish under the civilizing process which included subservience to the Christian church in Rome. The Irish, though "pagan" in the view of the English, were judged not to be permanently inferior. Nevertheless, conquest was the necessary first step towards becoming civilized. Civilization required that their backward culture be extirpated. With a firm government in control, the Irish could be reformed. At this time, the English argued that underneath their backwardness they were still human beings. The key was to remove their chiefs and and replace them with civilized English rulers and landlords. Giraldus' view of the Irish became deeply imbedded in the English mass culture for hundreds of years. (Cairns and Richards, 1988)

The official and popular view of the Irish changed during the Tudor period after 1540. The Irish were no longer perceived as simply a backward people in need of civilization and Christianity. The English began to portray them as *true barbarians*, a people who could not be civilized through normal processes but only by armed force. This was due to the fact, of course, that for hundreds of years they resisted English colonialism and imperialism. (Canny, 1976)

The new English position on the Irish was popularized by the poet Edmund Spenser in *A View of the Present State of Ireland* and *The Faerie Queene*, fashioned during his travels in Ireland in the late 16th century. Following Giraldus, Spenser argued that Ireland could not be brought to civilization except through the destruction of their indigenous culture, and this could only be done through famine and the sword.

The values of the Irish were incompatible with civilization and had to be purged. The refusal of the Irish to accept English ways demonstrated that they were barbarous and the whole population needed a root and branch treatment. (Cairns and Richards, 1988)

The establishment of the Protestant religion, separate from Rome, made this easier. The state religion of England was declared to be the only true Christian religion. Catholicism was now deemed to be based on superstition and idolatry. Thus the Anglo-Irish, who were Catholics, were now also placed in the camp of the inferior "Other." The world in Ireland was divided between the elect and the fallen, the colonizers and the colonized. As Edward Said has stressed, those colonized by the Europeans were regularly defined as barbarians, pagan, ape, female, and always subordinate and inferior. (Said, 1994)

The general case against the Irish developed into a racialist attitude. The pillars of this common sense English attitude were as follows:

(1) The Irish were described as pagans. It did not matter that they had been Christians for hundreds of years. Their religion had to be replaced by the imperial religion.

(2) The Irish were barbarians. The English believed that a people could be civilized without being Christian, but no one could be a Christian without first being civilized. English civilization was superior because it combined both. Once the Irish were identified as pagans, then the next step was to declare them barbarians.

Because the Irish were barbarians, an uncivilized people, the English armies in the field were absolved from all normal ethical restrains. The Earl of Leicester argued that there was a difference in fighting a war against civilized people and the Irish barbarians. "Savages and those rurall raskells are only by force and fear to be vanquished." Sir John Davies argued that "a barbarous country must be first broken by a war before it will be capable of good government." As Nicholas Canny concludes, the English of the Tudor period replaced the old view that the Irish were socially inferior with the view that they were anthropologically inferior. (Canny, 1973;1976)

(3) The Irish did not use the land. The English claimed that the Irish were just nomads who followed herds around. Therefore, it was justifiable to seize their land. Furthermore, the Irish clans held their lands in common. There was no private, individual ownership of land. Again, this was evidence that they were a

backward race. The Irish, of course, practiced agriculture across the island. The English knew this because they regularly burned their crops as part of their policy of the promotion of famine.

(4) The Irish were licentious. Spenser argued that the Irish in dress, hairstyle, and weapons were similar to the Scythians and had devious sexual practices. Incest was said to be common. The English were appalled by the Irish Brehon law and the extent to which it granted rights to women. They insisted that the Irish law be replaced by the Roman Christian law, where the man was the head of the household and had domain over everyone within. Women were not to own property, as under Irish law; women were to become the property of men. Women were to have no rights in marriage, especially rights to divorce, as they did under the barbarous Irish law. Civilization required the complete subordination of women. (Gillingham, 2000)

(5) The Irish had a barbarous form of government. There was no strong centralized government, ruled from the top down. They elected their chiefs. The decentralization of power and authority, the English argued, inevitably led to war and rebellion. Civilization required an absolute monarchy and hereditary class rule. (Warnock, 2001)

The English view of the Irish became deeply imbedded in the culture of common knowledge. Thus, during the Irish famine (1845-1848) the English managed to blame the Irish and not colonialism and the exploitative English landlord/Irish tenant system. It was at this time that the English began to describe the Irish as "an inferior race." Biological theories of racism were on the rise. Robert Knox in *The Races of Men* (1850) declared that "the source of all evil lies in *the race*, the Celtic race of Ireland." Nothing good could come from intermarriage between the Saxon and the Celts. The Union between the countries was a fraud: "Ireland is not a colony, but merely a country held by force of arms, like India; a country inhabited by another race." (Cited in Lengel, 1996)

English colonial policy was not just war, killing, seizing of land, and imposing an authoritarian and undemocratic system of government on a defeated people. It was combined with an *ideological racism* which categorized the defeated people as biologically inferior. English colonialism had material, economic roots, beginning with the seizure of land for agricultural purposes. This was the general policy that the English carried over to the imperial colonization project in North America.

## The Evolution of Racism in White Settler Capitalist Societies

Western European imperialism and colonialism was always closely connected with race and racism. In all the colonies the imperial powers instituted a range of policies which had the effect of created two different societies, one representing the colonizers and the European settlers and the other representing the colonized, indigenous peoples. Of course, skin colour was paramount: western European colonialism took the form of white imperialists and non-white subjugated indigenous peoples.

Thus colonies were segregated societies. White Europeans were the governors. European legal systems were imposed, and whites were subject only to European laws. Indigenous peoples were denied positions of power and authority. There was widespread job discrimination, with good jobs reserved for whites. Land was simply taken away from indigenous peoples and granted to white settlers. Very often slavery was a key institution in the colonial economy. Colonized peoples were forbidden from forming trade unions and political organizations which in any way advocated independence.

The colonized peoples were denied education provided to white settlers. There was a rejection of indigenous religions and the insistence that Christianity was the only true religion. There was a negation of tradition laws and customs with regard to marriage and sexual practices. In some societies, there was a formal caste system. For example, in Indonesia the Dutch passed laws making it illegal for indigenous people to wear European clothing. Intermarriage between whites and indigenous peoples was often prohibited. In French, Spanish and Portuguese colonies indigenous peoples could achieve the status of citizen but only by rejecting their own culture and completely becoming European. Colonial exploitation and economic domination was accompanied by formal systems of racism. (see Wallerstein, 1966; Marnier, 1949; Cox, 1948; Fanon, 1970; Memmi, 1965; Bodley, 1999)

When looking at racism in Canada, it is essential to remember Canada's history as a white settler society. An important work here is Stanley B. Greenberg's *Race and State in Capitalist Development; comparative perspectives.* Greenberg examines the origin and persistence of racism within four white settler communities: Alabama in the United States, the Union of South Africa, Israel and Northern Ireland. (Greenberg, 1980)

Greenberg is driven to his work by "the continuing reality of racial and ethnic domination." The divisions between Arabs and Jews, Catholics and Protestants, blacks and whites, Chicanos and Anglos in the American Southwest, Flemings and

Walloons in Belgium, English and French in Canada, Welsh, Scots and English in Great Britain continue to exist in "modern" industrial societies. Greenberg asks: why do we continue to find "such parochial and ascriptive loyalties" in social and political life "despite the growth of rationalism, nations, industry, and capitalism?"

This was not supposed to happen, whether the framework for analysis is mainstream liberal modernization theory or Marxism. As countries progressed and developed economically, these old allegiances were expected to disappear. But in the four countries he examines, bitter racial and ethnic divisions have continued down to the present in spite of "high levels of urbanization, mass communication, economic growth, wage labour, trade-union organization, bureaucratization, political mobilization, indeed, all the essentials of developing capitalist societies." Therefore, Greenberg concludes we have to look more closely at capitalist development. What has its impact been on historic patterns of racial and ethnic domination?

Being Irish or black is not the same as being a member of a particular farm group or political party. Many anthropologists have argued that race and ethnicity are "primordial" or part of a common origin. They are the result of ties of language, ethnicity, often skin colour, religion and culture. They have their origin in the family. They create a sense of affinity—of people who are "our kind."

Yet we know that group identities develop historically and socially. For example, how can one define the historical origin of the Scots as a nation? They evolved as an amalgamation of peoples who came to that area of northwest Europe. Or for that matter, the English, who for a very long time believed that they were the superior race. Is the English race the original Britons, the Celts, the Anglo-Saxons, or the Normans? Obviously, national identities are fluid and shifting. Even what we call "race" did not really appear as a central identification and ideology until the middle of the nineteenth century.

As Greenberg argues, both the mainstream liberal school of modernization as well as Marx and Lenin believed that the spread of capitalism and modern liberalism would break down the old "primordial" alliances and bring new forms of social conflict. Karl Deutsch, the American political scientist, noted the example of the Gaelic Highlanders in Scotland. Once they lost their language and moved to the cities to work, they were assimilated into the greater English culture of modern capitalism. It was thought that this would be the general pattern under capitalism. (Deutsch, 1965)

Marx and Lenin argued that the "national question" was limited to the backward areas of the capitalist world, like Ireland, the Ukraine and Poland. While the Marxists argued for the right of nations to self determination, they also believed that there is the "international unity of capital, of economic life in general," and that this powerful force will "break down national barriers, obliterate national distinction, and assimilate nations." As Marx wrote "Ties of personal dependence—of blood, education, caste, or estate—fall away before the progressive pre-eminence of 'free wage labour.'" (Marx and Engels, 1965)

The German sociologist Max Weber also believed that capitalism would not work unless there was "free wage labour," a large class of propertyless people, "a class compelled to sell its labour services to live." Race and ethnic divisions may exist in capitalist society, but Weber concluded that eventually they become a barrier to individual mobility and would decline in importance. (Greenberg, 1980)

The dependency or underdevelopment school of political economy and sociology has stressed that as capitalism has developed it has increased inequalities, unevenness, and even created underdevelopment. In its early period it expanded and enhanced production under slave labour, an archaic mode of production. In Central and South America, capitalist imperialism brought plantations with forced labour and the quasi-serf system of the hacienda and debt peonage. It created a class of landed commercial aristocrats, societies based on social inequities and informal caste systems. Many associate the development of racial and ethnic stratification with the arrival of European capitalism, imperialism and colonialism.

For the four white settler societies he studied, Greenberg notes that the period of imperialism and colonialism created *a state apparatus committed to a racial order*. This order developed as the state was used extensively to enforce the imposition of a system of exploitation based in agriculture. Greenberg concludes: "Commercial farmers, more than any other set of actors, set the tone for this intensification." Their status is founded on seizing the land from the indigenous population, creating commercial farming operations, and the use of the indigenous population (or imported slaves) for the production of product and rent. Thus, the key to racial systems in these white settler societies is "plundering the subordinate peasantry" who were dependent on subsistence farming. Those who own the stolen land become the strongest supporters of the racialized system.

The commercial owners of land have allies in support of the new state system. Businessmen, particularly in the extractive natural resource industries, depend on the state system to recruit labour. The new workers from the European countries support the racialized system by forming organizations to preserve their privileged place at the top, the aristocracy of labour, to the exclusion of the indigenous population, forced to remain in the lower working class strata. The trade unions of the privileged form an alliance with the state sector. These groups unite to call on the state to enforce the system of racial discrimination and exclusion.

Greenberg concludes that in the white settler societies there are changes. But the old system of class and ethnic exclusion does not disappear. There are strong class forces that carry forward and elaborate the traditional racial patterns. Rather than promoting change under capitalism, they use their control over the state apparatus and limit the "proletarianization of the subordinate population." Economic growth and change brings forward conflicts and can threaten to undo the old social order. Its survival depends on the ability of dominant groups to maintain their "primordial" identities. Greenberg finds this to be the case in the four areas he studied. (Greenberg, 1980)

Northern Ireland is one of Greenberg's case studies. Protestant workers formed an alliance with the business class, which was also Protestant. He details this alliance which was founded on the exclusion of Roman Catholics from all the skilled jobs and any role in the state apparatus. The business community even financed the Protestant paramilitary groups. Government policy, invoked by the Protestants with the support of the British government, consciously created residential segregation. The police force was completely dominated by the Protestant working class. (Greenberg, 1980)

Pamela Clayton notes that because of the Protestant inter-class alliance, the socialist and Marxist parties have never had success in Northern Ireland. Protestant solidarity is the rule, and appeals to working class solidarity "make little headway in the face of the overriding determination to retain settler power." Those who try to break this alliance are denounced as "traitors." (Clayton, 1998; Taylor, 1999)

Saskatchewan developed as a white settler society within Canada and the British empire. At an early date, the Aboriginal people of North America made it clear that they had no desire to become agricultural slaves or serfs. In the Carolinas, the English captured thousands of Indians and sold them into slavery. But almost always they were shipped to the Caribbean islands. To profit from the seizing of the land it was necessary for the European powers to import agricultural labour. The English had sold Irish rebels into slavery to work on plantations in the Caribbean, but they resisted at every chance. Other poor whites became indentured servants, many sold in the American colonies in slave markets and treated like slaves. But the best supply of labour came as slaves from Africa. With the legal end of slavery, agricultural labour was provided by "free labour." In Canada, agricultural labour was provided by men and their families from Europe, white settlers and independent farmers. (Nash, 2000)

The National Policy of post-Confederation Canada depended on the removal of the Aboriginal people from their historic lands, segregating those who survived the imperial onslaught on small rural reserves, and the immigration of European home-steaders who were to become commercial wheat growers. In this process the Aboriginal people of Canada were labeled "savages" and "barbarians," people who were destined to either die out or be assimilated into white European society. They were seen as a barrier to progress that had to be removed. The state, with strong popular support, created a political economy that marginalized and isolated the Aboriginal population for a long period of time. It was fundamentally a racist policy, and it became deeply entrenched in the popular culture.

While this system of subordination was based on seizing Aboriginal land by military force for the benefit of a class of European private property owners, Saskatchewan has changed over the years. The economy has become significantly diversified. Agriculture is still very important but it no longer completely dominates the economy. Aboriginal people have moved off the reserves, entered the labour force in large numbers and are becoming more highly educated. Yet this process of modernization and assimilation has not served to break down traditional social barriers and attitudes. Racialization and discrimination continue to exist. It is the basis of a pervasive discontent in the province.

## Conclusion

Within Europe, the ideas of superiority/inferiority developed in an early period in Greek and Roman advanced civilizations, well before capitalism, the modern territorial state and even class societies. The barbarians were identified as the Other who lived outside of civilization, and they were dark. Whiteness was seen in a positive light.

The Christian church developed a white/black, good/evil, Christ/Satan dichotomy at an early period. The barbarians were the infidels who live in the wild, had no moral sense, and were characterized by untamed sexuality. They were also deemed to be cannibals.

The earliest European explorers identified the new people as the Other, close to the "wild men of the woods" who were evil, just one step up from the apes. This view of the non-European, non-Christian quickly became part of the mass, popular culture.

The first case of *state sponsored racism* developed in the long campaign of the English to subjugate the Irish. Over hundreds of years of war and occupation, the English adopted a racist view of the Irish: they were pagans, barbarians, licentious, and an uncivilized people who did not know agriculture and had no system of government.

There was a *materialist base* to this racism. The goal of English colonialism in Ireland was to seize the land from the Irish, transfer ownership to the English and Scottish gentry, and to profit from the labour of the Irish tenant farmers and farm labourers. The English insisted that civilization was based on the private, individual ownership of land.

Racism became a world wide phenomenon during the expansion of European colonialism in the 19th and 20th centuries. Race discrimination was a central part of colonial policy in all the areas of the world conquered by the European states. It became deeply entrenched in those societies where there was a significant influx of European immigrants. As Stanley Greenberg has demonstrated, in white settler societies it is the *European settlers on the land* who originally form the core group which uphold racist ideology. The seizure of land from indigenous peoples by force or threat of force is justified by arguing that the colonized are inferior people, that they are not using the land, have no concept of private property, and are not Christians. The white settler societies construct a state system that embodies this racist ideology, and it becomes part of the mass popular culture, common sense. Canada and Saskatchewan have been part of this development.

## References

Banton, Michael. *Racial Theories.* 1987. Cambridge: Cambridge University Press.

Barot, Rawhide and John Bird. 2001. "Racialization: the Genealogy and Critique of a Concept." *Ethnic and Racial Studies*, Vol. 24, No. 4, July 2001, pp. 601-618

Benedict, Ruth. 1983. *Race and Racism.* London: Routledge and Kegan Paul.

Blaut, J.M. 1993. *The Colonizer's Model of the World.* New York: The Guilford Press.

Bodley, John H. 1999. *Victims of Progress.* Toronto: Mayfield Publishing Company.

Bolaria, B. Singh and Peter S. Li. 1988. *Racial Oppression in Canada.* Toronto: Garamond Press.

Cairns, David and Shaun Richards. 1988. *Writing Ireland: Colonialism, Nationalism and Culture.* New York: St. Martin's Press.

Canny, Nicholas P. 1976. *The Elizabethan Conquest of Ireland: A Pattern Established 1565-76.* New York: Barnes & Noble Books.

Canny, Nicholas P. 1973. "The Ideology of English Colonization: From Ireland to America." *William and Mary Quarterly*, Vol. 30, October, pp. 575-598.

Clayton, Pamela. 1998. "Religion, Ethnicity and Colonialism as Explanations of the Northern Ireland Conflict." In Miller, pp. 40-54.

Cox, Oliver C. 1948. *Caste, Class & Race.* New York: Monthly Review Press.

Curtis, Edmund. 1950. *A History of Ireland.* London: Methuen.

Curtis, Edmund. 1968. *A History of Medieval Ireland, from 1086 to 1513.* London: Methuen.

Cuthand, Doug. 2003. "Urban Reserve Finally a Reality." *Regina Leader-Post,* January 20, B-1.

Cuthand, Doug. 2002. "Indians of the Middle East? Palestinian Quagmire Essentially an Unresolved Land Claim," *Prairie Dog,* January 24, p. 6.

De Breffny, Brian. 1977. *The Irish World: the History and Cultural Achievements of the Irish People.* London: Thames and Hudson.

Deutsch, Karl. 1965. *Nationalism and Social Communication.* New Haven: Yale University Press.

Duffy, Sean. 1997. *Ireland in the Middle Ages.* New York: St. Martin's Press.

Fanon, Franz. 1970. *Toward the African Revolution.* Harmondsworth: Penguin.

Frame, Robin. 1998. *Ireland and Britain, 1170-1450.* London: The Hambledon Press.

Genovese, Eugene D. 1965. *The Political Economy of Slavery.* New York: Pantheon.

Gillingham, John. 2000. *The English in the Twelfth Century: Imperialism, National Identity and Political Values.* Woodbridge: The Boydell Press.

Greenberg, Stanley B. 1980. *Race and State in Capitalist Development: Comparative Perspectives.* New Haven: Yale University Press.

Hall, Stuart. 1980. "Race, Articulation and Societies Structured in Dominance." In UNESCO, *Sociological Theories: Racism and Colonialism.* Paris: UNESCO.

Jahota, Gustav. 1999, *Images of Savages: Ancient Roots of Modern Prejudice in Western Culture.* London: Routledge.

Jenkins, Richard. 1999. "Ethnicity etcetera: Social Anthropological Points of View." *Ethnic and Racial Studies,* Vol. 19, No. 4, October, pp. 807-822.

Jennings, Francis. 1975. *The Invasion of America: Indians, Colonialism, and the Cant of Conquest.* Chapel Hill, N.C.: University of North Carolina Press.

Laycock, David. 2002. *The New Right and Democracy in Canada: Understanding Reform and the Canadian Alliance.* Don Mills: Oxford University Press.

Lengel, Ed. 1996. "A 'Perverse and Ill-Fated People': English Perceptions of the Irish, 1845-52," *Essays in History.* Vol. 38, University of Virginia, pp. 1-10.

Macdonald, Laura. 1995. "Unequal Partnership: The Politics of Canada's Relations with the Third World." *Studies in Political Economy,* No. 47, Summer, pp. 111-141.

Marnier, Rene. 1949. *The Sociology of Colonies.* London: Routledge & Kegan Paul.

Marx, Karl and Frederick Engels. 1965. *On Colonialism.* New York: Progress Books.

Memmi, Albert. 1965. *The Colonizer and the Colonized.* Boston: Beacon Press.

Miles, Robert. 1989. *Racism.* London: Routledge.

Miller, David, ed. 1998. *Rethinking Northern Ireland: Culture Ideology and Colonialism.* New York: Longman.

Montague, Ashley, ed.1964. *The Concept of Race.* New York: Free Press.

Montague, Ashley. 1997. *Man's Most Dangerous Myth: the Fallacy of Race.* New York: Rowman & Littlefield Publishers.

Nash, Gary B. 2000. *Red, White and Black: The Peoples of Early North America.* Upper Saddle River, N.J.: Prentice Hall.

Quinn, David B. 1966. *The Elizabethans and the Irish.* Ithaca, NY: Cornell University Press.

Ranelagh, John O'Beirne. 1983. *A Short History of Ireland.* Cambridge: Cambridge University Press.

Rex, John. 1970. *Race Relations in Sociological Theory.* London: Weidenfeld & Nicholson.

Rolston, Bill. 1993. "The Training Ground: Ireland, Conquest and Decolonisation." *Race & Class.* Vol. 34, No. 4, pp.13-24.

Rolson, Bill. 1998. "What's Wrong with Multiculturalism? Liberalism and the Irish Conflict." In Miller, pp. 253-274.

Said, Edward W. 1993. *Culture and Imperialism.* New York: Knopf.

Saskatchewan Human Rights Commission. 2001. "Policy Relating to Aboriginal People as a Designated Group." *Equity,* March. http://www.gov.sk.shrc.ca

Taylor, Peter. 1999. *Loyalists.* London: Bloomsbury.

United Nations Economic, Social and Cultural Organization (UNESCO). 1978. *Declaration on Race and Racial Prejudice.* Adopted by the General Conference, Paris, November.

Wallerstein, Immanuel. 1966. *Social Change: The Colonial Situation.* New York: Wiley.

Warick, Jason. 2003a. "Outrage in Melfort." *Leader-*Post, September 5, A-1-2.

Warick, Jason. 2003b. "Why the Water Stopped Flowing." *Leader-Post,* August 16, A-1-2.

Warnock, John W. 2001. "The National Policy and Racism in Saskatchewan." Paper presented to the Territorial Grain Growers Association Symposium, University of Regina, November 24 and 25. Publication forthcoming.

Wellman, David. 1977. *Portraits of White Racism.* Cambridge: Cambridge University Press.

# Chapter 7

———○———

# THE ROOTS OF RACISM IN SASKATCHEWAN

Saskatchewan was created as part of the commercial and political plan of Canada's political and business leaders to create a national economy based on the production and export of wheat. But that domestic operation took place within the broader context of the European colonization project in North America. This is the major shortcoming of the classic and traditional explanations for the development of Canada as a "new country" based on European immigration. It is also the major factor left out of almost every account of the creation of Saskatchewan and the other western provinces.

In the early 15th century European powers began to expand abroad with the maritime states "discovering" the rest of the world and claiming areas for their new national states. Spanish and Portuguese merchants, traders and pirates moved into Africa, around the Cape of Good Hope to Asia, and then to the Americas. By the middle of the 16th century the Spanish and Portuguese had seized land in the Americas, were transforming the indigenous peoples into slaves for their mines and agricultural plantations, and beginning to import African slave labour. The British East India Company started to make India into the "Jewel of the Empire," and direct colonial rule was established by the British state after the failed rebellion of 1757.

The merchants of Bristol, who had been deeply involved in the colonization of Ireland, backed John Cabot in his voyage to Canada to try to find a passage to India. Jacques Cartier sailed up the St. Lawrence River in 1535 and claimed the whole country for the government of France. After a series of inter-imperialist wars, the English eventually came to dominate the European colonial occupation of North America.

By the middle of the 19th century, Great Britain, France, Spain, Portugal, Belgium, Denmark, and The Netherlands controlled most of the world, either directly as colonies or indirectly as spheres of influence. But the drive for colonies was not over. In the latter part of the century Africa was absorbed. The Great Depression of 1873-96 convinced European political and business leaders that colonies and dominated overseas territories were necessary for economic and political development. To a large extent World War I was a battle over colonies, and in its aftermath, Great Britain, France, Italy and Spain took North Africa and most of the Near East. The imperial thinking of the day was reflected by Cecil Rhodes in 1895:

> I was in the East End of London yesterday and attended a meeting of the unemployed. I listened to the wild speeches, which were just a cry for 'bread,' 'bread,' 'bread,' and on my way home I pondered over the scene and I became more than ever convinced of the importance of imperialism. My cherished idea is a solution for the social problem, i.e., in order to save the 40,000,000 inhabitants of the United Kingdom from a bloody civil war, we colonial statesmen must acquire new lands to settle the surplus population, to provide new markets for the goods produced by them in the factories and mines. The Empire, as I have always said, is a bread and butter question. If you want to avoid civil war, you must become imperialists. (Quoted in Maslowe, 1973)

The U.S. government was not going to be left out. In 1822 President James Monroe declared that the two continents of the Americas were off limits to European powers who could not colonize, extend their political systems, or directly intervene. As U.S. historian Richard Van Alstyne has written, "This is imperialism preached in the grand manner, for the only restrictions placed upon the directing power are those which it imposes upon itself. The Monroe Doctrine is really an official declaration fencing in the 'western hemisphere' as a United States sphere of influence." (Van Alstyne, 1960)

Various U.S. administrations declared the Caribbean and Central America to be their "back yard" where intervention and control was necessary. In 1867 the U.S. government purchased Alaska from Russia. British North America was their "front yard" to be brought under control primarily through the economic policies of the "Open Door" and "Dollar Diplomacy," by controlling trade and investment, although a number of prominent political leaders wanted annexation. The next move was the march into the Pacific, taking the Midway Islands, Hawaii, and the Philippines. (see Van Alstyne, 1960; Pratt, 1959; LaFeber, 1963)

All of the European imperial powers utilized similar strategies in controlling their colonial areas. Rule was enforced from the central state using military power. The economies of the colonized areas were controlled and fashioned to suit the interests of the "mother country." The indigenous populations were denied any control over their own affairs and denied rights as citizens. A key to colonial rule was the hegemonic ideology which argued that the Europeans were the advanced, modernizing force, representing the only true religion, Christianity, and that the indigenous populations, almost always non-white, were deemed to be inferior. Racism and racial segregation were the rule in the colonized areas. There was one law for the white Europeans and another for the non-white indigenous population. The authoritarian and brutal nature of the policies of colonialism were in direct contrast to the professed liberal and democratic rights for citizens found in the European countries. The general policies of European colonialism, including racist ideology, were central to British, French, Spanish, Portuguese and Dutch colonial policies in the Americas. (see Parry, 1961; Magdoff, 1978; Curtis, 1964; Rodney, 1974; Fanon, 1966; Memmi, 1965; Bodley, 1999)

## The English Colonize North America

The imperial countries and the colonists carried out "total war" against the indigenous peoples of North America. As Michael Stevenson argues, total war is "to lay waste a people and destroy their culture in order to undermine the integrity of their existence and appropriate their riches." This requires "the devastation of their material and spiritual economy," and it "continually recreates its mechanisms of justification." The result is a "structure of collective feeling, a way of thought and a language that facilitates its continuity from generation to generation." It demands an enemy that is not just defeated but eradicated. Those who are not physically destroyed are assimilated. (Stevenson, 1992)

The English who came to dominate North America had centuries of experience in Ireland. The war against the "savage Indians" was the same as the war against the "savage Irish." It was a war of terror and included the seizing of land by military force, the burning of crops, houses and villages, killing non-combatants as well as taking no prisoners, promoting war between Indian tribes, breaking promises and treaties, exterminating entire bands or tribes, and developing a propaganda of falsification.

Compared to the Spanish, French, and Dutch, the English were late arriving in North America. Historian David Quinn has stressed that many of the people who were directly involved in the English wars against the Irish as military officers, colonial government officials, and operators of plantations, were also involved in the earliest colonial efforts in North America. These included Walter Raleigh, Humphrey Gilbert, Francis Drake and Richard Grenville. (Quinn, 1962)

In 1578 Queen Elizabeth I officially authorized Sir Humphrey Gilbert to seize "remote heathen and barbarous lands." In 1583 he sailed into Placentia Bay in Newfoundland and claimed it for English. In 1584 Elizabeth gave a similar patent to Sir Walter Raleigh. Both had served as military commanders and plantation owners in Ireland. The focus of the royal charters was on seizure of property and the imposition of English government. Historian Richard Jennings points out that there was no mention at this time of an intent or obligation to convert the "heathens" to Christianity. (Jennings, 1976)

In recruiting Englishmen to go to the New World as colonists, Quinn points out that Sir Humphrey Gilbert "placed his main emphasis on land to arouse the cupidity of the land-hungry young men of his own social group." For a small investment they were led to believe that "gentlemen might find themselves suddenly transformed into feudal lords of great estates on which towns and tenancies might be multiplied quickly and cheaply." Sir Walter Raleigh, who sponsored the first attempted English settlement, described himself as "Lord and Governor of Virginia." The goal was free land, tenant farmers, and a good profit. (Quinn, 1976)

The first successful English plantation came with the Virginia Company which landed at Jamestown in 1607. While they were instructed in how to grow corn, the settlers suffered from dysentery, malaria and food deficiency diseases. Very often they survived only because of charity from the "heathen" Indians. The early settlers generally negotiated and traded with the Indians for the use of land. The Virginia Company had instructed the colonists to buy corn from the Indians when they were short. The strategy was not to provoke the Indians into a war. In this early period, Jennings notes, the Virginia company referred to the Indians as "native people," "naturals," and "country people." (Quinn, 1962; Jennings, 1976)

The change came when the colonists learned that a profit could be made from the production and export of tobacco. The Indians had taught the colonists how to grow tobacco. Now the colonists coveted more land to grow a commercial crop. They did not want to expend the labour clearing land of trees. Instead, they decided to annex the land cleared by the Indians for their agriculture. They began to use force to seize land, and the Indians began to resist. (Jennings, 1976; Nash, 2000)

The position of the Virginia Company and the colonists changed after the Indians began to use force to defend their land. Edward Waterhouse of the Company set the tone: the English were now justified by the right of war to "destroy them who sought to destroy us." The fact that so many of the settlers had escaped being killed by the Indians during the early uprisings seemingly had demonstrated that God was on the side of the colonists. Waterhouse instructed the colonists on how to deal with the "savage Indians" by following the Irish example:

> By force, by surprise, by famine in burning their Corne, by destroying and burning their Boats, Canoes, and Houses, by breaking their fishing Weares, by assailing them in their huntings...by pursuing and chasing them with our hourses, and blood-Hounds to draw after them, and Mastives to tear them, which take this naked, tanned, deformed Savages for no other than wild beasts. (Cited in Pennington, 1978)

The justification for imperialism and colonialism was the same as in Ireland. The colonists were going to inhabit and reform a "barbarian nation." Colonists were assured that the land was empty and free for the taking. What Indians there were survived by hunting in the bush, the prospective colonists were told, as they did not know agriculture. As Robert Cushman wrote at the time, "Their land is spacious and void. The Indians do but run over the grass, as do the foxes and wild beasts." Therefore, "it is lawful now to take a land, which none useth, and make use of it." Puritan leader John Winthrop argued, "God gave the earth to man—why should we stand starving here for places of habitation?" (Cited in Jones, 1967)

But of course this was false. Like the Irish, the Indians had a good understanding of their territory. As John Smith reported, the Indians knew exactly where the boundaries were between the territories of the tribes. The Indian communities the colonists encountered on the East Coast were primarily based on agricultural, using corn, beans, squash and sunflower as their basic foods, a system which had spread north from Mesoamerica. The agricultural villages had permanent buildings. Many bands moved around their land, practicing shifting cultivation to preserve the fertility of the soil. They always returned to land they had cleared. Individual Indians farmed land parceled out by their chiefs. As Jennings comments, "The Indian did not wander; he commuted."

To the Europeans the Indians were heathens. The colonists argued that the native religions were in reality worship of the devil. It was God's plan that the European should take the Christian religion to these pagan people.

Albert Gentili, professor of civil law at Oxford University, argued that seizing the land in North America was justified because the indigenous population "practiced abominable lewdness" and engaged in sins. He also argued that the law of nature "abhors a vacuum" and concluded that almost all of the New World was unoccupied. Hugo Grotius, often identified as the father of international law, argued that the war on the indigenous population in North America was a "most just war" because the people were "savage beasts." Amerigo Vespucci the great navigator reported that the people of the New World were not only cannibals, "the women are very libidinous, and when they had the opportunity of copulating with Christians, urged by excessive lust, they defiled and prostituted themselves." (Cited in Stevenson, 1992)

In a notable contrast to the Europeans the Indians along the Atlantic coast had a peculiar practice of taking a bath every day; nevertheless, they were characterized as "filthy." But this was because of their sexual practices. Most of the Aboriginal nations dependent on agriculture were matrilineal, with women in charge of agriculture and land and having considerable power and influence. In summer months the Aboriginal people wore almost no clothes, and some went entirely naked. They were not ashamed of nakedness. The practice of premarital sex was common. Women decided who they would marry. Divorce was relatively easy. Homosexuality was tolerated and even institutionalized. They had no concept of sin. It was easy for the English with their patriarchal Christianity to conclude that the Indians worshiped the devil. (Jennings, 1976; Trigger, 1969, 1985; Nash, 2000)

Nicholas Canny notes that the Indians, the blacks used as slaves in the Caribbean, and the Irish "were accused of being idle, lazy, dirty and licentious." Samuel Johnson proclaimed that the English had used the sword to bring "manners and civilization to the Scots" and they would "do the same in time to all barbarous nations including the Cherokees." (Canny, 1976)

Those who came to conquer America represented the Christians of western Europe. As Jennings points out, they were "not only holy and white but also *civilized.*" In contrast the "pigmented heathens of distant lands were not only idolatrous and dark but *savage.*" Mumford Jones has written: "The antithesis which opposed civilization and barbarism was a highly useful cliché, and one which served equally well as a means of self-congratulation and as a rationalization for aggression." (Jennings, 1976; Jones, 1967)

But the settlers were first of all coming to get free land and this meant displacing the indigenous population. In the early 17th century John Smith of the Jamestown colony waged total war against the tribes of the Chesapeake Bay area, burning their fields and villages, stealing their food, and slaughtering Indians of all ages and both sexes. By 1669 only 11 of the 28 tribes remained, and their population had declined from 20,000 to 2,900. By the late 17th century, Nathaniel Bacon led the colonists in a "war of extermination" against all Indians. As historian Gary Nash concludes, "The price of survival in Virginia, as in New England, was the sacrifice of an independent tribal identity and submission to white civilization as tenant farmers, day labourers, and domestic servants." (Nash, 2000)

In 1637 the Puritans launched a war on the Pequots, allies of the Dutch in New England. They surrounded their fort at Mystic River, burned it, and slaughtered most of the men, women and children who escaped the flames. Those who survived were sold as slaves to the West Indies market. Their allies, the Narragansett Indians, were shocked by the slaughter. As Roger Williams put it, while the Indians "might fight seven years and not kill seven men," the English were schooled in the wars of terrorism from their experience in Ireland. But the war of extermination against the Indians was not limited to the English. Between 1713 and 1731 the French waged war on the Natchez as they seized their land in the southern Mississippi region. In their final assault they killed 1,000, burned captives at the stake, and sold the remaining 400 into slavery.

In the Carolinas, many of the settlers had come from the West Indies where the plantation-slave economy was in place. They made a serious attempt to enslave the Indians to work on their Carolina plantations. They also engaged in the slave trade. In the 18th century tens of thousands of Indians were marched to Charleston and sold at the slave auctions and then sent to the other English colonies. (Nash, 2000)

In Canada there was less devastation of the indigenous population by the colonists. As many writers have pointed out, the main reason for this was the development of the fur trade, which was central to commercial and imperial interests. The fur trade depended on the indigenous population for labour, harvesting the furs and then transporting them to ports for export.

Secondly, the soil and climate of Canada was inferior to that south of the border. Farming was marginal, and it was not until the mid-19th century that commercial agriculture developed to any significant degree in Upper Canada. However, the indigenous population in Eastern Canada was decimated by the new European diseases and the wars to control the fur trade. The French were allied to the Montagnais, the Algonquin peoples and the Hurons. The Dutch and later the English were allied to the Iroquois. Only through the fur trade could the indigenous people obtain guns and ammunition. The French colonial regime developed as a commercial empire along the rivers that connected the west to Montreal. In 1649 this was disrupted when the Iroquois launched its successful war against the Hurons, then again in 1680 when they attacked the Illinois, and finally in 1689 when they launched an attack on the French. Early agriculture developed along the banks of the St. Lawrence River, on land which was not crucial to the livelihood of the indigenous population. Settler expansion into what is now Ontario took the form of treaties signed under duress that ceded the land owned by the indigenous tribes. (Innis, 1962; Eccles, 1969; Trigger, 1985)

## The Frontier in the 19th Century

The U.S. government and settlers continued the total war on the Indians through most of the 18th and 19th century. Across the continent there was the systematic destruction of villages and croplands to induce famine. By 1717 all the New England colonies offered bounties for Indian scalps, and it became a lucrative enterprise. Later, the practice was introduced in every state and the western territories. (Churchill, 1997)

In 1807 President Thomas Jefferson ordered that all Indians should be "exterminated or driven beyond the Mississippi." In 1830 the U.S. Congress passed the Indian Removal Act to do just that. In the West, the U.S. military killed Indian ponies and horses to destroy their ability to hunt and to induce famine. When the U.S. Army dispensed smallpox-infested blankets to the Mandans in North Dakota on June 20, 1837, they created an epidemic that spread as far as Saskatchewan and Alberta, killing around half of all the Blackfeet, Blood, Peigan, Pawnee, Crow and Assiniboine nations. As the buffalo were killed, the plains Indians faced starvation. (Denig, 1961; Churchill, 1997; Nash, 2000)

The fur trade created a different relationship between Europeans and the indigenous population in what is now Canada. The French could not carry out their fur trade enterprise without the labour of the indigenous peoples. French traders married Indian women, who provided them with invaluable labour and services as well as a family life. The North West Company, which moved into the prairie West in the 1770s, officially endorsed such unions. While the Hudson Bay Company officially opposed such relationships, because of practical needs this was ignored in Canada. (Van Kirk, 1980; Wolf, 1982)

At all the trading posts, mixed blood women were sought after as wives because of their many skills, especially as interpreters. This changed with the founding of the Selkirk Colony in 1811. The English came with white women and Christian missionaries. The churchmen denounced inter-racial marriages, and as Silvia Van Kirk concludes, "racism had arrived with a vengeance." Indian and Métis wives were shunned and stigmatized as were men with such relationships. Nevertheless, inter-racial relationships persisted on the Canadian prairies until the introduction of the agrarian economy after 1870, when they were "quickly shunted aside." (Van Kirk, 1980)

The settlement of the prairies by Europeans was very much part of the expansion of colonialism that took place around the world in the 19th century. Anthropologist John Bodley of Washington State University calls this "the uncontrolled frontier." Across the globe Europeans were seizing land and resources:

> Without the restraints of law, individuals used force or deception to ruthlessly and profitably obtain the land, labour, minerals, and other resources they sought. In the process, tribal societies were disrupted, weakened, and embittered, or simply exterminated. There is certainly no mystery to be explained here. (Bodley, 1999)

The patterns within the British empire were documented in the 1,000-page "Official Report and Minutes of Evidence of the British House of Commons Select Committee on Aborigines" released in 1837. The indigenous peoples were always classed as "savages." As they were less than human, it was all right to kill them. The Committee reported that in Canada it was long considered "meritorious" to kill an Indian. Settlers in South Africa regularly killed native people. In New Zealand the Maori were killed and their tattooed heads sold. In Australia it was common practice to kill Aborigines. It is not widely known but this practice was widespread in South America as well. (Bodley, 1999; Armitage, 1995)

In all areas being colonized the indigenous populations were being driven from their land by military force, most commonly by the European settlers. Africa was just the last continent to experience European imperialism, colonialism, and the invasion of the settlers. As Bodley points out, in all these cases there was "the unwillingness of governments to protect the rights of tribal peoples against the interests of intruding settlers." What was the cost in North America? There has been a serious academic debate about this. Bodley accepts the middle of the road view that the North American indigenous population probably totaled around seven million before colonization, dropped to a low of 390,000, resulting in a "depopulation" of around 6.6 million indigenous people. He documents some of the worst cases of extermination, the wars of "guns against spears." (Bodley, 1999)

The creation of Canada as a "new country" and the settlement of the prairies by Europeans takes place *within this world context*. The practices of the British and Canadian governments have to be seen as part of the general operation of the British empire at that time. That is the major shortcoming of traditional mainstream accounts of the development of the National Policy and the wheat economy.

Within the British empire, the "barbarism" of indigenous peoples meant the inferiority of moral worth. This was central to the ideological justification of colonial expansion. The English had established at an early time that the "wild Irish" were also the "savage Irish" and the enemies of England. So were the Scots of the highlands and the islands. Civilization, as the English argued, was not only a technological superiority but a moral superiority. The distant heathens were still in the state of savagery (band societies) or barbarism (tribal societies). But civilization was more than just a higher stage of economic and social development. Civilization required that a people embrace Christianity. As the view of the Irish and Indians as an inferior people became part of popular culture, or "common sense," it became an ideology of hierarchy and exploitation.

To invade a country, destroy its people, and to seize its land would have been a violation of European rules of international law and Christian concepts of a "just war." But there was no concern about such actions when they were imposed on non-civilized "savage" or "barbarian" people. Whether they were Irish, African, or American Indian, they were outside the law and outside the codes of morality of civilized countries.

## Colonization of Western Canada

Canadian political economists who have studied the National Policy and the wheat economy all conclude that the formation of Canadian Confederation was an essential first step. Without a national government of some sort, the British colonies in North America could not finance the integration of the western territories and start the process of settling the prairies.

Confederation was also necessary as part of the colonization process. As James S. Frideres stresses, "Prior to Confederation, the government was unable to effectively implement its policy of assimilation." There needed to be a national program, the formation of the Department of Indian Affairs, and a systematic way of utilizing the different Christian churches. (Frideres, 1988)

In 1869 the Parliament in England passed legislation to facilitate the transfer of Rupert's Land from the Hudson Bay Company to the Canadian government. The Canadian settlers in the eastern colonies were at least to some degree consulted over the formation of the Canadian Confederation. But it never would have occurred to the English to consult with the Indians and Métis on what was to be done with their land. They were the colonized indigenous peoples, non-whites, judged to be barbarians. Before the Métis of the Red River settlement even learned of the land transfer, land surveyor's arrived to document the change. The plains Indians learned of the transfer of land when the surveyors appeared setting the route for the Canadian Pacific Railway (CPR). (Carter, 1999)

The Métis resisted. They occupied Upper For Garry, established a provisional government, and began negotiations with the federal government to enter Confederation as a new province. With little options available at the moment, Ottawa passed the Manitoba Act in 1870 which created a very small province and granted 570,000 hectares of land to the Métis.

But the Canadian government was following the precedent of their English mentors. While supposedly negotiating in good faith, they sent a military force under the command of Lord Garnet Wolseley to reassert control over the Métis. Wolseley was a British imperialist, having served in the British army against indigenous peoples in a number of colonies. By 1872 the military were in control of Red River, the Manitoba Act had been repealed, and the Métis, robbed of their land, dispersed to the Northwest Territories. European settlers began to invade Manitoba, and the Indian and Métis population soon became a diminishing minority. (Dobbin, 1981; Friesen, 1987)

The Canadian government passed the Dominion Land Act in 1872, opening up the west to settlers from Europe and the United States. But first it was necessary to destroy the buffalo (bison) economy, defeat the resistance of the Indians and Métis, formalize the border with the United States, and establish a military/police force to control the Territories.

In 1818 the governments of Great Britain and the United States had agreed on a border from Lake of the Woods to the Rocky Mountains, and it was to follow the 49th parallel. As in Africa and the Near East, territorial state boundaries were drawn by the imperial powers without consulting the local people. Before land on the prairies could be distributed to corporations or individuals, the actual boundary had to be staked out. This was the work of the International Boundary Commission, first created by the two governments in 1816, and reconstituted for 1872-76 to survey the prairies. (Spry, 1963)

In the United States, the government and its military arm were slaughtering the buffalo as part of a policy of total war against the American Indians. After the U.S. Homestead Act was adopted in 1862 by President Abraham Lincoln, and the U.S. government gave 36 million hectares of land to the railway companies, the push began to clear the west of Indians. At one time the buffalo numbered 40 million on the Great Plains. The diseases brought by cattle killed most of them. The trade in buffalo hides, which greatly expanded after 1860, encouraged the Métis and others to massacre the herd for commercial reasons. For example, in 1873 Gabriel Dumont led a buffalo hunt out of Wood Mountain that was a brigade of one thousand Red River carts! It is generally agreed that by 1878 the buffalo were gone from the Canadian plains and the Indian and Métis people faced starvation. (Carter, 1999; Buckley, 1992; Potyondi, 1995; LaDuke, 1999)

The Indians of the Canadian plains had experienced the horrors of the plagues. The first smallpox epidemic (1780-2) killed around one half of the people. It was reported that the Chipewyans lost 90 percent of their population. The second pandemic came in 1837, moving up from the infamous biological warfare campaign of the U.S. army against the Mandan people. The Assiniboine lost entire bands, around 4,000. The Blackfoot population fell from 28,000 to 2,600. The remaining Mandans in the Dakotas dropped from 2,000 to 50, and they disappeared as a people. One third of the Crows died. They are part of what is now known as "The First Great Holocaust," the decimation of the indigenous population of the Americas. (Patterson, 1972; Buckley, 1992; Churchill, 1997; Miller, 1991; Wright, 1993)

The British Select Committee on Aborigines in 1837 argued that there were two policy lines available in the process of colonization. The first was the policy of extermination, the killing of Aboriginal people. This had been carried out in parts of the British Empire including the Caribbean, Newfoundland and Tasmania.

The second policy line was assimilation. First, the sword was necessary to demonstrate that the British government was in control and would determine the course of action. A military and police force would be created to enforce colonial policy. Their key role was to oversee the transfer of land ownership from Aboriginal people to Europeans. They would be supported by Christian missionaries. The Aboriginal people would cease to be "savages" and become civilized people, like Europeans. The key in the transformation process was to separate children from their families and communities and place them in European, Christian schools. Canadian government policy closely followed British colonial policy. (Armitage, 1995)

The Select Committee on Aborigines set forth the advantages of English civilization. In commenting on reports of their mission in North America, the Committee stated:

> True civilization and Christianity are inseparable: the former has never been found, but is a fruit of the latter. As soon as they [North American Indians] were converted they perceived the evils attendant upon their former ignorant wandering state; they began to work, which they never did

before; they perceived the advantage of cultivating the soil; they totally gave up drinking; they became industrious, sober and useful. (Cited in Armitage, 1995)

The first Indian Act was passed in 1876. Under this legislation the federal government took formal control over all First Nations in Canada. They were to be placed on reserves under the control of the federal government. Indian Agents were to administer the reserves and the financial affairs of all nations. Aboriginal people were not even informed that the legislation had been passed.

The goals of the Indian Act followed precedents established by the English and other European countries in their colonial practices. The Aboriginal people of Canada would be brought under the Christian church and educated in Christian church-run schools. They would be forced to learn English, to dress and behave like Englishmen. The Indian Act destroyed the rights of native women; the colonizers were determined to impose the Christian model, where the woman was the virtual property of her husband. Once they were assimilated Aboriginal people would leave the reserves, the system would no longer be needed, and the reserve land would be divided into personal holdings and disappear as common property. (Frideres, 1998; Wotherspoon and Satzewich, 1993)

The precedent had already been set in the Gradual Civilization Act (1857) of the United Canadas. It called for the eventual division of Indian land into individually owned private properties. Noel Dyck argues that while the Jesuits saw the Catholic faith as the primary gift to be given to the Indians, "the land speculators who held office in colonial Canada were determined that Indians should appreciate what they saw as the hallmark of civilized existence—private property." The Enfranchisement Act (1869) further reduced the degree to which the First Nations had any self government which could be used to block the colonizer's goals. Under this act the Indian ceased to be an Indian under law if he (it applied only to males) had either demonstrated that he could farm as a European or became a trained professional. The assimilation strategy had worked for the English with the rebellious Scots, and it would work with the North American Indians. Coercive tutelage would do the job. (Dyck, 1991; Armitage, 1995)

The Indians of the Canadian plains were not as ignorant as the Europeans believed. They knew that the buffalo were gone and that they had to shift to agriculture to survive. They were well aware of the fact that Indian Nations, even on the Great Plains, had engaged in agricultural practices for a long period of time. They knew they could make the change.

As Sarah Carter points out, "before European contact, agricultural products accounted for about 75 percent of the food consumed by North American Indians." The Mandan grew corn in the Dakotas and traded it with the Cree and Assiniboine. The Cree were familiar with agriculture through their long contact with the Hurons. Archaeological evidence shows that agriculture was present at Lockport, Manitoba in the fourteenth century AD. The Blackfoot cultivated along the Bow River. Tobacco was grown in Saskatchewan. The Ottawa cultivated corn and potatoes north of Lake Winnipeg and a variety of crops along the shores of the Lake of the Woods. Fur traders with the North West Company reported that many of the Indians bands "kept gardens" and even grew wheat. At Fort Clinton on the North Saskatchewan River Indians grew barley, potatoes, wheat and hops. As the fur traders and settlers came, Indians worked as hired hands. They were fully capable of making the transition to an agricultural economy. (Carter, 1990)

Big Bear, the leader of the plains Crees, believed that the best hope for survival would be if they were granted a large area of land where they could live together. The American government had originally agreed to this in treaties in the west. But the Indians were not in any position to make demands on the Canadian government. Furthermore, the priority of the government was to make the Northwest Territories safe for homesteaders and this meant that the surviving First Nations were to be dispersed to small, scattered reserves, where they would be segregated from white society. The Cree and the Assiniboine wanted a large settlement in the Cyprus Hills region, where they had historical roots. This was denied. Eventually they agreed to sign a Treaty after the Canadian government refused them rations in order to starve them into submission.

One test case showed the determination of the Canadian government. In 1876 Sitting Bull and around 2,000 people of the Lakota Sioux crossed the border into Canada to avoid being massacred by the U.S. army. This followed their victory over General George Custer at the Battle of the Little Bighorn in Montana. They wanted to stay in Canada. By 1878 their numbers had risen to 5,000. Seeing the presence of the Lakota as a threat to the policy of homesteading, the Canadian government drastically cut their food rations, forcing them to leave Canada in order to avoid starvation. (Carter, 1999; Thomson and Thomson, 2000)

## Surrendering the Land

The surrender of Aboriginal land through treaties rather than a prolonged war has been seen as the key difference between U.S. and Canadian policy. Noel Dyck argues that the government's strategy for removing the Indians from the land was pragmatic.

There was no basic principle which encouraged them not to follow general colonial policy. "The substantial costs incurred by the American army in fighting a series of protracted Indians wars horrified Canadian government leaders." (Dyck, 1992)

A necessary part of this strategy was the creation of a special military force to control the Indians and Métis. John A. Macdonald started making plans for such a force in 1869. He wanted the force to be mounted riflemen, a cavalry, and also trained in the use of artillery. William McDougall, who was appointed Lieutenant-Governor to administer the Northwest Territories, designed such a military force, based on the model of the Irish Constabulary that the English employed in rebellious Ireland. The plan was approved in 1870 by Macdonald. Captain D. R. Cameron wanted the new Northwest Mounted Police to be based on the model of the English force used in India, which included indigenous people, but this was rejected.

The NWMP was created in 1873 as a semi-military force to bring law and order to Indian country. Most of the men had considerable military experience. They were charged with the responsibility of moving the Indians to the soon-to-be-created reserves. Only whites would be employed. Scarlet coats were chosen, the colours of the military forces throughout the British empire. At the negotiations for Treaty 7, the NWMP brought cannons and fired them to remind the Indians who was in control. (Brown and Brown, 1973; Horrall, 1972)

The Indians of western Canada were removed from their land in a series of numbered treaties, negotiated between 1871 and 1899. The written texts were prepared in advance by the Canadian government. The existing texts of the treaties do not include the verbal agreements made at each treaty session. For the Indians, the verbal agreements were most important, as they included the concessions made by the government. They considered the verbal agreements to be as binding as the written text. For hundreds of years Indians had made treaties among themselves, and they were always verbal agreements, memorized and recounted by special historians.

In all of the treaties the Indians agreed to "cede, release, surrender, and yield up to the Government of Canada for Her Majesty the Queen" the land that had been theirs. The Indians had been astounded to learn that the Hudson Bay Company "owned" their land and had sold it to the Canadian government. All of the treaties guaranteed Indians land on reserves for agricultural use, cattle, farm implements, seeds, schools, and various annual monetary payments.

There were significant differences between the treaties. The size of family land grants differed. Treaty 6 included assistance if there were a famine or another pestilence. At Treaty 4 in 1874 at Fort Qu'Appelle most of the Cree and some other prominent leaders were not invited, including Chief Big Bear. For the Indians who had no notion of individual property ownership, they did not understand that they had "surrendered" the land. They thought they had agreed to joint use with the colonists. (Carter, 1999; Wotherspoon and Satzewich, 1993)

The Indians were desperate. They were on the verge of starvation and they had no alternative. They had no control over the process. There was no real understanding of what was happening because there were often no people to translate from English into the indigenous languages. They were not given the drafts in advance of the meetings to study. There was a gross inequality of bargaining power. When the Aboriginal people objected to certain parts of the draft treaties, the treaty commissioners would call on the missionaries and traders to push the government's position. Nevertheless, through hard bargaining the Indians managed to obtain some improvements in the drafts. The treaties were rushed through quickly as the settlers were on their way. (Buckley, 1991; Frideres, 1998)

The buffalo were gone, and Indians knew that they had to shift to agriculture. They petitioned the Dominion government numerous times asking for the agricultural equipment and cattle promised under the treaties. They needed temporary rations to survive until they were able to produce crops. Hunger and starvation were growing, yet this reality was denied by government officials and the local press. Settlers denounced the Indians as lazy and protested any emergency provisions they were granted. Bands began to defy government authorities and meet to plan strategies to deal with their poverty-stricken situation. Discontent peaked in 1884 and 1885. Their petitions were rejected by the governor general of the Territories and the Macdonald government. The Indians feared they would never be able to farm commercially, for the white settlers had capital and were purchasing threshing mills, mowers, reapers and rakes. (Carter, 1990)

The Métis were left out of this process completely. They had been promised 1.4 million acres of land in the Manitoba Act of 1870 but had not received it. In 1874 legislation offered "half-breed heads of families" $160 in script to purchase Dominion lands. But the location of the land to be granted or purchased was not identified. In 1875 a compromise promised that adult Métis script could be exchanged for cash, and that land for Métis children would be allotted in reserves. But speculators descended on the Métis, and much of this land was basically stolen. Around 75 percent of the "infant land" disappeared through illegal speculation. Métis lands on the river lot farms was expropriated on the grounds that the Métis were not sufficiently engaged in farming or were living in "unacceptable housing." Over 90 percent of this Métis land was confiscated.

The Métis were buffalo hunters. Every year they had traveled from the Red River to Wood Mountain and Cypress Hills for two hunts. After the debacle of 1870, most of the Métis moved to the Northwest Territories. In 1871 there were 175 families, around 1,000 people, living in Wood Mountain. The main settlements were at St. Laurent, Batoche and Duck Lake on the South Saskatchewan river. But without the buffalo, they needed security of land, and they did not have it. At the same time they saw the Canadian government making enormous grants of land to the Hudson Bay Company and the CPR. (Dobbin, 1981; Potyondi, 1995)

While the Indians eagerly awaited agricultural implements, seed, and instruction, very little came. On the reserves the Indian agent made all the decisions. As the agricultural system failed to develop as an alternative means of providing a living, the Indians became increasingly dependent on rations from the federal government. In the early 1880s the Indians began holding annual meetings to discuss the failure of the Canadian government to honour the treaties. The reaction of the Canadian government was to cut food rations. Indians at Crooked Lakes seized the government warehouse and distributed food. But the government insisted it was not going to renegotiate any of the treaties. (Dyck, 1991; Buckley, 1992)

The Indian and Métis were also treated badly by the incoming white settlers. As Patterson notes, "The white settlers frequently treated the Indian with scorn, ridicule, and contempt. They invaded his reserves, took timber off his lands, and grazed their cattle there, cutting fences to do so." Indian resentment grew, and hunger—even starvation—increased. (Patterson, 1972)

In 1884 a group of Métis went to Montana and asked Louis Riel to return to help them. Petitions to the Canadian government were denied. Big Bear, who was uniting the Cree, met with Riel in 1884. There was a crop failure that year, and they faced starvation. In March 1885 the Métis seized some guns and ammunition and declared another provisional government.

In the Northwest rebellion of 1885 few Indians participated. Some members of Big Bear's band ignored his pleas and killed six people at Frog Lake. His group was attacked by Major General T. B. Strange at Red Deer Creek, fled and then surrendered. At Battleford the whites panicked and walled themselves in the fort. Local Indians approached the fort not to lay siege but to beg for food. Some of Cree Chief Poundmaker's men had raided the town and burned some buildings. Several white men were killed. Colonel W. D. Otter launched an attack on Poundmaker and his camp at Cut Knife Hill and were driven off. Poundmaker stopped his men from killing them. Two white women had been taken prisoner at Frog Lake and were treated very well. But the Canadian white community went into a frenzy assuming that they would be sexually assaulted. (Howard, 1974; Stanley, 1970)

The Canadian government mobilized a large military force to defeat the rebellion, 3,300 from eastern Canada, 2,000 from Manitoba and the North West Territories, plus 500 from the NWMP. They had nine cannon and two machine guns. The men were the militia, almost all volunteers, who had never fired a shot in combat. They joined up to fight the "savages" and the Catholic French-speaking half-breeds. The "Jolly Boys" were going West to fight for England's flag. (Stanley, 1961; Howard, 1974)

They were commanded by General Frederick Middleton, an old imperialist who had fought for the British Empire in the famous Great Indian Mutiny in 1857 and then against the Maori in New Zealand after 1860. The total number of Métis and Indians in rebellion was around 1,000, but because of their very harsh treatment of the Métis and Indians, the Canadian government feared a general uprising. (Woodcock, 1975)

At Duck Lake in March Superintendent L. N. F. Crozier led a group of 100 Mounties and volunteers against the Métis but were soundly defeated. In a confrontation at Fish Creek Gabriel Dumont, with less then 100 men, held off an advance by Middleton's forces. But in May Middleton marched on Batoche with 850 men, cannons and machine guns. After three days of bombardment, the Métis, having run out of ammunition, fled into the woods. Shortly thereafter, Big Bear and his group were attacked and dispersed. The rebellion was over. (Stanley, 1961; Woodcock, 1975)

Reil was tried for treason and hanged. Eighteen Métis and 30 Indians were given jail sentences. Eight Indian men were executed at the NWMP barracks in Battleford before assembled Indians. Present were two full divisions of the Mounties, including a battery of regulars from Eastern Canada, 350 in all. Government militiamen and vigilantes burned and looted the homes and property of the Métis. They confiscated arms and horses from Indians who participated in the rebellion and withheld their annuities. As Sarah Carter has written, "If there was a shred of tolerance before, or the possibility of working towards a progressive partnership, it was shattered in 1885, as thereafter Aboriginal people were viewed as a threat to the property and safety of the white settlers."(Patterson, 1972; Carter, 1999)

Edgar Dewdney and Hayter Reed, who ran the Department of Indian Affairs, began the "assault on the tribal system." With the introduction of the pass system, where Indians could not leave the reserve without the permission of the Indian agent, the reserves became concentration camps. It was deemed necessary to isolate Indians from the Métis troublemakers and white society in general. Vagrancy laws were passed to segregate Indians from white areas. Reed referred to the Aboriginal people as a "foreign element" in Canadian society, a source of danger, who had to be broken up, disbanded and assimilated. (Carter, 1999; Bourgeault, 1988)

In a letter to the *Irish World* published just five days after he was hanged, Louis Riel set forth the case against the "blood-thirsty British Empire" in Canada and elsewhere:

> Our lands have since been torn from us, and given to landgrabbers who never saw the country...The riches which these lands produce are drained out of the country and sent over to England to be consumed by a people that fatten on a system that pauperizes us. The result is extermination or slavery. Against this monstrous tyranny we have been forced to rebel...
>
> The behaviour of the English is not singular. Follow those pirates the world over, and you will find that everywhere, and at all times, they adopt the same tactics, and operate on the same thievish lines. Ireland, India, the Highlands of Scotland, Australia, and the Isles of the Indian Ocean—all these countries are the sad evidences, and their native populations are the witnesses to England's land robberies. (cited in Bourgeault, 1988)

## Reserves and Indian Farming

The Indians faced many obstacles to farming on the reserves. Their situation was made even more difficult by changes that came after the rebellion. Under the 1876 Indian Act, Indians could not take homesteads. They were confined to farming on reserves.

The pass system was demanded by the white settlers. In fact, they wanted all Indians and Métis removed to the north, away from farming land. Indian children were segregated in industrial schools and later in residential schools run by the Christian churches. If their parents refused, they were subject to criminal penalties. Ceremonies like the Sun Dance were banned. They were required to comply with the Canadian game laws. Indian agents assumed even more power over Aboriginal people. (Buckley, 1992; Carter, 1999; Dosman, 1972)

Government support for the transition to farming was guaranteed in the Treaties. But there was a general reluctance to make this work. Indians found that there were no funds available to start farming or buy cattle. There were no animals for plowing. Reserve land could not be used to get a mortgage. There was a general ban on credit. The Indian agents were determined to keep their own costs low. Nevertheless, there were successes. Some bands acquired machinery and produced good crops. Aboriginal wheat farmers even won prizes at agricultural fairs. (Carter, 1990; Buckley, 1992)

The white settlers complained about competition from Indian farmers. They did not want to see Indians begin cattle ranching for this would threaten their markets. The settlers around North Battleford protested to the Indian Agency when local Indians became good wheat farmers and began to take their markets. The settlers put tremendous pressure on the Indian agents to surrender treaty land to whites for settlement. They demanded the right to cut hay on reserve land. They strongly objected when government agencies purchased any agricultural products from Indian farmers. The North Battleford *Gazette* insisted that the government give up the project of teaching the Indians "the ways of the white man." There were numerous incidents where white settlers entered Indian land to cut wood and hay. Pushed by the settlers, Hayter Reed and the Indian agents did their best to ease the process of surrender and sale of reserve land. (Carter, 1990)

Hayter Reed, who became Indian commissioner, had a dramatic impact on prairie Indians. He was a career military officer who moved into the Department of Indian Affairs in 1881 and set policy in the period following the rebellion. When he was an Indian agent, he described the Battleford Indians as "the scum of the plains" and "parasites" living off the work of others. He was adamant that he was making policy and did not believe the Indians should be consulted on anything. His goal was to assimilate the Indians into white society, break up the reserve system, eliminate tribalism, and introduce Indians to private property in land. His policies were strongly supported by Edgar Dewdney, the Indian commissioner.

Reed introduced the system of "peasant farming," where each Indian family would be given 40 acres of reserve land, hoes and scythes, and encouraged to farm on a subsistence basis. They were instructed to grow root crops. No Indian could sell a product or buy a farm input without the permission of the Indian agent. The peasant farming system would reduce government costs and eliminate competition with white farmers. As Helen Buckley has pointed out, the policy of subsistence farming was copied from the U.S. government, where its implementation was designed to continue segregation and poverty. Discouraged, many Indians gave up the attempt to farm. By 1896 reserve land under cultivation had declined by 50 percent. When the Liberals were elected in 1896, they increased the pressure on the bands to surrender their reserve land; in return, they introduced a new system of welfare. Because of poverty, disease and malnutrition, the Indian population on prairie reserves declined between 30 and 50 percent from the mid-1880s to World War I. (Buckley, 1992; Carter, 1990)

Sarah Carter stresses that the agricultural policies imposed on the Indians by the U.S. and Canadian governments were not unique. It was the pattern found throughout the British empire where white European settlers were farming in competition with indigenous peoples. In Kenya, the best land was taken from Africans and given to white settlers. The infrastructure was designed to aid the Europeans. Heavy taxes were imposed on indigenous farmers to encourage them to give up independent farming and work as farm labourers for the white settlers.

In South Africa, Europeans seized the best farm land from the Africans. Nevertheless, small African farmers expanded their production and began to compete with white farmers. The result was "a barrage of legislative measures designed to inhibit African farming, while white agriculture was aided by a massive program of grants and subsidies."

In Rhodesia (now Zimbabwe), the British colonial government adopted a range of policies to "ensure that African farmers were not in a position to compete with immigrant European farmers, who benefited from special tax measures and favourable marketing arrangements." (Carter, 1990)

In commenting on colonial agricultural policy in Africa, Montague Yudelman concludes: "The whole system of economic and social control was geared to protecting European incomes and maintaining high levels of living among the European minority at the expense of the African majority." How different was that from Canadian policy on the prairies? (Yudelman, 1964, cited in Carter, 1990)

European colonists introduced similar policies in Latin America. The governments of Brazil and Peru have been removing tribal people from their land in the Amazon Basin right up until the end of the 20th century. Dispossession from lands is still happening in Bolivia. In Columbia indigenous peoples who were not Christians were denied land rights. Indian rights were recognized in Venezuela in 1960 but have not been enforced against invasions. Governments in Chile and Argentina have pushed for individual ownership of lands originally guaranteed to indigenous peoples. (Bodley, 1999)

The Australian government never recognized any land right for the Aborigines, even though they had been there for 50,000 years. The first rights were granted in 1976, and subsequent governments are pushing to have the lands individualized. The British Treaty of Waitangi (1840) gave the Maori in New Zealand exclusive rights to most of the land. By 1940 the Maori had been stripped of 94 percent of this treaty land. The colonial pattern was clear around the world: indigenous peoples have had no rights to the land they occupy or owned by local laws, traditions and treaties. They were to be taken by colonists, usually with the acquiescence of the imperial and national governments. What was happening in Canada and on the prairies was the norm in the world of capitalist imperialism, and it was supported by British colonial policy. (Bodley, 1999)

The indigenous population of the Americas had a well developed agriculture before the arrival of the Europeans. In North America agriculture was the basic means of subsistence. All of the Indian bands and tribes in the Eastern United States had developed highly productive agricultural systems. The Iroquois and the Hurons were advanced, agricultural societies.

By around 600 A.D. the Mississippi Culture, based on the cultivation of corn, beans, squash and sunflowers, was spreading up the river valley. The development of the Flint variety of corn allowed the agricultural system to be adopted into North and South Dakota. The spread of this culture onto the Canadian prairies began but seems to have been abandoned after the beginning of a colder climate around 1500. But agricultural culture was well known to the Indians of the prairie provinces. (Bryan, 1991; Ward, 1995)

The indigenous peoples of Mesoamerica and the Andean highlands were among the most highly developed agriculturalists in the world. When Christopher Columbus and other Spanish explorers reached the American continents, they thought they had reached Paradise or Utopia. Indeed, one Spanish lawyer wrote a two-volume work arguing that the Garden of Eden was in South America. The diversified agricultural systems, based on irrigation, were far in advance of anything that existed in Europe. The Spaniards were in awe of the size and beauty of the cities they found, with their massive architectural centres, engineering achievements and complex irrigation systems. Their highly productive agricultural systems were developed without draft animals or the wheel. But the Europeans saw only a chance to seize the land, transform the peasants into slave labour, and maximize profits. (Warnock, 1987)

## Conclusion

There were obvious differences between the European colonists and the Aboriginal population. They came from different cultures. They had different levels of economic development. They had different religious beliefs. They had different concepts of community and family. They had different views of appropriate sexual behaviour. But at the core of all the disputes is the fact that the European and Canadian governments took the land and the resources from the Aboriginal people by force and threat of force and gave it to white, European settlers.

This is this central fact which distinguishes Aboriginal people from immigrants of colour. Aboriginal people are the First Nations. They were here before all the rest of us immigrants. This was their land, the home of their nations. By the time non-white immigrants started to come to Canada in large numbers, most of the Aboriginal population was being held on reserves in a form of internal colonialism.

That is why Canada is referred to as a "white settler society" or a "white Dominion." In contrast to most other areas of the world subjected to European colonialism, the white immigrants came to outnumber and marginalize the indigenous population. This is the most important characteristic to be listed when describing Canada's political culture. The racism towards Aboriginal people found in the popular culture or "common sense" is an outgrowth of our historical past. Aboriginal people did not disappear as expected. After World War I they began to increase in numbers and demand recognition as distinct people.

In most of the areas of the world under colonial control, the move towards independence came in the post World War II period and was virtually completed by the end of the 1960s. While these former colonies have not done well economically, they have at least ended the formal structure of racism that was a central part of colonial policy. In almost all of the former colonies, whites no longer rule over non-whites. But there has been no clear break in the policies of the countries like Canada where the European immigrants became the majority. Racist policies existed for many years. Racist attitudes towards indigenous populations persist to the present.

The National Policy and the wheat economy together established the plan for the western Canadian region after the collapse of the fur trade. The key to this was the removal of the indigenous peoples from their land and their segregation on the reserves. This aspect of the policy is generally ignored in the political economy studies on the National Policy. The government's program for the Aboriginal people closely followed patterns throughout the European colonial system.

In Canada the racist attitudes towards the Aboriginal population were well entrenched in the structures of society and popular culture before the wave of new European settlers arrived to homestead the prairies. The "savages" were a barrier to civilization and progress. The government's assimilation policies were similar to those found in other European colonies.

While social scientists and other scientists now agree that there is no such thing as a genetic link to a concept of race, it nevertheless remains a part of popular culture or "common sense." Stanley Greenberg, whose approach I have largely adopted as a theoretical model, argues that while racial domination is very close to class domination, we should not conclude that it does not have a status of its own. "Racial prejudice and group sentiment cannot be dismissed as superstructure or false consciousness." He argues that racial categories, commonly identified now as differences in skin colour, are real and rooted in "shared historical experiences, language facility, kinship ties, affinity in values and modes of behaviour." But this does not tell us when these sentiments will take a political form for group members. (Greenberg, 1980)

Racism directed against Aboriginal people in Saskatchewan has its roots in British imperialism and colonialism, the removal of the indigenous people from their land by military force and threat of force, and their segregation on rural reserves removed from mainstream society. The state, the business elite, the European settlers, and the common people all identified the indigenous people as "barbarians," barriers to civilization and progress.

Racism is not limited to the class of people who initially benefit from group stratification. As Eugene Genovese argues, and I agree, an ideology of racism emerges from a material condition but can assume an autonomous identity. It is re-enforced by the role of the state, the political elite, and the institutions of ideology. But it is also reproduced through the family, the community, the church and the society in general. As Greenberg has shown for Northern Ireland, Alabama, South Africa and Israel, a system of race hierarchy can be maintained through the process of transformation from a colonial system of land ownership and exploitation to a modern advanced capitalist system. In modern capitalist agriculture, racialization is often maintained through a system of land ownership by whites and non-white farm workers. (Genovese, 1965; Greenberg, 1980)

There is evidence that across Canada and in Saskatchewan we are witnessing a rise in racial antagonism towards Aboriginal people. Almost one-half of all First Nations people in Saskatchewan now live in urban centres and most are forced to locate in low income ghettos. All across Canada those who still live on reserves and in the rural communities are pushing their land claims and demanding access to the natural resources now reserved almost exclusively to whites and corporate interests. Under the Treaty Land Entitlement process in Saskatchewan, Indian bands are negotiating settlements, acquiring compensation, establishing urban reserves and buying farmland. In the past they leased out their farmland to whites. Now there are community demands to farm the land themselves.

The growing resentment towards Aboriginal people is commonly described by the media as "right wing populism." Once again, there is a push to eliminate reserves and divide up the land among individuals, to instill the ideology of capitalism and private ownership of property. This conflict will not disappear. It will continue to grow in political importance in Saskatchewan. The Aboriginal population is increasing, more young people are completing high school, and more are going to post-secondary institutions of learning. Aboriginal businesses are proliferating. In the future the economy will have to depend more on the Aboriginal labour force. Currently, this is an area of major discontent.

## References

Andrews, K.R., N.P. Canny and P.E.H. Hair, eds. 1978. *The Westward Enterprise: English Activities in Ireland, the Atlantic and America, 1480-1650*. Liverpool: Liverpool University Press.

Armitage, Andrew. 1999. "Comparing Aboriginal Policies: The Colonial Legacy." In Hylton, pp. 61-77.

Armitage, Andrew. 1995. *Comparing the Policy of Aboriginal Assimilation: Australia, Canada and New Zealand*. Vancouver: University of British Columbia Press.

Bodley, John H. 1999. *Victims of Progress*. London: Mayfield Publishing.

Bolaria, B. Singh and Peter S. Li, eds. 1998. *Racial Oppression in Canada*. Toronto: Garamond Press.

Bourgeault, Ron G. 1988. "Race and Class Under Mercantilism: Indigenous People in Nineteenth Century Canada." In Bolaria and Li, pp. 41-70.

Brown, Caroline and Lorne Brown. 1973. *An Unauthorized History of the RCMP*. Toronto: James Lewis and Samuel.

Bryan, Liz. 1991. *The Buffalo People: Prehistoric Archaeology on the Canadian Plains*. Edmonton: University of Alberta Press.

Carter, Sarah. 1999. *Aboriginal People and Colonizers of Western Canada to 1900*. Toronto: University of Toronto Press.

Carter, Sarah. 1990. *Lost Harvests, Prairie Indian Reserve Farmers and Government Policy*. Montreal: McGill-Queen's University Press.

Churchill, Ward.1997. *A Little Matter of Genocide: Holocaust and Denial in the Americas, 1492 to the Present*. San Francisco: City Light Books.

Churchill, Ward. 1997. "Nits Make Lice: The Extermination of North American Indians, 1607-1996." In Churchill, pp. 129-288.

Denig, Edwin T. 1961. *Five Indian Tribes of the Upper Missouri*. Norman: University of Oklahoma Press.

Dobbin, Murray. 1981. *One-And-A-Half Men*. Vancouver: New Star Books.

Dosman, Edgar J. 1972. *Indians: The Urban Dilemma*. Toronto: McClelland and Stewart.

Dyck, Noel. 1991. *What is the Indian 'Problem'": Tutelage and Resistance in Canadian Indian Administration*. St. John's: Memorial University of Newfoundland

Eccles, E.C. 1969. *The Canadian Frontier, 1534-1760*. New York: Holt Rinehart and Winston.

Fanon, Frantz. 1963. *The Wretched of the Earth*. New York: Grove Press.

Frideres, James S. 1998. *Aboriginal Peoples in Canada: Contemporary Conflicts*. Scarborough: Prentice Hall Allyn and Bacon Canada. Fifth edition.

Frideres, James S. 1988. "Institutional Structures and Economic Deprivation: Native People in Canada," in Bolaria and Li, pp. 71-100.

Friesen, Gerald. 1987. *The Canadian Prairies: A History*. Toronto: University of Toronto Press.

Genovese, Eugene D. 1965. *The Political Economy of Slavery*. New York: Pantheon.

Greenberg, Stanley B. 1980. *Race and State in Capitalist Development: Comparative Perspectives*. New Haven: Yale University Press.

Howard, Joseph. 1974. *Strange Empire: Louis Riel and the Métis People*. Toronto: James Lewis and Samuel.

Hylton, John H., ed. 1999. *Aboriginal Self-Government in Canada: Current Trends and Issues*. Saskatoon: Purich Publishing Ltd.

Innis, Harold A. 1962. *The Fur Trade In Canada*. Toronto: University of Toronto Press.

Jenkins, Richard. 1999. "Ethnicity etcetera: Social Anthropological Points of View." *Ethnic and Racial Studies*, Vol. 19, No. 4, October, pp. 807-822.

Jennings, Francis. 1975. *The Invasion of America: Indians, Colonialism, and the Cant of Conquest*. Chapel Hill, N.C.: University of North Carolina Press.

Jones, Howard Mumford. 1952. *O Strange New World*. New York: Viking Press.

LaDuke, Winona. 1999. *All Our Relations: Native Struggles for Land and Life*. Cambridge: South End Press

LaFeber, Walter. 1963. *The New Empire: An Interpretation of American Expansion 1860-1898*. Ithaca: Cornell University Press.

Magdoff, Harry 1978. *Imperialism: From the Colonial Age to the Present*. New York: Monthly Review Press.

Mandelbaum, David G. 1979. *The Plains Cree: An Ethnographic, Historical and Comparative Study*. Regina: Canadian Plains Research Centre.

Maslowe, John. 1972. *Cecil Rhodes: The Anatomy of Empire*. London: Eleck.

Memmi, Albert. 1965. *The Colonizer and the Colonized*. Boston: Beacon Press.

Miller, J.R., ed. 1991. *Sweet Promises: A Reader on Indian-White Relations in Canada*. Toronto: University of Toronto Press.

Nash, Gary B. 2000. *Red, White & Black: The Peoples of Early North America*. Upper Saddle River, N.J.: Prentice Hall.

Parry, J.H. 1961. *The Establishment of the European Hegemony 1415-1715*. New York: Harper & Row.

Patterson, E. Palmer. 1972. *The Canadian Indian: A History Since 1500*. Don Mills: Collier-Macmillian Canada Ltd.

Pennington, Loren E. 1978. "The Amerindian in English Promotional Literature, 1575-1625." In Andrews, pp. 175-194.

Poirier, Thelma, ed. 2000. *Wood Mountain Uplands: From the Big Muddy to the Frenchman River.* Wood Mountain, Sk: Wood Mountain Historical Society.

Potyondi, Barry. 1995. *In Palliser's Triangle: Living in the Grasslands, 1850-1930.* Saskatoon: Purich Publishing.

Pratt, Julius W. 1959. *Expansionists of 1898: The Acquisition of Hawaii and the Spanish Islands.* Gloucester, Mass.: Peter Smith.

Quinn, David B. 1962. *Raleigh and the British Empire.* New York: Collier Books.

Rodney, Walter. 1974. *How Europe Underdeveloped Africa.* Washington, D.C.: Howard University Press.

Satzewich, Vic and Terry Wotherspoon. 1993. *First Nations: Race, Class and Gender Relations.* Scarborough: Nelson Canada.

Stanley, George F.G. 1970. *The Birth of Western Canada: A History of the Riel Rebellions.* Toronto: University of Toronto Press.

Stevenson, Michael. 1992. "Columbus and the War on Indigenous Peoples." *Race & Class,* Vol. 33, No. 3, pp. 27-45.

Stonechild, Blair and Bill Waiser. 1997. *Loyal Till Death: Indians and the North-West Rebellion.* Calgary: Fifth House.

Thomson, Elizabeth and Rory Thomson. 2000. "The Lakota." In Poirier, pp. 66-85.

Trigger, Bruce G. 1969. *The Huron: Farmers of the North.* Toronto: Holt, Rinehart and Winston.

Trigger, Bruce C. 1985. *Natives and Newcomers: Canada's 'Heroic Age' Reconsidered.* Montreal: McGill-Queen's University Press.

Van Alstyne, Richard W. 1960. *The Rising American Empire.* Oxford: Basil Blackwell.

Van Kirk, Sylvia. 1980. *'Many Tender Ties': Women in the Fur-Trade Society in Western Canada, 1670-1870.* Winnipeg: Watson and Dwyer.

Ward, Donald. 1995. *The People: A Historical Guide to the First Nations of Alberta, Saskatchewan and Manitoba.* Calgary: Fifth House Publishers.

Warnock, John W. 1987. *The Politics of Hunger: The Global Food System.* Toronto: Methuen.

Wolf, Eric. 1982. *Europe and the People Without History.* Berkeley: University of California Press.

Woodcock, George. 1975. *Gabriel Dumont: The Métis Chief and His Lost World.* Edmonton: Hurtig Publishers.

Wright, Ronald. 1993. *Stolen Continents: The 'New World' Through Indian Eyes.* Toronto: Penguin Books.

Yudelman, Montague. 1964. *Africans on the Land: Economic Problems of African Agricultural Development in Southern, Central and East Africa, with Special Reference to Southern Rhodesia.* Cambridge: Harvard University Press.

# Chapter 8

————○————

# THE PERSISTENCE OF PATRIARCHY
# IN SASKATCHEWAN

---

The Mayor of Elbow, Saskatchewan pleads guilty to 11 incidents of sexual assault against women employed by the village. He "groped" seven women over a period of six years and made sexual advances. Those who file the charges against him are called "troublemakers," and there is an outpouring of sympathy for the man. Prayers are said for him in the Lutheran church, and he is described as "a very Christian man." A woman who is a village councillor sponsors a party for him and there is a move to petition the minister of justice for leniency. There is no support expressed for the women who have been molested. (Warick, 2003)

The NDP government of Lorne Calvert announces that they will not co-operate in any way with the federal government to enforce the Canadian Firearms Act, the gun registry program. Women's organizations pushed hard for this legislation. The Coalition For Gun Control expresses dismay. From the beginning, the NDP government strongly opposed the legislation and challenged it in court. They were supported by the Liberal Party, the Saskatchewan Party, the Conservative Party, the Canadian Alliance Party and men in right wing political and hunting organizations. Public opinion polls consistently show that across Canada there is strong majority support for the legislation. The lowest support is always in Saskatchewan, where ownership of firearms is considered a basic human right for men. (Hall, 2002a; Cuthand, 2003; Coalition for Gun Control, July 2003)

Deborah Higgins, the NDP Minister of Labour, announces that the government has "no intention of introducing wide-reaching pay equity legislation." For over ten years the Pay Equity Coalition and the Saskatchewan Federation of Labour have pushed for such legislation. Alberta is the only other province without such legislation. Between 1991 and 1995, Saskatchewan was the only province in Canada where the gap in income between men and women widened. The 2001 census found that Regina had the widest gap in income between men and women, $14,000, of any major city in Canada. (Hall, 2002b; Canada, 1997)

In their budget of March 2002, the NDP government of Lorne Calvert eliminates the Women's Secretariat and the Minister Responsible for the Status of Women. Women across the province are shocked and start a petition drive in protest. The government does not change its position. Furthermore, in the same budget they substantially cut the funding of the Saskatchewan Human Rights Commission, which defends the rights of disabled persons, marginalized women, visible minorities, the Aboriginal community, gays and lesbians, and people on social assistance. Again, protests have no affect on the government. (Bangsund, 2002)

Two public opinion polls taken in 2003 revealed that around 60 percent of Saskatchewan residents oppose same sex marriage, the highest opposition of any province. A public opinion poll conducted by the Social Research Unit of the University of Saskatchewan in 2001 found that 55 percent of those surveyed did not believe that "homosexual couples" should be able to adopt children. Fifty percent of respondents believe that religious instruction should be included in public school education, and 63 percent feel that the Christian Lord's Prayer should be part of the school day in public schools. (Centre for Research and Information on Canada, June 2003; *Leader-Post*, September 6, 2003; Klein, 2001)

In rural Tisdale three adult, white men sexually assault a 12 year old Aboriginal girl after giving her beer. The town rallies behind the men. Aboriginal organizations, the Saskatchewan Coalition Against Racism and the Saskatchewan Action Committee on the Status of Women demand strong action by the government and jail sentences. Two are acquitted and the third receives a short house arrest. (*Leader Post*, September 5, 2003)

These are just a few of the stories that we regularly hear in the province of Saskatchewan. Patriarchy and patriarchal values are deeply entrenched in the political culture. There has been an ebb and flow in the women's movement in the province. In the early 1970s there was a strong women's movement, and progressive changes were made. There was a bit of a revival during the 1980s, in reaction to the policies of the Tory government of Grant Devine, but after the election of the NDP government in 1991 the women's movement all but disappeared. Even the Saskatchewan Action Committee on the Status of Women began to fade away.

One good indicator of the low status of women in Saskatchewan is the provincial system of child care. When child care legislation was introduced by the NDP government of Allan Blakeney in 1974, they pledged to create 13,500 child care spaces in day care centres within five years. In 1994 Saskatchewan had by far the lowest per capita budget for child care in western Canada. By 1995 there were only 7,266 spaces, and of these, 36 percent were in private homes, by far the highest in Canada. Saskatchewan had the lowest ratio of spaces to children of working mothers, and in 2001 the province still ranked last in Canada. The basic subsidy for child care for low income families on social assistance remained at around $240 per month, and it had not risen since 1982. In 2003 a lone parent woman in Saskatchewan on social assistance had to find an additional $3000 per year to pay for child care. (Philip, 2002; Childcare Resources and Research Unit, 1995)

The most vulnerable people on social assistance in Saskatchewan are lone parent women with children. In 1998 around 66 percent lived below the official poverty line; of those under 25, 83 percent. As of early 2002, their basic social assistance rates were still stuck at the 1982 level. When the new Child Tax Benefit was introduced in 1998, it was designed by the provincial government to discriminate against lone parent families. No additional money was to go to support poor children if their mother had chosen or was forced to stay home and care for them after their male partners had left. (Saskatchewan, 1994; 1998)

Defenders of the policies of the Saskatchewan government argue that they reflect broad support among the population. And there is considerable evidence that there is public support for traditional patriarchal values. For example, in 1991 a plebiscite was held in conjunction with the provincial election. It asked: "Should the government of Saskatchewan pay for abortions?" They are covered under Saskatchewan medicare. A surprising 63 percent voted "no."

One of the most conservative women's organizations in Canada is REAL Women, and they claim that around one half of their 50,000 members are from Saskatchewan. They are strong supporters of traditional patriarchal values. Their role has been to oppose the National Action Committee on the Status of Women. They support "permanent marriage" and want divorce to be made more difficult, oppose abortion, oppose the gay rights movement and human rights commissions, oppose day care services and argue that women should be paid to stay at home and care for their children. They oppose premarital sex, do not want sex education taught in the schools, oppose planned parenthood clinics, oppose funding for homes for battered women, and insist that the father should be the head of the household. They oppose pay equity legislation, gun control, affirmative action programs, and they want prostitution to be made illegal. They are strongest in rural areas. As they are close to Christian fundamentalism, they support public funds for religious schools. While they want married women to stay home and care for their own children, like many conservative men, they think lone parent women on social assistance should be required to find child care and get out of the house and work. (Polachic, 1994; www.realwomenca.com)

How do women fare in the Saskatchewan economy? Around 240,000 women work, including 65 percent of all married women. In 1995 one-third of women earned less than $10,000 and another 32 percent earned between $10,000 and $20,000. A total of 70 percent of all part time workers were women, and Saskatchewan led the country in part time workers. Women were much more likely to be moonlighters than men, and again Saskatchewan was first in the country with the percentage of workers holding down two jobs. More than 60 percent of full time women workers were in clerical, sales, service and agricultural occupations, among the lowest paying jobs. (Saskatchewan Women's Secretariat, 1997a; 1997b)

Traditional patriarchal values are deeply entrenched in Saskatchewan. They are particularly strong in our rural areas and small towns. The inequalities between men and women, and male domination of the major institutions in our society, continue as a major social problem. The ongoing problem cannot be confronted in a serious way until the origins of patriarchy and how it came to be so pronounced in Saskatchewan are understood.

## What Is a Family?

In all human societies there are groups of people who call themselves members of a family. But there have been a wide variety of types of families across human history. In traditional western Christian societies, the core of a family has been a sexual union between a man and a woman, who form a household for purposes of producing and raising children. In most human societies, this basic union is given some permanence through the institution of marriage, a social contract. In state societies, marriage is supported by a range of legislation.

In North America the social ideal is the nuclear family of the husband, the wife and the children. But around the world we find a lot of different types of families. In

many societies we find extended families which include grandparents and other relatives. In East Africa, people commonly define their families in hundreds of people related through blood and marriage. In the Celtic Irish clan the basic unit consisted of a
four-generation family. The view that families have "clear boundaries," put forth by
British anthropologist Bronislaw Malinowski, has been challenged by modern anthropologists. Families do not always have fathers. They are not always nurturing. A
married couple and their children may live in a large house with other people, which
was common in North America among indigenous tribes based on agriculture. There
are quite a few examples of "hut societies" in Africa and South America where men
live in houses with other men and women and children live in separate houses. In
matrilineal societies it is common for a husband to live with his own kin and not with
his wife. How societies choose to raise their children is a cultural matter which
evolves historically. Many traditional family practices around the world were destroyed under the impact of western imperialism, colonialism and Christianity. (Collier *et al.*, 1997; Mies, 1986)

Anthropologist George P. Murdock categorized 1,179 band and tribal societies
in his *Ethnographic Atlas*. In sixty-nine percent of these the women who were married
left their families and kinship group and moved to the home of either the husband or
one of the husband's paternal relatives. This is called patrilocal residence. In thirteen
percent of these societies, the husband left his family and kinship group and moved
to the home of his wife or her maternal relatives. This is called matrilocal residence.
In only nine percent of these societies did a married couple have the free choice of determining whether they wanted to live with either the relatives of the husband or the
wife. There is also a close relationship between residence patterns and kinship systems. Patrilineal descent, where children are considered part of a male descent group,
is five times more common than matrilineal descent. (Murdock, 1967)

Band and tribal societies are commonly seen as egalitarian. Productive resources
are held in common, and all people have access to the means of production. Because
of the social commitment to reciprocity and redistribution, no one in these societies
suffers from an economic hardship. But this does not necessarily carry over to the
area of social organization for the purposes of reproduction. All societies construct
rules to regulate sexual behaviour, even band societies. Hierarchy and stratification
are culturally created and are found to exist within families. There is evidence that
even in the most egalitarian band societies, women have a lower status than men. In
making political decisions, for example, men in band societies have more authority
than women. We also see that as societies advance economically, and move to stratifi-

cation and the formation of the state, there is a decline of egalitarianism and fewer women have high status. For example, polygyny (one man and a number of wives) is much more common around the world than polyandry (one wife and several husbands). In a wide variety of societies it is common to find that men with wealth and power have more than one wife, and they may also have concubines and female slaves. (Miller, 1993; Harris, 1978)

The traditional father-led family with children remains the social ideal in Canada. But the actual family has been changing over the years, even in Saskatchewan. According to the 2001 Census, the traditional family of a married couple with children had declined to only 28 percent of all Saskatchewan households. The number of married couples who choose not to have children, or have them later in life, is rising; they constituted 22 percent of households. Single persons living alone accounted for 28 percent of all Saskatchewan households, lone-parent families 10 percent, and common law families, around six percent. Another three percent of households are "others," including gay and lesbian couples and friends living together. The official government definition of family has not kept up with social changes because of conservative pressure to maintain the father-led nuclear family as the ideal. (Census Canada, 1996, 2001)

## What Is Patriarchy?

Today in almost all states and societies around the world we find that the patriarchal family order is the norm. What do we mean when we refer to patriarchy or a patriarchal order? Feminists most often cite the definition provided by Heidi Hartmann, widely circulated during the second phase of feminism in the 1970s: "We can usefully define patriarchy as a set of social relations between men, which have a material base, and which, though hierarchical, establish or create interdependence and solidarity among men that enable them to dominate women." (Hartmann, 1981)

Thus, as Ellen Mutari argues, "even though men of different classes, races and ethnic groups have different places in the social hierarchy, they all benefit from being men." As one example, within the traditional household, "men benefit from women's unpaid domestic labour." And this has not changed much over the years. The 2001 Census revealed that women still do twice as much housework as men, even though both will probably we working outside the home. (Mutari, 2000; Anderssen, 2003)

Most people define patriarchy as a system where men dominate women and children. Originally patriarchy referred to the family system which developed in the Near East, North Africa, Greece and Rome, and formed the foundation of the European family. It had a rather narrow meaning, referring to the fact that in these societies the man was culturally and legally the head of his household and had almost complete economic and legal power over the wives, children, concubines and slaves who were considered part of his family. In Latin the word *familia* originally meant "the total number of slaves belonging to one man." Roman law defined the family as "the organization of a number of persons, bond and free, into a family under paternal power for the purpose of holding lands and for the care of flocks and herds." The patriarchal family had a material base. (O'Faolain and Martines, 1973; Engels, 1967; Lerner, 1986)

Sociologist Michael Mann calls this "traditional patriarchy." Power is held by the man, the head of the household, and there is a clear separation of spheres of life between public and private. Married women are to be confined to the house and cannot appear in public without a chaperone or without their faces veiled. The public sphere is the man's world. Many cultures around the world maintain this form of the patriarchal family. (Mann, 1986)

It is often argued that when this family structure changes patriarchy declines. Some social scientists insist that patriarchy ends with the legal recognition of women as persons in European societies. But others hold that the family remains hierarchically structured when men are still recognized as the head of the family, where patrilineal descent remains the dominant order, and when women surrender their family names on marriage. When married women are working out of the house, the man's job is still considered the most important. As in Canada today, women remain the primary care givers. (Armstrong and Armstrong, 1984; Mackie, 1983; Wilson, 1986)

But many social scientists argue that patriarchy is not just a question of the structure of the family. Male dominance over women is found in society in general. In industrialized countries today most women are working, but gender segregation remains in the workplace. Men's base of power remains in the ownership of private property, in the economic area. They own wealth and control corporations, businesses, and financial institutions. They also dominate the key institutions of state power: the military, the police, the legal and penal systems, and the state bureaucracies. Furthermore, they control the important institutions of ideological power: the universities, the educational system, the mass media and the religious orders. Social scientists call these "gendered institutions." The terms used to describe this broader system of gender stratification include "social patriarchy," "neo-patriarchy" or "public patriarchy." Control over these key institutions serves to support the continuation of patriarchal power within the family. These institutions all play a central role in the socialization process and re-enforce the patriarchal ideal. (Lerner, 1986; Clement and Myles, 1994)

## The Origin of Patriarchy

The first important general social science work on the family and the institution of patriarchy was Frederick Engels' *The Origin of the Family, Private Property and the State*. Published in 1884, it drew heavily on Lewis Henry Morgan's *Ancient Society* which was based on the evidence that was known from Australian, Iroquois, Aztec, Greek and Roman societies. Morgan was greatly influenced by the development of evolutionary theory in Europe, and in particular the work of Herbert Spencer and Charles Darwin. He followed their general classification of societies of his day as having moved from "savagery" (hunter-gatherer) to "barbarism" (horticultural and pastoral) to "civilization" (plow agriculture).

Engels was also influenced by J. J. Bachofen's book, *Das Mutterrecht* (Mother Right). Bachofen was also a social evolutionist who followed Darwin. He saw society evolving from a primitive state where there was no marriage and open sexuality to civilization which was based on patriarchy. He did an extensive study of mythologies from different pre-historic cultures and concluded that early human primitive societies were egalitarian and matrilineal. (Bachofen, 1967)

Engels' work was the first to argue that there was a direct link between how a society was organized for the purposes of production and distribution and the structure of family life and the status of women. He argued that in hunter-gatherer societies both women and men would have sexual relationships outside marriage. In societies based on horticulture and domestication of animals, Morgan and Engels both concluded that marriage became more structured. Parents play a role in the selection of marriage partners, and the union is cemented through the exchange of goods. In horticultural societies matrilineal descent is often found. Women provide most if not all of the labour in food production and have a significant role in decision making.

According to Engels the fundamental change comes with the development of state societies, stratification into social classes, and private ownership of property or property rights. In *all* state societies there is patriarchal rule, the domination of women by men, monogamous marriage with fidelity demanded of women, the double standard on pre-marital and extra-marital sex for men, prostitution, and male control of social power. In Engels' famous words: "The overthrow of the mother right was the *world historical defeat of the female sex*. The man took command in the home also; the woman was degraded and reduced to servitude; she became the slave of his lust and a mere instrument for the production of children."

Engels went on to add that "The first class opposition that appears in history coincides with the development of the antagonism between man and woman in monogamous marriage, and the first class oppression coincides with that of the female sex by the male." (Engels, 1967; Leacock, 1972; Silverblatt, 1991)

Engels' thesis and facts have been criticized by feminists and many anthropologists. But there is little doubt that under the system of private ownership or control of property in archaic state societies, women came under political domination of men. As Gerda Lerner points out, Engels "defined the major theoretical questions for the next hundred years" and "most of the theoretical work done on the question of the origin of women's subordination has been directed toward proving, improving, or disproving Engels' work." (Lerner, 1986)

While most Marxists accepted Engels' basic argument, many feminists do not. New anthropological evidence indicates that male domination over women, to one degree or another, existed in pre-state societies, before the introduction of private property. Thus over the last forty years other theories have emerged which attempt to explain the phenomenon of patriarchy.

Lila Leibowitz, an American anthropologist, has advanced one of the alternative theories of the origin of patriarchy. She argues that for thousands of years early humans lived in small bands where their survival depended on foraging for food. There was no sexual division of labour, life was hard and short, fertility was limited due to malnutrition, and what hunting occurred was by the group. This changed with the introduction of projectile hunting by spears and then bows and arrows. With this came food processing techniques associated with fire and the hearth. These technological developments brought about the first division of labour along the lines of sex and age.

However, the socialization of labour in these societies was a task of both men and women. With this new system of hunting, the first *gender* differences appear, as men taught boys to hunt and women taught girls gathering and processing of food.

For Leibowitz, the key to the beginning of patriarchy was the introduction of exchange between bands. First, there was the introduction of incest rules and marriage according to exogamy, where marriage must be outside the group. Incest rules define who one can and cannot marry. In band societies with a small population, it was generally the case that incest rules banned marriage within the band. Bands needed to exchange goods and marriage partners. Exchange relations between bands was formalized by the exchange of marriage partners. Either men or women were moved to other groups in order to regularize exchange in general. (Leibowitz, 1986)

Nicole Chevillard and Sebastien Leconte point out that exogamy has been practiced by almost all societies based on kinship. But exogamy is usually combined with a second rule—patrilocality, where the woman must leave her family and kinship group and live with the man's family in another band or tribe. This demonstrates that in early band societies men had more political power than women.

The ceremony of male adult initiation, often involving circumcision, commonly found in hunting societies, is to distinguish men from women. In many ceremonies this involves scorn of women, to make a boy part of a superior group. In almost every hunting society there are taboos that forbid women to have any weapons or even touch them. In many this taboo carries over to symbols of power, like drums and other musical instruments. Men are insistent that women should be disarmed for "it is well known that differential access to arms always reflects class relations." (Chevillard and Leconte, 1986)

Thus the inferior political position of women in lineage societies, reflected in men's absolute control over weapons, is reinforced by marriage rules for exogamy. Women are cut off from their families and friends. As foreigners in another lineage group they are alienated and atomized "and their subjection is more easily guaranteed." Chevillard and Leconte also argue that women have greater status and are not exploited in societies without exchange marriages, where residence rules are matrilocal, and where women have influence because of the key role they play in horticulture. The Hopi Indians are a good example. (Chevillard and Leconte, 1986)

Marvin Harris, the well-known American anthropologist, argues that in all human populations men in general are larger and stronger than women. In contests they generally outperform women in archery, javelin hurling and running. Thus it is not surprising that in hunter gatherer societies, where survival is precarious, men become the specialists in hunting and the manufacture of weapons like spears, bows and arrows, harpoons, clubs and boomerangs. Men also maintain a monopoly over the manufacture and use of weapons, which gives them political power and influence. Harris concludes that "in the realm of public decision-making and conflict resolution, men generally have a slight but nonetheless significant edge over women in virtually all foraging societies." He also agrees with those anthropologists who find that "wherever conditions favoured the development of warfare among bands and villages, the political and domestic subordination of women increased."

Harris has argued that men also have political power in matrilineal and matrilocal societies based on horticulture. For example, women in the Iroquois society had control over agriculture, crafts and the longhouse, and held political council. But this was a fierce warrior society, men monopolized weapons, and they regularly went on long distance wars. Men had the real power in Iroquois society, Harris argues. Iroquois society was not matriarchal because "Iroquois women did not humiliate, degrade, and exploit their men." Harris concludes that there are many patriarchies but no matriarchies because men monopolize weapons and the skills of war. (Harris, 1977; 1993)

The French structuralist anthropologists have generally concluded that in all human societies men have been in political control. Claude Levi-Strauss argued that this is directly associated with the incest taboo, common to all societies. Because of this taboo, linked to the small size of bands, from the beginning the exchange of women is the norm. As he argues, "The fundamental fact is that men exchange women and not the other way around." Therefore, in the very earliest of societies, men had authority, for it was they who exchanged women; it was men who gave away their daughters in marriage.

The structuralists argue that the central goal of the early hunter gatherer societies was the preservation of the group, its own reproduction. Thus, the incest rule was designed to increase the chances of having enough women to produce enough children. The incest rule promotes the exchange of women which is the first instance of trade. But the structuralists argue that this is where *women become a commodity*, a good to be traded. Women are also traded in order to build bonds of peace with neighbouring bands and tribes. When this happens, the status of women declines. Levi-Strauss argues that this is the beginning of the subordination of women. Men have certain rights in women but women do not have the same rights in men. Today's anthropologists and feminists are convinced that patriarchy was well established before the introduction of private property. (Levi-Strauss, 1969)

## Biological Determinism and the Rise of Neoliberalism

In the early 1960s the second wave of feminism began. Women demanded equality with men, the right to economic freedom, the right to control their own bodies, and sexual freedom. This was often combined with an attack on militarism and war.

A male reaction came in the form of a series of popular books by ethologists who argued that through biology and the evolutionary process of natural selection men were by nature more aggressive and that patriarchy was the natural human order. On a more sophisticated level, Steven Goldberg argued that male hormones, and in particular testosterone, led to male aggression, interest in weapons, and survival in a hostile, competitive world. Men are bigger and stronger because of genetic makeup and evolution. He argued that it was irrational for women to try to overthrow the natural, biological order. Thus our patriarchal culture *reflects* biology, and in all human societies men work out of the home and women stay home and care for children. Because this is genetic, it cannot change. (Goldberg, 1971)

The most influential work supporting biological determinism was Edward O. Wilson's *Sociobiology*, published in 1975. A well-known Darwinian biologist, he brought respectability to the debate. Wilson argued that males have dominated females in all hunter gatherer societies, and since this hierarchical sex order is also a common characteristic of most non-human primates, it must be biological in origin. Competition and a long period of evolution has resulted in male domination. He concluded that while women are being given equal access to education, men, because of their aggressive and competitive behaviour, are likely to continue to dominate economic life, politics and science.

Wilson, following other social Darwinists, argued that the basis for all human societies is the nuclear family, whether it is in the Australian desert or the modern American city. In both cases, women and children remain in the residential areas while men pursue game or money in the public area. This is the natural order. (Wilson, 1975; Sayers, 1982)

Sociobiologists argue that humans have a genetic strategy for attempting to maximize the survival of their genes. R. L. Trivers and Richard Dawkins popularized the arguments of investment in genetic success. Men's strategy is to try to spread their genes as widely as possible, and this leads to a strategy of sexual promiscuity. In contrast, since women must spend nine months labouring to produce a child, their strategy is "coyness" as they try to find a man who will provide support for their offspring. All this is a product of evolution. Different biological strategies cause the battle of the sexes. There is no such thing as altruism here, only the pursuit of self-interest. (Dawkins, 1976; Trivers, 1985)

Numerous social scientists attacked the theory of biological determinism. They have all pointed out that the theory ignores the wide variety of sexual life in human societies, both past and present. Many sociologists and political economists have argued that sociobiology is an ideological defence of right-wing political economy. In the nineteenth century it was identified with Social Darwinism, particularly with Herbert Spencer, and the defence of wealthy men and monopoly corporations. In the present era, its role is to defend neo-classical economics and the right wing politics of the free market and free trade, represented by Margaret Thatcher and Ronald Reagan. These two political leaders were strong supporters of neoliberalism as well as the traditional patriarchal order. They have many followers in Saskatchewan.

We know that competition is contrary to the basic values in hunter gatherer, horticultural or many peasant societies that existed before the rise and expansion of capitalism. Co-operation and reciprocity are the central values. What sets human beings off from other animal species is the fact that through social action and culture humans dominate and change nature. Humans are not bound by genetic inheritances. Biological differences do not seem to be the likely cause of the persistence of patriarchy in advanced, liberal democratic societies like Saskatchewan. (see Rose, Lewontin and Kamin, 1984; Lewontin, 1991; Fausto-Sterling, 1992)

Gerda Lerner's book, *The Creation of Patriarchy*, appeared in 1986 and was quickly recognized as the most important book on the subject since Simone de Beauvoir's *The Second Sex*. Lerner, a professor of history at the University of Wisconsin, based her analysis on the extensive work she did on historical developments in gender and political economy in the Ancient Near East plus a wide reading of anthropology. She starts from the assumption that "men and women built civilization jointly." She argues that we have to abandon the concept that women were "historical victims, acted on by violent men." Nevertheless, we have to explain "the central puzzle—woman's participation in the construction of the system that subordinates her." In doing so we must abandon "single factor explanations" and "assume that changes as complex as a basic alteration of kinship structures most likely occurred as a result of a variety of interacting forces."

In looking at the transition period when humanoids evolve from primates, the role of the woman in protecting the child was crucial. The human brain expands because of the cultural learning process. This sets humans off from other animals. Human babies require longer nurturance.

Following anthropologist Nancy Tanner, Lerner points out that for many thousands of years humans existed as foragers and gatherers. The earliest evidence of the existence of bow and arrow hunting dates only to 15,000 years ago. Given the need to support small children for many years, mothers were most likely to be gatherers and not big-game hunters. Thus, she argues, sex differences were based on reproductive differences, not strength and endurance. This division of labour is necessary at the earliest stages of human development. It is not necessary in later periods. Male domination is culturally created over time.

In hunting societies, Lerner notes, it is common for men to have segregated male initiation rites, same-sex lodges, and same-sex rituals. Hunting together increases male bonding, and this was obviously intensified by the expansion of warfare. Women also become the spoils of the warriors. As Lerner argues, it is not women who are being subordinated at this time—it is women's *reproductive capacity* that is being sought. When hunting and gathering or horticulture shifts to plow agriculture, kinship systems change from matriliny to patriliny, and private property develops. At this time we see the beginnings of patriarchy.

Early state societies, based on advanced agriculture, clearly subordinated women's reproductive capacities. Social systems based on a balanced complementarity between sexes collapse when confronted by the power of the militaristic patriarchal states and their ability to appropriate surpluses. Thus, Lerner argues, "the first appropriation of private property consists of the appropriation of the labour of women as *reproducers*." The agricultural revolution brought us the exploitation of human labour and the sexual exploitation of women. They are inextricably linked. (Lerner, 1986)

## The Patriarchal State, Religion and the Ownership of Land

The enduring strength of patriarchy is reinforced by our religions. All the major religions of the world assume that God is a man, that his disciples on earth are men, that the leaders of our religious institutions are men, and that the role of women is to bear children and maintain the household for men. Man, we are told, is made in the image of God, not woman. All the major religions of the world have historically supported the nuclear family headed by a man. Until recently all of them held that women were inferior to men and had no rights as citizens. As the major mainstream Christian churches moved to accept a greater equality for women, new fundamentalists churches expanded to reinforce traditional patriarchal values.

This discussion is very important to understanding the persistence of patriarchy in Saskatchewan. The churches which dominate the province have their historic roots in the culture of the Middle East, the Jewish religion and the origins of Christianity. The modern Christian church in Europe also has its cultural ties to patriarchal practices in ancient Rome and Greece. Religious doctrine has also been closely linked to the issue of the ownership of land and property. The Christian churches were originally embedded in the European states. Indeed, they were official state churches, and the kings and queens held that they ruled by divine right, chosen by the Christian God. These European churches, both Roman Catholic and Protestant, have played a central role in developing and maintaining the culture of patriarchy in Saskatchewan. (O'Faolain and Martines, 1973; Daly, 1973)

The most comprehensive study of the rise of the state and its impact on women has been done by Gerda Lerner. She chose to concentrate on the Near East, for this is where the first states emerged. The political, economic and social developments here had an enormous impact on the European political and state culture. By 3000

B.C. there were city states in the Tigris Euphrates area, commonly referred to as Mesopotamia. Sargon of Akkad had established an imperial kingship over Sumer, Assyria, Elam and the Euphrates valley in 2371 B.C.

But Lerner goes back before this time to try to determine how and why these patriarchal states developed. She looks first at the development of slavery, and in particular female slavery. In tribal and nomadic societies, conflict and warfare were common. So was the capture of women and children and their incorporation into the families of the conquering peoples. The rape of captured women is also the norm, expressing male power and dominance. In this early period it was the usual practice to kill all males captured in military exercises. Men were too difficult to control, they could not be policed, and they were a danger to the community. In contrast, women who had been transformed into slaves and sexual property were easier to control, particularly if they had dependent children. Women, seized in military episodes, were distributed among warriors as spoils of war. This practice was well developed before states had emerged. This was the general pattern in the Middle East.

Thus, as Lerner argues, *women were the first slaves*. They were converted to private property of men. The enslavement of women existed for several thousands of years before the enslavement of men was introduced. It was only when the state was created, and a permanent state military/police force created, that it became possible to enslave men and to use them as agricultural labourers. It was only after the development of the state that it became possible to introduce slavery as a *mode of production*. (Lerner, 1986)

The subordination of women advances with the development of the state and its role in creating laws to control property, marriage and sexuality. Lerner examines the laws regulating women, sexuality and property in the Code of Hammurabi (1752 B.C.), the Middle Assyrian Kingdoms (15th to 11th centuries B.C.), the Hittite Laws (13th Century B.C.), and the Hebrew Laws (1200-400 B.C.). These laws codified and reflected the practice at the time; the patriarchal order becomes institutionalized.

All of these laws confirm that the man was the head of the household and that he had political domination over the members of his household, which could include his wife or wives, concubines, female slaves and children. As Lerner argues, "a man's class station is determined by his economic relations and a woman's by her sexual relations."

In the Code of Hammurabi, which was a codification of general laws in the Mesopotamian area which had been in existence for several hundred years, we find patrilineal descent, patrilocal residence, inheritance of property by sons, male dominance in sexual and property relations, and male dominance of military, political and religious institutions. This state system was supported by the patriarchal family and in turn constantly recreated by it. Central to this system of laws was the private ownership of landed property and its preservation within the family.

It is not possible here to go into all these extensive and detailed laws. But in general, property went from man to man, male family head to male family head. But often it went through women. The wife had use-rights of her property while alive, but it went to her sons on her death. If she were divorced, or did not have sons, the dowry was returned to her father or brothers. Levirate was established, particularly in Hebrew culture, to try to preserve property in the male lineage. These laws and customs are the root of western patriarchy. They carry over to Canada and Saskatchewan. (Lerner, 1986)

Men had the right to exchange women and children before the creation of the state. But as Lerner argues, "with the development of private property and class stratification, this customary right became of crucial economic significance." *Marriage was a device for expanding family assets.* Women were important to the family economy as producers, but their sexual and reproductive abilities were central and became "marketable commodities."

Thus for a family with property in land and herds, the central purpose of marriage was to assure that the property stayed in the family through the production of sons. Thus, a dowry was only paid after it was proven that a woman given in marriage could produce a male heir. All the complex laws of this time were constructed around this primary goal. Men could easily get a divorce; women could not get a divorce. Heterosexual marriages could produce heirs, homosexual marriages could not.

If a wife could not produce a son, a second wife could be acquired. A slave woman could be elevated to the status of wife or concubine if she bore a son and the wife could not. Concubines, women acquired specifically for sexual services, had a higher social and legal status than mere female slaves; they were there primarily to provide sexual services. Women were to be virgins at marriage and were to be sexually faithful to their husbands. Men were free to commit adultery with prostitutes and slave women. Men were guilty of adultery only if they had sexual relations with another man's wife. As the laws made clear, this was *a violation of a husband's property rights.* For women committing adultery, the normal punishment was death.

In the case of rape, the injured party was the husband or the father of the woman who was raped. Laws were strict for miscarriage or abortion. The crime here was depriving a husband of a possible son and heir. The first state laws against abortion have their origin here. Abortion was a public crime, to be tried in the King's court. The punishment was in public as well. Under Middle Assyrian Law a woman who had an abortion was to be impaled in public and not buried. There was a *material base* to the laws against abortion.

The veiling of women is developed during this period and codified in the laws. It serves to distinguish between "respectable" and "non-respectable" women. Unmarried women, wives, and widows may not go into the street unless veiled. Neither can a concubine or a sacred slave. An unmarried slave and a prostitute may not wear a veil under severe public punishment. In Middle Assyrian Law, a slave who veils herself loses her clothing, is flogged 50 times in the street, and has pitch poured on her head. This is a major state offence. It sets the basic class division of women, based on their sexual status.

Lerner stresses that the control of women's sexuality was moved from the family and the kinship group to the state. The rights of men and the father are now "equated with the keeping of social order. For the wife to usurp such a right is now seen as equal in magnitude to treason or to an assault upon the king." The patriarchal family is mirrored in the archaic state, paternalism and unquestioned authority. "The archaic state," Lerner argues, "from its inception, recognized its dependence on the patriarchal family and equated the family's orderly functioning with order in the public domain." (Lerner, 1986)

As we have previously noted, the forms of religion change with the structure of society. In the pre-state societies, there was widespread reverence for fertility goddesses, the mother goddess, often identified with the moon. The mother goddess was also the goddess of creation. In the Near East we see the transition from a polytheism which has many goddesses of high status to a hierarchical polytheism headed by the male sun god, and then to the single male god who becomes the creator. As Sir J. G. Frazer put it, "Men make the gods; women worship them."

The mother goddess was apparently widely worshiped in Europe as well. Archeologists have recovered around 30,000 miniature goddess or fertility figures from 3,000 sites in southwest Europe alone and virtually no male god figures. Similar goddesses were common throughout the Near East and identified with fertility rites. As we move to plow agricultural societies, the sun god and the storm god are elevated. The Hittites transformed the sun goddess Estan into the sun god Istanu. With the development of the Mesopotamian state, the sun god Marduke becomes the king of the universe.

The complete transformation of state religious ideology occurs with the patriarchal Hebrew tribes. Given the influence of the Bible and the Jewish and Christian religions on the western European view of the status of women in society, Lerner goes into this in some detail. By the time of Moses (ca 1200 B.C.) Yahweh, a male god with no ties to goddesses, is to be worshiped as the only god, and this covenant is solidified through male circumcision. King David (1004-965 B.C.) unites the tribes into a national state and pursues an imperial policy of military expansion. Later religious revivals "introduced into Yahwism the revolutionary idea of intolerance toward other gods and cults." With the fall of Palestine to Babylon in 586 B.C. Jewish monotheism is established with an absolute faith in the one, invisible, ineffable, male God.

In an analysis of Genesis and other Biblical laws, Lerner traces the transition to a patriarchal social system entrenched in state law. "The Old Testament text shows a gradual restriction of women's public and economic role, a lessening of her cultic function and an ever increasing regulation of her sexuality, as the Jewish tribes move from confederacy to statehood." The evolution of religion to monotheism parallels the evolution of human societies from kinship based groups to the state. State power is buttressed by the state ideology, which in early times was almost exclusively that of the state religion. The state was also a patriarchal order, and the new state god was a male god, the creator, who supported a hierarchical system of power. But we should never forget that the early development of patriarchy is centrally linked to the private ownership of agricultural land. (Lerner, 1986)

## The Roots of Our Culture: European Patriarchy

Western patriarchal culture has its roots in the Near East and the Jewish religion, the Greek and Roman imperial state systems, and Christianity. In early Greece women had high status, particularly in the Minoan civilization at Crete. But by the time of Homer (ninth century B.C.) women were already subordinate to men, often slaves, and subject to death by the head of the household, as we learn from Odysseus. Women were the property of men.

In classical "democratic" Athens (480- 400 B.C.), respectable women were confined to the household, which included a wife, concubines, slaves and children. Marriage banquets were held to let the public know that the woman had entered the man's household as a wife and not as a concubine. Once married, the Greek wife did not eat with her husband and was generally confined to a part of the house known as the gynaeceum. Female children were not wanted and often they were "exposed," left outside to die when they were newborn infants. This power was given to the man. Children of slave women belonged to their master. Women who were adulterers were to be publicly shamed and beaten by any man. Only men could get a divorce, but in such cases they had to return the dowry. If there were no male heirs, and the husband died, levirate was invoked, and the widow was required to marry the eldest man in her husband's family. (O'Faolain and Martines, 1973; de Beauvoir, 1974)

Simone de Beauvoir points out that *the central purpose of marriage was to keep the family property*, therefore "woman escapes complete dependency to the degree to which she escapes from the family." This is aided when there is no private property. For example, in Sparta at this time all land was held in common. In spite of the fact that Sparta was a militaristic, hierarchical society dominated by men, women were treated almost equally to men. There was no concept of adultery. Children were considered to belong to the society as a whole and not a family. Women were not enslaved to one master. "The citizen, possessing neither private wealth nor specific ancestry, was no longer in possession of woman." (de Beauvoir, 1948)

Most influential to western culture was the enduring work of Aristotle. His views on procreation dominated European thought until the middle of the 19th century. The woman, he argued, was a mere vessel for the development of the offspring. The male seed was not just the material which produced the embryo but a spiritual contribution and was divine. Since man was made in god's image, the female was "a mutilated male" and was devoid of any soul. Aristotle consistently argued that the female was *biologically inferior* to the male, and this view was carried over to the European Christian tradition.

Aristotle believed that a hierarchical order was natural. Some men are born to rule. Some men are born to be slaves. The rule of man over animals is normal, as is the rule of man over his slaves, his wife and his children. It was natural for the Greeks as the highest civilization to rule over the barbarian foreigners and transform them into slaves. (Lerner, 1986)

The history of Rome illustrates that the status of women could change in more democratic societies. By the time of Tarquin (616-578 B.C.) Rome was a patriarchal state society. Patrician men, the class of land owners, had nearly complete control over those who lived in their households. Wives, concubines, slaves and children were the man's legal possessions. The man could legally kill his wife or daughter for sexual infidelity. Women could be killed for drinking wine, which was forbidden; it was believed that wine might cause an abortion. Women were expected to be veiled when they went outside the house.

A woman was always a dependent under the Roman tradition of *manus*, a man holding a woman or a child in his hand. Thus a woman, with the status of a child, was dependent on her father, given to her husband in marriage, and then to her son if her husband died. This tradition is also found in the Hindu Code of Manu and the Three Submissions in Confucianism. It is found in the traditional religious wedding ceremony, where a father or another male member of a family gives the daughter to another man.

Women achieved considerable independence as the state developed in Rome. The political and military elite built the state to counter the wealth and power of the land owners. The Roman state assumed the power to make laws and regulate marriage, adultery, divorce and property rights, subverting the absolute power of the man as the head of the family. During the decline of the empire, the status of women greatly improved. This trend was reversed when Christianity became the ruling state ideology in Rome. (O'Faolain and Martines, 1973; de Beauvoir, 1974)

We can easily see how Saskatchewan's patriarchal traditions are linked to our European past. The Christian churches are a key social institution and brought forth and re-enforced the patriarchal culture. The family structure is still patrilineal, patrilocal, with the man recognized as the head of the family. This remains the social ideal. This tradition has been particularly strong in the farming community. Right down to the present, land ownership normally goes from father to son. Farm organizations are organizations of farmers, who are men. The purpose of marriage is to produce male heirs. The traditional role of women, particularly in rural areas, has been to raise children and maintain the household.

It is common to identify patriarchy with western Europe and European colonialism. But that does not mean that it was not present in the Americas. Patriarchy was well established in the city states and empires before the arrival of the Europeans. These state systems had much in common with states in other parts of the world. They were patriarchal in that men controlled the political system. But the status and influence of women outside of the political area varied.

The Mayan society in Mesoamerica was matrilocal. Women had an important role in agriculture, took part in some important affairs, and had some property rights. But they could not hold public office or enter the religious temples. Marriage was monogamous, but if a women did not produce children, the man could dissolve the marriage. Kings had one wife to produce heirs and many concubines. As in Europe, kingship was hereditary and went from father to son. (see Von Hagen, 1960; Peterson, 1962; Ruz, 1993; Fox, 1988)

The history of the development of the Aztecs from a tribal society into an imperial state records the relative decline in the status of women. By 1345 it is recorded the men were in positions of authority as judges, executioners, and mediators. The leader of the Aztecs was called "father and mother of the people." (Nash, 1978)

By 1429 the Aztecs had emerged as a militaristic and imperialist state. It was a warrior society, and all boys were educated and trained to be warriors. There was a clear division of labour between men and women. Boys were trained for agriculture, fishing, public life, and crafts. Priestesses taught girls religion and how to weave, tend babies, and cook. (Nash, 1978; Peterson, 1960; Tarazona, 1991)

Inga Clendinnen argues that "rank did not mitigate female destiny: newborn females regardless of caste were all condemned, it would seem, to a destiny of unrelieved domesticity." Women were expected to be virgins when married and sexually faithful to their husbands. "Respectable" girls, unmarried women, and women in public performances as artists were "masked" with feathers and their faces painted when they went out of their house. In contrast, the prostitutes were to have bare faces. This is also seen as reflecting the Aztec view of the dual nature of women, the contrast between reproduction and sexual pleasure.

The Aztecs were an imperialist state, and women were always captured in war and taken as tribute. They were distributed to warriors and nobles as concubines and slaves. Moctezuma II was reported to have had 2,000 concubines. Aztec barracks in the provinces had brothels populated by captive women. "Tribute girls" from the provinces were often put in the state brothels, called "Houses of Joy." (Clendinnen, 1991)

The Inca society was also a militaristic imperial state. The Inca king was divine, a direct descendant of the Sun, the male creator god. He had a primary wife, secondary wives, and hundreds of concubines. Huascar, the last Inca before the Spaniards, was reported to have had 500 children.

Each year Inca administrators went around to villages within the empire and took girls under the age of eight who became known as the Chosen Women. As many as 15,000 were under the control of the Inca, and others were given to men of the upper classes and military leaders. A few were sacrificed in special religious ceremonies. As Pizarro and his Christians marched on Cuzco, they stopped for five days to rape the Chosen Women held at Caxas in the Sun Temple.

The status of non-elite women was mitigated by the system of land ownership. The *ayllu* or clan of extended families was the basic social unit, and it held land, animals and food in common. Every person had land use rights, but there was no formal usufruct, no particular piece of land which was linked to family by inheritance. Communal land was redistributed every fall. So there was no private ownership of land or land use rights, no male ownership, and thus no need to control female sexuality. Premarital sex was considered normal, as was homosexuality. Monogamous marriage was the rule for the lower classes, but there was no prohibition against extramarital sexual activity. However, there was still male political power on the local level; the male clan chief was elected, and there was a council of male elders.(See Schreiber, 1992; Von Hagen, 1961; Rowe, 1982; Moore, 1958; Silverblatt, 1978)

The extent of male domination among the plains tribes varied. The Hidatsa, Mandan and Arikara tribes were matrilineal and depended on agriculture, and women had high status. Women "owned" land rights, did all the farming, preserved the food, and were in charge of marketing surpluses. They also built and "owned" the earthen lodges, which housed extended families. (Wilson, 1987; Spector, 1983)

For the plains Indians which depended on the buffalo and not agriculture, the status of women differs in fact and opinion. Anthropologist Raymond DeMallie finds that the Lakota culture was almost Victorian, with men having political, economic and social power, and there were strict rules of masculinity, femininity and sexuality. Mary Jane Schneider argues that women's industrial arts brought honour, status and prestige because of their control over resources needed by men. Alan Klein details the decline in status of women in plains tribes with the introduction of the capitalist fur trade, the horse and the gun. (DeMallie, 1983; Schneider, 1983; Klein, 1983)

European colonialism strengthened the power of men across the world. Colonial administrators talked only to men, insisted that tribes be organized on a centralized, hierarchical structure, and negotiated with only men. They brought with them Christian missionaries who immediately demanded that indigenous people change their traditions of marriage and sexuality to conform to the Christian standard, which required the subjugation of women. (see Mies, 1986)

## The Persistence of Patriarchal Values in Saskatchewan

Patriarchy, generally described as a set of social relations that allows men to dominate women, has existed since humans lived in band societies. With the move to agricultural systems based on private ownership of land, patriarchy intensified. Marriage customs became primarily concerned with the ownership and transfer of land and property from father to son. The established religions provided an ideological justification for this system of domination. Throughout the world, patriarchy became deeply entrenched with the creation of the state. The state was the patriarchal state. Customs promoting patriarchy now also became state laws. In the west these traditions were a central focus of Christianity. Men were made in God's image and women were biologically inferior. This view was then re-enforced with the introduction of the theories of biological determinism and social Darwinism.

Given the rise of capitalism and liberalism, and then the development of egalitarianism with socialism and Marxism, how can we explain the persistence of patriarchal values and institutions into the twenty-first century? Why do patriarchal values remain so entrenched in the political culture of Saskatchewan?

The roots of patriarchy go back to the settlers who came to the prairies to establish family farms. They brought with them the culture of independent commodity production for the market, based on private ownership of land. All of the terms used by academics to identify the "family farm" tend to obscure the fact that this form of production has been deeply rooted in patriarchy. Men have historically owned the means of production, have been the managers and decision makers, pass on their property to their sons and not their daughters, and their women partners laboured very long hours for no pay. All of the structures and institutions in the rural and farm community have supported this entrenched patriarchal system. It is the core of rural culture.

The role of women on the family farm has been well documented over the last twenty years. Typically, women have been responsible for doing the household work, providing almost all of the care for children, subsidizing the family through their production of domestic food and clothing, working off the farm to bring additional income to the family, and doing much of the farm work. Thus there is no separation of labour on the farm between "domestic" and "productive" work. All of the work that the woman does provides a direct subsidy to the family farm as an economic unit. (Reimer, 1986; Hedley, 1981; Smith, 1988, 1992; Friedmann, 1988)

From the very beginning, men had a difficult time keeping the prairie homestead without the support of a wife. Pioneer women were "Canada's most wanted" because of their skills and abilities to make a farm operation successful. They were "hauling a double load." Christa Scowby and others point out that many farm women on the prairies did not agree with this social form of production and expressed their dissent in political forums, farm meetings, through farm publications, and by forming women's farm organizations. They attended meetings of the Grain Growers Association, but constituted only around 10 percent of the delegates. They were up against an "agrarian ideology" that held that the farm family worked in harmony as a production unit and that women's roles as mothers and housewives have been deemed "natural, divinely inspired, and biologically determined." (Rollings-Magnusson, 2000; Palmer and Sinclair, 1997; Scowby, 1996; Jahn, 1994; Strong-Boag, 1986)

As Max Hedley has pointed out, the ideology of the "family farm" assumes that it is a non-exploitative and egalitarian social relationship. Yet family farms have historically depended on the exploitation of labour by women and children. This ideology also obscures the fact that commercial family farms regularly exploit hired farm labourers, most often immigrants or minorities who are paid less than the normal non-farm wage. (Hedley, 1981)

Deborah Fink has analyzed the agrarian ideology that has persisted in North America. This is often traced to Thomas Jefferson, who argued that the hard working settler family was the backbone of democratic life in the New World. Rural people were healthier, happier, strong supporters of Christian morality, and their life and purpose was superior to that of those condemned to live in urban society. Fink notes that this mythology of the family farm served as the ideological justification for the imperial expansion of European immigrants across the North American continent. The focus on the moral superiority of the frontier family farm served to distract attention from the reality that the European strategy of colonialism led to the genocide of a great many indigenous nations and the decimation of those that survived. (Fink, 1992)

Farm women were idealized under the agrarian myth. They struggled for the frontier farm family, but they benefitted from living in the country with its fresh air, good food, freedom, and the absence of factory life. Men were the farmers, of course. But farm wives had a very high moral position as mothers and supporters of the family farm. These women made an unselfish commitment to remaining in the home and providing service to their husbands and children. Like urban middle class women, they were the defenders of traditional Christian morality and the heterosexual nuclear family. As Sarah Whatmore notes, sexual independence was "the least desirable characteristic" of a woman in rural North America. Women were to get married to a farmer and put their families first. They were privileged, compared to other rural women, because they were part of a family which owned property. Other women who were poor or working class were forced out of the house to do any kind of work. (Fink, 1992; Whatmore, 1991)

Ironically, with the coming of western, Christian "civilization" women in North America lost their access to land. In the eastern and southern part of the continent, Aboriginal women produced the majority of agricultural goods. Many of the Aboriginal societies were matrilineal, and the right to the use of land was inherited through the female line. This was the system among the Iroquois nations. Seneca women had rights to the land and did the farming. At one settlement they farmed over 1,000 acres and managed 1,500 fruit trees. Their farming operation was deliberately destroyed by a military attack ordered by George Washington in 1779. (Jensen, 1991)

On the prairies, in the Hidatsa, Mandan and Arikara tribes of North Dakota women were the farmers, and they had usufruct (or use) rights to communally owned lands. This was the system under the Mississippi culture which spread north from Mexico. They lost their land and were resettled on reservations where the U.S. government insisted that Indian farmers were to be men. The coming of European civilization ended the right of women to own farmland and be farmers. (Wilson, 1987)

The culture of patriarchy was emboldened by the legal system. Under English Common Law married women lost their right to hold property. Property would pass to a man's children. There were heavy penalties against women for promiscuity and adultery. In western Canada, women could not vote or run for elected office. Many jurisdictions limited voters to those who owned property. The Dominion Lands Act of 1872 provided homestead land to those who were over 21 and the "head of a family." Theoretically, women who were divorced, widows, or deserted heads of family with children could claim land, but this was hard to prove and rarely granted.

Under the Territories Real Property Act of 1886, a widow could claim up to one-third of her husband's assets. Some additional claims were included in the Saskatchewan Devolution of Estates Act of 1919. But a woman who was separated or divorced had little claim to property.

The federal criminal acts also enforced the patriarchal order by prohibiting abortion and access to birth control. Long jail sentences could be imposed for violations. Women could not even legally acquire birth control information.

The father was recognized as the head of the family and held authority over his children, including their religious upbringing, when they would leave school to go to work, and who would be their guardian in the event the father died. The Female Employment Act put restrictions on women's participation in the labour force. Inheriting the English Common Law, the husband was permitted to use a stick to discipline a wife, so long as it was no larger than a thumb. Women did not have the right to divorce until 1925, the right to equal pay for work until 1956, access to abortion and birth control until 1968, and no equal right to farm property until the Matrimonial Property Act of 1979. (Sach, 1996; Rollings-Magnusson, 1999)

With the rise of the women's liberation movement in the 1970s, farm women began to demand changes. Governments were quite reluctant to change matrimonial property laws to give farm women an equal share of the farm assets. Even in the 1970s and 1980s, the Supreme Court of Canada handed down several decisions which virtually denied women property rights after they had laboured on the farm for many years. The Saskatchewan Matrimonial Property Act of 1979 was a step forward in some ways but as women noted, merely reaffirmed the gender inequalities that existed prior to marriage, where women normally do not have assets to add to the farm. (Keet, 1988; Smith, 1988; Hedley, 1982)

Today women on North American farms have a legal right to a share of any increase in the value of the farm which occurs during the marriage or common law relationship. On divorce or death of the man, a woman can now expect to inherit a share of the farm. But has this produced any major shift in farm ownership? Joan Jensen argues that not much has changed. Farm women now play a role in the transfer of farms from father to son. Multigenerational farms are widely being promoted, farm partnerships and corporations involving fathers and sons. Farm women support this development even though this makes it more difficult for daughters to inherit land. Furthermore, if a farm wife inherits a farm on the death of her husband, the most common outcome is that she rents or leases the farm to one of her sons until she dies, and he inherits it. (Jensen, 1991; Shortall, 1999)

It does not seem that much is really changing in rural Saskatchewan. The cultural norm remains: the man is the "natural farmer." Look through the farm publications. Farmers are men. They are the only ones who can operate the modern farm machinery. Farming is a business, and it is a man's business. Lise Saugeres argues that farm machines have replaced women in the fields, and today the machinery is the symbol of male power. The land is seen as feminine. It is considered natural that men are still ploughing, penetrating and fertilizing the land, "an extension of men's biological functions." Men's control over the land parallels their control over animals, women and children. (Saugeres, 2002)

The women are there, of course, in a background supportive position, invisible. Farm publications give no indication that there has been any change. Carolyn Sachs argues that women played a greater role in the old populist general farm organizations. The new specific commodity organizations, like those so widespread today in Saskatchewan, are even more dominated by men. (Sachs, 1996)

New organizations for farm women have developed in the last few decades. Elizabeth Teather surveyed their histories in Canada, New Zealand and Australia. Despite the many changes, she found that the women's organizations were still strongly committed to the traditional family. In part this is an attempt not to be labeled radical or disruptive. But in this struggle they face a contradictory position. On the one hand they are challenging "male hegemonic control over land, labour and its product" while on the other hand fighting to keep the traditional family farm, which is "the site of reproduction of gender-based hierarchy." The hesitancy to push more feminist goals, Teather concludes, "is related to sensitive motives related to the male ego, to female support of long-established views about masculinity, and to an awareness of 'old-fashioned' attitudes of many rural residents." (Teather, 1996; see also Bell and Campbell, 2000)

The man is still regarded as the farmer and the head of the household. It is not surprising to find that farm organizations continue to be patriarchal organizations. In 1990 of the 237 positions on Canadian marketing boards and commissions, only 10 (4 percent) were held by women. In 1997 a survey in Saskatchewan found that of credit unions only 8 percent of delegates were women, and there were no women on the central board of directors. For the Wheat Pool, only six of 125 (5 percent) delegates were women and there were no women on the board. The Pool had never had a woman on the board of directors. Of the delegates to the annual general meeting of Federated Co-operatives Ltd., 76 of 379 (20 percent) were women but of the nineteen members on the board of directors, only one was a woman. The National Farmers Union was best, with women representing 39 of the 217 (18 percent) regional positions, six of 18 (33 percent) of the national board and three of six of the national executive. (Rogers, 1997)

The patriarchal tradition is certainly reflected in Saskatchewan politics. During the first sixty years of the legislature there were 450 MLAs and only six women. Thousands of men were appointed Justices of the Peace in the first 80 years as a province, but not one woman. (Higginbotham, 1968)

Women were granted the franchise in Saskatchewan in 1916. The women's movement pushed for reform of property rights, child custody and measures to protect women. They argued that giving the women the vote would allow them to extend their "maternal role" into the public sphere, to make the whole world "home-like." Why did they fail to achieve many of their goals? Elizabeth Kalmakoff suggests that "perhaps the 'social feminist' arguments used in the campaign for the vote prevented the suffragists from formulating a critique of the family structure which was the real source of their oppression." In the 1917 election little attempt was made to nominate women. Only Zoa Haight, running for the Nonpartisan League, was nominated. In 1918 Sarah Katherine Ramsland was nominated by the Liberal Party in a by-election called to replace her husband who had died, and she was the first woman elected to the legislature. (Kalmakoff, 1994)

Many thought the social democratic CCF and NDP would be different. Georgina Taylor reports that between 1934 and 1965 there were 429 contests for nomination for election to the provincial legislature, and of these only twelve (2.8 percent) were won by women. Of the 187 federal CCF and NDP candidates, only seven (3.7 percent) were women. Only three women were elected as CCF MLAs (Marjorie Cooper, Galdys Strum and Beatrice Trew). As CCF activist Gertrude Telford explained, "men are subconsciously unwilling to give up their age old prerogatives of dominance." Taylor notes that women had the easiest time getting nominations in seats where victory was remote. (Taylor, 1984)

Joan Sangster has documented the prominent role that women played in the organization of the CCF, doing the educational work, serving as local and regional organizers, forming women's auxiliaries and women's committees, and raising funds. As she concludes, the CCF did not see the "woman question" as an issue of priority. The complaints by women were voiced privately. She attributes the sex-segregation of the movement, and the under-representation of women in the leadership, as a reflection of the society as a whole, where there were unequal roles for women. Across Canada women's committees were created by the CCF, but not in Saskatchewan. (Sangster, 1984; Taylor 1992)

The NDP introduced constitutional and other changes to try to increase the number of women candidates. But in the 1982 provincial election they fielded not one woman candidate, and the same was true in the 1997 federal election. There was not a single woman in the caucus of the government of Allan Blakeney (1971-82).

Louise Carbert has argued that this is changing. In 1991 the NDP under Roy Romanow elected 13 women to the legislature. The other parties are also electing some women. In 1995 of 14 women nominated by the NDP, 10 were elected. But in the 2003 provincial election the NDP, under Lorne Calvert, nominated only ten women, of whom seven were elected.

The Romanow government passed some legislation which aided women. The Labour Standards Act was changed, but the key sections aiding part-time workers, who are mainly women, were not implemented. The Child Action Plan aided working women but not women on social assistance. The main success was the passage of the Domestic Violence Act. However, with the NDP government putting a priority on tax reductions, the cuts to health care and other social programs resulted in an increase in the responsibility for care giving being pushed back onto the family and women. (Carbert, 1997)

A somewhat different view has been expressed by Anne Smart, one of three NDP women elected in the 1986 provincial election. She made the mistake of expressing her opposition to uranium mining, a key project of the Blakeney and Romanow NDP governments. When she sought re-nomination in 1991, she was opposed by Eric Cline, a young lawyer in Roy Romanow's law firm. Although she was strongly pro-trade union, members of the Steelworkers, the United Food and Commercial Workers and the construction trades campaigned against her. They told members that she was "too old," a "radical feminist," too concerned with the interests of "fringe groups" like those on welfare and gays, and that "women are getting too much power" in the party. She was disappointed that some prominent women in the party worked against her. She did not win the nomination, and Cline entered the Romanow cabinet. (Smart, 1992)

The evidence is clear. As humans moved from egalitarian societies based on reciprocity to state societies based on social class, the status of women declined. In all state societies men are in control of the economy and the institutions of state power. The political state is a patriarchal state. Even in the advanced capitalist countries, where most women have paid employment and equal access to good education, the patriarchal state remains a reality. This is true in Saskatchewan after sixty years of the social democratic CCF-NDP as the dominant party, which from the beginning has been in principle committed to the equality of women.

Despite the fact that capitalism was originally linked to liberalism, there is no fundamental contradiction between capitalism and patriarchy. Indeed, many feminists argue that capitalism has benefitted from the patriarchal system. While doing unpaid work in the house, and raising children, the married woman helps to reproduce capitalism and the class system. Women maintain the workforce by doing unpaid labour. Their work allows men to provide more labour time for their employers. The family reproduces the labour force at no cost to the capitalist. The nuclear family consumes endless commodities and accumulates savings for the capitalists to use. The ties to family and family ideology are a conservative barrier to class alliances and class consciousness. The family socializes children into the present system. Sheila Rowbotham adds that the patriarchal family serves as a release for men who are powerless in their work environment and a release from the alienation of competitive life under capitalism. (Rowbotham, 1973)

## Conclusion: Power in Rural Societies

While the discipline of economics never discusses power, the concept is central to political economy. What is power? At its base level, it is the ability to implement decisions through force or coercion. This is the power we associate with authoritarian political regimes. But from the beginning, all ruling classes sought to acquire authority which brings legitimacy to their state regime, to create an understanding among the common people that they have an obligation to obey those who make the rules. This is the function of ideology.

Thus ideology is a system of beliefs which provide a moral justification for the established order, primarily to explain the existence of inequalities of wealth, power and social status. Morton Fried, a well known political anthropologist, argues that ideology serves "to explain and justify the existence of concentrated social power wielded by a portion of the community." (Fried, 1967)

Ideology is reproduced through religious institutions, the mass media, and educational institutions. It is the base of popular culture. From the beginning of the earliest states, the rock of ideology has been the religious order. Rulers were the son (always male) of the sun god, the givers of life. They had a mandate from heaven. They were the European Christian kings who ruled by divine right, having been chosen by God. In modern times, ideology become more complex as it has to justify socially constructed systems of domination: men over women, whites over non-whites, Europeans over non-Europeans, Christians over non-Christians.

From the beginning of agricultural societies and the early states, power first of all came to those with property. The land owners, the landlords, were the first ruling classes. They controlled the peasants, the serfs and the slaves. Of necessity, they had close ties to the political rulers. Of course, that is still true today. Those who own capital are the most powerful group in our modern industrial society. Those in political office have considerable power as well, but it is rare that they take a general position in opposition to the interests of those who hold economy power.

Most people are aware that Marx and Engels stressed that in class divided societies those who held power, the ruling class, were those who owned productive wealth. They argued that this ruling class also controlled the state and the superstructure which went with it: the political system and bureaucracy, the ideological system, the legal system, and the military and the police. Marxists generally argue that the ideology of the superstructure cannot be in contradiction to the basic economic system.

Sociologist Max Weber agreed that the most important source of power in a modern society is the ownership of property. But he also argued that within the capitalist system there were other bases of power, particularly at the individual level. Weber argued that those with state power had a greater degree of independence than that suggested by the Marxists. Within the working class (those who owned no property but sold their labour to gain a living), there were differentiations according to status and prestige. Men had more power than women. Whites had more power than non-whites. Protestants had more power than Catholics. Those with a British ethnic background had more power than those with Eastern European ethnic backgrounds. White collar workers had more status and prestige than blue collar workers. Those who had skills had more power, prestige and status than those who did not. Individuals would try to use any edge they had to increase their income and status over others. (Weber, 1968)

For those without status and power, they could gain influence by working together, forming co-operates and trade unions. Prairie farmers had some political power locally as small property owners. They attempted to exert greater power through joint action in both the political and economic area. The unskilled working class has brought many changes to the political and economic system through organization, collective bargaining, and general political activity.

Power is not only reflected in actions by those in positions of economic and political authority. Power is also revealed when important issues are excluded from the agenda of decision making. Power is seen when the majority of the people do not bother to vote, feeling it doesn't make any difference. Today there are no alternative models being advanced to the world capitalist system. The alternative of the centrally planned economy under the Soviet model has collapsed. There is widespread dissatisfaction with the system as it presently operates, particularly in the less developed world, but no one has put forth an alternate model which has any serious political support. This leads people to accept the present system of widespread inequality, domination and exploitation as more or less normal.

Sally Shortall argues that this *obstruction of choice* re-enforces prevailing social customs, particularly in rural areas. Property ownership by men is the basis for rural power. The fact that men are considered farmers is a social construction. Women are precluded from becoming farmers because of the social custom of land ownership by men. This is the combination—male land ownership and social custom—that limits the ability of women becoming farmers. (Shortall, 1999)

So if we are searching for a reason for the persistence of patriarchy in Saskatchewan, we should start with the system of property ownership and the prevailing social culture. Power comes from the ownership of property, in this case agricultural land, and by social custom men are the owners. Power is held by men who control public institutions and popular organizations. This distribution of power has been accepted as legitimate by society as a whole. The institutions of the state uphold the tradition of male ownership of land. This is the "taken-for-granted" characteristic of farming in Saskatchewan. Because of the history of the province, and the continued importance of farming to the economy, this culture of rural patriarchy carries over to the province as a whole. It is re-enforced by the ideological system, beginning with the Christian churches. There is change, but it comes slow because the women's movement is so weak. (see Shortall, 1999)

# References

Albers, Patricia and Beatrice Medicine, eds. 1983. *The Hidden Half: Studies in Plains Indian Women*. New York: University Press of America.

Anderssen, Erin. 2003. "Women Do Lion's Share At Home." *Globe and Mail*, February 12, A-7.

Armstrong, Pat and Hugh Armstrong. 1984. *The Double Ghetto: Canadian Women and their Segregated Work*. Toronto: McClelland and Stewart.

Arscott, Jane and Linda Trimble, eds. 1997. *In the Presence of Women: Representation in Canadian Governments*. Toronto: Harcourt Brace & Company.

Bachofen, Johann J. 1967. *Myth, Religion and Mother Right: Selected Writings of J. J. Bachofen*. Princeton: Princeton University Press.

Baiman, Ron *et al*. eds. 2000. *Political Economy and Contemporary Capitalism*. New York: M. E. Sharpe.

Bangsund, Adrienne. 2002. "Shakeup Causes Some Concerns for Women." *Leader-Post*, April 3, A-5.

Basran, Gurcharn S. and David A. Hay, eds. 1988. *The Political Economy of Agriculture in Western Canada*. Toronto: Garamond Press.

de Beauvoir, Simone. 1974. *The Second Sex*. New York: Vintage Books.

Bell, Michael M. and Hugh Campbell, eds. 2000. "Rural Masculinities." Special issue of *Rural Sociology*, Vol. 65, No. 4, December.

Brennan, J. William, ed. 1984. *Building the Co-operative Commonwealth: Essays on the Democratic Socialist Tradition in Canada*. Regina: Canadian Plains Research Centre.

Canada. Status of Women Canada. 1997. *Economic Gender Equality Indicators*. Ottawa: Federal-Provincial/Territorial Ministers Responsible for the Status of Women.

Carbert, Louise. 1997. "Governing on 'The Correct, the Compassionate, the Saskatchewan Side of the Border.'" In Arscott and Trimble, pp. 154-179.

Chevillard, Nicole and Sebastien Leconte. 1986. "The Dawn of Lineage Societies and the Origins of Women's Oppression." in Coontz and Henderson, pp. 76-107.

Childcare Resource and Research Unit. 1995. *Child Care in Canada: Provinces and Territories*. Toronto: University of Toronto, Centre for Urban and Community Studies.

Clement, Wallace and John Myles. 1994. *Relations of Ruling: Class and Gender in Postindustrial Societies*. Montreal: McGill-Queen's University Press.

Clendinnen, Inga. 1991. *Aztecs: An Interpretation*. Cambridge: Cambridge University Press.

Collier, George A., Renato I. Rosaldo and John D. Wirth. 1982. *The Inca and Aztec States, 1400-1800; Anthropology and History*. New York: Academic Press.

Collier, Jane, Michelle Z. Rosaldo, and Sylvia Yanagisako. 1997. "Is There a Family? New Anthropological Views." in Lancaster and di Leonardo, pp. 73-81.

Coontz, Stephanie and Peta Henderson, eds. 1986. *Women's Work, Men's Property: The Origins of Gender and Class*. London: Verso Books.

Crompton, Rosemary and Michael Mann, eds. 1986. *Gender and Stratification.* Cambridge: Polity Press.

Cuthand, Doug. 2003. "Gun Control Just Makes Sense." *Leader-Post,* January 6, B-1.

Daly, Mary. 1973. *Beyond God the Father: Toward a Philosophy of Women's Liberation.* Boston: Beacon Press.

Dawkins, Richard. 1976. *The Selfish Gene.* New York: Oxford University Press.

DeMallie, Raymond. 1983. "Male and Female in Traditional Lakota Culture." In Albers and Medicine, pp. 237-266.

Engels, Frederick. 1972. *The Origin of the Family, Private Property and the State.* New York: International Publishers.

Fausto-Sterling, Anne. 1992. *Myths of Gender: Biological Theories about Women and Men.* New York: Harper Collins Publishers.

Fox, John W. 1988. "Hierarchization in Maya Segmentary States," in Gledhill, Bender and Larsen, pp. 103-112.

Fried, Morton H. 1967. *The Evolution of Political Society: An Essay in Political Anthropology.* New York: Random House.

Gledhill, John, Barbara Bender and Mogens Trolle Larsen, eds. 1988. *State and Society: The Emergence and Development of Social Hierarchy and Political Centralization.* London: Routledge.

Goldberg, Steven. 1971. *The Inevitability of Patriarchy.* London: Temple Smith.

Hall, Angela. 2003a. "Sask Won't Help Enforce Gun Law: Axworthy." *Leader-Post,* January 8, A-1.

Hall, Angela. 2002b. "The Battle Continues: Pay Equity." *Leader-Post,* August 1, A-7.

Harris, Marvin. 1977. *Cannibals and Kings: The Origins of Cultures.* New York: Random House.

Harris, Marvin. 1993. "The Evolution of Human Gender Hierarchies: A Trial Formulation," in Miller, pp. 57-77.

Hartmann, Heidi I. 1981. "The Unhappy Marriage of Marxism and Feminism: Towards a More Progressive Union." In Sargent, pp. 1-41.

Hay, David A. and Gurcharn S. Basran, eds. 1992. *Rural Sociology in Canada.* Toronto: Oxford University Press.

Hedley, Max. 1982. "Normal Expectations: Rural Women Without Property, *Resources for Feminist Research,* Vol. 11, No. 1, pp. 15-16.

Higginbotham, C.H. 1968. *Off the Record: The CCF in Saskatchewan.* Toronto: McClelland and Stewart.

Jahn, Cheryle. 1994. "Class, Gender and Agrarian Socialism: The United Farm Women of Saskatchewan, 1926-1931." *Prairie Forum,* Vol. 19, Fall, pp. 189-206.

Kalmakoff, Elizabeth. 1994. "Naturally Divided: Women in Saskatchewan Politics, 1916-1919." *Saskatchewan History,* Vol. 46, No. 2, Fall 1994, pp. 3-17.

Keet, Jean. 1988. "Matrimonial Property Legislation: Are Women Equal Partners?" in Basran and Hay, pp. 175-184.

Klein, Alan. 1983. "The Political Economy of Gender: A 19th Century Plains Indian Case Study." In Albers and Medicine, pp. 143-174.

Klein, Gerry. 2001. "Pulse of a Province: An Opinion Poll on Life in Saskatchewan." *Leader-Post*, January 20, Section H.

Lancaster, Roger N. and Micaela di Leonardo, eds. 1997. *The Gender/Sexuality Reader: Culture, History, Political Economy*. London: Routledge.

Leacock, Eleanor Burke. 1972. "Introduction: The Origin of the Family." In Engels, pp. 7-67.

Leibowitz, Lila. 1986. "In the Beginning...: The Origins of the Sexual Division of Labour and the Development of the First Human Societies." In Coontz and Henderson, pp. 43-75.

Di Leonardo, Micaela, ed. 1991. *Gender at the Crossroads of Knowledge: Feminist Anthropology in the Postmodern Era*. Berkeley: University of California Press.

Lerner, Gerda. 1986. *The Creation of Patriarchy*. New York: Oxford University Press.

Levi-Strauss, Claude. 1969. *The Elementary Structure of Kinship*. Boston: Beacon Press.

Lewontin, Richard C. 1991. *Biology as Ideology: The Doctrine of DNA*. Toronto: Anansi for the Canadian Broadcasting Corporation.

Mackie, Marlene. 1983. *Exploring Gender Relations: A Canadian Perspective*. Toronto: Butterworths.

Mann, Michael. 1986. "A Crisis in Stratification Theory? Persons, Households/ Families/ Lineages, Genders, Classes and Nations," in Crompton and Mann, pp. 40-56.

Mies, Maria. 1986. *Patriarchy and Accumulation on a World Scale: Women in the International Division of Labour*. London: Zed Books.

Miller, Barbara Diane. 1993. *Sex and Gender Hierarchies*. Cambridge: Cambridge University Press.

Miller, Barbara Diane. 1993. "The Anthropology of Sex and Gender Hierarchies," in Miller, pp. 3- 31.

Moore, Sally Falk. 1958. *Power and Property in Inca Peru*. New York: Columbia University Press.

Murdock, George P. 1967. "Ethnographic Atlas: A Summary," *Ethnology*, Vol. 6, No. 2, pp. 109-236.

Mutari, Ellen. 1997. "Feminist Political Economy: A Primer." In Baiman, Bouskey and Saunders, pp. 29-35.

Nash, June. 1978. "The Aztecs and the Ideology of Male Dominance," *SIGNS*, Vol. 4, No. 2, pp. 349-62.

O'Faolain, Julia and Lauro Martines, eds. 1973. *Not in God's Image: Women in History from the Greeks to the Victorians*. New York: Harper & Row.

Palmer, Craig and Peter Sinclair. 1997. *When the Fish Are Gone: Ecological Disaster and Fishers in Northwest Newfoundland*. Halifax: Fernwood Publishing.

Peterson, Frederick. 1962. *Ancient Mexico: An Introduction to the Pre-Hispanic Cultures*. New York: Capricorn Books.

Philip, Margaret. 2002. "National Daycare Plan Being Hammered Out." *Globe and Mail*, December 12, A-4.

Polachic, Darlene. 1994. "Rural Views Are Major Element in REAL Women's Group," *Western Producer*, January 30, p. 55.

Rogers, Diane. 1997. "Prairie Organizations Explore New Ways to Attract Women," *Western Producer*, December 4, p. 87.

Rollings-Magnusson, Sandra. 2000. "Canada's Most Wanted: Pioneer Women on the Western Prairies." *Canadian Review of Sociology and Anthropology*, Vol. 37, No. 2, pp. 223-238.

Rollings-Magnusson, Sandra. 1999. "Hidden Homesteaders: Women, the State and Patriarchy in the Saskatchewan Wheat Economy, 1870-1930." *Prairie Forum*, Vol. 24, Fall, pp. 171-183.

Rose, Steven, R. C. Lewontin and Leon J. Kamin. 1984. *Not in Our Genes: Biology, Ideology and Human Nature*. Toronto: Penguin Books.

Rowe, John Howland. 1982. "Inca Policies and Institutions Relating to the Cultural Unification of the Empire," in Collier *et al.*, pp. 93-118.

Rowbotham, Sheila. 1973. *Woman's Consciousness, Man's World*. Harmondsworth: Penguin.

Ruz, Alberto. 1993. *El Pueblo Maya*. Mexico City: Salvat Ciencia y Cultura Latinoamerica.

Sangster, Joan. 1984. "Women and the New Era: The Role of Women in the Early CCF, 1933-1940," in Brennan, pp. 69-97.

Sangster, Joan. 1989. *Dreams of Equality: Women on the Canadian Left*. Toronto: McClelland and Stewart.

Sargent, Lydia, ed. 1981. *Women and Revolution*. Boston: South End Press.

Saskatchewan. Department of Social Services. 1994. *Breaking New Ground in Child Care*. Regina: Government of Saskatchewan.

Saskatchewan. Department of Social Services. 1998. *Building Independence: Investing in Families*. Regina: Government of Saskatchewan.

Saskatchewan. Saskatchewan Women's Secretariat. 1997a. *The Economic Status of Saskatchewan Women*. Regina: Saskatchewan Women's Secretariat, May.

Saskatchewan. Saskatchewan Women's Secretariat. 1997b. "The Wage Gap: The Difference in Earnings between Men and Women," *The Source*, Vol. 1, No. 2, Winter, pp. 1-23.

Saugeres, Lise. 2002. "The Cultural Representation of the Farming Landscape: Masculinity, Power and Nature." *Journal of Rural Studies*, Vol. 18, pp/ 373-384.

Sayers, Janet. 1982. *Biological Politics: Feminist and Anti-Feminist Perspectives*. London: Tavistock Publications.

Schneider, Mary Jane. 1983. "Women's Work: An Examination of Women's Roles in Plains Indian Arts and Crafts." In Albers and Medicine, pp. 101-122.

Schreiber, Katharina J. 1992. *War Imperialism in Middle Horizon Peru*. Ann Arbor: University of Michigan.

Scowby, Christa. 1996. "I am a Worker, Not a Drone: Farm Women, Reproductive Work and the *Western Producer*, 1930-1939," *Saskatchewan History*, Vol. 48, No. 2, Fall, pp. 3-15.

Shortall, Sally. 1999. *Women and Farming: Property and Power*. Toronto: Macmillan.

Silverblatt, Irene. 1978. "Andean Women in the Inca Empire." *Feminist Studies*, Vol. 4, No. 3, October, pp. 37-61.

Silverblatt, Irene. 1991. "Interpreting Women in States: New Feminist Ethnohistories." In di Leonardo, pp. 140-171.

Smart, Anne. 1992. "Introducing the Feminine into the Body Politic—And Experiencing Its Allergic Reaction." *Canadian Woman Studies*, Vol. 12, No. 3, Spring, pp. 59-63.

Smith, Pamela. 1992. "Beyond 'Add Women and Stir' in Canadian Rural Society," in Hay and Basran, pp. 155-172.

Smith, Pamela. 1988. "Murdoch's, Becker's and Sorochan's Challenge: Thinking Again About the Roles of Women in Primary Agriculture," in Basran and Hay, pp. 157-174.

Spector, Janet. 1983. "Male/Female Task Differentiation Among the Hadatsa: Toward the Development of an Archaeological Approach to the Study of Gender." In Albers and Medicine, pp. 77-100.

Strong-Boag, Veronica. 1986. "Pulling in Double Harness or Hauling a Double Load: Women, Work and Feminism on the Canadian Prairie." *Journal of Canadian Studies*, Vol. 21, No. 3, pp. 32-52.

Tanner, Nancy M. 1981. *On Becoming Human.* Cambridge: Cambridge University Press.

Tarazona, Silvia Garza. 1991. *La Mujer Mesoamericana.* Mexico City: Editorial Planeta Mexicana.

Taylor, Georgina M. 1992. "Gender and the History of the Left," *Saskatchewan History*, Vol. 44, No. 1, Spring, pp. 31-34.

Taylor, Georgina M. 1984. "The Women...Shall Help to Lead the Way: Saskatchewan CCF-NDP Women Candidates in Provincial and Federal Elections, 1934-1965," in Brennan, pp. 141-160.

Teather, Elizabeth Kenworthy. 1996. "Farm Women in Canada, New Zealand and Australia Redefine their Rurality." *Journal of Rural Studies*, Vol. 12, No. 1, pp. 1-14.

Trivers, R.L. 1985. *Social Evolution.* Menlo Park, California: Benjamin/Cummings.

Ursel, Jane. 1992. *Private Lives, Public Policy.* Toronto: Women's Press.

Von Hagen, Victor W. 1960. *The World of the Maya.* New York: The New American Library.

Von Hagen, Victor W. 1961. *Realm of the Incas.* New York: The New American Library.

Warick, Jason. 2003. "When the Mayor's Hands Wander." *Leader-Post*, January 25, G-1.

Weber, Max. 1968. *Economy and Society: An Outline of Interpretive Sociology.* New York: Bedminister Press.

Whatmore, Sarah *et al.* eds. 1994. *Gender and Rurality.* London: David Fulton Publishers.

Wilson, Edward O. 1975. *Sociobiology: The New Synthesis.* Cambridge, Mass.: Harvard University Press.

Wilson, Gilbert. 1987. *Buffalo Bird Woman's Garden: Agriculture of the Hidatsa Indians.* St. Paul: Minnesota Historical Society Press.

Wilson, S. J. 1986. *Women, the Family and the Economy.* Toronto: McGraw-Hill Ryerson.

# Chapter 9

————○————

# POPULISM
# OF THE POLITICAL LEFT AND RIGHT

What is populism? The mass media declared the Reform Party and its leader Preston Manning to be "populists," although they always said that they were representative of "right-wing populism." But populist parties have traditionally represented ordinary workers and farmers who denounced the "special interest" groups representing big business and their political allies. How could the Reform Party be populist? It represented the most right-wing of business interests, particularly the oil corporations.

In Saskatchewan the term "populism" was always linked to the farmers' movements and the political forces that created the Co-operative Commonwealth Federation (CCF). Populism meant the politics of "the people" who opposed the domination of the economy and the government by the rich and powerful. It was a broad movement that wanted the system of government changed, to make it possible for the popular majority to actually influence government, if not direct it. Thus it demanded reforms that included popular initiatives for new legislation, popular referendums on bills passed by legislatures, and the right to the recall of elected representatives when they sold out to corporate interests. But today populism often has a different meaning.

In the 1990s we have seen the rise of far-right political parties in Europe, and most of them support openly racist policies. Yet the press and many academics call these parties "populist." The most important issue for these parties is immigration, and particularly Muslim and Arab immigration from North Africa and the Middle East. Thus, Jean-Marie Le Pen, head of the National Front in France, has established that he is anti-Semitic, following the traditional European right. But at the same time he gives strong support to Prime Minister Ariel Sharon and the Likud Party of Israel for its hard-line militaristic actions against the Palestinians. These European parties are deemed "populist" because their supporters are usually not from the traditional upper classes but are generally the poor, the marginalized working class, and the insecure middle class. They are opposed by the liberal establishment and the political left, including the Green parties.

Patrick J. Buchanan, the Christian fundamentalist and a leading Republican Party voice in the United States, is usually called a "populist" although almost always a "right-wing populist." He is considered a populist because he opposes free trade that threatens the jobs of American blue collar workers, and free trade is the political agenda of big business. The One Nation political party in Australia, which supports strict limits on non-white immigrants, is also called "populist" although almost always "right-wing populist." It is considered populist because it appeals to ordinary workers who feel threatened by Asian immigrants who are most likely to be highly trained and skilled but willing to work for lower wages and salaries.

The term "populism" has been used for many years to describe certain political leaders in Latin America. The first was Getulio Vargas, who ruled as dictator of Brazil from 1930 to 1945. He jailed the leaders of the Fascist Party, survived a 1935 coup attempted by an alliance of socialists and communists, was removed from office by a military coup in 1945, but was overwhelmingly elected President in 1950. In Argentina, Juan Peron ruled from 1945-1955, leading an authoritarian government that was often called fascist but also "populist." Both of these governments had strong support from a major trade union movement that rejected socialism and communism. The government of General Lázaro Cárdenas in Mexico (1934-40) is also called "populist." He was strongly opposed to the development of socialism but introduced a range of policies designed to provide better economic conditions for peasants and workers. He also mobilized a large majority to support his presidency.

Hugo Chavez, at present the leader of the Bolivarian Revolution in Venezuela, is characterized by the press as the modern-day Latin American populist. An army colonel, he was elected President with mass support from the poor. He introduced radical democratic changes to the structure of government, all of which were endorsed by large majorities in official referendums. He has been strongly opposed by the wealthy and the relatively small middle class, big business interests, the social democratic party Accion Democratica, and the mainstream trade union movement which has close ties to the AFL-CIO in the United States. He is also strongly opposed by the U.S. government and American business interests. His goal is to change the economy in order to benefit the poor majority but to oppose socialism.

In Latin America today, populism is associated with what we might call Keynesian government policies: progressive tax policies, government intervention in the economy, state ownership of key industries like oil, the expansion of the welfare state, support for small farmers, protection of the right of workers to form trade unions, and policies which try to deal with poverty and unemployment. The populist leaders and parties appeal to the majority who are poor and underemployed. Populists oppose the free trade and free market policies imposed on these countries by the World Bank, the International Monetary Fund, the U.S. government and their local allies, the political and business elite. Authoritarian governments are often called "populist" if they pass legislation that tries to improve the status of the poor majority.

The key characteristic of Latin American populism in the past and the present, and populism in general, is that *it has rejected a radical change in the capitalist economy.* All of the populist movements in Latin America have opposed the creation of a socialist or communist alternative political economy. What they want is a reformed capitalist system, with less control by foreign corporations, less control by the U.S. government, and less control by their local oligarchies. They advocate increased democracy. Populist leaders and governments have tried to improve the conditions of workers, farmers and the poor. The main problem they have faced is trying to get the middle class, the wealthy and business interests to pay taxes. In this part of the world, populism has usually been associated with authoritarian leaders and not with real democratic participation.

But in the industrialized countries of the north, populism today is commonly associated with right wing parties that are racist, oppose immigration, are strongly committed to the patriarchal order, and oppose rights for gays and lesbians. Those who feel that these are the most important issues today are giving support to the right wing parties and groups like the Reform-Alliance Party. Because they seem to have wide support on some of these issues, they are commonly called "right wing populists" by the mass media.

Populism is deeply rooted in the ideological history of Saskatchewan. It is present today in different forms. To understand this political tradition it is necessary to examine its roots.

## The Impact of Capitalism on Agriculture

Populism only developed with the rise of the capitalist mode of production. As a political movement for reform, it is most identified with the struggle of peasant and independent family farmers to survive within the new economic system. The traditional peasant economy, with emphasis on local production for primarily local or national markets, experienced the penetration of agriculture by capital, the rise of corporate agribusiness and its increasingly dominant role in the overall food system.

The first capitalist state was Great Britain. The classical liberal political economists were not that concerned with the impact of capitalism on agriculture. They did not focus on the changes in the class system brought by capitalism. But Karl Marx and Frederick Engels believed that how agriculture had changed in Great Britain would be the model for agriculture under capitalism in general.

The capitalist class is divided into class fractions representing merchant capital, finance capital, industrial capital, and capital in land and resources. In early 19th century England the peasant and the independent family farmer had all but disappeared. Agricultural land was owned by capitalists, the landlords. The actual farming was done by "farmers" who rented the land from the landlords, hired men and women as farm labour, and sought to make a profit on their operation. The landlord would extract rent from the tenant farmer, and he in turn would extract his profit and rent from the wage labourers.

Marx commented on agriculture in Great Britain in his major work, *Capital: A Critical Analysis of Capitalist Production* (1867). But at an earlier period he assessed the plight of the peasantry in revolutionary France. In 1798 the old feudal order was replaced and peasant farmers now owned their own land. Louis Napoleon Bonaparte was elected President in 1848, but seized absolute power in a coup d'état in 1851. The coup and the creation of an absolutist empire was supported by the peasants. However, the new regime did not protect the peasants but solidified the control of the new bourgeois class. In *The Eighteenth Brumaire of Louis Bonaparte* (1852) Marx commented on the plight of the peasant following the rise of the capitalist mode of production. The peasant farmer no longer paid a rent to the feudal lord, but the surplus he created was now taken by the urban usurers and the capitalists who held mortgages to the land. The sixteen million French peasants were now "enslaved by capitalism," he wrote. The new economic system allows "the capitalist to draw profits, interest and rent from the soil, while leaving it to the tiller of the soil himself to see how he can extract his wage." The other burden on the peasant was the new tax imposed to support the state and army. The result was the steady flow of dispossessed peasants to the city, the new landless proletariat. Capitalists invested in land vacated by peasants, and large new farms devoted to producing for the market emerged.

The peasants, closely tied to their religion, found that the local priest "appears as only the anointed bloodhound of the earthly police," Marx wrote. The army, which the peasants originally saw as necessary to defend the fatherland, became the army of the capitalists, hounding the peasants when they mobilized to defend their class position. Thus for Marx and Engels, capitalist penetration of agriculture would lead naturally to large capitalist farms, and the vast majority of peasants and small farmers would be forced off the land. Technological change and the introduction of machinery gave capitalist farmers a great advantage over peasant farmers in producing for the market.

Engels also described the changes that capitalism was bringing to the system of agricultural production. While the peasant farmer produced most of his farm inputs, the independent farmer under capitalism bought almost all of his farm inputs. This increased the indebtedness of farmers in general and accelerated their flight from the land. Of those remaining on the land, their relative income would fall. The control of the food system by capitalists ensured that they would get an increasing share of the economic surplus created by the farmers producing for the market. It was inevitable that peasants and small farmers would rebel against the new system. Marx and Engels hoped that they would see what was happening and align themselves with the working class. (Marx and Engels, 1968; Goodman and Redclift, 1991)

## Modern Populism Develops First in Russia

In the latter part of the 19th century the major agrarian populist movements developed in Russia and the United States. In both countries the peasants and small farmers mobilized to try to defend themselves from the impact of capitalist penetration of agriculture. The problems they faced were intensified by the first great world depression between 1873 and 1896 during which prices for primary products, and in particular agricultural products, fell substantially.

In 1861 Tsar Alexander II issued an edict emancipating the serfs from feudalism. However, the land was not given to individual farmers but to the village commune, known as the *mir*. The village commune in turn distributed the land to the peasants according to the size of the family. In addition, the land was re-distributed every ten years to ensure that their was equality. This new system was backed by the Zemstov Law of 1864, which organized local governments on a corporate basis, representing different classes and groups.

But the reforms served to open the door to capitalist penetration of agriculture. The life of peasants did not improve and many became paupers. The system of *artel* cultivation, where work was commonly done and the product equally shared by the farm workers, was disappearing. Capitalism was appearing in the form of the *kulak* or rich peasant who was acquiring an unequal share of the land.

The populist movement began in the mid 1870s as a secret society known as Land and Liberty. It stressed the democratic rights and power of the people and strongly supported the collective life of the commune. They opposed the values of capitalism, based on individualism and greed. The movement involved "going to the people," where intellectuals, students, professionals, and others went to work at the local level to try to spread their political message. However, their efforts were not that well received by the peasants. Many were turned over to the police, and in 1877 there were mass public trials and imprisonments.

Alexander III repressed the populist movement, but it arose again in 1901 with the formation of the Social Revolutionary Party, the populist party of the farmers and peasants. In 1906 the Stolypin reform was introduced, ending the *mir* commune system. Each *mir* could by majority vote abolish the communal system and grant each peasant private ownership of land. This system favoured the growth of the *kulaks* and reflected the development of capitalism in Russia. The Social Revolutionary Party advocated radical democratic changes and nationalization of land as the way to preserve the peasants on the land. (Wortman, 1967)

John Conway of the University of Regina has shown the similarities between 19th century populism in Russia and the United States. In both countries populism was "the characteristic response of the independent commodity producer, or the agrarian petit-bourgeoisie, to the threat of capitalist industrial modernization." Small producers must constantly get larger or else be forced off the land. The small manufacturer who uses a labour-intensive process finds he cannot compete with the large industrial factories.

Furthermore, the process of capitalism is the process of capital accumulation. Capital accumulation moves into every area of the world, and in every area of society where investment can make a profit. Food production is no exception. As Conway notes, the capitalist revolution in England was founded on a structural change in agriculture which produced a larger surplus to feed the urban population, the movement of labour off the farms and into the industrial cities, and a new area of investment. The burden of the change to industrial capitalism fell heaviest on the agrarian petit-bourgeois class of producers. (Conway, 1978)

The most extensive data on peasant and independent farming came from Russia. In the 1870s sociologists and social scientists by the thousands spread out through the country collecting statistics and writing articles and books on rural society and the impact of capitalism. As Daniel Thorner notes, this provided "the richest analytical literature we have on the peasant economy of any country in the period since the Industrial Revolution." The most prominent of these writers was Alexander Vasilevich Chayanov, whose followers were called "neopopulists" because they opposed both capitalist agriculture and socialist collectivist agriculture. (Thorner, 1986)

The Russian scholarship on populism was also the most prominent because of the political struggle between the Marxists and the populists, represented by the Social Revolutionary Party, over which political movement would replace the old regime of the Tsars. Polish sociologist Andrezej Walicki argues that the most serious work on populism at the time was done by V. I. Lenin. Russian populism, Lenin argued, was a struggle against serfdom but also a struggle against the capitalist system. It supported the thrifty, productive small farmer against big capital, which the Russian populists regarded as foreign, un-Russian. Capitalism brought gross inequalities to rural communities and promoted the ideology of greed. Lenin saw the populist as a Russian Janus, with one face looking to the past and the other to the future.

The populists in Russia opposed commercialized agriculture with its capitalist landlords and money lenders. They supported the system of small farms using family labour. They organized protests, formed farmers unions and association, and put a high emphasis on the creation of producer and consumer co-operatives. They pushed government to put controls on capitalism, urged progressive tax measures, and demanded a range of democratic political reforms, including free, universal education. The populists argued that western capitalism did not have to be adopted in Russia and that the general principles of the commune could be applied to industrial production. (Walicki, 1969; Conway, 1978; 1981)

## Agrarian Populism in the United States

In North America the populist tradition began in the United States after the Civil War and then spread into Canada. The great rush to settle the American west came after the passage of the Homestead Act of 1862. Any person over 21, the head of a family, a citizen or landed immigrant, could acquire 160 acres by living on the land for five years. Soldiers, their widows, and their children could claim 160 acres within the land granted to the railways. Those who did not want to wait five years on the land could exercise the "right of commutation" and after six months on the land pay $1.25 per acre and obtain title. This clause greatly encouraged land speculation. There was a great rush to the Western land because it was much easier to farm as there were no forests to be cleared.

Eastern money from banks, mortgage companies and individuals flooded to the west to provide mortgages, normally for five years paying eight percent interest. Mortgages carried a lien on the land, but with good crops, relatively high prices and steadily rising land prices, how could anyone lose? Farms were mortgaged to the hilt. By the late 1880s, land prices were up to $17 per acre on the frontier. The railways overbuilt branch lines, sold their free land to land development companies, and more settlers and land speculators came. But in 1887 the bubble burst. The abundant rainfall ended, and for five of the next ten years there was almost no crop. Deflation set in and the boom ended. Settlers and speculators defaulted on their mortgages and many moved back to the east.

In the American south the plantation system was destroyed by the Civil War. Bankrupt owners sold their land for between three and five dollars per acre. Tenant farming became the norm, with the share cropper giving one half of his crop to the proprietor. Merchants advanced credit to farmers and took liens on their land. They also advanced credit, sold supplies for 20 to 50 percent above normal prices, and attached liens on the forthcoming crop. Farmers defaulted and merchants became large land owners. Former slaves were now share croppers on land owned by whites as they had no money to purchase land. Poverty was widespread, among both black and white farmers. (see Hicks, 1961; Hofstadter, 1955; Pollack, 1966; Goodwyn, 1978; McMath, 1975)

The world depression began in 1873 and lasted until 1896. Over that period of time the average price of a bushel of wheat fell from $1.06 to $.63, a bushel of corn from $.43 to $.30, and a pound of cotton from $.15 to $.06. Farmers could not pay their mortgages nor could they pay the merchant for the advances on the crop. The freight rates charged by the railroad were relatively high and appeared to be discriminatory. Long haul rates were lower than small shipments on short line routes. Farmers discovered that it was cheaper to ship wheat from Chicago to Liverpool than from North Dakota to Minneapolis. The owners of the railroads, the grain companies and the flour mill corporations worked within the Republican Party and set government policy. The farmers protested the higher interest rates on their mortgages and operating loans, the high railway rates, and the monopoly power of the grain and milling industry. They criticized the high tariffs introduced after the Civil War.

Supporters of the Greenback and free silver movements argued that the plight of the farmer was made worse by the actual shortage of currency in circulation, which, they believed, led to the appreciation of the value of the dollar and their debts. (Hicks, 1961; Goodwyn, 1978)

The farmers responded by forming organizations. There was the Patrons of Husbandry, the Grange movement, the National Greenback Party, and then the National Farmers' Alliance. In the South there was the Southern Farmers' Alliance of small white farmers, and over one million black tenant farmers joined the Colored Farmers' Alliance. In 1887 the Farmers' Alliances held a national convention in Minneapolis, and they approached the Knights of Labor and the Laborers' Union of America to form a political coalition. The American Federation of Labor rejected any affiliation because farmers were "employers of labour."

In 1889 the Knights of Labor signed a coalition with the National Farmers' Alliance and Industrial Union. They agreed that there were just demands "of labor of every grade" and that "producers should unite in a demand for the reform of unjust systems and the repeal of laws that bear unequally upon the people." (Cited in Hicks, 1961)

The American farmers, of course, were strongly committed to private ownership of land. Their attacks were primarily on the "monopoly conditions" that they faced, and they demanded reforms to the economic system which would make it more competitive. They also began creating a range of co-operative enterprises which they would own and control. Some sought a system to pool grain to ship to markets. Farmers organized to pressure governments to regulate the railroads, the banking system and the grain handling system.

The farm movement also attacked the control of the Republican and Democratic parties by business interests and what they saw as the undemocratic nature of the government. In 1890 a convention was held in Lincoln, Nebraska to consider the creation of an independent party. It included delegates from the Granges, the Knights of Labor, and the Union Laborites. In the election of 1890 the candidates they supported did quite well, and they elected several governors and many state legislators. On July 4, 1892 farmers met in Omaha to create the national Peoples Party (also known as the Populist Party) and nominate General James B. Weaver of Iowa for president and General James G. Field of Virginia for vice president.

The platform reflected the political ideology of agrarian populism. It called for government ownership of the railroads and communications, reform of the banking system, reduction of the tariff, free coinage of silver, and a graduated income tax. Under no circumstances should government ever provide subsidies to private corporations. They demanded democratic reforms including suffrage for women, direct election of the President and Vice President while limiting office to one term, the direct election of Senators, the Australian preferential ballot, and the introduction of direct democracy through the use of the initiative and referendum.

While the emphasis was on problems facing farmers, the People's Party sought an alliance with ordinary workers. The first principle of the party called for the "union of the labor forces" and the second principle declared that "wealth belongs to him who creates it" and proclaimed that those who take it from the farmer and labourer were guilty of "robbery." The People's Party declared that "the interests of rural and civic labor are the same; their enemies are identical." The party supported the eight hour day, the minimum wage and the abolition of the "large standing army of mercenaries, known as the Pinkerton system" used to repress labour, the "hired assassins of plutocracy." But critics did not find the populists always on the side of progress. In many of their platforms the Farmers Alliance had called for an end to immigration by "the pauper and criminal classes of the world," the prohibition of alien ownership of land and the opening of land on Indian reservations to homesteading. (see Hicks, 1961 for texts of platforms.)

The American populists insisted that society was divided between those who worked hard and created the wealth and those who lived off their work. The "productive majority" included the farmers, the workers, and small businessmen. They opposed the "small parasitic minority in the highest places of power." "Sockless" Jerry Simpson, one of the leading populist organizers, argued that it was a struggle between "the robbers and the robbed." As the populist manifesto stated, "on the one side are the allied hosts of monopolies, the money power, great trusts and the railway corporation" and on the other side were those "who produce wealth and bear the burdens of taxation." General Weaver declared that "it is a fight between labor and capital, and labor is in the vast majority." (Hofstadter, 1955)

As in Russia, Populism in the United States had the face of Janus. Richard Hofstadter and others have pointed out its "rhetorical anti-Semitism." There was the general attack on the banks and those upholding the gold standard. Often they were identified with Baron Rothschild and other Jewish bankers. Mary Ellen Lease, one of the most famous populist leaders, regularly attacked Wall Street and the Jewish bankers. The populists were also strong advocates of American nationalism and expressed hatred of Great Britain, the home of imperialists, money lenders, and supporters of the gold standard. (Hofstadter, 1961)

The populist movement was undermined in the south by the race issue. The political and business forces of the right denounced the white farmers for co-operating with the Colored Farmers' Alliance. There was a class issue as well, as many black tenant farmers were share croppers and labourers for white farmers. In 1891 the national strike by the cotton pickers was initiated by the Colored Farmers' Alliance, and the white Southern Farmers' Alliance stood on the other side. In 1896 the defeat in the south came when the Populist Party joined in a fusion ticket with the Democratic Party which strongly supported racism and racial segregation. (Dickson, 1999; McMath, 1975)

The People's Party did not do very well in 1892, winning only 8.5 percent of the national vote. They did very well in the states where wheat was the primary crop and silver mining was important. They did fairly well in the south given the racist attacks by supporters of the Republican and Democratic parties. They did not receive many votes from the urban working class. The Knights of Labor was dying, the American Federation of Labour was just getting started, and the labour movement was weak. (Hicks, 1955; Hofstadter, 1961)

There were a number of reasons for the general decline of populism in the United States. In 1896 the People's Party had only one major issue that was generally popular, free silver, and this was adopted by the Democratic Party. Instead of fielding their own candidate, the People's Party voted at convention to back William Jennings Bryan of the Democrats for President. This signaled the end of the third party strategy. After 1897 there was a general upturn in farm prices and farm discontent dropped off. Farmers declined in political influence with immigration, urbanization, and the growth of the labour movement. The most important third party became the Socialist Party, backed by labour, but which recruited significant popular support from farmers in the wheat belt states. In the progressive period in the early 20th century, many of the populist demands for regulation of business were adopted. Finally, there was the formation of the Farm Bureau Federation which reflected the interests of the conservative and prosperous farmers. It became the favoured vehicle of the Republican and Democratic parties. (Hofstadter, 1961; Lipset, 1971)

## The Nonpartisan League in North Dakota

The populist movement was very strong in North Dakota, where the ticket of Weaver and Field obtained 49 percent of the vote in 1892. The political experience of populism in this state carried over the border into Canada. Census figures show that over 900,000 Americans crossed the border after 1896 and came to the Canadian prairies to obtain cheap land. In 1909 farmland in North Dakota sold for 50 dollars an acre and comparable land could be purchased in Saskatchewan for only two dollars an acre. (Sharp, 1997; Robinson, 1966)

In 1892 the Populists ran a full slate for North Dakota state offices, and because of fusion with the Democrats, won every office except secretary of state. In 1894 the Democrats ran a separate slate, and the Republicans swept the state. Populism faded away. (Robinson, 1966)

However, the radical tradition was not dead. There was wide support for Theodore Roosevelt and Robert LaFollette and the Progressive movement in the early 20th century. The metropolitan-hinterland reality brought discontent to farmers in North Dakota, for the banks, railroads, wholesale dealers, and the grain and flour industries were controlled from Minneapolis-St. Paul. In 1908 the Progressive Republicans and the Democrats gained control of the state Assembly, and in 1910 the Democrats and Progressives controlled the Governor and both houses of the legislature. A full slate of reform legislation was passed.

In 1912. Arthur C. Townley, a Minnesota farmer who had gone bankrupt in 1912, worked in North Dakota as an organizer for the Socialist Party. He quit the party and began to organize the Nonpartisan League, a new farmers' organization. The League worked as an organized group within the Republican Party, and its candidates swept the nominations in the primaries. In the election of 1916 candidates endorsed by the League swept state office. Their more radical program was blocked in the state Senate, but the legislature still passed a range of economic and political reforms.

The Republicans, Democrats and business interests, with strong support from the media, created the Independent Voters Association (IVA) to oppose the Non Partisan League. In 1916 they organized a single slate to oppose them in the state elections. With the all-out attack from business and the political right, the Nonpartisan League was defeated and faded away. (Robinson, 1966; Sharp, 1997; Lipset, 1971)

## Contradictions Within the Populist Movement

John Conway has commented on the "two-sidedness" of the populist movement in the United States, which was both progressive and "backward looking and confused." American scholarship, trapped in liberal theoretical analysis, could only see populism as either progressive or reactionary. (Conway, 1978; 1984)

It was not just the progressive face of populism that crossed the border into Canada. In the 1920s there was a revival of the Ku Klux Klan in the United States, and it moved onto the Canadian prairies where it gained considerable influence. In

1929 the Klan was very influential in the provincial election in Saskatchewan, where it was aligned with the Conservative Party. It focused its attack on Roman Catholics and immigrants. A faction of the Progressive Party participated in this campaign. (Brown, 1997)

Yet the contradictions in the populist position can be understood in a modern political economy framework. Populism began as an agrarian movement, advancing the perceived interests of the petit bourgeois class, farmers and small businessmen who are trapped by the expansion of capitalism and its move to a monopoly stage. The original populism represented the economic interests of small property owners. But their attack on inequality and the domination of big business, and demands for democratic reforms, was supported by large sectors of the working class, professionals and intellectuals who had rejected socialism and communism. Thus the appeal to populism has never been limited to those who are formally in the petit bourgeois class. It has always included those who approve of its political and ideological orientation, the reform of capitalism.

We know very well that people have never voted solely along lines of economic self interest. It is common that people feel that other political and social issues are more important. Historically, many people have primarily identified with the political position of the leaders of their church. The hostility of farmers in North America to Aboriginal people is rooted in the fact that they have their land because of imperialist colonial policy. The populist tradition, rooted in the family farm, has always been strongly patriarchal, supporting the belief that the farm or family business is rightly owned by the father as the head of the family and passed on to a son. This ideological position has been strongly supported by the major religions. Conservative parties have stressed the attachment to the traditional patriarchal family, and for many this guides their political party orientation. Populism has also been strongly identified with nationalism and national culture. It is no surprise that American populists were nationalists, often supporters of white supremacy, and were hostile to non-white immigration. (see Bode, 1971; McMath, 1975)

The contradictions within populism can be illustrated through the example of Lyman Frank Baum. Born in New York in 1856 he moved to Aberdeen, South Dakota in 1887 to become editor of the *Aberdeen Saturday Pioneer*. He wrote a number of editorials calling on the U.S. government to "finish the job" and exterminate all the remaining Aboriginal people. "The Whites, by law of conquest, by justice of civilization, are masters of the American continent, and the best safety of the frontier settlements will be secured by the total annihilation of the few remaining Indians," he wrote following the U.S. military assault on the women and children of Wounded Knee Creek in December 1890. Yet Baum also wrote "The Wizard of Oz" in 1900, a story of the plight of the western farmer in the struggle against big business, the bankers who controlled the monetary system, the corrupt political leaders, and the Cowardly Lion, the weak William Jennings Bryan. The Tin Woodsman, once an independent worker, was so oppressed by the Wicked Witch of the East (the industrial capitalists) that he had lost his heart, was incapable of love, and ceased to be human. Baum strongly supported the creation of a progressive farmer-labour populist party. (Churchill, 1997; Rockoff, 1990)

## The Development of Prairie Populism

The populist movement in the United States had a major impact on farm and political movements in Canada. The problems faced by farmers in Canada were almost the same as in the United States. American farm organizations operated on both sides of the border. The Grange moved into Ontario in 1872 and then into Manitoba in 1876. The Patrons of Industry, with its strong commitment to building co-operatives, moved into Manitoba in 1891. They also entered politics, winning seats in the Ontario legislature and taking a few federal seats. The U.S. Farmers' Alliance was the inspiration behind the Manitoba and North West Farmers' Union. In 1908 the Society of Equity formed a Canadian branch and was particularly influential in Alberta. They focused on building producer co-operatives. The U.S. Nonpartisan League moved into the prairies and was particularly influential in Alberta. In 1917 they elected Louise McKinny to the legislature, the first woman elected in the British Empire. (Brown, 1997)

In 1901 the Territorial Grain Growers' Association was formed, and after 1905 it divided into Alberta and Saskatchewan organizations. A similar organization was formed in Manitoba in 1903. In 1909 the three organizations joined the newly formed Canadian Council of Agriculture (CCA). Prairie farmers joined the co-operative movement with the formation of the Grain Growers Grain Company in 1906, the Saskatchewan Co-operative Elevator Company in 1911 and the Alberta Farmers' Co-operative in 1913. (Sharp, 1997; Morton, 1967; Conway, 1981; Finkel, 1989; Laycock, 1990; Brown, 1997)

The struggle of the prairie farmers was against eastern big business and the National Policy. They campaigned against the plutocracy, money power and "the New Feudalism." They attacked the "special interests" who were able to dominate the political establishment in Ottawa. The Grain Growers Guide and their readers railed against the monopolies and the combines which exploited the producing classes, both farmer and worker. The dominant political parties were characterized by graft and corruption. The farmers' protest movement was led by men who came from the British Labour Party, the trade unions, socialism, the co-operative movement, and the American populist movement. In contrast to the United States, the prairie protest movement was greatly influenced by the "social gospel" movement within the mainstream churches. During the First World War many of the progressive farmers joined the crusade for peace and denounced militarism.

The Farmers' Platform of 1910 came after the CCA mobilized a "siege on Ottawa" to directly press their demands on the federal legislature. They wanted free trade and not the National Policy Tariff. They advocated progressive taxation, government owned railroads, government owned grain terminals, changes in the Bank Act to provide cheaper credit, support for the formation of co-operatives, and even government intervention into the meat packing industry. The revised Farmers Platform of 1918 became known as the "New National Policy." It was more progressive, demanding democratic reforms, graduated income and inheritance taxes, a progressive tax on corporate profits, suffrage for women, and more direct government action to defend and support farmers. (Sharp, 1997; Morton, 1967)

During the war the farmers movements demanded the "conscription of wealth" and attacked "war profiteering" by big business. Inflation raised farming costs. Interest rates on mortgages and farm loans went up substantially. There were numerous political scandals which involved all of the prairie governments. By the end of the war, the farmers' organizations and periodicals were attacking militarism, imperialism, calling for disarmament, and urging a World Court and support for the League of Nations to prevent future wars. Farmers were demanding a new "free trade party."

In mid-1920 a depression struck the farm community. Prices for farm products fell dramatically over the next few years. Yet costs of production kept increasing. Many on the prairies concluded their plight was caused by the abolition of the Canadian Wheat Board, the federal marketing agency created during the war.

The proposed alliance with labour in a movement of producers was shaken by the revolution in Russia, the militancy of the new One Big Union, the Winnipeg General Strike, and the Red Scare. The majority of farmers opposed the radical turn of organized labour in Canada. Many feared that a socialist or communist government would implement the nationalization of land. As Paul Sharp notes, the *Grain Growers' Guide* took a hostile editorial position towards the labour left, strikes, sympathy strikes, and decried all industrial violence as undemocratic. "Thereafter, the *Guide* seldom called for any alliance with labour." (Sharp, 1997) .

The new farmers political movement grew rapidly. In October 1919 the United Farmers of Ontario, formed by the Dominion Grange and Farmers' Association, contested the provincial election and won 45 seats. In alliance with the leftist Independent Labour Party, which won 11 seats, they formed the government. In 1921 the United Farmers of Alberta swept into office and governed the province for fourteen years. In Manitoba in 1920 farmers had joined with various labour parties in election saw-offs and to back joint candidates. There were many notable successes. But in 1922 the United Farmers of Manitoba entered the provincial election independent of labour, won 27 seats, and formed a majority government.

In Saskatchewan, the Liberal Party and government was successful in containing the farmers. Premiers W. M. Martin and C. A. Dunning were leaders of the Saskatchewan Grain Growers Association. They co-opted the farmers'policy ideas and leaders and supported the Saskatchewan Co-op Elevator Association. The Liberals backed co-operative ventures, which were non-partisan and non-political. They were determined to keep the farmers' movement a "privileged pressure group" and not a separate political party. (Laycock, 1990)

In the federal House of Commons a number of MPs joined together to officially form the Progressive Party. In the federal election of 1921 they contested 149 seats and won 65 of them. Of the 43 MPs from the prairies, only four were not Progressives. But the populist farmers movement failed to become a political party and collapsed. They were the second largest party in the House of Commons, but they refused to take on the role as Official Opposition. Many members were opposed to political parties, convinced the political and electoral system was inherently corrupt and undemocratic. Many felt that they should be only a farmers' party, not admitting non-farmers as members. They were unable to build any relationship with the rising labour movement with its trade unions, labour and socialist parties. As Paul Sharp concludes, they evaded their political responsibility, had ineffective leadership, and were incapable of implementing any kind of party discipline. Many of their Members of Parliament took the position that they were there simply to hold a "balance of power" between the two old parties and not to advance a separate progressive agenda. They fell apart over 1922 and 1923 and dropped to 24 seats in 1925 and 20 in 1926. Agrarian populism had reached the end of the line in Canada. (Sharp, 1997; Morton, 1967)

## Different Prairie Populism

Nevertheless, as Lorne Brown has argued, the populist farmers movement had a enduring impact on the political culture of the prairies. The two party system would never return. The farmers' movements contributed greatly to the development of the regional political culture. But it was more than just regionalism; the farmers movement was based on class identity and class conflict. The prairie populist movement paved the way for the development of the Co-operative Commonwealth Federation (CCF) and the Social Credit Party in the 1930s. It was still there in some form when John Diefenbaker and the federal Progressive Conservative Party were elected in 1957. (Brown, 1997)

David Laycock has been critical of the political economy analysis of populism which puts an emphasis on class relations and the economics of the capitalist market. He argues that this approach does not explain the difference between the kinds of populism that developed on the Canadian prairies. He argues that political culture on the prairies has been greatly influenced by the existence of provinces, their different economic composition, and their different historical experiences. He classifies prairie populism between 1910 and 1945 under four headings.

"Crypto-Liberalism" describes the populist movement that was closely linked to the Liberal party. It was primarily a farm reform movement which believed that necessary change could come about through reform of the Liberal Party. This populism was found in the National Progressive Party, the United Farmers of Alberta government between 1921 and 1935, the Saskatchewan Grain Growers' Association and the Saskatchewan Liberal Party, and the Liberal party and governments in Manitoba. According to Laycock, "crypto-Liberalism generated the lowest common denominator—rurally oriented hinterland regionalism."

A second version of prairie populism is identified with the Social Credit movement in Alberta. Laycock calls this "plebiscitarian populism." The Alberta Social Credit movement was characterized by mass support for a popular but authoritarian leader, in this case William Aberhart, who was both political leader and religious evangelist. Political mobilization and election became "plebiscites" for obtaining a government which would implement the "general will" of the people. This was combined with the technocracy movement on the prairies, a belief that if government was being run by the right people, technology would bring prosperity for all. There was a basic contradiction in the Social Credit phenomenon, for while it advocated popular, participatory democracy, in office it was dominated and manipulated by an authoritarian leadership.

"Radical democratic populism" represented a third stream in prairie populism. Laycock identifies this with the American populist movement, the Nonpartisan League, the demands for a co-operative and not a competitive society, and a rejection of party politics. This is best illustrated in the United Farmers of Alberta and with its two prominent intellectual leaders, Henry Wise Wood and William Irvine.

"Social democratic populism" is the fourth populism, the one which is of most interest to us. It came from the socialist wing of the Nonpartisan League, the labour parties which had emerged in the prairie cities, left wing activists in the United Farmers organizations, and many settlers of British or Scandinavian background with experience in social democratic parties. They carried on the populist belief in the necessity of a farmer-labour political alliance. They supported a reform of political parties by using democratically controlled governments to promote the interests of the majority. They were gradualists, supported the development of co-operatives, and the majority were not socialists. (Laycock, 1990)

## Peasants, Farmers and Household Production

Political economists, sociologists and anthropologist have argued that there is a fundamental difference between peasants and farmers working within the capitalist system. Eric Wolf, a renowned American anthropologist, insists that peasants are not the same as independent farmers. "The peasant does not operate an enterprise in the economic sense; he runs a household, not a business concern." But peasants are also different from rural cultivators who live in pre-capitalist societies. In these societies production is for use and for obligations to the band, tribe or kinship group. Relations of economic coercion and exploitation do not exist. Exchange is minimal and there is no incentive to try to maximize production for a market.

This egalitarian system of agricultural production changes with the development of hierarchy, centralization of power and then state societies. As Wolf argues, "In primitive societies, surpluses are exchanged directly among groups or members of groups; peasants, however, are rural cultivators whose surpluses are transferred to a dominant group of rulers that uses the surpluses both to underwrite its own standard of living and to distribute the remainder to groups in society that do not farm but must be fed for their specific goods and services in turn." Peasants in more advanced societies are primarily concerned with maintaining their position on the land and perpetuating their ability to operate the farm. This is a *family economy*, where the household depends on the labour of the man who is the head of the household, his wife, and his children. (Wolf, 1966)

The best data on peasant life was collected in Russia in the 19th and early 20th centuries. Of the many who wrote about the Russian peasant, Alexander Chayanov was the most widely known. From 1919 to 1930 he was recognized as the leading authority on economics and agriculture and the role of the peasant. In 1925 he published *The Theory of Peasant Economy.*

For Chayanov, one of the central distinctions between peasants and a farm as a business enterprise was the use of labour to accumulate profits. In Russia data indicated that over 90 percent of peasant farms hired no labour. Since the peasant farm hired no labour, it paid no wages. In a family or domestic enterprise, wages are irrelevant. Peasants never calculated the value of unpaid family labour. They treated the farm as a family operation, a single economic unit. The family did what was necessary to stay on the farm and pass it on to an older son. Thus the family would produce crafts to sell or exchange and do farm work and trades for additional income. But it did this not to acquire a surplus to invest but to guarantee the survival of the farm family.

The Russian peasant was only too aware of the drudgery of labour on the farm. Family members were able to work more hours and work more intensively if it was necessary to sustain their household. This was all based on the "self-exploitation" of family labour. Chayanov argued that Russian peasants carefully considered how hard and long they had to work. If a crop was good, they would reduce the hours of labour they worked. They would increase their labour activity if they wanted to increase family consumption or expand investment in the farm. He called this the "labour-consumer balance" between satisfying family needs and the drudgery of labour. In times of poor crops or poor prices, the farm family would cut consumption. The peasant farm could survive in hard times when a commercial farm could not.

Indeed, Chayanov argued that in most cases in Russia a peasant was willing to pay more for land or a higher rent than a commercial farmer because they were not oriented toward maximizing a profit and were more capable of resisting the cost-price squeeze. The data collected showed that landowners were getting out of production themselves and instead renting their land to peasants. This brought them a good income without having to do the work. Chayanov argued that the peasant would eventually be drawn into the capitalist mode of production through the "circulation process," the buying and selling of commodities, and the formation of co-operatives. Co-operatives would grow, become more controlled by bureaucracies, and then begin to make demands on their peasant owners. Household farm production would have to change.

But the peasant farm was not an egalitarian operation. The man was unquestionably the head of the household. When decisions were made on what to do with the gross farm income, it was made by him. He decided which son would inherit the farm. The woman of the household and the children were in a clearly subordinate position. This *patriarchal order*, certainly not limited to Russia, was strongly supported by the established churches.

The independent farmer in Russia operated on a different basis. He was driven by the values of the capitalist system. Money was borrowed to buy land, machinery and to pay wages for hired labour. Farm debt was higher, and it was easier to go bankrupt. The family farm operation was oriented to profit or maximizing absolute rent in the value of farm land. But it was similar to the peasant farm in that it was still based on household production. The head of the family unit was the man, and his wife and children worked for no wages. It was still a patriarchal domestic operation. But it was specifically producing commodities for the market. (Thorner *et al.*, 1986; Kitching, 1982)

With the spread of capitalism around the world, and its rapid advancement to a mature or monopoly stage, it was assumed that production in agriculture would be similarly transformed. As noted above, Marx and Engels believed that the petit bourgeois farmer, often referred to in political economy and sociology as the "independent commodity producer" or the "simple commodity producer," would basically disappear. The spread of capitalism would lead to the introduction of capitalist farming as had developed in Great Britain. But this did not happen. Even in the advanced capitalist world of the north, the dominant social form of farming remained the petit bourgeois family farmer. How can this be explained?

The small farmer who owns his own land has some things in common with the capitalist farmer. They both own the means of production, the land and the tools. Both produce commodities for the market. Both are concerned with maximizing profit or the private accumulation of capital. They both employ the same technology. But there are social differences. The petit bourgeois farm is characterized by a *unity of capital and labour*, whereas capitalist production is based on the separation of capital and labour. There are many examples of capitalist farms around. They are owned by investors. They hire the managers and farm labour who are paid salaries and wages. But there are many cases where large agribusiness corporations directly entered the farming business and then after a number of years got out. There are good examples in fruit and vegetable production. (Warnock, 1978)

A number of explanations have been put forth to account for the persistence of the petit bourgeois farm. The first reason advanced was the self-exploitation of farm labour in this form of production. Farmers and family members do not have to earn wages for the management and labour they provide. In recent times men and women on farms have taken off-farms jobs to earn income to subsidize the farm's operation. Capitalist farms cannot compete because they have to pay wages for management and farm workers. Secondly, it has been argued that agricultural machinery has allowed individual families to farm without having to hire any or many farm workers. But capitalist farms use the same technology, so this cannot be the defining reason. Social scientists have concluded that these explanations have not proven to be satisfactory.

Karl Marx and his followers in political economy have advanced an alternative explanation based on the key characteristics of the capitalist system of production and accumulation. Why would a capitalist want to invest in a farm when he could invest in General Motors? The *turnover time* for invested capital greatly affects the rate of profit. For many farm commodities (like those crops grown on the prairies) there are only annual harvests. Capital comes from the accumulation of surplus value, labour value extracted from workers. For wheat and other commodities, the labour turnover time is only annual. If the same amount of capital is invested in manufacturing, more surplus value is extracted because it is extracted in each production cycle.

Farmers must invest in machinery and other capital goods which lie idle for long periods of time. Marxists argue that capitalists will avoid this kind of investment. Many farm commodities are perishable or subject to losses due to changes in the weather. Thus farming appears to be a high risk investment compared to General Motors. The trend in North America is for farmers to hire more labour as they get larger. Yet most farm work is periodic, and there are long periods of time when labour is not needed. This creates either higher than necessary labour costs, if labour is retained on the year-round basis, or an unstable farm labour market. This form of business operation will not attract capital. (Mann and Dickinson, 1978; Warnock, 1978; Magdoff, 1998; Goodman and Redclift, 1991; Goodman and Watts, 1997)

There is no doubt that corporate agribusiness is invading the area of farming. The most common development is the vertical integration of corporate agribusiness and family farms through a contract. But these contracts specify what is to be produced and how. It transforms the individual family farm operator into a modern serf. Even at the level of industrial food production, capitalists are reluctant to directly enter at the farm level.

In contrast, we can see in Saskatchewan that local capitalists, including many large farmers, are willing to invest in giant hog barn operations and feedlots for cattle. But these operations are capitalist factories, not family farms. They are getting extensive government support and subsidies which make investing more secure. But most important for the capitalists is the fact that their investment is producing surplus value and economic rent every hour of the day, every day of the year. (Warnock, 1986; Denis, 1979)

Wallace Clement, a sociologist and political economist at Carleton University, has done extensive research into simple commodity production in Canadian farming and fishing industries. He argues that petit bourgeois or family production survives because it is beneficial to the capitalist system. The high risks of investment in farming and fishing, the lower profit rates, and the necessity for the supervision of labour are thus passed on to the producers themselves. But through the vertical contract the corporation maintains access to the product and is able to define all the parameters of the production system. (Clement, 1983; also, Davis, 1980)

Thus the family farmer and the independent fisherman keep the old petit bourgeois *form* of production, but the *content* has been set by the capitalist mode of production. While the man as the head of the family production unit retains formal ownership and possesses the means of production (land, machinery, fishing boat, etc.), capital captures economic ownership and control. Clement insists that this is part of the proletarianization process, for the family producers lose economic control. "Capital progressively appropriates the property rights of independent commodity producers, thereby increasingly reducing them to performing exclusively the obligations of labour." Proletarianization is a process and only the end result is the loss of ownership of private property in the means of production. Family production units in the era of monopoly capitalism have only the facade of independence. (Clement, 1983)

Harriet Friedmann has argued that a stable system of agricultural production by the family farm requires the existence of a developed capitalist economy. Households produce commodities which they must sell, and they buy all the commodities that they consume. But a developed labour market must also exist. Members of households must be able to go into the labour market, at least on a temporary basis, to earn money to support the farm. Underemployed members of farm families must also enter the labour force to earn money in order to establish new household enterprises. Often this involves the exchange of labour between farms, but other employment must also be available. Thus her survey of wheat farmers in Cass County, North Dakota in 1920 demonstrates that specialized commodity production by households requires a labour market that only exists under a fully developed capitalist system. (Friedmann, 1978)

Some sociologists and political economists prefer to use the term "domestic commodity production" to define the class of petit bourgeois producers. Craig Palmer and Peter Sinclair, who have studied the fishery industry on Canada's east coast, don't like the term "independent commodity production" because the small operators have no autonomy in the production process and no control over prices and returns. They don't like the term "simple commodity production" because it implies that the main purpose is reproducing the economic unit and not the accumulation of capital or expanded reproduction. "Petit bourgeois" or "petty commodity production" implies small scale, and this is certainly not the case with many producers today. Palmer and Sinclair prefer the term "domestic commodity production" because it recognizes "the importance of kin, usually living in the same or neighbouring households, in supplying and organizing labour." In the Newfoundland fishery, domestic commodity production recognizes the traditional form of the producing household, "the patrilocal extended family." This type of production unit "is formed when sons continue to work and live with or near their father, even after reaching adulthood." Most of the fish caught is salted by the fishers and their families with men, women and children participating in the curing process. These family operations are also producing for the market. But as largely inshore fisher family operations, they are being replaced by the introduction of longliners and trawlers, small capitalist enterprises depending on hired labour. The parallels with farming on the prairies are obvious. (Palmer and Sinclair, 1997)

## Conclusion

Populism is closely linked to agrarian ideology, the struggle of men and women to make a living on family owned farms. In the world of advancing capitalism they sought to survive on the land in the face of the power of capitalist agribusiness: the finance industry, the farm supply industry, the food processing industry, and the wholesale and retail industry. The capitalist section of the food chain has been far more powerful and influential than the independent family farmer trying to make a living while competing against the neighbours. The share of the consumer's food dollar that goes to the farmer has been steadily falling over the years despite the political struggles of the farmers and some government support. While the family-owned farm remains the dominant producer of agricultural products in Canada, the majority of farms have disappeared, with families moving to the city and their land absorbed by other farmers. The farmers who remain are large land owners and have little in common with the farmers of the classic populist period.

Populism was historically a battle to extend democracy. Farmers and their supporters could easily see that big business interests, the "special interests," had little difficulty dominating the major political parties. Everywhere, populism was identified with demands for a more democratic political system. In North America in particular there was the demand for direct participation through the initiative, referendum and recall. Many populist farm groups and political parties demanded proportional representation. Others had no faith whatsoever in the political system as it existed and demanded some form of corporate "group government." This position was strong among supporters of the Nonpartisan League which had considerable influence in Alberta, less so in Saskatchewan.

The populist movement was not limited to farmers. Its demands for curtailment of the power of big business and democratic reforms had significant support in other popular groups in society, beginning with workers and trade unionists who were interested in reforming capitalism and not replacing it. At the same time, of course, not all farmers supported the populist movements. The populist movement in Canada had little support from farmers in the east who were farming primarily for the domestic market. More well-to-do farmers did not join the movement. And farmers, like every social group, had a variety of ideological orientations. The emphasis on the building of farmer-owned co-operatives demonstrates the reform nature of the movement. The co-operatives were "people's capitalism" not the basis for a socialist alternative.

So what does it mean when it is said that the Reform-Alliance Party today is right wing populist? At this point it may be useful to review the terms "left" and "right." They emerged in Europe after the French Revolution when men without property were first allowed to be elected to parliaments. In France, and elsewhere in Europe, the national legislature is in the form of seats in a half circle, with the Speaker facing them sitting at a table. From the beginning, parties on their own aligned themselves in the half circle of seats according to their political ideology. Those representatives and parties sitting to the left of the Speaker were committed to expanding democracy and equality. They became known as "the left." Those to the right of the Speaker opposed democracy and stood for inequality, particularly the control of wealth by the few. They also supported traditional privileged institutions, like the state church, and rule from the top down. They became known as "the right." In Canada only the Manitoba legislature has this physical structure, with the seats in a half circle facing the Speaker; the rest have the British parliamentary structure with government and opposition members facing each other and the Speaker at one end of the legislative room.

Thus, traditional populism was always classified as "left" because it supported democracy and a greater movement toward equality of condition. The right has always included big business, property owners, the hierarchies of the established churches, those who historically opposed the expansion of democracy.

So in some respects the Reform-Alliance Party has claimed a populist identification because in rhetoric it has supported a move towards more direct democracy by endorsing the initiative, referendum and recall. But this is problematic. Under Preston Manning the party itself functioned more like the populism of William Aberhart, for the leader made all the fundamental decisions and controlled the party platform and those nominated as candidates. In its subsequent form as the Canadian Alliance it was still run from the top down, as we can see in the move by the leadership in 2003 to merge with the Progressive Conservative Party.

The Reform-Alliance is similar to the classic populists in that its membership and voter support has been strong in the rural sector of Canada. But it also has strong support among the representatives of big business in Canada, particularly those on Bay Street. In this respect, it has nothing in common with classic populism. In Alberta, from the beginning the party has been closely aligned with the oil industry. As Lorne Brown points out, "They represent radical individualism rather than communitarian populism." (Brown, 1997)

The Reform-Alliance also shares the old populist commitment to patriarchy and other conservative social causes. This places the party on the political right, for when women, visible minorities, Aboriginal people, immigrants, French Canadians, and gays and lesbians demand equality, they are taking up a left wing cause. (see Laycock, 2002; Dobbin, 1991; Harrison, 1995; Patten, 1996)

Traditional populism is all but gone from North America. The class base of that political movement no longer exists. The large majority of individual family farms no longer exist, having been driven out of business by the impact of corporate capitalism. The rural movement that attacked the "special interests" of big business, finance and their political allies has been greatly reduced. There remains a minority of farmers in Saskatchewan who are members of the National Farmers Union and the New Democratic Party, and they carry on the left populist tradition. But because of their small numbers, they are not in a position to spearhead any serious political movement.

Some may conclude that populism today is best represented by the Reform-Alliance Party and the neo-fascist parties of the right in Europe. Their supporters in Saskatchewan include many of the remaining farmers. But these farmers tend to be large land owners, belong to special commodity groups which advance their own particular interests, and are supporters of a more free market approach to farming. Their farm organizations are closely linked to agribusiness corporations and interests. The Reform-Alliance Party is supported by people who live in the small towns, who generally have lower incomes, but who are strong supporters of traditional patriarchal values. They also have an extensive base in the Christian fundamentalist churches. Overall, provincial and federal elections have shown that they have wide popular support in Saskatchewan. That is another reason why they are deemed populists.

David Laycock shows that the new right wing populists are still attacking the "special interests." But the enemy has changed. It is now the modern welfare state and those who are seen to benefit from it. These include "feminist lobby groups, Native organizations, ethnic and cultural minority groups, state-aided arts and cultural organizations, providers of state-subsidized legal assistance to the poor or traditionally disadvantages, the management and employees of virtually all Crown corporations and state agencies, and all public-sector unions." The agenda of the new populists in Canada has been adopted from the new right in the United States which has captured the Republican Party. Business interests never fall under the category of special interests. This right wing populism strongly opposes all state involvement in redistributing income, wealth or power. (Laycock, 2002)

But there is another thrust of populism in Saskatchewan and around the world. This is found in the new popular movements and political alliances that oppose the free trade and free market agenda of neoliberalism. Today they are linked together through the World Social Forum. This is commonly referred to as the "anti-globalization" movement. It has its strong supporters in Canada and Saskatchewan, a collection of groups which originally came together to oppose the Canada-U.S. Free Trade Agreement and the North American Free Trade Agreement. There is more on this development in Chapter 14.

The anti-globalization movement is populist in that people from community groups, farm organizations, trade unions, and a wide variety of popular organizations, are demanding greater democracy and oppose the domination of governments by big business interests. They are opposed to the policies of the International Monetary Fund, the World Bank, and the World Trade Organization, which primarily represent the interests of international capital. They are populist in that they advocate reforms to the existing capitalist system. The movement as a whole does not see the root cause of their problems and discontents in capitalism as an economic system. Therefore, they only propose reforms and do not demand that capitalism be replaced by some other mode of production.

# References

Basran, Gurcharn S. and David A. Hay, eds. 1988. *The Political Economy of Agriculture in Western Canada*. Toronto: Garamond Press.

Bechofer, Frank and Brian Elliott, eds. 1981. *The Petit Bourgeoisie*. London: MacMillan.

Brown, Lorne A. 1997. "Introduction" to the 1997 Reprint of Paul F. Sharp, *The Agrarian Revolt in Western Canada*. In Sharp, pp. xvii-xxviii.

Buttel, Frederick H. and Howard Newby, eds. 1980. *The Rural Sociology of the Advanced Societies: Critical Perspectives*. London: Croom Helm.

Canovan, Margaret. 1981. *Populism*. New York: Harcourt Brace Jovanovich.

Chevalier, Jacques. 1982. "There is Nothing Simple about Simple Commodity Production." *Studies in Political Economy*, No. 7, Winter, pp. 89-124.

Churchill, Ward. 1997. *A Little Matter of Genocide: Holocaust and Denial in the Americas 1492 to the Present*. San Francisco: City Light Books.

Clement, Wallace. 1983. *Class, Power and Property: Essays on Canadian Society*. Toronto: Methuen.

Clement, Wallace. 1983. "Property and Proletarianization: Transformation of Simple Commodity Producers in Canadian Farming and Fishing." In Clement, pp. 225-43.

Conway, John. 1978. "Populism in the United States, Russia and Canada: Explaining the Roots of Canada's Third Parties." *Canadian Journal of Political Science*, Vol. 11, No. 1, March, pp. 99-124.

Conway, John. 1981. "Agrarian Petit-Bourgeois Responses to Capitalist Industrialization: The Case of Canada," in Bechofer and Elliott, pp. 1-37.

Conway, John. 1984. "The Nature of Populism: A Clarification." *Studies in Political Economy*, No. 13, Spring, pp. 137-84.

Davis, John Emmeus. 1980. "Capitalist Agricultural Development and the Exploitation of the Properties Laborer." In Buttel and Newby, pp. 133-153.

De Janvry, Alain. 1980. "Social Differentiation in Agriculture and the Ideology of Neopopulism." In Buttel and Newby, pp. 155-168.

Denis, Wilfred B . 1982. "Capital and Agriculture: A Review of Marxist Problematics." *Studies in Political Economy*, No. 7, Winter, pp. 127-54.

Denis, Wilfred B. 1979. "Exploitation in Canadian Prairie Agriculture, 1900-1970." Paper presented to the Annual Meetings of the Canadian Sociology and Anthropology Association, University of Saskatchewan, Saskatoon, June 4.

Dickson, Patrick. 1999. "A Brief History of the Colored Farmers' Alliance Through 1891." *Kalamu Magazine*, June, Cornell University. http://www.kalamumagazine.com

Dobbin, Murray. 1991. *Preston Manning and the Reform Party*. Toronto: James Lorimer & Co.

Fairbanks, Carol and Sara Sundberg. 1983. *Farm Women on the Prairie Frontier*. New Jersey: Scarecrow Press.

Finkel, Alvin. 1989. *The Social Credit Phenomenon in Alberta*. Toronto: University of Toronto Press.

Friedland, William H. *et al.*, eds. 1991. *Towards a New Political Economy of Agriculture*. Boulder: Westview Press.

Friedmann, Harriet. 1980. "Household Production and the National Economy: Concepts for the Analysis of Agrarian Formations." *Journal of Peasant Studies*, Vol. 7, pp. 158-84.

Friedmann, Harriet. 1978. "World Market, State and Family Farm: Social Bases of Household Production in the Era of Wage Labour." *Comparative Studies in Society and History*, Vol. 20, pp. 545-86.

Goodman, David and Michael Redclift. 1981. *From Peasant to Proletarian: Capitalist Development and Agrarian Transitions*. Oxford: Basil Blackwell.

Goodman, David and Michael Redclift. 1991. *Refashioning Nature: Food, Ecology and Culture*. London: Routledge.

Goodman, David and Michael J. Watts, eds. 1997. *Globalizing Food: Agrarian Questions and Global Restructuring*. London: Routledge.

Goodwyn, Lawrence. 1978. *The Populist Movement: A Short History of the Agrarian Revolt in America*. New York: Oxford University Press.

Goss, Kevin F. *et al.* 1980. "The Political Economy of Class Structure in U.S. Agriculture: A Theoretical Outline." In Buttel and Newby, pp. 83-132.

Haney, Wava G. and Jane B. Knowles, eds. 1988. *Women and Farming: Changing Roles, Changing Structures*. Boulder: Westview Press.

Harrison, Trevor. 1995. *Passionate Intensity: Right-wing Populism and the Reform Party of Canada*. Toronto: University of Toronto Press.

Hay, David A. and Gurcharn S. Basran. 1992. *Rural Sociology in Canada*. Don Mills: Oxford University Press.

Hedley, Max J. 1981. "Rural Social Structure and the Ideology of the 'Family Farm.'" *Canadian Journal of Anthropology*, Vol. 2, No. 1, Spring, pp. 85-9.

Hedley, Max J. 1981. "Relations of Production of the 'Family Farm': Canadian Prairies." *Journal of Peasant Studies*, Vol. 9, pp. 71-86.

Hedley, Max J. 1976. "Independent Commodity Production." *Canadian Review of Sociology and Anthropology*, Vol. 13, pp. 413-21.

Hedley, Max. 1982. "Normal Expectations: Rural Women Without Property." *Resources for Feminist Research*, Vol. 11, No. 1, pp. 15-16.

Hicks, John D. 1931. *The Populist Revolt: A History of the Farmers' Alliance and the People's Party.* Lincoln: University of Nebraska Press.

Hofstadter, Richard. 1955. *The Age of Reform: From Bryan to F.D.R.* New York: Vintage Books.

Ionescu, Ghita and Ernest Gellner, eds. 1969. *Populism: Its Meaning and National Characteristics.* London: Weidenfeld and Nicolson.

Janiewski, Dolores. 1988. "Making Women into Farmers' Wives: The Native American Experience in the Inland Northwest." In Haney and Knowles, pp. 35-54.

Jensen, Joan M. 1991. *Promise to the Land: Essays on Rural Women.* Albuquerque: University of New Mexico Press.

Johnson. Leo. 1981. "Independent Commodity Production: Mode of Production or Capitalist Class Formation?" *Studies in Political Economy*, No. 6, pp. 93-112.

Keet, Jean E. 1988. "Matrimonial Property Legislation: Are Farm Women Equal Partners?" In Basran and Hay, pp. 174-184.

Kitching, Gavin. 1982. *Development and Underdevelopment in Historical Perspective: Populism, Nationalism and Industrialization.* London: Methuen.

Kohl, Seena. 1976. *Working Together: Women and Family in Southwestern Saskatchewan.* Toronto: Holt, Rinehart and Winston.

Laclau, Ernesto. 1977. *Politics and Ideology in Marxist Theory.* London: Verso.

Laxer, Gordon, ed. 1991. *Perspectives on Canadian Economic Development: Class, Staples, Gender and Elites.* Toronto: Oxford University Press.

Laycock, David. 2002. *The New Right and Democracy in Canada.* Don Mills: Oxford University Press.

Laycock, David. 1990. *Populism and Democratic Thought in the Canadian Prairies, 1910 to 1945.* Toronto: University of Toronto Press.

Lind, Christopher. 1995. *Something's Wrong Somewhere: Globalization, Community and the Moral Economy of the Farm Crisis.* Halifax: Fernwood Publishing.

Lipset, Seymour Martin. 1971. *Agrarian Socialism: The Co-operative Commonwealth Federation in Saskatchewan.* Berkeley: University of California Press.

McMath, Robert C. 1975. *Populist Vanguard: A History of the Farmers' Alliance.* Chapel Hill: University of North Carolina Press.

Magdoff, Fred *et al.*, eds. 1998. *Hungry for Profit: Agriculture, Food, and Ecology.* New York: Monthly Review Press.

Mann, Susan A. and James M. Dickinson. 1978. "Obstacles to the Development of Capitalist Agriculture." *Journal of Peasant Studies*, Vol. 5, No. 4, July, pp. 466-81.

Martinson, Oscar B. and Gerald R. Campbell. 1980. "Betwixt and Between: Farmers and the Marketing of Agricultural Imputs and Outputs." In Buttel and Newby, pp. 215-253.

Marx, Karl and Frederick Engels. 1968. *Selected Works.* New York: International Publishers.

Morton, William L. 1967. *The Progressive Party in Canada*. Toronto: University of Toronto Press.

Palmer, Craig and Peter Sinclair. 1997. *When the Fish Are Gone: Ecological Disaster and Fishers in Northwest Newfoundland*. Halifax: Fernwood Books.

Patten, Steve. 1996. "Preston Manning's Populism: Constructing the Common Sense of the Common People." *Studies in Political Economy*, No. 50, Summer, pp. 95-132.

Pollack, Norman. 1966. *The Populist Response to Industrial America*. New York: Norton.

Reimer, Bill. 1986. "Women as Farm Labour." *Rural Sociology*, Vol. 51, No. 2, pp. 143-55.

Robinson, Elwyn B. 1966. *History of North Dakota*. Lincoln: University of Nebraska Press.

Rockoff, Hugh. 1990. "The 'Wizard of Oz' as a Monetary Allegory." *Journal of Political Economy*, Vol. 98, No. 4, August, pp. 739-748.

Sachs, Carolyn. 1983. *The Invisible Farmers: Women in Agricultural Production*. Ottawa Rowman and Allanheld.

Sharp, Paul F. 1997. *The Agrarian Revolt in Western Canada: A Survey Showing American Parallels*. Regina Canadian Plains Research Centre, University of Regina. Originally published in 1948. New introduction by Lorne A. Brown.

Sinclair, Peter R. 1972. "Populism in Alberta and Saskatchewan." Unpublished Ph.D. dissertation, University of Edinburgh.

Stirling, Bob and John Conway. 1988. "Fractions among Prairie Farmers." In Basran and Hay, pp. 73-86.

Thorner, Daniel *et al.*, eds. 1986. *A. V. Chayanov on the Theory of the Peasant Economy*. Madison: University of Wisconsin Press.

Walicki, Andrezej. 1969. *The Controversy over Capitalism: Studies in the Social Philosophy of the Russian Populists*. Oxford: Clarenden Press.

Warnock, John W. 1986. *The Politics of Hunger: The Global Food System*. Toronto: Methuen.

Warnock, John W. 1978. *Profit Hungry: The Food Industry in Canada*. Vancouver: New Star Books.

Warnock, John W. 1975. "Free Trade Fantasies: The Case of the Farm Implements Industry." *This Magazine*, Vol. 9, Nos. 5/6, pp. 36-40.

Wartman, Richard. 1967. *The Crisis of Russian Populism*. Cambridge: Cambridge University Press.

Whatmore, Sarah. 1991. *Farming Women: Gender, Work, and Family Enterprise*. London: Macmillan.

Wolf, Eric. 1966. *Peasants*. Englewood Cliffs: Prentice Hall.

Wood, L.A. 1924. *A History of the Farmers' Movements in Canada*. Toronto: Ryerson Press.

Wortman, R. 1967. *The Crisis of Russian Populism*. New York: Cambridge University Press.

# Chapter 10

——○——

# FOREST RESOURCES
# IN ECONOMIC DEVELOPMENT

The creation of Canada as a modern nation state and the settlement of the prairies involved a massive privatization of natural resources. The land and its resources had been seized from the Aboriginal people through military force and threat of force. At that point it became Canadian state property, owned by the people as a whole through their government. The unification of both the United States and Canada involved a westward expansion, driven by the building of the railways and the immigration of Europeans to settle as farmers on the land. The federal government retained control over natural resources on the Canadian prairies in order to implement the National Policy.

The major railways in both the United States and Canada were built by private capitalists. They received a variety of state subsidies, and the most important was the granting of public land. The railway companies sold the land and used the capital to finance their expansion. The homestead acts in both countries involved the transfer of public land to private individuals at virtually no cost. Thus a substantial number of immigrants to the Canadian prairies took up homesteads with the goal to selling out after the three year occupation requirement in order to take a capital gain and move on to some other enterprise or occupation. Many farmers in the United States sold their land and used the cash to buy larger holdings on the Canadian prairies. Indeed, that is still happening. Farmers from other provinces and countries are selling their land and moving to Saskatchewan, where land is cheaper. Those who now own the land are pressing the provincial government to repeal the legislation which places restrictions on foreign and non-resident ownership of agricultural land hoping that this will lead to even higher land prices. (Briere, 2002)

The settlement of the west in North America led to the development of a liberal reform movement around the question of economic rent from natural resources. This is most identified with Henry George (1839-97), the founder of the "single tax" movement. Since land is a scarce resource, and population continues to rise, the price of land is driven up by the law of supply and demand. People can buy land, hold it for a few years, and then sell it for a capital gain. George and his followers denounced this practice. They argued that this was an unearned surplus or transfer of capital which was received without performing any productive services. Following Adam Smith, George believed that wealth was created by individual entrepreneurs and family farmers who worked hard, ran their enterprises efficiently, and produced a surplus from their labour. Thus George proposed that this unearned wealth be confiscated through a tax by governments. Indeed, George believed that his "single tax" could become the primary source of revenue for governments. While he was a journalist and political activist in California, his movement spilled over the border into Canada. (Keiper, 1961)

Thus the settlement of the prairies places the issue of *economic rent* at the centre of economic development. The classical liberal political economists established the debate. Economic rent is the term used to describe income derived from the use of land and its resources. This includes land, all the resources it contains including the subsoil minerals and water, and indeed just the space or "standing room." Natural resources are a free gift from nature. Human beings did not have to apply any capital or labour to produce them. Furthermore, there is no reciprocity involved in this gift.

From the beginning of the European nation-states, it was argued that natural resources were a free gift from God, and they were given to human beings (more specifically, "men") in common. Governments hold these gifts as a trust for the public as a whole. In the early period kings and queens would grant these valuable resources to their male friends and family members. In the modern period of capitalism, elected governments allocate them to a small group of private corporations. Today, it is expected that "royalties" or "resource rents" will be returned to the people as a whole as a compensation for privatization. In Canada some resources (like hydro electric power) have been developed by state owned enterprises. But given the capitalist system, privatization of resources is the norm. All governments in Canada want to expand and fully use natural resources for economic development. In the not-too-distant past, the extraction of natural resources by private corporations and the rates of royalties and resource taxes were a matter of wide public debate. But by the 1990s none of the major political parties wanted to open any debate on the issue. Royalty rates are set in behind-closed-doors meetings with private industry officials.

Nevertheless, Saskatchewan's economy is based on natural resource extraction. At first, of course, the agricultural sector completely dominated the economy. But like all provincial governments, Saskatchewan sought ways to diversify the economy through the development of natural resource industries. Today, the extraction of oil, natural gas, potash, uranium, coal and other minerals is very important to Saskatchewan's economy. Forestry, a renewable resource, could become very important. Given that very little tax revenue comes from the agricultural sector, economic rents from resource extraction are increasingly important to provincial government revenues.

## Resource Rents under Capitalism

In pre-capitalist societies land and resources were owned by the society as a whole. Whether in Ireland, the Americas or Africa, ownership rested with the clan or tribe. Individuals who farmed the land had usufruct (or use) rights. In early state societies with class systems, rent for the use of land was clearly defined, a share of the crop or labour from the direct producers, whether serfs, slaves, peasants, or tenant farmers. The economic rent went to the owners of the land, or those who had legal control over state land. Rent was the surplus over and above the subsistence and reproduction needs of the agricultural producers.

The concept of economic rent that we are familiar with in economics was developed during the early period of capitalism, and it focused on the use of land for agriculture. The classic liberal political economy approach was first set forth in the writings of John Locke, in *Two Treatises on Government* (1690) and *Some Considerations on the Consequences of the Lowering of Interest and Raising the Value of Money* (1691). This has been discussed in Chapter 3. Barbara Arneil's comprehensive study of Locke rightly concludes that his primary concern was to establish a moral and legal justification for the seizing of land from the Aboriginal peoples in the Americas. His theory of private property and individual rights, as well as the labour theory of value, developed out of his defence of England's colonial policy. (see Arneil, 1996; Laslett, 1960; Kelly, 1991)

Most commentators on Locke's work have concentrated on how he defends the labour theory of value, the right of a man to take private possession of common land

and enclose it for his own use, and the lack of any obligation to compensate the common owners. The English had the right to seize the land of the American Indians because it was "not being used." Individuals had a similar right to seize "unoccupied" and "unused" land. Once the land had been appropriated by individual men, then this ownership would be defended by constitutional law. (Arneil, 1996)

Locke's key argument was that individual farmers, corporations or capitalists did not owe the people as a whole anything for seizing a piece of land, enclosing it with fences, and claiming it as private property as long as they used it productively. Applying their own labour to the land, or the labour of others, improved it and the general condition of the society as a whole. That was an adequate payment. Thus Locke was the first major political economist to argue that God did not create the resources of the earth for humans in common but only for those men who had a capitalist spirit and were fortunate to get to the land before others. But he also established the capitalist political economy principle that resource rents in all natural resources should go to the individual and not to society as a whole.

Adam Smith, who drew heavily upon the work of Locke, took up the issue of economic rent where it is seen as a return on the use of land, one of the necessary factors of all production. During the 17th and 18th centuries, rent captured from agricultural production was relatively high in England, and it went to the class of land owners. But Smith, writing in the period of mercantile capitalism, was not concerned about economic rents from agriculture. He saw land owners and farmers as productive people, helping to build the national economy. He believed that farm production would continue to improve. Furthermore, he felt that industry would expand even faster. Rents in agriculture would not hinder the development of capitalism.

This was the period when the landed aristocracy was the dominant class and controlled the government. With the rise of the new capitalist class, the question of economic rent became a hot political issue. The Corn Laws, passed by the landed oligarchy, protected agricultural producers from cheap imports. Capitalists were strongly opposed to the Corn Laws.

Thomas Malthus, a prominent political economist in his time, was a defender of the Corn Laws, and he argued that rents rose because there was a scarcity of fertile land. Farm operators required that the prices for their produce cover the cost of the land. In contrast, David Ricardo, his friend and fellow political economist, was strongly opposed to the Corn Laws. He argued that tariff protections for land owners artificially increased the cost of bread. Since the wages for workers, set at the subsistence level, had to include the price of bread, high land rents resulted in higher-than-necessary wages and as a result lower profits. Following the arguments of the capitalists, he advocated the elimination of the Corn Laws, free trade in agricultural products, and the import of cheaper grain. Ricardo concluded that the interests of the landlords were always opposed to the interests of the capitalist class and society as a whole. (Heilbroner, 1961; Robbins, 1998; Buchholz, 1989)

The concept of *differential rent* was formulated by Ricardo. He recognized that there were different grades of land depending on their fertility. In Canada today we classify land according to an agro-climatic index; the higher the rating, the more valuable the land for agriculture. Ricardo argued that commercial farmers would first farm the most fertile land. As the population grew, the demand for food would increase as would its price. In this market more marginal land would then be farmed. If demand increased further even more marginal land would be brought under the plow. Thus if a farmer could make a profit on the least fertile land, then the farmer on the most fertile land not only would make the normal profit he would also make a surplus profit. Ricardo called this surplus profit *differential rent*, that which is in excess of the normal rent that tenant farmers paid to their absentee landlords. It should be remembered that the English system of agriculture at the time consisted of large absentee landlords who owned the land, "farmers" who were tenant farmers who paid a rent to the landlord for the use of the land, and farm workers, men and women who were paid a wage to do the actual farm labour.

Ricardo's theory has formed the basis of the mainstream economic theory of resource rents since this time. Economic rents are defined as a payment *over and above* what is necessary to keep labour and capital on the land producing farm products, and that includes making a normal profit. Anyone who has farmed knows the validity of this argument. When buying farm land, the first thing a farmer looks at is what the farm has produced in the past. A quarter section of Saskatchewan land that produces on average thirty bushels of wheat will command a higher price than one that on average produces only fifteen bushels.

Ricardo also pointed out that land can claim a differential rent if it is close to a market. Thus a dairy or market garden close to a city would command a higher economic rent than one farther away. Land in general is higher in price the closer it is to a city. The difference in the cost of transportation creates a differential rent reflected in the price of land. This principle can be seen in the settlement of the Canadian prairies under the Dominion Lands Act of 1872. Homesteads, a quarter section of land (160 acres) for $10, were available only outside the 20-mile belt of land adjacent to the Canadian Pacific Railway. Within the belt, the government would sell land for $2.50

per acre. The CPR and the Hudson's Bay Company sold their land within the belt for even more. Land was slow to be taken by homesteaders, for it was difficult and costly to haul a grain crop twenty miles to a grain elevator by horse and wagon. (see Norrie and Owram, 1996)

Karl Marx added to the classical political economy view of economic rent. First, he argued that economic rent occurred only under capitalism, where there was private ownership of land and resources. In pre-capitalist societies, agricultural production was for use, to provide a fundamental need. Because land was not privately owned, no economic rent existed as it is defined by Ricardo. (Marx, 1966)

Marx did not disagree with Ricardo on the issue of differential rents. Soil fertility and access to markets were real differences in the value of land. But Marx argued that differential rent in more advanced capitalist agriculture would be determined by the application of capital to the land. As Marx noted, the most productive agriculture was that which was under irrigation. He argued that the fertility of the land was less important than the investment of capital. Gerald Friesen has stressed that the prairie settlers who were most successful in staying on the farm were those who had capital to buy more land, hire more labour, use more fertilizer, and were able to acquire the new farm machinery. (Friesen, 1987)

Marx is most associated with the concept of *absolute rent*. This exists in a capitalist society where there is private ownership of land. Private ownership creates a monopoly situation. As the majority of people cannot own land, they must pay for the right to use the land and its products. This economic rent arises from the ability of owners to exclude others from the resource. Thus corn is sold not at the highest price of production but at an even higher price which also includes a monopoly factor. The monopoly factor is capitalized in the price of land. This is why a number of the classical liberal political economists, including David Ricardo and John Stuart Mill, opposed private ownership of land. (Robbins, 1998; Bucholtz, 1989)

If there were significant capital investments in agriculture, Marx argued, there could be a crisis of overproduction. This would be caused by the inequalities of income and wealth, where many people were hungry but could not afford to buy food. Under capitalism, food is not distributed according to need but according to ability to pay. Thus with farmers having similar means of production, it is possible for the cost of production to exceed the prices for farm products. Under these circumstances, Marx argued that those on the more marginal lands would be the first to go out of business. Historically, this has proven to be true. (Hindness and Hirst, 1975; Perelman, 1996)

Marx's analysis led to the use of the term *quasi-rents*. This refers to a return to the use of the land or a resource like forestry which is not really a return to the land itself but to the capital goods invested in the land. These investments are seen as a "sunk cost." There has been considerable debate about the nature of this form of rent. In general, quasi-rents are identified as returns from past investments and management. In farming, obvious examples would include the installation of irrigation, the application of fertilizers, or a series of crop rotations that have improved the quality of the soil and increased its productivity. (Fine, 1982; Marx, 1966)

The existence of absolute rent explains why farmers as an economic class support private ownership of land and oppose social ownership. As they used to say in Saskatchewan, "farmers live poor and die rich." In recent years farm prices have stagnated and the costs of agricultural production have risen much faster. But while net farm income was falling, and the number of farmers was steadily declining, there have been relatively few farm bankruptcies. Indeed, the annual number of bankruptcies in Saskatchewan steadily fell from 225 in 1991 to only 60 in 2001. When farmers decide to quit farming, they sell their land to others, usually local farmers. They rarely go bankrupt because of their substantial capital assets, particularly in land.

The price of farmland today includes the capital value of absolute rent. All farmers know this very well. The first day we were on our orchard in the spring of 1974, our neighbour, one of the largest orchardists in the Okanagan, came over to welcome us. As he left he said to me: "John, don't forget. We're not in the business of raising food for hungry people. We're in the business of land speculation." In spite of the B. C. Agricultural Land Reserve, he made a lot of money buying and selling agricultural land.

Today, farmers in Saskatchewan are among the most wealthy people in the province. Statistics Canada's Census of Agriculture reports that between 1996 and 2001 the size of an average farm in Saskatchewan increased from 1,146 acres to 1,277 acres. The average capital value of a farm increased from $523,470 to $661,368. Farmers know how to capitalize their income, buying additional land, new machinery, etc. They have been encouraged to do this; from the beginning the capital gains tax rate was much lower than the income tax rate. There is an even greater incentive now, as new legislation has granted farmers a $500,000 lifetime capital gains exemption. (Statistics Canada, 2002)

The traditional theory of economic rent was designed to encourage the development of the capitalist class, capital accumulation and private ownership of natural resources. The classic theory, expounded by David Ricardo, did not include the payment of any compensation or royalty to the general public for the privatization of public resources. It also assumed that land and resources which were not used in the capitalist production process were "waste" lands.

## Rent in Forestry

Forests are a free gift from nature. Historically, they have been held as common property of a society. In most advanced capitalist societies, forest land has been privatized. The extent of public ownership varies: Canada, 96%; Russia, 90%; United States, 45%; Finland, 29%; Sweden, 13%; New Zealand, 4%. Where forests are publicly owned, as in Canada, economic rent is paid to the government in the form of royalties and taxes. Where forests are privately owned, the rent accrues to the individual owner. (Van Kooten and Bulte, 2000)

The issue of economic rents in forestry has been a prominent political issue over the past ten years or so. Canada exports around 80 percent of its lumber and most of its pulp and paper to the United States. Lumber exports are worth $10 billion and comprise one-third of the U.S. market. The U.S. forest industry, supported by environmental and Aboriginal organizations on both sides of the border, insists that Canadian governments subsidize the forest industry through very low stumpage fees (royalties), direct state subsidies to private corporations, non-enforcement of environmental regulations, infringement on Aboriginal title to land and resources, and granting large trans-national corporations long term tenures on public land for no cost. (Green and Matthaus, 2001)

In Canada forest land is held by the Crown and then granted to large corporations through long term leases. The government is supposed to get some return from this system through resource royalties, commonly referred to as "stumpage fees." Stumpage fees are set by the government to allow the corporation to make the average profit. In calculating this fee the government commonly excludes normal costs of harvesting, building roads, costs of replanting, and sometimes the costs of disease and insect management. A number of basic approaches have been implemented to try to collect some of the economic rent for the general public.

Beginning in the 19th century provincial governments simply gave the trees away to private interests hoping that they would create some economic activity and employment. All economic rent went to the companies, their employees and perhaps to some consumers. But with the extension of democracy, political pressure demanded that the public receive some compensation for the privatization of the Crown resource.

A full royalty tax tries to capture all of the Ricardian economic rent for the government. Under this approach the forest corporations are expected to earn only the normal rate of return on investment. This is difficult to implement as governments have incomplete information of company operations, particularly if they are trans-national corporations that engage in intra-corporate transfer pricing between branch plants and head offices in another country.

A second approach is to apply a uniform fixed royalty. The earliest royalties were a flat fee per tree felled and a fixed fee per cubic metre of wood harvested. This resulted in "high grading" where the company only takes the best wood from the site and abandons the other trees.

A third approach is the *ad valorem* royalty on resource revenues, a proportion or percentage of the selling price. This also encourages high grading.

The fourth method is to apply an *ad valorem* tax or royalty to the profits of the corporation. This does not work well, for governments have incomplete knowledge of company operations and large corporations have many ways of hiding profits. Over the last fifteen years provincial governments in Canada have been shifting all resource royalties to this approach, which has been pushed by private industry associations.

A fifth method is used in the public forests in the United States. A particular forestry site is put up for general bidding. Competition supposedly sets a truer market value. The province of British Columbia has used this method in the Small Business Enterprise Program and the Minor Timber Sale Licenses. However, large corporations can outbid small businesses for forest sites, even purchasing them at a loss, knowing that this can be evened out by their larger operations. Thus relatively small markets are not an accurate reflection of "market prices." (Van Kooten and Bulte, 2000; Schwindt, 1987; Warnock, 2001)

It would be very difficult to determine the profit level of the forest industry in Saskatchewan because of the overwhelming domination by one entity, Weyerhaeuser Corporation of Tacoma, Washington. It would be impossible to create a "market price" in the province. Indeed, this is widely recognized by the industry and governments. In 2002 the U.S. government imposed import duties of 27 percent on lumber from Canada because of alleged export subsidies. In the government/industry negotiations that followed, the U.S. decided to exempt Saskatchewan from proposed new marketing systems because of the domination of one company. Indeed, the industry refers to Saskatchewan as "The Province of Weyerhaeuser." With its dominant position, it gets whatever it wants from the provincial government. The corporation also has a special status in Washington, D.C. because of its long commitment to the Republican Party and most recently to George W. Bush. (Saunders, 2003)

The difficulties in setting a royalty can be seen in Saskatchewan. One company, Weyerhaeuser, has around 85 percent of forest cutting rights and exercises monopoly power and influence. The provincial government has demonstrated that it is not willing to challenge the power of this corporation. Around 80 percent of their pulp and paper products and 60 percent of their construction grade lumber is exported to the United States. When Weyerhaeuser Canada sells its product to Weyerhaeuser U.S.A., this is a managed price and not a market price. When Weyerhaeuser Canada buys goods and services from its head office, they are not market prices but managed prices. Intra-corporate transfers are not market choices. It is impossible to determine the difference between normal corporate profit and economic rent from the extraction and use of a public resource under such a situation.

In Canada the highest stumpage fees are charged in British Columbia. Tom L. Green and Lisa Mattaus, resource economists, have tried to calculate the extent to which the B.C. government subsidizes the forest industry. They compared stumpage fees over a 12 month period between 1999 and 2000. In a competitive market in western Washington, the stumpage fee was $84.31 per cubic metre. On the B.C. coast, the stumpage paid was $18.74 per cubic metre. In a competitive market in Idaho, the stumpage fee was $63.25 per cubic metre. In the B.C. Interior it was $28.26 per cubic metre. Stumpage fees are lower in coastal B.C. because harvesting costs there are the highest in the world. They concluded that over this period of time the annual provincial subsidy to the industry in the form of low stumpage fees was $2.835 billion. (Green and Mattaus, 2001)

Even a superficial examination reveals that much of the Ricardian economic rent in forestry is going to the corporations and not the public treasury. But as many commentators have noted, governments will give away public resources for nothing to create other social objectives, in this case employment in more remote areas. Rents from forestry can also go to the unionized workers in the industry who are able to capture wages and benefits that are higher than industry in general. They also go to upper middle class Americans who pay less for lumber when they build their 3,000 square foot houses. (Schwindt, 1987)

From the beginning, forests in Canada have been allocated to private individuals, companies and corporations to exploit in order to accumulate capital. Whether one looks at the history of forestry in British Columbia or Saskatchewan, it is clear that governments have agreed with the dominant business interests: forests are to be transformed into wood for construction and pulp and paper. Other uses for forests have always been ignored or dismissed. There are many across Canada who want a different forest policy, but they have almost no influence over governments. (see Swift, 1983; Drushka, 1985; May, 1998)

In more recent times economists have subjected competing demands for public forests to cost benefit analysis and the allocation of the social discount rate. An assessment can be made of the opportunity costs of alternate uses. What is the value of the forests for the protection of the fishing industry? Recreational use? The tourist industry? How can we assess the costs of environmental degradation? How can we include the cost of the loss of a resource to future generations? Which use of the forest will create the most jobs? How can we put a price on the preservation of endangered species? What of lost Aboriginal rights? But when it comes to making decisions on development, governments have ignored these issues. (see van Kooten and Bulte, 2000)

There are also the questions about equity. Who benefits and who loses? Professors Cornelis Van Kooten and Erwin Bulte argue that "most economists do not consider it proper to include income distributional considerations within the cost benefit analysis framework." These are considered to be "subjective value judgements" which would water down the contribution of cost benefit analysis. But for political economists, they are central. (Van Kooten and Bulte, 2000)

There is the fact that mainstream economic analysis cannot put a price or value on many *non-market functions* of natural resources. How does one put a value on the preservation of wilderness or an endangered species? What is the value of maintaining a forest and its biodiversity in contrast to the plantation monocultures that replace them? How can we put a price on the value of forests for preserving and cleaning water? For moderation of weather? For the role they play in the carbon cycle? Or the role of forests in the creation of oxygen? How can we put a value on their role as part of the natural ecosystem which recycles human-created wastes?

## An Overview of Saskatchewan's Policy

Under the English law that Canada inherited, all natural resources—air, water, land, sub-surface minerals, and forests—are held for the population as a whole by the Crown. It is up to the government to decide how it will dispose of these public assets and what prices it will charge when they are sold. In Canada, the British North America Act of 1867 granted authority over natural resources to the provinces. But due to the federal government's National Policy for the promotion of the wheat economy, Saskatchewan was not granted control over natural resources until 1930, and the first Forest Act was not passed until 1931.

The new CCF government of T. C. Douglas, elected in 1944, was primarily concerned with the destruction of the forests by extensive fires during the drought years of the 1930s and high-grade cutting by private interests. A Royal Commission on Forestry was appointed to provide advice on conservation. The government created the Timber Board in 1945 as a marketing agency for the hundreds of small saw mills, but it soon became an instrument of the Department of Natural Resources for managing the commercial forest. While all pulp wood cut was exported to Manitoba and the United States, the lumber was consumed almost entirely in the province.

However, the Douglas government's resource policy was not fundamentally different from those pursued by other governments in other provinces. They were interested in expanding a commercial forestry industry, including the building of a large saw mill and a pulp mill, and they were quite willing to use economic incentives to attract foreign or domestic capital. A pulp mill was announced in 1958, but the agreement fell through.

The first major forest industry project was announced by Ross Thatcher's Liberal government in 1965. They negotiated an agreement with Karl Landegger, owner of Parsons and Whittemore, a U.S. corporation, to build a pulp and paper mill at Prince Albert (PAPCO). Of the $65 million originally invested in the project, $50 million came from a government-guaranteed loan and $5 million from the federal Department of Regional Economic Expansion (DREE). Landegger got 70 percent ownership with an investment of only $7 million. The provincial government took a 30 percent equity position. The corporation was guaranteed a supply of wood at a low stumpage fee for a long period of time. Landegger specialized in operations in Third World countries with weak governments. (Eisler, 1987)

The NDP government of Allan Blakeney, elected in 1971, pursued a policy of trying to increase the royalties on the extraction of natural resources and promoting Saskatchewan ownership. But this did not carry over to the forestry sector.

However, in 1980 Parsons and Whittemore decided to sell their 70 percent share in PAPCO to another American corporation. Invoking a clause in the original agreement, the Blakeney government borrowed $162 million in New York, bought the outstanding stock, and transformed PAPCO into a provincially-owned Crown corporation. For a company not doing well, it was a high price to pay. With the onset of the recession in the 1980s, PAPCO began to lose money. Between 1982 and 1986 the company lost $44 million. (see Richards and Pratt, 1979; Gruending, 1990; Glor, 1997; Barron, 1997)

Grant Devine's Tory government was elected in 1982. In 1986 they arranged to sell PAPCO to Weyerhaeuser Corporation for $248 million. But the Washington corporation put up no money. The government lent them the sum via a 30-year debenture. Any losses incurred for the first three years could be deducted from the purchase price. For its part, Weyerhaeuser agreed to construct a paper mill in Prince Albert, which required an investment of $250 million. The government guaranteed $83 million of the debt of the new paper mill.

Management at Weyerhaeuser knew they had a good deal. A new Forest Management Licence gave them cutting rights on a huge area of land for a stumpage fee that was a small percentage of what they had to pay in the United States. They did pay back the government for the original purchase and made further investments in the mill in 1999.

A second mill was promised for the Meadow Lake area, and in 1971 Parsons and Whittemore was again chosen by the Thatcher government. However, the incoming NDP government paid a penalty and canceled the agreement. They did not believe that the province and the market could support two paper mills. But in 1990 the Tory government of Grant Devine put up one half of the capital ($246 million) to create the mill, a joint venture with Millar Western Industries of Alberta. Today that mill still operates but only because of annual subsidies of around $40 million from the Saskatchewan government. (Pitsula and Rasmussen, 1990; May, 1998)

In 1991 the New Democratic Party was elected, and many believed that there would be a return to the province-building strategies of the Blakeney government. But the new government led by Roy Romanow continued the neoliberal strategy introduced by the Tory government of Grant Devine.

The CCF government of Tommy Douglas had created Sask Forest Products in 1949, a successful Crown corporation, which built and operated a plywood plant and a saw mill. In 1995 Roy Romanow's NDP government "merged it" with MacMillan Bloedel and in 1999 completed the privatization. There was a payoff: MacBlo was to build a new oriented strand board (OSB) plant at Hudson Bay, Saskatchewan. (see Brown *et al.*, 1999)

Just one month later MacBlo sold out to Weyerhaeuser. The NDP government immediately announced that it would transfer MacBlo's forest management license areas to Weyerhaeuser. Janice MacKinnon, the NDP Minister of Economic Development, proclaimed that the government had no fear of Weyerhaeuser's near monopoly position in Saskatchewan because of their "track record as a good corporate citizen in Saskatchewan." (Lyons, 1999)

Weyerhaeuser Corporation's record was somewhat different in British Columbia, Oregon and Washington. George Draffan of the Public Information Network in Seattle, Washington argues that the corporation has a poor record in the Pacific Northwest. The founder of the corporation, Frederick Weyerhaeuser, "was castigated as the classic cut-and-run timberman." In June 1992 the Council on Economic Priorities released a comprehensive environmental profile of the corporation, documenting widespread environmental violations. It noted that in 1984 Weyerhaeuser was named to the "Filthy Five" by Environmental Action. While running advertisements promoting intensively managed "forest" operations, the corporation replaced natural forests with "genetically-engineered, single-species plantations." In 1998 Weyerhaeuser had the highest number of violations of the Forest Practices Code in British Columbia. (*Globe and Mail*, July 2, 1999; "A Profile of the Weyerhaeuser Corporation" at www.endgame.org)

## Managing the Forest Resources

In 1965 the Simpson Timber company from Seattle was invited to Saskatchewan to establish a major sawmill to produce lumber. They received the usual long term agreement to cut timber on Crown land, and they were supposed to reforest the areas cut. The company did not replant, arguing that the costs were too high. Neither the Liberal, NDP nor Tory governments took any action against the company. Simpson Timber closed the plant in 1990 and fled. The taxpayers are paying for the reforestation of the Northeast area of the province.

Today most of the harvested forest areas in Saskatchewan are considered to be understocked, basically deforested. Those areas left to regenerate on their own have not done well. Plantations have had a high failure rate. Around 600,000 hectares of harvested forests are classified as "not satisfactorily restocked," harvested forest land which is "partially or completely barren of its potential." This amounts to 66 percent of the forest land harvested since 1975. Nationally, the comparative figure is 17 percent. (Global Forest Watch, 2000; Brady and Appleby, 2000)

Saskatchewan forest policy has been consistent regardless of what party has been in office. In April 1999 the Romanow Government announced a massive expansion plan for the forest industry. Twelve new processing facilities were to be built or expanded, $850 million was to be invested by private corporations, and 10,000 new jobs were to be created. The NDP government stressed that the comparative advantage of the Saskatchewan industry was the growing share of the market in the United States and the province's exemption from the Softwood Lumber Agreement. The plan is summarized below:

## Basic Facts on Saskatchewan's Commercial Forest Zone

Commercial forest region: 15.89 million hectares

Total standing volume of wood: 179.7 million cubic metres

Annual harvest volume schedule: 6.6 million cubic metres
        Softwood: 3.6 million cubic metres
        Hardwood: 3.0 million cubic metres

Current harvest rate: 3 million cubic metres

Surplus wood available 3.6 million cubic metres

Projected harvest volume schedule: 27 years of original forest wood

Source: KPMG study of the Forest Industry in Saskatchewan, prepared for Saskatchewan Environment and Resource Management, August 1998.

In the Commercial Forest Zone, the boreal forest in central Saskatchewan, the NDP plan is to increase the allowable annual cut of wood from three million cubic meters to 6.6 million. At this new rate of harvest, all the commercial timber would be cut in just 27 years. In fact, the NDP government raised the annual allowable cut to 7.7 million cubic metres in 2000. In the boreal area it takes 70 years to grow a hardwood tree to maturity and 90 years for a softwood tree. The new policy was supported by the Liberal and Saskatchewan parties. The only opposition came from the province's environmental groups and the fledgling New Green Alliance. The Aboriginal community was split, with support coming from some band leaders and Indian corporations and opposition from Natives who oppose clear-cut logging. The opponents supported sustainable logging and diversified forest use.

The Romanow government also brought in a new Forest Resources Management Act in 1999. Corporations are to negotiate 20-year Forest Management Plans with the province. Forest corporations are now required to pay for reforestation and roads where they are harvesting. But there is to be no policing of the implementation of plans by the provincial government; this will be left to the private corporation, with an outside review to be held every five years. The new act was consistent with the government's general budget and staff cuts in the area of environmental enforcement.

The NDP government pushed hard for an expansion of the forest industry, and there was considerable investment. Weyerhaeuser upgraded their pulp mill in Prince Albert, completed a sawmill at Big River, and built the new oriented strand board mill at Hudson Bay. Wapawekka Lumber built a new sawmill at Prince Albert, L &

M Wood Products built a new sawmill at Glaslyn and Norsak Forest Products expanded their mill at Dillon. The Zelensky Brother and the Lac La Ronge Indian Band expanded the capacity of their sawmill. The Green Lake Métis Wood Products sawmill was redeveloped. Norsak Forest Products began construction of a new planer mill at Meadow Lake. Construction began on a new oriented strand board plant at Meadow Lake. Other new operations were in the planning stage. (Saskatchewan Industry and Resources, spring 2002)

The success of this major new forest development rested on several assumptions. First, after 2001 the province would remain exempt from the Canada-US Softwood Lumber Agreement. There would be no quotas or duties imposed. Second, the provincial government would continue to provide the forest industry with timber at give away prices. The province would also continue to provide other extensive supports for the industry, like control of forest fires, financed out of general revenues. Third, global warming and climate change would have little effect on Saskatchewan. There would be no massive forest fires or insect infestations. Fourth, Aboriginal land claims would continue to be unresolved. Private capital would continue to have access to the forests under provincial government ownership and management.

## What Is a Fair Stumpage Fee?

What about stumpage fees, royalties received by the Crown in return for selling provincial natural resource assets? In 1990 a study for the UN Food and Agriculture Organization by Minoru Kumazaki, professor of forestry at Tsukuba University in Japan, concluded that Canada had the lowest overall stumpage rates in the world, even lower than Malaysia and Thailand. In 1998 a study by Reid Carter for First Marathon Securities concluded that the stumpage rates in British Columbia were the lowest in the world except for the other provinces. In 1999 B.C.'s stumpage fees for coastal areas averaged $33 a cubic meter and $27 a cubic meter for the interior. The Transborder Conservation Project concluded that B.C.'s stumpage fees in 1999 were "about one half of what companies in the U.S. are paying for similar wood." (see Rainforest Action Network, http://forests.org; Carter, 1998; Marshall, 1999; Transborder Conservation Project, 1999)

How low can stumpage fees get? Take a look at Saskatchewan. In 1996 companies in the forest industry paid between $0.28 and $0.60 for a cubic meter of hardwood and between $1.02 and $1.77 for a cubic meter of softwood. (see Canadian Council of Forest Ministers: http://nfdp.ccfm.org)

The present Saskatchewan stumpage fees are included in the Forest Resources Management Act passed in 1999. For softwood used for lumber, the base rate is $2.00 per cubic metre of timber with a diameter greater than 14 centimetres, with a formula for recovering more if the price of lumber exceed $350 per thousand board feet (mbf). For smaller softwood timber, the fee is only $0.75. Thus, at $2 per cubic metre for softwood for lumber, the stumpage would be $4.72 for a thousand board feet of lumber, the standard of measurement used in the United States.

Hardwood used to be considered a "weed" species in Saskatchewan, but it is now used widely for pulp and paper, oriented strand board, chipboard, and particle board. The new prices for hardwood range from $6.00 per cubic metre for ash, birch, elm and maple timber greater than 14 centimetres to only $0.75 for smaller wood. For other hardwood timber, including the widely used aspen, the larger trees earn $1.00 a cubic metre and the smaller $0.50.

How does this compare to the stumpage resource royalty system in the United States? Environmental groups in the United States say that the U.S. National Forest Service is selling timber to private companies at below market value. Let us look at one example, sales from the Chippewa National Forest, as reported by the U.S. Forest Service and the U.S. General Accounting Office. In 1996 the U.S. Forest Service sold 62.3 million board feet of timber from this forest for $3.390 million U.S., for an average of $54.41 U.S. per thousand board feet (mbf). In 1994 the average from this forest was $42.86 U.S. mbf and in 1995 it was $80.37 U.S. mbf. (USDA Forest Service, http://www.fs.fed.us)

## The Balance Sheet on the Forest Industry

Given the very low stumpage fees in Saskatchewan, it is no surprise to learn that over the 1990s the provincial government averaged only around $3.5 million a year in total revenues from forestry operations. The NDP government is so embarrassed by the low returns that it has buried the figures in all the published reports. In 1992, for example, the province received $3.1 million from all forestry dues, fees and royalties, but received $3.7 million from licenses from big game hunters! Industry sales were $335 million in 1992 but rose to $654 million in 1997, thanks to increased exports to the United States. Provincial revenues rose to only $4.9 million in 1997. Since then the industry has been hard hit by the imposition of the tariffs on Canadian softwood lumber exports by the U.S. government. Total sales fell to $355 million in 2002. (Saskatchewan Environment and Resource Management, annual reports; Natural Resources Canada, 2003; Cartwright, 1999)

Saskatchewan government forestry expenditures, which include management, replanting, and fighting fires have averaged around $66 million per year over the 1990s. Data from the Canadian Council of Forest Ministers shows that only British Columbia takes in more revenues each year than it spends in forest management. In Saskatchewan, the citizens are paying the forestry corporations to take away the wood!

There are, of course, other government subsidies to the industry which are not found in the accounts of the forestry department. All the resource extraction industries have been assisted by government and Crown corporation infrastructure spending. One example will illustrate the point. As part of the 1999 NDP plan for expansion, Ainsworth Lumber of Vancouver agreed to build a new sawmill at Deschambault Lake. This was to be in partnership with the Peter Ballantyne Cree Nation. Ainsworth wanted Sask Power, the Crown utility, to pay for a new power transmission line. The total cost was to be $16 million, but when Sask Power asked Ainsworth to put up $2.9 million as its share, they refused and pulled out of the project. The company also complained that the province was not spending enough on expanding roads in the area. (*Leader Post*, April 5, 2001)

What we have in Saskatchewan, and across Canada, is a neo-colonial industrial forestry model. The provincial governments freely give very large corporations, domestic and foreign, long term leases to harvest the trees. The trees, which are owned by the people as a whole, are sold to the corporations for a very low stumpage fee. In addition, the provincial and federal governments undertake to facilitate this resource extraction policy through a range of subsidies and supports. A few large firms dominate a highly concentrated industry. Foreign ownership and control is welcomed and on the increase.

The trade unions in the forest industry have bought into this system. Technological changes have greatly reduced the number of workers in the industry. However, those remaining earn wages well above the average for industrial workers. In Saskatchewan in 2001 the average hourly wage for logging and forestry was 40 percent above the average for industrial workers in the province. These workers and their trade unions are seen as part of the "wood exploitation axis." (see *Saskatchewan Economic Review*, 2003)

There are drawbacks to this model. As Roger Hayter of Simon Fraser University stresses, the large forestry firms spend virtually nothing on research and development in Canada, and there is a loss of those high income jobs. It results in extensive importation of equipment and payments for licenses and services from parent corporations. There is a loss of manufacturing export potential. (Hayter, 2000)

The neo-colonial industrial model results in a heavy emphasis on exporting low value added wood products, lumber and pulp and paper. The corporations and their allies are always pressing governments to allow an increase in the export of logs. Secondary manufacturing in wood products is very weak compared to European and Japanese industry, and the Canadian industry provides relatively few jobs. In 2001, the Saskatchewan industry consisted of 283 logging, wood product manufacturing and paper manufacturing establishments providing 5,100 jobs. (Natural Resources Canada, 2003)

Under this exploitation model there is only one use for our forests: cheap wood for the building and pulp and paper industries. The role of forests in providing pure water, pure air, climate moderation, protection from wind, flood control, production of topsoil, cycling of elements through the ocean and the atmosphere, the storehouse for wild genes, biological diversity, and aesthetic or spiritual value are ignored.

Opponents of the present capitalist industrial forestry policy stress multiple economic uses for the Saskatchewan forests. These include ecological forestry, wild food industries, commercial fishing, outfitting, trapping and tourism, and the maintenance of the forests and their diversified species.

The environmental impact of the industrial model is devastating. Clear cutting is the norm and accounts for 90 percent of the harvesting in Saskatchewan. At best, forests are replaced with plantations without structural diversity. Forest fires increase. Soil erosion increases and soil quality declines. Fish habitat is destroyed. Lakes experience a rise in acidity and high rates of mercury contamination. Pest infestations increase. Water tables decline and wetlands dry up. Biological diversity declines. The carbon balance is changed. The Saskatchewan government is promoting a massive increase in the allowable annual cut for the boreal forests right at the time when the scientific evidence is mounting that this forest region is under severe threat from global warming and climate change. Clearcut logging under these conditions will just promote ecological and economic disaster. (Wittbecker, 1999; Schlinder, 2000; Forest Stewardship Council, http://canadian-forests.com)

The social costs of this approach to forestry are externalized from the private firm to the general public. These include the costs of fossil fuel use, transportation costs, environmental degradation and clean-up costs, damage to fish habitat, loss of aesthetic appeal to recreation and tourism, loss of employment, and health costs.

## There Is a Viable Alternative

There are, of course, alternative systems of forest use. They emphasize local ownership and control by communities, value added wood production, reduction of waste and emphasis on recycling, protection of the environment, selective logging, and a shift to labour-intensive production. Many of the organizations promoting this model can be found in the International Network of Forests and Communities. (http://forestsandcommunities.org)

Supporters of the alternate model helped found the international Forest Stewardship Council in 1993, which has established forest management criteria and certifies production systems. They are actively involved across Canada. Certification is a way to ensure that logging and timber management protects the forests, encourages recycling, allocates full costs to industry, protects the ecosystem, and provides community stability. In Saskatchewan, of the four political parties, only the New Green Alliance supports the adoption of these principles as forest policy. (see Forest Stewardship Council-Canada, http://antequera.antequera.com/FSC)

There are a lot of good examples of the alternative system of forest management. Merv Wilkinson's operation at Wildwood on Vancouver Island is well known. Orville Camp bought over cut land in Oregon and nursed it back to a natural forest. Herb Hammond did the same in British Columbia. In Alberta and Saskatchewan there are a number of small business operations following these practices, using selective cutting, small skidders, farm tractors, some with horses, and small local mills hiring local people. (see Western Canada Wilderness Committee, 2000)

In November 1995 the Lumby Log Market in Vernon, B.C. became Canada's first certified eco-forestry operation. Contractors log the forest site according to the plan and then the B.C. Forest Service auctions the wood on the open market. Revenue to the government has been three times as high as the stumpage fee. The logging plans were developed by the B.C. Forest Service in consultation with forester Herb Hammond and the Silva Forest Foundation, chosen by the Forest Stewardship Council to certify B.C. operations.

## The Menominee First Nation Alternative

The forestry operations of the Meadow Lake Tribal Council are hardly different from the industrial practices of Weyerhaeuser. In 1992 there was a struggle between the Protectors of Mother Earth and the Tribal Council. Elders, men, women, and children, First Nation and Métis from the Meadow Lake area tried to stop clear cut logging by the Council on their historic lands. The NDP government called in the RCMP SWAT team to end their non-violent protests. Forest policy, implemented by Weyerhaeuser and the Meadow Lake Tribal Council, and supported by Eldon Lautermilch, the NDP Minister of Resources, backed clear cut logging at the expense of other forest uses.

In New York in 1995 the United Nations presented a special award to the Menominee of Wisconsin for their contribution to the world's environment through sustainable forestry development. The Menominee forest, 235,000 acres in Wisconsin close to Green Bay, is the only true forest left in the Great Lakes area, or for that matter, in the Eastern United States. People from all over the world come to see how it is possible to maintain a traditional forest, with all its original diversity, and still carry out logging. Between 1865 and the early 1990s, over two billion board feet of saw timber had been harvested with no reduction in the existing saw timber stock. Biodiversity has been maintained. The Menominee Forest stands in direct contrast to the Nicolet National Forest on its northern border, which has been managed in the "business as usual" way. Many studies have compared the two forests. (see Davis, 2000)

This was not an easy process. The Menominee people originally had historic rights to around two-thirds of what is now Wisconsin. They survived the colonialism of the French and the British and adapted to the fur trade. But they could not resist the American invasion. Between 1817 and 1856 the U.S. government forced eight treaties on the Menominee, with the Lake Pagan Treaty of 1848 forcing them to cede all of their land to the U.S. government. They protested, went to the Congress, and managed to obtain the Treaty of Wolf River in 1864, which restored to the Tribe their present forest and reservation. The Wisconsin "pine barons" moved in and began to cut their trees.

The struggle for the survival of the Menominee took two phases. First, they fought to get ownership rights to their land. Then they fought to end clear cutting. They were able to achieve this because they found an ally in "Fighting Bob" LaFollett, the Progressive Party leader from Wisconsin, who worked with the Menominee. The result was the LaFollett Act of 1908, which gave them control over their land and specifically required selective logging in the Menominee forest.

The principles of sustainability are the foundation for the Menominee Tribal Enterprises, which administers the forest. There is a tribal consensus agreement on three basic operating principles. "First, the system must be sustainable for future generations. Second, the forest must be cared for properly to provide the needs of the people. Third, we keep all the pieces of the forest to maintain diversity." Forestry must be "ecologically viable, economically feasible, and socially desirable." All species must retain use of the forest, and the forest must be maintained for all uses, not just the harvesting of trees.

As the Menominee insist, "The Earth is your mother, and you do not purposely set out to wound your mother." But they always add that "your mother must also provide for you." The Menominee practice forestry using the best of new science and technology, while doing the very minimum of damage to the forest in the harvesting process. For example, the forest has been classified into 884 habitat-type plots which are all carefully monitored for growth, pests and diseases, and planned harvest. Selective harvesting is used, and those trees harvested are past maturity, have a poor quality, or are not likely to survive until the next scheduled cutting. After these trees are cut, then it is decided whether others can be cut as well. For the few species which reproduce best without shade, clear cutting is used, but no clear cut may be larger than 30 acres. There is still strong opposition within the community to even this minimal clear cutting. (Davis, 2000)

Central to the tribe's dramatic success in forestry is their commitment to collective ownership of the forest and land. There is strong consensus that the product of the land, the natural resources, are for the benefit of all of the people and not just for those who may be fortunate enough to have enough income or power to own land. Secondly, the earth is too important to be privately owned. It is basic to life. They know that the survival of the Menominee as a people depends on their historic ties to the land. The Menominee have avoided the "tragedy of the commons" described by Garret Hardin because they have not applied the principles of capitalism to land and its resources.

The political structure of the Menominee Tribe makes this possible. The key is the practice of participatory democracy, based in the Tribal Council meetings. All interested members of the tribe attend Council meetings, and everyone is guaranteed a chance to speak. On important questions debate may go on for days. The purpose is to reach a *consensus*. After a long debate it usually appears that a good majority has developed on one side of an issue. At this point the opponents recognize that they must bend to the will of the growing majority. Once a policy is established through such a decision making process, it becomes entrenched in tribal policy and is very hard to change. This is the basis for the Green Party belief in consensus decision making through participatory democracy.

The other basic characteristic of the Menominee First Nation is the diversity of interests and balance of power within the community. The Menominee themselves are a diversified people. Power is decentralized and no group, family or clan is able to dominate the local government. Women have considerable power and status going back to the pre-colonial period when the Menominee were a matrilineal society. Ada Deer, Sylvia Wilbur, and Shirley Daly, known as the "three sisters," led the fight for restoration of Menominee rights. No group remains in office or in power for more than a short time. There is wide agreement that this is best for the community. The Menominee were the first wood producers in the United States to obtain Green Cross certification by the Scientific Certification System and Smart Wood certification from the Rain Forest Alliance. This has helped them secure sales.

For the people of Saskatchewan, the Menominee experience is an example of an alternative way to development. One can visit the forest and even attend the College of the Menominee Nation which has a Sustainable Development Institute. (Davis, 2000; Bernard and Young, 1997; also, Menominee Nation at http://www.menominee.edu)

## The Threats to the Boreal Forest

Between 1996 and 2001 the Canada-U.S. Softwood Lumber Agreement used a quota system to manage Canadian wood exports to the United States. All exports above 14.7 billion board feet per year were taxed on a sliding scale. Only B.C., Alberta, Ontario and Quebec were limited by quotas and penalties; the other provinces were exempt. When the agreement expired, the U.S. forest industry, represented by the Coalition for Fair Lumber Imports, asked the U.S. Department of Commerce to impose countervailing duties against the Canadian industry. They argued that if Canadian provincial governments wish to subsidize their forest industry, that is their choice. But under international trade rules set forth in the Canada-U.S. Free Trade Agreement, the North American Free Trade Agreement and the World Trade Organization, such subsidies cannot be used to promote exports. The U.S. forest companies are supported by a long list of Members of Congress, trade unions and environmental groups. In 2001 a coalition of U.S. and Canadian environmental groups and First Nations demanded that government subsidies to the industry be abolished. In July 2000 the World Resources Institute petitioned the G-8 Summit of major industrial countries to end "destructive forest subsidies which cause forest loss or degradation and have no lasting positive impact on economic development." (text at http://www.wri.org; Coalition for Fair Lumber Imports, http://www.fairlumbercoalition.org)

The U.S. industry accused Canadian provincial governments of providing subsidies to the forest industry through very low royalties on timber, non-enforcement of forestry rules, mandating forest firms to comply with minimum cut requirements, providing tax benefits to private firms, bailing out firms in financial difficulty, and providing extensive infrastructure, clean up and reforestation. Direct financial subsidies have been given to forest corporations to encourage local employment. They argue that our forestry policy encourages over-harvesting and wasted wood resulting in environmental damage. By granting very large corporations long term cutting rights on huge areas of land, the provincial governments have hurt small independent forestry companies and have denied Aboriginal Canadians, who actually live in the forests, access to forest resources. The response by our political leaders, government spokesmen, trade union leaders, the mass media and most of the Canadian industry has been to emphatically dismiss the charges out of hand.

In 2001 the U.S. Department of Commerce ruled that Canadian provincial governments subsidize the forest industry, and that their subsidies promoted exports to the United States. The resulting inflow of Canadian wood products caused injury to the U.S. industry. They imposed a 27 percent countervailing duty on Canadian imports of wood products. This has been very hard on the Canadian industry.

The Canadian government challenged these duties before dispute panels of the World Trade Organization and the North American Free Trade Agreement. In May 2003, the WTO ruled in favour of the U.S. position, agreeing that forest companies "receive a financial contribution from their government," and that the U.S. government could impose countervailing duties. However, they ruled against the methodology used by the U.S. Department of Commerce, which compared stumpage fees in Canada with those in the United States.

As one example, U.S. Department of Commerce figures showed that forest companies in Saskatchewan in 2001 paid on average only $1.64 for a cubic metre of softwood. In Montana, forest companies in that same year paid on average $30.58 per cubic metre for softwood. The WTO ruled that the U.S. industry and the Department of Commerce would have to provide new data showing comparisons with the private market in Canada, which only really exists in the Atlantic provinces where 75 percent of forests are on private lands. The NAFTA panel which issued its decision in July 2003 reached a similar conclusion.

In the face of this stalemate, the forest industry in Canada has been working to get the two governments to create a new agreement. The draft proposals have provided that Canadian exports would be limited to a share of around 32 percent of the U.S. market, and that individual provinces would receive a particular quota for exports. The big corporations have generally supported this compromise position.

Under the previous Canada-U.S. agreement, Saskatchewan was excluded. The NDP government responded with increased subsidies to the industry and promoted greater exports to the United States. In 2002 around 70 percent of all Saskatchewan wood products were exported to the United States. If there is a new international agreement based on a new quota system, it is unlikely that Saskatchewan would again be exempted. Weyerhaeuser does not have that much influence in Washington. If quotas were imposed, the provincial export industry would most likely shrink. Many of the new operations built after the new forest policy of 1999 would probably have to go out of business.

Another threat to the Saskatchewan boreal forest comes from the effects of global warming and climate change. The year 2003 was the eleventh consecutive year in which temperatures were higher than average. Environment Canada reported that 25 of the last 26 seasons have had temperature warmer than the average. This year was the third warmest on record since records began in 1861.

The impact on the Canadian prairies is well known. From 2001 through 2003 there was a prolonged drought. With it came hordes of grasshoppers. Across western Canada forest fires were profound. In Saskatchewan the government had to spend over $100 million in both 2002 and 2003 fighting fires.

With warmer weather, insect pests move north, and they are not killed over the winter. In the first few years of the 21st century British Columbia has had a major infestation and loss of forests due to the mountain pine beetle. The winters are no longer cold enough to control their growth. A similar infestation could well occur in Saskatchewan. (Natural Resources Canada, 1999, 2002)

## Conclusion

The wood exploitation axis of the large corporations, the provincial governments and the industry's trade unions have no interest in an ecological alternative. In Saskatchewan they have had the support of some leaders in the Aboriginal communities. The neo-colonial industrial system that operates in Saskatchewan was established precisely to maximize the return on capital investment. The driving force has always been capital accumulation by big corporations, domestic and foreign.

Local community control means more local value added, more capital is retained in local communities, and ownership is more diversified. Less capital is spent on imported machinery, such as the feller-bunchers used in clear cutting. One feller-buncher replaces 15 workers. Small operations, such as the non-industrial private forestry operations in Europe, employ many more people. However, the workers who benefit from the existing Canadian industrial system of forestry do not want to see their high wages reduced to the average found in manufacturing. (see the role of the Industrial, Wood and Allied Workers of Canada on these issues at www.iwa.ca)

As the study by Global Forest Watch Canada pointed out, around 55 percent of Canada's large, intact forests lie within First Nation historic treaty areas. Yet they do not benefit from this resource. Aboriginal communities within the forest areas have lower incomes and lower employment rates than Aboriginal communities in Canada's inner city areas. There is also a greater disparity in socio-economic status within the communities in the forest areas compared to the urban areas. (Global Forest Watch, 2003)

Our provincial governments, regardless of what party is in office, cannot contemplate moving from the present system to a radically different alternative. Not even the populist social democratic CCF in Saskatchewan was willing to try a different approach. The alternatives have been advocated by environmental groups and Aboriginal people living in the forests. In Saskatchewan all the political parties have always been hostile to the environmental movement and have a long record of ignoring Aboriginal concerns. Only the small New Green Alliance supports the alternative strategy of sustainable forestry. It appears that it will take a crisis situation before public pressure will force the provincial government to take a different course on forestry policy.

## References

Arneil, Barbara. 1996. *John Locke and America: The Defence of English Colonialism.* Oxford: Clarendon Press.

Baltgailis, Karen and Gray Jones. 1993. *A New Leaf: Real Sustainability for the Boreal Forest.* Edmonton: Western Canada Wilderness Committee.

Barron, F. Laurie. 1997. *Walking in Indian Moccasins: The Native Policies of Tommy Douglas and the CCF.* Vancouver: University of British Columbia Press.

BC Coalition for Sustainable Forest Solutions. 2001. *Getting Beyond the Softwood Lumber Dispute: Solutions in BC's Interest.* Vancouver: B.C. Coalition for Sustainable Forest Solutions, September.

Benton, Ted, ed., 1996. *The Greening of Marxism.* New York: The Guilford Press.

Bernard, Ted and Jora Young. 1997. *The Ecology of Hope: Communities Collaborate for Sustainability.* Gabriola Island, B.C.: New Society Publishers.

Brady, Allyson and Alan Appleby. 2000. *Deforestation: Lack of Regeneration in Saskatchewan Forests.* Saskatoon: Saskatchewan Environmental Society, March 6.

Briere, Karen. 2002. "Outdated Law Stifles Growth: Report." *Western Producer*, May 30, p. 10.

Brown, Lorne A. *et al.* 1999. *Saskatchewan Politics from Left to Right '44-'99.* Regina: Hinterland Books.

Bucholtz, Todd G. 1989. *New Ideas from Dead Economists.* Toronto: Penguin Books.

Canada. Natural Resources. 1999. *Climate Change and Forests: Context for the Canadian Forest Service's Science Program.* Ottawa: Natural Resources Canada.

Canada. Natural Resources. 2001. *Climate Change Impacts and Adaptations: A Canadian Perspective: Forestry.* Ottawa: Natural Resources Canada, October.

Canada. Natural Resources. 2002. *The State of Canada's Forests.* Ottawa: Natural Resources Canada. http://www.nrcan.gc.ca

Canada. Statistics Canada. 2002. *2001 Census of Agriculture.* Ottawa: Government of Canada.

Carter, Reid. 1998. *Death of an Industry? British Columbia's Wood Products Industry.* Vancouver: First Marathon Securities, April 6.

Cartwright, John. 1999. "The Price of Compromise: Why We Should Wind Down Our Forest Industry." *Canadian Public Policy,* Vol. 25, No. 2. http://www.utpjournals.com

Davis, Thomas. 2000. *Sustaining the Forest, the People, and the Spirit.* Albany: State University Press of New York.

Drengston, Alan and Duncan Taylor, eds. 1997. *Ecoforestry: The Art and Science of Sustainable Forest Use.* Gabriola Island, B.C.: New Society Publishers.

Drushka, Ken. 1985. *Stumped: The Forest Industry in Transition.* Vancouver: Douglas and McIntyre.

Fine, Ben. 1982. *Theories of the Capitalist Economy.* London: Edward Arnold.

Friesen, Gerald. 1987. *The Canadian Prairies: A History.* Toronto: University of Toronto Press.

Global Forest Watch. 2000. *Canada's Forests at a Crossroads: An Assessment in the Year 2000.* Washington, D.C.: Global Forest Watch.

Global Forest Watch. 2003. *Aboriginal Communities in Forest Regions in Canada: Disparities in Socio-Economic Conditions.* At http://www.globalforestwatch.ca

Glor, Eleanor D., ed. 1997. *Policy Innovation in the Saskatchewan Public Sector, 1971-82.* North York: Captus Press of York University.

Green, Tom L. and Lisa Matthaus. 2001. *Cutting Subsidies, or Subsidized Cutting?* Vancouver: Report prepared for the B.C. Coalition for Sustainable Forestry Solutions, July 12.

Gruending, Dennis. 1990. *Promises to Keep: A Political Biography of Allan Blakeney.* Saskatoon: Western Producer Prairie Books.

Gunton, Thomas and John Richards, eds. 1987. *Resource Rents and Public Policy in Western Canada.* Montreal: The Institute for Research on Public Policy.

Hayter, Roger. 2000. *Flexible Crossroads: The Restructuring of British Columbia's Forest Economy.* Vancouver: University of British Columbia Press.

Heilbroner, Robert L. 1961. *The Worldly Philosophers: The Lives, Times and Ideas of the Great Economic Thinkers.* New York: Simon and Schuster.

Hindess, Barry and Paul Q. Hirst. 1975. *Pre-capitalist Modes of Production.* London: Routledge & Kegan Paul.

Keiper, Joseph S. *et al.* 1961. *Theory and Measurement of Rent.* New York: Chilton Company.

Kelly, Patrick, ed. 1991. *Locke on Money.* Oxford: Oxford University Press.

Laslett, Peter, ed. 1960. *Two Treatises of Government by John Locke.* Cambridge: Cambridge University Press.

Lyons, Murray. 1999. "Province Says Weyerhaeuser's Record is Good." *Leader Post,* June 22.

Marshall, Dale. 1999. *Follow the Money: Understanding the Crisis in BC's Resource Sector.* Vancouver: Canadian Centre for Policy Alternatives.

May, Elizabeth. 1998. *At the Cutting Edge: The Crisis in Canada's Forests.* Toronto: Key Porter Books.

Norrie, Kenneth and Douglas Owram. 1996. *A History of the Canadian Economy.* Toronto: Harcourt Brace Canada.

Northwest Ecosystem Alliance. 2002. *Canada's Softwood Lumber 'Advantage' Taking Toll on Environment.* At http://www.ecosystem.org.

Perelman, Michael. 1996. "Marx and Resource Scarcity." In Benton, pp. 64-80.

Pitsula, James M. and Ken Rasmussen. 1990. *Privatizing a Province: The New Right in Saskatchewan.* Vancouver: New Star Books.

Rainforest Action Network. 1993. *Canada Accused of Dumping Forest Products.* Seattle, December. Text at Forest Networking Project, http://www.ecosystem.org

Richards, John and Larry Pratt. 1979. *Prairie Capitalism: Power and Influence in the New West.* Toronto: McClelland and Stewart.

Robbins, Lionel. 1998. *A History of Economic Thought: The LSE Lectures.* Princeton: Princeton University Press.

Roberts, Joseph. "State, Class and Development Strategy." *Canadian Review of Sociology and Anthropology.* Vol. 17, No. 3, pp. 287-97.

Saskatchewan. Bureau of Statistics. 2003. *Economic Review.* Regina: Government of Saskatchewan.

Saunders, John. 2003. "U.S. Set to Make Final Lumber Demands." *Globe and Mail,* February 24, B-1, B-10.

Schindler, David W. 1998. "A Dim Future for Boreal Waters and Landscapes." *BioScience,* Vol. 48, No. 3, March, pp. 157-64.

Schlindler, David W. 2000. "Boreal Mayhem: The Effects of Human Activities on Boreal Landscapes." Edmonton: Western Canada Wilderness Committee.

Schwindt, Richard. 1987. "The British Columbia Forest Sector: Pros and Cons of the Stumpage System." In Gunton and Richards, pp. 181-213.

Swift, Jamie. 1983. *Cut and Run: The Assault on Canada's Forests.* Toronto: Between the Lines.

Van Kooten, Cornelis and Erwin H. Bulte. 2000. *The Economics of Nature: Managing Biological Assets.* Oxford: Blackwell Publishers.

Warnock, John W. 2001. "Saskatchewan's Neo-colonial Forestry Policy." *Policy Options,* Vol. 22, No. 5, June, pp. 31-6.

Wittbecker, Alan. 1999. "How Much is a Forest Worth?" *International Journal of Ecoforestry.* Vol. 14. No. 2, pp. 7-12.

# Chapter 11

─────○─────

# THE STRUGGLE OVER RESOURCE ROYALTIES

A ll governments in Saskatchewan have sought to diversify the economy beyond food and agriculture. Because of its hinterland status, from the perspective of geography as well as the centralization of the Canadian economy, the future for manufacturing has always been limited. The most likely avenue for new development was in the area of natural resource extraction. But activity in this area did not begin on a serious level until the CCF under T. C. Douglas was elected in 1944.

Well before it took office, the CCF had been preparing plans for the resource industry. Once in office, it introduced new legislation and directives. In 1944 the new Mineral Taxation Act assessed taxes on private mineral rights that had been granted by the federal government. Amendments in 1947 allowed the provincial government to set regulations for the industry and to change the royalty rates set by previous governments. The CCF was establishing the principle that natural resources belong to all the people and their development and use would be determined by their elected governments.

While there was a desire by many in the party to develop natural resources under state ownership, the CCF government chose a pragmatic approach once in office. They did not have the capital for the investment required and little chance to obtain it. They did not have the expertise to undertake oil, natural gas, and mineral developments. The policy goal they chose was not to nationalize existing resource extraction industries but to raise royalties. In 1946 they decided to leave mineral exploration to private interests while the government would provide research, mapping and financial assistance. Incentives would be offered to private oil and gas corporations. They sought federal government support for the development of potash, but this was not forthcoming.

Corporations were reluctant to invest in Saskatchewan with a new government many saw as socialist. How could capital be attracted? Government policy changed again. In 1947 they announced reductions in royalties on non-renewable resource extraction. In the 1948 provincial election Douglas pledged that the CCF government would not expropriate or socialize the mining or petroleum industry in the province. Royalties would be fixed, to help corporations plan, and to guarantee the province a "fair return" for the extraction of their public assets. They pledged "fair play" and financial assistance as long as the large corporations in these industries did not abuse their power. The Saskatchewan Research Council and the Industrial Development Fund were created to assist corporations. (Larmour, 1984; Johnson, 1963; McLeod, 1946)

The Prospectors Assistance Plan of 1948 provided licences, free assays, free recording and transfer of claims, equipment to be lent free of charge, free aerial transportation and resupply, training courses and other support. The provincial geological survey was created to assist exploration. Companies were encouraged to explore through licenses which gave them monopoly control over specific areas. The CCF government was following the resource strategy adopted by the other provinces: state support for capital accumulation.

The province's resource extraction policy was basically set by the CCF government. Since this time, all Saskatchewan governments have given extensive subsidies to private corporations extracting non-renewable resources. These have included technical research and support by the provincial government, the Saskatchewan Research Council, and the two universities. Infrastructure has been provided through extensive road construction, streets in northern mining towns, and paving access highways. Saskatchewan Government Airways was created as a Crown corporation in 1947 to aid northern resource development. Airfields were constructed. Saskatchewan Power Corporation, a Crown corporation, created power generating plants and transmission lines to serve the mining and forestry corporations. Sask Power and then Sask Energy have provided low-cost natural gas. The Department of Natural Resources created the first communications network in Northern Saskatchewan, including the first radio stations. Saskatchewan Telephone, another Crown corporation, has provided telephone services. The province built the Gardiner Dam on the South Saskatchewan River and then spent $13 million to construct the canal system, pipelines and reservoirs for the potash mines.

The provincial government has played a key role in providing a trained labour force. The Industrial Towns Act of 1964 provided services for mining families in the north, paying for schools, hospitals, housing, streets and other facilities. In contrast to the United States, employees of resource corporations are covered by state health and medicare services. (Murray, 1978; Warnock, 1974)

Saskatchewan governments have long been involved in raising capital for private corporations. The Douglas government provided generous land disposition regulations, tax incentives, and established low tax and royalty rates. All Saskatchewan governments since the end of World War II have provided direct government grants, loans, and guaranteed loans to large corporations in all sectors of the economy. In the resource extraction sector, it was hoped that the private corporations would in turn invest more of the profits and economic rent in the province.

The ability to collect resource rents is also greatly influenced by policies of the federal government. A key factor here is the wide range of tax expenditures (indirect subsidies) granted to natural resource extraction industries. For example, in 1970 mining companies received resource depletion allowances to be deducted as a cost of production, exemption of mining profits from taxation for the first three years of operation, immediate write offs of future exploration expenditures, and accelerated depreciation allowances (capital cost allowances). These subsidies were designed to help investors recover all of their investment during the first three years of a mine's construction and operation. McGill University economist Eric Kierans reported that in 1970 this allowed the mining corporations in Manitoba to reduce their provincial taxes and royalties to only 7.9 percent of book profits and 1.9 percent of the value of their output. In Canada as a whole, he reported, the mineral fuels industry taxable income was only six percent of book profits and for metal mining only 19 percent. In contrast, manufacturing, construction, services, wholesale and retail trade had taxable income which was around 85 percent of book profits. Hugh Aitken, an American economist who wrote extensively on Canadian resource policy, once stated that Canadian economic development was based on government financing of infrastructure and unrestricted access to natural resources. He left out capital subsidies. (Kierans, 1973; Aitken, 1961)

## How Do We Collect Economic Rents from Non-renewable Resources?

The concept of economic rent used in the petroleum and mining industries today is that set forth by David Ricardo in 1817. If all mines have the same degree of ore concentration, and the same costs of production and transportation, then the value of the extracted resource would depend only on the quantity of labour needed to bring the resource to market. Following from his argument on rent in agricultural land, Ricardo's thesis is that the resource extracted from the poorest mine, sold in the market, and returning the normal rate of profit will yield no rent. Rent only comes from those mines which have the higher grade of ore or mineral fuel. Rent is a surplus income over and above normal profit.

An example of this would be uranium. Saskatchewan has 31 percent of world uranium production, by far the highest grade ore deposits, and modern efficient mining operations. Under free market conditions, it should bring in a high level of economic rent. Markets have been somewhat limited because of uranium's key role in nuclear weapons; other governments maintain extensive subsidies to less efficient operations and national security controls. The domestic nuclear industry is also limited. Nuclear power plants are very expensive to build, and because of the hazardous nature of the entire nuclear fuel cycle, there is strong opposition around the world to further development. Nevertheless, the profit margin of the Saskatchewan mines should be high. This may be the case, but we do not really know. A high level of Ricardian rent extraction in Saskatchewan is definitely not reflected in the provincial royalties and taxes the corporations pay. (Anderson, 1987; Whillans, 1997; Pembina Institute, 2001; Prudhomme, 1998)

It is very difficult to determine the economic rent for the extraction of mineral resources in Canada's political economy. Natural resources are in theory owned by the public as a whole and managed by our elected provincial governments. It is presumed that the public as the owners of the resources should get a return when they are privatized. The mining and fossil fuel industries are dominated by large trans-national corporations which are granted licenses to extract and use natural resources. There are many different resource royalty systems which vary between provinces, and they vary between projects in the same industry. However, there are a few basic approaches to rent extraction that are in use today. (see Gunton and Richards, 1987)

First, a government can try to capture some of the economic rent through a *flat rate* which is usually a quantity-based royalty. This was the system used originally in the coal mining industry. A flat rate per tonne was charged. This approach does not take into consideration ore grades or the costs of production. The reasoning behind this approach is the belief that when a private company takes a natural resource from the public for its own use and profit they owe the people some basic return. The purchase of the raw material should be considered a cost of production. However, under the flat rate system inflation reduces the value of the royalty. This system is not widely used today, although it is still common for construction materials. Other similar royalties include a property tax, usually a percentage of the value of the land for mineral or oil extraction, or a lease fee, an annual fee on land leased for mineral purposes. These are used in Saskatchewan.

Second, an *ad valorem* royalty is widely used, usually a percentage of the sales price or gross revenues that the operator receives. This approach should be easy to calculate. However, it is very difficult to determine when "sales" are in fact intra-company transfers by trans-national corporations. These "sales" are not market transactions but administered prices. This situation is the norm in Saskatchewan.

Third, a *net profits* royalty is used. This also takes the form of an *ad valorem* rate, usually a percentage of the profits, which can increase as the rate of profit increases. This is the approach favoured by the private corporations and has been widely adopted in Saskatchewan in more recent years. This tends to result in low royalty payments, sometimes approaching zero. Michael Cartwright, a U.S. specialist in this field, has commented that "there are virtually no buyers for this type of royalty [in the United States] because of the creative accounting that the mining operator can use to depress the royalty payment account." When the Blakeney government enacted a net income royalty on potash, the private corporations refused to provide data on their operations. This provoked the NDP government into nationalizing part of the industry. (Cartwright, 1999; Gunton and Richards, 1987)

Fourth, a government can introduce a *marketing board* with monopoly power to purchase all the output from the corporations and market the product. This approach gives the government additional power when dealing with large trans-national corporations. It can increase the ability of the government to assess the real costs of resource extraction. Ross Thatcher's Liberal government set up the Potash Conservation Board in 1969, a marketing board with monopoly power to sell potash. The government was trying to capture a royalty in a situation of over investment and excess capacity, but it was also trying to create a cartel which could set prices and production quotas. In 1973 Peter Lougheed's Conservative government in Alberta created the Petroleum Marketing Commission, a Crown corporation which had broad control over the production and marketing of oil. It held ownership of all oil in the province until it was sold to the consumer. It was quite successful in capturing economic rent. (Warnock, 1974; Richards and Pratt, 1979)

Finally, there is the use of the state through *joint ventures* with private corporations and the use of state-owned corporations. Through a number of joint ventures between the Saskatchewan Mining and Development Corporation (SMDC) and private corporations, the government of Saskatchewan was directly involved in the extraction of uranium and was able to determine the real costs of uranium production. Through the Potash Corporation of Saskatchewan (PCS) and the Saskatchewan Oil and Gas Corporation (Sask Oil) they appropriated all the rent from some resource extraction and paid it into the provincial treasury.

A very good example of the benefits of state ownership can be seen in Mexico. Petróleos Méxicanos (PEMEX), a state owned enterprise, has had monopoly control over the extraction, refining, processing and distribution of oil since 1938. The government of Lázaro Cárdenas, facing a capital strike by the foreign-owned oil companies, responded by nationalizing all of them. PEMEX has been criticized by mainstream economists as inefficient, hiring too many workers, hiring too many high paid executives, and being under the control of patronage. These criticism are certainly true. But it is the largest employer in Mexico, pays the highest wages and salaries, and over the years has provided around 40 percent of all federal government revenues. Students going to state owned universities in Mexico pay no tuition. This is provided by grants from the federal government, economic rent from the extraction and sale of oil. The vast majority of the people in Mexico are determined to keep state ownership of this industry. State ownership of the oil industry is entrenched in the constitution. The economic rents stay in Mexico, and they do benefit ordinary people. However, this approach to capturing economic rent is out of fashion in the new era of globalization, free trade and the private enterprise economy. State ownership certainly benefits the population as a whole, but not private investors. (see Teichman, 1988)

The case for public ownership of natural resource extraction industries was advanced by Eric Kierans in his report on the mining industry to the government of Manitoba in 1973. He argued that it is extremely difficult to devise a system of capturing economic rents when the mining industry is dominated by large trans-national corporations. Even when there is some revenue in the form of royalties, it is usually not enough to "finance the costs of the highways, schools, hospitals and other services that are required to make a new community livable." With the wide range of subsidies found in mineral extraction, "the social costs will exceed the returns and the resource development, far from yielding a net income to the province, becomes a burden on the whole community."

Kierans argued that "it is vital to the growth and development of a province or nation that it retain these super-returns [the Ricardian economic rent] as a means of ensuring its growth and lessening its dependence on others." The former president of the Montreal Stock Exchange went farther:

> To be satisfied with the new jobs created and to forego the surpluses and profits inherent in the development of its own endowment is hardly the mark of a strong and mature government. It accepts the role of "hewers of wood and drawers of water" for its people when they are capable of much more. That role provides wages and salaries and little else. The profits, which direct and finance the future, belong to those who have been invited in, and this capital formation...does nothing for [government] priorities in the fields of agriculture, health, education or whatever. A developing nation, a province or a colony may be rich in its beginnings but when that wealth is depleted through the poverty of its policies, nothing remains of the original endowment but the instability, dissatisfaction and political unrest arising from poorly conceived policies. (Kierans, 1973)

## The History of Extracting Resource Rents

How successful have Canadian governments been in extracting a rent from the natural resources that we have given the private corporations? Of course, this is a political and ideological question. Supporters of the private industry say that royalties are too high. Those who want to see the government improve social programs believe they are too low.

In 1987 Tom Gunton and John Richards of Simon Fraser University published *Resource Rents and Public Policy in Western Canada*, a collection of case studies. They covered a period when governments were still to some degree following Keynesian economic and welfare policies. Today elected governments are even less likely to feel the need to act on behalf of the public interest as opposed to private corporate interest.

Nevertheless, the general thrust of all the case studies was that our governments were not collecting much of the economic rent. The preponderance was going to the private corporate sector. Crown corporations creating hydroelectric power in British Columbia and Manitoba were passing rents off to industrial and residential consumers. (Bernard and Payne, 1987) Manitoba failed to capture rents in nickel because of the monopoly power of the International Nickel Company (INCO) and the generous mineral royalty system introduced by the Conservative government in 1977. (Gunton, 1987)

Minerals and fuels are relatively new to the Saskatchewan economy. Coal was discovered and was being mined before Saskatchewan became a province in 1905. The volume of production has steadily increased over the years. Oil extraction was under way in the 1950s, but the industry did not take off until after the Oil Producing and Exporting Countries (OPEC) increased prices after 1973. Natural gas expanded in the 1980s, and exports rose rapidly after the Canada-U.S. Free Trade Agreement in 1989 and the dismantling of the National Energy Board.

Uranium was discovered near Lake Athabasca, where it was developed by Eldorado Nuclear, a federal Crown corporation, beginning in World War II. The nuclear arms race led to a boom in the industry in Saskatchewan. Additional high grade deposits led to a second boom after 1976 as government subsidies encouraged the development of nuclear power plants.

In 1943 an oil drilling rig at Radville found high concentrations of potash. It was soon learned that Saskatchewan had the most extensive reserves in the world and the highest grade ore. In the 1950s commercial extraction began. Expansion took place in the 1960s, and the volume sold has remained relatively stable since the mid-1980s.

In the early period of the development of the resource extraction industry little of the economic rent that was created went to government revenues because of provincial and federal direct subsidies and other economic incentives. Royalties and taxes, set low to attract capital investment, provided considerably less than 10 percent of government revenues down through the 1960s.

The change came with the election of the NDP government under Allan Blakeney (1971-82). Between 1972 and 1975 royalties and taxes from resource extraction went from 8.8 percent of government revenues to 32.3 percent. In the second term of the government resource royalties and taxes provided on average 28 percent of total revenues. The third term (1979-1982) was even better with resource revenues providing on average 37 percent of government revenues. The additional revenues allowed the government to expand social programs and make a real effort to tackle poverty. (Saskatchewan Bureau of Statistics, 2001)

The NDP government emphasized "province building," gaining some significant control over economic development and capturing resource rents. In 1973 the

Saskatchewan Oil and Gas Corporation (SaskOil) was created. In 1976 SaskOil bought the reserves of Atlantic Richfield Canada and began to expand its role in the provincial industry. The Crown corporation became a partner in the consortium planning a heavy oil up grader for Lloydminister.

Following the 1973 decision by OPEC to increase prices, there was strong public support across Canada for nationalizing the entire industry. In December 1973 the NDP government introduced legislation to nationalize all freehold oil and gas rights and charge a royalty for all Crown oil extraction. The government, in league with Peter Loughheed's Tory government in Alberta, proposed a 100 percent tax on all the windfall profits stemming from the rise in world prices caused by the OPEC oil cartel. The oil industry in Canada went to court to challenge the legislation, supported by the federal government. The courts ruled against the province, but the Blakeney government did not surrender. They passed new laws and regulations. The Lougheed government in Alberta created the petroleum marketing board. By the last term of the Blakeney government the province was collecting over 50 percent of the value of oil extraction as royalties and taxes. (see Richards and Pratt, 1979)

The potash industry in Saskatchewan developed overcapacity due to the extensive provincial and federal government subsidies, and royalties were only around three percent of gross industry revenue. A major confrontation developed when the NDP government under Allan Blakeney moved to collect more of the economic rent. When the Potash corporations jointly refused to co-operate, the NDP government nationalized four of the mines and acquired an interest in a fifth, controlling 40 percent of the industry. Greater returns came to the province after these acquisitions were transformed into the Potash Corporation of Saskatchewan (PCS), a Crown corporation. (Richards, 1987)

In 1974 the Blakeney government created the Saskatchewan Mining and Development Corporation (SMDC) to participate in hard rock mining. The legislation gave the province the right to claim 50 percent ownership of any new mine. The province increased its share of the rents from uranium mining through a new royalty regime. The public also benefited directly from Crown corporation equity participation in the new highly profitable mines at Cigar Lake, Key Lake and Cluff Lake. (Anderson, 1987)

The Saskatchewan Heritage Fund was created in 1978. It was the recipient of economic rents from resource development. In 1981 it became linked to the Crown Investment Corporation (CIC), a provincial Crown corporation which was a holding corporation overseeing all Crown corporations. During the Blakeney government resource revenues increased provincial government revenues which financed social programs. But the primary focus of this development was the expansion of capital and assets under the control of the province. (see Glor, 1997)

The policy direction of the Blakeney government was reversed during the Conservative government of Grant Devine (1982-91). One of the very first things the Tory government did was reduce the royalties and taxes on the oil industry. Between 1981 and 1989 the revenues from the sale of oil went from $821 million to $1,170 million, but royalties dropped from $532 million to $254 million. The "Open for Business" campaign pledged to restrict the development of Crown corporations and bring in the private sector, large trans-national corporations, for economic development of the resource industry. The Devine government canceled the right of SMDC to claim a percentage of all new mines and began the privatization process. Royalties on other resources were lowered. Provincial revenues fell, and budget deficits and the provincial debt increased. (see Pitsula and Rasmussen, 1990; Biggs and Stobbe, 1991; Thatcher, 1985)

It takes some training as an economist and access to inside information to make a precise evaluation of the question of economic rents for natural resource extraction. However, general trends can be seen by looking at the volume of the resource extracted, revenues from sales, and royalties and taxes paid to the provincial government. These can also be measured in relation to the provincial gross domestic product.

In 1990 Doug Elliott, who publishes *Sask Trends Monitor*, assessed the resource industry over the period from 1981 to 1989, when the Devine government reduced royalties and taxes on the resource extraction corporations. He noted that the volume of extraction of all the key non-renewable natural resources increased significantly: oil 57 percent; natural gas, 466 percent; coal, 69 percent; potash 12 percent; and uranium 291 percent. Overall resource sales increased from $2.182 billion to $2.950 billion or by 35 percent. But royalties and taxes going to the government fell from $797 million in 1981 (34 percent of resource sales) and $1,031 million in 1982 (43 percent of resource sales) to only $397 million in 1989 (13 percent of resource sales). Royalties and taxes from natural resources provided 33 percent of all government revenues in 1981 but only nine percent by 1989. Elliott concluded that "even with the declining prices, had the royalty and taxation levels remained at their earlier levels, the current provincial debt of $4 billion would simply not exist." This was the debt inherited by the NDP government in 1991. (Elliott, 1990)

## Oil and Natural Gas Extraction under the New NDP Government

The extraction of minerals and mineral fuels is an important part of the Saskatchewan economy. Sales in 2001 were over $7 billion, and as a share of provincial gross domestic product, had risen from 12 percent in 1990 to around 22 percent in 2001. But this sector of the economy is very capital intensive and employs only around 13,500 people, or 2.6 percent of the labour force. (Saskatchewan Bureau of Statistics, 2001)

It was widely believed that when the NDP was elected in 1991 there would be a return to the policy direction of the Blakeney government. Indeed, when Grant Devine's government started to privatize the Crown corporations in the resource sector, the NDP, then the official opposition, pledged that if they were elected in the next election they would "buy back or expropriate any Crown corporations or government assets sold by the Tories." (Pitsula and Rasmussen, 1990)

While it was not a part of the formal election platform, throughout the 1991 election campaign NDP candidates regularly proclaimed that when they were elected they would raise the taxes and royalties in the resource sector to balance the budget and pay down the provincial debt. The NDP caucus made a similar pledge in their official policy position, *Tax Fairness for the 1990s*, released in January 1991. However, once in office, the new NDP government, led by Roy Romanow, chose instead to complete the job started by the Devine government. The NDP government sold the remainder of the province's shares in Sask Oil, the Potash Corporation of Saskatchewan, Saskatchewan Mining and Development Corporation (now Cameco), and the Lloydminister Heavy Oil Upgrader. In addition, they kept the low resource royalty structure. Indeed, during the NDP governments of Roy Romanow and Lorne Calvert, from 1991 to 2003, resources royalties and taxes were even further reduced.

What is a proper rate of royalty for resource extraction? The rule of thumb which is sometimes cited by Saskatchewan government officials in recent years has been fifteen percent. Where did this figure come from? Cyrus Bina, a resource economist, says this arbitrary standard stems from the contracts made between the Seven Sisters international oil cartel and the Middle East and Venezuelan governments during the period 1901-1950. The standard royalty in the contracts between the transnational oil corporations and the local governments was a fixed rate which translated into 12.5 percent of the market price of oil. These agreements were imposed on weak Third World governments.

After World War II all of the colonies in the Middle East achieved independence. With the onset of the Cold War, these new governments forced the private corporations to replace the concessions with new agreements that shared the returns from oil extraction on a fifty/fifty basis. When the Organization of Petroleum Exporting Countries (OPEC) was formed in 1970, these agreements were replaced by a system where the national governments receive *all the rents* from oil production. The Arab states chose to operate the oil industry as a state owned enterprise. The private corporations are left to make their profits on refining and sales. Yet natural resource extraction corporations in Canada see the old neo-colonial 15 percent figure as a guideline or a maximum for royalties. In the present era of globalization, our governments agree. (see Bina, 1985)

For many in Saskatchewan, it was hoped that the Crown corporation Sask Oil would become a major factor in oil and gas extraction and increase government revenues and provincial control over the industry. A successful model here is found in Norway where Statoil, a state owned enterprise, has brought much higher returns than in Canada where the private corporations completely control the industry. Statoil is a partner in all Norway's oil and gas developments. It contributes a share of the capital investment and the costs of production but also gets an equivalent share of profits and economic rent. The people of Norway have received a greater return from North Sea oil development than would otherwise be the case. A study by the Parkland Institute in Alberta found that Norway's return from oil and gas extraction was 2.7 times that received by the province of Alberta under the Tory government of Ralph Klein. (Parkland, 1999)

The royalties paid by the individual resource corporations have varied greatly between industries and over time. In 1981 and 1982 the royalties and taxes paid by the oil industry exceeded 50 percent of the value of all sales. This dropped to a low of 18 percent under Grant Devine's government and then to 16 percent under the NDP governments of Roy Romanow and Lorne Calvert. Our own Crown corporation, Sask Oil, which was only a small player, was privatized by the governments of Grant Devine and Roy Romanow. The renamed Wascana Oil was then bought by Continental Oil. (Warnock, 1990b)

In the fall of 2002 the NDP government of Lorne Calvert announced major tax breaks and cuts in royalties for the mining, oil and gas industries. This came at a time when oil and gas prices were steadily rising and shortages were developing. In 2002 over 3,500 new wells were drilled in the province, and in 2003 over 4,000. Profits in the oil and gas industry were skyrocketing. For example, Husky Oil, with a major refining operation in Lloydminister, formerly in partnership with the Saskatchewan government, reported a 13 percent increase in production but a 438 percent increase in earnings. (*Globe and Mail*, February 7, 2003)

The natural gas industry in Saskatchewan has paid very low royalties, less than four percent of sales prior to 1981, rising to 13 percent in 1990, and then peaking at 15 percent in the later years of the Romanow government. Natural gas, a non-renewable resource, is rapidly disappearing in western Canada. At the time of the Canada-U.S. Free Trade Agreement in 1989, Canada had a 20 year proven reserve. That was down to only eight years in 2003. Over 50 percent of all Canadian natural gas is now exported to the United States. Yet at the Western Premiers' Conference in 2002 Premier Lorne Calvert gave support to President George W. Bush's call for a new continental energy agreement which would increase Canadian energy exports. (*Leader-Post*, June 7, 2002)

With the new tax breaks and reductions in royalties, the private sector drilled 2,100 gas wells in Saskatchewan in 2003. Land sales for the rights to drill oil and gas wells reached their second highest level in history, bringing in $159 million. Natural gas prices were on the rise, from $3.85 per thousand cubic feet (mcf) in 2002 to $6.80 in 2003. However, for the new gas wells that were drilled in 2003, the average flow of gas was only 41 percent of the flow recorded in the mid-1990s. The fact is, we are fast running out of natural gas. In the past the National Energy Board required the private sector to retain a 20 year proven supply for Canadian needs. Sask Power bought gas fields to protect the future needs of the province. But in the era of free trade and neoliberal economic policies, this is no longer the case. (Jang, 2003)

Oil and gas royalties are quite low for both Saskatchewan and Alberta. The Parkland Institute at the University of Alberta compared the rent collected from the oil and gas industry by the governments of Alberta, Alaska and Norway over the period 1992-7. On the sale of a barrel of oil the Alberta government collected $2.41, the Alaska government $3.74 and the government of Norway, $6.41. They also compared the returns during different Alberta governments. Peter Lougheed's government (1972-85) collected on average $4.67 per barrel, Paul Getty's government (1986-92) $2.06, and Ralph Klein's government (1992-7) $2.10. The authors concluded that if Ralph Klein's government had continued to collect energy rents at the same level as the Lougheed government, the province would have collected on average another $3.78 billion per year over the 1992-7 period. (Parkland Institute, 1999)

The problem with having governments heavily subsidize private resource corporations through very low royalty structures, economic incentives, and direct subsidies is it leads to overinvestment in the industry, surplus capacity and overproduction. This has been one of the characteristics of the potash and uranium industries in Saskatchewan. It leads to overproduction of oil and gas as well. (Gunton and Richards, 1987)

This view is endorsed by Cyrus Bina, who has conducted a detailed study of the oil industry. When there are very low taxes and royalties, the result is a very inefficient extraction process that artificially increases the cost of recovery. Firms have a tendency to intensify exploration in the same areas, or to "simply concentrate on investing in the *existing oil fields* for further recovery." Even on government owned lands, this leads to a great deal of "speculative activity" and fragmentation of ownership. This situation increases the capital expenditure per barrel in the extraction process. (Bina, 1985)

At the end of 2003 Eric Cline, NDP minister for industry and resources, was proudly proclaiming how much investment there was in the oil and gas industry and how many jobs had been created. It was claimed that this was the result of the lowering of taxes and royalties on the industry. Just before the provincial election in the fall of 2003, the NDP government announced even further royalty reductions. New oil and gas wells would be subject to a maximum royalty of 2.5 percent on Crown land and 0.0 percent on freehold (private) land. This new production may help improve Canada's relations with President George W. Bush. But we might remember the critique of Grant Devine's royalty reduction policy by Mark Stobbe, long time NDP party official:

> Oil is a finite, non-renewable resource. If left in the ground, it increases in value. While giving oil away may not result in any immediate drop in revenue, in the medium and long-term the province has given away a nonrenewable resource without receiving any compensation in return. Further, by making the production from new wells royalty-free, the government encourages oil companies to artificially shift production from old wells to new ones. This creates a few drilling jobs, but makes no long-term economic sense. The royalty structure encourages waste and inefficiency by giving an incentive to producers to restrict output from existing wells while drilling new wells in the same field. (Biggs and Stobbe, 1991)

## Who Profits from the Extraction of Non-renewable Resources?

The royalties received from coal extraction in Saskatchewan have been fairly steady, between 15 and 17 percent of sales since the early 1980s. The Sask Power Corporation originally owned the Souris Valley mine and used the coal for the production of electricity, capturing all of the economic rent for the province. However, in 1982 Grant Devine's government sold the mine and its equipment to Manalta, a private Alberta firm, and granted them the SPC coal contract. The mine is now owned by

Sherritt Gordon, a Canadian trans-national corporation. The economic rent from this production of coal now goes out of the province. When I first read about this privatization it reminded me of Karl Marx's commentary on "primitive accumulation of capital," which he noted was just a form of piracy. The Devine government's policy decision, later supported by the NDP government of Roy Romanow, illustrates the degree to which Saskatchewan governments are committed to the accumulation of capital by private interests. (Warnock, 1990a; Shapiro, 1998)

Given the high grade of the ore, the volume extracted, and the high value of sales, the province has received precious little from the potash industry. In 1981, the last year of the Blakeney government, royalties and taxes were 18 percent of sales. This dropped to 5.7 percent in 1982 and stayed below 10 percent for all of the years of the Devine government. They have slowly risen to 10 to 12 percent of sales under the Romanow/Calvert governments.

In August 2003, right before the provincial election, Premier Lorne Calvert announced that there would be further reductions in the royalties paid by the potash industry. The base payment has been 35 percent of profits, with a minimum and maximum payment. The effective base rate has been between 2.1 and 4.5 percent of profits since the royalty system was created in 1990. In addition, there was an second "profit tax." This was not onerous because of the 35 percent capital depreciation allowance granted to the industry. In order to "stimulate investment" and "create jobs," Premier Calvert announced that the second "profit tax" would be removed as part of a new plan to lower potash royalties and taxes. In addition, the province announced that any new investments in the industry would be eligible for an "accelerated 100-percent depreciation." Immediately after this the now private Potash Corporation of Saskatchewan announced it would spend $80 million to upgrade its Rocanville mine. Since privatization by the Devine and Romanow governments, the dividends that the Potash Corporation of Saskatchewan used to pay to the Saskatchewan government now go primarily to U.S. investors. Again, privatization has not been in the interests of the Saskatchewan public. (Warnock and Checkley, 1990; Charlton *et al.*, 1996)

The uranium industry has a similar record. The present royalty regime is four percent of gross sales with a tiered system which goes up with the price of a pound of uranium oxide. But the tiered structure of royalties established by the NDP government in 2001 is a bad joke. The four percent base royalty rate applies when the market price of uranium oxide is below $15 per pound. In the first tier above $15, the total royalty is set at only 4.3 percent of the sales price. There are four higher tiers, with the total royalty rising to a maximum of 10 percent of sale price when a pound of uranium oxide exceeds $35. But over the period between 1988 and 2002, there were only a few months when the world price was above $15 per pound! So the effective royalty on uranium oxide is the absurdly low rate of only four percent of sales. (Cameco Corporation, *Annual Report*, December 12, 2002)

Royalties and taxes on uranium extraction were 12 percent of sales in 1981, fell to a low of three percent in 1988, rose to 10 percent in 1995, and then fell to less than seven percent in 1997 and 1998. In 2000 and 2001 they were under five percent. With the privatization of SMDC by the Devine and Romanow governments, the province has lost the dividends from its equity position in the major uranium projects. Those profits now leave the province. Paul Hanley, a reporter for the Saskatoon *Star Phoenix*, did an analysis of the industry in early 1992. He concluded that the subsidies provided to the industry exceeded its royalties and taxes. This is certainly still true today. But this policy has been good for the owners of the Cameco and Cogema who live in comfort elsewhere. (Hanley, 1992)

The right wing Fraser Institute, in its annual survey of mining executives, reported in 2002 that Saskatchewan ranked 10th out of 47 political jurisdictions around the world on "factors which encourage exploration investment." Saskatchewan ranked high for its "mining friendly labour regulations" and its low level of taxation. Saskatchewan was ranked as more friendly to mining interests than most of the Third World governments, with a more pro-business tax regime than countries like Colombia, South Africa, Ghana, India, Indonesia, the Philippines and Papua New Guinea. (Fredricksen, 2002)

It seems fairly clear that the people of Saskatchewan are receiving a bare minimum for the exploitation of non-renewable natural resources by the large transnational corporations. The NDP governments in office after 1991 have had no interest at all in raising royalties or in re-establishing any of the Crown corporations in the resource sector. Indeed, as one reads the Annual Report of the Ministry of Energy and Mines (now part of Industry and Resources), one gets the feeling that the provincial government is just a junior partner serving the private sector. The emphasis is on providing a "competitive climate" with the lowest cost producer anywhere in the world. The department is continually "consulting with industry" (behind closed doors) over their belief that our taxation and royalty system is too high. The ministry is always boasting about the special incentives and subsidies given to oil corporations to try to extract more oil from old pools. With all the tax incentives and subsidies, an excessive number of wells are being drilled every year. The provincial government acts like Saskatchewan is a semi-colonial Third World country.

## Problems with the Resource Extraction Industry

As Tom Gunton and John Richards have argued, provincial governments need to remove subsidies which promote overcapacity and result in a reduction in the rent being captured for the people of the province. John Burton, former NDP Member of Parliament and executive with the Potash Corporation of Saskatchewan, points out that for some resource industries low royalties and taxes and other subsidies are granted to promote early economic development, before the market needs those more marginal resources. That judgement would apply to much of the oil extraction in Saskatchewan today. (Gunton and Richards, 1987; Burton, 1997)

However, the subsidies given resource extraction industries always seem to increase. A recent study by the Pembina Institute concludes that tax breaks and subsidies are very much central to the mining industry in Canada, a "public generosity, often exercised on the public's behalf without their knowledge or consent." Canada's taxation of the industry ranks low to middle range on a world basis, "especially when allowable accelerated capital cost allowances, tax deferrals, tax credits and tax holidays are taken into account." More recently "flow-through share programs," a new tax shelter, has been added by both federal and provincial governments, including Saskatchewan. Another support for the industry is found in the environmental assessment systems, which are heavily pro-industry. Subsidies include "low-cost access to land and to the mineral resource, but most jurisdictions go well beyond just giving away the public resource—government actually pays the mining companies to take it!" Saskatchewan leads the way in providing "incentives." (Pembina, 2001)

Taxes on the resource extraction industry are among the lowest in Canada. The 1998 report by the Minister of Finance's Task Force on Business Taxation concluded that the *effective corporate tax rate* (what is actually paid) on the mining industry in Canada was only six percent. This was the lowest rate for all the sectors of the economy that were studied. (Canada, Technical Committee, 1998)

Nevertheless, in 2003 the federal government's budget included a reduction of the formal corporate tax rate for the resource sector from 28 percent to 21 percent. Originally, the resource sector had been excluded from the corporate tax reductions begun in 2000 because they have particular benefits from "incentives" in mineral exploration and development, depletion allowances, and many other special deductions. The resource corporations will now also benefit from the ability to deduct all provincial royalties and taxes from their federal taxes. In addition, they were to receive a new 10 percent Investment Tax Credit based on exploration expenses. The federal government also proposed the removal of the Capital Tax on resource corporations in 2008. Apparently, there will be no end to the concessions offered by Canadian governments to the resource industries until they pay no taxes at all.

MiningWatch Canada and the Green Budget Coalition strongly opposed these new tax reductions. They stressed the position taken by the Organization for Economic Cooperation and Development (OECD) in their survey of the Canadian economy. The OECD recommended that "preferential tax treatment of conventional resource sectors, such as oil and gas and minerals and metals be eliminated." This was put in the context of their conclusion that "all major global ecosystems are in decline."

The OECD noted that the 1992 Rio Declaration committed Canada and others to "the elimination of unsustainable patterns of production and consumption." The material intensity of each economic unit needed to be reduced by 50 percent, and for Canada it would have to fall by a factor of between four and 10. Recycling of materials was absolutely necessary. Canada's tax policies on the resource sector undermines economic efficiency and promotes environmental degradation. (MiningWatch Canada, 2003; Pembina Institute, 2003)

When governments have to defend the use of taxpayers' money to subsidize resource corporations, they inevitably fall back on the argument that they are creating employment and economic activity. But as Dale Marshall and other economists have pointed out, while the volume of extraction continues to increase, employment has been steadily falling across Canada in coal mining, oil and natural gas extraction, and the production of electricity. In addition, the resource extraction industries are very capital intensive. The oil industry is renowned for this. In Canada in 1994 it took an investment of $790,000 in the oil and gas industry to create a single job. As one examines the resource industry over the years, the number of people working in particular Saskatchewan mines has regularly declined as new machinery is installed. Investment in any other sector of the economy would create more jobs. (Marshall, 2002; Stanford, 1999; Russell, 1997)

It may be that hinterland areas have few options but to develop resource industries. But the way that they are developed under the present capitalist system leaves much to be desired. Following the criticism of many academics and political leaders from the less developed countries, the United Nations Conference on Trade and Development (UNCTAD) recently pointed out the continuing impact of these industries. They noted that mining and oil export economic development usually creates "an isolated capital-intensive enclave development." The rising overall per capita gross domestic product "does not often lead to poverty reduction." Enclave development usually creates greater inequality between the minority who work in the industry and the large majority outside the industry, who continue to live in poverty. (UNCTAD, 2002)

This can certainly be seen in northern Saskatchewan. The dominant economic development in the north has been uranium mining. Those working in the industry are often "long distance commuters" flown in for seven days and then flown back home for seven days. The better paying jobs go to outsiders. Some "northerners" may get employment as labourers in the industry. But like all of these resource industries, the uranium industry relies heavily on the importation of expensive machinery, equipment and technology from outside the province. There is very little processing of the resource in the local area. Thus, the Canadian staple theory of development produces few local benefits, for there are weak backward and forward linkages to the local economy. In the period of the oil boom in Mexico in the 1970s, the country imported expensive machinery and equipment needed in oil production, but exported a relatively inexpensive raw material, oil. The imbalance in terms of trade produced a major balance of payments problem which eventually crashed the economy. (see Teichman, 1988; Warnock, 1995)

There is one other major issue concerning resource exploitation that rarely gets mentioned. Who pays for the social and environmental costs of these operations? Who pays for the high rate of injuries to workers? There is a debate going on in Alberta today over the cost of the oil and gas industry, which produces widespread pollution and seriously affects those living in the rural areas. The oil industry uses one-third of all water in a time when drought is making everyone think about conservation. In addition, the oil and gas industry uses considerable fossil fuels in the extraction process and creates a great deal of air pollution and greenhouse gases.

The norm in Canada has been for the mining company to simply abandon a mine when it is depleted without rehabilitating the site. Most mines are only operated between 15 and 25 years. There are around 7,000 abandoned mines in Canada, including over 500 in Saskatchewan, and it is estimated that it would cost $6 billion or more to clean them up. The environmental costs are very large, including open pits and shafts, dam collapses, ground subsidence, and environmental hazards. There is drainage from mines, metal leaching, contamination from agents used, and fuels and other pollutants used on the site. As they say, clean water goes in and toxic water comes out. The Canadian mineral industry creates on average 950,000 tonnes of tailings and one million tonnes of waste rock per day. The runoff from tailings needs to be carefully monitored, but this is not done; it would cost too much. (Mining Watch Canada, 2003; Pembina Institute, 2001)

There are also the social costs of mining, including the health effects on workers and people in the mining communities, injuries on the job, the boom and bust economic cycles, the changes to rural communities, and the antagonisms of the social relations, particularly between imported skilled miners from the south and the local indigenous peoples. It is easy to conclude that for those communities who must live near mining operations, the costs of mining outweigh the benefits. (Pembina Institute, 2002; Gullickson, 1990; Gunn, 1982; Parrott, 1996; Hesch, 1980)

## Uranium Mining in Northern Saskatchewan

Some of the worst examples of environmental mining disasters have occurred in the extraction of uranium. Probably the worst example in Canada is found in Saskatchewan in the uranium mines around Lake Athabasca and Uranium City.

Uranium was discovered in 1936, but it was not developed until the U.S. government began to build nuclear weapons. Fifty mines were developed during the Cold War period, and the uranium was processed at mills at the Beaverlodge, Gunnar and Larado mines. Uranium City was founded in 1952 to house the miners and their families, and at its peak it was home for 5,000 people. Beaverlodge, the last mine, was closed in 1982 and Uranium City was almost completely abandoned. Forty-five mines, under contract with Eldorado Nuclear and Uranium Canada, a federal Crown corporation, were simply abandoned. (McIntyre, 1993)

The mining area at Lake Athabasca is the worse toxic environmental site in Canada. Millions of tonnes of radioactive waste have been left by the mines, and the tailing pits are exposed to the open environment. A report by the provincial government states that the 4.4 million tonnes of tailings over 75 hectares from the Gunnar mine alone have been migrating into Lake Athabasca since this mine was closed in 1964. The three unconfined tailings pits are on the ground surface and wind blows them around, creating acids and leaching metals into the surrounding area. Most of the tailings at this site were at first bulldozed into a small lake. The water in the lake near the mill is heavily contaminated, with uranium levels 31 times higher than the acceptable limits set by Environment Canada.

The tailings from the Larado mine and mill site south of Uranium City, 0.6 million tonnes over 14 hectares, are leaching into local lakes. The area around this site was found to have radioactive levels 208 times the acceptable levels set by Health Canada. There are 6 million tonnes of tailings over 25 hectares at the Beaverlodge mine and mill. They were originally dumped into Beaverlodge Lake. The report records that these unconfined tailings "pose a gamma radiation concern." Both the provincial and federal government have concluded that these radioactive tailings "pose an immediate threat to people and the environment." The tailings still contain 85 percent of the radioactive materials from the original ore. Radioactive dust covers the environment around Uranium City. Cameco has done some cleanup under contract at Beaverlodge, but neither the provincial nor federal government wants to take on the task of cleanup, which would run at least $15 million. (MiningWatch Canada, 2002; Sierra Club of Canada, 2001; Saskatchewan Environment, 2002; Gelinas, 2002)

Uranium mining and milling has been a very hazardous occupation. It is well known that uranium miners have higher rates of lung cancer than the general population. Some have suffered from beta and gamma radiation exposure. The new uranium mines are much better in limiting the exposure of workers, but there has been no epidemiological study of the impact of radon exposure and lung cancer among workers at the new Saskatchewan uranium mines. Finally, in February 2003 the Canadian Nuclear Safety Commission announced that a two year study was to be undertaken. (Lung Association of Saskatchewan, February 6, 2003)

The main problem has come from inhaling alpha particles, from uranium, thorium and the dust that they contaminate. Exposure to radon gas is also a serious hazard. Workers at the old uranium mines in Saskatchewan experienced a range of illnesses from radiation exposure. A group who call themselves "The Survivors of Uranium City" meet every year in Prince Albert to discuss their health problems and to remember their colleagues who have passed away.

Those working the mines and mills in the early period were generally non-Native miners from the south. The Déline Dene worked at the Eldorado mine at Great Bear Lake in the Northwest Territories, the mine which produced the first Canadian uranium, the material that was in the atomic bomb dropped by the U.S. government on the Japanese at Hiroshima. As they put it, "the Dene were employed as 'coolies' packing 45-kilogram sacks of radioactive ore for three dollars a day, working 12 hours a day, six days a week for four months of the year." They have suffered extensive illnesses, cancers and early deaths from radiation exposure. In 1998 six survivors went to Hiroshima for the August 6 memorial, to honour the survivors of the bomb made from Canadian uranium. The Dene from the Athabasca Lake area in Saskatchewan and Alberta did the same kind of work for their local mines, and they have experienced the same kinds of illnesses and deaths. (Barbour, 1998)

During the NDP government of Allan Blakeney there was a major battle with the public over a proposal to build a uranium refinery at Warman, close to Saskatoon. A broad coalition of public interest groups, including representatives from Saskatchewan's major Christian churches, carried out a vigorous campaign against the government. But aside from this example, the operations of the uranium industry and the mines in northern Saskatchewan are almost completely outside public debate. Few people know anything about the industry. It is ignored by the mass media. The industry is strongly supported by the three major political parties. Only the small New Green Alliance is in favour of phasing out the industry.

The new mines are not without their problems. Several have very high levels of concentrations of uranium and are the most hazardous mines in the world. They threaten the local environment. In January 1984 there was a major spill of 100 million litres of radioactive water at the Key Lake mine. This mine had experienced numerous other small spills. In June 1989 the mine at Wollaston Lake spilled one million litres of radioactive water. Before this time it had reported 48 smaller spills. (see Harding, 1995; Prebble, 1991)

In the spring of 2003 Cameco's mine at McArthur River, the largest uranium mine in the world, started to flood. Pumps were extracting radioactive water from the mine at the rate of 1,000 cubic metres per hour for months on end. While the water was being run through settling ponds, even the Canadian Nuclear Safety Commission expressed concern about the toxic threat to the environment from gamma radiation and radioactive bioaccumulation through the food chain. (Stueck, 2003)

In August 2003 Cameco proposed major changes to its Rabbit Lake operation, which included breaching the dike in the middle of Wollaston Lake. There was to be no environmental assessment of the project. There was no consultation with local communities. The local Aboriginal community met and expressed strong opposition to the proposal. But, as usual, their concerns were ignored. (Kuyek, 2003)

There has always been opposition to the extraction of uranium in Saskatchewan. Many were morally opposed to selling uranium to the U.S. government, knowing that it was being used to produce nuclear weapons. Then after the disasters at Three Mile Island and Chernobyl, there developed a strong public opposition to providing uranium for nuclear power reactors. Environmentalists are still very concerned about the toxic wastes from the entire nuclear fuel cycle. Now there is growing worldwide concern over the use of depleted uranium in modern weapons, particularly by the U.S. and UK governments.

Depleted uranium (DU) is produced during the uranium enrichment process. The U-235 has been extracted, leaving the U-238 isotope. The material is extremely dense, greatly increases the penetration ability of weapons, and is used to coat shells and warheads on missiles and bombs. On impact the shell, with its uranium and traces of americium and plutonium, vaporizes and becomes very tiny particles of radioactive dust. It blows around in other dust. When it is inhaled, it can stay in the body, emitting radiation.

In the first Gulf War in 1991, DU was delivered almost exclusively with shells from tanks and ammunition used by the aircraft of the United States and its allies. In the bombing of Bosnia and Kosovo in the Balkans in 1999, the NATO allies added DU missiles and bunker busting bombs. Thousands of DU bombs and missiles were used in the war against Afghanistan and in the second Gulf War. A typical bunker busting bomb used by the U.S. and UK air forces contains 1.5 tonnes of depleted uranium. An estimated 320 tonnes of DU were used in the first Gulf War, primarily around Basra. It has been estimated that the U.S. and UK forces have dropped more than ten times this amount of DU in the second Gulf War. In August 2003, Scott Peterson of the *Christian Science Monitor* used a Geiger counter to test several sites in Bagdad near where bunker buster bombs and missiles had fallen. He found radiation readings which were between 1,000 and 1,900 times higher than normal background radiation readings. (Herold, 2003; Johnson, 2003; Taylor, 2003; *Express* [London], September 1, 2003)

The United Nations Children Fund (UNICEF) and other organizations have recorded the fact that tens of thousands of children in Iraq, primarily around Basra, are suffering from leukemia and birth defects. Similar medical reports are coming from Kosovo. Veterans of the first Gulf War and operations in Bosnia and Kosovo refer to their range of illnesses as "Gulf War Syndrome." As of 2003, over 208,000 U.S. Gulf War veterans or their families have filed claims seeking compensation for death, illnesses or disabilities from exposure to DU. By the middle of 2003, the U.S. Veterans Administration had granted compensation for over 8,000 deaths and 168,000 disabilities due to "service related exposure" incurred while serving in the first Gulf War. Officially, none of the NATO governments will admit that the deaths and illnesses are related to exposure to DU. As Chalmers Johnson has pointed out, the U.S. government has now recognized that the casualty rate for serving in this war is "a staggering 29.3 percent." (Johnson, 2003; Parsons, 2002; http://www.gulfwarvets.com; http://www.gulfweb.org)

How many Canadians know that in 1996 the United Nations General Assembly adopted a resolution that declared DU weapons to be illegal "weapons of mass destruction?" Scott Taylor, editor of *Esprit de Corps* magazine, who covered the Gulf

War, reminds us that in August 2002 at the UN Human Rights Convention meeting a resolution was passed urging a ban on the use of any DU weapons until a full-scale medical survey could determine the impact on humans and the environment. Only the governments from the United States and the United Kingdom voted against the resolution. This is Saskatchewan's contribution to the Anglo-American war machine. (Johnson, 2003; Taylor, 2003)

## A Green Alternative

There is an alternative strategy for resource development in Saskatchewan. It would begin by going back to the goals set by the NDP government of Allan Blakeney. A new approach would start by raising royalties and taxes on resource extraction corporations back to the levels they were in 1982. The province would steadily cut back on the public subsidies to the resource extraction industry. New Crown corporations could be introduced. The Romanow government originally proposed to create a Saskatchewan Economic Development Corporation to mobilize local savings for local investment. This is still a good idea. The objective would be to gain ownership and control over natural resources. Royalties collected from resource extraction would be shared with the Aboriginal population.

Under this new strategy the volume of resources extracted would undoubtedly be reduced. But they would increase in value and would be utilized when the market was right. In the meantime there would have to be a system of just transition for workers who lost their jobs. The Communications, Energy, and Paperworkers Union of Canada has developed a program for such a transition. The government would have to look for alternative areas of investment and employment. (see "Kyoto Smart," www.cep.ca)

There is an obvious alternative job creation strategy which is well known. The "soft energy path" could be developed to replace dependence on fossil fuels. This industry is labour intensive, creates far more jobs than the fossil fuel and mining industry, involves skilled labour and high technology, and has much greater backward and forward linkages to the local economy. Furthermore, the industries created would most likely be locally owned and controlled. Much more of our economic surplus would be retained in the province. Furthermore, this industry is far less polluting and contributes greatly to the reduction of greenhouse gasses and global warming.

The alternative energy economy was clearly set forth by the Saskatchewan Energy Conservation and Development Authority (SECDA) during the early 1990s. Its studies and proposals so embarrassed the NDP government that it abolished the agency in 1995. (For an overview see SECDA, 1994)

Currently, Sask Power has a generating capacity of about 3500 megawatts (MW) of energy. Studies by SECDA project that an energy conservation plan could create 400 MW of equivalent energy savings, and more efficient residential utilities could save another 150 MW. Better design and equipment could produce a 30 percent energy saving in industrial operations. All across North America such programs are sponsored by local public utilities. Sask Power and Energy could be forced to do the same. Co-generation of power with existing industrial firms could create 500 MW. Small hydro in the north could create 150 MW. Wind power farms in the Swift Current area alone could create 1200 MW.

Then there is the potential for passive and active collection of solar energy. Saskatchewan has one of the best solar energy regimes in North America. SECDA rightly noted that solar energy "will be the energy of the 21st century." The Netherlands and Denmark have developed and are exporting solar and wind generation installations for individual residences and commercial buildings. There is no reason why similar industries cannot be developed in Saskatchewan. Some already exist, but they get little government support.

There is a great potential for biomass energy. SECDA concluded that there was a potential of 850 MW from crop residues and 1,600 MW from forest product wastes. The U.S. government and the UK are moving ahead with the development of energy crops like willows, hybrid poplars, elephant grass and switchgrass (native to the prairies). They are introducing power generation facilities which use these crops as a replacement for coal. They are grown on marginal lands, are perennial crops, improve fragile environments, and bring returns to farmers that greatly exceed the growing of food crops. Why can't this be done in Saskatchewan? A community solar greenhouse for food production exists in Inuvik; why can't Saskatchewan develop food production in the north?

The sad reality is that there is no will in the NDP government nor in the major opposition parties. Only the New Green Alliance promotes this alternative. While the NDP government says it supports energy conservation and wind power, and has its token programs, it devotes almost all its resources to renovating existing coal fired generating plants, promoting a major new "clean coal" project, and channeling millions of dollars into enhanced oil recovery. They constantly brag about the Weyburn carbon dioxide injection and storage project, designed to help Saskatchewan industry extract and burn even more fossil fuels.

It is not that the NDP government and their supporters are just stuck in time in the mid-19th century. They stay on this treadmill because that is where big capital and the transnational corporations want them to be. The policies in place in Saskatchewan for resource extraction are designed to help them maximize capital accumulation.

## Conclusion

The entire debate around rents in natural resources takes place within the parameters of the capitalist mode of production. The very concept of rent in resources has its foundation in John Locke's defence of taking the land from the Aboriginal people of the Americas. David Ricardo built the standard theory of rent on Locke's argument. Thus, under competitive capitalism, it is assumed that there is no rent from the use of resources. Rent is only monopoly profit or surplus over and above the normal profit. Those private individuals or corporations who exploit a natural resource owe nothing to the community for their appropriation of nature. There is no reason to preserve any wilderness areas or any species other than human beings. All natural resources are there to be used free of charge in the drive to accumulate capital. Natural resources are a free gift from nature, but under the capitalist system the benefits of use are restricted to those with a direct interest.

Following Adam Smith, Karl Marx agreed that the driving force behind capitalism is the law of accumulation. Capital expands in every sector, in every corner of the world, in the drive to accumulate new capital. This includes the natural world. Thus a seam of coal or uranium under ground, or the trees in the forest, have no value in the capitalist system until transformed into a commodity to expand capital accumulation. Natural resources always had an historic use value in pre-capitalist societies. Under capitalism they are commodities that have a key role in the accumulation of capital. Thus governments exist primarily to help individual capitalists and corporations appropriate natural resources for the production of more capital. They are not there to make sure that natural resources are used for the best interests of the society as a whole while protecting the environment and non-human species. (see Fine, 1982; Benton, 1996; O'Connor, 1994)

The present system of extracting and using non-renewable natural resources does create some economic development. In Saskatchewan around 13,500 good paying jobs have been created in the mining and mineral industries. Some businesses do well servicing the resource extraction industries. Some royalties and taxes go to the provincial government, although this most likely does not exceed the subsidies and social costs involved.

But to a political economist, resource development in Saskatchewan looks very much like a classic case of "enclave development" under western European colonialism. The natural resource is extracted by transnational corporations who sell the product abroad and claim the profits and most of the economic rent. The capital is accumulated in the metropolitan centres. Very little is paid to the local government, and precious little stays in the local community. The key high-paying jobs go to outside workers. Some local workers get relatively good paying jobs, but in hinterland areas like northern Saskatchewan, the vast majority of the local people remain unemployed or underemployed. There is little diversification of the local economy, as the major backward and forward economic linkages lead out of the province. The provincial government provides extensive infrastructure support and manages the labour force. Local communities have no control over development. There is no sharing of the royalties with the local communities or the Aboriginal people. The adverse health and environmental effects will be managed by the provincial government. This appears to be a classic example of mercantile capitalist accumulation. But this is not Bolivia in the 17th century, it is Canada in the 21st century. Is Saskatchewan trapped in this system of exploitation? Is there nothing better?

The use of natural resources is a political question involving value judgements. There are clear alternatives to corporate-style farming. There are alternatives to clear-cut logging which work very well. Uranium mining by large transnational corporations with extensive support from the government is not the only road to economic development in northern Saskatchewan. It is not necessary to depend on the extraction of a mineral ore which creates so many serious hazards around the world. Saskatchewan has shown that there is a viable alternative to private corporate exploitation of the potash resource. Many who are fearful of the impact of global warming on Saskatchewan and our children and grandchildren think it would be wise to shift to conservation, wind power, solar energy, biomass energy and to cut back on the extraction, export and burning of oil and natural gas. They also believe it would be wise to phase out coal mining and production of electricity from coal-fired generation plants. These are political choices. They require that people and governments understand and confront the capitalist law of accumulation and the modern system of imperial domination. There is an alternative to business as usual.

# References

Aitken, Hugh G.J. 1951. *American Capital and Canadian Resources*. Cambridge: Harvard University Press.

Anderson, David L. 1987. "Innovation in Public Rent Capture: The Saskatchewan Uranium Industry." In Gunton and Richards, pp. 147-180.

Barbour, Ronald B. 1998. "Dene Mining Tragedy." *First Nations Drum*. Fall issue. http://www.firstnationsdrum.com

Barron, F. Laurie. 1997. *Walking in Indian Moccasins: The Native Policies of Tommy Douglas and the CCF*. Vancouver: University of British Columbia Press.

Benton, Ted, ed. 1996. *The Greening of Marxism*. New York: The Guilford Press.

Bernard, Jean-Thomas and Raymond W. Payne. 1987. "Natural Resource Rents and Hydroelectric Power: The Case of British Columbia and Manitoba." In Gunton and Richards, pp. 59-87.

Biggs, Lesley and Mark Stobbe, eds. 1991. *Devine Rule in Saskatchewan: A Decade of Hope and Hardship*. Saskatoon: Fifth House Press.

Bina, Cyrus. 1985. *The Economics of the Oil Crisis*. New York: St. Martins Press.

Brennan, J. William, ed. 1984. *"Building the Co-operative Commonwealth": Essays on the Democratic Socialist Tradition in Canada*." Regina: Canadian Plains Research Centre, University of Regina.

Britton, John N.H. 1997. *Canada and the Global Economy: The Geography of Structural and Technological Change*. Montreal: McGill-Queen's University Press.

Burton, John S. 1997. "Resource Rent and Taxation—Application of New Principles and Approaches in Saskatchewan." In Glor, pp. 59-77,

Canada. Department of Finance. Technical Committee on Business Taxation. 1998. *Report*. Ottawa: Department of Finance.

Cartwright, Michael R. 1999. "Mineral Production Royalties and Related Property Payments." Mineral Business Appraisal. http://www.minval.com

Charlton, Aydon *et al*. 1996. "The Privatization of the Potash Corporation of Saskatchewan: A Case Study." Regina: Saskatchewan Institute for Social and Economic Alternatives. Unpublished paper, June. 16 pp.

Elliott, Doug. 1990. "Resource Industry Statistics." *Sask Trends Monitor*, Vol. 7, No 4, April, pp. 7-8.

Fine, Ben. 1982. *Theories of the Capitalist Economy*. London: Edward Arnold.

Fredricksen, Liv. 2002. *Annual Survey of Mining Companies 2002/2003*. Vancouver: The Fraser Institute.

Gelinas, Johanne. 2002. *Abandoned Mines in the North*. Ottawa: Auditor General of Canada.

Glor, Eleanor D., ed. 1997. *Policy Innovation in the Saskatchewan Public Sector, 1971-82*. North York: Captus Press of York University.

Gruending, Dennis. 1990. *Promises to Keep: A Political Biography of Allan Blakeney.* Saskatoon: Western Producer Prairie Books.

Gullickson, David P. M. 1990. *Uranium Mining, the State and Public Policy in Saskatchewan, 1971-1982. The Limits of the Social Democratic Imagination.* Regina: Unpublished MA Thesis, University of Regina.

Gunn, Joseph. 1982. *The Political and Theoretical Conflict over Saskatchewan Uranium Development.* Regina: Unpublished MA thesis at the University of Regina.

Gunton, Thomas. 1987. "Manitoba's Nickel Industry: The Paradox of a Low Cost Producer." In Gunton and Richards, pp. 89-117.

Gunton, Thomas and John Richards, eds. 1987. *Resource Rents and Public Policy in Western Canada.* Montreal: The Institute for Research on Public Policy.

Gunton, Thomas and John Richards. 1987. "Political Economy of Resource Policy." In Gunton and Richards, pp. 1-57.

Hanley, Paul. 1992. "Full Cost Accounting Needed for Uranium Industry." Saskatoon *Star Phoenix*, February 24.

Harding, Jim. 1995. "The Burdens and Benefits of Growth: Mineral Resource Revenues and Heritage Fund Allocations under the Saskatchewan NDP, 1971-82." In Harding, 1996, pp. 341-374.

Harding, Jim, ed. 1995. *Social Policy and Social Justice: The NDP Government in Saskatchewan During the Blakeney Years.* Waterloo: Wilfred Laurier University Press.

Herold, Marc W. 2003. "Uranium Wars: The Pentagon Steps Up its Use of Radioactive Munitions." Whittmore School of Business and Economics, University of New Hampshire. http://www.cursor.org

Hesch, Rick. 1980. *The Policy Making Process in Northern Saskatchewan, 1972-77.* Regina: Unpublished MA thesis at the University of Regina.

Jang, Brent. 2003. "As Wells Sputter, Gas Prices Spurt." *Globe and Mail*, December 15, B-8.

Johnson, Allan W. 1963. "Biography of a Government: Policy Formulation in Saskatchewan, 1944-1961." Unpublished Ph.D. dissertation, Harvard University.

Johnson, Chalmers. 2003. "Empire of Sorrows." *The Times* (London). www.temesonline.co.uk

Kierans, Eric. 1973. *Report on Natural Resources Policy in Manitoba.* Winnipeg: Government of Manitoba.

Kuyek, Joan. 2003. "Presentation to the Canadian Nuclear Safety Commission RE Cameco Corporation's Rabbit Lake Operation." MiningWatch Canada, August 25. http://miningwatch.ca

Larmour, Jean. 1984. "The Douglas Government's Changing Emphasis on Public, Private and Co-operative Development in Saskatchewan, 1944-1961." In Brennan, pp. 161-80.

McIntyre, Bernard G. 1993. *Uranium City: The Last Boom Town.* Mill Bay, B.C.: Driftwood Publishers.

McLeod., Thomas H. 1946. *Industrial Development in Saskatchewan.* Regina: Research Division, Economic Advisory and Planning Board, November.

Marshall, Dale. 2002. *Making Kyoto Work: A Transition Strategy for Canadian Energy Workers.* Vancouver: Canadian Centre for Policy Alternatives, April.

MiningWatch Canada. 2003. *Presentation on Bill C-48 Regarding the Taxation of Industry and Natural Resources.* Ottawa: Senate Banking, Trade and Commerce Committee, with Green Budget Coalition, November 5. http://miningwatch.ca

Murray, Ronald C. 1978. *Provincial Mineral Policies, Saskatchewan 1944-1975.* Kingston: Centre for Resource Studies, Queen's University, Working Paper No. 6, September.

O'Connor, Martin, ed. 1994. *Is Capitalism Sustainable? Political Economy and the Politics of Ecology.* London: Guilford Press.

Parkland Institute. 1999. *Giving Away the Alberta Advantage: Are Albertans Receiving Maximum Revenues from the Oil and Gas?* Edmonton: Parkland Institute, November.

Parrott, Dan. 1996. "Criticisms of Development Theory with Northern Saskatchewan as an Example of Forced Underdevelopment." Paper presented to the Joint Federal-Provincial Inquiry on Uranium Mining Development in Northern Saskatchewan, June 10.

Parsons, Robert J. 2002. "America's Big Dirty Secret: Depleted Uranium in Bunker Bombs." *Le Monde diplomatique,* March. http://mondediplo.com

Pembina Institute. 2002. *Looking Beneath the Surface: An Assessment of the Value of Public Support for the Metal Mining Industry in Canada.* Ottawa: Pembina Institute and Mining Watch Canada.

Pembina Institute. 2001. *The Boreal Below: Mining Issues and Activities in Canada's Boreal Forest Region.* Calgary: Pembina Institute for Mining Watch Canada, October.

Pembina Institute. 2003. *Mining Industry Criticism of "Looking Beneath the Surface: An Assessment of the Value of Public Support for the Metal Mining Industry in Canada": A Response from the Authors.* Calgary: Pembina Institute and Mining Watch Canada, February.

Pitsula, James M. and Ken Rasmussen. 1990. *Privatizing a Province: The New Right in Saskatchewan.* Vancouver: New Star Books.

Prebble, Peter. 1991. "Protecting God's Country," in Biggs and Stobbe, pp. 11-136.

Prudhomme, Michel. 1998. "Potash." In *Canadian Minerals Yearbook.* Ottawa: Ministry of Public Works and Government Services, pp. 41.1-41.15.

Richards, John. 1987. "The Saskatchewan Potash Industry: An Exercise in What Could Have Been." In Gunton and Richards, pp. 119-46.

Richards, John and Larry Pratt. 1979. *Prairie Capitalism: Power and Influence in the New West.* Toronto: McClelland and Stewart.

Russell, Bob. 1997. "Rival Paradigms at Work: Work Reorganization and Labour Force Impacts in a Staple Industry." *Canadian Review of Sociology and Anthropology,* Vol. 34, No. 1, February, pp. 25-52.

Saskatchewan. Bureau of Statistics. 2001. *Economic Review.* Regina: Government of Saskatchewan.

Saskatchewan. Department of Energy and Mines. 2001. *Annual Report.* Regina: Government of Saskatchewan.

Saskatchewan. Department of Energy and Mines. 2002. *Crown Royalty and Tax Systems.* Available at: http://www.gov.sk.ca/enermine

Saskatchewan. Department of Energy and Mines. 2001. *Mineral Statistics Yearbook.* Regina: Government of Saskatchewan.

Saskatchewan Energy Conservation and Development Authority. 1994. *Electric Option 2003-2020.* Regina: Government of Saskatchewan.

Saskatchewan Environment. 2002. *An Assessment of Abandoned Mines in Northern Saskatchewan.* Regina: Government of Saskatchewan.

Shapiro, Lisa. 1998. "Coal." In *Canadian Minerals Yearbook.* Ottawa: Ministry of Public Works and Government Services, pp. 19.1-19.7.

Sierra Club of Canada. 2001. *Establish a Clean Canada Fund: A Report by the Sierra Club of Canada and MiningWatch Canada.* July 1.http://miningwatch.ca

Stanford, Jim. 1999. *Paper Boom: Why Real Prosperity Requires a New Approach to Canada's Economy.* Toronto: James Lorimer & Co.

Stobbe, Mark. 1991. "The Selling of Saskatchewan." In Biggs and Stobbe, pp. 81-110.

Stueck, Wendy. 2003. "Flooding Puts Damper on Cameco's Showcase Mine." *Globe and Mail,* April 17, pp. B-1, B-2.

Taylor, Scott. 2003. "The Weapons We Gave Iraq." *Globe and Mail,* February 17, A-11.

Teichman, Judith. 1988. *Policymaking in Mexico: From Boom to Crisis.* Boston: Allen and Unwin.

Thatcher, Colin. 1985. *Backrooms: A Story of Politics.* Saskatoon: Prairie Books.

United Nations Conference on Trade and Development. 2002. *Least Developed Countries Report 2002: Escaping the Poverty Trap.* Geneva: UNCTAD.

Warnock, John W. 1995. *The Other Mexico: The North American Triangle Completed.* Montreal: Black Rose Books.

Warnock, John W. 1974. "Potash in Saskatchewan: Keeping It Safe for the 'Multi-Nationals.'" *This Magazine,* Vol. 7, No. 4, January, pp. 3-9.

Warnock, John W. 1990a. "Privatizing the Coal Mines." *Briarpatch Magazine,* Vol. 19, No. 4, May, pp. 13-15.

Warnock, John W. 1990b. "Turning Off the Gas: Sask Oil Privatization." *Briarpatch,* Vol. 19, No. 4, May, pp. 18-20.

Warnock, John W. and Shauna Checkley. 1990. "The Potash Rip-Off." *Briarpatch Magazine,* Vol. 18, No. 10, January, pp. 11-13.

Whillans, Robert T. 1998. "Uranium." In *Canadian Minerals Yearbook.* Ottawa: Ministry of Public Works and Government Services, pp. 59.1-59.11.

# Chapter 12

————O————

# SOCIAL DEMOCRACY ON THE PRAIRIES

The first socialist or social democratic government in North America was elected in Saskatchewan in 1944. But everywhere in the industrialized world, socialist, social democratic and communist parties have had their base in the organized working class. In many countries, like Australia and New Zealand, the Labour Parties were created by the national trade union movement. Why was a left-wing government elected in a province which had a very small class of people working for wages and salaries and a weak trade union movement? Where the majority of people in the labour force were farmers and farm workers?

Furthermore, this party, the Co-operative Commonwealth Federation (CCF), became the dominant party in the province. It has formed the government of Saskatchewan for 44 of the 60 years since 1944. While its original base was in the community of the more radical grain growers, it has continued to survive, and dominate the political scene, after the disappearance of around 60 percent of the farmers! The CCF has been transformed into the New Democratic Party (NDP), and while it has been formally aligned with the labour movement since 1962, it continues to have wide support in other classes.

Today the NDP has a dominant (or hegemonic) role in most of the progressive popular and community groups in the province of Saskatchewan. If one is opposed to right-wing politics, the natural home is in the NDP. It never occurs to people that there is any other choice. The political opposition formally changes, from the Liberal

Party to the Conservative Party, to the Saskatchewan Party, to the Reform-Alliance Party. But the common denominator is a loose coalition of forces on the political right brought together to oppose the NDP.

Aside from the dominant position of the CCF and the NDP in the formal political system, the party has had a tremendous impact on the political culture of Saskatchewan. The principles of the Keynesian welfare state are deeply entrenched. The majority believe that social programs should be available to all who live here. There is widespread concern about the persistence of poverty. There is strong support for a mixed economy and public ownership of utilities. But since 1991 the NDP has been moving to the right, adopting most of the political agenda of neoconservatism or neoliberalism. Who would have believed that an NDP government would adopt a package of policies most often identified with Ronald Reagan, Margaret Thatcher and Brian Mulroney? Will this mean that the people will give up on the NDP and seek a new party on the left? Or will there be a shift to the right in the political culture? Are the people of Saskatchewan well enough off today that they no longer have any concerns about the way the capitalist system operates? The province is currently going through a transition period.

## Social Democracy Develops in Europe

The political movements for trade unions, co-operatives, socialism and social democracy developed as a reaction to the horrors brought by the capitalist system as it developed in Europe. Millions of people were poor and unemployed with no social support. Peasants were driven off the land, and families, communities and towns were destroyed. Skilled craftsmen lost their trades and the new factory work was mechanical, oppressive and required no skills. Women and children worked long hours in the factories and the mines. Urbanization led to slums characterized by pollution, lack of sanitation, poor housing, and epidemics of cholera and typhoid. Life expectancy declined. Wages were at the subsistence level, just enough to allow workers to avoid starvation. The government, controlled by men with property, ruled for the benefit of the relatively small capitalist class. Workers responded by riots and rebellions and were repressed by the state.

The early critics of capitalism blamed all of this on the institution of private property and competition. The key value of capitalist ideology is selfishness. William Thompson, one of the early English critics, argued that the new economy required the nuclear family and the systematic oppression of women who were required to work in factories and then go home and perform domestic drudgery. He supported a planned co-operative society.

Perhaps the most influential British critic was Robert Owen, who managed a textile mill at New Lanark in Scotland. He argued that capitalism was contrary to basic Christian principles. As an alternative, he pushed for workers' co-operatives in agriculture and industry and became one of the earliest proponents of the rights of workers. In the 1830s he created the Grand National Consolidated Trades Union.

The early radicals were also opposed to the state and governments, as they were dominated by rich men who used power to coerce the common people. The anarchist movement grew out of this state oppression. Pierre Joseph Proudhon argued that "property is theft" from those who produce and that "every state is a tyranny." Some, like Gracchus Babeuf, argued that change could only come through revolution given the control of the state apparatus by the capitalist class.

In the period down to 1848 a wide variety of movements for change emerged across Europe. The trade unions began to develop. Co-operatives were created to try to defend workers and farmers. A range of political parties emerged, from radical liberalism to anarchism to socialism. In all European countries the working class demanded democratic rights and the end to the control of governments by men with property. The term "socialism" arose around 1830 as a radical alternative to the individualism associated with capitalism. The emerging socialists called for the rejection of economic liberalism and the expansion of democracy to include not only political rights but social and economic rights. They sought a new community with emphasis on equality, which many linked to Christian principles. (see Lichtheim, 1968; Mackenzie, 1949; Radice, 1965)

The year 1848 was a turning point in the history of European politics. In Great Britain the People's Charter, a petition signed by three million, was rejected by the British Parliament. Its six principles simply called for a liberal democratic government. Defeated in this moderate proposal, workers shifted their efforts to forming trade unions and co-operative societies. Politically they attached themselves to the Liberal Party, electing the "Lib-Labs" to Parliament.

On the continent of Europe the surging capitalist class was demanding rights as was the new middle class. But the revolts against the old monarchist order were quickly joined by the mass of the unorganized, hungry poor. Governments were overthrown or immobilized in ten countries. There was a series of rebellions, beginning in Switzerland in November 1847 and in January 1848 in Italy. In March 1848 soldiers in Berlin shot demonstrating workers, as revolts spread across Germany. In

June 1,500 protesting workers were shot by soldiers in Paris. After the street conflict ended, another 3,000 workers were slaughtered and 12,000 were sent to labour camps in Algeria. The bourgeoisie and the small proprietors quickly joined with the old classes to restore order in the face of the possibility of a real social revolution. The workers struggle for democratic rights was repressed, leaders were arrested, jailed and exiled, and laws were passed banning socialist organizations and workers associations.

But there was one other important event in that year. Karl Marx and Frederick Engels published *The Communist Manifesto*, the most widely read political tract in history. It described the class system under capitalism and called for its overthrow by the organized working class and the creation of a socialist society. The Communist League supported the creation of anti-capitalist workers' parties in all countries. (Abendroth, 1872; Caute, 1966; Mackenzie, 1949; Lichtheim, 1968)

The period between 1848 and the beginning of World War I in 1914 saw the development of left-wing political parties across Europe and the formation of the First and Second International Working Mens Associations. All were strongly influenced by Marxism, but their political orientation varied greatly, including Christian socialists, anarchists, pacifists, reformers, and those who wanted to create co-operative societies. Many believed that capitalism could be replaced through electoral politics and reforms; others believed that the capitalist class would never surrender its power and that armed conflict would be necessary to create a new society.

The most important event in this period was the formation of the Paris Commune in 1871. Following the defeat of France in the short war with Prussia, popular uprisings tried to establish people's communes in a number of cities. The Paris Commune, which lasted the longest, was proclaimed on March 19, to be defended by the citizens' army. The Commune introduced a radical, democratic decentralized government based on workers' control of economic enterprises. Politically, it was a broad left wing pluralist government with almost no Marxists present. The French army, now under Republican control and with Prussian support, attacked Paris on May 21, and in the week-long conflict killed 20,000 men and women defending the Commune. Another 30,000 were arrested, executed, imprisoned and deported. In *The Civil War In France* published just after the slaughter, Karl Marx described the Commune as the model for a socialist society, with a pluralist, democratic political government alliance headed by workers. He called for the formation of a major workers political party in all states. The Second International promoted this development. (Leith, 1978; Marx, 1967)

Reform socialism was strongest in Great Britain. The Independent Labour Party was formed in 1891, calling for widespread nationalization of the economy. While it was basically Marxist in ideology, it opposed change by force of arms. It was influenced by the Fabian Society, founded by intellectual socialists in 1884, which advocated piece-by-piece reforms which would transform capitalism into a more humane social and democratic system. The present Labour Party was formed in 1906. The more left wing workers party, the Social Democratic Federation, was firmly committed to Marxism but was always a much smaller political organization.

The strongest workers party was the German Socialist Party (SPD) formed in 1875, an alliance between the more moderate followers of Ferdinand Lassalle and those committed to Marxism. It was within this party that much of the intellectual debate occurred on the meaning of socialism, communism and how to achieve power. At the beginning of the Great War they had over one million members. In France the Second International brought the Radical Socialists and the Socialist Party together to form the French Section of the Workers' International (SFIO), one of the largest European parties.

Socialist parties, Marxist but committed to the parliamentary road and reform, developed in the Scandinavian countries while more radical and revolutionary parties were founded in the countries of southern Europe. In Russia the Social Democratic Party, founded in 1898, was divided between the Bolsheviks who advocated armed revolution and the Mensheviks who advocated following the parliamentary route. They were opposed by the Socialist Revolutionary Party, which was basically a populist peasant organization.

The first great world depression (1873-96) intensified the struggle between the European national states, their capitalist classes, and the struggle for overseas colonies. The workers parties feared the onset of a world war. At the Stuttgart Congress of the Second International in 1907, they agreed to a resolution which called on the workers to use all of their powers, including demonstrations and strikes, to prevent and end any war. The workers agreed that they would be the primary victims of any war between imperialist powers. When war broke out there were numerous spontaneous protest demonstrations by workers across Europe. But the leadership of their parties and trade unions did not oppose the war. Indeed, the majority of the workers supported their right-wing governments, swept up in national patriotism. Dick Geary reminds us that in August 1914 "there was popular rejoicing on the streets of London, Paris, Berlin, Vienna and St. Petersburg when war was declared." Workers began killing workers. (Abendroth, 1972; Geary, 1981; 1989; Fainsod, 1966)

The success of the Bolshevik revolution in Russia in 1917 was welcomed and supported by workers throughout Europe, even in Great Britain. An attempt at a similar revolution in Germany failed. In this case, the majority wing of the Socialist Party played a key role in crushing the workers' and soldiers' councils and murdering key left wing leaders. Other revolutionary efforts were crushed in Finland and Hungary.

The conflict between right-wing reformist social democrats, the centrist socialists and left-wing Marxists was fought out in the Second International. In February 1919 the Second International met in Berne and adopted resolutions denouncing Bolshevism. The new Soviet regime in Russia demanded the creation of a new workers association that would be purged of reformist influences. In March 1919 the Russian leaders created the Third International Workingmen's Association under the control of Moscow. The European socialist parties split. The reconstructed social democratic and socialist parties united in a new Second International, rejecting armed revolution and control of the movement from Moscow. The left wing in the existing socialist parties formed communist parties which then became members of the Third International.

One of the key political differences between the two groups was the stand on imperialism and colonialism. The Third International called for active support of national liberation movements in the European colonies. They also were committed to establishing communist parties in all the colonies and semi-colonies. The social democratic parties of the Second International, all of whom (except the Italian party) had supported their right-wing governments during World War I, refused to call for the end of the colonial system. As an example, George Bernard Shaw, a leading member of the British Fabian Society, argued that the European countries had a right to conquer "backward people" as a way of bringing them progress and efficient government. (Abendroth, 1972; Mackenzie, 1949)

The most conservative of the socialist parties was the British Labour Party. Based in the most industrialized country, they had higher wages and less unemployment. They were able to benefit from the trickle down effects of the exploitation of colonial labour. Dick Geary argues that the capitalist class in Great Britain was more open to the formation of trade unions. On the continent, the capitalist class used the power of the state to ban and repress trade unions, which contributed to a more militant working class. (Geary, 1981)

There were other social forces which led to divisions within the working class. Skilled workers formed the first trade unions and sought higher wages; they ignored the interests of the unskilled workers. The 19th century saw the development of a new middle class and a white collar sector of the working class. The strong opposition of the Roman Catholic Church to socialism weakened support for socialist and labour politics in key areas. Ethnic conflicts were widespread. English workers hated Irish workers. German workers looked down on Polish and Slavic workers. State employees were forbidden from belonging to trade unions and socialist parties. Women were largely excluded from trade union and socialist party participation. Peasants, even poor peasants, were hostile to the parties advocating socialism; only in Russia did many support the radical parties. Finally, it should be remembered that the great majority of working class people in Europe did not belong to either a trade union or a political party. As a result, the working class, their trade unions, and the socialist parties did not have the power to halt the First World War. The social divisions were intensified after the success of the Bolshevik revolution in Russia. (Geary, 1981)

In the first part of the 1920s the world economy stagnated, but by the middle of the decade the economic situation was good, wages rose, and governments expanded social programs. The general standard of living increased. Yet the electoral strength of the social democratic and labour parties steadily increased. Many became the largest single political party in their country, and some participated in coalition governments. The communist parties increased their influence among the unskilled working class and the unemployed. The onset of the depression in 1929 brought a dramatic change. While the socialist and communist parties grew much stronger, they were not able to stop the rise of fascism and authoritarianism across Europe.

## The Rise of Canadian Socialism

Canada is a so-called "new country" populated by immigrants. A colony with a limited and declining indigenous population, it was the place where one could acquire cheap land and become a farmer and a property owner. While this was the goal of a great many immigrants, other immigrants made a living as self-employed entrepreneurs. For a long period of time those who were working for a wage or a salary were a small percentage of the population. At the beginning of the 20th century workers in the resource extraction industry, manufacturing and transportation represented less than 20 percent of the labour force. The fledgling working class was politically weak because it was spread across a very large territory. The existence of Quebec and the French language, and the religious division between Roman Catholics and Protestants, divided working class loyalties. Prior to World War I most immigrants were from Great Britain and Ireland. Following the war the new wave of immigrants came from Central and Eastern Europe.

As in Europe, the labour force in Canada at first backed the demands of the new propertied class for political and social reforms. Trade unions developed in Lower and Upper Canada in the 1830s, and they supported the democratic uprising of 1837-8. Craft unions were beginning to develop, and many had official ties with similar unions in the United States. Strikes were on the increase, the best known being that of 1872 which demanded the nine hour work day. This particular struggle led to the formation of the Canadian Labour Union. The Workingman's Progressive Political Party was formed at the same time and demanded the abolition of property qualifications for candidates, election of the Senate, a liberal land policy, and the extension of the vote to men without property.

In the 1880s the Knights of Labour moved into Canada from the United States. It focused on the unskilled worker, organized at the plant level, and rejected the craft basis of existing trade unions. When the American Federation of Labour (AFL) was formed in 1887, based in the craft unions, its affiliated unions extended into Canada, where it came into conflict with the Knights of Labour. However, two years later the Trades and Labour Congress (TLC) was formed in Canada, a merger of the craft unions and the locals of the Knights of Labour. It was closely tied to the AFL. Like its U.S. parent, it opposed the creation of a Canadian labour party and instead tried to work with and influence the Liberal and Conservative parties. (Lipton, 1967; Palmer, 1983; Williams, 1975)

Many of the activists in the new labour unions were immigrants from Great Britain and continental Europe, and they brought with them their political experience and ideologies. In the 1890s socialists were active in trade unions and political movements in Canada. The new labour press reported on political and trade union developments in Europe. The industrial unions in the west, the Western Federation of Miners, the American Railroad Union, and the Industrial Workers of the World all combined union organizing with the propagation of socialism. Socialists were elected to leadership positions in the TLC, and in 1913 the federation passed a resolution urging union locals to hold classes in Marxism. At their 1917 convention they endorsed the formation of a Canadian Labour Party.

Eventually elements of the more radical trade union movement sponsored the development of socialist and labour parties. In 1903 the Socialist Party of Canada was formed, and it was explicitly Marxist in theory and program. It elected members to the legislature in British Columbia. In 1911 some of its members split and formed the Social Democratic Party, also Marxist in orientation, but affiliated with the Second International Workingmen's Association in Europe.

In 1902 the Winnipeg Trades and Labour Council entered the political arena and started a trend which resulted in the formation of several Independent Labour Parties on a provincial basis. Based on the ILP in Great Britain, they were reformist social democratic parties which nevertheless were significantly influenced by Marxism. Their slogan was "Property rights have had precedence over human rights. This position must be reversed."

The Russian revolution had a major impact on labour and socialist groups in Canada. In 1918 the TLC was split between more conservative trade unions and the more radical western industrial unions. The TLC went back to its conservative U.S. roots, and the more radical elements at the Western Labour Conference of 1919 formed the One Big Union, a militant industrial organization. The Winnipeg General Strike of 1919 radicalized the working class. In the election of 1920, eleven Labour Party members were elected to the Manitoba legislature.

Canadian workers and political activists were also influenced by developments in Great Britain In 1918 the British Labour Party adopted a new manifesto which stated specifically that their goal was the creation of a socialist society. Within a year Independent Labour Parties with a similar political orientation were created in Ontario, Quebec, British Columbia, Alberta, and Nova Scotia. Saskatchewan followed in 1926. The more radical socialists formed the Communist Party of Canada in 1921 and sought affiliation with the Third International

In 1919 the United Farmers of Ontario won 43 seats in the provincial election and formed a governing alliance with the ILP which had won 12 seats. In a provincial election in Manitoba in 1920, the United Farmers of Manitoba formed an electoral alliance with the Labour Party and elected seven farmer-labour candidates in rural ridings. In Winnipeg all the labour candidates were elected, receiving 42 percent of the vote. Four of those elected had been prominent leaders in the General Strike.

The alliance between labour, socialist groups and farmers continued. The United Farmers of Alberta swept into office in 1921 in alliance with the Dominion Labour Party, which won four seats in Calgary and Edmonton. (Avakumovic, 1978; Penner, 1977; Robin, 1968; Lipton, 1968)

The particular characteristics of Canada heavily influenced the development of socialism and social democracy. As many social scientists have argued, Canada was founded on Toryism: loyal to Great Britain, tied to the Empire, conservative, elitist and opposed to democracy, while supporting a strong state and a strong central government. The early liberal reaction in Canada was not the same as in the United States; it was Whig liberalism, the English version, with its emphasis on private property rights. The democrats in the liberal movement were symbolically crushed in the rebellions of 1837-8. It was only after the rise of the trade union movement, agrarian populism, and the development of socialism and social democracy that Mackenzie King moved the Liberal Party to reform liberalism.

Socialism and social democracy were brought to the United States and Canada by immigrants. South of the border, where the political economy and political ideology of liberal capitalism was deeply entrenched, it was denounced as "alien" and "un-American." In Canada, socialism arrived at first from Great Britain, and British immigrants were not "aliens." Immigrants from the UK had first hand experience in trade unions, co-operatives and socialist parties. Canadian socialism and social democracy were heavily influenced by the Christian tradition of the social gospel. But as Norman Penner stresses, British labour parties and trade unions were also greatly influenced by Marxism, and this carried over to Canada. Many in the new wave of immigrants from continental Europe after World War I were also followers of Marxism. (Penner, 1977)

The Bolshevik revolution in Russia had an enormous impact in Canada. The more left wing groups and trade unionists chose to form the Communist Party of Canada. The more conservative socialists committed to the British tradition of social democracy and chose to build an alliance with agrarian populism. Both struggled for political leadership of the growing working class. (see Horowitz, 1968; Penner, 1977; Roberts, 1991)

## The Formation of the Co-operative Commonwealth Federation

The first major third party in Canada was the Progressive Party formed in the 1920s. But as David Laycock has stressed, they were "crypto-Liberals" who primarily sought to pressure the Liberal Party to adopt policies more favourable to farmers. After the 1921 election, James S. Woodsworth of Winnipeg and William Irvine of Calgary formed the "Labour Group" in the House of Commons. In 1924 they forced the caucus of the Progressive Party to decide whether they were going to support the principles of their party or support the Liberal government of Mackenzie King. In a the key vote, only fifteen of the sixty-five Progressives stood by their party's principles, and they became known as the "Ginger Group." Subsequently, they became members of the Co-operative Commonwealth Federation (CCF). (Laycock, 1990)

J.S. Woodsworth played a central role in the formation of the CCF and the creation of social democracy in Canada. He was one of a number of prominent

Protestant ministers who preached Christian socialism and backed the labour movement, including the 1919 Winnipeg General Strike. He was influenced by Marxist political economy, but he strongly opposed the use of violence, the Soviet form of government created in Russia, and the Communist Party in Canada. Like most Canadian socialists and social democrats, he was a committed supporter of the British system of Parliament and representative government. As the leader of the Ginger Group in Ottawa, he led their common fight against an entrenched system of special privilege.

In 1926 Woodsworth took the initiative to try to unite the various non-communist labour and socialist organizations in Canada. One result was the formation of the Western Conference of Canadian Labour Parties, which first met in Regina in 1929. Their initial statement called for social reforms and the public ownership and development of natural resources. At their third conference, held in Winnipeg in 1931, delegates went further demanding the replacement of capitalism with socialism. While rejecting a proposal to work with the Communist Party, they proclaimed that workers throughout the world should seek the "abolition of capitalism and the establishment of a co-operative commonwealth."

The Great Depression led farmers, workers and intellectuals to begin to seriously question of the capitalist system. The League for Social Reconstruction (LSR) was formed in January 1932, based on the British Fabian Society and the League for Industrial Democracy in the United States. This was the first time academics and other intellectuals had joined together to actively participate in socialist politics in Canada. Their charter called for the "the establishment in Canada of a social order in which the basic principles regulating production, distribution and service will be the common good rather than private profit." They played a key role in drafting the Regina Manifesto, the founding platform of the CCF.

The fourth conference of the western labour group was held in Calgary in August 1932 at the invitation of the United Farmers of Alberta. There were delegates from the various labour parties, the United Farmers of Alberta, Manitoba and Ontario, the Socialist Party of Canada, the Saskatchewan Farmer-Labour Group, and the Canadian Brotherhood of Railway Employees (CBRE). While there was a range of political ideologies present, there was a common bond that brought them together, a belief that capitalism was the cause of their problems. The eight points of the platform which were adopted called for the socialization of the banking and finance system and the social ownership of all public utilities and natural resource development. The social welfare system was to be maintained during the period of transition to a socialist state, after which it would not be needed. The provisional national council expanded on this to provide the outline of the Regina Manifesto to be presented at the founding meeting of the CCF in Regina in 1933. J. S. Woodsworth, the first national leader of the CCF, argued that "I am convinced that we may develop in Canada a distinctive type of socialism. I refuse to follow slavishly the British model or the American model or the Russian model. We in Canada will solve our problems along our own lines." (Young, 1969b; Penner, 1977, 1992; Lipset, 1971; McNaught, 1963)

In his study of the CCF Walter Young concludes that the party was "less socialistic than either the Labour Party or the Fabian Society, and less so than its American counterpart under the leadership of Eugene Debs and Norman Thomas." It was committed to the defence of family farms and private ownership of land and "made much of promises of more property for all." Thus, Young argues, the party had created "a doctrine with no flaws—one consistent with Christian societies, liberal democracy, bourgeois ideals, and the North American myth of prosperity for all." (Young, 1969a)

If the CCF was to become a socialist or social democratic party on a national level, it had to make links with the trade union movement. All major socialist, social democratic and communist parties had their foundation in the trade union movement. The CCF had to recruit the support of labour east of Manitoba. Farmers in this part of the country were conservative and had little interest in the CCF. At this time, most of the trade unions were craft unions affiliated with the TLC. They would not affiliate with the CCF and denounced the party's fraternal links to the Canadian Brotherhood of Railway Employees and the All Canadian Congress of Labour, which stood for independent Canadian trade unions. The only eastern base for the CCF was in Ontario, among trade unionists and socialists. During the 1930s, the Communist Party began a major campaign to organize the industrial trade unions in Canada. As the industrial unions developed, there was a deep political struggle between supporters of the CCF and those who backed the Communist Party. The conflict which had split European workers' trade unions and parties came to Canada. The CCF benefitted, particularly in Ontario. (see Horowitz, 1968; Zakuta, 1964; Abella, 1973; Penner, 1977; Avakumovic, 1975; Archer, 1990)

## Saskatchewan and the Founding of the CCF

In federal election of 1921 the Progressive party had done well in Saskatchewan winning 15 of the 16 seats and taking 63 percent of the vote in the rural areas. But the Saskatchewan Grain Growers Association (SGGA), the dominant farm organization, was closely linked to the Liberal Party, and the provincial Liberal government headed by William Martin was skillful in co-opting farm leaders. Thus there was no Progressive government in Saskatchewan.

In 1921 the more radical farmers formed the Farmers Union of Canada (Saskatchewan Section). They were led by farmers who had close ties to the industrial One Big Union. The FUC opposed party politics and concentrated on trying to build the "100 percent pool." The broad campaign for the Wheat Pool established the FUC as the most progressive and active farm organization. In 1924 they endorsed the demand by the Independent Labour Parties for the nationalization of the banks and the financial system. In 1926 they absorbed the faltering SGGA and became the United Farmers of Canada (Saskatchewan Section). Between 1927 and 1929 they sent J. S. Woodsworth on speaking tours around the province.

In 1926 the Independent Labour Party of Saskatchewan was formed, led by M. J. Coldwell, then a Regina alderman. It was based on the British model, stressing Fabian socialism. The Weyburn Labour Association was formed by a Baptist minister, T. C. Douglas, and in 1932 it became a Weyburn local of the ILP. Coldwell was well known throughout the province through his weekly radio talks on economics and socialism.

George Williams, a prominent socialist, was elected president of the UFC in 1928. Many farmers seemed to be content with the building of the Wheat Pool and other co-operatives, but this ended with the onset of the Great Depression. E. A. Partridge, the father of the Wheat Pools and the honorary president of the UFC, told the convention in February 1930 that "true co-operation has its final goal in socialism, which is the continual observance of the Golden Rule." While the delegates narrowly failed to give approval to independent political action, following the convention the Farmers' Political Association (FPA) was founded. This new organization called for a political alliance between farmers and workers. It was socialist in its orientation, calling for "the abolition of the competitive system and substitution of a co-operative system of manufacturing, transportation and distribution." Specifically, it proposed the nationalization of the railways, utilities, and natural resource development. In 1930 the FPA and the ILP met in a joint convention and nominated 13 candidates for the 1930 federal election. They received 23 percent of the vote and elected two MPs.

In July 1932 the UFC, the FPA and the ILP met in Saskatoon and founded the Farmer-Labour Group to run in provincial elections. They represented the political left in Saskatchewan in the deliberations leading up to the foundation of the national CCF. In 1935 the Farmer-Labour Group changed its name to the Co-operative Commonwealth Federation (CCF). (Lipset, 1971; Young, 1969a; Laycock, 1990; Avakumovic, 1978; Spafford, 1968; Brown, 1997)

The first test for the Farmer-Labour Group in Saskatchewan was the provincial election of 1934. Given the depression and the drought, many farmers faced foreclosure on their land. The new party pledged to implement a moratorium on debt foreclosure. But it also put forth a proposal where farmers could voluntarily surrender their land to the state in return for a use-lease title. This policy had been first proposed by the United Farmers of Alberta. Farmers facing bankruptcy would be able to stay on the land. With government eventually owning most of the farm land, there would be an end to land speculation and the population in rural areas would stabilize. The political right, the newspapers, and the Liberal and Conservative parties denounced this as a Bolshevik policy imported from Russia. It was also attacked by the Roman Catholic Church, which regularly proclaimed that Catholics should not be members of the Farmer-Labour Group or its successor, the CCF. Farmers were wary of the system, for it would eliminate capital gains in the ownership of land, or absolute rent. In the election the Farmer-Labour Group received 27 percent of the vote and elected only five Members of the Legislative Assembly. Given that the Farmer-Labour Group was new and had no money to carry out a campaign, this could be seen as a great breakthrough; but the leaders and activists saw it as a defeat. At the 1936 convention of the CCF, the delegates backed away from the use-lease policy.

The forward march of the CCF was complicated by the emergence of the Social Credit Party in Alberta and its move into Saskatchewan. As Alvin Finkel has documented, the party under William Aberhart started out as a progressive reform party, with a strong base in the urban middle class and the working class. The key organizers for the party in the rural areas came from their urban members. It was only after Ernest Manning took over the leadership in 1943 that it swung to the right and built its close ties with big business.

The early Social Credit party strongly opposed the banks, mortgage companies, and the powerful "vested interests." The party's promise of a social credit payment to everyone, the end of interest on debts, and the abolition of the Winnipeg Grain Exchange brought it many supporters in Saskatchewan. For farmers who were not sure about the socialism of the CCF, they offered another option. (Finkel, 1989)

The federal election in 1935 stunned the CCF. Their share of the vote in Saskatchewan was only 19 percent and they carried only two of the 21 ridings. Social Credit took 20 percent of the vote and two seats. In 1936 the CCF convention adopted a new provincial platform which did not mention socialism. As Seymour Martin Lipset points out, "The Saskatchewan CCF was the only provincial section of the national party to modify its socialist policies significantly at this time and to favour political alignments with other parties." (Lipset, 1971)

The national CCF opposed working in alliance with other political parties. The Saskatchewan party negotiated with Social Credit, the Communist Party, and even the Conservatives in an effort to dislodge the Liberal government. In the 1938 provincial election they nominated candidates in only 30 of the 52 ridings. In six electoral districts, Unity candidates were selected. Social Credit nominated 41 candidates. The Liberals were re-elected, the CCF won 11 seats to two for Social Credit and two for the Unity effort. But the CCF won 19 percent of the vote compared to 16 percent for Social Credit. The CCF was back on track as the official opposition and the alternative to the Liberals.

In the 1940s the CCF began to grow. In Ontario, a major effort was made to get trade unions to affiliate with the party. This was strongly opposed by both the federal Liberal government under Mackenzie King and the Communist Party, which had been outlawed by the Conservative government of R. B. Bennett in 1931. Norman Penner points out that there was a formal agreement that the Liberal government would permit the CP to again become a legal party if it assumed the name of the Labour Progressive Party, and the two parties would work together to try to prevent trade unions from affiliating with the CCF. In the Ontario election of August 1943, the CCF received 32 percent of the vote and 34 seats in the legislature. Nineteen of these MLAs were trade unionists. (Penner, 1992)

The time seemed right for socialism and social democracy. In New Zealand the Labour Party was elected government in 1935, 1938, 1943 and again in 1946. The Australian Labour Party, also the dominant national party, was elected in 1929, then lost, but was returned in 1941 and 1946. In July 1945 the Labour Party swept to office in Great Britain.

In Canada during World War II the government completely managed the national economy, unemployment disappeared, rates of economic growth were at an all time high, and progressive taxation had resulted in greater equality. Canada had demonstrated that social democratic economic planning would work, and for many, this was better than free market capitalism which had brought the Great Depression. The trend throughout the Commonwealth was to the left. On June 15, 1944 the CCF won big in Saskatchewan, taking 53 percent of the popular vote and 47 of the 52 seats. The Social Credit Party disappeared. (Lipset, 1971; Penner, 1992; Avakumovic, 1978)

Why did democratic socialism first appear in Canada in a province which was heavily agricultural and had a relatively small urban working class? Some historians and political scientists have stressed the cultural differences between the prairie provinces. Manitoba was settled mostly by people from Ontario, Alberta by immigrants from the United States, and in Saskatchewan there was a heavy influx of immigrants from Great Britain with its socialist, co-operative and trade union traditions. Most commentators have noted the more radical politics of wheat growers, heavily dependent on the foreign export market, facing tremendous variations in price, which created greater instability than was found in other branches of farming. Wheat growers were typically deeper in debt. They were very aware of the economic power of the railways, the grain industry, and the flour and baking industries. They also knew how these powerful economic interests were closely tied to the major political parties. In the United States, the Socialist Party had its greatest electoral success in Oklahoma, where it had strong support from wheat growers. The Farmer-Labour Party of Minnesota had an important base in the wheat growers. The socialist Non-Partisan League in North Dakota was formed by wheat growers.

Chester Martin traces the antagonism between wheat growers and business interests in the small towns back to the homestead days and the fraudulent manipulation of the system by land companies and local land speculators. "Only too frequently [the land speculator] was the village lawyer or doctor or store-keeper himself." The Saskatchewan Resources Commission reported that as farmers defaulted on their homesteads, they were taken over by the local non-farmers living in the towns: the printer, the grocery owner, the manger of the lumber yard, the school principal, the dentist, insurance agents, the druggist, the doctor, and even local tradesmen. Settlers were resentful of those in the towns who were acquiring farm land without farming. They also believed that they were being exploited by these groups and formed consumer co-operates to defend their interests. The political polarization in Saskatchewan had begun. (Martin, 1973)

In his classic study of the CCF in Saskatchewan, Seymour Martin Lipset details the sectors of the province which supported the party. They received support from the poorer Anglo-Saxon Protestants who had previously supported the Conservative Party. They were supported by the more well-to-do farmers with Anglo Saxon and Scandinavian backgrounds, particularly those who had been active in the Wheat

Pool and the other co-operatives. Around one half of all adults in the province were members of co-operatives. Members of the United Church voted strongly for the CCF. Their urban support was higher in areas populated by the upper strata of the working class.

While members of the Roman Catholic Church generally continued to support the Liberal Party, the CCF did well among Ukrainians. Both Lipset and Andrew Milnor say this was because they were less influenced by the Catholic Church, and a strong minority belonged to the Greek Orthodox Church not under the domination of Rome. In addition, they were angry with Mackenzie King who had pushed through legislation during World War I that made it more difficult for Eastern Europeans to obtain Canadian citizenship. Milnor argues that because they faced wide discrimination, Ukrainians were attracted to the CCF with its commitment to equality. By 1944 Social Credit had disappeared in Saskatchewan, and this protest vote largely went to the CCF. (Lipset, 1971; Milnor, 1968)

## The CCF Government

By the early 1940s the CCF was expecting to form the next government, and they had undertaken some serious planning. Over a period of several years they had carried out research and consultation with popular groups to develop a program that could be implemented even in a poor hinterland province. Academics who have studied the CCF in Saskatchewan have been impressed by the professional manner in which they ran the government. The Civil Service Act was designed to end the worst aspects of the patronage system. They appointed an Economic Advisory Committee of Vernon Fowke, George Britnell and F. C. Cronkite, three highly respected professors from the University of Saskatchewan. In 1945 they created the Economic Advisory and Planning Board which provided research and advice on all major legislation. The Government Finance Office was created to oversee the Crown corporations, which were also monitored by the legislative Crown Corporations Committee. A Cabinet Secretariat was established to co-ordinate policy development and implementation. Given the wide scope of the political attacks on the CCF, they were determined to demonstrate that they could effectively run the government.

The first problem they had to face was the debt left by the Liberal governments. In 1944 Saskatchewan had the highest per-capita debt of any province. But the government, the MLAs and the party were determined to undertake social and economic reforms, and they were not willing to make the reduction of the debt a high priority. Nevertheless, under the direction of the Minister of Finance, Clarence Fines, they reduced the provincial debt from $145 million in 1944 to $79 million in 1952, and by 1960 it was down to only $17 million. They did this while greatly expanding spending on social services and social programs. The debt was paid off by issuing Saskatchewan bonds and introducing a more progressive tax system, based on ability to pay. (see Johnson, 1963; Cadbury, 1971; Brownstone, 1971; McLeod and McLeod, 1987)

The CCF was committed to diversification of the economy through natural resource exploitation, rural development, and the expansion of Crown corporations. The Economic Advisory and Planning Board, under the direction of Tommy McLeod, prepared a major report on the potential for industrial development. Saskatchewan had the least industrial development of the three prairie provinces, a reality of their hinterland status. Loans from the federal Industrial Development Bank were only $67 million, the lowest of all the provinces, behind $410 million in Manitoba and $742 million in Alberta. The provincial Liberal government had clearly failed to attract much investment from their supporters in the business community or their political allies in Ottawa.

Where would the CCF find capital? The Planning Board noted that "less than one percent of all families in Saskatchewan receive incomes of $10,000 or more." Progressive income and wealth taxes, while successfully used by the federal Liberal government during World War II, would not raise much capital. The relatively small businesses in existence in Saskatchewan were not capable of accumulating much internal capital. There were two solutions proposed. First, co-operative development was seen as a better option given the relatively egalitarian distribution of income. Credit unions could be used to mobilize small savings. The CCF counted on the co-op movement to carry much of the load of economic diversification. Second, for major industrial development, money would have to be borrowed in capital markets, and such investments would be guaranteed by the provincial government. Later, the Industrial Development Office was created along with the Industrial Development Fund. Inland Cement and the Inter-Provincial Steel Company (IPSCO) were created in this manner. (Saskatchewan, 1946; Johnson, 1963)

The CCF government was not deterred from taking action, and a whole range of policies were enacted. There was the Farm Security legislation, the most progressive Trade Union Act in North America, actually designed to encourage unionization, and the first Bill of Rights in Canada. There was reorganization of school administration and other innovations, including adult education and recreation.

Within three years they created the Health Services Planning Commission, the air ambulance service, the first hospitalization program in North America, and the Swift Current Health Region as a pilot project for full medicare.

Strong support was given to the co-operative movement. They established the first Department of Co-operatives in North America and assisted the co-ops to move into the oil business. In the rural areas there was a major investment in roads, the Crown corporation bus service, the expansion of power through the new Saskatchewan Power Corporation, and the consolidation and improvement of the Government Telephone corporation. A compulsory automobile insurance system was enacted.

The CCF government always stressed that the reason it was providing services was to make them available to everyone and at a lower cost. They argued that very often governments could do things more efficiently and effectively than private enterprise. They rarely argued that these developments mobilized capital for investment in the province and the creation of local jobs. The CCF was implementing a reformist, social democratic improvement in the capitalist economy. It was not a socialist political economy strategy. (Larmour, 1984; Higgenbottom, 1968; MacPherson, 1984)

The Saskatchewan Teachers Federation was close to the CCF, and the first Minister of Education was the president of the organization, Woodrow Lloyd. The CCF raised teachers' salaries, created larger school districts to spread out and equalize the costs of education, introduced free text books, set up vocational high schools, and expanded scholarships to the University of Saskatchewan. (Lipset, 1971)

Tommy Douglas and the CCF never tired of proclaiming their commitment to "humanity first." But in contrast to politicians today, this was not just empty rhetoric. They raised the minimum wage to the highest in Canada. Those forced to live on social assistance received a major boost in their standard of living. Recipients of Mothers' Allowances received medical, dental and other services free. The Social Aid Act of 1959 established the right of all citizens to economic support based on need. Social assistance rates were to equal 95 percent of a person's normal wage or salary, to a maximum of $200 per month. People unable to work or unable to find work were never expected to have to live below the poverty line. The concern and actions to support the health and well being of lone parent women and their children was radically different from today's governments. In 1944 when the CCF took office the average per capita income in Saskatchewan was $637. By 1963 it had risen to $1,890, the third highest in Canada, and well above the national average. (Pitsula, 1984; Higgenbotham, 1968; Tyre, 1962)

Saskatchewan was highly polarized during the twenty years of the CCF government. Business interests and their allies in the Liberal and Conservative parties and
the local press denounced almost every policy implemented by the "socialists." They
proclaimed that the CCF government was chasing away capital investment, not providing enough jobs for young people, driving people out of the province, bankrupt-
ing the province with high taxes, and creating a totalitarian type government with
"state medicine." The high minimum wage and social assistance rates, the Work-
men's Compensation rates, the Labour Standards legislation, requirements for holi-
day pay, were all making the province "uncompetitive" with Alberta and Manitoba.
(For a good example of this, see Tyre 1962)

In 1961 the national CCF was transformed into the New Democratic Party.
Tommy Douglas retired from provincial politics to assume the leadership of the new
national party. He was replaced as premier by Woodrow Lloyd, who piloted the provincial government through the introduction of the first universal health care program in North America. It was a bitter fight against business interests, the medical
associations, the Liberal Party, and other right wing groups.

In the 1964 election the CCF was narrowly defeated by the Liberal Party under
the leadership of Ross Thatcher, a former CCF Member of Parliament. They lost
again in a tight race in 1967. Perhaps after twenty years in office people thought it was
time for a change. The CCF had not yet adjusted to the growing urbanization of the
province. They did not present the electorate with a new vision for the future. But
the changes they had introduced enjoyed wide popular support. The Liberal government, despite its right wing rhetoric and promotion of "free enterprise," did not reverse any of the major CCF innovations. When the federal Liberal government
began to offer new social programs based on 50-50 cost sharing, the Thatcher government signed on without a whimper.

## The CCF Evolves into the NDP

When the CCF won in Saskatchewan it seemed to indicate that Canada would follow the other Commonwealth countries and move toward social democracy. Those
hopes were dashed in 1945. In the Ontario election the vote for the CCF fell from 32
percent to 22 percent and its seats fell from 34 to eight. In the federal election the
same year the party's vote increased from eight to 16 percent, and it won 28 seats
compared to eight in 1940. But this was seen as a tremendous defeat. It did not win a
single seat in Ontario and only one east of Manitoba. And it did not get better. Its

popular vote in federal elections fell to 13 percent in 1949, 11 percent in 1953, 10 percent in 1957, and down to only nine percent in 1958.

Why did this happen? For political activists on the left, it was widely attributed to the lack of support in the trade union movement. All social democratic parties in the industrialized capitalist world had their base in the trade union movement. Indeed, many of the social democratic and labour parties had been formed by the trade union movement. This had not happened in Canada. Many said it was due to the domination of the trade union movement by U.S. unions, and their head offices strongly opposed any direct political involvement in political parties. There was the additional division caused by Quebec. The Communist Party and the Liberals had joined forces to try to block affiliation with the CCF. But in the end, workers themselves did not vote for the CCF. Even in those unions where the leadership was committed to the party, the majority of the rank and file continued to support the Liberal and Conservative parties.

The onset of the Cold War was another factor, with the U.S. government leading the attack against communism, socialism and trade unionism. The Cold War was welcomed by the Liberal and Conservative parties, the business community, and the mass media. The CCF leadership followed suit, embracing the Cold War, militarism and re-armament, and abandoned the United Nations and the peace movement for NATO, NORAD, military alliances, and defence production integration of Canada into the United States. Its political platform moved steadily to the right and ended up simply endorsing the limited Keynesian welfare state. The problem here was that the Liberal Party, and the Tories under John Diefenbaker, could just as readily adopt similar policies, and they did. The CCF no longer offered a clear alternative to the "old line parties."

The militarism associated with the Cold War led to increased government expenditures and the Long Boom in economic growth from 1945 to 1975. The real standard of living of working people rose steadily. In addition, the political culture of Canada, based in a North America dominated by the much larger United States, was different from Europe, Australia and New Zealand. All this seemed to mitigate against building a major party on the left.

In 1956 the trade union movement in the United States merged, the American Federation of Labour (the craft unions) and the Congress of Industrial Organizations (industrial unions) becoming the AFL-CIO. The Canadian unions, most of which were branch plants of U.S. unions, followed suit, forming the Canadian Labour Congress (CLC). This development encouraged CCF labour activists to try to forge a real partnership with the trade union movement. A National Committee for a New Party was formed with 10 representatives from the CCF and 10 from the CLC. In July 1961 2000 delegates met in Ottawa to found the New Democratic Party. (Penner, 1992; Archer, 1990; Horowitz, 1968)

But there were other opportunities for growth as well. The NDP was formed just as there was a revival of the left throughout the world. The peace movement against nuclear weapons expanded, even within Canada. The civil rights movement was mobilizing in the United States. In the Third World there was a strong movement against colonialism and imperialism. With the intervention of the United States into the civil war in Indochina in 1961, a new radical but populist left movement took off in North America. Within the New Democratic Party, the old left was bolstered by an influx of activists from the new left, formed the Waffle group, and issued the manifesto "For an Independent Socialist Canada" in 1969. This was a "new left," different from the old left of the communist and social democratic parties.

## The Blakeney Government and Hinterland Social Democracy

In Saskatchewan, Woodrow Lloyd, now leader of the NDP in opposition, backed the Waffle Manifesto at the 1969 federal NDP convention in Winnipeg. The right wing of the provincial party, led by Roy Romanow and his close associates, forced Lloyd to resign as leader, and a new leadership convention was called. Allan Blakeney was elected over Romanow, with Don Mitchell, the candidate of the Waffle, coming third with 25 percent of the vote. The policy of the provincial NDP, adopted at the 1970 convention, was greatly influenced by the Waffle group and shifted strongly to the left. In the 1971 provincial election the NDP won 55 percent of the vote and 45 of the 60 seats. This was the highest vote that any party had ever achieved in a Saskatchewan election. The NDP platform, "A New Deal for People," called for major reforms.

The NDP was no longer primarily a political party of agrarian protest. It was now an urban party, but not a traditional labour party. It included many from the middle class, with a leadership dominated by lawyers and professionals. It was no longer a populist party; with its long stint in office, it was becoming more and more like any other political party and government. Nevertheless, the Blakeney government was an active social democratic government, and they were committed to making progressive changes. As we have seen, they sought greater control over the resource economy.

The first term of the Blakeney government saw the introduction of a wide range of new social programs. Increased revenues from resource extraction, and a more progressive tax system based on ability to pay, enabled the government to expand social programs. They introduced a prescription drug plan, brought in a dental program for children, significantly expanded public housing in co-operation with the federal government, and improved the occupational health and safety program. The Trade Union Act and the Labour Standards Act were improved. The provincial JOBS program provided subsidies to businesses to hire unemployed workers. The minimum wage was consistently the highest in Canada while unemployment remained relatively low. Social assistance rates allowed recipients to live well above the poverty line. Saskatchewan was becoming a more equal society.

There was an attempt to help the ordinary family farmer in the struggle against agribusiness interests. Programs included the Family Farm Protection Act, Farmstart, the Land Bank and the Farm Land Ownership Act which restricted the amount of land non-residents of the province could own. The NDP helped create a hog marketing board. The Saskatchewan Beef Commission was an attempt to stabilize the marketing system. The Sask Trading Corporation was created to try to promote the export sales of farm products. (Glor, 1997; Richards and Pratt, 1979; Brown, 1999; Gruending, 1990; Harding, 1995)

Nevertheless, not everything was smooth sailing. In 1973 the Waffle was expelled from the Ontario NDP. David Lewis, leader of the federal NDP, announced that the Waffle would no longer be permitted to exist within the party as an organized group. In response, the Saskatchewan wing of the Waffle voted at a convention to withdraw and work outside the formal party structure. The left disappeared within the party.

The first significant world-wide recession since World War II came in the summer of 1975. In the June election of that year the NDP was returned but their popular support fell to 40 percent, and the revived Conservative Party began to emerge as the new provincial right wing alternative. In October 1975 the federal government imposed wage and price controls, and this was enthusiastically supported by Premier Allan Blakeney. In 1976 the Blakeney government introduced a budget of restraint and began to cut back on social programs. The child care program did not really develop. Spending on Health, Education and Social Services began to decline. There was a shift in spending from social services to police and corrections services. The Department of Northern Saskatchewan, originally a very promising innovation with broad support in the North, was steadily downsized and power shifted back to Regina. (Harding, 1995)

The second term of the Blakeney government (1975-8) was a period of rapid expansion of the resource sector and government participation in its development. However, the biggest single political problem for the NDP government was their decision to expand the extraction of uranium ore, process it in the province, and then send it to France and the United States where it was used to fuel nuclear power plants and make nuclear weapons. The NDP had created the Department of the Environment in 1972, and now many popular groups were demanding environmental assessments for all proposed new uranium mines. Strong opposition developed to the proposal for Eldorado Nuclear to create a uranium refinery at Warman, near Saskatoon.

It has been argued that the popular support for the Blakeney government began to fade after they won the October 1978 election. But the dissatisfaction began in 1976 with the growing public division over uranium mining. At the November 1976 NDP annual convention, the party leadership manipulated the process to try to head off a direct confrontation. Most popular groups opposing uranium development had strong ties to the NDP. They objected to the entire Cluff Lake Board of Inquiry process after February 1977. The Key Lake inquiry was appointed in December 1978. The NDP government and the mining corporations proceeded with development before the reports were released. Public opposition increased during the hearings in January 1980 over the proposed Warman refinery. There was strong opposition to this policy from many within the NDP, the peace movement, environmentalists, major elements of the Christian churches, and even the Saskatchewan Federation of Labour. The Blakeney government doggedly held to this policy as their key economic development strategy for northern Saskatchewan. (Gruending, 1990; Harding, 1995)

In the last term of the Blakeney government little progressive new legislation was passed. Furthermore, the Blakeney government came into conflict with one of its key supporting groups, organized labour. The trade union movement and others were dismayed when Premier Blakeney supported the federal Liberal government's wage and price control policy in 1975. In the late years of the Blakeney government, there were constant conflicts with public sector workers. Just before the 1982 provincial election the NDP government forced hospital workers to end their strike and go back to work. Many trade unionists and their supporters did not campaign for the NDP in the election and even stayed home and did not vote. Between 1971 and 1982 the NDP vote fell from 249,000 to 201,000. The Conservatives under Grant Devine won the election, receiving 54 percent of the popular vote. (Brown, 1999)

## The Keynesian Welfare State

The social democratic approach to political economy is always linked to the Keynesian welfare state. This is a package of social and economic reforms that were introduced by governments during World War II and the era of the post-war long economic boom, down to around 1980. They are identified with the famous English political economist, John Maynard Keynes (1883-1946). Keynes focused his research on the causes of the Great Depression of the 1930s. His theories of political economy had a major impact on Canadian academics and government officials, and by the beginning of World War II they were becoming the new mainstream view. They formed the basis for the policy of the social democratic governments in Saskatchewan.

Keynes, the son of a well known economist, went to Eton and Cambridge and quickly established himself as a brilliant economic thinker. He earned $2 million speculating in the money and commodities markets. As Todd Buchholz notes, "Keynes felt quite comfortable as a member of the high intellectual bourgeoisie." He was a Tory who feared the rise of socialism and communism. A new government economic policy was needed to protect the capitalist system. This program would convince the working class that capitalism was a good economic system which promised full employment, greater social and economic equality, stability with no depressions, and steadily increasing economic growth. (Keynes, 1960)

Keynes studied depressions, recessions and business cycles. He concluded that Jean Baptiste Say and his followers in the economics profession were stupid fools: supply did not create its own demand. He agreed with Thomas Robert Malthus who in the 18th century had argued that inequality of income and wealth would lead to "general gluts" which would produce economic depressions. The historical record was clear: capitalism is characterized by booms and busts of the business cycle and periodic depressions.

Capitalists will not invest in a depression as they can see no reason to expect to make a profit. Thus, Keynes argued, governments must intervene in the economy during depressions and use a number of techniques to stimulate spending and encourage investment. These include controlling interest rates, implementing a fiscal policy of borrowing and spending to stimulate demand, and actively promoting capital investment. Governments need to have control over capital and the monetary system in order to pursue a policy of full employment. Individual capitalists cannot be trusted, as they are only interested in maximizing their own profits. Governments have a responsibility to represent the interests of society as a whole and the capitalist class as a whole.

Keynes felt it was necessary to support a more egalitarian society as a form of *social control*, keeping the working class from embracing socialism, communism and militant trade unionism. Thus Keynes supported a progressive taxation system to promote greater equality, higher wages and full employment, a comprehensive social security system, and world peace. (see Heilbroner, 1961; Buchholz, 1990; Gonick, 1987)

The National Policy, promoted by John A. Macdonald, ended around 1930 after the prairies had been completely settled, the branch lines of the railways had been completed, and the wheat economy was well developed. Then came the Great Depression, and Canada was without a national development strategy. R. B. Bennett's Tory government reluctantly accepted some reform policies in 1935, but they were strongly opposed by the Liberal Party. A new Liberal government headed by Mackenzie King appointed the Royal Commission on Dominion Provincial Relations in 1937 and asked it to set forth a new national economic policy to deal with the depression. The classic liberal policies of balancing the budget and letting the private sector do its work had completely failed.

The Royal Commission headed by Newton Rowell and Joseph Sirois held extensive hearings across Canada, even in rural areas, and actually listened to what people were saying. The final report was presented in 1939. John Maynard Keynes had published his *General Theory on Unemployment, Interest and Money* in 1936. Keynes' policy approach to depressions was favourably received by governments around the world. The principles were accepted by the Bank of Canada and those working with the Rowell Sirois Royal Commission. (see Phillips and Watson, 1984; Gonick, 1987; Kaliski, 1966)

The commissioners, following the direction they had received at their public hearings, concluded that all Canadians had basic human and economic rights no matter where they lived. All provinces should provide the same level of social services. This is a right of citizenship, and Canada could afford it. The federal government, with broad taxing power, should assume primary responsibility for general social welfare. The depression had demonstrated that the provinces could not do this.

The commission argued that the federal government should also take primary responsibility for infrastructure. This was an obligation under their charge to provide "peace, order and good government," building Canadian unity. Governments had a responsibility to aid local communities. In contrast to the liberal, individualistic United States, Canadians knew that community, family and friends were important and not to be left to the free market. Canadian regional and local community diversity was important and to be preserved. Equalization grants and regional development programs would help.

In order to undertake these obligations, taxation should be progressive, based on ability to pay. All social programs should be universal to avoid stigmatization and drawing arbitrary poverty lines. Ordinary people were not responsible for recessions and depressions. Why should they be penalized? (Canada, 1939)

Keynesian economic and social policy worked very well for Canada during World War II. Unemployment fell from 18 percent to only 1.4 percent in 1944, and women were pressed into the labour force. Economic growth skyrocketed, peaking at 18.6 percent in 1942. Under government planning and the mobilization of capital, manufacturing exploded from 22 percent of gross domestic product in 1939 to 32 percent in 1944. Private investment and profits went up with government expenditures. Inflation was controlled by managing money and financing debt from within the country. A progressive taxation policy was introduced which included an income tax, luxury taxes, inheritance taxes, corporate taxes, and excess profits taxes. During wartime the capitalist class had no alternative but to accept the democratically directed economic policy. They greatly benefitted from the general policy of state supported capitalism. But would they accept government involvement in the economy when there was peace? (Wolfe, 1980; Phillips and Watson, 1984)

Vernon Fowke of the University of Saskatchewan called the Keynesian welfare state the Second National Policy. With the relative decline of the wheat economy, the new reliance of Canada on the export of other natural resource staples to the United States, and the growing American corporate domination of industry, it was hoped that Canada's commitment to full employment and a compassionate, universal welfare state would tie the country together on an east-west axis. It would serve to set Canada off from the United States. (Fowke, 1952)

For Keynes and many of his supporters in government, the welfare state was a system of social control. Nevertheless, for the working class in the industrialized countries, the welfare state was seen as basic human rights. Liberal, conservative and social democratic governments worked to entrench these policies as rights in various United Nations covenants. However, when electoral support for the socialist and communist parties began to decline, and it was evident that the mainstream of the working class was not interested in a socialist alternative, the capitalist class concluded that it was no longer necessary to support the Keynesian welfare state as a social control mechanism. It was more profitable for them to go back to the old system of military and police repression and the penal system. (see Djao, 1983; Mishra, 1990; Johnson, 1994; Rice and Prince, 2000)

## Conclusion

Social democracy developed in the advanced industrial states. The working class movement split into those who wanted to see the capitalist system replaced by a new socialist or communist order and those who simply wanted a series of reforms. Both these political elements were present in Canada, but the reform branch emerged as the dominant political movement on the left. In contrast to Europe, Australia and New Zealand, the social democratic movement in Canada did not have its base in the trade union movement. Farmers and other middle class elements had a much more pronounced influence.

In Saskatchewan the CCF and then the NDP was the home of social democracy and the Keynesian welfare state. The party had it base in the radical wing of the farmers' movement, supported by the leadership of the trade union movement, the teachers, the co-operative movement and other urban elements. The CCF and the NDP has always had strong support in the urban working class ridings, but the labour movement has had little influence at the party leadership level.

The governments of T. C. Douglas, Woodrow Lloyd and Allan Blakeney established the Keynesian welfare state in Saskatchewan. It has become part of the province's political culture. There is still strong support for the "mixed economy," the private sector, co-operatives and a government sector. Public opinion polls regularly show majority support for taxation needed to finance health, education and other social programs. The 2003 election demonstrated that there was still strong popular support for keeping the Crown corporations in the utility sector. People are ready to back universal programs which are more efficiently run by the government than private, profit-seeking interests.

While the CCF was originally a populist party with a strong commitment to democratic participation, this changed over the years. Within the party there was a long struggle between the government, the caucus of elected members of the legislature, and the rank and file members at party conventions. The leadership of the party was always more conservative than the active members. As Bob Sass has rightly pointed out, in the institutions under its control, the NDP was not interested in replacing the authoritarian structures found in private industry with a more democratic or socialist way of doing things. (Sass, 1995)

This conflict became more pronounced during the government of Allan Blakeney (1971-82). The government became more tied to agribusiness interests. It did not carry through on promises to northern Saskatchewan. It alienated its labour wing by supporting wage and price controls and using legislation to break the strike by hospital workers. It fought hard to make sure that those nominated by the NDP to run for the legislature were loyal to the leader. Not one woman served in the three NDP caucuses under Allan Blakeney. Many traditional NDP supporters sat out the election in 1982, the NDP government was swept from office, and they lost working class seats that they had held for decades. They were defeated in the rural areas, the historic base of the party. In opposition, the party would have to rebuild and change.

# References

Abella, Irving M. 1973. *Nationalism, Communism, and Canadian Labour: The CIO, the Communist Party, and the Canadian Congress of Labour 1935-1956*. Toronto: University of Toronto Press.

Abendroth, Wolfgang. 1972. *A Short History of the European Working Class*. New York: Monthly Review Press.

Archer, Keith. 1990. *Political Choices and Electoral Consequences: A Study of Organized Labour and the New Democratic Party*. Montreal: McGill-Queen's University Press.

Avakumovic, Ivan. 1975. *The Communist Party in Canada: A History*. Toronto: McClelland and Stewart.

Avakumovic, Ivan. 1978. *Socialism in Canada: A Study of the CCF-NDP in Federal and Provincial Politics*. Toronto: McClelland and Stewart.

Bennett, John W. and Cynthia Krueger. 1971. "Agrarian Pragmatism and Radical Politics." In Lipset, pp. 347-63.

Brennan, J. William. 1984. *"Building the Co-operative Commonwealth": Essays on the Democratic Socialist Tradition in Canada*. Regina: Canadian Plains Research Centre, University of Regina.

Brown, Lorne A., Joseph K. Roberts and John W. Warnock. 1999. *Saskatchewan Politics from Left to Right '44 to '99*. Regina: Hinterland Books.

Brown, Lorne A. 1997. "Introduction." Sharp, *ix to xxviii*.

Brownstone, Meyer. 1971. "The Douglas-Lloyd Governments: Innovation and Bureaucratic Response." In LaPierre, pp. 65-80.

Buchholz, Todd G. 1990 *New Ideas from Dead Economists: An Introduction to Modern Economic Thought*. New York: Penguin Books.

Cadbury, George. 1971. "Planning in Saskatchewan." In LaPierre, pp. 51-64.

Canada. 1939. *Report of the Royal Commission on Dominion-Provincial Relations*. Ottawa: The King's Printer.

Caute, David. 1966. *The Left in Europe since 1789*. London: Weidenfeld and Nicolson.

Cross, Michael S. and Gregory S. Kealey, eds. 1984. *Modern Canada: 1930-1980s*. Toronto: McClelland and Stewart.

Djao, A.W. 1983. *Inequality and Social Policy: The Sociology of Welfare*. Toronto: John Wiley and Sons.

Eager, Evelyn. 1980. *Saskatchewan Government: Politics and Pragmatism*. Saskatoon: Western Producer Prairie Books.

Fainsod, Merle. 1966. *International Socialism and the World War*. New York: Octagon Books.

Finkel, Alvin. 1989. *The Social Credit Phenomenon in Alberta*. Toronto: University of Toronto Press.

Fowke, Vernon C. 1952. "The National Policy—Old and New." *Canadian Journal of Economics and Political Science*, Vol. 18, No. 3, August, pp. 271-86.

Geary, Dick. 1981. *European Labour Protest 1848-1939*. New York: St. Martin's Press.

Geary, Dick, ed. 1989. *Labour and Socialist Movements in Europe Before 1914*. New York: St. Martin's Press.

Glor, Eleanor D., ed. 1997. *Policy Innovation in Saskatchewan Public Sector, 1971-82*. North York: Captus Press.

Gonick, Cy. 1987. *The Great Economic Debate*. Toronto: James Lorimer & Company.

Gruending, Dennis. 1990. *Promises to Keep: A Political Biography of Allan Blakeney*. Saskatoon: Western Producer Prairie Books.

Harding, Jim, ed. 1995. *Social Policy and Social Justice: The NDP Government in Saskatchewan during the Blakeney Years*. Waterloo: Wilfred Laurier University Press.

Heilbroner, Robert L. 1961. *The Worldly Philosophers: The Lives, Times and Ideas of the Great Economic Thinkers*. New York: Simon and Schuster.

Higginbotham, C.H. 1968. *Off The Record: The CCF in Saskatchewan*. Toronto: McClelland and Stewart.

Horowitz, Gad. 1968. *Canadian Labour in Politics*. Toronto: University of Toronto Press.

Johnson, Albert F. *et al.*, eds. 1994. *Continuities and Discontinuities: The Political Economy of Social Welfare and Labour Market Policy in Canada*. Toronto: University of Toronto Press.

Johnson, Albert W. 1963. *Biography of a Government: Policy Formulation in Saskatchewan, 1944-1961*. Unpublished dissertation, Harvard University.

Kaliski, S.F., ed. 1966. *Canadian Economic Policy Since the War*. Toronto: University of Toronto Press.

LaPierre, Laurier *et al.* eds. 1971. *Essays on the Left: Essays in Honour of T. C. Douglas*. Toronto: McClelland and Stewart.

Larmour, Jean. 1984. "The Douglas Government's Changing emphasis on Public, Private and Co-operative Development in Saskatchewan, 1944-1961." In Brennan, pp. 161-80.

Laycock, David. 1990. *Populism and Democratic Thought in the Canadian Prairies, 1910 to 1945*. Toronto: University of Toronto Press.

Leith, James A., ed. 1978. *Images of the Commune*. Montreal: McGill-University Press.

Lichtheim, George. 1968. *The Origins of Socialism*. London: Weidenfeld and Nicolson.

Lipset, Seymour M. 1971. *Agrarian Socialism: The Co-operative Commonwealth Federation in Saskatchewan, a Study in Political Sociology*. Berkeley: University of California Press.

Lipton, Charles. 1968. *The Trade Union Movement of Canada 1827-1959*. Montreal: Canadian Social Publications.

Mackenzie, Norman. 1949. *Socialism: A Short History*. London: Hutchinson's University Library.

McLeod, Thomas H. and Ian McLeod. 1987. *Tommy Douglas: The Road to Jerusalem*. Edmonton: Hurtig Publishers.

MacPherson, Ian. 1979. *The Co-operative Movement on the Prairies, 1900-1955*. Ottawa: Canadian Historical Association.

MacPherson, Ian. 1984. "The CCF and the Co-operative Movement in the Douglas years: An Uneasy Alliance." In Brennan, pp. 181-203.

McHenry, Dean E. 1950. *The Third Force in Canada: The Co-operative Commonwealth Federation, 1932-1948*. Berkeley: University of California Press.

McNaught, Kenneth. 1959. *A Prophet in Politics: A Biography of J. S. Woodsworth*. Toronto: University of Toronto Press.

Martin, Chester. 1973. *"Dominion Lands" Policy*. Toronto: McClelland and Stewart.

Marx, Karl. 1967. *The Civil War in France: The Paris Commune*. New York: International Publishers.

Milnor, Andrew. 1968. "The New Politics and Ethnic Revolt: 1929-1938." In Ward and Spafford, pp. 131-177.

Mishra, Ramesh. 1990. *The Welfare State in Capitalist Society*. Toronto: Harvester Wheatsheaf.

Palmer, Bryan D. 1983. *Working-Class Experience: The Rise and Reconstitution of Canadian Labour, 1800-1980*. Toronto: Butterworth (Canada) Ltd.

Penner, Norman. 1977. *The Canadian Left: A Critical Analysis*. Scarborough: Prentice-Hall of Canada.

Penner, Norman. 1992. *From Protest to Power: Social Democracy in Canada 1900-Present*. Toronto: James Lorimer & Company.

Phillips, Paul and Stephen Watson. 1984. "From Mobilization to Continentalism: The Canadian Economy in the Post-Depression Period." In Cross and Kealey, pp. 20-45.

Pitsula, Jim. 1984. "The CCF Government in Saskatchewan and Social Aid, 1944-1964." In Brennan, pp. 205-225.

Radice, Giles. 1965. *Democratic Socialism: A Short Survey*. London: Longmans, Green & Co.

Rice, James J. and Michael J. Prince. 2000. *Changing Politics of Canadian Social Policy*. Toronto: University of Toronto Press.

Richards, John and Larry Pratt. 1979. *Prairie Capitalism: Power and Influence in the New West.* Toronto: McClelland and Stewart.

Roberts, Joseph K. 1991. *Canadian Socialism: Invitation to Assessment.* Regina: unpublished manuscript.

Robin, Martin. 1968. *Radical Politics and Canadian Labour 1880-1930.* Kingston: Queen's University.

Saskatchewan. Economic Advisory and Planning Board. 1946. *Preliminary Report: Industrial Development in Saskatchewan.* Regina: Government of Saskatchewan, November.

Sass, Robert. 1995. "The Work Environment Board and the Limits of Social Democracy." In Harding, pp. 53-84.

Sharp, Paul S. 1997. *The Agrarian Revolt in Western Canada: A Survey Showing American Parallels.* Regina: Canadian Plains Research Centre.

Spafford, Duff. 1968. "The Left Wing 1921-1931." In Ward and Spafford, pp. 44-58.

Thomas, L.H., ed. 1982. *The Making of a Socialist: The Recollections of T. C. Douglas.* Edmonton: University of Alberta Press.

Tyre, Robert. 1962. *Douglas in Saskatchewan: The Story of a Socialist Experiment.* Vancouver: Mitchell Press.

Ward, Norman and Duff Spafford, eds. 1968. *Politics in Saskatchewan.* Don Mills: Longmans Canada.

Williams, Jack. 1975. *The Story of Unions in Canada.* Toronto: J. M. Dent & Sons (Canada) Ltd.

Wolfe, David A. 1980. *The Delicate Balance: The Changing Role of the State in Canada.* Dissertation, University of Toronto.

Young, Walter D. 1969a. *The Anatomy of a Party: The National CCF 1932-61.* Toronto: University of Toronto Press.

Young, Walter D. 1969b. *Democracy and Discontent: Progressivism, Socialism and Social Credit in the Canadian West.* Toronto: Ryerson Press.

Zakuta, Leo. 1964. *A Protest Movement Becalmed: A Study of Change in the CCF.* Toronto: University of Toronto Press.

# Chapter 13

————————O————————

# THE NDP AND STRUCTURAL ADJUSTMENT

Over the past twenty five years we have witnessed a major transformation of the capitalist system of production. In the popular press this is termed the shift from the Keynesian welfare state to globalization. Political economists refer it as the restructuring of the capitalist system, a change in the general system of capital accumulation.

The old capitalist system is described as the "industrial paradigm," "organized capitalism," or "Fordist production." It was closely identified with the nation state and its support for capital accumulation, mass production and consumption, the rise of the trade union movement, and the Keynesian welfare state. The old system emerged during World War II as the capitalist system began to recover from the second great international depression in the 1930s. It involved varying degrees of national planning to try to moderate the boom and bust swings of the business cycle. With a goal of full employment, and an expanded welfare state, the Fordist system of mass production and mass consumption was seen as an attempt to create "capitalism with a human face."

As we have seen in the previous chapter, in the First World of the advanced, industrialized capitalist states, almost all of the main political parties endorsed and participated in this system of political economy. It was not just the social democratic and labour parties, like the CCF-NDP, that implemented this broad program. In the period after World War II and down to around 1980, liberal and conservatives parties agreed with this general direction. Aside from the communist parties, there was a virtual consensus in support of this general program. In Canada we can think of the implementation of the welfare state by the Liberal governments of Lester Pearson and Pierre Elliott Trudeau and the Progressive Conservative government of John Diefenbaker. All three expanded the role of the government in the economy. They also sought to mitigate poverty and inequality, including the inequality between the different regions in Canada. There was broad popular support in Canada for this policy direction.

## The Collapse of the Keynesian Welfare System

Why did this end? There have been a lot of reasons set forth. Academics who are part of the new Canadian political economy attribute it to the very nature of the capitalist system. Because of the inequality of income and wealth, which is basic to the system, there are the recurring business cycles and even depressions. The capitalist system inevitably leads to the accumulation of excessive capital; outlets for profitable investment begin to disappear. The rate of profit begins to fall. The result is a crisis of overproduction which leads to a bust in the business cycle. After a recession or depression, which clears out a great deal of "inefficient" productive capacity, the cycle of growth begins again.

After World War II there was a long boom with no real recessions. Government spending on the military absorbed much of the excess capital. But the Vietnam War ended in 1974, and a major world recession began in the summer of 1975. It coincided with the increase in oil prices and inflation in general. From 1973 to 1980 the general rate of profit fell quite dramatically in all the advanced capitalist states. The result was a major demand by the capitalist class and groups representing big business for a restructuring of the system. This began in earnest in 1979 at the meetings of the World Bank and the International Monetary Fund in Belgrade, Yugoslavia. Here the central bankers of the advanced industrialized capitalist states agreed to increase their interest rates and brought on the 1980-1 deep world recession. The push for major political change came with the election of Margaret Thatcher's Tory government in Britain in 1979 and Ronald Reagan's Republicans in the United States in 1980. (see Harrison and Bluestone, 1988; Kolko, 1988; and Warnock, 1988)

## The Neoliberal System of Capital Accumulation

The new system of capital accumulation is popularly referred to as "globalization" in North America. In most areas of the world it is called "neoliberalism" because it is a return to the political economy system of the free market, free trade, and the re-establishment of the rights of private property. Political economists have called the new system "post-industrial capitalism," "disorganized capitalism," "flexible accumulation," or "neoliberalism." On the political level it has entailed the shrinking of the welfare state, a return to regressive taxation systems which promote inequality, and a broad attack on the rights of organized labour. Capital has benefitted from the introduction of deregulation by the state, privatization of public assets, cuts in corporate taxes, and direct and indirect government support for business enterprises.

Similar neoliberal policies were imposed on almost all of the states in the Third World through "structural adjustment programs" (commonly called SAPs) imposed by the International Monetary Fund (IMF), the World Bank (WB), the World Trade Organization (WTO) and regional economic institutions. These institutions are all controlled by the governments of the advanced capitalist states. Over the years, this policy package became known as "The Washington Consensus" because the IMF and WB are located in Washington, D.C. and the policy had the strong support of the U.S. government.

A key to the SAPs is the elimination of any state control over capital investment. Capitalists now demand the right to invest wherever they choose, repatriate capital without any constraints, and sell their products anywhere in the world without facing import controls or restrictions. Decentralization of production to peripheral regions has enhanced flexibility for investors. The industrialized states, led by the U.S. government, have insisted that less developed countries may not put restrictions on the export of natural resources and other primary products.

Many political economists have stressed the increased power of finance capital under the new system. There is now one international market for money and credit plus a world system of investment in stock markets and commodity exchanges. Profits are increasingly sought in the manipulation of stocks and bonds; there has been less interest in direct investment and profit from production. Money quickly flows in and out of national stock markets around the world. *Business Week* magazine termed this new system "Casino Capitalism."

In practical terms the new system of capital accumulation has led to more power for large transnational corporations. They are assisted by the new political institutions which oversee the general process: the G-8 representing the dominant capitalist countries, the Organization for Economic Co-operation and Development (OECD) which represents all the advanced capitalist states, and various regional development organizations. After the collapse of the Soviet bloc in 1989 the U.S. government emerged as the unchallenged leader of the advanced capitalist states in the military and political area. The United Nations, via the Security Council and the office of the Secretary General, has become another instrument of U.S. policy and the First World in general.

Table I: The Contrast Between Organized Capitalism and Flexible Capitalism

| Organized Capitalism—The Fordist System | Flexible Capitalism—Neoliberalism |
| --- | --- |
| Mass production of homogeneous goods | Decentralized small batch production |
| Uniformity and standardization | Variety of product types |
| Economies of scale and large plants | Dispersal, sub-contracting |
| Large industrial cities | Deconcentration to peripheral areas |
| Mass consumption of consumer goods | Individualized "yuppie" culture |
| National brand advertising | U.S. fashion promoted world wide |
| National collective bargaining | Dispersal to non-union plants |
| Payment by wages and salaries | Personal payments, bonus systems |
| High degree of job specialization | Elimination of job demarcation |
| Full time unionized jobs | Part time, temporary, contract, home/work |
| Regulations for health and welfare | Deregulation and new regulation systems |
| National welfare state | Privatization of collective needs |
| National policies on regionalism | Free market policies in depressed regions |
| Capital support for a national agenda | Capital support for internationalization |
| Liberal system of social control | Emphasis on repression and prison system |
| Ideological and class political parties | New religious and racialist parties |
| Inclusive religious organizations | Rise of fundamentalist religions |
| Socialization | Individualization and promotion of greed |
| Modernism | Postmodernism |

Source: Drawn from David Harvey, *The Condition of Postmodernity*                .

The United States also remains the dominant world economy and is the leading force in all the international economic and financial organizations. (For more detail on the transition, see: Dasgupta, 1998; McBride and Shields, 1997; Hoogvelt, 1997; Teeple, 1995; and Harvey, 1989.)

## Globalization Comes to Canada

The shift in the national political economy in Canada began with the Royal Commission on the Economic Union and Development Prospects for Canada, headed by Donald S. Macdonald, a former Liberal finance minister, appointed by Prime Minister Pierre Elliott Trudeau in 1982. Its report, issued in 1985, was a total rejection of the Keynesian welfare state and its economic policies. Of the twelve commissioners, only Gerard Docquier of the Steelworkers union issued a dissenting report. Jack Messer, the lone Saskatchewan commissioner, a long time NDP activist and close friend of Roy Romanow, sided with the majority position.

There was a profound polarization in presentations to the Macdonald Royal Commission. Business interests mobilized for the hearings and supported a move towards the free market, free trade, a drastic reduction of the welfare state, privatization of state owned enterprises, deregulation of the economy, opposition to programs to address regional disparities, the end to universal social programs, an end to all controls over foreign ownership in Canada, and an end to subsidies to farmers and marketing boards. They advocated a radical change in tax policy, shifting the burden off corporations and the upper classes towards consumption taxes, like a goods and services tax. Big business was supported by the right-wing "think tanks" and many mainstream economists.

In contrast, the community and popular organizations which presented briefs to the Royal Commission all supported the retention of the Keynesian welfare state. The final report followed closely the positions advocated by the big business organizations. The commission issued a special interim report advocated a free trade agreement between Canada and the United States. (Drache and Cameron, 1985; Gonick, 1987; Warnock, 1988)

The conflict intensified when the Tory government of Brian Mulroney negotiated the Canada-U.S. Free Trade Agreement (CUFTA) in 1987. A major political battle was fought over this agreement. Again it was a conflict between big capital, the dominant business organizations, their political "think tanks" and academic supporters, and the popular groups which mobilized to form the Action Canada Network. In 1994 they mobilized again to oppose the North American Free Trade Agreement (NAFTA). The federal New Democratic Party did not take a strong stand against so-called "free trade."

The most important aspect of the free trade agreements, the regulations of the World Trade Organization, and the proposed and then suspended Multilateral

Agreement on Investment (MAI) concern government regulation of investment. The free trade agreements and the WTO rules are specifically designed to protect the interests of capital. They are to prevent governments from using Keynesian policies to promote national economic development which in any way might impede the right of foreign capital and corporations to maximize profits.

Thus elected governments now find that their sovereign powers are limited by these international agreements. Canadian governments, both federal and provincial, can no longer legally give preference to Canadian firms, limit foreign ownership, require any performances standards for American firms which take over Canadian firms, offer compensation in government bonds if a foreign company is nationalized, subsidize firms as part of a regional development program, offer protection to farmers, restrict energy exports in order to conserve reserves for Canadian consumers, etc. (see Warnock, 1988; Cameron, 1988; Cameron and Watkins, 1993; Cohen, 1987; Teeple, 1995; Clarke and Barlow, 1997)

In the 1993 federal election the voters overwhelmingly rejected the Tories. The Liberals under Jean Chretien won the federal election promising to renegotiate the free trade agreements. But once in office they reverted to their historic position and became even stronger supporters of continental integration. The NDP, having further alienated their supporters by backing the very unpopular Charlottetown Accord in the national referendum in 1992, saw their support fall to a dismal seven percent.

Domestically, the federal government and almost all provincial governments have been pursuing neoliberal policies. The federal governments of Brian Mulroney and Jean Chretien cut the federal budget as a percentage of gross domestic product, particularly program expenditures. They raised interest rates resulting in higher unemployment. They cut taxes on corporations, cut the income taxes of those in the highest brackets, and eliminated inheritance taxes. They shifted revenues to the goods and services tax and increased unemployment insurance premiums, both of which fall heaviest on those in the lower income brackets. Federal financing of health, education and welfare was cut. Programs dealing with regional disparities were slashed. Federal fiscal contributions to health, education and welfare were cut and unemployment insurance was gutted.

A wide range of Crown corporations have been privatized, including Air Canada, Petro Canada, and Teleglobe Canada. Via Rail was almost eliminated. Most important, the Foreign Investment Review Act and the National Energy Policy were eliminated and the airlines were deregulated.

Both the Mulroney and Chretien governments pursued a policy of devolving the powers of government from the federal level to the provinces, further balkanizing the country. The Meech Lake Agreement and the Charlottetown Accord were both designed to promote decentralization. When they failed, the replacement was the New Social Union.

In 1995 Premier Roy Romanow of Saskatchewan initiated the federal provincial talks on a new Social Union. In 1997 the premiers met in Calgary and came up with a proposal for constitutional change. In August 1998 they met in Saskatoon and agreed on a Framework Agreement on Social Union. The focus was to limit the Keynesian welfare state. Provinces would now have the right to opt out of new social programs with full compensation. The final agreement stated that no new social programs could be introduced by the federal government without the support of six provinces. There are to be no national standards for any new programs, only "national principles." If the New Social Union had been in place in the past Canada might never have had a federal medicare program. When the Liberal government originally brought in medicare, only two provinces agreed. At the beginning of the 21st century, at least among Canada's political leaders, neoliberalism was deeply entrenched. (see McBride and Shields, 1993; Shields and Evans, 1998; Jackson and Robinson, 2000; Johnson, McBride and Smith, 1994)

## Saskatchewan and the Shift in World Capitalism

In Saskatchewan the Fordist system of production and the Keynesian welfare state was established after World War II by the CCF government headed by T. C. Douglas. The state was used to help diversify the economy in hopes that capital would be created and invested in the province. Economic growth would increase incomes and wealth, the ability to increase government revenues, and permit the expansion of the welfare state. This was the direction of the government from 1944 to 1964. Even during the right-wing Liberal government of Ross Thatcher (1964-71) the Keynesian welfare state and progressive taxation were not really challenged.

As we have seen, the NDP government under Allan Blakeney (1971-82) expanded the role of the government in the economy. Resource extraction industries were enhanced, and the government used higher taxation, private-government joint ventures and Crown corporations to significantly increase the share of resource rents going to the provincial government. New social programs were introduced. The minimum wage was set as the highest in Canada. Social assistance rates were raised significantly. Trade union membership increased.

Support for the Blakeney government and the Keynesian welfare state faded after the deep recession of 1980-1. The Progressive Conservative Party replaced the Liberals as the new right-of-centre party in the province. The Tories had the support of small business interests, the core of the political right in Saskatchewan. It also had the support of most of the new land-rich farmers who belonged to the new special commodity groups. The party formed links with those elements which supported the traditional patriarchal family, opposed feminism and equal rights for women, and supported traditional marriage and sexual behaviour. They developed support among the rising numbers of Christian fundamentalists, those who harboured racist attitudes towards Aboriginal people, and those who disliked the new ethnic composition of Canada brought by recent immigration. PC supporters were also generally hostile to Quebec national aspirations and official bilingualism. Supporters of this "social conservatism" were strongest in rural Saskatchewan.

Grant Devine, a populist agricultural economist, led the revived Progressive Conservative Party to a major victory in 1982. He promised to get rid of the socialists, provide government subsidies to middle class home owners, and back the farmers. (see Biggs and Stobbe, 1991; Baron and Jackson, 1991)

The Saskatchewan Tories identified with the governments of Margaret Thatcher in the United Kingdom and Ronald Reagan in the United States. During their first term in office they launched a broad attack against organized labour. With close ties to the business interests and those in the higher income brackets, they moved away from the progressive tax system. Royalties and taxes on resource extraction were cut, business and corporate taxes were reduced, and a flat tax on income was introduced. Reducing grants to municipalities led to an increase in local property taxes. The cuts to government revenues led to eight consecutive budget deficits which resulted in a large provincial debt.

The Tories were narrowly re-elected in 1986. The NDP actually got more votes, but the Tories swept rural Saskatchewan. In the second term they followed the script of Margaret Thatcher, even using her consultants, to move toward the privatization of Crown corporations. This included all or part of SaskMinerals, the Saskatchewan Mining and Development Corporation, the Saskatchewan Oil and Gas Corporation, the Potash Corporation of Saskatchewan, and sectors within the Saskatchewan Government Insurance and SaskTel. The Prince Albert Pulp Mill was sold to the U.S. giant Weyerhaeuser. They even privatized services in the provincial parks. Following the example of Margaret Thatcher's government, these corporations were initially sold at well below their market value. It was a major raid by private interests on public assets, a new form of piracy. The goal, of course, was to promote the private accumulation of capital. (Biggs and Stobbe, 1991; Pitsula and Rasmussen, 1990; Brown, 1999)

People were dissatisfied with the limited opposition provided by the NDP. Under their new leader, Roy Romanow, criticism of the Devine government was confined to speeches in the legislature. In 1987 the trade union movement and over 50 popular groups joined together to form the Saskatchewan Coalition for Social Justice to engage in extra-parliamentary activities to oppose the Tories. In June of that year around 8,000 people demonstrated against the government at the Legislature, the largest demonstration in the history of the province. (Warnock, 2002)

Nevertheless, the Tories did not retreat to the passive, neoliberal state. They used the economic power of the state to help bankroll major economic developments in the province. They believed that it was perfectly legitimate to use the state to promote capital accumulation by corporate interests. The recipients of government largesse included Saferco Fertilizer (Cargill), Crown Life Insurance, Intercontinental Packers, the Bi-Provincial Upgrader (Husky Oil), Weyerhaeuser, Miller-Western Pulp, Peter Pocklington's Gainers Meats, and the Co-op Refinery. Loans and grants were given smaller businesses through the Saskatchewan Economic Development Corporation (SEDCO). Over $1 billion was spent on the Rafferty and Alameda Dams and the Shand Power Plant, basically a local Tory patronage operation, but a grossly expensive and polluting energy project. The Devine government represented the beginning stage of capitalist restructuring in Saskatchewan.

The Tory government ended in disgrace. In the October 1991 election the NDP won 51 percent of the vote and 55 seats. The Tories won only 25 percent of the vote and ten seats. Around a dozen Conservative MLAs were indicted for petty fraud in handling offices expenses. After 1995 its remaining MLAs abandoned the party to form the core of the new Saskatchewan Party. (see Brown et al., 1999; Biggs and Stobbe, 1991; Pitsula and Rasmussen, 1990)

## Restructuring Saskatchewan

Following their electoral defeat in 1986, the NDP began the process of choosing a new leader. Roy Romanow, who had always been on the right wing of the party, was the most obvious choice. The party membership apparently decided that the most important objective was to once again gain office. The handsome lawyer from Saskatoon seemed to have the right image for this task. Neither the left nor the trade union sectors of the party chose to put forth an alternate candidate, and Romanow was crowned as leader at the November 1987 party convention. It was a bizarre ceremony, Hollywood style, in obvious contrast to the 1971 leadership convention, which focused on party policy and social democratic principles. It was a sign of a change in direction for the NDP.

While in opposition (1982-91) the NDP developed a policy position that was clearly to the left of the Tories. They opposed all the major policies of Grant Devine's government and promised a return to the social democratic orientation of the Blakeney government. They strongly opposed the privatization of Crown assets and were extremely critical of the Tory's regressive tax policies. They promised to raise the royalties and taxes on the resource industries back to the levels they were under the Blakeney government. They would end poverty in Saskatchewan and close the food banks. Public opinion polls in 1991 showed that the general population wanted a return to "The Saskatchewan Way," a mixed economy with a progressive and caring welfare state.

As the Tory government of Grant Devine began to collapse, the NDP prepared to take office again. Early in 1991 the party caucus released a position paper, *Tax Fairness in the 1990s*, calling for a return to the social democratic tradition of a progressive tax policy. They were supported by the Saskatchewan Coalition for Social Justice and the Saskatchewan Federation of Labour.

In the summer the party leadership revealed its brief platform for the 1991 election: repeal the provincial sales tax, a new health care system based on the "wellness model," improve the Gross Revenue Insurance Program (GRIP) and Net Income Stabilization Fund (NISA) to aid farmers, create an Environmental Bill of Rights, implement a comprehensive energy conservation strategy, improve the prescription drug plan, restore the school-based dental program, improve access to legal aid, implement pay equity legislation, increase funding for education, and eliminate poverty and food banks in the first term of office. However, their campaign stressed that the first priority would be to balance the budget in four years and eliminate the $5.2 billion general provincial debt over 15 years. In the October 1991 provincial election, the NDP won by a land slide.

A November 1991 public opinion poll conducted for the NDP government revealed that the electorate wanted a return to the social democratic traditions of the Douglas, Lloyd and Blakeney governments. The top priorities should be the creation of jobs and combating hunger and poverty. A strong majority opposed cutting public services, and there was no great concern over the debt and budget deficit. But it was soon clear that the new NDP government headed by Roy Romanow was going in a different direction. (Brown, 1999)

The key turning point for the new NDP government came in early 1992 with the formation of the new budget. The Saskatchewan Coalition for Social Justice, the Saskatchewan Federation of Labour, and the party itself pressured the government to keep their election promise and the tradition of social democracy. But they were defeated.

In contrast to the T.C. Douglas government, which inherited a relatively larger debt as a percentage of the annual operating budget, the Romanow government made balancing the budget and paying down the debt the central government priority. They abandoned their tax fairness policy and instead chose to carry on with the neoliberal direction established by Grant Devine's Tory government. They even lowered taxes and royalties on the resource sector. Without those revenues, in the billions of dollars, the NDP could not balance the budget except by making serious cuts to important social programs, and it could not implement its party platform. The budget imposed further cuts in the provincial grants to municipalities, which led to even greater increases in the regressive property tax, which falls heaviest on low income people. In a surprise move, the Romanow government introduced government-sponsored gambling, long opposed by the party, as a way of finding new revenues. But gambling is another regressive tax and creates new social problems. (see Hansen, 2003; MacKinnon, 2003; Brown *et al.*, 1999)

## Romanow and Calvert Endorse Neoliberalism

The NDP has now been in office in Saskatchewan for over thirteen years. The major thrust of the government has been the implementation of the global program for the restructuring of capitalism. In this process the NDP government has followed the patterns set by the Labour governments in New Zealand and Australia. They have not gone quite as far as Tony Blair's Labour government in Great Britain. These policies can be summarized as follows.

(1) Taxation policy. The stated goal of both Roy Romanow and Lorne Calvert has been to reproduce the tax structure that exists in Ralph Klein's Tory Alberta. There have been income tax cuts, particularly for those in the highest income brackets. A major three year tax cut program was set forth in the 2000 budget; despite budget deficits, Lorne Calvert completed their implementation. Business and corporate taxes have been cut. Users taxes have been increased everywhere. Cutting provincial grants to school boards and municipalities has re-

sulted in higher property taxes and users fees. The NDP removed the municipal business tax. Royalties and taxes on resource industries have been steadily reduced to about one-third the level they were during the Blakeney government. The introduction of government-sponsored gambling has only made up for part of the lost revenues.

(2) Privatization and deregulation. In its 1992 special report, *Partnership for Renewal*, the Romanow government announced that it would not try to regain control of the privatized Crown corporations and would not use Crown corporations for economic development. The NDP has carried out a piecemeal privatization of the Crown utility corporations, including an increase in contracting out. They removed cabinet ministers from Crown corporations and ordered them to operate as a commercial venture. When the Devine government had proposed a similar policy, they strongly opposed it. The Crown public utilities, now operating as independent companies without government policy direction, engaged in privatization and investment outside the province. The last three Sask Power corporation projects for power generation were done as joint ventures with ATCO and TransAlta, two large private Alberta energy firms. Right before the 2003 election, Lorne Calvert turned all of the investments of the Crown Investments Corporation in private companies, $600 million, over to an outside board of seven businessmen to manage.

The NDP government sold the remainder of the government's equity in the Potash Corporation of Saskatchewan, Sask Oil, and Cameco. They removed the limits on foreign ownership for the privatized corporations imposed by Grant Devine's Tory government. They sold all of the government's equity in the Lloydminister Heavy Oil Upgrader. The very successful Sask Forest Products was sold to MacMillan Blodell Corporation. Budgets were cut and the number of government employees was reduced. Deregulation at the municipal level, the disappearance of city planning, has enhanced urban sprawl, allowed large capitalists to determine development, and enhanced capital accumulation by the trans-national corporations who control the large shopping centres and box stores.

(3) Agriculture and rural development. The NDP government broke with its traditional allies, the National Farmers Union. They endorsed the closing of grain elevators, the abandonment of branch railway lines and the construction of large elevators. They openly supported the move by the management of the

Saskatchewan Wheat Pool to become a private grain company raising capital on the stock market. They supported the decision by management not to let the Pool members vote on the issue. This alienated another group of traditional NDP supporters in rural Saskatchewan.

The NDP government expressed no opposition to the move by U.S. corporate giant Archer Daniel Midland to take over the United Grain Growers (UGG) and the Alberta and Manitoba Pools. The NDP minister of agriculture welcomed the expansion into Saskatchewan of foreign agribusiness giants Cargill, ConAgra and Dreyfus, arguing that the competition would help farmers. They abolished the Gross Revenue Insurance Program (GRIP) designed to assist farmers in need. Breaking existing legislation, they unilaterally abolished the hog marketing board and have actively promoted, supported and financed corporate hog megabarns. Large subsidies and other supports were provided the huge foreign-owned chemical corporations developing genetically engineered crops. They gave these corporations, including Monsanto, permission to develop secret test plots; such testing was banned in Europe. Additional grants were given to Intercontinental Packers; the NDP then stood aside as it was bought out by U.S. giant Smithfield Foods. They gave Cargill, the largest company in the world, a grant to build an oilseed crushing plant. The NDP announced it would put up 40 percent of the capital to help Broe Industries of Denver to establish four ethanol plants in the province; in doing so, they undermined the well-advanced plans by local people to create five such enterprises.

(4) Northern development. In spite of promises made while in opposition, the NDP government refused to share resource royalties with the Aboriginal communities in northern Saskatchewan. Northern development continues to focus on the extraction and export of uranium, owned and controlled by two corporations, Cogema and Cameco, both heavily subsidized. Mineral royalties and taxes have been further reduced. U.S. giant Weyerhaeuser bought MacMillan Blodel, a move endorsed by the NDP government, creating a virtual monopoly in the forest sector. The new Forest Resources Management Act grants the forest giant access to over 12 million acres of forest land with virtually no regulation or monitoring by public servants. Royalties and taxes are minuscule, far smaller than the costs of maintaining the forest. Massive clear cutting remains the mode of wood extraction. The NDP has refused to implement the principles of the Forest Stewardship Council.

(5) Downsizing social programs. With the cuts to government revenues it was inevitable that programs would be slashed. Provincial spending on K-12 and higher education was cut. There was a major streamlining of health services, the closure of 52 hospitals, cuts to the budget, and a decentralization of services with a centralization of budgeting power. They passed weak labour legislation, imposed wage restraints, and used government power to break strikes by public sector workers. The minimum wage was allowed to fall to one of the lowest in Canada. Basic social assistance rates were frozen at 1982 levels. Food bank dependence increased. The one exception to downsizing has been the corrections services. The province has the highest crime rate in Canada, and it also has the highest rate of incarceration. It has the highest rate of youth incarceration. Unemployed Aboriginal people fill the jails. The only issue on which the NDP tried to mobilize public opinion was in opposition to gun control legislation.

(6) The environment. The NDP government abolished Grant Devine's Energy Options Panel, and in 1995 they abolished the Saskatchewan Energy Conservation and Development Authority (SECDA). They had both produced studies advocating soft energy paths rather than the use of oil, natural gas, coal and nuclear power. The NDP opposed the 1997 Kyoto conference on global warming, refused to send a delegation, and announced that only voluntary guidelines were necessary to deal with global warming and climate change. The NDP government spent $75 million to refurbish coal generating plants rather than introduce energy conservation and efficiency measures. The Pembina Institute surveyed government legislation and projects on global warming and climate change and concluded that the Saskatchewan government had done the least of any province to comply with the goals of the Kyoto Protocol. Water pollution remains a serious problem outside major urban centres. Budget cuts to the Environmental Protection Service led to the serious water quality problem at North Battleford. While the NDP government has been praised by the right wing Fraser Institute, it has regularly been given a failing grade by the Sierra Club, the Pembina Institute and the World Wildlife Fund.

The shift to the neoliberal order has had a major impact on Canada. It has clearly benefitted the large corporations and those in the upper income brackets. But it has had a negative impact on nearly everyone else. Over the 1990s most families had no real increase in their living standards. Families made up for the decline in real wages and salaries by working longer hours and having more family members working. The job market has not improved. There has been a significant expansion of "precarious work:" part time, casual, temporary, contract, and self employment. In general, these jobs have little security, few if any benefits, and are less well-paid. Over the 1990s Saskatchewan had the highest percentage of the work force in part-time jobs and the highest number of people "moonlighting," working two jobs to try to make ends meet. (see Poverty Action Group, 1998; Saskatoon District Health, 1996)

In the past, the people of Saskatchewan could expect that their CCF-NDP government would side with them against corporate interests and the political right. Their government would do what it could given the confines of a provincial government and the North American economy. But they would try. That completely changed with the advent of the Romanow and Calvert governments. They not only went with the flow of the Conservative and Liberal governments across Canada, they actively supported the shift from the Keynesian welfare state to the neoliberal order. Their approach to taxation and social services illustrates this different approach.

## Taxation Which Promotes Inequality

At the federal level, the Canadian government has been steadily shifting the burden of taxation onto those in the middle and lower income brackets. In the mid-1980s Brian Mulroney's government reduced corporate taxes, brought in the $500,000 capital gains tax exemption for farmers and businessmen, reduced the number of income tax brackets from ten to three, and the tax rate for those with higher incomes was dropped from 34 percent to 29 percent. The Manufacturers' Sales Tax, which was designed to cope with tax evasion by foreign owned corporations, was replaced with the Goods and Services Tax.

Further cuts were made after 1993 by Paul Martin, the Minister of Finance in Jean Chretien's Liberal government. Payroll taxes for unemployment insurance became a tax grab, as benefits were radically cut, resulting in huge surpluses which went into general revenues. In 1994 Martin gave the very rich a special capital gains tax loophole. In his infamous budget of 2000, he introduced a five year tax cut program of over $100 billion, of which 65 percent would go to those in the highest income brackets. Corporations and banks benefitted from new capital gains tax exemptions. Cuts were made in federal transfers to the provinces for health, education and welfare. By 2002 the effective average tax rate in Canada for an individual had fallen to 18 percent, which was lower than all the other G-8 countries except Japan. (Jackson and Robinson, 2000; Shields and Evans, 1998; McBride and Shields, 1997)

On assuming office in 1991, the Romanow government appointed the Financial Management Review Commission, chaired by Donald Gass, a Saskatoon chartered accountant. The Gass commission concluded that the debt accumulated by the Tory government was so great that there was no alternative but to reduce expenditures, downsize the government, and cut expectations. They argued that the provincial government could "no longer support the public sector infrastructure that we have built to serve the quality of life and standard of living that we have come to expect." The NDP government established as their primary goal the balancing of the budget and reduction of the debt. There were major cuts to social programs, including health and education, off loading to municipalities and school boards, higher sales taxes and a 10 percent surcharge on income taxes. They conveniently ignored the fact that the Tory debt was created by the reduction of taxes and royalties on the resource industries. The tax revenue system chosen by the NDP government was that advocated by corporate Canada and the political right.

In 1998 federal finance minister Paul Martin decided to allow the provinces to directly level taxes on incomes. Business interests pushed endlessly for more tax reductions. Ralph Klein's Tory government in Alberta reduced income taxes and announced that their goal was a flat income tax, one where every income earner, regardless of what they earned, would pay the same rate. This flat income tax had been proposed by the right wing of the Republican Party in the United States but had been rejected.

Business and right wing political interests in Saskatchewan demanded that all taxes be brought into line with those in Alberta. Without this, it was argued, Saskatchewan would be "uncompetitive" and investors and businesses would leave. In 1999 the Romanow government responded by appointing the Personal Income Tax Review Committee, again accountants, headed by Jack Vicq. The committee was only to review taxes on income and consider personal income tax strategies. They were to examine "fairness" and "competitiveness."

Phil Hansen has described the contrast between this commission and the Saskatchewan Royal Commission on Taxation appointed by Premier Woodrow Lloyd in 1963. The earlier commission was headed by Thomas H. McLeod, the Dean of the College of Commerce at the University of Saskatchewan. But he had long links to the CCF government. The Lloyd government knew full well that who was appointed to a commission largely determined the results. The McLeod report strongly supported the Keynesian welfare state, supported a tax policy designed to reduce inequality, saw the role of government in the economy as beneficial for the community as a whole, and promoted taxation based on ability to pay. They advocated provincial government grants to local communities for education and social services to replace local property taxes, which fell most heavily on low income households. (Hansen, 2003)

In contrast, the Vicq committee took the view that taxation was a barrier to well being, a burden on individuals and families. This view was that of the business community and the political right. Paul Martin, while he was still the Minister of Finance, often said that taxes were money taken from individuals which resulted in a loss of benefit. The McLeod commission had concluded that this view was "palpably nonsensical." The Keynesian view was that the government and public spending were positive for the economy and could be used to promote equity. (Hansen, 2003)

The Vicq commission proposed a range of changes in the tax system to align it more closely to the system in Alberta. The biggest cuts would go to those in the upper income brackets. Low income individuals and families who earned enough to pay income taxes would receive a small tax cut. But as many critics pointed out, these cuts would be more than offset by the increases in user fees for services that would inevitably follow. The proposed income tax cuts would amount to $427 million. The sales tax would be expanded to cover areas not included, and it would fall most heavily on low income households. (Saskatchewan Tax Committee, 1999; Hansen, 2003)

In the 2000 budget the NDP government adopted most of the recommendations of the Vicq report. Over a three year period there would be a combination of broader sales taxes, a sales tax credit system and income tax cuts. The personal income tax brackets would be flattened. The tax on "Canadian-controlled private corporations," sometimes called "small business," was cut from 10 percent to six percent. As Premier Roy Romanow argued, the largest tax cuts should go to those who make more than $85,000 per year. In Saskatchewan, that is the upper one percent of income earners. (see Canadian Centre for Policy Alternatives—Saskatchewan, 2003)

The Vicq committee reported that most of those who gave testimony were for retaining the Keynesian system of taxation based on ability to pay. Their views were ignored. Since 1994 EKOS Research Associates has been conducting a broad survey of public attitudes in their Rethinking Government series. The results have been consistent over the period, showing a major difference between "ordinary Canadians" and the political and economic elite. Business and political leaders support "minimal government" while ordinary Canadians want to keep the Keynesian welfare state. The survey in 2003 showed that Canadians ranked spending on health care, education, ending child poverty, and the environment highest. Out of 20 ranked topics, tax cuts ranked 15th. The NDP government has lined up with elite opinion in Canada and has opposed the values of ordinary Canadian citizens. (Ekos, 2003)

In 2003 the Calvert government introduced a new public relations campaign, "Wide Open Saskatchewan," almost identical to the campaign run by Grant Devine's Tory government in the 1980s. On the government web site viewers are greeted with a large box proclaiming that Saskatchewan had the highest corporate profits from 1990-2000. The tax rates for manufacturing were only 10 percent. Investors are promised a variety of tax incentives, very low land costs and "loyal employees." The Crown utilities corporations provide very low, competitive rates for business and industry. The NDP government concludes that they are "committed to continue reducing taxes." How different is this government from that of Grant Devine? (www.gov.sk.ca)

## The Fallout from NDP Policy

In 1989 the House of Commons resolved to "seek to achieve the goal of eliminating poverty among Canadian children by the year 2000." In November 2003 Campaign 2000 released its annual report on child poverty in Canada. The poverty rate has been in steady decline since 1996, but in 2001 it was still above the level it was in 1989. Over one million Canadian children (or 15.6 percent) lived in poverty. The child poverty rate in Saskatchewan was 17.6 percent, higher than the Canadian average and higher than all but three provinces. (Campaign 2000, 2003)

Part of the problem with persistent poverty is very low social assistance rates. Saskatchewan was criticized for clawing back the National Child Benefit. But Campaign 2000 focused its concern on the growth of low wage jobs in Canada. Of the industrialized countries, only the United States had a higher percentage of low wage jobs, defined as paying less than two thirds of the national median hourly wage. In Canada that is less than $10 per hour. Other causes of child poverty were identified as the fall in the real minimum wage, the lack of affordable housing, and the lack of child care for lone parent families. They noted that Aboriginal people are most vulnerable, with employment and income levels even lower than those of visible minorities and new immigrants. (Campaign 2000, 2003)

The poverty figures for Saskatchewan are understated because First Nations people living on reserves are excluded from the survey. According to the 2001 census there were around 83,000 First Nations people in Saskatchewan, with roughly one half living on reserves. The Aboriginal population in the province has a relatively high level of unemployment, dependence on social assistance, and low incomes. Between 1992 and 1998 the number on social assistance on Saskatchewan reserves increased by 7,500. (Gilmer, 2002; Lee, 1999)

The child poverty rate in Saskatchewan has fluctuated over the years. In 1980 it was only 11.6 percent. It rose to 24.8 percent in 1986, fell, but then peaked again at 21.7 percent in 1996. Garson Hunter has shown that the rate of poverty is closely tied to the business cycle. It falls in Saskatchewan and across Canada as the economy recovers from recessionary periods. The focus of recent surveys has been on low wages and the increase in the number of children in two parent families living below the poverty line. In Saskatchewan in 2001, 56 percent of First Nations and 36 percent of Métis children lived in families whose incomes were below the poverty line. (Hunter and Douglas, 2003; Hunter, 2002)

The absolute failure of Canadian governments to deal with the issue of poverty can be seen in the survey of poverty among rich countries conducted by the Innocenti Research Centre of the United Nations Children Fund. These figures are for 2000:

| Country | Child Poverty (%) | Low Wages* (%) |
|---|---|---|
| Sweden | 2.8 | 5.2 |
| Finland | 4.3 | 5.9 |
| Belgium | 4.4 | 7.2 |
| France | 7.9 | 13.3 |
| Germany | 10.7 | 13.3 |
| Japan | 12.2 | 15.7 |
| Australia | 12.6 | 13.8 |
| Canada | 15.5 | 23.7 |
| UK | 19.8 | 19.6 |
| USA | 22.4 | 25 |
| Saskatchewan | 22.3 | 29 |

Source: UNICEF: Innocenti Report Cards Issue #1, June 2002 (From Hunter and Douglas, 2002)

*The UN defines low wages as two-thirds of the median wage.

The poverty rate in Saskatchewan remains very high by international standards. One of the key reasons for this is the expansion of low wage jobs, encouraged by the steady drop of the real minimum wage since the end of the NDP government of Allan Blakeney in 1982. As the Innocenti report concludes, the above statistics "represent the unnecessary suffering and deprivation of millions of individual children. They also represent a failure to hold faith with the developed world's ideal of equality of opportunity." (Cited in Hunter and Douglas, 2002)

Basic social assistance rates in Saskatchewan have been frozen since 1982. They were cut by Grant Devine's Tory government, then raised back to the 1982 level by the NDP government in 1993. Today they are well below the poverty line, indicating the depth of poverty that has set in since 1982. The Canadian Council on Social Development has documented the impact of the change in policy. The table which follows lists Saskatchewan's annual social assistance rates for 2001, the poverty line as set by Statistics Canada, and the rates as a percentage of the poverty line. As a reference point, it should be remembered that during the NDP government of Allan Blakeney, social assistance rates were above the poverty line.

| Category | $Rates | $Poverty Line | % Poverty Line |
|---|---|---|---|
| Single employable | 5,978 | 16,167 | 37% |
| Disabled person | 8,662 | 16,167 | 54% |
| Lone parent & child | 12,367 | 20,209 | 61% |
| Couple, 2 children | 18,201 | 30,424 | 60% |

Source: Canadian Council on Social Development, 2002

It is quite clear that neither the Tory government of Grant Devine nor the NDP governments of Roy Romanow and Lorne Calvert have been concerned about the persistence of poverty in the province. They have consciously allowed the minimum wage to fall in real terms, and they have allowed social assistance rates to fall well below the poverty line. The system of child care in Saskatchewan is the poorest in Canada. Almost no social housing has been built since 1992; inadequate slum landlord housing is seen as acceptable for low income families. These governments have abandoned the social democratic objectives of Saskatchewan's pre-1982 governments.

How can we explain this? Garson Hunter and Dionne Miazdyck have done an excellent job of putting the Saskatchewan policy in the context of the international move towards neoliberalism. They have gone further than this by comparing the policies of the NDP government with the "work-first approaches" of the United States under President Bill Clinton and the "Third Way" policies of Tony Blair's Labour government in Great Britain.

The policies of neoliberalism stress the end to social programs with citizenship entitlement and their replacement by limited programs targeting a narrow group. Part of this strategy is to get people off social assistance and into the labour force. There have been two basic approaches used. First, there is the Human-Capital Development (HCD) approach which involves significant training and education and placement in jobs which pay a living wage. This approach has been used in a number of European countries. The second approach is the Labour-Force Attachment (LFA) model that stresses moving people off welfare quickly through low cost programs and into jobs which pay near the minimum wage. This approach is used in the UK and the USA.

The Clinton administration in the United States ended the federal Aid To Families with Dependent Children program in 1996. This was the last program left from the New Deal of Franklin Roosevelt, and it was based on government aid as an entitlement of citizenship. The new legislation, called the Personal Responsibility and Work Reconciliation Act, decentralized all welfare to the states and removed the right to entitlement to social assistance. States may set their own systems and limits. (Hunter and Miazdyck, 2003)

The federal Liberal government followed suit in 1996. The Canada Assistance Plan was abolished, replaced with the Canada Health and Social Transfer program. The new program for social assistance does not include national standards, a statement of the right to assistance, or the prescription for voluntary workfare. Following the U.S. precedent, provinces can now run different welfare systems. This has been an objective of the political right.

The NDP government in Saskatchewan has developed a new program designed to get people off social assistance, Building Independence—Investing in Families. In this they have adopted the LFA model designed to provide a new labour pool which has little option but to work for near minimum wages and to fill the corporate need for part time and temporary workers.

As Hunter and Miazdyck point out, this new welfare strategy is fully consistent with the Third Way policy identified with Tony Blair's Labour government. There is a rejection of equality of outcome as a goal, preferring instead the notion of equality of opportunity. There is a general attack on rights and entitlements. Those without employment must seek work. But they must be willing to accept any kind of work;

they cannot limit their search to quality work or work which pays a living wage. Today there is a large private sector that is seeking workers willing to work for a low wage, and Building Independence is designed to fill that corporate need. This general policy approach is one of the reasons that Saskatchewan has such a high percentage of low wage jobs and such a high level of inequality. (see Hunter and Miazdyck, 2003)

## The Decline of Support for the NDP

Roy Romanow and his supporters changed the Saskatchewan NDP. Romanow was always on the right of the party, but he was quick to embrace the general social democratic move to the right. He openly admired the neoliberal policies of the Labour government in New Zealand (1986-90), which was the first government in an industrialized country to virtually repeal the welfare state. Later he became an strong supporter of Tony Blair, leader of the so-called "New" Labour Party in Great Britain, who finished the job started by Margaret Thatcher. In an interview with Paul Adams of the *Globe and Mail* (September 17, 1999) Romanow recounted that from the beginning in 1991 the Saskatchewan government had chosen to follow a similar policy direction to that of Tony Blair. He stated that the political philosophy of Tommy Douglas and the CCF had become "a straitjacket" for his NDP government, limiting the changes it wanted to make, particularly in health care.

What we have seen in Saskatchewan is the general shift away from the political economy of the Keynesian welfare state to the neoliberal political economy of the free market and free trade. This process was begun by the Tory government of Grant Devine. But the transition to neoliberalism was completed by the NDP governments of Roy Romanow and Lorne Calvert (1991-2004). Provincial government spending fell from 30 percent of provincial gross domestic product under the Devine government to only 22 percent in 2002. Budget deficits and the debt began to increase due to the cuts in government revenues. The NDP was following the script set by the Labour parties in New Zealand, Australia and Great Britain.

The strong move to the right by the Romanow government disillusioned many people. Electoral participation by enumerated voters, normally around 80 percent, fell to 63 percent in 1995 and to 56 percent in 1999. NDP party membership dropped from 46,000 to 16,000 by the year 2000. To offset this lack of member support, the party shifted to actively soliciting financial contributions from banks and large corporations. It skirted the electoral law and solicited anonymous donations from local businesses through the T. C. Douglas House Foundation. (Brown, 1999)

In the fall 1999 election voter support for the NDP fell to under 38%, and they failed to obtain a majority of the seats. Their vote fell from 275,780 in 1991, to 192,320 in 1995 to only 156,243 in 1999. When they were routed in 1982, they still received 201,390 votes. The 1999 vote was by far their lowest total since the Douglas government was elected in 1944.

Following the 1999 election the Romanow government signed a formal alliance with their historic political enemies, the Liberal Party. A number of prominent Liberals remarked that this was not of any real concern because the NDP had abandoned its traditional position on the left. They had moved right to join the Liberals. However, support for the NDP continued to fall in a series of by-elections. Voter turnout continued to fall. People told enumerators that they did not even want their name of the voter's list.

Prominent cabinet ministers began to leave and government and resign their seats. Others stated that they would not run for re-election. In late 2002 Roy Romanow stepped down as leader of the NDP. The party chose to select the new leader by a vote of all party members. The voting members chose Lorne Calvert, even though public opinion polls indicated that NDP voters, and the public in general, wanted them to choose Chris Axworthy. The choice of Calvert indicated no change of direction for the party. Calvert had been elected in 1991 and had served as Minister of Social Services. He had been tough on those forced to depend on social assistance. He had been Associate Minister of Health when the major cut backs were introduced and hospitals were closed. While he had not sought re-election in 1995, he stayed on to be Roy Romanow's key political adviser. His first act as Premier was to announce that Eric Cline would remain as Minister of Finance, and the tax cut plan would be fully implemented. He received praise from the usual right wing business organizations.

When Lorne Calvert took over as leader of the NDP the prospects for re-election were not good. Public opinion polls put them slightly behind the Saskatchewan Party. In a series of by-elections voter turn out was low, and a significant number of voters shifted from the NDP to the Liberal Party. The party was also afraid that the New Green Alliance would attract many on the left of the party. In the 1999 election the newly formed NGA had won five percent of the vote where it ran candidates. It received 10 percent of the vote in the Regina Dewdney by-election and 6.5 percent in the Wood River by-election. Two polls in the spring of 2003 put support for the "other party" at five and seven percent.

Calvert took action. He fired the Phoenix Advertising Group and hired Now Communications from Vancouver to be his new advisers. First, they decided to run as a "green party" to try to limit the vote for the New Green Alliance. They even used green as the major colour on their campaign material! The new advisers determined that the best hope for re-election was to focus on Elwin Hermanson, the leader of the Saskatchewan Party. Hermanson was a Christian fundamentalist educated at a Bible college, who worried many urban voters. On many social issues he and his party were quite right wing. The NDP launched an American-style negative campaign attacking Hermanson. In this they seemed to have the support of the mainstream media. The election was turned into a referendum on Hermanson as leader. This was convenient for the NDP avoided having to defend its record in office. While organizations representing small business supported the Saskatchewan Party, the large corporations offered no criticism of the NDP government what so ever.

The strategy worked. The election called for November 2003 became totally polarized, and support for the Liberals and the New Green Alliance dropped. The NDP won re-election with 44 percent of the vote but have only a margin of two seats. Their vote total went up to 189,742 but was still far below what they were accustomed to receive. Only 58 percent of eligible voters (those 18 and over) bothered to vote. Few were in any way enthusiastic about voting for the NDP. They were seen by a great many as only the lesser evil. Given that the Calvert government is only promising more of the same, most political commentators are predicting that the Saskatchewan Party, with a new more urban leader, is almost certain to win the next provincial election.

Why has there been such a fundamental change in the policy orientation of the Saskatchewan NDP? For years many NDP supporters argued that the party had been betrayed by Roy Romanow and his right-wing allies. They believed that if they could remove Romanow the party would go back to being the old CCF-NDP. In the 2001 leadership campaign, Nettie Wiebe, past president of the National Farmers Union and a long-time NDP activist, ran for the leadership offering a progressive social democratic alternative. Despite an active campaign by her supporters, she received only 25 percent of the votes cast by members. Her supporters melted back into the NDP or disappeared from politics.

Ken Rasmussen, who teaches in the School of Administration at the University of Regina, offers other explanations. He argues that fiscal conservatism has always been a characteristic of CCF and NDP governments and that the public wanted the Romanow government to make this a first priority. In addition, the scope of activity for provincial governments has been limited by the international free trade agreements, the free trade agreements between provinces, and constitutional changes. (Rasmussen, 1994; 2000)

The nature of the party itself has led to changes, according to Rasmussen. Gone is the old farmer-labour alliance. Farmers today are "agribusiness entrepreneurs." The labour movement has been "marginalized, shunted aside in the party's quest to appeal to the centre of the spectrum." It is a coalition of professionals, public sector workers, trade union activists, and progressive farmers. But it is also characterized by "elite control and a lack of intellectual vigour." As such, it has "failed to articulate a new economic or social vision." (Rasmussen, 2000)

Howard Leeson, a political scientist with close links to the NDP, stresses the changes in rural Saskatchewan. The CCF had its base in the rural communities, among the wheat growers. But the forces of the market resulted in a significant depopulation of the rural areas. A new generation of larger farmers has no direct links to the old co-operative tradition and are much more likely to pursue "private sector measurements and methods, to view the role of government less positively." These farmers were already "socially conservative, they became more economically conservative, identifying less and less with urban economic interests." The Tories were skillful in exploiting this new development. The result, Leeson argues, is a "change in the political culture of rural Saskatchewan" which has carried over to the urban-rural polarization which now characterizes the province. (Leeson, 2001)

These arguements are true, but they only tell part of the story. The leadership of the NDP consciously chose to follow the neoliberal path set forth by other social democratic governments. There was, and still is, another road to follow. There is the large, marginalized sector of the Saskatchewan population which basically has opted out of the political process, in urban, rural and northern Saskatchewan. They could be mobilized. But at this time in history, this is not the political route being adopted by social democracy.

## Conclusion

Since the 1980s, we have seen a restructuring of international capital in an effort to increase the rate of profit. At the federal level in Canada this restructuring is reflected in the free trade agreements with the United States and support for an expansion of the powers of the World Trade Organization.

Resistance to the new system of "flexible accumulation" has been widespread. However, opposition has been contained in the formal political realm. All liberal democratic governments have become more authoritarian. The corporate mass media has given unchallenged support to the new system. Liberal and conservative parties shifted their policies to follow the neoliberal agenda set by capital. In Canada the new politics of neoliberalism has been implemented by the Tory government of Brian Mulroney and the Liberal government of Jean Chretien.

The majority, who oppose these changes and are the victims of the shift from the old Keynesian welfare state system, have been unable to mobilize effective resistance. They have lost the organizations which traditionally advocated their cause. The communist parties have disappeared, and no new large left wing parties have emerged to take their place. Communist, socialist and social democratic trade unions are under attack, and their influence and membership has declined. The social democratic and labour parties and governments, increasingly run on an authoritarian basis, have also shifted to the right to support the new world order. This began with the Labour governments in New Zealand (1984-90) and Australia (1983-1996). Tony Blair's Labour government in Britain (1997- present) has gone far beyond Margaret Thatcher in implementing the neoliberal agenda of deregulation and privatization. Other social democratic governments in Europe followed. The Green parties emerged to challenge neoliberalism and the ecological crisis, but they have been unable to move beyond the status of relatively small opposition parties. Where they have joined governing coalitions with social democratic parties (as in Germany, Italy and France), they have ended up supporting neoliberal programs and militarism.

In the less developed world the communist, socialist and nationalist movements and parties were repressed by a variety of dictatorships and quasi-democracies backed by the U.S. government. Because of this, popular movements of resistance turned to extra-parliamentary organizations, coalitions and local mobilizations to try to hold back the tide. In many places they have won local victories, but they have been notably unsuccessful in blocking structural change. Furthermore, in a great many less developed countries the collapse of "modernist" political movements and parties has been replaced by the rise of "post modern" movements and parties which represent fundamentalist religions. Political repression has helped to produce the politics of terrorism.

In Saskatchewan the restructuring of capitalism began with the Tory government of Grant Devine. In the 1991 election the citizens indicated that they wanted to return to the social democratic traditions of the past. But the NDP governments headed by Roy Romanow and Lorne Calvert have continued the policy direction begun by the Progressive Conservatives. This has resulted in a major transformation of the structure of the private sector in the province. One of the side effects has been the significant increase in foreign ownership and control by large corporations and their increasing monopoly power within the province. As well, social programs have been cut back due to wide ranging tax cuts and the loss of government revenues.

Following international trends, resistance in Canada to these changes has been significant. But this resistance has been ineffective in stopping or even slowing the change. In the past, those opposed to the agenda of big business turned to the CCF-NDP as their vehicle for political mobilization. However, the NDP in Saskatchewan has followed the pattern of other social democratic parties and has become more authoritarian, and its leadership has endorsed the policies central to the restructuring process. The opposition Liberal and Saskatchewan Party have not offered any policy alternatives. Only the new, very small New Green Alliance offers a different approach, but as yet it has no ability to influence or change government policy.

Support for the NDP has been falling since the 1991 election. Some of these voters came back to support the party in the polarized election of 2003. But 308,000 eligible voters chose not to go to the polls. With the Calvert government continuing to push even more tax cuts and budget cuts, there is little hope that any new policy direction will develop. Disillusionment, cynicism, and the withdrawal of so many people from politics will not change until either the NDP reverses direction or a new progressive movement is formed. There is no indication to date that the NDP leadership is about to change its policy direction.

## References

Alliance for Responsible Trade. 1998. *Alternatives for the Americas: Building a People's Hemispheric Agreement*. Halifax: Fernwood Books.

Baron, Don and Paul Jackson. 1991. *Battleground: The Socialist Assault on Grant Devine's Canadian Dream*. Toronto: Bedford House Publishing.

Biggs, Lesley and Mark Stobbe, eds. 1991. *Devine Rule in Saskatchewan: A Decade of Hope and Hardship*. Saskatoon: Fifth House Publishers.

Brown, Lorne A., Joseph K. Roberts and John W. Warnock. 1999. *Saskatchewan Politics from Left to Right '44 to '99*. Regina: Hinterland Books.

Cameron, Duncan. 1988. *The Free Trade Deal*. Toronto: James Lorimer & Company.

Cameron, Duncan and Mel Watkins. 1993. *Canada Under Free Trade*. Toronto: James Lorimer & Company.

Campaign 2000. 2003. *Honouring Our Promises: Meeting the Challenge to End Child and Family Poverty*. Toronto: 2003.

Campbell, Bruce *et al.* 1999. *Pulling Apart: The Deterioration of Employment and Income in North America Under Free Trade.* Ottawa: Canadian Centre for Policy Alternatives.

Canada. Royal Commission on the Economic Union and Development Prospects for Canada. 1985. *Report.* Toronto: University of Toronto Press.

Canadian Council on Social Development. 2002. *Statistics on Poverty.* Ottawa: Canadian Council on Social Development.

Canadian Centre for Policy Alternatives—Saskatchewan. 2003. *Saskatchewan Alternative Budget of Choice: A Budget for Communities, by Communities.* Saskatoon: CCPA-SK.

Clarke, Tony and Maude Barlow. 1997. *MAI: The Multilateral Agreement on Investment and the Threat to Canadian Sovereignty.* Toronto: Stoddard.

Cohen, Marjorie Griffin. 1987. *Free Trade and the Future of Women's Work: Manufacturing and Service Industries.* Toronto: Garamond Press.

Dasgupta, Biplab. 1998. *Structural Adjustment, Global Trade and the New Political Economy of Development.* London: Zed Books.

Drache, Daniel and Duncan Cameron, eds. 1985. *The Other Macdonald Report: The Consensus on Canada's Future that the Macdonald Commission Left Out.* Toronto: James Lorimer & Company.

Ekos Research Associates. 1994. *Rethinking Government '94.* Ottawa: Ekos Research Associates; annual reports to 2003.

Gilmer, Peter. 2002. *Saskatchewan Anti-Poverty Alternatives: Where Are We At?* Regina: Regina Anti-Poverty Ministry, October 24.

Gonick, Cy. 1987. *The Great Economic Debate: Failed Economics and a Future for Canada.* Toronto: James Lorimer & Company.

Hansen-Kuhn, Karen and Steve Hellinger, eds. 2003. *Lessons from NAFTA: The High Cost of "Free Trade."* Ottawa: Canadian Centre for Policy Alternatives.

Hansen, Phillip. 2003. *Taxing Illusions: Taxation, Democracy and Embedded Political Theory.* Halifax: Fernwood Books.

Harrison, Bennett and Barry Bluestone. 1988. *The Great U-Turn: Corporate Restructuring and the Polarizing of America.* New York: Basic Books.

Harvey, David. 1989. *The Condition of Postmodernity.* London: Basil Blackwell.

Hoogvelt, Ankie. 1997. *Globalization and the Postcolonial World: The New Political Economy of Development.* Baltimore: The Johns Hopkins University Press.

Hunter, Garson. 2002. *Social Assistance Caseload Impact of the Building Independence Program in Saskatchewan: A Time-Series Analysis.* Regina: Social Policy Research Unit, University of Regina. SPR Occasional Papers, No. 15, March.

Hunter, Garson and Dionne Miazdyck. 2003. *Current Issues Surrounding Poverty and Welfare Programming in Canada: Two Reviews.* Regina: Social Policy Research Unit, University of Regina, SPR Working Papers, No. 21, August.

Hunter, Garson and Fiona Douglas. 2002. *Saskatchewan Child Poverty Report*. Regina: Social Policy Research Unit, University of Regina, November.

Hunter, Garson and Fiona Douglas. 2003. *Saskatchewan Child Poverty Report*. Regina: Social Policy Research Unit, University of Regina.

Jackson, Andrew. 2003. *From Leaps of Faith to Hard Landings: Fifteen Years of "Free Trade."* Ottawa: Canadian Centre for Policy Alternatives, December.

Jackson, Andrew and David Robinson. 2000. *Falling Behind: The State of Working Canada, 2000.* Ottawa: Canadian Centre for Policy Alternatives.

Kolko, Joyce. 1988. *Restructuring the World Economy*. New York: Pantheon Books.

Lee, Kevin. 1999. "Measuring Poverty Among Canada's Aboriginal People." *Perception*, Vol. 23, No. 2, Fall, pp. 9-12.

Leeson, Howard A., ed. 2001. *Saskatchewan Politics in the Twenty-First Century*. Regina: Canadian Plains Research Centre, University of Regina.

McBride, Stephen and John Shields. 1997. *Dismantling a Nation: The Transition to Corporate Rule in Canada*. Halifax: Fernwood Publishing.

MacKinnon, Janice. 2003. *Minding the Public Purse: The Fiscal Crisis, Political Trade-offs, and Canada's Future*. Montreal: McGill-Queen's University Press.

Merrett, Christopher D. 1996. *Free Trade: Neither Free Nor about Trade*. Montreal: Black Rose Books.

Pitsula, James M. and Ken Rasmussen. 1990. *Privatizing a Province: The New Right in Saskatchewan*. Vancouver: New Star Books.

Poverty Action Group. 1998. *The Growing Depth of Poverty: A Brief to the Saskatchewan Cabinet*. Regina: Poverty Action Group, October 1.

Rasmussen, Ken. 1994. "Economic Policy in Saskatchewan, 1991-1994: The Politics of Declining Expectations." Canadian Political Science Association, Calgary, June 12.

Rasmussen, Ken. 2000. "Saskatchewan: From Entrepreneurial State to Embedded State." Regina: School of Public Administration, University of Regina.

Saskatoon District Health. 1996. *Poverty, Health and the Minimum Wage*. Saskatoon: Saskatoon District Health, January.

Shields, John and B. Mitchell Evans. 1998. *Shrinking the State: Globalization and Public Administration "Reform."* Halifax: Fernwood Publishing.

Stanford, Jim. 1999. *Paper Boom: Why Real Prosperity Requires a New Approach to Canada's Economy*. Toronto: James Lorimer & Company.

Teeple, Gary. 1995. *Globalization and the Decline of Social Reform*. Toronto: Garamond Press.

Warnock, John W. 1988. *Free Trade and the New Right Agenda*. Vancouver: New Star Books.

Warnock, John W. 2002. "Coalitions, Labour and the New Democratic Party." Paper presented to the Symposium on the Labour Movement in Saskatchewan, University of Regina, November 24. Publication forthcoming.

# Chapter 14

————○————

# BUILDING AN ALTERNATIVE
# TO NEOLIBERALISM

This ought to be a time for reflection. We have just entered the twenty-first century, and occasions like this usually inspire us to think about the past and what we expect in the future. In 2005 Saskatchewan will celebrate its centennial. A wide variety of new publications will be appearing, many of which will focus on the history of the province.

The collapse of the Soviet system in 1989 was widely celebrated in the west. The capitalist system had triumphed in the struggle with state socialism. But in the following years, many became uneasy as the U.S. government and its large corporations pushed hard to be sure that they remained the dominant world political and economic power. Then came the shock of the attack on the World Trade Center and the Pentagon by political dissidents from Saudi Arabia. U.S. President George W. Bush responded with the now famous National Security Council paper of September 2002 declaring that the U.S. government would do everything within its power to keep its position as the world's leading military and political force. China, and the U.S. allies in Europe, were warned not to challenge the United States.

Since the collapse of the Soviet bloc, the U.S. government has insisted that the North Atlantic Treaty Organization (NATO) be maintained so that they could continue their influence over Europe. They pushed for the creation of the Asia-Pacific Economic Co-operation Council (APEC) in order to prevent the rise of an autonomous economic group in the area which could be dominated by either Japan or China. They demanded the creation of the Free Trade Area of the Americas (FTAA) to try to create a zone of special interest in the western hemisphere, a new version of the Monroe Doctrine. The U.S. government, backed by its political allies, expanded the power and influence of international institutions to enforce neoliberalism, including the International Monetary Fund, the World Bank, the G-7, the Bank for International Settlement, and the Organization for Economic Co-operation and Development (OECD). These were to be enhanced by the Multilateral Agreement on Investment (MAI) and the World Trade Organization (WTO).

But as we know, the new "unipolar world" of U.S. military and economic domination produced resistance. Opposition to the U.S. project is growing across the world in the less developed countries. But to the surprise of the political and economic elite, it also appeared in the First World as the new anti-globalization and anti-capitalist movements. In every country there are political movements and often new political parties starting to demand an alternative.

Major political changes have happened in history during major wars and world economic crises. There have been a series of economic crises in recent years: Mexico in 1994, Asia in 1997, Russia in 1998, Argentina in 2002, and a major North American recession in 2001-3. Japan has experienced economic stagnation for over ten years. Economic growth in Europe has stagnated. But the world capitalist system has muddled through without another world depression. Governments and international agencies are quick to use the techniques of the Keynesian economics when necessary. Despite regular regional economic problems, a major world depression does not seem likely.

We are still having wars, of course. But they are not major wars that could trigger social change as happened in Russia and China. They are largely wars of the new imperialism, as the U.S. government uses its extensive military power to try to maintain its control and domination over less developed areas of the world. In this the U.S. government has been able to recruit the support of its NATO allies and the Security Council of the United Nations. So far they have managed to prevent the rise of major new anti-imperialist or socialist movements.

In this situation, what are the alternatives? In Mexico, to use one example, the people struggled from 1988 to 2000 to replace the virtual dictatorship of the Institutional Revolutionary Party (PRI), run by the wealthy elite with their degrees from Ivy League universities, committed to the neoliberal regime of the free market and free trade. What they got as a replacement was President Vicente Fox of the National Action Party (PAN); there were no policy changes. In the July 2003 off-year election, only 42 percent of those on the electoral lists bothered to vote.

Under the first ten years of the North American Free Trade Agreement (NAFTA) Mexico's trade increased by over 300 percent. But per capita economic growth was on average only 0.96 percent per year, and environmental degradation increased dramatically. Eight million new jobs were created, but 14 million people entered the labour force. Of the new jobs created, only 55 percent provided the meagre benefits required under Mexican law. During this time real wages and benefits fell by 36 percent. Unemployment in rural areas increased by 1.78 million as the influx of food imports drove Mexican farmers out of business. How many Mexicans would consider NAFTA a success? (see Hansen-Kuhn and Hellinger, 2003; Audley *et al.*, 2003)

Given this situation, the average Mexican hopes for a job which pays a wage or a salary of at least two minimum wages (i.e., US$8 per day). Working in the informal economy means very long hours for little income. It is hoped that a family member can get a job with a large corporation or the government, for this is the only way to get health insurance and a pension. The alternative proposed by the Party for the Democratic Revolution (PRD) is to break with the free trade regime, create a national economy, and work towards a First World welfare state. This was basically the Mexican economic strategy before 1980. They oppose the Free Trade Agreement for the Americas and support the Hemispheric Social Alliance (HSA) which advances the policies we identify with the Keynesian welfare state. This is the best alternative there is. There used to be socialist and communist parties in Mexico, advocating a different system, but they are gone.

What are the options in the United States? For most Americans the choice is between the Republicans and the Democrats. The American political system was best described by Joseph Schumpeter, the famous liberal economist at Harvard University. It is not democracy but "polyarchy." He defines this as "a system in which a small group actually rules, and mass participation in decision making is confined to choosing leaders in elections that are carefully managed by competing elites." This is an "institutional arrangement" for elites to acquire power "by means of a competitive struggle for the people's vote. Democracy means only that the people have the opportunity of accepting or refusing the men who are to rule them." The Green Party offers the only alternative, but it can't even get on the ballot in many states, and because it is opposed to U.S. imperial wars, it is considered almost treasonous by most U.S. citizens. It is no wonder that the turnout is only 50 percent in presidential elections and 35 percent in off-year elections. (Robinson, 1996; Schumpeter, 1961)

The choice for Canadians does not seem much better. We now have a Liberal Prime Minister, Paul Martin, who is the wealthiest political leader in Canada. He strongly supports neoliberalism and closer integration with the United States. The major opposition party is the new Conservative Party, a collection of right wingers with strong links to the oil corporations in Alberta. The CP (!) wants to go even faster than Martin down the neoliberal road to integration with the United States. The federal New Democratic Party has a new leader, Jack Layton. He is trying to attract left-leaning Liberals to the party. Many political commentators describe the NDP today as the real Liberal Party. They refuse to adopt a platform that calls for an independent Canada. This leaves only the small Green Party as the alternative, and it doesn't even run candidates in most provinces. There are no socialist or communist parties around today which call for an alternative to capitalism.

Is there any reason to believe that there is a possibility for an alternative to develop in Canada and elsewhere? Perhaps, for the world must eventually confront the ecological crisis. And this crisis is caused by the capitalist system and its need to constantly grow and expand.

There are practical reasons for doing some serious thinking about our society and where it is headed. In 2003 there was a major political fight over whether the Canadian government should endorse the modest first steps set forth by the Kyoto Protocol to try to address the growing threat posed by greenhouse gas emissions, global warming and climate change. There was strong opposition to ratifying the protocol and strong opposition from particular interests to do nothing that would in any way impede the ability of the private sector to maximize profits. In Saskatchewan the NDP government, the opposition Saskatchewan Party and the Liberal Party vigorously opposed the original Kyoto Protocol.

In the end the Liberal government of Jean Chretien ratified the protocol, but since then governments across Canada have been doing everything possible to avoid taking actions to fulfill the commitments that our government made. Some, like Lorne Calvert's NDP government, have announced a few token programs. But this is for public relations purposes. No governments in Canada are taking this issue seriously.

Yet in Saskatchewan the effects of climate change can already be seen. For three years running (2000-2003) there has been a drought. Researchers at the Prairie Adaptation Research Collaborative at the University of Regina have warned the public that in the past there were "megadroughts" on the prairies. One lasted from 1690 to 1730. Similar droughts have been recorded for Mexico and the western United

States. Rainfall was 83 percent of normal for over thirty years between 736 and 765. Peter Leavitt, a biologist at the University of Regina, has estimated that over the next 30 years there is a 45 percent chance of having a drought that lasts between five and twelve years.

Dave Sauchyn, head of the University of Regina group, reminds us that drought is the norm for the prairies and that the period from 1960 to 1990 was unusually wet. Thirty year periods of drought are not unusual. Prairie cities rely on the water running from glaciers in Alberta's mountains, and the glaciers are disappearing. But few people seem to care. (*Globe and Mail*, November 2, 2002; *Western Producer*, October 23, 2003)

For two of the last three years, Saskatchewan had the lowest rate of economic growth of any of the provinces. This was attributed to the drought and its impact on agriculture. Across the prairies the hot, dry climate has been the cause of a major increase in fires in the boreal forests. During the drought of the 1930s there were widespread forest fires in northern Saskatchewan. Scientists believe that global warming and climate change will involve a major, negative impact on Canada's boreal forests. As the University of Regina group stresses, climate change will have the greatest impact on the centre of the continents.

But it is business as usual in Saskatchewan. Our government, political and business leaders, and the mass media are not concerned. They seem obsessed by the fact that Saskatchewan's population has remained steady at around one million people since the 1930s and that the province has not become some industrial giant. Most people are comfortable in their lives and want it to stay that way. Sales of half-ton trucks, SUVs, and new homes are at record levels. No one seems to care at all about what kind of the world they are going to leave their children and grandchildren.

Margaret Thatcher is perhaps best known for her comment "There Is No Alternative." TINA as it is known, arguing that there is no alternative to free market capitalism. This is often cited along with her assertion that "there are no communities." Great Britain, she declares, is nothing more than a collection of individuals all seeking to maximize their own self interest. Francis Fukuyama proclaims that we have reached "the end of history," and the best we have is savage capitalism and authoritarian governments. In such a political atmosphere, how is it possible to build a movement for an alternate society? In the postmodern era, can we even think of a better future? (Fukuyama, 1992)

## The Failure of "Actual Existing Socialism"

In Canada, few were sad to see the fall of the centrally planned economies in the So-viet Union and Eastern Europe. They were all one party states, ruled by an oligarchy of men with special privileges. The repressive state was all powerful, with the secret police, gulags and prisons, and the absence of fundamental liberal rights. There was no political democracy, and even trade unions in this "workers' state" could not mo-bilize to defend the interests of their members. In all of the revolutionary states, once the men had seized power they found it difficult to lay down their guns.

But there were some notable successes. Despite the destruction of two world wars, the Soviet governments rapidly built advanced industrialized states. Poverty, hunger and destitution were all but eliminated. There was real full employment and a relatively good system of social services. Women had full educational opportunities, almost all of them were working and paid a living wage, and there was a good state system for child support. There was a serious attempt to invest in rural and farm com-munities and to bring the standard of material and cultural life up to urban levels.

But the state socialist countries remained strongly patriarchal and militaristic. Environmental destruction was worse than in the capitalist west. They copied U.S. corporate agriculture. Wilhelm Reich described the Stalinist state as "red fascism" for its opposition to sexual freedom, commitment to the patriarchal family, opposition to birth control and abortion, and hostility to gays and lesbians. (Reich, 1969)

Critics on the left referred to these regimes as "Stalinist state capitalism." Under the direction of Stalin, they had retained all the institutions of the capitalist and pre-capitalist states. The system of production in industries and factories retained the capitalist system of hierarchy, with bosses ruling workers. What was called "socialist accumulation" appeared to be the same as under capitalism, the extraction of the eco-nomic surplus from the labour of employees. The economic surplus did not go to pri-vate capitalists, of course, but to a state bureaucracy which decided how it would be spent. But there was no democratic participation in this process.

This was a very different society from the one envisioned by Karl Marx and Frederick Engels. As we have seen, Marx commented favourably on the Paris Com-mune of 1871 as an example of a future communist society. The goal of socialist soci-ety, Marx insisted, was the "full and free development of every individual" and the end of alienation. This could not be achieved under capitalism. (Draper, 1971)

Today when the subject of communism comes up, everyone automatically thinks of the old Soviet system. Who wants that system of government and society?

As desperate as people are in Africa today, the communist parties that do exist have virtually no support. In the former USSR and Eastern Europe, the vast majority of the people have experienced a dramatic fall in their standard of living as they have moved to embrace capitalism. A large percentage of the population wants to bring back the full employment and relatively good standard of living they used to have, but they are even more fearful of bringing back the old Soviet totalitarian state.

China is still ruled by the Communist Party. But the government is replacing the centrally planned economy which emphasized egalitarian development with capitalism. Gross inequalities are evident everywhere. Unemployment is a serious problem. But the totalitarian state refuses to allow any dissent, and it crushes with state power any attempt by workers to strike or use trade unions to try to protect their interests. There is horrendous exploitation of workers who in many industries are little more than slaves. That is why the student leaders demanding democratic reforms at the Tiananmen Square marches in 1989 referred the their government as "fascist," a totalitarian state imposing capitalism, much like Italy under Mussolini.

The model of revolutionary socialism put forth by Marx and Engels and their followers no longer seems to have any relevance. It depended on the blue collar working man in the industrial sector of the economy. In the western industrialized countries, this sector has been declining for decades. Furthermore, the work force in these countries has basically been divided into two broad sectors, the organized working class with trade unions, relatively good wages and benefits, and the marginalized workers who are not unionized, which includes women, youth, immigrants, minorities, and the handicapped. There is a new body of workers who have only precarious work: part time, temporary, contract, casual and self-employment. As Alain Lipietz points out, modern capitalism is creating new Third Worlds within the advanced capitalist countries. Today one would have a hard time finding much working class solidarity. (Lipietz, 1992)

Revolutionary Marxism still has appeal in some of the less developed countries. But the organized working class is a relatively small minority in these countries, far outnumbered by those working in the so-called "informal economy" without a wage or a salary. Today, the Marxist appeal is linked to the politics of anti-imperialism. The class struggle, many argue, is not the major form of conflict, but race and ethnicity, gender, religion, and the new imperialism of First World globalization. However, it may be too early to write off revolutionary Marxism. (For example, see Burbach, 1997; Lipietz, 1992)

## The Failure of Social Democracy

The original socialist project was to replace the capitalist system with one based on equality, democracy and co-operation. It was the profound belief of all socialists that capitalism, based on competition and greed, was contrary to the interests of the vast majority as well as basic humanistic values. It strengthened patriarchy, racism and colonialism. On a world scale, it produced horrific working conditions and gross inequalities. It was a barrier to the full development of the human personality.

The socialist project was split between those who argued that an armed revolution was necessary, believing that the capitalists and their state would never give up power without a fight, and those who believed that socialism could be achieved through the electoral process. As they shifted to the electoral route, socialists in Europe argued that social reforms would be cumulative and eventually socialist governments would lead to a socialist state and society, achieved without the use of armed force.

Marx and Engels urged workers of the world to unite, for "you have nothing to lose but your chains." But workers had much more to lose, and this has been demonstrated a great many times. In the 19th century, after every major political demonstration and general strike in Europe, there was widespread repression by the state. These were massive following the demonstrations for democracy in 1848 and the defeat of the Paris Commune in 1871. Demonstrating workers were easily shot by the military and the police, murdered, tortured, imprisoned, exiled, blacklisted from jobs, and their families threatened and attacked. The capitalist state is not a paper tiger. Given the reality of state repression, it is no wonder that workers leaned toward the electoral process. This kind of brutal repression is the still the normal order of the day in many Third World countries. It has a long history in Mexico, our NAFTA partner.

The rise of the new middle class undermined the hope that industrial workers would become the majority and elect socialist governments. The expansion of white collar workers and the government bureaucracy split the working class, even the organized working class. The reformist social democratic parties and trade unions became bureaucratized, controlled by a self-perpetuating elite, generally committed to a moderate status quo. There was no class unity. (see Przeworski, 1985)

The key turning point came during and after World War I, when the European socialist parties split between those loyal to their conservative governments and those who chose to follow the leadership of the new Soviet Union. During the Great Depression of the 1930s and World War II, the social democratic parties adopted the economic and social policies of John Maynard Keynes as their basic political orientation. As Adam Przeworski points out, the problem with this was that the social democratic project did not differ from the reforms offered by other parties and governments. (Przeworski, 1985)

During the Cold War against communism, the social democratic parties in the First World supported the military alliances against the Soviet bloc, large standing armies and war budgets, and the development and introduction of nuclear weapons. They put these allegiances above their commitment to the United Nations and building peace. They limited their definition of democracy to electoral politics within the existing parliamentary and presidential systems. When in office they continued with the executive domination of government, placed power in the hands of their leaders, and ruled from the top down in a hierarchical manner. The co-operatives they created, and their state owned enterprises, have operated like private corporations.

Thus, as Adam Przeworski and other have argued, social democratic parties and governments have not offered any *qualitatively* different state or society. At best, they tried to provide "capitalism with a human face." Here they have been least successful in the Anglo-Saxon countries: the United Kingdom, Canada, New Zealand and Australia. When they formed the government, they were unwilling to do what was necessary to eliminate poverty and hunger. On environmental issues, social democratic parties and governments have been no different from the traditional capitalist parties. In office they have not even better on gender issues. (Przeworski, 1985; Riches, 1997)

## Social Democrats Embrace Neoliberalism

Margaret Thatcher once said that the greatest achievement of her years in office was transforming the Labour Party into another conservative party. The move by social democracy to embrace the political economy of neoliberalism started earlier and elsewhere. In 1984 the New Zealand Labour Party was elected to government on a traditional Keynesian platform promising full employment, a fair tax policy and expanding social programs. But once in office there was a virtual coup, and the parliamentary party rushed through a dramatic change in policy. Over the opposition of the general public and resolutions passed by Labour Party conventions, the Labour government undertook a far reaching program of privatization, deregulation, cuts to spending on social programs, imposed high interest rates, and moved to free trade. They cut taxes on corporations and the rich and imposed a 15 percent goods and services tax. They removed all controls on foreign ownership and helped promote the foreign takeover of the largest private companies and state assets. The new right-wing policy direction by the Labour Party was praised by Bob Rae, the leader of the NDP in Ontario, and Roy Romanow, the new leader of the NDP in Saskatchewan. (see Kelsey, 1995; Warnock, 1996)

A similar policy direction was implemented in Australia under the Labour governments of Bob Hawke and Paul Keating, in office between 1983 and 1996. As a result, Australia became one of the most unequal countries in the world. The Aboriginal population experiences the "severest poverty and hunger." Compared to other industrialized countries, Australia's public sector and social expenditures fell to well below average. As John Wiseman argues, the slower pace of the move to neoliberalism was "only a kinder road to hell." (Wilson, 1997; Wiseman, 1996)

In recent years Tony Blair and the Labour Party in Great Britain have been the unabashed leaders of the move by social democracy to embrace the world of neoliberalism. Blair and his supporters have called this the "Third Way," which is supposed to avoid the old polarization of left and right. Yet the policies of the Labour government have been described as "Thatcherism pursued by other means" or "Thatcherism with a smirk." The move away from the welfare state begun by the Tory government of Margaret Thatcher has been carried much further by Blair's government. Cuts in social services fell heaviest on lone parent women, the elderly and the disabled. The administration of schools in low income neighbourhoods was turned over to private corporations. Margaret Thatcher would never have dared to privatize the National Health Service like Blair did, creating a cruel two-tier public-private system. Poverty and inequality greatly increased. The policy direction of "New Labour" in Great Britain was to appeal more to upper middle class voters and reduce ties to the trade union movement. In Canada, Blair's strongest supporter was Roy Romanow, although some of his cabinet members were close behind.

It is not just in domestic policy that Blair's Labour government has followed the direction set by Margaret Thatcher. In the international arena, the Blair government has been the strongest supporter of the U.S. government's military and economic policies. When George W. Bush went to war in Afghanistan and Iraq, Tony Blair was at his side. (see Giddens, 1998, 2000; Callinicos, 2001)

Across Europe the social democratic parties are moving steadily to the right. In Great Britain Tony Blair changed the structure of the party so that he could block the nomination of socialist and feminist candidates. In Germany, Gerhardt Schroeder has crushed the left within the Social Democratic Party. In France and Italy, the left within the socialist parties chose to quit and go elsewhere. Even in the

Scandinavian countries the leadership of the social democratic parties is now strongly committed to the political economy of free trade and the move towards the market economy.

All the social democratic and labour parties in Europe, with the exception of the Labour Party in Norway, have followed Blair's lead. Similar policies have been implement by Labour coalition governments in Germany, Italy, France, Denmark, Sweden and the Netherlands. In Canada provincial NDP governments also largely followed suit. As we enter the 21st century, there is no reason to believe that the social democratic parties can offer any alternative to the politics of neoliberalism. (see Howell, 2001; Yates, 2002; Sheldrick, 2002; Bradford, 2002)

The general establishment of neoliberalism in the advanced capitalist countries does not mean that alternatives are not possible. New movements are developing. New parties are being formed. There is still a majority of the population in the advanced industrialized world that remains strongly committed to the goals of the Keynesian welfare state. There are strong elements in all countries that are opposed to U.S. military and economic domination of the world. We have not yet reached the end of history.

## Combating Neoliberalism on an International Level

The anti-globalization movement has emerged as a broad network of groups around the world who are resisting the implementation of the neoliberal project. The horrors of this policy are most apparent in the less developed countries, and it is here that the resistance is strongest.

Neoliberalism is not just a case of expanding the power of capital against the democratic rights of the majority. It is also Northern economic warfare against the poor of the less developed countries of the South. Our Canadian governments support these policies, including our social democratic governments. (see Danaher, 1994; Rich, 1994; Bandow and Vasquez, 1993)

Canadians are most aware of the anti-globalization movement in the Northern countries. To a large extent the movement has grown out of the opposition to the North American free trade agreements, the Maastricht free trade treaty in Europe, and the proposed Multilateral Agreement on Investment (MAI). The first major confrontation was in Seattle in 1999 at the Third Ministerial Conference of the World Trade Organization. Other demonstrations have been at the APEC meeting in Vancouver, the IMF and World Bank meetings in Washington, the WTO and Group of

Seven (G-7) meetings in Europe, the Summit of the Americas at Quebec City, and at the Davos meetings in Switzerland. All the demonstrations and their counter conferences have focused on the role of these institutions in oppressing the majority of the people in less developed countries. Even in the North, groups and movements have mobilized against what they see as the new imperialism.

The anti-globalization movement has been led by popular coalitions of community groups, trade unions and non-governmental organizations. Their presence at these international meetings, both as mass mobilizations of people and in the well-organized alternative meetings and presentations, has served to bolster resistance by the governments of the less developed countries. Many of the NGOs have provided expert advice to the poorer less developed countries. This was a key factor in the breakdown of the WTO meetings in Seattle and the strength of the less developed countries at the Fifth Ministerial Conference of the WTO at Cancun, Mexico in September 2003.

In the past these international meetings have been dominated by the Quad Four: the governments of the United States, the European Economic Community, Japan and Canada. They normally decided all key matters behind closed doors, excluding the other governments. At Cancun they were confronted by the Group of Twenty-Two (G-22) led by Brazil, India and China, the African, Caribbean and Pacific Alliance (ACP), the African Union (AU), and the group of Least Developed Countries (LDC). An alliance of 70 countries from Africa, Asia and Latin American democratically and openly created an alternative plan and presented it to the Cancun meetings. It was rejected by the delegates from the industrialized countries, and the conference collapsed.

The Canadian delegation, headed by the Minister of Trade, Pierre Pettigrew, was the focus of anger from the less developed countries. As at the Fourth Ministerial meeting at Doha, Qatar in 2001, Pettigrew was the unabashed front man for the U.S. government. At Cancun he chaired the meeting where he and the U.S. government tried in vain to get the less developed countries to accept the Singapore principles, the constitutional rights for capital which are embedded in the North American free trade agreements. (see Third World Network, special issue of *Third World Resurgence*, 2003; Ballve, 2003)

The principles of fair trade, as opposed to so-called "free trade," have been set forth since the mobilization against the Structural Adjustment Programs in the Third World and the free trade agreements in the First World. They call for decision making which involves all the nation states that are going to be affected, democratic and participatory decision making at all levels, transparency of the content of all policy proposals, full representation of affected parties in debate and decision making, equity between all the affected parties, decentralization of power and authority, the sovereign right of all countries to democratically choose their own policies, the need for sustainability and the reduction of inequality, respect for human and labour rights, the right of governments to their own policies on agriculture and rural development, and respect for the diversity of people and nations. These are all rights set forth in the UN Declaration on Human Rights and UN Covenants on Economic and Social Rights. But they are in contradiction to the policies of neoliberalism. (see CCPA, 1999; Dawkins, 1993)

The meetings of the World Social Forum (WSF) have reflected this reality. The primary political and economic conflict in the world today is between the rich, industrialized First World and the less developed countries. It is the new Cold War. At the WSF meetings in Brazil in 2001, there were few participants from the United States, even from the groups officially opposed to free trade. There was almost no coverage of the meetings in the American and Canadian press. The concurrent meeting of the Legislative Forum was attended primarily by legislators from the Third World. The focus was on the "continuum of colonization, centralization and loss of self-determination." While the first two meetings were held in Brazil, the WSF is decentralizing, and regional meetings are being held. There was a huge meeting in Italy in 2002 that drew about 400,000 in a mass demonstration. (Klein, 2001; Houtart and Polet, 2001)

The anti-globalization movement is not a unified group. There are those who believe that capitalism has to be replaced, and this requires the formation of political parties and electoral struggle. But the general thrust of the movement is towards grass roots organization and action by "civil society." That is certainly the orientation of the Council of Canadians, the most prominent activist group in Canada, which has played a widely recognized leadership role. At Porto Alegre there was concern that the leadership of the new movement has been too heavily influenced by activists from France, academics and men. The youth are more openly anti-capitalist. The more established organizations, like the First World trade union movements, push for reforms rather than outright rejection of neoliberalism and its institutions.

A group of intellectuals at Porto Alegre in 2001 issued a declaration noting that the anti-globalization movement is divided between social movements, non-governmental organizations, and left wing political parties. There are the "neo-Keynesians" who want reforms to the market economy and those who demand an entire new post-capitalist order. While the groups from the Third World are insistent that the movement must be strongly anti-imperialist, supporters in the First World stress other issues. (Amin, 2001; Mander and Goldsmith, 1996; Biel, 2000)

The WSF has come under attack for its general position rejecting the mobilization of people into political parties. The movement distances itself from the centres of power. With its emphasis on localism and decentralization, it has no strategy for confronting corporate and state power. Its major financial supporters have been trade unions and non-governmental organizations which accept capitalist society. Thus at Porto Alegre there was no celebration of the political, economic and social revolution that the Bolivarians are implementing in Venezuela. (see Hardt, 2002; Mertes, 2002; Sader, 2002; Milstein, 2002)

Over the fall of 2002 and into early 2003 a broad coalition of extra-parliamentary groups in the First World was able to create the largest peace movement in history in opposition to the U.S. war against Iraq. It produced a public opinion that was heavily opposed to the war. But it was not able to stop the war. And it was not able to convince many governments to oppose the war. The Spanish government joined in the war in spite of opposition from 90 percent of its citizens. The government in Turkey gave extensive direct aid to the U.S. forces in spite of opposition from 85 percent of its citizens. There are limits to extra-parliamentary politics.

## First World Alternatives

Samir Amin, the internationally renowned political economist from Egypt, has argued that the primary division in the world came with the formation of the "social democratic alliance" between the organized working class and their national capitalists. As Europe industrialized and developed, the working class became divided between the organized sector, with many special privileges that came with collective agreements, and the marginalized workers. The organized workers, and their social democratic parties, made an informal accommodation with capital, particularly with regard to managing overseas interests. This alliance was strengthened by the imperialist ideology of nationalism. This First World social democratic alliance allied itself with the ruling political and business interests in the Third World. Thus, Amin argues, the world capitalist system is characterized by an ever rising reserve army of the unemployed and marginally employed in the less developed world and the split in the working class in all the advanced industrialized states. It is no surprise, then, that the social democratic parties in the First World have supported colonialism, imperialism, Cold War militarism, and now the exploitation of the Third World through neoliberalism and the new imperialism called "globalization." Given this basic division in the world, can there be any change in the First World? (Amin, 1980)

The first response to the collapse of the communist parties and the move to the right by the social democratic parties has been widespread withdrawal from politics. For example, in the June 2001 elections for Parliament in Great Britain only 59 percent went to the polls. In the spring 2002 election for President in France 72 percent voted, and in the subsequent elections for the Assembly, only 65 percent voted. In the 2000 federal election in Canada only 64 percent voted.

In Eastern Europe the communist parties changed their names, claimed they were now democratic socialists, and pledged their commitment to the principles of the Second International. As Peter Gowan argues, public opinion polls in these countries show continued strong support for "socialist social values, particularly egalitarianism and support for nationalized property." With the dramatic decline in the standard of living in the former Soviet bloc after the switch to capitalism, the enthusiasm for the right-wing free enterprise and nationalist parties declined, and many of the former communist parties increased their representation in the legislatures and participated in governing coalitions. But because of the pressure from their coalition partners, the international financial institutions, and the U.S. and German governments, they have been unable to reverse the tide towards neoliberalism. Disillusionment set in.

Gowan points out that one of the responses to this lack of real choice in government policy is the refusal of a large sector of the population to bother to vote. In the parliamentary election in Poland in 2001, the turnout was only 46 percent. In the 2002 parliamentary election in the Czech Republic, the turnout was only 58 percent. In Romania in the 2000 presidential election 50 percent voted and 56 percent in the parliamentary elections. In 2001 the turnout for the presidential election in Bulgaria was 54 percent. Political commentators in Europe insist that the low turnout is due to the fact that the major parties are so similar in policy that when in office there is no difference in how they govern. (Gowan, 1999)

There are new left wing parties in most of the European countries today. In the European Parliament they operate under a coalition known as the European Unitary Left. They include the remaining communist parties (as in France) and those which have been transformed into the Parties of Democratic Socialism. In the French elections in 2002 there were *three* candidates for President who claimed to be Trotskyist, all running for different parties; between them they received 10 percent of the vote. This was seen largely as a protest by young people against the neoliberal policies of the coalition government led by the Socialist Party. There are also a range of new socialist parties. The Scottish Socialist Party is one of them, a merger of various left wing elements, and its vote is steadily increasing. These parties do not have a uniform ideology but range from left wing Keynesianism to those which insist that the capitalist system must be replaced.

The move to the right by the Labour Party has begun to change the political landscape in Great Britain. In the regional assemblies in Scotland and Wales, Labour and the Liberal Democrats govern as the coalition of the right, and the Scottish National Party and Plaid Cymru are the official opposition parties, providing a critique which is social democratic left. Sinn Fein is also making a breakthrough in electoral politics in Ireland and Northern Ireland as a party of the socialist left.

## The Emergence of the Green Parties

One major change in Europe has been the development of the Green parties. The first Green parties were the United Tasmanian Group in Australia and the Values Party in New Zealand, both formed in 1972. The Ecology Party was founded in Britain the following year. The other Green parties grew out of the mass demonstrations against militarism and nuclear power over the 1970s. Most prominent was the Green Party in Germany, founded in 1979 by a broad coalition of environmentalists, communists, new left activists, feminists, libertarians, peace activists, gay rights activists, youth movements, and Third World solidarity groups. There was a wave of Green parties formed after 1983, which included the Green Party of Canada.

All of the Green parties have experienced internal divisions between environmentalists and ecologists, those who want to stress electoral politics and those who favour extra-parliamentary movement politics, those who want to be purely an ecology party and those who want to include a broader social agenda, and those who want to participate in coalition governments and those who want the parliamentary party to remain independent. Petra Kelly, for example, a co-founder of the German Greens, insisted that the Green movement should not help maintain other parties in office or accept any coalitions or alliances with them. (see Richardson and Rootes, 1995; Pepper, 1993; Kelly, 1994; Merchant, 1992; Manes, 1990)

The ecologists have stressed that the planet is in danger of radically changing because of industrialization, economic growth and rampant consumerism. They argue that the Green movement must stress the necessity of reducing economic growth and environmental destruction. They advance a Green future without consumerism.

The mainstream parties, which are committed to economic growth, are referred to as the "grey parties." The ecologists argue that Green means going beyond the old divisions between left and right. The survival of the planet must come first, they argue, and this can only happen in a conserver society. In contrast, environmentalists are seen as those who believe we can solve the biological problems of the world created by industrialization through better technology. They believe that all that is needed is a reform of capitalism. Most environmentalists are willing to work within mainstream political parties, including the social democratic parties. The Greens have been criticized by the left and other progressive groups for failing to understand the nature of capitalism and ignoring class divisions in society.

At the same time, the ten basic principles of the international Green Party movement today include a commitment to peace and nonviolence, participatory democracy and decentralization, racial and gender equality, strong support for human rights, social justice, and equality and justice for people in the Third World. To actually achieve this requires broadening the movement beyond ecologists to include other progressive movements. The serious problems we face cannot be solved by technological changes.

These divisions have even led to the Greens being split into two separate political parties in the same country. For example, in Switzerland there was the Grune Bundnis (Red Greens) which then changed to become the Alternative Green Alliance, a left green party. They were separate from the Green Party of Switzerland, which opposed them in a number of elections. In Austria, the United Greens of Austria (VGO) was opposed by the more radical left leaning Alternative List of Austria (ALO) which then became the Green Alternative/Green (GAL). In both these cases, the different parties later merged. (Richardson and Rootes, 1995; Anderson, 1996)

This division can be seen in Finland today. The Left Alliance is a left green party which is a member of the European United Left/Nordic Green Left in the European Parliament. In the 2003 election it received 9.9 percent of the vote and 19 seats in the legislature. But there is also the Green League, a mainstream Green party which won eight percent of the vote and 14 seats in the 2003 election. Both participated in the coalition governments with the conservatives and social democrats between 1995 and 2003.

The German Greens have had a long, bitter division over these differences. There was a major split over the decision of the parliamentary party to participate in a coalition government supporting Gerhard Shroeder's Social Democratic Party. The SPD government pursued the same general neoliberal policy of Tony Blair's

Third Way. The parliamentary Greens (the "realists") had to abandon key fundamental Green party positions to participate in the coalition government. This included support for the NATO bombing of Serbia and sending the German military abroad. When the parliamentary group broke with party policy on nuclear power, and issues around globalization, many in the left of the party quit to work with instead with extra-parliamentary organizations. (Wolf, 2003)

The more traditional Green parties grew in popular support and peaked near the end of the 1980s. In the 1990s the green left parties did better in elections, winning between nine and 12 percent of the vote. These include the Left Green Alliance in Iceland, the Socialist Left Party in Norway, and the Left Alliance in Finland. The left green parties are more dominant in Denmark (Unity List—Red Green) and The Netherlands (Green Left Party). In the European Parliament they operate as a bloc, the European Federation of Green Parties. But several of the Green left parties have chosen to affiliate with the European Unitary Left.

Over the past twenty years the European Green parties have moved steadily to the left as they have embraced a range of social justice issues. In Great Britain the Ecology Party never won two percent of the votes, but as a progressive Green Party it has done much better and won a high of 15 percent of the vote in the 1989 elections to the European Parliament. The Green Party of Sweden began with its base in the upper middle class. But as the Social Democratic Party moved more to the right, it found it was more often allied with the Left Party. Throughout Europe, including Sweden, big business pushed for the expansion of the European Community with its commitment to internal free trade and neoliberalism. The Green Party and the Left Party were the only parties in Sweden who opposed the business agenda, and this drew them together. The same phenomenon was repeated in the other Nordic countries and elsewhere in Europe. The Green parties are now seen as being to the left of the social democratic parties.

However, this move to the left is not uniform across Europe. The German Greens, under the domination of the parliamentary party, have moved to the right to accommodate the alliance with the Social Democratic Party (SPD). In Austria in early 2003 the Green Party was considering joining a governing coalition with the conservative Austrian Peoples Party. Like the German party, the Austrian Green Party has abandoned is historic opposition to militarism and is starting to water down its commitment to social justice policies.

In Australia and New Zealand the Greens moved steadily to the left as they embraced social justice issues. Today in both countries the Green Party is to the critical left of the Labour party as well as the only party taking a strong position on environmental issues.

While the Green parties were leaders in the Eastern European countries in the movement to end the Soviet regimes, after the breakup of the Soviet bloc they have all but disappeared. The electorate decided that other issues were more important, and they were undermined by the rise of right-wing nationalism. The Green parties have not done well in the less affluent European countries, like Greece, Spain and Portugal. It remains to be seen whether the environmental crisis will lead voters to shift their political allegiances. (Richardson and Rootes, 1995; Merchant, 1992)

All of the Green parties accept the basic "four pillars" of the movement: a sustainable ecology, social and economic equity, grass-roots participatory democracy, and peace, nonviolence and disarmament. These are the foundations of the Green Party of Canada. Other basic principles include community-based economics, feminism, and respect for biological and social diversity. (see www.greenparty.ca)

The Green Party in the United States is a party of the left. Under the leadership of Ralph Nader and Winona LaDuke, it has emphasized social justice, elimination of poverty, the end to racism, the promotion of feminist values, opposition to free trade agreements, as well as a sustainable environment. In the widely diverse United States, it is the one organization which unites people from coast to coast. In the fall 2002 election Stanley Aronowitz, a well known socialist and labour activist, was its candidate for governor in New York. In Texas, it ran Rahul Mahajan for governor, an American of East Indian descent, a physicist and anti-war activist, who has written extensively attacking George W. Bush's "War on Terrorism." (www.greenpartyus.org)

In Canada, the federal Green Party, which has a left orientation on the questions of militarism, trade policy and Canadian independence, is relatively conservative on many other issues. Although it has been around for quite a few years, to date it has failed to develop a policy on social justice. The Green Party of British Columbia has been the most successful of the provincial parties in the electoral area. But it also has the historic division. Under the leadership of Stuart Parker it stressed social justice issues and on the municipal level joined electoral alliances with the NDP in Victoria and the Committee of Progressive Electors (COPE) in Vancouver. But under the new leadership of Adrianne Carr it has moved to the right, dropped these alliances, and has been mild in its criticism of the right wing policies of the provincial Liberal government under Gordon Campbell.

None of the Green Parties in the industrialized world has managed to attract more than 15 percent of the vote. Unlike successful electoral parties, the Greens have no base in a social class, religious or ethnic group, nor can they represent regional interests. It might take a serious ecological crisis before people will accept them as a major party.

## The Road to North Dakota

Within Saskatchewan, the move towards a free market and free trade economy has been supported by the NDP, the provincial Liberal Party, and the Tories and their successors, the Saskatchewan Party. Business and right-wing interests like the Saskatchewan Chamber of Commerce, the Federation of Independent Business and the Canadian Taxpayers Federation want the province to move even more rapidly down this path. We can see how such policies work in hinterland areas by looking across the border into the United States.

Saskatchewan is a hinterland province and will always be so. In this we are much more like North Dakota than we are like Alberta or Manitoba. The model for Saskatchewan advanced by our political and business leaders is North Dakota, where the policies of the free market, free trade, and limited state government have been in place for decades.

North Dakota today is still very much a hinterland of Minneapolis-St. Paul. Its population peaked in 1930 at 680,000. The largest city, Fargo-Moorhead, is only 90,000. The progressive farmers' movements, which began in 1915, brought in many reforms including state control of the banks, flour mills, grain elevators and the insurance business. While this resistance movement was still strong in the 1930s, following World War II it was defeated by "free market" forces behind the Republican Party. More orthodox state governments brought privatization and pro-business policies. (Robinson, 1995)

North Dakota has been pursuing a right wing revenue and expenditure policy for years. Resource royalties are even lower than in Saskatchewan. In 2002 corporate taxes provided only three percent of revenues compared to 7.5 percent in Saskatchewan. Individual income taxes provided only seven percent compared to 19 percent. Sales and use taxes provided 25 percent of revenues compared to only 13.6 percent. North Dakota has done better in obtaining revenues from the federal government; 32 percent of their revenues came from the federal government compared to only 21 percent for Saskatchewan.

But what has this free market policy direction done for North Dakota? Their manufacturing sector is much smaller than Saskatchewan's. Their co-op system has steadily declined. The farmers grain elevators have been replaced by a virtual monopoly by Cargill. Their state government trumpets their "right-to-work" legislation and the fact that only 6.5 percent of employees are in trade unions. But they have the second lowest per-capita income of the 50 states, 18 percent below the U.S. average. Their state budget is smaller because there is almost no state involvement in the health sector. Public utilities are not state owned and costs are higher.

Agriculture still accounts for 25 percent of North Dakota's economy and provides 24 percent of the labour force. But the agricultural sector is much less diversified than in Saskatchewan, and very little slaughtering and food processing is done in the state. It doesn't even have a feed lot industry, as almost all of its cattle are shipped down to Kansas or Nebraska.

Take a drive down through North Dakota some time. Here one finds the real wide open spaces between farms and tiny towns. The differences with Saskatchewan are obvious. North of the border there are no large military bases, B-52 bombers or ICBMs. But Saskatchewan has long had a strong co-operative sector and modern, efficient, publicly owned utilities. Marketing boards have provided important help for farmers. State intervention has produced greater economic development in Saskatchewan. The traditional "mixed economy" has provided a base for a larger, better paid population.

In contrasting Saskatchewan with North Dakota it is possible to see how human activity can modify the metropolitan-hinterland relationship, even within the capitalist system.

Saskatchewan is more highly populated and more industrialized than North Dakota. Both are hinterland areas dominated by outside metropolitan centres and their capitalists. Why are there such notable differences?

Saskatchewan has had much more successful grass roots political movements which have produced progressive parties. Provincial governments have been able to use the state to take actions to retain more of the economic surplus in the province. Marketing boards permit higher returns to farmers. There are poultry and dairy operations. Co-operatives remain stronger and return part of the economic surplus to producers and consumers. The public utilities are Crown corporations and retain the economic surplus or rent in the province. Even before the election of the CCF government, there was a stronger tradition of government intervention in the economy, including state subsidies, Crown corporations, and joint public-private ventures.

Legislation was used to promote economic diversification. For example, breweries which sold beer in the province were required to manufacture in the province. The regulation requiring the use of bottles promoted local production and reduced imports. Much of this is being lost in the move towards the free market and free trade.

The farmers and the CCF gave Saskatchewan a tradition of caring about the weakest members of society. A policy of compassion towards other human beings, and other species, requires government taxation and intervention in the economy. Over the last twenty years that tradition has been weakening under the policies of the Tory and NDP governments. Is this the way Saskatchewan really wants to go? Is Saskatchewan destined to become North Dakota?

## What Are the Political Alternatives?

Since its formation in 1933 the CCF and then the NDP has been the party of the Canadian left. The federal New Democratic Party peaked in popular support during the summer of 1987. Under the leadership of Ed Broadbent its support in national public opinion polls reached 40 percent, equal to that of the Liberal Party. At this time they promoted the Keynesian welfare state. Then came the 1988 "free trade election." The NDP all but eliminated that issue from their campaign, allowing the Liberals under John Turner to take the leadership role in opposing the Canada-U.S. Free Trade Agreement. But NDP supporters were strongly against the free trade agreement. As a result, in the 1988 election support for the NDP fell to a disappointing 25 percent and did not recover.

In 1992 there was the national referendum on the Charlottetown Accord, designed to advanced decentralization, promoted by the Mulroney Government and strongly supported by all the big business organizations. The NDP under the leadership of Audrey MacLaughlin supported the Accord, which was strongly opposed by their membership and working class Canadians across the country. Roy Romanow and the Saskatchewan NDP also supported the Accord. Only two ridings in Western Canada voted "yes" on the referendum, both upper middle class ridings. Every NDP riding voted heavily against the Accord. To no one's surprise, support for the NDP fell to 15 percent and then drifted down to less than 10 percent in 2001. The party's members and historic voters became disillusioned and gave up on them. Many, particularly those in British Columbia, shifted their support to the Reform Party.

In 2001 a group of progressives within the NDP founded the New Politics Initiative (NPI). It included two Members of Parliament from British Columbia, Svend

Robinson and Libby Davis. Some within the group saw the NPI as the beginning of a move to form a new political party, merging the NDP with a range of popular groups. Others saw it only as a group to modernize the NDP. Its focus was on reforming the structure and operation of the party, to make it more democratic and open, and it chose not to take a strong stand on policy issues. The NPI had a real presence at the 2001 federal party convention in Winnipeg but faded after that. When Alexa McDonough stepped down as leader of the NDP in 2002, and a leadership campaign began, the NPI chose not to advance or back a candidate. The new leader of the NDP, Toronto alderman Jack Layton, is in the tradition of the reform bloc within the party. But under his leadership the NDP has not adopted a new policy direction. (www.newpolitics.ca)

Many political commentators compared the NPI to the Waffle movement within the NDP in the 1960s and early 1970s. The Waffle gained immediate support both within and outside the NDP because it issued a strong manifesto calling for an independent Canada and a move towards socialism. In contrast, the NPI chose to dodge the historic central issue in Canadian politics: does the party support further continental integration or a move towards an independent Canada? With none of the other parties nor the incumbent leadership of the NDP standing for an independent Canada, they chose to avoid taking a stand on an issue which could have brought them much greater influence and support. On a whole range of issues, the campaign by David Orchard for the leadership of the federal Progressive Conservative Party was to the left of the NDP and the NPI.

Working within the NDP to try to promote a move towards socialism or a more left wing social democracy has not succeeded in the past. But the campaigns for Jim Laxer, the Waffle candidate for leader, and then Rosemary Brown, did invigorate the party. But such attempts now are highly unlikely to succeed because of the general swing to the right by all of the social democratic parties. It is no longer even possible to look to Sweden as an ideal social democratic country, for the Swedish SDP has moved to accept neoliberalism and as the government led the fight for free trade and entrance into the European Economic Community. It is just not feasible today to try to transform the NDP into a Canadian social democratic party that is different from all the others. Alternative social democratic policies are still around, but there is no will by the parties or their leaders to change direction. (see Drache, 1992)

Others across Canada believe that the way to change politics is to work outside the political party system through various social movements and political coalitions.

The Council of Canadians is perhaps the most prominent independent political organization. The new social movements represent women, poor people, seniors, the disabled, gays and lesbians, and others. They have worked with the traditional groups like trade unions and farm organizations. These popular organizations built the coalitions that continue to fight against the free trade agreements, the Action Canada Network and Common Frontiers. In opposing the neoliberal corporate agenda, they have worked with similar groups elsewhere, like the Alliance for Responsible Trade in the United States and the Mexican Network against Free Trade (RMALC). As a world movement they were successful in blocking the introduction of the Multilateral Agreement on Investment (MAI), at least for the time being.

These organizations have also worked through the social justice coalitions that have existed in recent years in almost all of the provinces. Other coalitions have been formed around more specific issues, such as the Canadian Health Coalition which is fighting to maintain and improve medicare. Coalitions are also organized around local issues, such as Hog Watch, individuals and organizations opposed to corporate pig factories. These organizations are trying to save what is left of the Keynesian welfare state economy. On the whole, they have not been all that successful. Furthermore, because they are defensive by nature, they have been unable to set forth an alternative vision of a better society. (see Carroll, 1992; Wharf and Clague, 1997)

## Is There a Saskatchewan Alternative?

The NPI had little support in Saskatchewan. The NDP has been the natural governing party since 1944, and it was still in office, although in a coalition with MLAs from the Liberal Party. The leadership of the NDP in Saskatchewan had strongly opposed the Waffle movement, and they would not in any way support the NPI. They were not interested in democratic reform of the party or its transformation into a new party.

The left tried once again to gain influence within the Saskatchewan NDP during the 2001 leadership campaign. An informal group backed Nettie Wiebe's campaign. They received 25 percent of the vote of the membership. However, unlike the Waffle group, they had no ongoing organization, and they have since faded away. Few new people were able to obtain NDP nominations for the 2003 election, and the party took a step backward by only nominating ten women candidates. There seems to be little hope of changing the NDP from within.

In Saskatchewan there is a long history of popular groups pressuring governments. Many have also been closely connected to one of the political parties. In the early period the grain growers were involved with the provincial Liberal Party. Beginning in the Great Depression the major farm organizations helped create the CCF. In the 1960s and the 1970s the Saskatchewan Farmers Union, the Saskatchewan Federation of Labour and the Saskatchewan Teachers Federation met jointly on an annual basis to plan strategies on how to influence the NDP. These major popular organizations were very close to the party.

During the Tory government of Grant Devine over 50 organizations representing workers, farmers, seniors, students, women, Aboriginal people, and others joined together and formed the Saskatchewan Coalition for Social Justice (SCSJ). Through demonstrations and other actions the Coalition mobilized opposition to the neoliberal policies of the government. They played a significant role in convincing the Tory government not to proceed with the privatization of the Crown public utilities, but in general they had little influence on government policy. There is no doubt, however, that they played a major role in swinging public opinion against the Tory government and contributed to their defeat in the 1991 provincial election.

At the Coalition's Peoples' Conventions, the delegates vowed to maintain their organization and keep pressing the government even after the NDP was elected. But this did not happen. After the election in 1991, the Coalition faded away in a few short years. The leadership of the various community organizations all had long ties to the NDP, and they could not see their organizations or the Coalition operating in the same manner with a "friendly" government. Thus at no time while the NDP government of Roy Romanow was implementing neoliberal policies did the Coalition ever mount a public campaign in opposition. To begin with, their most prominent organization, the Saskatchewan Federation of Labour, would not hear of it. They had official ties to the NDP. (Warnock, 2002)

In more recent years in Saskatchewan the locals of the Council of Canadians have mobilized people. However, they have almost always focused on federal or international issues, rarely provincial issues. Their leaders were very hesitant to criticize the NDP government for supporting the free trade agreements. There are limitations to this type of political organizing. For the vast majority of people, the only time they engage in politics is when they go to the polls to vote. If a political movement is not involved in electoral politics, most people believe that they are wasting their time, and they are not taken seriously.

There is one alternative choice in Saskatchewan today, the New Green Alliance (NGA), a new political party. In 1983 a group of people, primarily in Saskatoon, began the process of trying to create a provincial wing of the federal Green Party. But this project was suspended. In 1994 political activists in Regina who had been in the Saskatchewan Coalition for Social Justice and in the leadership of the Young New Democrats began informal meetings about the possibility of forming a new political party. As the NDP government moved farther to the right after the 1995 election, the group went public. Meetings were held, principles were drafted, and a constitution was created. In October 1998 a founding convention was held. By January 1999 the provincial electoral requirements were fulfilled, and the New Green Alliance became an official party. In the June 1999 by-elections their candidate in Saskatoon Fairview obtained 2.5 percent of the vote and their candidate in Regina Dewdney received 10 percent. In the 1999 provincial election, the new party managed to field 16 candidates who received on average five percent of the vote. It has continued to grow in membership and develop regional locals. In the 2003 election it fielded 27 candidates but was pushed aside in the political polarization. In contrast to the other political parties, the NGA has joined with community groups in extra-parliamentary actions.

The NGA has its divisions similar to all the international Green parties. There are those who advocate the Green ecology position developed in Europe. But most of the founding members looked with greater favour to the progressive left Green alliances with their emphasis on social justice. They were also influenced by Green party developments in New Zealand and Australia. (see Brown, 1999; www.nga.sk.ca)

Today Saskatchewan is going through a transition period. Since the 1991 election the support for the NDP has dropped significantly. The trade unions are not providing the membership, campaign organizers and funds that they have in the past. There is a great deal of cynicism over the political process. Around 40 percent of eligible voters are not bothering to go to the polls. Only around 25 percent of people in their 20s are voting. The competition between the three dominant parties focuses on which one can promise the most support for business interests. They ignore policy preferences recorded in numerous public opinion polls.

## Is Any Alternative Possible?

The world capitalist system is going through an economic and political crisis. It seems to be the worst crisis since the Great Depression and the Second World War. It is characterized by a declining rate of growth, increasing inequality, and a crisis of overproduction and under consumption. Overcapacity and declining corporate profits are the norm around the world. The economy in North America struggles on due to a steady expansion of corporate and personal debt. A horrendous crisis of drought, despair, AIDS, hunger and famine continue to plague Africa, and the rich countries in the North just sit back and watch. Assistance is very limited.

There is a mounting ecological crisis. It is caused by overproduction and over consumption in the First World. Scientific evidence indicates that the world is already experiencing the effects of global warming and climate change. Global warming is a major contributor to the problem of drought and famine in Africa. While governments in Europe are taking action, those in North America, Japan and Australia seemed determined to do nothing.

But as Walden Bellow and others from the Third World Network stress, neoliberalism is also going through a crisis of legitimacy. The policies of the free market and free trade no longer have any popular appeal among the people of the less developed countries. The structural adjustment programs and the constant financial crises give a lie to the promise of better times. In 2002 the top corporate elite in the United States were exposed as criminals for their massive fraud and deception. This corruption has included many of the most prominent political leaders in the United States, beginning with President George W. Bush and Vice President Dick Cheney. (Bellow, 2002)

There is also a crisis for liberal democracy itself. This system of government, usually identified as the natural system for capitalism, has proven to be anything but democratic. It is at best "elite democracy" or "techno-democracy." It is characterized by rule by privileged elites backed by corporations, big money, and the mass media. It is widely believed that George W. Bush and his powerful supporters in the oil industry stole the U.S. presidential election in 2000. In addition, the political and economic elite have been promoting the transfer of power from democratically elected national governments to supra-national institutions like NAFTA, the World Trade Organization and the European Economic Union which are unelected bodies, are not accountable to anyone, and make decisions behind closed doors. This may be liberalism, but it is not democracy.

While the U.S. government has enormous economic power, and uncontested military power, it is becoming less able to control the world. There was widespread opposition to the military intervention and bombing of Yugoslavia. Following the first Gulf War in 1991, there were years of constant bombing of Iraq by U.S. and British forces, and the economic boycott which cost of the lives of hundreds of thousands of children was widely denounced. The war against the Taliban and al-Qaida in Afghanistan has not enhanced U.S. influence in Asia. The all out support for the right-wing government of Israel and its assault on the Palestinian people has cost the

U.S. enormously in the Middle East and parts of Asia. The U.S. and British war against Iraq in 2003 was overwhelmingly opposed by world public opinion. Even in Europe opposition was over 80 percent. The unilateralism of the U.S. government has made it more difficult for European governments to keep supporting U.S. policy initiatives, particularly the "war on terrorism."

Major political and economic changes have occurred in history during profound crises: civil wars, international wars, and world depressions. It may take another major crisis for the majority of the people in the First World to conclude that serious changes need to be made. This may come with global warming and climate change. But a grass roots resistance to neoliberalism and U.S. domination is developing throughout the world.

It is easy to conclude that there is no possibility for any change in direction in the politics and political economy of Saskatchewan. Indeed, the defenders of the NDP's move to the right argue that no alternative course is possible. They insist that what was possible twenty years ago when Allan Blakeney was premier can no longer work today.

It is also argued that the ideology of neoliberalism has become hegemonic in Canada, and there is no strong support for a policy of active government and the welfare state. However, public opinion polls indicate that this is not true. Michael Adams of Environics argues that their public opinion polls indicate the opposite, that Canadian values are moving away from the general conservative and patriarchal values held in the United States. Canadians, he argues, are much more committed to democracy. (Adams, 2003)

Most people know that there is a great deal of discontent in Saskatchewan at this time and a great deal of cynicism about politicians and governments. Despite the continuous propaganda from the mass media in support of neoliberalism, Saskatchewan residents remain largely unconvinced. For example, business interests have been pushing for the privatization of the Crown corporation utilities. But public opinion polls show a strong majority in opposition to such a policy.

The main barrier to the development of a political alternative has been the materialist framework. Canadians in general are among the richest people in the world. In general, they identify with the advanced industrialist capitalist states. Canada is also a white settler society, historically in a basic conflict with the non-white Third World. There may be a lot of problems, but Canada is not Mexico or an African country. Canadians in principle support giving aid to less developed countries, but they do not seem to be prepared to accept a reduction in their conspicuous consumption in order to eliminate poverty and despair. Historically, Canadian political leaders have always lined up with the western imperial powers against rebellions in colonial and semi-colonial countries. In these cases they appear to have been following public opinion.

This brings us back to Samir Amin and other political economists and commentators from the Third World. They insist that the major conflict in the world today is between the industrialized First World and the less developed countries. Given the reality of this polarization, many political commentators believe that the alternative vision of socialism or communism is simply not on the agenda in the First World. Workers have opted for collaboration with the capitalists. The best that can be hoped for is some commitment to a left wing or progressive social democracy. But this assumes that the status quo will persist and there will be no economic, political, social or environmental crisis or breakdown.

Nevertheless, within Saskatchewan there are serious problems with the status quo and the thrust toward the North Dakota model. The free market model being advanced by our political and business leaders assumes that everyone is "economic man," pursuing their own self interest at the expense of everyone else. But this is not true. People still remain primarily committed to their personal relationships, their families, their friends and even their community.

Under the capitalist economic system, people are forced to work wherever they can find employment. When they do find employment, it is invariably within the authoritarian command system. Employees are told what to do. They have no say in what they produce or how they produce it. There is no democracy in the place of employment; it is run like a military organization, from the top down. Employees follow orders.

Karl Marx made a distinction between "work" and "labour." What distinguishes humans from other animals is our ability to transform natural resources by physical and mental labour. "Work," as Marx argued, is "life-maintaining," part of our creative being. Whether it is producing food, producing goods for use, or writing classical music, it is creative work. The key is that "work" is under our control. In contrast, "labour" is performed under the control of someone else, the lord of the manor, the landlord, the slave-owner, or the capitalist. This is the root of alienation.

While this labour is carried out under the forms of capitalist production, the economic base of society, the same alienation carries over to employment in the superstructure, that part of the economy that services capitalism, provides ideological control, and provides social control via state institutions. While labour here may not produce surplus value for capital accumulation, the structure of this labour mirrors labour in the economic base. It is also alienated labour. For example, recently the *Globe and Mail Report on Business* surveyed 8700 readers via e-mail to find where they find fulfillment in life. Only 10 percent said it was found in their employment. The rest cited family and friends, doing charity and community work, leisure activities and spiritual pursuits. This records the alienation that the majority of working people experience in their labour, even when they are highly skilled. (*Globe and Mail*, February 20, 2003)

For Adam Smith and all his defenders of capitalism, employment was never seen as a fulfilling experience. It was never "work." Labour was necessary to obtain an income to exist. Pleasure came *outside labour* in leisure, family, and the consumption of material goods. Labour was not considered to be a creative process; most often it was just something that had to be endured. Marxists called this "wage slavery."

From the very beginning people have seen capitalism as destructive of the human spirit. Critics have argued that capitalism blocks the full development of human beings. Personal development can only be achieved through productive and useful work, in co-operation with other human beings, respecting the environment and other species. This has not changed as we have moved to the advanced, consumer society. Buying endless "things," commodity fetishism, is no substitute for the full development of the self and community.

Thus any real political alternative must include a *qualitative change* in how we work and live. We have examples of co-operative enterprises in Canada where workers control what and how they produce. Any new political movement must emphasize a transition to end the alienation of labouring under the capitalist command society. We must also gain control over the institutions that we once created, the existing co-operatives, credit unions and Crown corporations. Today they operate just like capitalist institutions. Democracy has to extend to the workplace, which is so central to our lives and existence.

We do not have a democratic political system. We have virtually no control over what our governments do. The resistance to authoritarian governments started in Saskatchewan with the agrarian populist movement in the late 19th century. Nothing has changed since then. Any new political movement for an alternative must include a more democratic structure of government, with local control, and actual participation.

There is a great need to reverse the process that has depopulated our rural communities by driving people off the land and creating corporate-style farms. The industrial model of farming is not sustainable, and it is polluting our food, land, water and air. As David Suzuki argues, it is a suicidal approach to providing food for humans. Any shift in direction will require major support from the government to counteract the pressures of the agribusiness corporations and the market. But governments around the world have long histories of successful rural development programs. European governments are giving new financial support to expand organic farming and the preservation of small farms. It can be done. Popular support is there. What is lacking here is the will by political leaders.

For Saskatchewan, gaining ownership and control over natural resources is essential for any real development. In the 1980s the NDP government demonstrated that this is feasible. Without control over natural resources and the returns from their exploitation there can be no real change.

Saskatchewan has a history that provides guidance for political action. For over a hundred years people have been involved in non-governmental organizations that have mobilized and brought pressure on governments. But this is not enough. As our farmers demonstrated, real changes will only come when popular organizations are combined with political parties to gain control of government. When faced with the power of corporations and the federal and U.S. governments, popular movements need the support of the democratic state.

Any real change in direction may require a crisis. The Great Depression brought the CCF government. It also came with the drought of the Dirty Thirties. The next crisis may well be the worsening of the environmental crisis caused by global warming and climate change. Capitalism as a system requires endless growth of commodity production to produce new capital. It cannot exist in a "steady state" economy with no economic growth. Capitalism is the root cause of the ecological crisis, and it is the root cause of human alienation. When the next crisis comes, it will be time to mobilize and demand a new political economy. (see Kovel, 2002)

There is a model for an alternative system that is recognized in both the First World and the less developed countries. It starts with a return to local ownership and control of the economy, one that is based on human need and not private profit for a small minority. As Ralph Miliband has pointed out, from the time of the rise of liberalism through the development of the socialist alternatives there has been the belief that "human beings are perfectly capable of organizing themselves into co-operative, democratic, egalitarian and self-governing communities, in which all conflict would certainly not have been eliminated, but where it would become less frequent and acute." There is no fixed human nature that rules that this is impossible. The new left and Green movements have emphasized that a new society would no longer be based on racism, sexism, and exploitation of others. It would have to be an ecologically balanced world where other species are recognized as having a right to exist in nature. This can only happen in a post-capitalist and post-patriarchal society. A growing number of people in Saskatchewan are beginning to think this way. (Miliband, 1994; Anderson, 1996)

## References

Adams, Michael. 2003. *Fire and Ice: The United States, Canada and the Myth of Converging Values.* Toronto: Penguin Books.

Amin, Samir *et al.* 2001. *Declaration of a Group of Intellectuals in Porto Alegre.* Porto Alegre: World Social Forum. www.forumsocialmundial.org

Amin, Samir. 1980. *Class and Nation.* New York: Monthly Review Press.

Anderson, Jan Otto. 1996. "Fundamental Values for a Third Left." *New Left Review,* No. 216, March/April, pp. 66-78.

Audley, John J. *et al.* 2003. *NAFTA's Promise and Reality: Lessons from Mexico for the Hemisphere.* Washington, D.C.: Carnegie Endowment for International Peace.

Ballve, Teo. 2003. "Globalizing Resistance in Cancun." *NACLA Report on the Americas,* Vol. 37, No. 3, November/December, pp. 16-19.

Bandow, Doug and Ian Vasquez. 1993. *Perpetuating Poverty: The World Bank, the IMF and the Developing World.* Washington, DC: The Cato Institute.

Bello, Walden. 2002. "A Fundamental Loss of Confidence Means the World Could Be Entering a Great Depression-Style Era." The Philippines: Focus on the Global South.

Biel, Robert. 2000. *The New Imperialism: Crisis and Contradictions in North/South Relations.* London: Zed Books.

Burbach, Roger *et al.* 1997. *Globalization and its Discontents: The Rise of Postmodern Socialisms.* London: Pluto Press.

Bradford, Neil. 2002. "Renewing Social Democracy? Beyond the Third Way." *Studies in Political Economy,* No. 67, Spring, pp. 145-161.

Brown, Lorne A., Joseph K. Roberts and John W. Warnock. 1999. *Saskatchewan Politics from Left to Right '44-'99* Regina: Hinterland Publications. .

Callinicos, Alex. 2001. *Against the Third Way: An Anti-Capitalist Critique.* London: Polity.

Canadian Centre for Policy Alternatives. 1999. *Alternatives for the Americas: Building a Peoples' Hemispheric Agreement.* Ottawa: Canadian Centre for Policy Alternatives and Common Frontiers.

Carroll, William K. 1992. *Organizing Dissent: Contemporary Social Movements in Theory and Practice.* Toronto: Garamond Press.

Danaher, Kevin, ed. 1994. *50 Years Is Enough: The Case Against the World Bank and the International Monetary Fund.* Boston: South End Press.

Dawkins, Kristin. 1993. "Principles of Fair Trade and a Just Foreign Policy." *Third World Resurgence*, No. 29/30, January-February, pp. 40-1.

Drache, Daniel, ed. 1992. *Getting on Track: Social Democratic Strategies for Ontario.* Montreal: McGill-Queen's University Press.

Draper, Hal, ed. 1971. *Writings on the Paris Commune.* New York: International Publishers.

Fukuyama, Francis. 1992. *The End of History and the Last Man.* New York: Avon Books.

Giddens, Anthony. 1998. *The Third Way.* Cambridge: Cambridge University Press.

Giddens, Anthony. 2000. *The Third Way and Its Critics.* Cambridge: Cambridge University Press.

Gorz, Andre. 1994. *Capitalism, Socialism, Ecology.* London: Verso.

Gowan, Peter. 1999. *The Global Gamble: Washington's Faustian Bid for World Dominance.* London: Verso.

Hansen-Kuhn, Karen and Steve Hellinger, eds. *Lessons from NAFTA: The High Cost of "Free Trade."* Ottawa: Canadian Centre for Policy Alternatives.

Hardt, Michael. 2002. "Porto Alegre: Today's Bandung?" *New Left Review*, 14, March-April, pp. 1-5.

Houtart, François and Francois Polet, eds. 2001. *The Other Davos: The Globalization of Resistance to the World Economic System.* London: Zed Books.

Howell, Chris. 2001. "The End of the Relationship between Social Democratic Parties and Trade Unions?" *Studies in Political Economy*, No. 65, Summer, pp. 7-37.

Jackson, Andrew. 2003. *From Leaps of Faith to Hard Landings: Fifteen Years of "Free Trade."* Ottawa: Canadian Centre for Policy Alternatives, December.

Kelly, Petra K. 1994. *Thinking Green! Essays on Environmentalism, Feminism, and Nonviolence.* Berkeley: Parallax Press.

Kelsey, Jane. 1995. *Economic Fundamentalism.* London: Pluto Press.

Klein, Naomi. 2001. "A Fete for the End of the End of History." *The Nation*, March 19, 2001. www.forumsocialmundo.org

Kovel, Joel. 2002. *The Enemy of Nature: The End of Capitalism or the End of the World?* Halifax: Fernwood Books.

Lipietz, Alain. 1992. *Towards a New Economic Order: Postfordism, Ecology and Democracy.* New York: Oxford University Press.

Mander, Jerry and Edward Goldsmith, eds. 1996. *The Case Against the Global Economy and For a Turn Toward the Local.* San Francisco: Sierra Club Books.

Manes, Christopher. 1990. *Green Rage: Radical Environmentalism and the Unmaking of Civilization.* Boston: Little, Brown and Company.

Merchant, Carolyn. 1992. *Radical Ecology: The Search for a Livable World.* London: Routledge.

Mertes, Tom. 2002. "Grass-Roots Globalism." *New Left Review*, 17, September-October, pp. 101-110.

Miliband, Ralph. 1994. *Socialism for a Sceptical Age*. London: Verso.

Milstein, Cindy. 2002. "Another World Is Possible, But What kind, and Shaped by Whom?" Plainfield, VT: Institute of Social Ecology.

Panitch, Leo. 1996. *Are there Alternatives? Socialist Register 1996*. New York: Monthly Review Press.

Pepper, David. 1993. *Eco-Socialism: From Deep Ecology to Social Justice*. London: Routledge.

Przeworski, Adam. 1985. *Capitalism and Social Democracy*. Cambridge: Cambridge University Press.

Reich, Wilhelm. 1969. "The Struggle for the 'New Life" in the Soviet Union." *The Sexual Revolution*, Part II. New York: Farrar, Straus and Giroux.

Rich, Bruce. 1994. *Mortgaging the Earth: The World Bank, Environmental Impoverishment and the Crisis of Development*. Boston: Beacon Press.

Richardson, Dick and Chris Rootes, eds. 1995. *The Green Challenge: The Development of Green Parties in Europe*. London: Routledge.

Riches, Graham, ed. 1997. *First World Hunger: Food Security and Welfare Politics*. London: Macmillan.

Robinson, Elwyn B. 1966. *History of North Dakota*. Lincoln: University of Nebraska Press.

Robinson, William I. 1996. *Promoting Polyarchy: Globalization, U.S. Intervention, and Hegemony*. London: Cambridge University Press.

Sader, Emir. 2002. "Beyond Civil Society." *New Left Review*, 17, September-October, pp. 87-99.

Schumpeter, Joseph A. 1961. *Capitalism, Socialism and Democracy*. London: George Allen & Unwin.

Sheldrick, Byron. 2002. "New Labour and the Third Way Democracy, Accountability and Social Democratic Politics." *Studies in Political Economy*, No. 67, Spring, pp. 133-43.

Third World Network. 2003. "The Cancun Collapse." Special issue of *Third World Resurgence*, Nos. 157/158, September/October.

Warnock, John W. 2002. "Coalitions, Labour and the New Democratic Party." Paper presented at the Symposium on the Labour Movement in Saskatchewan, University of Regina, November 25. Publication forthcoming.

Warnock, John W. 1996. "Social Democracy's Failure: The New Zealand Experience." *Our Times*, December, pp. 18-20.

Wharf, Brian and Michael Clague, eds. 1997. *Community Organizing: Canadian Experiences*. Don Mills: Oxford University Press.

Wilson, John. 1997. "Australia: Lucky Country/Hungry Silence." In Riches, pp. 14-45.

Wiseman, John. 1996. "A Kinder Road to Hell? Labour and the Politics of Progressive Competitiveness in Australia." In Panitch, pp. 93-117.

Wolf, Frieder Otto. 2003. "Whatever Happened to the German Greens?" *Red Pepper*, No. 110, August, pp. 24-25.

Yates, Charlotte. 2002. "In Defence of Unions: A Critique of the Third Way." *Studies in Political Economy*, No. 67, Spring, pp. 123-31.

# INDEX

# also by John Warnock

## OTHER MEXICO
### The North American Triangle Completed

A harsh program was imposed on Mexicans, creating a Mexico characterized by the highest unemployment in its history, a dramatic increase in poverty, and gross inequalities in income and wealth, all the while making illicit drugs an important industry. President Carlos Salinas was praised by politicians, bankers and foreign investors for bringing a right-wing revolution to Mexico.

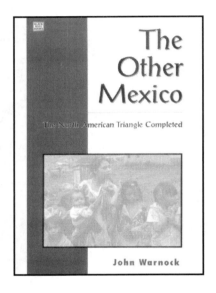

The Other Mexico describes how two presidents brought the neoliberal revolution to Mexico: the free market, foreign investment, privatization of state enterprises, deregulation, cuts in social spending, and free trade with the United States and Canada, and how Mexicans, who have a long history of resistance to domination and exploitation, fought back in an effort to create an alternative, more humane society.

A well-written study...one of the best that's been published about NAFTA and its impact. —*Canadian Book Review Annual*

In-depth research and a superb collection of photos. —*Briarpatch*

People frequently ask me what book they should read to gain an understanding of Mexico. I confidently recommend John Warnock's volume. —*Canadian Forum*

Situates Mexico within its own history, as well as both the North American and global context...here is fascinating reading. —*Canadian Dimension*

*Photographs by Elaine Brière*

321 pages, photographs, index
Paperback ISBN: 1-55164-028-7          $23.99
Hardcover ISBN: 1-55164-029-5          $52.99

# of related interest

## REQUIEM FOR A LIGHTWEIGHT
### Stockwell Day and Image Politics
*Trevor W. Harrison*

From his days as an Alberta politician, to the transformation of the Reform party into the Alliance party, to the high-point of Day's coronation as Alliance leader, to the 2000 federal election, to the debacles of early 2001 that shattered the Alliance dream: this book chronicles it all—the people, personalities, and politics.

> Throws a nifty one-two combination—a quick, accurate history of Stockwell Day's bumpy journey as Canadian Alliance party leader, followed by a solid commentary on the nature of populism in Canadian politics. —*Edmonton Journal*

TREVOR W. HARRISON, University of Alberta, is the co-editor of *The Trojan Horse: Alberta and the Future of Canada.*

> 204 pages, 6x9, bibliography, index
> Paperback ISBN: 1-55164-206-9       $19.99
> Hardcover ISBN: 1-55164-207-7       $48.99

## TOWARD A HUMANIST POLITICAL ECONOMY
*Harold Chorney, Phillip Hansen*

A collection of essays written between the late 70s and the present day that focus on the neglected cultural side of society in order to chart the progress of political change.

> ...the later essays have a remarkably perceptive quality. This is particularly true of essays on Keynes and ideology. —*Chartist*

> ...the themes are relevant for those trying to fathom the post-Reaganite political world of the 1990s. —*Canadian Book Review Annual*

> ...their publication in one volume is a welcome addition to both Canadian political economy literature and literature on western Canada. —*Prairie Forum*

HAROLD CHORNEY teaches public policy and social theory at Concordia University, Quebec. PHILLIP HANSEN teaches social theory at the University of Regina, Saskatchewan.

> 224 pages, index
> Paperback ISBN:1-895431-22-0       $19.99
> Hardcover ISBN:1-895431-23-9       $48.99

# of related interest

## TRIUMPH OF THE MARKET
### Essays on Economics, Politics, and the Media
*Edward S. Herman*

The unifying theme of the essays in this volume is the increasing national and global power and reach of the market and its growing impact on all aspects of human life.

A non-fiction horror story, where what is good for private profit is hailed as good for the public. —Fairness and Accuracy in Reporting (FAIR)

Demystifies the many ways that giant global corporations have worked to replace democratic and community values with market exchange.
—Elaine Bernard, Harvard University

EDWARD HERMAN is an economist and media analyst, Professor Emeritus at the Wharton School, University of Pennsylvania, author of *Beyond Hypocrisy*.

286 pages, 6x9, bibliography, index
Paperback ISBN: 1-55164-062-7        $19.99
Hardcover ISBN: 1-55164-063-5        $48.99

### *send for a free catalogue of all our titles*

BLACK
ROSE
BOOKS

C.P. 1258, Succ. Place du Parc
Montréal, Québec
H2X 4A7 Canada

### *or visit our website at http://www.web.net/blackrosebooks*

### *to order books*
In Canada: (phone) 1-800-565-9523 (fax) 1-800-221-9985
email: utpbooks@utpress.utoronto.ca

In United States: (phone) 1-800-283-3572 (fax) 1-651-917-6406

In UK & Europe: (phone) London 44 (0)20 8986-4854 (fax) 44 (0)20 8533-5821
email: order@centralbooks.com

Printed by the workers of
MARC VEILLEUX IMPRIMEUR INC.
Boucherville, Québec
for Black Rose Books Ltd.